Edexcel BTEC National Public Services (Uniformed)

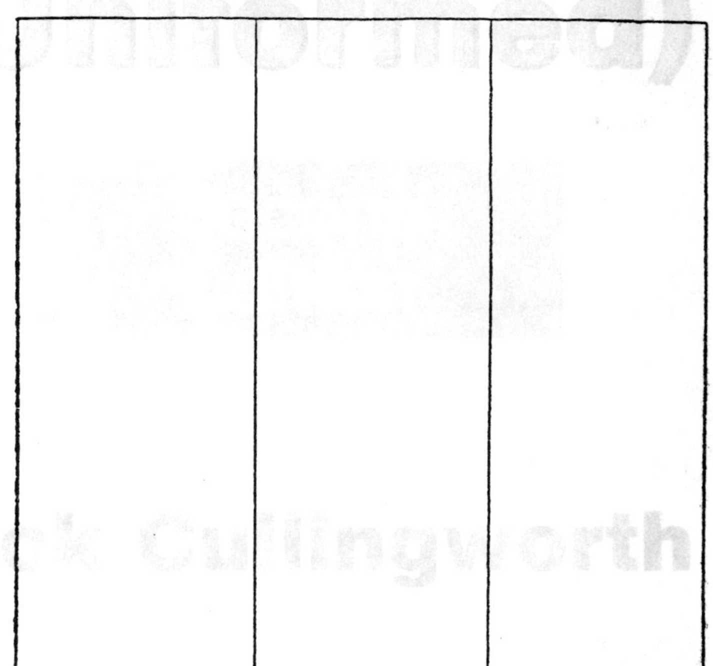

Nick Cullingworth

Published in 2004 by:
Nelson Thornes Ltd
Delta Place
27 Bath Road
CHELTENHAM
GL53 7TH
United Kingdom

04 05 06 07 08 / 10 9 8 7 6 5 4 3 2 1

A catalogue record for this book is available from the British Library

ISBN 0-7487-8514-0

Illustrations by Alex Machin

Page make-up by GreenGate Publishing Services, Tonbridge, Kent

Printed and bound in Great Britain by Scotprint

Contents

Units available on the Web:

Introduction

Foreword

This book is for students doing any of the BTEC Nationals in Public Services (uniformed) programmes designed by the Edexcel Foundation. It follows the new Specifications: *BN011697 Guidance and Units for the Edexcel Level 3 BTEC Nationals in Public Services – Issue 1 – May 2002*.

The book covers:

- all the core units
- the following specialist units:
- 9 Physical Preparation for the Uniformed Services
- 10 Democratic Processes
- 11 Expedition Skills
- 12 Human Behaviour
- 14 Understanding Discipline
- 16 Dealing with Accidents
- 17 Teamwork in the Public Services
- 18 Health and Fitness
- 20 Outdoor Activities
- 21 Criminology
- 24 Major Incidents.

Chapters covering the five remaining specialist units – 13, 15, 19, 22 and 23 – are freely available on the Nelson Thornes website: www.nelsonthornes.com/vocational/public_services/

Subject areas are dealt with outcome by outcome. Students will find information, ideas and skills guidance for all parts of the syllabus. There is also information and guidance on assessment and grading, and on the integrated vocational assignments (IVAs) for Unit 3 Leadership and Unit 4 Citizenship and Contemporary Issues.

Introduction for students

The aim of this book is to help you to succeed on your BTEC National Public Services (Uniformed) course. The book covers:

- all the outcomes for each unit
- the content of the units
- how you will be assessed.

In addition it gives you guidance on how to carry out research and develop your study skills.

Though this book contains plenty of information, it has not been written to do your work for you, but to help you to do your own work. At BTEC National level you are expected to do your own research, ask your own questions, and find your own answers. You will achieve the highest levels of success by being active and motivated, and by getting up-to-date information from as many different sources as possible.

How the book is organised

As in the Specifications, the book is divided into core units and specialist units. The numbering of the units is the same as in the Specifications. Each unit begins with a grid showing the grading criteria (referred to as 'outcomes' in the text) for that unit. Most grading criteria are dealt with individually – though where they are very closely linked, they have been dealt with together.

Content is covered with the relevant outcomes, and links with other units are clearly signposted.

Special features

Special features are included to make the book easier to use. These are:

FOCUS – definitions, facts, figures and useful quotations

CHECKPOINT – questions to make you think, or ideas for research

SKILLPOWER – advice on how to understand or cover outcomes

PASSGRADE, MERIT AND DISTINCTION – sections which deal with the outcomes and tell you how to get these grades

PROFILE – examples of how you could approach certain tasks

LINK! – directs you to another part of the book to find relevant information

COOL SITES – good websites with free, useful information and links to the units on the Nelson Thornes website

COOL BOOKS – recommended books.

About the BTEC Nationals in Public Services

BTEC Nationals in Public Services (Uniformed) are courses designed to prepare you for:

- advancement in your work, if you are already employed in a uniformed public service
- successful entry at an appropriate level into a uniformed public service
- university-level study in a public service related subject.

BTEC Nationals in Public Service do not guarantee entry into any public service. Public services have their own entry tests. But the Nationals *increase your chances of acceptance* by showing that you have interest, ability and commitment – and by giving you valuable skills and knowledge.

The BTEC Nationals in Public Services (Uniformed) comprise:

Qualification	Number of core units	Number of specialist units
BTEC National Award	3	3
BTEC National Certificate	5	7
BTEC National Diploma	8	10

For each qualification, the core units are compulsory – but there is a range of choice for the specialist units. For the exact details of this choice see *BN011697 Guidance and Units for the Edexcel Level 3 BTEC Nationals in Public Services – Issue 1 – May 2002*. (available at http://www.edexcel.org.uk/VirtualContent/23855.pdf – or ask your tutor).

The Award is designed mainly for mature learners who wish to know more about specific aspects of uniformed public service work. The Certificate covers more units and is suited for learners who have already decided which career they wish to follow. The Diploma is the most demanding of the qualifications, and gives learners a wide range of choices.

The Award, Certificate and Diploma all encourage active, practical, job-related learning. They also promote personal development and are designed to make learners more aware of spiritual, moral, ethical, social and cultural aspects of life. These elements are built into the content of the units.

Equal opportunities apply to both recruitment and progress on the courses.

FOCUS

- The Edexcel Foundation is an 'awarding body' which sets examinations and supervises courses.
- BTEC stands for the Business and Technology Education Council, an awarding body which merged with Edexcel in 1996.

http://www.edexcel.org.uk/aboutus/WhatWeDo.aspx?id=59380

Units

Each unit is an area of study related to the public services. Learners are expected to need 60 hours of guided study (lessons) to cover each unit. Your college will offer a full choice of units to enable you to get your qualification.

Content

The content of the unit is the subject areas you have to study in order to achieve the outcomes, or grading criteria for that unit. The content is listed in the Specifications – and is covered in this book. You will find the content for each outcome after the outcome itself.

Assessment

The assessment (marking) of BTEC Nationals is based on the grading criteria shown at the beginning of each unit in this book. These criteria show clearly what you need to do to achieve a pass, merit or distinction for each 'outcome' (part of the unit). You get merits and distinctions for doing *better* work, not for doing more work. Quality matters more than size.

There are two types of assessment:

- **internal assessment** This is marking done by your tutors. It is based on 'evidence' – produced by you – that you have met the grading criteria for the unit. Evidence is work or activities such as assignments, case studies, presentations, role plays, tests and practical activities. Tutors assess this evidence using the grading criteria.

Though you may be assessed on each piece of work or activity, the assessment which really matters is the overall assessment for the unit. This may be reached by averaging out your assignment grades, or by some other method. But whatever method is used, it has to be based on the work done and the grading criteria – nothing else.

- **external assessment** This is marking done by outside experts chosen by Edexcel. At present this applies to only two units: Unit 3 Leadership and Unit 4 Citizenship and Contemporary Issues. (See IVA below.)

The points system

The grade you get for each unit – pass, merit or distinction – carries points which go towards your total number of points for the qualification. The points for internally-assessed units are:

Pass – 2
Merit – 4
Distinction – 6.

The points available for each of the externally assessed units (Units 3 and 4) are double those for all the other, internally-assessed units. Thus for Leadership, for example, a Pass brings 4 points, a Merit brings 8 points, and a Distinction brings 12 points.

Overall grades for the qualification

Under the new Specifications, you get overall grades for the qualification you are doing. These are arrived at by adding up the points you score for each unit. Your tutors have full details of the overall grading system and will give them to you at the start of your course.

Appeals on grades

As a BTEC student, you have a right to appeal against any internally-assessed grade which you feel is unfair. The appeal will normally be dealt with on the basis of whether your work fulfils or does not fulfil the relevant grading criteria. If you are ill, or have personal or family problems which could affect your college work, let your tutor know about these problems as soon as you can.

Checking systems (quality control)

BTEC has systems to ensure that you are graded fairly. These are:

- **internal verification** Experienced assessors within your department or college cross-check the grading of your assignments to make sure that it is fair, and fits the grading criteria. If internal verifiers think a tutor has graded work unfairly, the grades will be changed.
- **external verification** Specialists from outside the college, employed by Edexcel, sample graded work from your college to ensure that work is being both graded and internally verified according to the right standards. If they think something is wrong with the grading at your college, they can then look at a lot more work and reach a decision.

Tutor to students. 'If the external verifier asks you a question, just pretend to be dead!'

Units and points needed to pass National qualifications

	Number of units that learners must complete	Minimum number of units that learners must pass	Minimum number of points needed for an overall pass
BTEC National Award	6 units	6 units	12 points
BTEC National Certificate	12 units	10 units	24 points
BTEC National Diploma	18 units	16 units	36 points

FOCUS

The integrated vocational assignment (IVA)

For Unit 3 Leadership and Unit 4 Citizenship and Contemporary Issues, the work you are assessed on will be set by Edexcel and will take the form of an integrated vocational assignment (IVA). For more information about the IVA, please go to Edexcel's website: www.edexcel.org.uk.

COOL SITE:

http://www.edexcel.org.uk/qualifications/QualificationAward.aspx?id=47163 – see for yourself the full Specifications and all the other official information for BTEC Nationals in Public Services

Accreditation

This means getting credit (or grades) for work you have done before or outside your course, which covers outcomes in the units you are studying. For example, if you had been in the army and had carried out expedition-type exercises, these might give you accreditation for parts of Unit 11 Expedition Skills. But to get accreditation you need to supply valid evidence to your tutors that you really have covered the outcomes. If you think you deserve accreditation for any part of the course, discuss it with your tutors.

Key Skills

Key Skills are not part of your BTEC Nationals, but you may well be gaining Key Skills qualifications alongside your BTEC qualification. The same pieces of work may be used for both qualifications. This means that it is possible to pass your BTEC qualification and fail Key Skills, and it is possible to pass your Key Skills and fail BTEC. It is best to pass both.

Contacting the public services

For nearly all units, you will benefit if you can meet, talk to or listen to people who work in the public services. Your tutors will arrange many visits and visiting speakers. They may also arrange placements and work shadowing.

But it is also possible to contact and get help from the public services yourself, if you do it in the right way. This means:

- phoning or writing to public services to make appointments
- keeping any appointments you make
- planning your approach, and the reasons for asking for help, information, etc.
- thinking carefully about the questions you ask and the information you want
- taking plenty of notes, so you don't forget what you found out
- being polite, interested, and thanking whoever has helped you.

Remember that the public services are busy. Don't waste their time, e.g. by going in lots of small groups when you could all go in one bigger group.

Never forget that:

- good public service contacts increase the chances of landing a job, or getting a good grade
- you are representing yourself and your college – so always try to give the best possible impression.

If you arrange a work placement yourself, check with your tutors that it will not clash with important events on your course, such as residentials or IVA deadlines.

How to get the most out of your course

- Set out with a positive, purposeful attitude, and a determination to succeed.
- Attend all lessons and participate in all course activities.
- Do all your assignments on time.
- Tell tutors if you have any problems (personal, money or study) that might affect your progress on the course.
- Get special help from your college if you think you need it.
- Set out to make friends.
- Work on your health and fitness.
- Develop your communication, study and thinking skills.

You have three aims on the course:

- to pass the course
- to enjoy the course
- to improve your employability.

Good luck with all of these!

Acknowledgements

The author and publishers would like to thank the following for permission to reproduce material.

BBC News Online; Alan Chapman Consultancy; Lancashire Fire and Rescue Service; CompactLaw Ltd, Hertfordshire; National Search and Rescue Dog Association; Citizens' Advice Bureau; Samaritans; Leeds University; West Yorkshire Police; Fire Brigades Union; United Nations; Jane's Information Group; Human Rights Watch; Metropolitan Police; The Maritime and Coastguard Agency; Association of Graduate Careers Advisory Services; Sussex Police; Gloucestershire Police; Hampshire Fire and Rescue Service; Prison Service, Ministry of Defence; Labour Party; Ramblers' Association; Countryside Agency, Cheltenham; Team Technology, Wirral; Arab Press Freedom Watch; British Standards Institution; New Scotland Yard; Institute of Electrical Engineers; Lancashire Combined Fire Authority; Dr Meredith Belbin; TMS Devt International Ltd, York; Top End Sports; DRS Data and Research Services plc, Milton Keynes; The Crime and Disorder Partnership; Victim Support West Yorkshire; Institute of Race Relations; Northern Ireland Office.

Chris Collins/Corbis (p 128), Tim Hawkins/Corbis (p. 197), Bisson Bernard/Corbis Sygma (p. 278), McLeod Murdo/Corbis Sygma (p. 369), Shout/Alamy (p. 141), Scotland/Wild Corel 28 (NT) (p. 222), Corel 120 (NT) (p. 289), Corel 414 (NT) (p. 236), Digital Vision XA (NT) (p. 312), Digital Vision XA (NT) (p. 330), Corel 262 (NT) (p. 57), Corel 170 (NT) (p. 80), Photodisc 31 (NT) (p. 98), Photodisc 67 (NT) (p. 182), David Parker/Science Photo Library (p. 345), Getty/Colin Davey (p. 4), Getty (p.255), Science Photo Library (p. 43), David Hoffman Photo Library (p. 167).

Many people have helped me with the preparation of this book. I would like to thank Carolyn Lee, who started the project off and gave me valuable help and encouragement, and Eve Thould, who continued the process and kept the book on track. I am also grateful to Stephanie Richards and George Moore, who improved the book's organisation and accuracy, and Chris Wortley, who piloted it through its later stages. I received significant help from Keith Courtney and Cris Cullingworth, particularly on boats, navigation and radio communication: special thanks go to them. Above all I should like to thank Loretta – for everything.

Nick Cullingworth

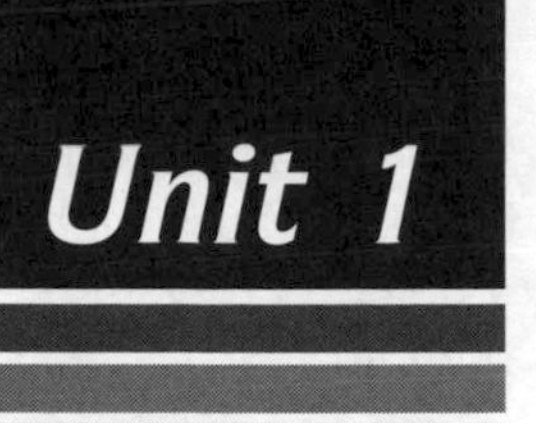

Understanding the Public Sector

Grading criteria

PASSGRADE	Merit	Distinction
To achieve a pass grade the evidence must show that the learner is able to:	To achieve a merit grade the evidence must show that the learner is able to:	To achieve a distinction grade the evidence must show that the learner is able to:
• demonstrate a basic understanding of the development, structure and scale of the public sector 2 • provide a limited explanation of the effects of the internal and external environment on public sector organisations 15 • display an understanding of the effects of socio-cultural and technological changes on a public sector organisation 20 • display an understanding of the effects of political ideology and government economic policy on a public sector organisation 24 • use a limited range of information to reach simple conclusions 27 • demonstrate the use of a range of specialist terminology 27	• demonstrate a sound knowledge of the development, structure and scale of the public sector 2 • provide detailed explanations of the effects of the internal and external environment on public sector organisations 16 • show a detailed understanding of the effects of political ideology and government economic policy on a public sector organisation 23 • show a detailed understanding of the effects of socio-cultural and technological changes on a public sector organisation 25 • use a range of information sources to present and analyse your answers and provide some valid conclusions 27 • communicate fluently, using a wide range of specialist terminology 27	• demonstrate a comprehensive knowledge of the development, structure and scale of the public sector 8 • provide a detailed analysis of the effects of socio-cultural and technological changes on a public sector organisation 20 • provide a detailed evaluation of the effects of the internal and external environment on public sector organisations 23 • provide a detailed analysis of the effects of political ideology and government economic policy on a public sector organisation 26 • use a wide range of sources of information to present and analyse information effectively, reaching well-reasoned conclusions 27

The aim of this unit is to give you the background to our modern public services, and to explain some of the challenges, opportunities and problems they face in the early twenty-first century.

DEVELOPMENT AND STRUCTURE OF THE PUBLIC SECTOR

PASSGRADE

Demonstrate a basic understanding of the development, structure and scale of the public sector.

Merit

Demonstrate a sound knowledge of the development, structure and scale of the public sector.

For these outcomes, you need to:

- explain what the public sector is
- outline its history, growth and recent changes
- describe how the public sector is organised
- show how big the public sector is, and what it costs the taxpayer.

What is the public sector?

There are three sectors in the British economy:

- **The private sector** These are individuals, businesses and organisations which sell goods or services to their customers or clients. They aim to make a profit. They are not owned by the government. Examples include: British Aerospace, McDonalds, the Shahenshah Takeaway, HBOS, Fred's taxis.
- **The public sector** The public sector is all the organisations which are paid for by the government, with money which comes from the taxpayer. These organisations are non-profit-making. Examples include: the police, fire, ambulance and prison services, the armed forces, the NHS, the Civil Service, state schools.
- **The voluntary sector** These are organisations whose workers are mostly unpaid. They include charities and volunteer organisations such as Mountain Rescue. They are paid for by their members or by government grants.

The distinction between public and private sector is not always as clear as it used to be, because many public sector organisations now have partnerships with the private sector, or are organised as 'corporations'.

Development of the public sector

The table below summarises the main stages in the development of Britain's public sector.

The main stages in the development of Britain's public sector

Dates	Public sector development
Stage 1: before 1800	
	Parliament
	Law courts
	A few universities
	The stock market
	Mail deliveries
	Army
	Navy
	Customs
Stage 2: 1800–99	
1806	Dartmoor Prison built
1823	Customs and Excise Board established (to organise Customs and Excise more effectively)
1824	Trade unions started
1829	Metropolitan Police set up
1832	Reform Bill (allowed many more men to vote – but no women)
1833	Liverpool Fire Brigade started
1835	Municipal Corporation Act (set up local government)
1837	Compulsory registration of births, marriages and deaths
1840	Penny Post set up – first national postal service
1841	First full British census (18.5 million people)
1842	Introduction of income tax. First Factory Acts to ensure that people's working conditions began to improve.
1848	Board of Health set up – to improve public health

1853	Compulsory smallpox vaccination
1858	East India Company dissolved (i.e. the British government had to take over the colony)
1863	Start of the London Underground
1871	Legalisation of trade unions
1872	Licensing hours fixed
1880	Compulsory education from 5–10-year-olds
1888	County councils set up (expansion of local government)
1894	Local Government Act setting up local councils
1897	National Insurance begins. London Ambulance Service set up
1899	Board of Education (forerunner of present Ministry of Education) set up

Stage 3: 1900–79

1902	Balfour Education Act – setting up public sector (government-owned) secondary schools
1903	Suffragettes (women campaigning for the right to vote)
1906	Labour Party formed
1907	School medical service set up
1908	Juvenile courts started
1911	MPs paid for the first time
1912	Telephone service nationalised (taken over by the government)
	RAF started (as Royal Flying Corps)
1914–18	World War I – massive development of the armed forces
1916	Compulsory military service introduced
1918	Votes for women over 30
1919	48-hour working week introduced
1921	Railways amalgamated (joined up) into four companies
1922	BBC set up
1928	Votes for all men and women over 21
1929	Abolition of the Poor Law (after this the government started tackling poverty more seriously)
1931	Great Depression – mass unemployment in Britain, Europe and America
1935	Green belts and speed limits set up
1938	The right for all workers to have a paid holiday introduced
1939	Introduction of compulsory military service (National Service)
	Start of World War II – big increase in armed forces
	British Airways nationalised
1941	Rationing of food, clothes, petrol, sugar, soap, etc.
1944	Education Act – secondary education for all children up to 15
1945	United Nations started
1946	Coal mines nationalised
1948	Railways nationalised. National Health Service (NHS) started
	Gas nationalised. Electricity nationalised
1949	British Citizenship Act. British and Commonwealth citizens allowed British passports. Immigration from Caribbean and Indian sub-continent begins.
1956	First nuclear power station at Windscale (now Sellafield)
1959	First motorway (M1)
1960	End of National Service. MOT tests started
1961–9	Eighteen new universities set up
1965	British Airports Authority nationalised
1967	British Steel nationalised
1969	Voting age lowered to 18
1973	Britain joins the Common Market – later called the European Union
	Water authorities nationalised
1975	Equal Pay Act, Sex Discrimination Act
1976	Race Relations Act
1979	British Airways privatised

Stage 4: 1980–2003

1982	Heavier lorries allowed on roads
1984	Miners' Strike. BT privatised
1985	British Airports Authority privatised. British Gas privatised
1986	Greater London Council (GLC) abolished. Water privatised
1987	Electricity privatised
1988	Rover Group privatised
1989	Poll Tax tried in Scotland
1992	Privatisation of the coal industry. First privatised prison
1996	Railtrack privatised

1997	Bank of England freed from government control
2001	Latest British census
2003	Reform of the NHS – allowing more competition

In 1984, police and striking miners faced each other in one of the worst strikes in living memory. The coal industry was later privatised, and the government passed laws limiting the powers of trade unions.

FOCUS

Some definitions

- Nationalisation – the taking over of a private industry or service by the government
- Privatisation – the selling of a nationalised industry to a private buyer

CHECKPOINT ...

What did people do before 1800 if:

- a woman was raped?
- a man was murdered?
- someone's house was on fire?
- the government needed more soldiers?

Stage 1: before 1800 – the beginnings of the public sector

Before 1800 the public sector as we now know it hardly existed. Health and education were paid for by the individual. There were no professional police or fire services.

Stage 2: 1800–99 – a century of development

Reasons:

- The Industrial Revolution caused many people to move to towns and cities to work in factories and mills. Some mill-owners realised that healthy and well-cared for workers made more profit – and so began to provide public services.
- Britain became powerful and rich. The profits of industry were ploughed back into better local government organisation and into public services such as the police and fire brigades.
- Workers organised to improve their own living conditions through Chartist and socialist movements. They wanted better health care and public hygiene.

Stage 3: 1900–79 – the golden age of the public sector

Reasons:

- This was a time of collectivism, i.e. working together. Industries such as steel, coal, water and railways were nationalised because people believed they would make more profit or give a better service if they were in the public sector.
- The first half of the twentieth century saw two World Wars, in which Britain could have been defeated if the nation had not made a huge collective effort. The armed forces developed enormously, along with a powerful government-owned arms industry.
- Mass education meant that there was a big enough educated workforce to staff a National Health Service, a full education service, a huge civil service and a big police force. The public sector provided useful and constructive employment for large numbers of people.
- People thought the government should care for everybody, including the poor, the weak and the old – in what was known as the Welfare State.

Stage 4: 1980–2003 – rethinking the public sector

Reasons:

- The public sector was costing the taxpayer a lot of money, and grew unpopular as a result.
- The government could make huge sums of money by privatising nationalised industries and public services, while at the same time cutting taxes.
- Many politicians believed that people worked harder and better in the private sector, while public sector workers were lazy and complacent.
- Strikes (e.g. the Miners' Strike of 1984) made the government feel that public sector trade unions were getting too powerful. They decided privatisation would restore order and discipline in the workplace.
- Privatisation in America brought low taxes and good public service.
- Public sector workers supported Labour, which the Conservative government of Mrs Thatcher didn't like!
- The Labour government elected in 1997 by a landslide promised the British people that they would not raise taxes. So they had to continue privatising (in part) the NHS and other public sector areas, in order to help keep taxes down.
- The EU discourages nationalisation.

'Get a move on. You're not in the public sector now, you know!'

Structure of the public sector

The public sector has a very complex structure, because:

- it costs billions of pounds each year
- millions of people work in it
- it does a huge number of different jobs.

Large public sector organisations, such as the armed forces, the police, the teaching service and local government are all linked to different government departments – which are called ministries.

> **!** CHECKPOINT ...
> Think of as many public sector bodies as you can. Then, using the internet, find out which government ministry they are responsible to.

Links with local government

Local government, like central government and the public services, is part of the public sector. Most public services have links with local government. The police and fire services are monitored and advised by committees of local citizens, called the Police Authority and the Fire Authority. Most members of these authorities are local councillors, elected by local people to serve them and represent their interests.

Health authorities and primary care trusts get their money from central government. However, like the police and fire service they have local committees which make sure they satisfy the health needs of local people.

> CHECKPOINT ...
> Find who sits on your local police or fire authority. Why do you think those people were chosen?

Examples of links between the public sector and government ministries

Public sector organisation	Ministry in charge
Police	Home Office
Fire service	Office of the Deputy Prime Minister
NHS	Department of Health
Armed forces	Ministry of Defence
Prison service	Home Office

FOCUS

Structure of the NHS

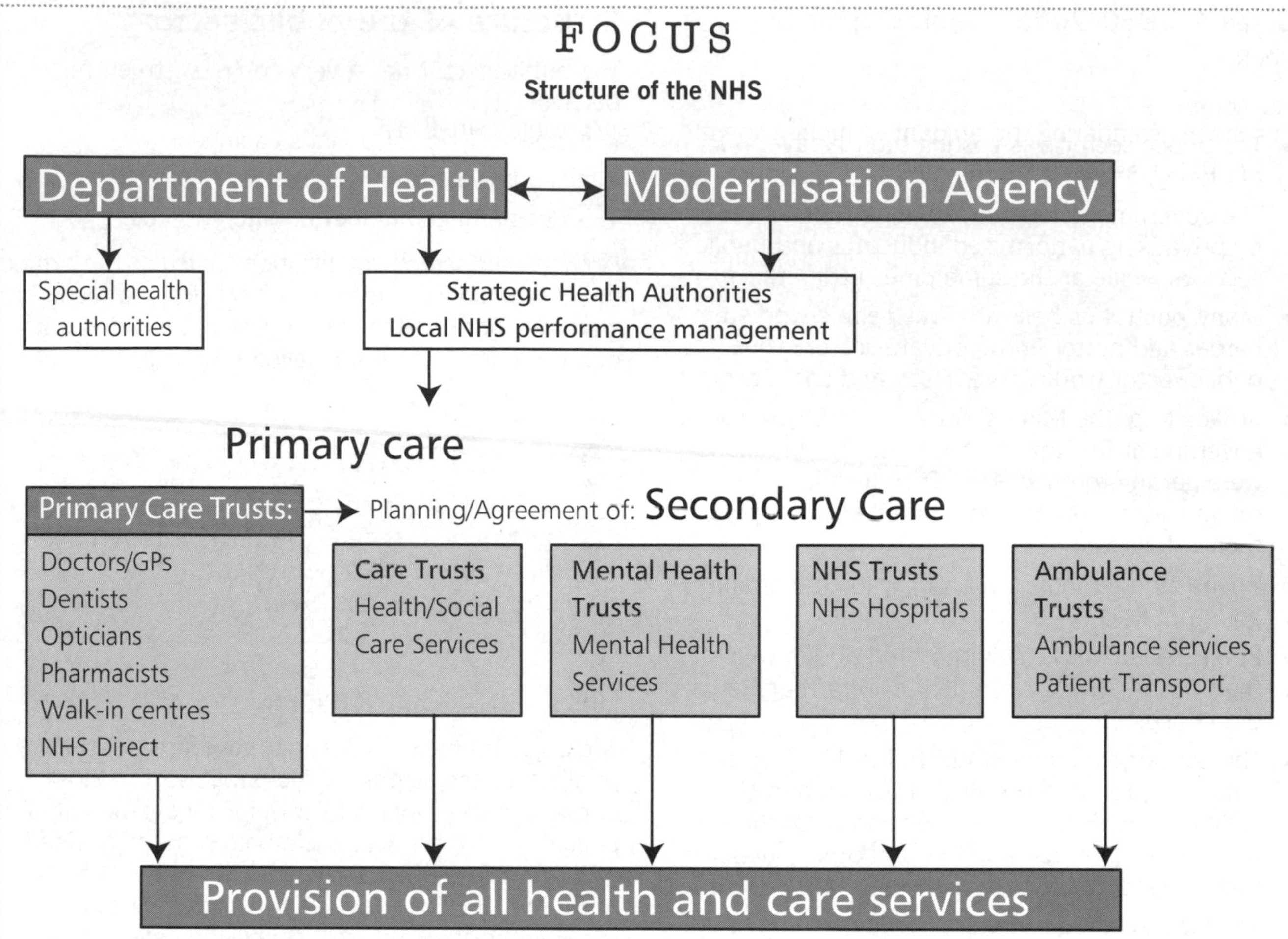

Source: www.nhs.uk

How the NHS works

In this diagram the government is at the top and the patient is at the bottom. Each NHS organisation has its own roles:

- **Department of Health** This government ministry oversees all publicly-funded health care in the UK. Major decisions are made by MPs in Parliament and within the Department of Health. The rest of the work is done by civil servants.
- **Strategic health authorities** oversee the local planning and organisation of health care. There are 28 of them and they are regionally based. They develop the local health services and manage the primary care trusts and NHS trusts in their areas.
- **Primary care trusts** These local organisations are run by local people such as councillors who know the needs of the area. They try to make sure that local primary care – doctors, dentists, etc. – is good enough, and gets enough government money.
- **Secondary care** This is the specialist care carried out by hospitals, which are managed by secondary care trusts
- **NHS Direct** opened in March 1998 and offers fast and free 24-hour advice about personal health care.
- **Ambulance trusts** These organise local ambulance services.

Scale of the public sector

To understand the scale (size) of the public sector it needs to be compared to the country as a whole. This means comparing the amount of money spent by the public sector with the amount of money produced by the country in any one year. This amount of money is called the Gross Domestic Product (GDP). The earnings come from consumer spending, investment and exports.

> **FOCUS**
>
> **GDP**
>
> GDP is the total market value of goods and services produced within a given period after deducting the cost of goods utilised in the process of production.
>
> *Source: New Zealand Institute of Economic Research*

Britain's annual GDP is £1,000,000,000,000 (£1 trillion). It goes up by about 2 per cent each year, and is the fourth biggest in the world.

In 2003–4, £407 billion, less than half of GDP, went to the government.

The amount of money the government intended to spend in 2003–4 was £263,500,000,000 (£263.5 billion). This was the total amount of money available for the public sector.

Key public sector spending figures for 2003–4

Part of public sector	Spending in £billion
Education	58.6
National Health Service	74.9
Local government	40.7
Defence	30.9
Transport	15.4
Housing	5.5
Criminal justice (police and courts)	16.4

Public spending as a proportion of GDP

Although billions of pounds are spent on public services, the proportion of GDP spent on them is surprisingly small.

Trends

Trends are long-term changes in spending, employment or anything else concerned with the way the public sector works.

The government estimates that in the next few years there will be a yearly average growth of spending on the public sector of 5.2 per cent. But remember this is only an estimate: the actual figure will depend on government policies, and the economic progress of the country – and both these can change!

> **CHECKPOINT ...**
>
> Look at the table below showing public sector expenditure as a percentage of GDP. What public sector spending trends does it show?

Employment trends

Spending trends are closely linked to employment trends. This is because the main cost in running the public sector is paying salaries. The more people the public sector employs, the more money it needs.

The diagram at the top of the next page shows how police numbers have fluctuated in recent years. Possible reasons include:

- changes in salaries
- political changes in the value that society and politicians give to law and order
- the need to recruit more women and members of ethnic minority groups into the police.

Public sector expenditure as % of GNP (NB the figures for 2002/3 are estimated.)

	1985–6	1990–1	1995–6	2000–1	2001–2	2002–3
Education	4.6	4.7	4.9	4.6	4.9	5.1
Social services	5.8	6.0	6.8	6.9	7.3	7.8
Health	5.0	5.0	5.6	5.6	6.0	6.3
Transport	1.9	1.7	1.6	0.9	1.1	1.2
Housing	1.1	0.9	0.7	0.3	0.5	0.4
Environment	1.1	1.2	1.2	1.1	1.1	1.2
Law and order	1.8	2.0	2.2	2.1	2.3	2.4
Defence	5.0	3.8	3.0	2.6	2.4	2.4

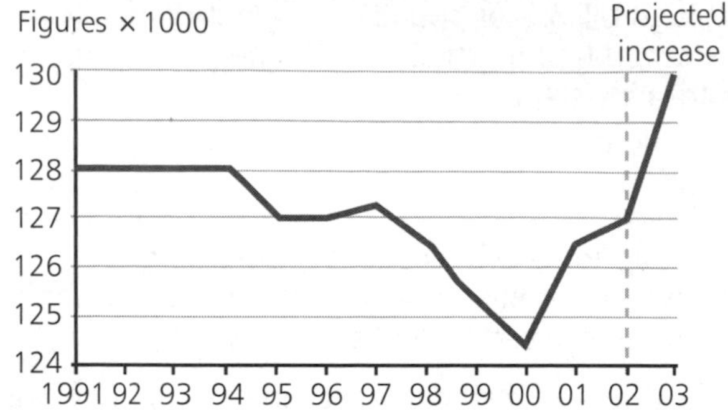

Police employment trends, 1991–2003
Source: Home Office

COOL SITES:

http://www.redbox.gov.uk/Teachers/index.html

http://www.hm-treasury.gov.uk/media – the Treasury – in charge of government spending

http://www.hm-treasury.gov.uk/media//C6E3A/pesa_03_indexed.pdf – annual spending – always use the most recent one!

Distinction

Demonstrate a comprehensive knowledge of the development, structure and scale of the public sector.

For this outcome, you need to show wide knowledge and understanding about:

- how and why the public sector grew up and changed with time
- how the public sector is organised
- how many people work in the public sector and how much it costs to run.

Your knowledge and understanding need to be backed up by accurate, up-to-date and relevant facts.

You will find information on government websites: Home Office, the Office of the Deputy Prime Minister and the Ministry of Defence.

For information on funding you should go to the Treasury website. The table below is an example of the information you will find there.

Total Managed Expenditure by function, 1997–98 to 2002–03

	Cash, £ million				Resources, £ million	
	1997–98 outturn	**1998–99 outturn**	**1999–00 outturn**	**2000–01 outturn**	**2001–02 outturn**	**2002–03 estimated outturn**
Law, order and protective services						
Administration of justice	3,242	3,281	3,393	3,923	4,159	4,614
Prisons and offender programmes	2,535	2,730	2,746	2,649	2,898	3,258
Police	8,677	8,862	9,189	9,692	11,158	12,130
Immigration and citizenship	256	217	797	1,398	1,729	1,801
Fire	1,720	1,799	1,879	1,943	2,086	2,334
Civil defence	28	6	6	6	6	6
Constitutional and community services	114	114	243	90	82	99
Central and miscellaneous services	435	466	513	606	682	707
Total law, order and protective services	17,007	17,475	18,766	20,307	22,800	24,949
Defence						
Defence budget	21,646	22,634	22,717	24,899,	24,098	24,990
Receipts from sale of married quarters	–700					
Total defence	20,946	22,634	22,717	24,899	24,098	24,990
International development assistance and other international services						
International development assistance	1,772	2,042	2,276	2,747	3,198	3,368
Other international services	1,097	1,123	1,154	1,308	1,929	3,164

Source: Public Expenditure Statistical Analyses 2003, page 44, May 2003 (www.hm-treasury.gov.uk/media/81937/pesa_03_652.pdf)

http://www.homeoffice.gov.uk/

http://www.mod.uk/

http://www.odpm.gov.uk/

http://www.hm-treasury.gov.uk/

> **CHECKPOINT ...**
>
> The table above shows that spending on law and order is rising quickly – but not as fast as spending on immigration and citizenship.
>
> Look at the first five rows of figures, and note down as many reasons as you can why government spending in these areas is rising.

Points to consider for this outcome:

- What impact is privatisation having on the public sector?
- What problems do the spending trends pose for the future?

Four aspects of present-day public service development

Partnerships

The public sector is increasingly being expected to work in partnership with both the private and voluntary sector. One example is in local crime and disorder partnerships, where the police and other agencies work together to tackle youth crime. Another example is the cooperation between the prison service and organisations such as Group 4 which transport prisoners and run 'privatised' prisons (though with a good deal of government help and control).

Accountability

The public sector has to be much more accountable than it was in the past. This means it let the public know how much money is being spent on it, and whether they are getting value for money. Public services such as the police have to publish accounts of how they spend their money and what the public get in return.

Targets

Performance targets are used to try to improve the quality, effectiveness and efficiency of public services. They are set by central government, local government or by the public sector organisations themselves.

Competition

The public sector is traditionally made up of monopolies – huge organisations which have no competition. However, since 1990 there has been more and more competition within and between public sector organisations. This is especially the case in the NHS and in education, where governments have aimed to improve efficiency and quality by allowing competition. The NHS 'internal market' system between 1991 and 1999 was designed to make hospitals and doctors' practices compete for patients. The new system of health trusts similarly encourages competition – something which used to only exist in the private sector of competitive businesses.

> **CHECKPOINT ...**
>
> Obtain a copy of your local policing plan, and find examples of their targets. What are:
>
> (a) the advantages and
>
> (b) the disadvantages of setting targets?

More on the structure of the public sector

As we have seen, the public sector consists of

- the government itself (both central and local)
- the Civil Service (which puts government into practice)
- all public services – uniformed and non-uniformed – which are paid for by the taxpayer. (This includes the police, fire and rescue services, Customs and Excise and the armed forces. It also includes health, education, etc.)
- any other public corporations (e.g. your college, unless it is a private, fee-paying institution).

The structure of the public sector can be defined as the way the sector is organised. This can be looked at from four points of view:

(a) the way government itself is organised
(b) the relationships between the government and different bodies in the public sector
(c) the internal structure of different public sector organisations

and

(d) partnerships between different public sector organisations

Together, public sector organisations employ millions of people and carry out a huge range of jobs. For this reason the structures are very complex, and only the main points can be described here.

(a) Organisation of government

This is described in Unit 10: Democratic processes, pages 199–208. The structural features of government which are most relevant to the public services are:

- government in Britain is arranged on democratic lines, the purpose of which is to allow ordinary people to choose the way they are governed
- central government has departments or ministries which oversee the public sector in general, and public services in particular (see page 5)
- local government controls local public services using committees called 'authorities' (see below)
- government spending on public services is controlled by the Treasury (the government department headed by the Chancellor of the Exchequer). Other departments negotiate with the Treasury to get funding (money) for their public services.

(b) Relationships between government and public services

Money
Most of the money that pays for public services comes from the taxpayer. Taxes for central government are collected by the Inland Revenue Service (income tax) and by HM Customs and Excise (VAT, excise duties and customs duties). These taxes go to the Treasury, and are then shared out among the various government departments. Taxes for local government are collected locally as council tax. Council tax is added to Treasury grants and spent on local services.

The amounts of money spent by central government on public services are very large. Examples are given on page 8.

Power
Each of the main public services is attached to a central government department, or ministry. For example the police are attached to the Home Office, the Fire and Rescue service is attached to the Office of the Deputy Prime Minister, Customs and Excise is attached to the Treasury, the NHS is attached to the Department of Health and the armed forces are attached to the Ministry of Defence.

Normally, central government departments do not directly tell the public services what to do. There is a two-way relationship between the departments and the services attached to them. They exchange information and advice, and the government has the last word – but it rarely interferes in the day-to-day running of public services. This is to avoid accusations of political bias and control, which would undermine the respect of many ordinary people for the public services – and for the government. Most police officers would not want to think that they were running a 'police state'!

Local government operates tighter controls on local public services. It does this through the use of committees called 'authorities' (e.g. police and fire authorities). Most police authorities are made up of 17 members: 3 magistrates, 9 local councillors and 5 independent members. Their job is to:

- appoint the Chief Constable
- consult local people about the kind of local policing they want
- publish reports, plans and targets for local policing
- set a budget for local policing, stating how the money should be spent
- monitor the performance of their police force
- deal with some discipline and complaint problems

Fire authorities and health authorities are organised in much the same way, and have similar roles in supporting local fire and ambulance services.

Customs and Excise, and the armed forces do not have this type of local control. This is because much of their work is confidential or secret, and they do not serve local people in the way that the police, fire or ambulance services do.

http://www.apa.police.uk/apa_home.htm

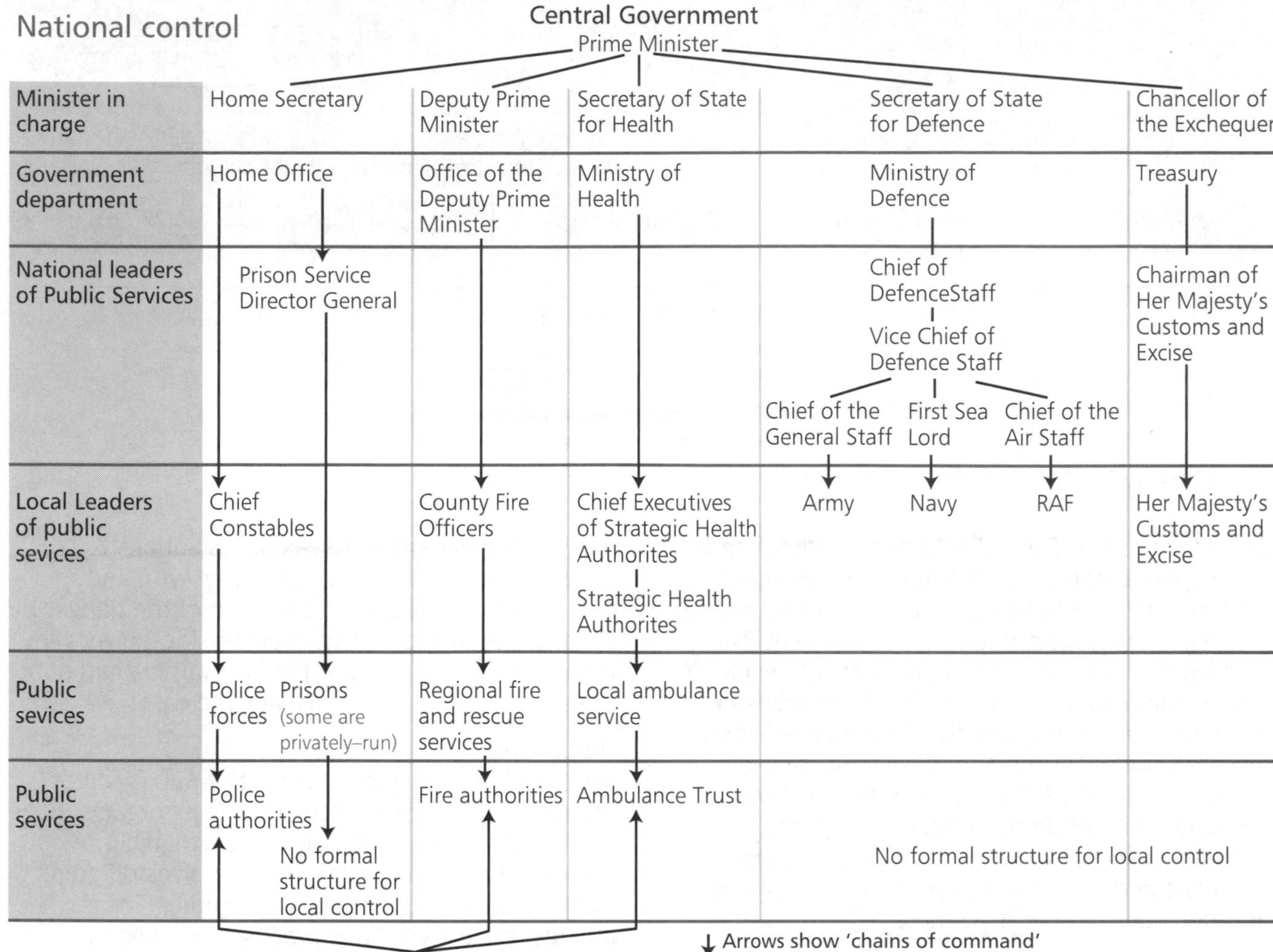

Local Government and Local People
(There may be changes when or if the new regional assesemlies are brought in.)

Local control

↓ Arrows show 'chains of command'

Most of the money spent on the police and fire services comes from locally–elected councillors; decide how the money is spent. Ambulance trusts are funded through the NHS, which gets mone from both central and local government

The relationship between government and the public services

(c) Internal organisation of public sector organisations

Regional organisation

The main civilian public sector organisations are divided into regional or local bodies. For example, in England and Wales there are 43 regional police forces (e.g. Avon and Somerset Police) and five 'non-geographic' forces:

- British Transport Police
- Ministry of Defence Police
- UK Atomic Energy Constabulary
- Port of Dover Police
- The National Crime Squad

There are 48 public sector fire and rescue services in England and Wales and – in England alone – there are 33 ambulance trusts.

The aim of having a regional organisation is to make these services accessible to the public, and responsive to local needs.

Within each region

Each regional civilian public service has a complex organisational structure. The structure (sometimes described as a matrix) is based on two principles:

- specialisation of work
- seniority of employee

The extract on the following page from the organisation chart of Avon and Somerset Police shows these two principles in operation. A high-ranking officer, the Assistant Chief Constable, is in charge of 'Specialist Operations'. Part of these specialist operations come under the control of a Detective Chief Superintendent who has the title of 'Crime Manager'. Directly responsible to the Crime

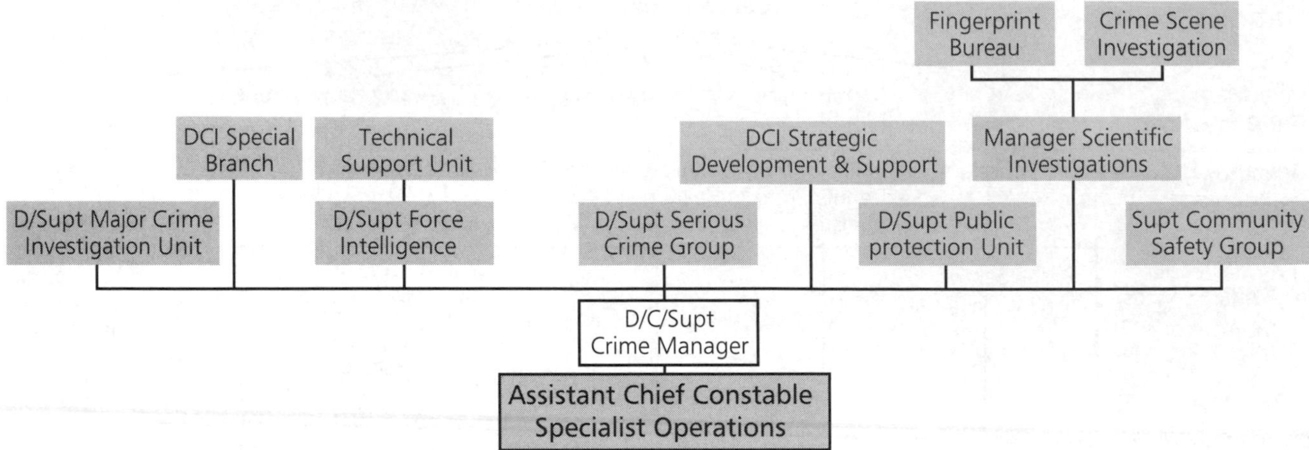

Extract from the organisation chart of Avon and Somerset Police

Manager are four Detective Superintendents and one Superintendent. Each of these officers does work of a managerial type and rank, but specialises in a particular aspect of crime management. The next layer of the organisation consists of people of slightly lower rank: Detective Chief Inspectors or the equivalent. An example is the 'Manager Scientific Investigations'. This person is in charge of two teams: the Fingerprint Bureau and Crime Scene Investigation. Within these teams sergeants, constables and civilian experts such as forensic scientists and technicians work on the investigation and detection of specific crimes.

In this part of the organisational structure there is a hierarchical organisation (people or teams ranked in order of status – and pay) but also a specialisation in a particular kind of work: the investigation of crime. None of the people in this part of the organisation patrols a beat or handles dogs.

The complexity of public service work means that there are many structures like this within the overall structure of a regional public service. The advantages of such structures are:

- they enable people to specialise in the work they do best
- they provide encouragement for people lower down the structure to work hard and seek promotion
- they make it clear who is managing whom, and who has responsibility for different aspects of the organisation's work
- they enable communication to pass up and down the chains of command.

The disadvantage of such a structure is that it is traditional and can lead to authoritarian styles of management, which make it difficult for people to use their imagination or seek new solutions to old problems. However, in this example Avon and Somerset Police show a recognition of the danger by placing their management 'tree' upside-down, with the most senior person at the bottom, instead of at the top of the chart as is usually the case!

Partnerships

An increasingly important aspect of public sector organisation, which particularly affects organisations such as the police, is that of the partnership. A partnership is any system which involves different public services working closely together. The emergency services have practised working in partnership for many years – for example in their joint response to serious road traffic accidents. Many more partnerships involving the police have sprung up following the Crime and Disorder Act of 1998. These multi-agency partnerships, involving the police, schools, probation officers and local authorities, work together to combat the 'low-level' crime – often by young people – which is becoming such a problem in some areas. A new kind of partnership which is planned for dealing with organised crime is the Serious Organised Crime Agency. This 'will bring together world-class experts including hi-tech and financial specialists and those with criminal intelligence and investigative skills. It will exploit hi-tech 21st century technology to uncover the new wave of crime bosses whose lucrative illegal enterprises range from drug trafficking and people smuggling through to fraud and money laundering' (Home Office). Partnerships are proving to be an effective way of tackling difficult problems, such as crime, from a number of angles. Their drawback is that they are time-consuming to operate, require special training – and it may not always be clear who is responsible for what. (See more on page 351.)

FOCUS

Rank Structures (civilian)

Police	Fire Service
Police Constable	Fire-fighter
Sergeant	Leading fire-fighter
Inspector	Sub-officer
Chief Inspector	Station Officer
Superintendent	Assistant Divisional Officer
Chief Superintendent	Divisional Officer
Assistant Chief Constable	Senior Divisional Officer
Deputy Chief Constable	Assistant County Fire Officer
Chief Constable	County Fire Officer

Armed forces structures

The armed forces' organisational structures are based on

- specialisation of work
- groups of people of manageable size
- rank.

Specialisation

Because armies have to be self-sufficient they need specialists in every conceivable kind of work needed for survival in a hostile environment. Transport, artillery, communications, infantry, catering – all are essential in the armed forces. These specialised jobs are carried out by 'corps' – 'bodies of people' – who have special training.

Groups of manageable size

As with civilian public services, teamwork and obeying orders is vital in the armed forces. People are grouped in the armed forces so that they can obey orders and work effectively together. Different sizes of groups are needed for different tasks, and this is reflected in the way people are grouped in the army. The groupings, together with rough numbers, are given in the table below:

Name of grouping	Approximate number of people
Platoon or troop	90
Company or squadron	200
Battalion or regiment	600
Brigade	1800
Division	5400

The central grouping is the regiment. Regiments are groups of soldiers recruited from a geographical area (for example the Duke of Wellington's Regiment recruits from West Yorkshire) and have a long history. They are important in building morale and giving soldiers and their officers a sense of belonging to a caring and well-established organisation.

Rank

The armed forces have a rank system sometimes called the 'chain of command'. This resembles the system used in the police and fire service, except that the names are (on the whole) different.

There is a two-tier system in the armed forces – 'officers' and 'the ranks'. Army ranks are shown below:

FOCUS

Rank Structure – the Army

Officers	Soldiers
Brigadier	Warrant Officer I
Colonel	Warrant Officer II
Lieutenant Colonel	Staff Sergeant
Major	Sergeant
Captain	Corporal
Lieutenant	Lance Corporal
	Private

The job of officers is a managerial one – motivating the troops, organising their work, and giving commands.

The job of soldiers is essentially an operative job – 'doing the work' – though all except privates have to give orders and command those of lower rank. Soldiers who can give orders are sometimes called 'non-commissioned officers'.

CHECKPOINT ...

Research the ranks in the RAF and the Royal Navy.

Scope and role of public services

Scope

The scope of a public service is the extent of its powers and the range of work that it does. Partly this is to do with the physical area in which the public service works. The armed forces, for example, can operate anywhere in the world, but the Greater Manchester Police can normally only operate in Greater Manchester. This gives the armed forces a wider scope – in this sense. On the other hand the Greater Manchester Police do a vast range of crime prevention and detection which the army can never hope to do, even if on a 'policing' mission of the type carried out in southern Iraq in 2003/4. So in this limited sense the police have more scope than the army.

Taking a general view, it could be said that of the armed forces, the army has the widest scope, because of the range of tasks it has to perform. Of the civilian public services, the police have the widest scope – again because of the varied and far-reaching nature of their work.

The scope of a public service is reflected in the number of people it employs, and the amount it costs the government to run it. Here are a few relevant figures:

Public service	Number of employees	Annual cost (2003)
Armed forces	304,000	£25.0 billion
Police	199,237	£12.1 billion
Fire	50,000	£2.3 billion
Prison Service	43,800	£3.2 billion

For example the police service is bigger than the fire service, employs more people, and does more varied work. This is why it costs so much more!

Role

The role of a public service is the work it does (see more about this in Unit 8, page 156).

The roles of public services change over time. Preventive roles are becoming much more important than they used to be – mainly because they are more cost effective. Crime and fire prevention are growth areas of the police and fire service respectively. Peacekeeping – which can be seen as 'war-prevention' – is a more important role of the armed forces than it ever used to be.

Roles also change with changing public perceptions of society's needs. Fifty years ago, the police were extremely reluctant to involve themselves in any kind of 'domestic' crime – e.g. spouse or child abuse.

The table on the opposite page outlines the main roles of the main public services.

FOCUS

Role of the Royal Navy

1 Contribute to the security of the UK and its citizens world-wide in peacetime, including providing military aid to civil authorities.

2 Contribute to the internal and external security of the UK's Overseas Territories, e.g. Bermuda, Gibraltar and the Falklands.

3 Participate in the Defence Diplomacy initiative through the building of international trust.

4 Support British interests, influence and standing abroad extending to the support of defence exports.

5 Participate in Peace Support and Humanitarian Operations.

6 Provide forces required to counter a strategic attack on NATO.

7 Maintain capability to mount a response to a regional conflict outside NATO which could adversely affect European Security or UK interests.

8 Provide forces needed to respond to a regional conflict inside NATO where an Ally calls for assistance under Article 5 of the Washington Treaty.

http://www.royal-navy.mod.uk/static/pages/168.html

CHECKPOINT ...

Read the FOCUS on the role of the Royal Navy. Then consider these questions:

(a) Give examples of the way the Royal Navy can help the civil authorities in peacetime.

(b) What was the role of the Royal Navy in the Falklands Islands conflict in 1982?

The roles of the main public services

Service	Roles
Central Government	To enable the country to become secure and wealthy To collect taxation and spend the money to provide maximum benefit to as many people as possible To improve both standard of living and quality of life for everybody To provide high quality public services for all who need them
Local Government	To support and protect everybody living in a local area To provide good local public services at the lowest possible cost
Police	To make places safer To cut crime and the fear of crime To uphold the law
Fire and Rescue Service	To promote fire safety and provide a highly responsive, caring and efficient fire and rescue service.
Ambulance Service	To give high quality patient care in emergencies, and transport people to hospital
Customs and Excise	To collect VAT, other taxes and customs duties. To protect society from illegal imports of drugs, alcohol, tobacco and prohibited goods To help combat other forms of organised international crime
Prison Service	To keep people in custody when sent there by the courts. To look after them with humanity and help them lead law-abiding and useful lives in custody and after release.
Army	To protect the security of the UK To protect the interests of Britain and its close allies To carry out peacekeeping missions To give humanitarian aid
Royal Navy	As with the army – but see the FOCUS below
RAF	To generate air power to meet the Defence Mission.

(c) In what ways can the Royal Navy build 'international trust'?
(d) What is NATO and what is its purpose?
(e) Name ten countries which are allies of Britain, and five countries which are not allies. In the case of the five which are not allies, explain why they are not allies.

INTERNAL AND EXTERNAL ENVIRONMENTS

Provide a limited explanation of the effects of the internal and external environment on public sector organisations.

For this outcome, you need to give basic explanations on how public sector organisations are influenced by:

- the nature of the organisation itself
- pressures acting on it from outside, e.g. political and economic pressures.

Internal environment

The internal environment is the **structure** and **culture** of an organisation.

Structure

The structure of an organisation is the way that an organisation is divided up, and the way power and responsibility are used within it. The structure can normally be found in the form of a diagram (see the organisational structure of the NHS in England and Wales on page 6).

Culture

The culture of an organisation is the way people who belong to it think and behave. It consists of **norms** (accepted ways of behaving) and **values** (accepted ways of thinking).

Organisational culture is often difficult to pin down, since people are not always aware of what they are thinking or how they behave. For example, an organisation may be racist, but the people who work in that organisation may not know it. After the murder of Stephen Lawrence the Metropolitan Police were accused of 'institutionalised racism' in the Macpherson Report of 1999, but most officers in the Metropolitan Police believed that they were not racist.

FOCUS

Definitions of organisational culture

Organisational culture is ...

'the way we do things around here' – Sackman, 1991

'An organizational culture is the environment of beliefs, customs, knowledge, practices, and conventionalized behavior of a particular social group' – Cleland, 1994

'... commonly held and relatively stable beliefs, attitudes and values that exist within an organisation' – Baron and Walters, 1994

Source: quoted from Gray, R. (1998), Organisational Culture: A Review of the Literature, Anglia Business School

External environment

The external environment is all those factors which influence the organisation from the outside. It includes:

- people, including other organisations:
  - the media
  - politicians
  - central and local government
  - governments of other countries (either friendly or hostile)
  - monopoly provision, i.e. whether there is competition from other organisations or not
  - customers or users of the organisation
  - the general public
- money – economic conditions, funding, costs, salary levels, etc.
- other outside influences:
  - transport infrastructure
  - nature of area served – e.g. inner city, rural area, etc.

www.nelsonthornes.com – Unit 13 Media and the Public Services – lots more on media pressure

Different public sector organisations are affected by their internal and external environments in different ways. The recent firefighters' strikes (2002–3) provide an interesting case study on the effects on a public service organisation of the internal and external environment at a particular time. The table at the top of the next page outlines these environments and their effects.

Merit

Provide detailed explanations of the effects of the internal and external environment on public sector organisations.

For this outcome, you need to build on the previous outcome by:

- providing more information
- giving more, or more complex, reasons behind the effects of internal and external influences on organisations
- stating clearly what the 'effects' can be.

If we look at public sector organisations in general, here are some of the explanations which could be made of the effects of internal and external environments.

Internal and external influences on the fire service, 2002–3

Internal environment	External environment
• Firefighters follow a traditional system of working, using teams called 'watches'. *Effect:* They have high levels of loyalty, but can be inward-looking. • Firefighters work long shifts (sometimes 15 hours at a stretch). *Effect:* They can work four days on and four days off, and even take on part-time jobs outside working hours. But it is hard for firefighters' families. • Firefighters have a strong union – the Fire Brigades Union. *Effect:* They can go on strike, unlike the police who have no union and are banned from striking. • Firefighters are not racist or sexist, but over 95 per cent are white males. *Effect:* There are few ethnic minority or female applicants.	• Over the years firefighters suffered a steady decrease in pay compared with people in other emergency services, and with male workers as a whole. *Effect:* Firefighters decided to strike for more pay. • The fire service has a monopoly of fire-fighting work – no competition. *Effect:* Firefighters felt able to strike because there was no one to take over their work on a permanent basis. • Sir George Bain wrote an independent report on the fire service (2002) recommending that the organisation needed modernising if firefighters were to get more pay. *Effect:* The government decided to modernise fire service working practices. *Effect:* Firefighters didn't like this, and decided to strike.

Internal environment: structure and culture

Structure

The effects of structure on public sector organisations

Feature	Effects
Rank structure	This provides a clear 'chain of command' for passing instructions down an organisation to the 'front line'. The rank structure also enables feedback to be passed back up the chain of command, so that those who are in charge know whether their policies are working or not. On the basis of this feedback, the organisation can, if necessary, change its priorities or methods. A further advantage of a rank structure is that it provides a career path for new, ambitious recruits. It encourages good people, who have been trained at great expense, to stay in the service and try for promotion.
Functional and division structures	Many public sector organisations, e.g. hospitals, have a **functional structure**. This means that teams and sections specialise in particular jobs and functions, e.g. surgery, orthopaedics, sexually transmitted diseases. Advantages of functional structures: • enable specialisation • a clear chain of command • easy for the public to understand

Disadvantages of functional structures:

- can lead to smugness and lack of competition
- sometimes less aware of the consumer (i.e. the public)

Other organisations, such as the fire service, have **divisional structures**. In this kind of organisation each team can do many different jobs or functions.

Advantages of divisional structures:

- encourage competition and excellence
- may be better team spirit
- more aware of the public

Disadvantage of divisional structures:

- harder to manage

Divisional structures tend to be seen as more modern and forward-looking than functional structures.

Culture

The effects of culture on public service organisations

Feature	Effects
Morale	This can be defined as 'a strong sense of enthusiasm and dedication to a shared goal that unifies a group'. Morale is often used in relation to the armed forces. If the morale of an army is good, it can fight much more effectively, and will not easily give way under pressure. Good morale in the civilian public sector leads to efficiency, good relations with the public, good relationships between staff, high success rates (e.g. in solving crimes and meeting targets), good staff retention, low rates of absenteeism and stress, and high job satisfaction. Low morale leads to poor work, low productivity, low job satisfaction, poor relations with the public and with workmates, high staff turnover, high absenteeism and stress rates, racism, sexism, bullying, 'skiving', faking or missing targets, sabotage of an organisation, strikes, etc.

Determinants of culture

You can see from the above that the culture of an organisation can be either good or bad – both for the organisation and for the individuals working in it. Experts believe that the culture of an organisation can be improved by changing the determinants, i.e. the factors which create or influence a culture.

Determinants of public sector organisational cultures include:

- strategy: the long term planning and development of the organisation
- structure: if the organisation rewards merit through promotion, this motivates employees to work harder and more effectively
- teamwork: the way people are encouraged to work together to achieve agreed aims
- leadership: good leadership, which respects diversity, sets appropriate goals and instils enthusiasm and discipline is good for the organisational culture
- ethos: this is the 'spirit', 'atmosphere' or 'traditions' of an organisation.

CHECKPOINT ...

Culture consists of norms and values.

1 Choose a group which you belong to (it may be your class, a team, a group of workmates or a public service you work for) and list all the norms and values of that group.

2 Distinguish between the organisation's official norms, and the informal norms which may be at odds with those of the organisation.
3 Suggest determinants which would 'improve' the culture of your chosen group.

External environment

The effects of the external environment on public sector organisations

Feature	Effects
Local government committees such as police and fire authorities	• Give local people a say in how the public sector is run. • Set funding for the local services they control. Where the funding comes from, and how it is allocated, is shown in the FOCUS below.
National government	• Sets standards and targets to try to make public sector organisations more effective. • Acts as a forum for new ideas, collecting and disseminating information. • Expresses the views of the public about public sector organisations. • Controls funding, giving more money where there is greater need (or where the public wants it to go). • Criticises errors or poor policy-making in public sector.
European Union	• Tries to standardise the public sector and public services in all member countries, while allowing a degree of independence for each country (called 'subsidiarity'). • Develops communication and cooperation between the public sectors of member states. • Tries to ensure that the public sectors of member states observe human rights, give value for money and care for the environment. • Works to achieve a shared level of security in all member states – especially in issues linked to asylum, immigration, cross-border crime and terrorism.
Key stakeholders	Stakeholders are people or organisations who put money or effort into a project, and therefore have a stake, or interest, in the success of the project. In a partnership, all members are stakeholders. The system of stakeholders breaks down the boundaries between the public and private sectors. An example is seen in local Crime and Disorder Partnerships, which were set up under the 1998 Crime and Disorder Act to fight youth crime. See page 350.

FOCUS

Surrey Police budget for 2003–4

'Who sets the budget?
The budget is drawn up by the chief constable working with officers from the police force and Surrey Police Authority. The members of the police authority agree the budget at a public meeting – it is one of their main responsibilities.

Who are the members of the police authority?
Surrey Police Authority has 17 members:

- nine county councillors
- three magistrates
- five independent members.

Where does the money come from?
Police authorities are funded partly by central government grants and partly through the local government finance system – revenue support grant, business rates and council tax. Last year council tax made up about 35 per cent of Surrey Police's funding.

Surrey Police Authority has set a budget for 2003/4 based on expenditure of £154.2 million. Most of this, almost 70%, is spent on the people who provide policing services – their salaries, training and other costs. This year Surrey Police will employ 1,928 police officers, 1,404 civilians and 241 specials. Some 90% of officers will be employed on front line duties – one of the highest rates of any police force.

This means the cost per person for policing services in Surrey is £146.70 – about 40p a day.

Where this money comes from
Council Tax £60.26
Police Grant £50.92
National business rates £14.27
Revenue Support Grant £15.40
Special grants £5.85'

Source: Surrey Police Authority website www.surreypa.gov.uk

Distinction

Provide a detailed evaluation of the effects of the internal and external environment on public sector organisations.

For this outcome, you need to build on the previous two by drawing conclusions, and reaching reasoned judgements about which effects are good, and which may be harmful, both for the public sector organisations and for their users.

'Evaluation' means:

- explaining the good and bad points of an idea, system, scheme or action
- saying who gains and who loses from this idea, etc.
- looking at implications (hidden or long-term effects, benefits or drawbacks)
- giving convincing reasons and explanations for what you think
- giving relevant and accurate examples from two or more public sector organisations
- reaching an overall conclusion (if you can) about the value or usefulness of whatever you are discussing (in this case 'the effects of the internal and external environment on public sector organisations').

'Detailed' means:

- giving as much information as you reasonably can
- showing the sort of in-depth understanding that might be expected of a new recruit to a public service.

Detail is not the same thing as length. Flannelling and waffling are not as good as being clear, concise and relevant!

EFFECTS OF POLITICAL AND ECONOMIC POLICY

PASSGRADE

Display an understanding of the effects of political ideology and government economic policy on a public sector organisation.

For this outcome, you need to explain the effects of the government's political ideas, and economic pressures (the amount of money allowed by the government) on one particular public sector organisation.

FOCUS

Definitions of ideology

Ideology is ...

'a coherent set of beliefs that characterises the thinking of a group or nation.'

'the ideas and values of the ruling class' – Marxist definition

British political parties, such as Labour or the Conservative Party, have systems of ideas and beliefs which are called ideology. Ideology is linked to policy – the plans for putting ideology into practice.

Policy and ideological differences affecting the public sector – Labour and Conservative

Labour Party policy and ideology	Conservative Party policy and ideology
Policy (2001)	**Policy (2003)**
Improving basic skills	Reward quality schools
More investment in transport	More private/independent schools
Raise minimum wage	Longer sentences for young offenders
Recruit more teachers	Compulsory treatment for drug addicts
Expand the health service	More police on the beat
Reduce unemployment	Encourage personal saving
Neighbourhood renewal	Sell council houses
Tackling crime, especially drugs	Less government control over NHS
Help for the poor and for pensioners	More freedom for schools
Tackle global warming	Scrap AS levels
Ideology	**Ideology**
Active government	Minimal government
Free state education	Fee-paying private education
Free health care	Health privatisation is OK
Public services kept in public sector	Some public services should be privatised
Benefits for the poor	Poor people must work
In favour of diversity	Mistrustful of diversity
Distrustful of privatisation, likes public ownership	In favour of privatisation, dislikes public ownership
Pro-European; distrustful of USA	Pro-USA; distrustful of Europe
Tendency towards pacifism and internationalism	Tendency towards nationalism; less pacifist
Anti-racist	Non-racist
Environmentalist – anti-nuclear, anti-'blood sports'	Country-loving but not environmentalist – pro-nuclear, pro-'field sports'
Town-based and biased towards public sector	Strongest support in the country, in the private sector, and in banking
Traditionally on the side of workers and poor people	Traditionally on the side of landowners, factory-owners and the rich
Believes in government control	Believes in 'free enterprise'
Traditionally linked to socialism	Traditionally linked to capitalism

The post-war consensus and the New Right

Under the so-called 'post-war consensus' which lasted from 1945 up to the late 1970s, the idea that there should be a large public sector was generally accepted. This was therefore a period of growth and development in the public sector.

But public ownership was questioned after the Conservatives came to power in 1979, and there was an ideological shift towards private ownership, even of organisations such as prisons and hospitals. The post-war British idea of the Welfare State, and of the government looking after people 'from the cradle to the grave' was replaced by American ideas of running public services as competitive businesses, to save taxpayers' money and to get a better, more efficient service.

Ideology is not as clear-cut in the UK as it is in some other countries, and in practice is more a set of underlying feelings in politicians and party members, rather than a rigid system of beliefs.

Effects of ideology on a public sector organisation

Every public sector organisation has been deeply affected by ideology in recent years. Examples (which you could research in more detail) include:

- the privatisation of the coal industry in 1994
- the privatisation of public utilities – water, electricity, gas and telephones – in the 1980s
- the privatisation of prisons
- the effect of Labour's idea of 'joined up government' on crime and disorder partnerships
- ideological arguments underlying the Iraq War 2003
- recruitment problems in the fire service, relating to women and people from ethnic minorities
- response of police forces to the Macpherson Report of 1999, and accusations of 'institutionalised racism'.

Economic policy

Economic policy can be defined as the plans and ideas of the government, with regard to the creation and distribution of wealth.

The main players in deciding British economic policy are two big government departments:

- the Department of Trade and Industry, which is the ministry responsible for creating wealth
- the Treasury, which has overall control over spending.

The government gets money by taxing individuals (through income tax and National Insurance), goods (through VAT and excise duties), services (also through VAT) and industries (through Corporation tax, etc.).

Spending on public services is the responsibility of ministries such as:

- the Home Office
- the Ministry of Defence
- the Department of Health
- the Office of the Deputy Prime Minister.

These ministries try to get as much money as possible for the public services under their control, and also try to control how the public services spend the money they get.

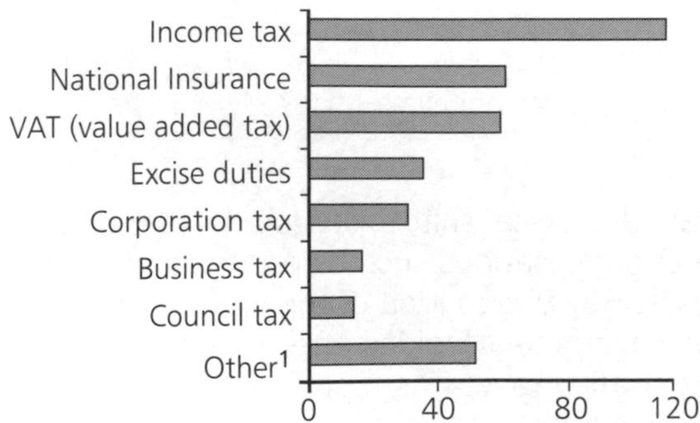

[1] Includes capital taxes, stamp duties, vehicle excise duties and some other tax and non-tax receipts (such as interest and dividends).

Projections of UK government receipts 2002–3
Source: HM Treasury, Budget 2002

Profile

Effects of political ideology and government economic policy on the prison service

- **The opening of privatised prisons**
  In 1992, under a Conservative government the first privatised prison, the Wolds, in East Yorkshire, was opened. It was run by the security company, Group 4.
- **Worse pay and conditions for some prison officers**
  According to *Prison Privatisation Report International*, 'Wages and benefits for most staff in private prisons in England and Wales lag behind their public sector counterparts. Starting pay for operational support grades and prison officers in the private sector is around 15 per cent and 22 per cent less than the public sector and ... average pay for prison officers and senior officers is over 50 per cent less than the public sector.'
- **Prison disturbances**
  In Scotland there have been higher rates of disturbances and prison deaths at privately-run prisons. The Member of the Scottish Parliament, Roseanna Cunningham said in 2002: 'There have been 26 fires at Kilmarnock in the last year, compared with 41 across the rest of the prison estate (16 prisons) and 5 deaths compared with a total of 16 at all other Scottish Prison Service prisons (12 prisons).'

- **Prison profits**
  Despite the fires, Kilmarnock prison made a profit of £1 million in two years.
- **Cheapness**
  It costs £24,000 a year to keep a prisoner in a prison service gaol. Private prisons are 10 per cent cheaper.
- On average, prisoners at private prisons spend more time out of cell, and do more purposeful activity.

COOL SITE:

www.nelsonthornes.com/vocational/public_services – Unit 23 Custodial Care

Merit

Show a detailed understanding of the effects of political ideology and government economic policy on a public sector organisation.

Distinction

Provide a detailed analysis of the effects of political ideology and government economic policy on a public sector organisation.

For these outcomes, you need to develop the explanations and arguments used for the passgrade.

To meet these objectives you need:

- detailed information about one public sector organisation, and the ways in which it is trying to save money, make money or become more accountable
- explanations – preferably given by the organisation you are researching – on how much money it is saving, and why it is saving it
- explanations on how the organisation you are researching ensures that it is accountable. For example does it publish financial reports or audits of its activities? Is it clear how much money it gets, and how it spends it?
- your own reasoned opinions about the advantages and disadvantages (there are some!) of saving money and of having greater accountability.

The last point is essential if you are aiming for a distinction grade!

! CHECKPOINT ...

Your college is a public sector organisation.

1 Make a survey of all the charges it makes to students. These have all been brought in because of government economic policy: the need to save money in the public sector. Comment on:
   (a) how much of the college's budget is covered by these various charges or ways of making money
   (b) how much the college's service to the community or its users is undermined by the need to make these charges.
2 Find out about limits to class sizes in various parts of your college. Make notes on how these limits affect the college's spending. Then comment on the advantages and disadvantages of these class size limits.

Merit and demerit goods

Merit goods are products and services which are generally agreed to benefit the population. They include things like education, health care, good sewerage, clean water, electricity and good public transport. These are all goods which before 1980 were provided by the government, through the public sector.

Demerit goods are products and services which people want, but which are not considered to be good for them. These include things like fast food, sweets, cigarettes, alcoholic drinks, recreational drugs and private transport.

Though merit goods are now provided by the private sector, for example privatised water companies, the government recognises their social, economic and moral importance, and takes steps to ensure that they are of adequate quality. It does this partly through its own inspections, and partly through independent organisations called regulators. Examples of regulators are Ofsted (the Office of Standards in Education) and Ofwat (the Office of Water Services), which checks that water companies are producing clean water at a fair price – and caring for the environment. Environmental health inspectors, employed by local authorities, and the Health and Safety Executive are public services which also have a vital role to play in keeping up the quality of merit goods.

Demerit goods have always been provided by the private sector. The government regulates them with semi-independent organisations ('quangos') such as the Food Standards Agency and the Office of Fair Trading.

Since demerit goods such as tobacco and alcohol are bad for health, they provide extra work for the public sector, especially the National Health Service. They are also taxed through excise duty levied by HM Customs and Excise. Illegal demerit goods such as recreational drugs and pornography make extra work for the police, Customs and Excise and the courts. In this sense, demerit goods are costing the country money and undermining the economy.

SOCIO-CULTURAL AND TECHNOLOGICAL CHANGES

Display an understanding of the effects of socio-cultural and technological changes on a public sector organisation.

For this outcome, you need to research and explain the effects of two kinds of changes on one public sector organisation:

- changes in society, e.g. changes in people, and the way they think and behave
- changes in technology which affect the way the public sector organisation does its job.

Profile: Effects of socio-cultural and technological changes on the police

Changes	Effects on the police
Demographic changes These are changes in population. They include:	
• changes in overall population of the country, from about 57 million in 1991 to 59 million in 2001	• Little obvious short-term effect
• changes in the social class of people living in certain areas. For example, most C2 people who would have been living in the inner cities in the 1950s now live in suburbs of the main towns.	• Changed crime patterns in these areas will change police patrolling systems
• changes in the average age of the population	• More government money spent on pensions and in caring for older people – so perhaps less funding available for the police
• changes in ethnicity, either of regions or of the whole country. These changes have been fast in some inner-city areas, but are slow in the country as a whole. The percentage of people from ethnic minorities living in Britain went up from 7 per cent to 9 per cent between 1991 and 2001.	• Some changes in crime patterns. The police need to recruit more ethnic minority staff

Societal pressures These are the expectations that people have of their public services. They include things like:	
• increased levels of public dissatisfaction with the police	• Policing methods changed in line with public wishes
• expecting the police to deal with domestic incidents, which they used to consider as 'family matters' and none of their concern.	• The police have had to develop this work, and form partnerships with social work departments of local authorities
• unhappiness at the low numbers of ethnic minority employees in some public services	• Changing recruitment methods; building links with local communities
• public concern about asylum seekers, illegal immigrants or the threat of terrorism	• Finding ways of handling the problem which respect human rights and international obligations, yet also allay people's worries
• fears linked to racism or religious discrimination.	• Sensitive policing needed; changes in the law
Lifestyle changes The ways we spend our time, both in work and in leisure, affect the public services. These include:	
• increasing use of the car	• More work for traffic police
• changing patterns in alcohol consumption and recreational drug use	• Changes in licensing laws; reclassification of cannabis
• increased tourism and air travel	• Problems for police, customs, immigration service and NHS (due to global spread of diseases such as HIV/Aids, malaria or SARS)
• use of IT – especially the internet.	• Greater police response to on-line crime
• changing attitudes to sex and to the family.	• New policing skills needed to deal with rape, abuse and domestic crime. Acceptance of gays and transsexuals into the police.
Technological changes These changes relate to the development of new equipment, machinery, weapons or consumer goods. They include:	
• new equipment used by public services, for riot control, surveillance, information storage, etc.	• New policing methods; increased effectiveness of security services; effects of Data Protection Acts
• new communication systems	• These help the police, but require training
• weapons of mass destruction	• Police training needed to try to combat this threat
• mobile phones.	• Monitoring by intelligence services may help police in anti-terrorist work

Merit

Show a detailed understanding of the effects of socio-cultural and technological changes on a public sector organisation.

For this outcome, you need to develop your response to the pass grade.

An example of a possible approach to this outcome for 'Demographic changes' is given on the next page.

Profile

Description of changes	Explanation of changes	Analysis of changes
Demographic changes		
The slow rise in the British population does not affect the police much. But changes in the population of local areas affect community policing and the priorities for each 'beat'. In areas with large ethnic minority populations, the police have to make links with community leaders, and need to recruit from the community, so that the proportion of ethnic minority officers in the police matches the proportion of ethnic minority people in the local population.	Where the police force is predominantly white and the people being policed are predominantly non-white, the police may develop racial prejudices and start to stereotype the people they deal with. In any case they are open to accusations of racism, and the failure of the police to recruit enough ethnic minority officers reflects badly on race relations in the country as a whole. On average, ethnic minority groups have lower crime rates – though this is not true of African-Caribbean people, who are more likely to be arrested than white people.	Following the 1999 Macpherson Report on the police response to the murder of Stephen Lawrence in 1993, the Metropolitan Police (and by implication all police forces in Britain) were labelled as 'institutionally racist'. This meant that racist thinking – which they were often not even aware of themselves – underlay their thinking and their actions. The police have had to review their recruitment of, and relations with, ethnic minority groups, and have had to try to change their white middle-class culture to reflect the growing diversity of British society.

For this outcome you need:

- information on a range of socio-cultural and technological changes
- a description of how they affect one particular public sector organisation
- an explanation of why the changes affect the organisation (e.g. they lower its public image, they increase the amount of work it has to do, they cause planning or funding problems, etc.).

Distinction

Provide a detailed analysis of the effects of socio-cultural and technological changes on a public sector organisation.

For this outcome, you need to provide detailed and thoughtful ideas explaining the effects of social and technological changes on a public sector organisation.

skill POWER

1 For this outcome, you need to do everything you do for a merit and analyse (look in depth at) the effects. For example, if you were looking at technological changes in the armed forces you could consider:
   - the morality of using cluster bombs

- the questionable effects of injections to protect soldiers from chemical and biological weapons
- the problem of whether Britain should do its own military research and development of new weapons, or whether it should try to buy everything from the Americans
- whether the development of overwhelming fire power makes it inevitable that enemies will try to use WMD (weapons of mass destruction) against the British and allied armies.

2 In this unit, you should pay close attention to the requirements for getting passes, merits and distinctions. These are spelt out in the outcomes we have already covered, and in five additional grading criteria given below and on page 36 of the 2002 Specifications.

STUDY SKILLS FOR THIS UNIT

PASSGRADE

- Use a limited range of information to reach simple conclusions.
- Demonstrate the use of a range of specialist terminology.

Merit

- Use a range of information sources to present and analyse your answers and provide some valid conclusions.
- Communicate fluently, using a wide range of specialist terminology.

Distinction

Use a wide range of sources of information to present and analyse information effectively, reaching well-reasoned conclusions.

These grading criteria tell you that you will get higher grades if you:

- use more information sources. Suitable sources include:
  - people who work in the public sector
  - your tutors
  - leaflets and documents produced by public services
  - magazines such as *Police Review* and *Fire* which give an in-depth insight into the work of the police and fire service
  - newspapers
  - TV news and current affairs programmes
  - the internet
  - relevant and up-to-date books.

Bibliographies and references

You should make it clear that you have used these sources by listing them. Websites should be written in full. Information about books, newspaper articles and magazine articles should be listed in the following order:

- **books:** author, initial, (date), title, (edition), publisher
- **magazines:** author, initial, (date), title of article, name of magazine, issue number of magazine, relevant page numbers.

- analyse your information. 'Analyse' means:
  - explain
  - show what factors are more and which are less important
  - give causes and reasons for what you describe (e.g. speaking on hand-held mobile phones while driving was made illegal in 2003 because it had been shown to cause accidents and cost lives)
  - give your own reasoned opinions (e.g. this law places restrictions on individual liberty and enforcing it could divert the police from other more important duties)
- express yourself clearly and fluently, using appropriate specialist terminology. This means:
  - if you are speaking or giving a presentation, speak clearly and loudly and make eye contact with your listener(s)

- use the words the professionals would use, and make distinctions between words or phrases which could be confused. For example, if you are talking about immigration, show that you know the differences in meaning between 'illegal immigrants', 'asylum-seekers' and 'economic migrants'.

> **!** CHECKPOINT ...
>
> Contact a public service and try to:
> (a) visit their control centre, if they have one
> (b) look at any new technology they use
> (c) ask what the main changes in their work have been in, say, the last 20 years.
>
> Alternatively, ask your tutors to invite visiting speakers to cover these topics.

Unit 2 Law and the Legal System

Grading criteria

PASSGRADE	Merit	Distinction
To achieve a pass grade the evidence must show that the learner is able to:	To achieve a merit grade the evidence must show that the learner is able to:	To achieve a distinction grade the evidence must show that the learner is able to:
• explain, with reference to appropriate legislation, how police activities are controlled by the law **30** • explain, using appropriate examples, the effects of civilian and military law on armed forces personnel **34** • accurately describe the institutions and legal process of the criminal courts in England and Wales **36** • compare the features of the English legal system with those of other national legal systems **40** • explain the differences between common and statute law, and criminal and civil law **42** • explain how courts deal with three types of criminal offence **42** • explain how courts deal with civil matters **45** • explain the role of the police in the English legal system **45** • explain the roles of at least two other public services in the English legal system **46**	• explain, with detailed reference to appropriate legislation, how police activities are controlled by the law **30** • explain in detail the institutions and legal process of the criminal courts in England and Wales **36** • compare in detail the features of the English legal system with those of other nations **40** • compare the roles of the police and at least two other public services in the English legal system **46**	• analyse, with detailed reference to appropriate legislation, how police activities are controlled by the law **30** • analyse and compare the features of the English legal system with those of other national legal systems **40** • analyse the role of the police and the roles of at least two other public services in the English legal system **46**

All public service work requires some knowledge of the law. This is particularly true of the police, but any public service work, whether it's in the armed forces or in a civilian service, is closely controlled by laws.

This unit looks at different types of law, how they operate and the impact they have on public service work

PUBLIC SERVICE LAW

PASSGRADE

Explain, with reference to appropriate legislation, how police activities are controlled by the law.

Merit

Explain, with detailed reference to appropriate legislation, how police activities are controlled by the law.

Distinction

Analyse, with detailed reference to appropriate legislation, how police activities are controlled by the law.

For these outcomes, you need to:

- research and describe the laws which outline the powers of the police
- explain how and why they are used.

Police officers are citizens like the rest of us, and are bound by the same laws. They are not allowed to steal, assault people, drop litter or sell cocaine. But they are also bound by special laws which tell them how to do their job.

The main law of this kind is the Police and Criminal Evidence Act 1984. Its aim is to control the way the police deal with the public – especially people they suspect of committing offences.

This Act, often known as PACE for short, is updated from time to time as policing needs and public attitudes change. Its **codes of practice** cover the following aspects of police work – all of which relate to collecting evidence of crimes:

Code A: Stop and search
Code B: Searching premises and seizing property
Code C: Detention, treatment and questioning
Code D: Identification
Code E: Audio recording of suspects
Code F: Visual recording of suspects.

Explanation and analysis of PACE codes

Code A: Stop and search

Explanation	Analysis
This code deals with stopping and searching pedestrians and vehicles. All searches must be fair, reasonable, conducted with respect and without discrimination, and as brief as possible.	The PACE Act replaces the old 'sus' laws, when people could be stopped 'on suspicion'. These led to riots (Brixton 1981) and accusations of police racism. PACE reflects the increased awareness of human rights in the 1980s.
There must be 'reasonable grounds for suspicion' that 'an unlawfully obtained or possessed' article or an offensive weapon is being carried. This could be a tip-off, or suspicious behaviour.	People can't be stopped because they have long hair, brown skin or scruffy jeans. Appearance is not a 'reasonable ground'. The PACE Act is designed to respect diversity. It also protects the police, by helping them to act fairly.
Police must seek cooperation for a search, though they can forcibly search if consent is not given. They can only remove the person's coat, jacket and gloves in public view. Other clothes can be removed at police station.	Many people will allow themselves to be searched. Even if they are not innocent, the fact that they cooperated with the police will be in their favour. The PACE Act is designed to avoid embarrassment and ensure that even suspects are treated with respect.

Information must be given to the searched person about the aims of the search. There must be a written record kept of the search.	Wherever possible the public services – including the police – should be open in their dealings with the public. 'Putting it in writing' also reduces the risk of victimisation and falsification of evidence.
Supervisory officers must monitor stop and search operations.	Keeping statistics of stop and search, and ethnic monitoring, will help the police to ensure that they are not unfairly 'picking on' any section of the public.

Code B: Searching premises and seizing property

Explanation	Analysis
This code deals with searching premises (buildings, vehicles, etc.) for property and people. An application for a search warrant is normally made by a senior officer to a Justice of the Peace.	Search warrants are needed to justify an invasion of privacy, and to discourage unnecessary searches. But searches can be made without a warrant if the case is urgent or someone is at risk. The warrant is then obtained afterwards.
The application must state the premises to be searched, the object and the grounds for the search.	The code of practice respects the rights of the suspect. Some people feel the PACE Act is *too* helpful to suspects.
The search must be made within one month of the warrant being issued, at a reasonable hour. Reasonable force can be used to enter. If the occupier gives consent, it should be in writing.	Making the search at a reasonable time reduces the risk of the police being accused of harassment. 'Reasonable force' is defined by the police: they can break the door down if they think a person, or evidence, is at risk.
Searchers must explain the search and give details of compensation arrangements in case of damage.	There must be the 'assumption of innocence' of the person whose property is being searched.
They must only search to the extent needed to find what they are looking for. They must allow a friend/ neighbour of the occupier to act as witness.	These rules protect the suspect's dignity. They mean, for example, that the police should not search a chest of drawers for drugs, if they have said they are looking for stolen televisions.
Evidence can be seized and kept for trial or – if stolen – returned to the owner.	Proper treatment of evidence (a) helps the case to succeed and (b) protects the police from accusations of slackness and dishonesty.
A full record of the search must be kept.	This could well be evidence in court.

Code C: Detention, treatment and questioning

Explanation	Analysis
This code is about keeping people in police custody. A custody officer not linked to the case must look after the detainee, and keep a full record.	The custody officer should be a sergeant or a higher rank. The custody record contains full details of the time of detention, and the detainee's possessions, treatment, visitors, etc.
There are special arrangements for detainees under 17, people who are mentally ill or who cannot speak English.	In most cases an 'appropriate person' must be at the police station to protect the vulnerable person, e.g. from confessing to crimes they didn't commit.

Detainees have a right to have someone informed of their arrest, and to have a free solicitor.	Human rights must be respected. Everybody, rich or poor, is supposed to be equal under the law
Interviews normally take place at the police station. There must be no oppression or threats.	Police stations are properly equipped for interviews. A confession that results from bullying would not be admissible in court.
Accommodation must be clean and warm, and suspects can have three meals a day, and 8 hours' continuous rest in every 24.	In countries where human rights are not respected, detainees are kept under harsh conditions until they confess. In Britain this is not allowed.
The police are allowed to detain suspects for 24 hours without charge, and 36 hours in all. But in serious cases they can get an extension from a magistrate and keep the suspect up to 96 hours.	Depriving someone of their freedom goes against a basic human right. Detention and questioning should take as short a time as possible. In the case of possible murderers or terrorists detention is extended.
Questioning must not go on for more than 2 hours without a break. A solicitor can be present. The caution must be given before questioning, and a proper record, usually audio or visual, must be kept.	Too much questioning at once is inhumane and may lead to invalid answers. The solicitor can listen and make notes, but must not disrupt the questioning unnecessarily. There are strict rules for record-keeping so that evidence is not falsified.

Code D: Identification

Explanation	**Analysis**
This code concerns evidence of a suspect's identity. It covers video ID, ID parades, voice ID, fingerprints, body samples, other impressions and photographs.	People have been wrongly sentenced, or prosecutions have failed in the past, due to bad identification evidence, e.g. through biased ID parades or mixed-up DNA samples.

CHECKPOINT ...

1. Look up the detailed guidance for running ID parades. What safeguards does the suspect have?
2. Students can often get paid to take part in identity parades. Consider registering with the local police for interesting and well-paid occasional work!

Code E: Audio recording of suspects

Explanation	**Analysis**
This code concerns tape-recording interviews. The main regulations for police interviewers are: • to say the interview is being recorded • to give their names and rank • to ask suspect, solicitor, etc. to identify themselves • state date, time and place • explain security arrangements for the tapes • caution the suspect.	The purpose of all these practices is to ensure that the tapes give a truthful record of the interview, and that they cannot be tampered with. The words of the caution were changed in 1994 to: 'You do not have to say anything. But it may harm your defence if you do not mention when questioned something which you later rely on in Court. Anything you do say may be given in evidence'. This change removes the ancient right to silence – and has been condemned by human rights organisations.

Code F: Visual recording of suspects

Explanation	Analysis
This code sets out the approved method of making video recordings during questioning of suspects.	The aim of this code is to provide a clearer record of what happens in police interviews – and reduce the number of disagreements about police interviews in court.

! CHECKPOINT ...

With a friend, discuss the wording of the caution. The old caution was 'You do not have to say anything but anything you do say can be taken down and may be used in evidence.' What, in your opinion, are the advantages and disadvantages of this old caution?

http://www.yourrights.org.uk/your-rights/chapters/the-rights-of-suspects/police

http://www.homeoffice.gov.uk/crimpol/police/system/pacecodes.html – sound!

The Police and Criminal Evidence Act is not the only Act which controls police activities – though it is the most important because it is the most widely used. Here are some more:

- Anti-Terrorism, Crime and Security Act 2001
- Aviation Security Act 1982
- Badgers Act 1992
- Conservation of Seals Act 1970
- Crime and Disorder Act 1998
- Criminal Justice Act 1988
- Criminal Justice and Public Order Act 1994
- Customs and Excise Goods Management Act 1979
- Deer Act 1991
- Firearms Act 1968
- Knives Act 1997
- Misuse of Drugs Act 1971
- Public Stores Act 1875
- Road Traffic Act 1988
- Sporting Events Act 1985
- Terrorism Act 2000
- Vehicles (Crime) Act 2001
- Wildlife and Countryside Act 1981, s19.

'We got him under the Deer Act, 1991!'

Police powers and traffic offences

Police have wide powers in relation to road traffic. These are set out in the Road Traffic Act of 1988. Any constable in uniform can require a driver or cyclist to stop. Any driver who fails to stop when told to do so by the police is committing an offence.

The police can demand to see the licence of any driver. They can also demand to see the licence of anyone who they think was driving and involved in an accident, or anyone who they think was driving in connection with a crime. And they can demand to see the licence of anyone supervising a learner driver. The main purpose of this is to find out the identity of the person being checked.

The police also have powers to obtain insurance documents and test certificates by the same methods.

They can only carry out breath tests for alcohol if they have 'reasonable cause to suspect that the person':

- 'has alcohol in their body'
- has 'committed a moving traffic offence'
- has been involved in accident.

The police have powers to give out fixed penalty notices for parking offences, speeding and other motoring offences such as driving in a bus lane or jumping a red light.

> **!** CHECKPOINT ...
>
> 1 Have a look at the Crime and Disorder Act 1998, and list the powers it gives the police and courts to deal with the so-called 'yob culture'
>
> 2 What other ways, besides increased police powers and new laws, could be helpful in tackling this problem?

The armed forces and the law

> Explain, using appropriate examples, the effects of civilian and military law on armed forces personnel.

For this outcome, you need to:

- show how people in the armed forces are controlled by two systems of law
- give examples of how the laws work on armed forces personnel.

Civilian law is the laws which control all of us. Military law is a collection of laws and systems of laws which are only used to control people who work in the army, Royal Navy and RAF. People who work in the armed forces are subject both to civilian and military law.

> **FOCUS**
>
> **Outline of the main points of British military law**
>
> 'Military law is the body of law governing the rights and duties of soldiers.
>
> All serving British soldiers are subject to it.
>
> The foundation for military law is the Army Act 1955, backed up by a range of rules and regulations, including the Queen's Regulations 1975.
>
> The Army Act 1955 sets out the law in respect of enlistment, discipline, the trial and punishment of offences and forfeiture and deductions from pay, as well as provisions applicable in time of war, such as billeting and requisitioning of vehicles.
>
> It applies to British soldiers on duty anywhere in the world.
>
> The principal object of military law is to maintain order and discipline amongst members of the Army and, in certain circumstances, those who accompany them.
>
> It does so by creating a special disciplinary code and procedure that supplants the ordinary criminal law of England.
>
> The Army Act 1955 provides that soldiers are liable for any criminal offences in English law committed by them. In addition, they may be dealt with for a range of offences unique to the military, such as absence without leave.'
>
> *Source: www.army.mod.uk/servingsoldier*
> *© Crown Copyright*

Acts covering military law:

- Army Act 1955,
- Air Force Act 1955
- Naval Discipline Act 1957
- Armed Forces Discipline Act 2000
- Armed Forces Act 2001.

Under military law there are two main procedures:

- summary dealing – used for minor offences, and completed within 30 days of the offence being committed
- courts martial – used for serious crimes.

Summary dealing

Summary dealing is used for offences such as those listed below. It can be used for both military and civil offences. Sentencing is done by the commanding officer (CO).

Examples of military and civil offences which can be dealt with summarily in the army include:

- **military offences**
  - offences concerning sentries
  - failure to attend for duty, neglect of duty, etc.

- taking stores, etc., abandoned by the enemy
- using/offering violence to a superior officer
- threatening/insubordinate language
- disobeying lawful commands
- Failure to provide a sample for drug testing
- s.38 AWOL

- **civil offences**
  - common assault or battery
  - driving without due care and attention or driving without reasonable consideration
  - dangerous riding of a cycle
  - taking a conveyance without the consent of the owner
  - criminal damage not exceeding £2000
  - unlawful possession of a controlled drug
  - theft
  - driving a motor vehicle with excess alcohol
  - making off without payment not exceeding £100.

Awards (i.e. sentences) include:

- detention up to 28 days
- fine up to 28 days' pay
- severe reprimand
- reprimand
- reversion to the ranks
- stoppages of pay
- minor punishments
  - admonition
  - restriction of privileges (up to 14 days)
  - extra guards or picquets (up to three).

In summary dealing, the severity of the penalty is linked to the circumstances of the offence. An example is the loss of the identity card MOD Form 90 (see below).

FOCUS

Loss of identity card

'The initial decision should be based on an assessment of the operational and security consequences of the loss; the apparent degree of negligence or wilfulness involved in the loss; and the apparent degree of culpability of the individual. ... Where there are no significant potential operational or security consequences, and no aggravating factors, the loss of MOD Form 90 should normally be dealt with informally. ... When the loss appears to be culpable, for example through negligence or wilful destruction, or where there are other aggravating factors such as an unreasonable delay in reporting the loss – but no significant security or operational implications – then the matter may require formal disciplinary action. The circumstances of each case must be considered on its individual merits. ... When the operational or security implications of a loss might merit severe punishment, it should be a prerequisite that the requirement for greater vigilance be effectively publicised and that guidelines to promote consistent sentencing be provided by formations.'

Source: http://www.army.mod.uk/linked_files/ag/servingsoldier/termsofserv/
© Crown Copyright

CHECKPOINT ...

1 What do you think is meant by 'dealing informally' with the loss of MOD Form 90?

2 What are the similarities and differences between a soldier losing their Ministry of Defence identity card, and a student losing their college identity card?

Courts martial

A court martial is a military court at which armed forces personnel can be tried for relatively serious crimes (carrying up to two years' imprisonment). More serious crimes, e.g. murder, are tried in a civilian Crown Court.

The procedure for courts martial in the army is as follows:

1. Arrest – which must be carried out by a soldier of higher rank, or a member of the Royal Military Police (RMP)
2. After arrest, the soldier may be put in military custody. The soldier has a right to writing materials, a legal adviser and a phone call to a friend to say they are in custody. (But these rights are not allowed if it is thought they would interfere with the investigation.) Custody without charge can last up to 48 hours (96 hours in special cases) and is determined by the soldier's Commanding Officer.
3. An Assisting Officer, normally a civilian lawyer, helps prepare the soldier's defence.
4. Questioning, ID parades, etc. are carried out by the RMP.
5. A Judicial Officer (JO) is in charge of the investigation of the case and the suspect's background.

6 When the evidence is gathered the prosecution is prepared by the Army Prosecuting Authority (APA).

7 The defence is organised by the Unit Defending Officer – usually a civilian lawyer. The accused also has their own legal adviser.

8 The judge is called a Judge Advocate. He or she can arrange a preliminary examination in the court to get at the basic facts of the case.

9 The trial takes place, using witnesses, etc. It usually happens some months after the original offence.

Examples of court martial sentences include:

- imprisonment or custodial order (maximum two years)
- dismissal (with/without disgrace) from HM Service
- forfeiture of seniority
- reduction in rank
- fine
- severe reprimand or reprimand
- stoppages of pay.

The future of courts martial is in some doubt, following appeals to the European Court in 2002. The European Court ruled that the court martial system was incompatible with Article 6 of the European Human Rights Convention, which states that everyone has the right to a fair and public hearing by an independent and impartial tribunal.

! CHECKPOINT ...

1 To what extent do you think the European Court should be allowed to influence the English legal system?

2 Research a case where the laws of the EU have had an impact on English laws. In the case you have chosen, do you think the impact was good or bad?

3 What would be the advantages and disadvantages of having the same legal system in all the countries of the European Union?

4 Do you think it is fair to have a separate system of justice for civilians and for people in the armed forces?

Other kinds of military law

Other laws which can affect armed forces personnel, especially when on active service, include:

- human rights law
- the Geneva Convention
- rules of engagement (specific Ministry of Defence regulations for specific conflicts, which are not published for the public).

COOL SITES:

http://www.unhchr.ch/html/menu3/b/91.htm

http://www.us-israel.org/jsource/History/Human_Rights/geneva1.html

http://news.bbc.co.uk/1/hi/uk/383102.stm

http://www.un.org/aboutun/charter/index.html

http://www1.umn.edu/humanrts/instree/chapter5.html

ENGLISH LEGAL INSTITUTIONS

Accurately describe the institutions and legal process of the criminal courts in England and Wales.

Merit

Explain in detail the institutions and legal process of the criminal courts in England and Wales.

For these outcomes, you need to:

- describe the kinds of court which specialise in dealing with criminals
- explain the kinds of work they do
- explain the different jobs of the people who work in these courts.

Your explanations need to be accurate and sufficiently detailed.

The court system in England and Wales is different from the system in Scotland and Northern Ireland. That is why we never talk about the 'British court system' – there is no such thing!

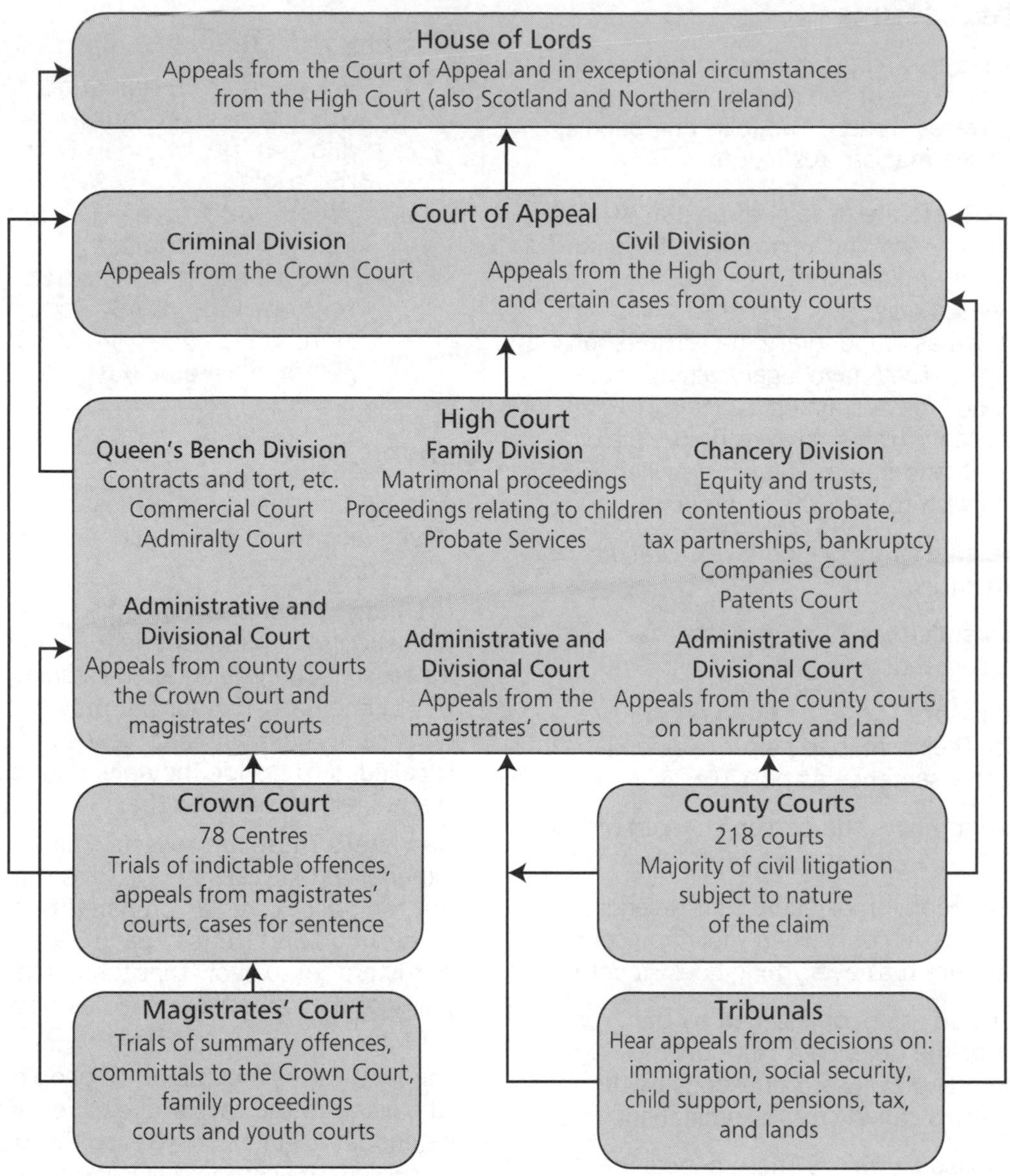

The English court system
Source: http://www.courtservice.gov.uk

The diagram above shows both civil and criminal courts. The difference between these is explained on page 43.

The main criminal courts are the magistrates' court and the Crown Court. People accused of crime go first to the magistrates' court to discover if there is 'a case to be answered' – in other words so that the court can find out what the crime is and whether it should be tried at the magistrates' court or the Crown Court. Any case likely to result in a fine of less than £5000 or imprisonment of six months or less is tried at the magistrates' court. Cases which *might* be more serious are called 'triable either way', and here the defendant has the choice of being tried at the magistrates' or the Crown Court.

Really serious cases, such as those involving murder and rape, are always tried at the Crown Court.

If someone thinks they have been wrongly convicted of a crime, they can appeal against their conviction. If they were convicted at a magistrates' court, the appeal is heard at the Crown Court. If they were convicted at the Crown Court the appeal is usually held at the High Court. If they have been convicted at the High Court, the Court of Appeal will hear their appeal – if there is one. If even they seem to have got it wrong, the appeal can be heard in the House of Lords – 'the highest court in the land'.

A convicted person will not be given the right to appeal unless there is new evidence, or a clear reason for believing that there has been a mistake (a 'miscarriage of justice') in their original trial.

Magistrates' courts

There is a magistrates' court in most large towns, and about 95 per cent of all criminal cases are heard in magistrates' courts. The following people are involved in the magistrates' court:

- **magistrates** There are usually three magistrates, collectively known as 'the Bench'. Most are not paid; they take time off from their jobs and receive expenses only. The magistrates who are paid are known as 'stipendiary magistrates' or 'district judges'. They have legal training: other magistrates only have training in being magistrates. Magistrates have to be people of common sense and integrity, aged between 27 and 65, who wish to help the community.
- **clerk of the court** This person gives legal advice to the magistrates.
- **prosecution solicitors** These put the case *against* the accused.
- **defence solicitors** These are lawyers acting *for* the accused. Their aim is to help the defendant get as lenient a sentence as possible.
- **the defendant** This is the person charged with a crime.
- **ushers** These people make sure that defendants and solicitors are in court when they are needed, and try to ensure that everything goes smoothly.
- **witnesses** These are people called by the prosecution or the defence to support their cases. They can be asked awkward questions by the other side: this is called cross-examination.
- **police and prison officers** These people are in court if the defendant has come straight from custody. They make sure the defendant doesn't try to escape, and that there is no trouble in the court. Sometimes they protect witnesses.
- **probation officers and social workers** They write pre-sentence reports about the crimes and defendants. The magistrates read these reports to help them decide the guilt of the defendant, and the sentence they should hand down.
- **journalists** They sometimes come to court and write reports for (usually) the local paper.
- **the public** The public can sit in the public gallery to watch the trial.

! CHECKPOINT ...

1. Why is it so important that members of the public should be allowed into the courts to watch the trials?
2. When and why are the public not allowed into trials?
3. Visit a magistrates' court yourself (either alone or in a group) and watch what goes on. What do you like or dislike about what you see?

Crown Court

The Crown Court is found in most cities. It is used for trying people for serious crimes. The people involved are:

- **the judge** He or she is a highly qualified lawyer with successful past experience in criminal law as a barrister. The judge has to listen to the case, as put by the barristers for the prosecution and the defence. If the defendant pleads not guilty, a jury is called in to decide the defendant's guilt – and the judge has to advise them.
- **barristers** These are lawyers trained and experienced in criminal law. Prosecution barristers put the police case, as prepared by the Crown Prosecution Service (see page 39). Defence barristers try to show that the defendant is not guilty of the crime he or she has been charged with.
- **the jury** This is a panel of 12 people aged 18–70 who listen to the case and decide whether the defendant is guilty. They reach this decision by discussing the case in a closed room, until they have an agreement of at least 10:2. They are selected at random from the electoral rolls (lists of voters) – but some professions, e.g. police and doctors, are exempt. Barristers are allowed to reject or change some jurors if they think they might be biased. Though the judge advises the jury, they do not have to follow this advice.
- **solicitors** These are in court to help the barristers prepare their arguments, and to supply legal information.
- **stenographer** This person types out everything that is said in court, even though the proceedings are also taped.
- **witnesses, the defendant, police, prison officers, probation officers, social workers, ushers, journalists and the public** have the same role in the Crown Court as they have in a magistrates' court.

CHECKPOINT ...

What happens if a jury cannot reach a decision?

The adversarial system

This is the English type of trial where there are two sides – the prosecution and the defence.

The prosecution

The aim of the prosecution in an English criminal court is to prove beyond reasonable doubt that the defendant has committed the crime they are charged with. The police collect the evidence for the prosecution. They then pass their information to the Crown Prosecution Service (CPS).

FOCUS

The Crown Prosecution Service

The Crown Prosecution Service is a body of lawyers headed by the Director of Public Prosecutions. It was formed in 1985, with the aim of taking over the work previously done by the police in preparing prosecutions. The reasons for this were:

- 'the police should not investigate offences and decide whether to prosecute. The officer who investigated a case could not be relied on to make a fair decision whether to prosecute
- different police forces around the country used different standards to decide whether to prosecute
- the police were allowing too many weak cases to come to court. This led to a high percentage of judge-directed acquittals.'

Source: CPS website

The defence

The aim of the defence is to act in the interests of the accused person. Ideally a defence lawyer can show that the accused is not guilty, and should therefore be acquitted (let off). This can be done by finding errors in the prosecution's arguments, or in the testimony of the prosecution's witnesses. It can also be done by showing that the police acted improperly while collecting evidence for the case. More often, though, the aim is to reduce the sentence by pointing out the personal or other problems which led to the accused committing a crime.

Presumption of innocence

This is an ancient but very important idea: that the person accused of committing a crime must be considered innocent unless they can be shown to be guilty beyond reasonable doubt.

Cross-examination

This is the right of the defence's lawyers to question the prosecution's witnesses, and vice versa. Cross-examination helps to find out if witnesses are lying, or mistaken in their evidence.

Trial by jury

This is used in the Crown Court when the defendant has pleaded not guilty. As stated above, the jury consists of 12 people aged 18–70, picked at random from the electoral rolls. Their job is to sit in the courtroom, listen carefully to the evidence on both sides, and to the advice of the judge, and then decide in a closed room whether the defendant is guilty of the crime they are charged with or not. Normally they only decide the guilt, not the sentence, which is set down by law. The exception to this rule is in libel cases, where the jury can fix the amount of damages.

The jury system ensures that defendants are tried 'by their peers', and that the outcome of most cases is what the public as a whole would want.

! CHECKPOINT ...

1 It has recently been suggested that some cases, such as complicated frauds, should not be tried by jury. What are the reasons for this? What is your own opinion about this suggested change to the system?
2 Why are some public service professionals never chosen for jury service?
3 What is 'jury nobbling' and what steps are taken to prevent it?

Evidence under oath

When witnesses give evidence it is normal for them to put their hand on a holy book such as the Bible or the Qu'ran and say something like 'I swear by Almighty God to tell the truth, the whole truth and nothing but the truth'. But they do not have to use this form of words, and if they prefer not to swear, they can 'affirm' that they will tell the truth.

CHECKPOINT ...

Why would some people rather affirm than swear?

PASSGRADE

Compare the features of the English legal system with those of other national legal systems.

Merit

Compare in detail the features of the English legal system with those of other nations.

Distinction

Analyse and compare the features of the English legal system with those of other national legal systems.

For these outcomes, you need to:

- show the similarities and differences between the English legal system and the legal systems of two – or more – other countries
- carry out a detailed comparison and analysis for higher grades (see below).

For a **pass**, you need to

- research legal systems from England and from at least two other nations (since it says 'nations' in the grading criterion for merit)
- state the similarities and differences between the legal systems you have chosen.

For a **merit**, you need to do what you've done for a pass, but include more information, preferably from a wider range of sources. (This does not mean, however, that you need to pick more than three nations in all.)

For a **distinction** there needs to be analysis. You have to show the differences, suggest the advantages and disadvantages of different systems, and explain the resemblances in greater detail and depth. You can make reasoned criticisms about all or any of the systems. Points you can consider include:

- How well does each system protect the human rights of the accused?
- How well does each system protect the victim of crime?
- What methods are used to ensure that the courts are reliable and consistent in their sentencing?
- Which systems seem more expensive, or appear to give better value for money?
- How specialised are the functions of each court – and what might be the advantages and disadvantages of such specialisation?
- Are the systems open and accountable, and do they include mechanisms for correcting their own mistakes (e.g. appeal courts)?

FOCUS

Scottish Courts

The **High Court of Justiciary** is the supreme criminal court in Scotland and may deal with virtually any crime or offence committed in Scotland and in addition it has exclusive jurisdiction over the following crimes: murder, treason, rape, and breach of duty of magistrate.

The **Sheriff Court** sits either with a jury of 15 lay people (in what is known as solemn procedure) or without jury (summary procedure). Summary procedure deals with most crimes and offences which occur within its local sheriffdom.

The **District Court** is usually presided over by one or more Justices of the Peace and deals with cases considered not serious enough for the Sheriff Court.

Civil cases are dealt with either in the Sheriff Court or in the Court of Session (the civil name for the High Court of Justiciary).

> In Scotland there are three possible verdicts: Guilty, Not Guilty and Not Proven. The verdicts of Not Guilty and Not Proven are verdicts which have exactly the same effect; acquitting the accused, who can never again be tried for the same offence.
>
> *Source: Lothian and Borders Police website*

www.lbp.police.uk

! CHECKPOINT ...

What differences do you notice between the Scottish and the English justice system from this short extract?

The French System

The French have three jurisdictions, or areas of law. These are civil (*Juridictions civiles*), special (*Juridictions spécialisées*) and criminal (*Juridictions pénales*). The table below shows the courts falling under the three jurisdictions.

There are three courts for children and young people:

- the *Juge des enfants* looks at children at risk, or children carrying out petty crimes
- the *Tribunal pour enfants* deals with minor crimes committed by children under 16
- the *Cour d'assises pour mineurs* tries more serious crimes committed by young people over the age of 16.

The highest court, to which major appeals go, is called the *Cour de Cassation*.

COOL SITES:

http://www.justice.gouv.fr – in French

http://www.dcba.org/brief/aprissue/2001/art50401.htm – English outline of French system

http://www.ntu.ac.uk/lis/otherjurisdictions.htm – legal systems of other countries

The courts in the French legal system

Juridictions civiles	Juridictions spécialisées	Juridictions penales
Juge de proximité (district judge) Small claims up to €1500, neighbours' disputes and other minor lawsuits	*Conseil des prud'hommes* Disputes between employees and employers relating to work contracts and apprenticeships	*Juge de proximité* Deals with low-level crimes committed by either adults or children
Tribunal d'instance Lawsuits involving less than €7600, often dealing with debt or rent arrears	*Tribunal des affaires de securité sociale* Lawsuits involving state benefits	*Tribunal de police* Crimes which can be punished by fines or other non-custodial sentences, such as withdrawal of driving licence
Tribunal de grande instance Lawsuits of more than €7600, divorce, inheritance, parental authority, property	*Tribunal de commerce* Lawsuits involving businesses or companies	*Tribunal correctionnel* Crimes which carry sentences of up to 10 years' imprisonment and other penalties such as community service
	Tribunal paritaire des baux ruraux Lawsuits involving landowners, tenants and farm buildings	*Cour d'assises* Very serious crimes which carry life sentences

Profile

Comparison of English and French legal systems

Similarities

Both systems have existed for a long time and are considered effective by most of the people who they serve. They are evolving and changing as technical, political, social and economic pressures change people's ideas of crime and punishment. They have similar views about the relative seriousness of different crimes, and follow the same principle of trying crimes of different levels of seriousness in different courts.

Differences

There are obvious differences between the English and French legal system in the types of courts at which different cases are tried. There are more courts for minor offences in France, whereas in England almost all minor offences are tried in the magistrates' courts. The specialisation in French courts may enable the lawyers and officials working in them to develop a larger body of knowledge and skill than English magistrates, who hear a wide variety of cases. On the other hand, when there are more courts it is more difficult to standardise their judgments, and some French courts have been accused of being too lenient.

French courts are considered less likely to make serious errors than English ones. Since the 1980s there has been a string of cases in England where people have turned out to be wrongly imprisoned (see below).

FOCUS

Miscarriages of justice in England

1989 The Guildford Four are released by the Court of Appeal. The detectives at the centre of the case are later cleared of fabricating evidence.

1991 The Birmingham Six are freed. Prosecutions against officers accused of tampering with evidence are halted because of 'adverse publicity'.

1997 The Bridgwater Four – minus Patrick Molloy, who died in prison – are released after 17 years in prison.

2000 The M25 Three are freed by three Court of Appeal judges who say there had been a 'conspiracy' to give perjured evidence.

A miscarriage of justice can result from non-disclosure of evidence by police or prosecution, fabrication of evidence, poor identification, over-estimation of the evidential value of expert testimony, unreliable confessions due to police pressure or psychological instability and misdirection by a judge during trial.

Source: http://news.bbc.co.uk/hi/english/static/in_depth/uk/2001/life_of_crime/miscarriages.stm BBC News Online

Miscarriages of justice happen in French courts as well. Patrick Dils was imprisoned from 1986–2002 for the murder of two 8-year-old boys, which he confessed to out of 'timidity'. But miscarriages of justice are considered less likely in France because the way they investigate serious crimes there is different. A skilled magistrate called a *juge d'instruction* leads the investigation of the crime. The aim is not to try to collect evidence proving the suspect's guilt, but simply to get at the truth. This type of investigation is called the 'inquisitorial system', and many experts think it is more even-handed than the English 'adversarial system' which sets out to prove the suspect's guilt.

LEGAL PROCESSES

PASSGRADE

Explain the differences between common and statute law, and criminal and civil law.

For this outcome, you need to explain what these kinds of law are (shown in the table on the next page), and how they differ.

Criminal offences

PASSGRADE

Explain how courts deal with three types of criminal offence.

For this outcome, you need to choose three different kinds of offence, say which kind(s) of court will deal with them, and explain how the offender will be tried.

Common, statute, civil and criminal law

Common law	Statute law	Civil law	Criminal law
Common law is the ancient law of the land. It covers crimes which have always existed such as murder, rape, assault and theft. Murder has always been illegal, and the sentencing for it has evolved over the ages. The idea of precedent (what sentences have been passed before for similar crimes) is used to this day in determining the sentence for a common law crime.	Statute law is law which is written down by a law-making body. In Britain this law-making body is Parliament. All new laws are statute laws and they are drafted (planned) and debated (discussed) in Parliament before they 'enter the statute book', i.e. become official laws. New laws such as the Race Relations Act 1976 or the Data Protection Act 1998 are statute laws.	Civil law includes the law relating to property, contracts and wrongs. For example the laws relating to buying and selling, to education for young people, and compensation and damages are all civil law. Civil law is practised by solicitors, and cases are normally heard at small claims courts or county courts. Civil law cases are brought by individuals or organisations, not by the police.	Criminal law is the law used by the police to prosecute offenders. The police bring the prosecution on behalf of the Queen (i.e. the public). Criminal law concerns crimes such as murder, theft, driving offences, etc. and the penalties they carry. Criminal cases are tried in the magistrates' and Crown courts.

The following are types of criminal offences:

- **summary offences** – crimes which can be tried at a magistrates' court. The maximum sentence is six months' imprisonment or a £5000 fine
- **each-way offences** – offences which are of 'moderate seriousness', in that they could be tried at either a magistrates' court or Crown Court
- **indictable offences** – more serious offences, which must be tried at the Crown Court. The maximum penalty is life imprisonment
- **offences against the person** – involve physical attacks (or the threat of physical attacks) and include assaults, rape, robbery, manslaughter and murder
- **offences against property** – thefts or criminal damage in which nobody is threatened or hurt
- **drug offences** – offences which involve the processing, selling or possession of prohibited drugs
- **fraud** – offences in which money is stolen by trickery or deception
- **sex offences** – offences involving under-age sex, or sex without a person's consent
- **traffic offences** – offences involving motor vehicles, especially to do with bad driving.

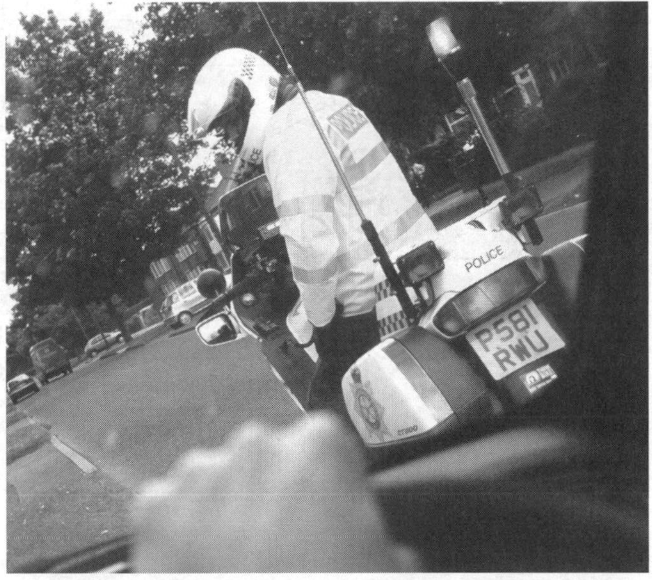

Most driving offences are tried at a magistrates' court.

! CHECKPOINT ...

Look at the crime statistics in *Social Trends* or your local police force's annual policing report to find other types of criminal offence.

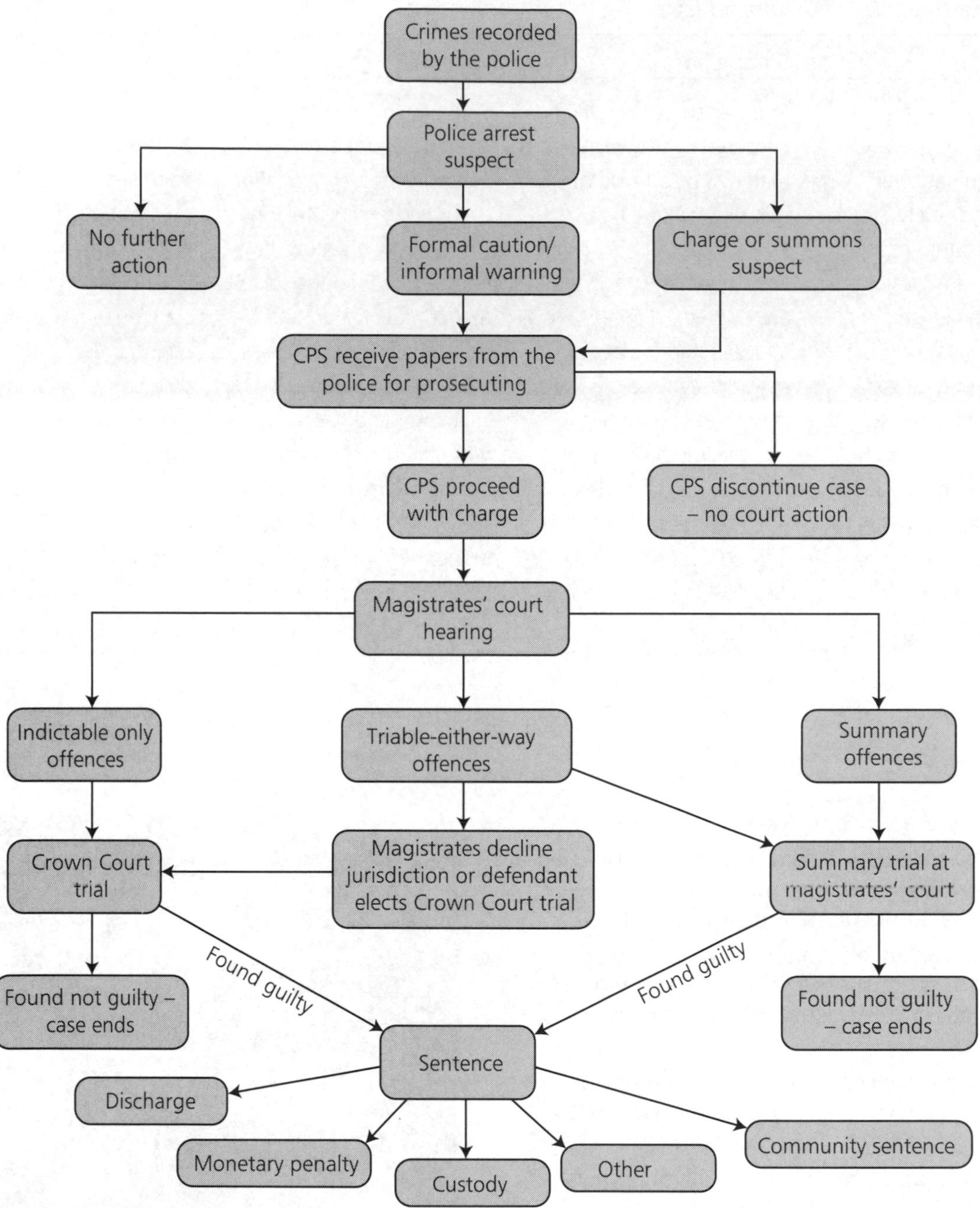

How offenders are prosecuted
Source: Home Office RDS

FOCUS

Some definitions

- charge – the police tell the suspect exactly what their offence is
- police bail – a promise made to the police that the suspect will turn up for their trial. Sometimes a sum of money is demanded to make sure the offender turns up. Offenders who are considered dangerous can be kept in prison, on remand, until trial
- legal aid – people charged with an offence are entitled to free representation by a solicitor

Further information on this outcome can be obtained from your local magistrates' court, Crown Court, or from the website below.

http://www.cjsonline.gov.uk/citizen/typical/sentence.html

Civil matters

Explain how courts deal with civil matters.

For this outcome, you need to explain how civil courts work, and the kind of things they deal with.

You will find the information you need for this outcome at your local county court, at a Citizens' Advice Bureau, or on the website below.

http://www.courtservice.gov.uk/you_courts/index.htm

The matters which are dealt with in civil courts include:

- making a claim – getting money which someone owes you
- defending a claim – if someone is wrongly trying to get money out of you
- getting a divorce
- adopting a child
- decisions about children
- disputes over family money and property
- protecting victims of domestic violence.

In a civil court, the police are normally not involved, and it is up to you, the complainant (or your solicitor) to get the ball rolling.

If you want to make a claim:

1. You go to the county court and 'issue' the claim. This means filling in a claim form. You then make three copies – one for yourself, one for the court and one for the defendant (the person you are claiming from).
2. The court sends your claim form and a 'response pack' to the defendant(s).
3. If the claim is admitted you get your money. If the claim is defended (i.e. the defendant says they do not owe you money), then the case may go to court.

Fourteen days before the court hearing you have to send all papers about the case to the court. The judge may hold a preliminary hearing, to try to find out more about the case, or because the case is likely to be difficult in some way. The judge may also try to settle the case out of court.

In most cases the court hearing is public, but it can be made private if the judge agrees that there is good reason for a private hearing, e.g. if a child is involved.

County court hearings are much less formal than those in the magistrates' court or Crown Court. The strict rules of evidence do not have to be followed if the judge thinks it isn't necessary. At the end of the hearing there is a judgment, and the judge explains the reasons for it.

If you win the case you will get your money; if you lose it you may have to pay 'costs'. If you lose the case you can also appeal – if you have 'good reason'.

ROLE OF THE PUBLIC SERVICES

PASSGRADE

Explain the role of the police in the English legal system.

For this outcome, you need to explain what the police do, how it relates to what the courts do, and how it helps to uphold the law.

Police roles in the English legal system include:

- collecting evidence about crimes, with a view to prosecuting an offender
- sending the evidence to the Crown Prosecution Service
- enforcing civil court orders, e.g. a non-molestation order from a county court for an abusive husband to keep away from his wife
- escorting offenders who are in police custody to and from court, or from court to prison
- running or assisting witness protection and victim support schemes (see Unit 21, page 348)
- ensuring security in the courtroom and, if necessary, in the neighbouring area.

The aims of these roles are to:

- combat crime
- gain successful prosecutions
- enable the courts to function without disturbance
- protect juries, witnesses and crime victims.

PASSGRADE

Explain the roles of at least two other public services in the English legal system.

For this outcome, you need to show what two other public services do, in relation to upholding the law.

The prison service, the probation service, HM Customs and Excise, the Crown Prosecution Service and the Forensic Science Service are all public services with a role to play in the English legal system. We will look briefly at two of them.

The prison service

The main roles of a prison officer are given below.

FOCUS

The main duties and tasks of a prison officer

'As a Prison Officer you will be expected to undertake varied duties and tasks, such as:

- carrying out security checks and searching procedures
- supervising prisoners, keeping account of prisoners in your charge and maintaining proper order
- employing authorised physical control and restraint procedures where appropriate
- taking proper care of prisoners and their property, taking account of their rights and dignity and their personal responsibility
- providing appropriate care and support for prisoners at risk of self harm
- promoting Anti-Bullying and suicide prevention policies
- taking an active part in rehabilitation programmes for prisoners
- assessing and advising prisoners, using your own experiences and integrity
- writing fair and perceptive reports on prisoners.'

Source: Prison service website

Prison officers supervise custodial sentences, whose purposes are to:

- punish the offender
- deter others from committing crime
- protect society from offenders who are dangerous
- rehabilitate the offender.

! CHECKPOINT ...

1 Put the purposes of sentencing listed above in what you think is the order of their importance.

2 Does society give us any rewards for obeying the law?

Customs and Excise

Customs and Excise have a role similar to that of the police. They work closely with the police, and they fight crime. The crime they fight is of specialised types, and includes:

- bringing banned goods into the country, e.g. drugs, illegal firearms, child pornography, endangered species
- tax evasion, either by importing goods without paying duty, or by not paying VAT.

Customs are also involved in the fight against terrorism and against sex tourism.

Customs officers work mainly in ports and airports, where illegal goods are likely to enter the country. Like the criminals they are combating, they have close international links – with police and customs agencies in many countries, and with Interpol.

www.hmce.gov.uk/index.htm (packed with good information – check it out!)

Merit

Compare the roles of the police and at least two other public services in the English legal system.

Distinction

Analyse the role of the police and the roles of at least two other public services in the English legal system.

For these outcomes, you need to:

- examine carefully what the police and two or more other public services do to uphold the law, and to support the work of the courts
- explain the similarities and differences between what they do and how they work.

For the **merit** outcome you need:

- good, up-to-date information on the police and two other public services with a role in the English legal system
- a clear statement of the similarities and differences in the roles of the three public services you have chosen. This statement could include:
  - the similarities in their aims, e.g. to serve the public, to combat crime, to provide prosecution evidence for the CPS and the courts
  - the similarities in their ways of working, e.g. patrolling, acting on 'intelligence', using informers, using computers and high-tech surveillance
  - the similarities in the crimes they target, i.e. crimes which are against the person, and which the public are fearful or angry about
  - the ways in which they cooperate.

But you must also mention differences in your comparison, such as:

- reasons why they operate in different places
- why some services catch offenders, while others are involved in sentencing and rehabilitation.

For the **distinction** outcome you need everything you would put in for a merit plus:

- an assessment of how the organisations you have chosen are affected by changing crime trends
- an evaluation of the role of technology and IT in their investigations, surveillance, security arrangements, etc. (as appropriate)
- observations about the effects of globalisation and international links, either in crime or in ways of dealing with crime (as appropriate)
- observations on the human rights dimension of the work of your chosen public services
- a mention of any wider contribution made by your chosen public services towards a more diverse or a just society
- a criticism of where your chosen public services have, perhaps, failed to support the legal system as well as they should have done
- any other observations which show that you have researched and thought about the question in depth.

You stand a better chance of getting these higher grades if you:

- contact the public services of your choice and ask their opinion on the subject
- ask your tutors to find speakers who can throw light on these questions
- study relevant internet sites
- increase your general knowledge by watching TV news or reading a good newspaper!

www.hmprisonservice.gov.uk

www.hmce.gov.uk/index.htm

Unit 3 Leadership

Grading criteria

PASSGRADE To achieve a pass grade the evidence must show that the learner is able to:	*Merit* To achieve a merit grade the evidence must show that the learner is able to:	*Distinction* To achieve a distinction grade the evidence must show that the learner is able to:
• outline the different styles of leadership and describe the use of at least two different styles in two of the public services **49** • describe three different theories of motivation and relate their relevance to at least two public services **53** • suggest and explain three appropriate methods of maximising the productivity of groups in the public services **59** • identify qualities of leaders in public services explaining how these are applied in at least four different situations **61** • undertake a review of personal leadership qualities **70**	• compare and contrast at least two different styles of leadership and their use in two of the public services **49** • analyse and contrast different motivation theories as applied to at least two of the public services **57** • establish and analyse different ways in which leaders are selected or emerge **67** • analyse personal leadership qualities and identify needs for personal development **71**	• assess the effectiveness of at least two different styles of leadership and justify their use in two of the public services **52** • draw conclusions relating to the different applications of motivation theories in at least two of the public services **57** • critically evaluate the selection process of a public services leader **68** • monitor and evaluate personal leadership development in relation to specified targets and objectives **72**

Public service work is all about teamwork. But teams have leaders. If you work in a public service and do well, you may soon find yourself leading a team.

This unit will help you to find the leader inside yourself.

The unit is externally assessed, through an IVA.

LINK! See page ix for more about this.

FOCUS

Definitions of leadership

Leadership is 'winning the hearts and minds of people' – Major General Tim Cross, UK's chief representative in Iraq 2003

'A leader is a man who has the ability to get other people to do what they don't want to do and like it' – President Truman (1945–53)

'The leaders' responsibility is to elicit, by example and direction, all the qualities of soldiering in their subordinates, so as to achieve their purpose. Leaders must develop these qualities in themselves by practice and study, reinforced by experience. The leader must inculcate confidence in commanders, equipment and administration, and foster mutual trust, respect and understanding. He [*sic*] must personally sustain morale and motivation; the leader must know his soldiers and they must know him. Soldiers must know where they stand with their commander, and where he is leading them. They must know their part in every plan. The leader must possess special qualities of willpower, intelligence, imagination, humanity, decisiveness and, above all, the ability to inspire.' – *The Military Covenant*, Chapter 3; http://www.army.mod.uk/servingsoldier/usefulinfo/valuesgeneral/adp5milcov/ss_hrpers_values_adp5_3_w.html#ldrshp

© Crown Copyright

CHECKPOINT ...

1 Write your own definition of leadership.
2 What qualities would you look for if you were choosing:
   (a) a class representative for a staff–student committee?
   (b) the leader of a youth club?
   (c) the leader of a football (or other sports) team?
   (d) the leader of a platoon of soldiers?
   (e) a police sergeant to run a team of community constables?

STYLES OF LEADERSHIP

PASSGRADE

Outline the different styles of leadership and describe the use of at least two different styles in two of the public services.

For this outcome, you need to:

- identify styles of leadership
- show how two (or more) are used in two public services.

There are three main styles of leadership: authoritarian, democratic and *laissez-faire*. These are described in the table on the next two pages.

Merit

Compare and contrast at least two different styles of leadership and their use in two of the public services.

For this outcome, you need to:

- pick out similarities and differences between two or more leadership styles
- show how these leadership styles are used in two public services
- show any differences in the ways they are used.

Comparison of leadership styles

What follows is an outline of authoritarian and democratic leadership styles in the army and in the police.

The main styles of leadership

Authoritarian leadership	**Democratic leadership**	***Laissez-faire* leadership**
1 *Leader-centred.* All the planning and thinking is done by the leader: the team's role is to follow orders. The leader is expected to set an example.	1 *Team-centred.* The leader is a facilitator and organiser, but depends on the team to come up with the plans and ideas. These are discussed and agreement is reached, by consensus or vote. True democratic leaders will not go against the majority opinion. The leader need not set an example.	1 *No particular centre.* The leader may inspire, motivate or produce plans and ideas, but makes no effort to ensure that the team uses or follows these ideas. The leader may set an example but nobody has to follow it if they don't want to.
2 *Motivation.* This comes from the leader's status, charisma, expertise or power to reward and punish. The team struggle to please, or satisfy, the leader.	2 *Motivation* comes from the collective wishes of the group and the fact that they have all been consulted, and their ideas listened to and taken into account.	2 *Motivation* comes from the fact that the individual is free to do what he or she likes, and that no one has to waste time explaining their actions.
3 *Sanctions (rewards and punishments).* The main sanction is the approval or disapproval of the leader.	3 *Sanctions* come from the group rather than the leader. The reward is the acceptance of the individual's ideas by the group after a democratic discussion; the punishment is the rejection of those ideas.	3 *Sanctions.* There are no sanctions from the leader, and none from the group, since everybody can do their own thing.
4 *Situations when this kind of leadership works:* when decisions are a matter of life and death and have to be made quickly. If there is no time for questions and discussion, and everybody has to act together, this kind of leadership is very effective.	4 *This kind of leadership works where everybody has ideas and decisions do not have to be made immediately.* It allows ideas to be 'thrashed out'. The leader manipulates the team so that all members contribute their ideas and help to the general effort.	4 *This kind of leadership works with individualists:* people like academics and artists who need to be free to work in their own way, and don't like teamwork. The 'leader' can inspire or encourage but does not try to influence individual decisions.
5 *The main drawback of this style of leadership is that team members have to take all their ideas from the leader.* If the leader makes a mistake, everybody can suffer, because no one else is allowed to have their say.	5 *A drawback of this style is that it can lead to long, tedious meetings.* People who disagree with the majority feel rejected and demotivated. Majority decisions can sometimes be unimaginative and uninspiring.	5 *This style of leadership offers no support to team members,* and can often give an impression of being 'shambolic'. It only motivates people who are self-motivated, and group decisions are almost impossible.
6 *Accountability.* In this style of leadership, the leader takes responsibility if things go wrong. Where money is	6 *The whole team has an input in decision-making.* The leader may choose to take responsibility, but in reality there	6 *Under this style of leadership, it is hard for a team to be accountable.* Everybody is a law unto

involved, it is hard to keep a clear track of how money is being spent, since spending is all the responsibility of one person. Authoritarian leaders are often not interested in book-keeping – they are too busy leading!	is a group responsibility if things go wrong.	themselves, and can spend as much money as they like provided they can get away with it.
7 *Symbols of authority*. Stripes, badges and other signs of rank are associated with authoritarian leadership. So are formal clothes, e.g. a suit and tie. Even office furniture, or a name or title on a door, may reflect an authoritarian attitude.	7 *Subdued symbols of authority*, such as a darkish suit and tie may be used by democratic leaders, but they prefer a civilian image.	7 Laissez-faire *leaders rarely wear anything which suggests rank or authority.* They prefer informality – it's less effort.
8 *Followers* are expected to be disciplined and obedient.	8 *Followers* are expected to cooperate with the will of the majority.	8 *Followers* are expected to do what they want, and not ask for guidance or permission.

Authoritarian leadership

In the army
Where quick decisions have to be made on matters of life and death, the authoritarian style of leadership is still the norm. Leaders are expected to understand soldiering, and how to motivate and care for those they command.

In the modern army, leadership is less authoritarian than it used to be. In World War I (1914–18) bad orders went unquestioned and hundreds of thousands of lives were needlessly lost. In the modern army lessons have been learned and planning is much more democratic (this gives everybody a chance to contribute ideas). The use of tough entry procedures and demanding training exercises enables the best leaders to be identified and fully trained in their job, and in the skills of authoritarian leadership. The other side of the coin is that soldiers are fully trained in how to understand and obey orders. When a unit is on active service, orders can be given and obeyed at once and without question. This makes the army efficient, swift and firm in its responses.

In the police
There are times when authoritarian leadership is used in the police – but usually only in an emergency. In an operation such as a drugs raid, the raid is planned democratically beforehand, with the officers taking part able to give their ideas. But when the plan is put into practice, there is no time for discussion, and leadership becomes authoritarian.

Even in routine duties there is an authoritarian element in police leadership: this is shown in the rank order, the use of uniforms, and sometimes in formal modes of address such as 'sir' or 'madam'.

Democratic leadership

In the army
Democratic leadership is used in small non-combatant groups (such as the Army Youth Teams who may take you on residentials). The atmosphere is informal and there is a good deal of discussion before the leader makes decisions.

Democratic styles of leadership are valuable in meetings, especially those held for planning purposes. Authoritarian leaders hold briefings; democratic leaders hold meetings. The purpose of a democratically-led meeting is to find out what everybody thinks about a particular issue. These meetings are far more effective for generating ideas than a briefing would be.

In the police
The police are an information-gathering organisation, and democratic styles of leadership make information gathering easier and more effective at all levels of an organisation. Democracy

is about listening, and democratic leadership is essential if ideas are to pass up the chain of command as well as down it.

Meetings run on democratic lines usually have a secretary, and minutes are taken to record everything that has been said. This takes time, but ensures that good ideas are not forgotten or lost. Majority decisions are made, and people who agree with the majority are motivated by these.

The democratic style of leadership spreads responsibility for both good and bad decisions. Badly used, it can lead to 'passing the buck'. And sometimes it results in 'leadership by committee', with safe, unimaginative decisions. But on the whole it works well, is good for communication and helps provide a more professional service.

Comparison of the use of two leadership styles in the army and the police

When comparing these two leadership styles, you could mention the following points:

- The army is more authoritarian than the police.
- Authoritarian leadership styles suit operations where there is immediate physical danger, or no time to be democratic.
- Authoritarian leadership leaves soldiers free to concentrate on the demands of fighting.
- Under an authoritarian system, officers have to take the blame for mistakes, and soldiers are not to blame for killing people: they are following orders.
- The police are more democratic than the army.
- Police work with the public is often democratic in nature, involving consultation and cooperation – partnerships should always be democratic.
- Democratic leadership works slowly and involves a lot of paperwork, but the police are more accountable to the public than the Army are, so paperwork is needed anyway.
- Authoritarian leadership is a good way of keeping secrets – which is essential in the army. Confidentiality is vital in the police too, but they have to hold meetings and practise democracy in order to communicate information within the organisation.
- Authoritarian leadership is suited to organisations where orders are passed down, e.g. the army.
- Democratic leadership is needed in organisations where the planners need to know what is happening on the streets, e.g. the police.

! CHECKPOINT ...

This is the sort of topic you should ask serving soldiers, police officers, etc. about.

Either:

1 Contact your local public services and make some appointments to see them to discuss leadership styles.

or:

2 Ask your tutor to arrange some visiting speakers.

skill POWER

When interviewing people on this sort of subject:

- Write down the questions you want to ask beforehand.
- Take your assignment brief with you.
- Take a pen and notebook with you and make notes on what your interviewee says.
- Don't forget to thank your interviewee at the end!

Distinction

Assess the effectiveness of at least two different styles of leadership and justify their use in two of the public services.

For this outcome, you need to build on the previous outcome by saying, with reasons, how effective your chosen leadership styles are, in the public services where they are used.

To 'assess' means to judge, estimate or evaluate. In other words you must give your *reasoned* opinion as to how well your two chosen styles of leadership work within the two public services you have chosen.

For this outcome, you should be well-informed about leadership in two public services. Much the best way of getting information is to ask the views of people who actually work in public services. (NB If you want to work in a uniformed public service, people who work in uniformed services would be the best to ask. But if you get stuck, ask a tutor: teaching is a public service too!)

When you have your information you should ask some questions, for example:

- Does the style of leadership help to get the job done?
- Does it motivate people?
- Are plans, targets and aims made clear?
- Does the leadership style create imaginative and effective solutions?
- What kinds of sanctions (rewards and punishments) are used to motivate people (these don't have to be formal: they can be small gestures and remarks)?
- Does the leadership style allow mistakes to be corrected?
- Are some styles of leadership more expensive than others?
- Does the leadership style have drawbacks (e.g. by using or permitting discrimination or bullying)?
- Who has the responsibility? Who takes the blame if things go wrong, and who gets the praise if things go well?
- How does the leadership style cater for different types of team members?
- Are there times when the organisation should consider different leadership styles?
- Is it a good idea to mix leadership styles in a public service?

Commanding officer: What's going on here?
Corporal: We're voting whether to blow up that tank, sir.

CHECKPOINT ...

Discuss this statement: 'The weakness of democratic leadership is that the majority are not always right.'

THEORIES OF MOTIVATION

Describe three different theories of motivation and relate their relevance to at least two public services.

For this outcome, you need to:

- outline three ideas (based on research) about what makes people work hard
- show their relevance to two or more public services.

http://chiron.valdosta.edu/whuitt/col/regsys/maslow.html

FOCUS

Definitions of motivation
Motivation is ...

'the arousal, direction, and persistence of behavior' – Franken (1994)

'an emotion, desire, physiological need or similar impulse that acts as an incitement to action' – *Webster's Dictionary*

'the art of helping people to focus their minds and energies on doing their work as effectively as possible' – Gellerman, S.W. (1992), *Motivation in the Real World*, Dutton Books: New York

Drive theories

Many psychologists who have studied motivation have assumed that we are pushed, or driven, to do what we do by instincts within us. These theories, which were developed by people like McDougall (1932) and Morgan (1943), take the view that most of us are motivated whether we want to be or not. For example, we are motivated by hunger to eat, and by the sex drive to have children.

Maslow's hierarchy of human needs

In 1954 Abraham Maslow put forward a motivation theory based on what he called the 'hierarchy of human needs'.

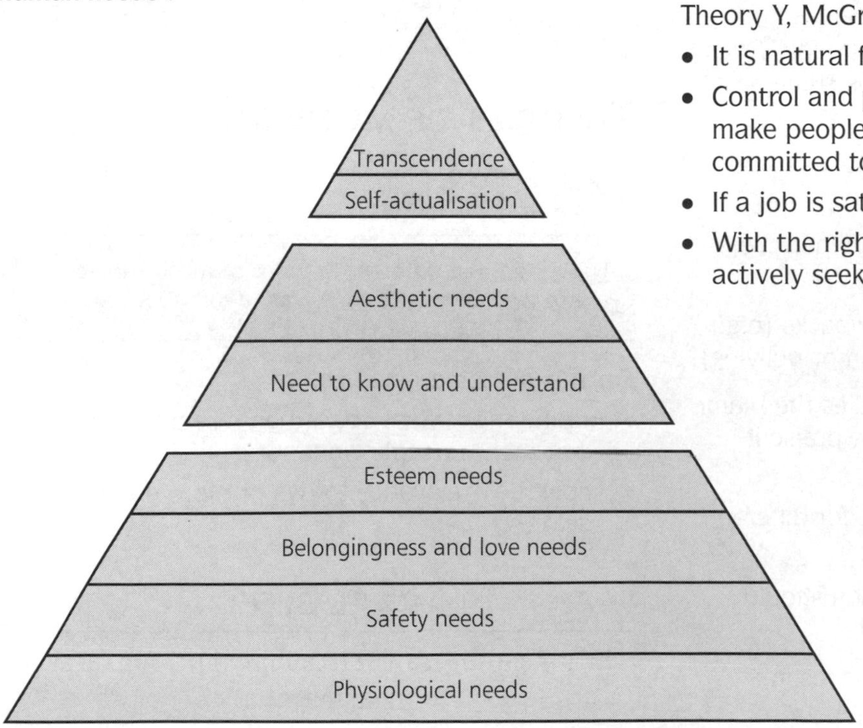

Transcendence
Self-actualisation
Aesthetic needs
Need to know and understand
Esteem needs
Belongingness and love needs
Safety needs
Physiological needs

Maslow's hierarchy of human needs

This is perhaps the single most influential theory of motivation. It states that the needs at the bottom of the pyramid are the most basic and essential. Only when we have satisfied these needs, which include food and sleep, can we move up the pyramid to the second layer, which includes shelter and security. The third layer is the need for human relationships such as friendship and love; the fourth layer represents the respect of our fellow citizens. The fifth and sixth layers are the needs we have for knowledge and beauty and the top two layers are to do with self-fulfilment and spiritual happiness.

McGregor's X and Y theories of management

Douglas McGregor, an American who was interested in motivation and management, put forward his ideas in 1960. They are really a simplification of Maslow's system, put in practical terms which everybody can understand.

For McGregor the X theory of management is traditional authoritarian management. It states:

- Most people dislike work and need to be forced to do it.
- Most people prefer to be told what to do, dislike responsibility and need security more than anything else.
- These beliefs lead to a tough, controlling style of management, or one which offers no choice or challenge to employees.

Theory Y, McGregor's alternative, states:

- It is natural for people to want to work.
- Control and punishment are not the only ways to make people work; they will also work if they are committed to the aims of the organisation.
- If a job is satisfying, people will work harder.
- With the right encouragement, workers will actively seek responsibility.

- Many workers want to use their imagination, creativity and problem-solving abilities.
- Many employers do not try hard enough to use the abilities of their workforce.

CHECKPOINT ...

Are there any ways in which Theory X is actually better than Theory Y? What do you think?

Herzberg's motivation–hygiene theory

In 1959 Frederick Herzberg wrote an influential book called *The Motivation to Work*. This puts forward his 'motivation-hygiene' theory. Herzberg interviewed large numbers of workers to find out what gave them job satisfaction and job dissatisfaction. The table below gives a simplified list of his results.

Results of Herzberg's research

Factors leading to dissatisfaction	Factors leading to satisfaction
Company policy	Achievement
Supervision	Recognition
Relationship with boss	Work itself
Work conditions	Responsibility
Salary	Advancement
Relationship with peers	Growth

The left-hand column of the table lists consists of incentives, rewards or punishments which have nothing to do with the work itself. Herzberg called these 'KITA' factors, KITA being short for 'kick in the a***'. He also called them 'hygiene' in the sense that they maintained conditions which made the job possible. The true motivators are in the right-hand column – they lead to better fulfilment of workers as human beings, by developing their abilities and self-respect. Herzberg believed that 'job enrichment' – making work more challenging and interesting – was the key to better motivation in the workplace.

Adair's theory of motivation

John Adair has a background in teaching motivation and motivation theory, notably at the top military college, Sandhurst. His rules are:

- Be motivated yourself.
- Select people who are highly motivated.
- Treat each person as an individual.
- Set realistic and challenging targets.
- Remember that progress motivates.
- Create a motivating environment.
- Provide fair rewards.
- Give recognition.

Source: John Adair, 2002; www.johnadair.co.uk

His ideas belong to the same general school of thinking as Maslow, McGregor and Herzberg, but he has brought them up-to-date and expresses them in straightforward practical terms which people find easy to understand and use. They are clearly applicable to public service work.

LINK! See page 61 for Adair's theory of Action-Centred Leadership.

Alderfer's ERG theory

These ideas of motivation also stem from Maslow. In 1972, C.P. Alderfer classified human needs as:

1. Existence needs – basic necessities, such as food and shelter
2. Relatedness needs – the needs for human companionship
3. Growth needs – the development of individual potential and the satisfaction of personal ambitions.

Intrinsic and extrinsic motivators

It is worth mentioning that Herzberg's 'hygiene' and 'motivating' factors are 'extrinsic' and 'intrinsic' respectively.

- Extrinsic motivators are motivating factors outside the job itself, such as salary, working regulations and working conditions.
- Intrinsic motivators are factors connected with the work, e.g. the pleasure of solving problems or planning operations.

Profile

Relevance of one theory of motivation to two public services

Theory	Fire service	Army
Herzberg's motivation-hygiene theory	Herzberg's 'hygiene' motivating factors are very relevant to the fire service, especially in relation to the 2002–3 firefighters' strikes.	Herzberg's motivation-hygiene theory is also relevant to the army.
	Company policy The employers were seen as high-handed and unreasonable.	**Company policy** There is a recruitment problem, which implies that some aspects of the government's approach needs changing.
	Supervision At the local level, this was OK, but there had been some bad inspectors' reports about fire service working practices.	**Supervision** Soldiers sometimes have difficulties with the discipline, and there have been cases of bullying.
	Relationship with boss OK at the local level, but a poor relationship with the Office of the Deputy Prime Minister.	**Relationship with boss** Relationships between soldiers and their officers are generally good – but this is not the reason why soldiers join the army!
	Work conditions Firefighters liked them, because they could work four days on and four days off.	**Work conditions** Very variable. Work conditions just before the Iraq war (e.g. poor food) led to complaints.
	Salary Very demotivating – far too little for an emergency service doing a tough job.	**Salary** Possibly too low, in view of the recruiting problems mentioned above.
	Relationship with peers Good on the whole, though a few accusations of bullying and discrimination.	**Relationship with peers** Good on the whole, but bullying has been a problem in the past.
	Motivators: *Achievement* – high levels of achievement by the fire service in rescues, response times, fire prevention and other aspects of public safety. *Recognition* – high recognition by the public, which is why the firefighters' strikes enjoyed more public support than most strikes. *Work itself* – the work itself is challenging and varied.	**Motivators:** *Achievement* – high levels of achievement: the British army is very effective as the Iraq War and its aftermath have shown. *Recognition* – held in high public esteem (shown by opinion polls around the time of the Iraq War). *Work itself* – hard, challenging and varied.

	Responsibility – high levels of responsibility in saving lives and property.	*Responsibility* – high levels of responsibility.
	Advancement – there is a clear career structure which provides opportunities for promotion.	*Advancement* – clear career structure which provides opportunities for promotion.
	Growth – firefighters achieve personal and professional satisfaction from the intrinsic motivators in their work, but less from the extrinsic motivators.	*Growth* – good personal and professional development but there is a problem when it comes to returning to civilian life.

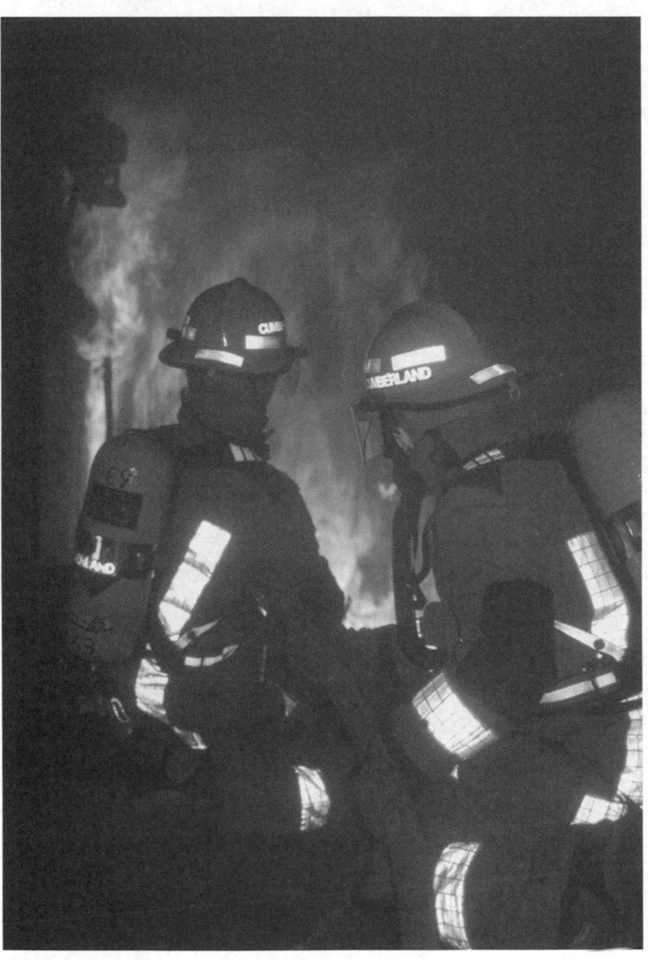

The challenge of putting out fires and rescuing people is a powerful intrinsic motivator for firefighters.

Merit

Analyse and contrast different motivation theories as applied to at least two of the public services.

For this outcome, you need to:

- pick out the main points of different motivation theories
- highlight the differences
- show how they are used in at least two public services.

skill POWER

For this outcome, 'analyse' means 'pick out and comment on the main points' and 'contrast' means 'give the main differences'.

The outcome does not say how many motivation theories you should consider. The profile on the next page is given as a guide.

Distinction

Draw conclusions relating to the different applications of motivation theories in at least two of the public services.

! CHECKPOINT ...

Relate the relevance of two more theories of motivation to two public services.

Profile

McGregor's X and Y theories and Alderfer's ERG theory applied to the prison service and the army

Theory and summary	Prison service	Army
McGregor X and Y theory Theory X = authoritarian management – tough and controlling, with penalties for poor performance, i.e. driving the workforce Theory Y= humanistic management offering encouragement, challenges and opportunities for self-development and self-fulfilment	With difficult prisoners, the X style of management was traditionally used, but now it can lead to prison riots and violence. Because a small number of staff control many prisoners, more subtle methods – Theory Y – must be included. The caring and rehabilitative side of prison work uses Theory Y, offering incentives for good behaviour and prisoner achievement. Theory Y also works better with prison officers, since it facilitates the flow of information and makes for better staff relations. It offers rewards and incentives for good work, such as promotion.	McGregor's X theory of management owes something to traditional army discipline, which was tough and authoritarian. This kind of management shows itself in the strict and complex army discipline regulations. On the whole, though, the 'square-bashing' mentality of the old army is giving way to a more humane style of leadership which rewards merit as much as it penalises faults. Theory Y encourages subordinates to give of their best, and to see the army as a career with prospects, rather than a type of prolonged suffering.
Alderfer's ERG theory 1 Existence – the satisfaction of basic needs such as food and shelter 2 Relatedness – the satisfaction of social needs such as friendship and working together with colleagues 3 Growth – the development of personal and professional abilities leading to self-fulfilment and job satisfaction. These abilities include skill, knowledge and confidence	Alderfer's motivation theory is again a humanistic variant of Maslow's. In a prison, if prisoners are hungry and cold, for instance, they can never expect to develop their social attitudes because their existence needs are not fulfilled. Only after existence needs are fulfilled can a person step up to the next level – relatedness needs. It is on this social level that many prisoners are inadequate human beings. Alderfer's theory implies that, to develop prisoners' social skills, and rehabilitate them for free society, they should live under good conditions, well fed and in comfort. Its basic message is similar to that of McGregor's – people should be treated humanely and encouraged to develop.	Alderfer is relevant to the army. As Napoleon, one of the world's greatest ever motivators said, at the beginning of the nineteenth century, 'an army marches on its stomach'. Alderfer confirms this idea: that an army's existence needs must be fulfilled before it can come together through relatedness needs and develop fighting skills and courage in the 'growth' phase. The organisation of the army, which satisfies soldiers' social needs (at least at a professional level), has developed over the centuries into a complex system based on power relations between different ranks, and *esprit de corps* between soldiers of the same rank. This strong social organisation provides a setting which motivates soldiers to develop their skills.

For this outcome, you need to:

- explain how different types of motivation theories are put into practice in at least two public services
- reach reasoned judgements as to how, why and whether they are effective.

This outcome calls for information on the range of methods used by public service organisations to motivate their staff. The best source of this information would be a manager who works, or has worked, in a public service.

You need to be able to relate practical methods of motivation used in public services with the theories (see above) which explain them, or which they originate from.

To draw conclusions you need to pick out the main points, and to suggest which kinds of motivation are most effective in different services, and in different contexts (situations) within those services.

You should remember that different kinds of motivation work better with different people, or in different situations. There is no such thing as a 'perfect' way of motivating people!

Points you could make include:

- **group motivation** Theories of social facilitation, based on the work of social psychologists such as Zajonc (1965) and Cottrell (1968) suggest that people who work with their peers, in groups, perform many tasks better than people who work alone. This is one reason why so many people share offices in the public services – the other is lack of space!
- **money** A salary scale with increments and grades is the normal one used in the public services – it motivates people to stay and get more money next year. A rank structure with clear pay differentials also motivates keen employees to work hard and strive for promotion.
- **job satisfaction**, which comes both from achievement, and from motivation to do better. It is also linked with the satisfaction of relatedness needs, and the social facilitation mentioned above.
- **status**, like money, is an incentive to work hard: public service workers enjoy the raised status which comes with promotion, and the fact that they have more freedom to develop their skills and fulfil their activities.
- **equality with other groups of workers** can be a motivating factor. When a group of workers falls behind, as the firefighters did in the 1990s compared with other emergency workers, it led to strikes.
- **accountability** This is what Herzberg would call a 'hygiene' factor. Accountability may be a good thing from the taxpayer's or customer's point of view, but the paperwork and target-setting can be demotivating from the point of view of a worker in a public service.
- **fast-tracking** This is practised in the army and in the accelerated promotion schemes of the police and prison service. It motivates able young people to take up these careers in the hope that they will be quickly promoted to rewarding and interesting jobs. But it may demotivate people who are not on these schemes.
- **job-rotation** One demotivating factor is boredom: doing the same thing for too long, so that we feel we are not progressing to a higher level of motivation, and our 'growth needs' are not being met. Job-rotation (e.g. moving from traffic police to CID) is normally motivating because it enables people to develop their skills and fulfil their potential. But for officers who liked their job, it might be demotivating.
- **government restraints on public sector pay** are clearly demotivating, not least because public sector workers' families may suffer as well. People who feel undervalued cut down on their work-rate, and lose their commitment to the organisation that employs them. The able ones leave for better paid jobs; the rest remain – bad news for the public sector.

Maximising productivity

Suggest and explain three appropriate methods of maximising the productivity of groups in the public services.

FOCUS

Definitions of productivity

Productivity is ...

'achievement per dollar spent' – Professor Caroline Hoxby, Harvard University, USA

'the ratio between output and the total input of factors required to achieve it' – International Labour Organisation (a branch of the UN, 2002)

Explanation

'Productivity' is a word more associated with the private sector than the public sector. If 1000 workers in Factory A produce 30 cars a day, and 1000 workers in Factory B produce 25 cars a day, then Factory A is more productive – because they work faster.

But if the cars made in Factory A sell for £10,000 and the cars made in Factory B sell for £20,000 then Factory B is more productive, because the total value of the cars they produce each day is greater.

But then again, if the workers at Factory B are paid twice as much per hour as those at Factory A (and there are the same number of workers) that might make Factory A more productive.

Productivity is the total value of what comes out, divided by the total value of what goes in, in a given period of time.

In the public services, productivity can be described as the quantity and quality of the work done, divided by the time and money needed to do that work. 'Maximum productivity' from the public service's point of view (or the government's) is to get as much work done as possible, of the highest possible quality, by the fewest possible people, at the lowest possible cost, in the shortest possible time.

One can therefore maximise productivity of groups in a public service by altering factors such as salary, numbers of employees and time allowed for the job. This has been tried – and done – on a large scale in the public services over the years, so these are not unrealistic suggestions.

But from a leadership viewpoint, a better way to look at this outcome is to look at the motivating factors which might maximise the productivity of a group in the public services – without laying people off or cutting their salaries.

Some 'appropriate' methods of maximising the productivity of groups, involving leadership and motivation, are summarised in the table below.

Some ways of maximising productivity

Method	Leadership or motivation theory	Explanation of possible effects
Change style of leadership and management, giving more responsibility to the group	This is linked to McGregor's Theory X and Theory Y styles of management. People will be given more responsibilities, and their tasks will be made more varied. They will make their own decisions instead of merely following orders.	The group – especially if working in a 'people-centred' public service such as the police or prison service – will be able to communicate better, both up and down the organisation and between themselves. Time will be saved because information will flow more freely.
Set realistic and challenging targets	This is one of the rules for good management set out by Adair, and it is already being widely used in the public services, to motivate groups and give them a clear idea of how successful they are in their work. A target is motivating, and can increase 'productivity' without increasing costs. Target-setting is useful to the wider organisation, and to the public, who can see that service is getting better.	Target setting works if the targets set are realistic (i.e. achievable and reasonable) and challenging (capable of inspiring the group to greater efforts). Targets which are too difficult are demotivating and can lead to falsification of paperwork. Targets which are too easy are simply ignored. There are drawbacks to target-setting: the employers are trying to get something for nothing, and public service workers can suffer 'target-fatigue' and become cynical about them.

> **!** **CHECKPOINT ...**
>
> Some public services such as the police make people share open-plan offices to improve productivity (i.e. work-rate and performance). Comment on this, in relation to 'social facilitation', 'relatedness needs' and ease of communication.

FOCUS

Methods of maximising the productivity of groups (Action-Centred Leadership – Adair)

'Your responsibilities as a manager for achieving the Task are:

define the task

make the plan

allocate work and resources

control quality and rate of work

check performance against plan

adjust the plan

Your responsibilities as a manager for the Group are:

set standards

maintain discipline

build team spirit

encourage, motivate, give a sense of purpose

appoint sub-leaders

ensure communication within group

train the group

Your responsibilities as a manager for each Individual are:

attend to personal problems

praise individuals

give status

recognise and use individual abilities

train the individual'

Source: http://www.businessballs.com © Alan Chapman 2004. Taken from www.businessballs.com free resources and used with permission. Adapted by Alan Chapman

Qualities of leadership

> Identify qualities of leaders in public services explaining how these are applied in at least four different situations.

For this outcome, you need to:

- find out what makes a person a good leader
- explain how different leadership qualities can be used in different situations.

For this outcome, you should try to talk to someone who recruits for a public service. A good place to start might be your armed forces information office. Alternatively, make an appointment with someone at a public service of your choice, or ask a visiting speaker about leadership qualities.

You are not told how many leadership qualities you have to identify, but you do need to look at the application of those qualities in four or more situations.

NB Leadership qualities are *not* the same as leadership styles. Some leadership *qualities* are underlined in the FOCUS below.

FOCUS

Leadership qualities required in public services

This is from an advertisement for the National Crime Squad:

'In your role as Operational Sergeant you will be required to supervise, direct and co-ordinate a team of officers engaged in all aspects of proactive intelligence-led investigation and prosecution of complex, serious and organised crime at a national and international level.

Profile

How leadership qualities are applied in four different public service situations

The table takes one leadership quality from the FOCUS above and applies it to four different public service situations.

Quality	Situation 1	Situation 2	Situation 3	Situation 4
Good written and verbal communication skills	When a probation officer is writing a pre-sentence report for someone accused of a crime	When a police officer is advising a group of youths in a bus station to go home	When a worker for Victim Support is comforting a crime victim	When a firefighter is reading instructions about the safe handling of a dangerous chemical

You will possess good written and verbal communication skills and proven investigative/interview ability. In addition to a positive and interventionist style, you will be a good motivator, stimulating and encouraging others to make positive contributions.

A sound knowledge of technical and conventional investigation techniques, and an ability to analyse information and intelligence in conjunction with other organisations is essential for these roles.'

Source: www.ncs.police.uk

CHECKPOINT ...

Make a list of as many leadership qualities as you can. Then check it with your friends or with a tutor to make sure that what you have written down really are leadership qualities.

Successful leaders

It is widely believed that successful leaders, in the public services or anywhere else, have certain qualities which help to make them good leaders. Some of these qualities may be partly inborn or innate – for example good looks or academic ability. But all leadership qualities can be developed to some extent by people who have the motivation and self-discipline.

Nearly everybody has some leadership qualities. These qualities are important in public service work, and all effective public service employees – whatever the service – will use them from time to time. This is especially true in the uniformed public services.

However, the leadership qualities needed at any given time vary according to

(a) the situation. This means the nature, aims and urgency of the work to be done. A soldier commanding a platoon under enemy fire will use different leadership qualities and skills from a police officer chairing a meeting of community leaders.

(b) the personality of the leader. Different leaders will deal with the same situation in different ways. A half-time pep talk by Sir Alex Ferguson (Manager of Manchester United) will not be the same as one by Sven-Goran Eriksson (Manager of England) – even if the scoreline of their teams is the same!

(c) the people being led. Soldiers and social workers expect different styles of leadership, and therefore different leadership qualities in their leaders.

What is a successful leader?

A successful leader is a person who motivates and enables a number of people to achieve an agreed aim. A successful leader is not necessarily a famous leader – for example the leader of a small team of customs officers may have a high success rate in drug seizures and other activities without ever becoming known to the public.

Example of a successful leader in a public service

Each of the paragraphs in the FOCUS below demonstrates Mr Clarke's leadership traits (qualities) which have helped him rise to the position of Chief Constable in the Ministry of Defence Police.

FOCUS

Chief Constable's Biography

Lloyd Clarke joined the Ministry of Defence Police (MDP) as Chief Constable on 13 November 2000. He was previously Assistant Chief Constable (Designated Deputy) at West Yorkshire Police.

Mr Clarke joined West Yorkshire in 1969 and served as a cadet until 1971. He is particularly proud of the fact that all his police service was in West Yorkshire prior to joining MDP.

In 1982 he gained a Masters Degree in Peace Studies from Bradford University, having studied conflict resolution and mediation techniques, including hostage negotiation. He attended both the National Training Course for Hostage Negotiators as well as the National Prison Service course in Siege Management.

Between 1989 and 1992 he was the Police Commander at Dudley Hill, an inner city sub division of the City of Bradford. Whilst in this post, he presided over a number of initiatives aimed at enhancing partnerships and community policing techniques on large inner city estates, and with the minority ethnic community of Bradford.

In March 1993 he attended the Strategic Command Course for Chief Officers and was promoted Assistant Chief Constable in December 1993 with specific responsibility for Management and Information Support.

From January 1995 to June 1998 he had functional responsibility for Divisional Operations, which encompassed all aspects of policing for the 17 operational divisions in West Yorkshire. He introduced robust performance management in the Force through Performance Reviews with senior officers.

Mr Clarke was appointed the designated Deputy to the Chief Constable in June 1998 and also had specific functional responsibility for the Force's Management Support Department, Media and Press Relations and the Information Technology Department.

He has studied policing models in other European countries and North America, and has provided a teaching input on Contemporary and Community Policing at the International Law Enforcement Academy in Budapest, as well as in the Netherlands, Canada and Fiji.

From March 1997, he was the officer in overall command of a Multi-Force Enquiry, Operation Lynx, enquiring into offences of attempted homicide, abduction and rape across the country committed over a 15-year period. A man was given eight life sentences for these offences in October 1999.

In October 1999, Mr Clarke became the Investigating Officer for Operation Lancet, an investigation supervised by the Police Complaints Authority into alleged police corruption in Cleveland.

He was the Secretary of the Association of Chief Police Officers (ACPO) Race and Community Relations Sub Committee between 1996 and 1999. He prepared the ACPO written submission and gave oral evidence to the Macpherson Inquiry. He retains a deep interest in race relations issues.

Between 1997 and 2000 Mr Clarke was a Board Member of an Independent Housing Association which provides more than 20,000 units for social housing throughout the North of England.

He was awarded the Queen's Police Medal for Distinguished Police Service in the 1999 New Year's Honours.

http://www.mod.uk/mdp/aboutus/cc.htm Ministry of Defence website)

Paragraph	Leadership qualities shown
1	Loyalty – he stayed with West Yorkshire police for many years.
2	Willingness to study and learn – he studied Peace Studies at Bradford University Fearlessness – willing to train in hostage negotiation and siege management (both risky activities!)
3	Willingness to innovate – he developed new policing techniques in Dudley Hill, Bradford Keen to work with others – he enhanced partnerships with other agencies and groups
4	Interested in leadership – he trained himself, for example by attending a strategic command course (thus showing an interest in theory as well as practice)
5	Willingness to take on wide responsibilities – 'all aspects of policing' - when in charge of divisional operations Interested in management – he brought in new techniques for reviewing performance
6	Willing and able to talk to the press – responsible for media and press relations (shows he could be trusted to give a good impression to the public, and would not make irresponsible remarks) Computer literate – he was in charge of the IT department
7	Outward-looking – he has studied policing in other countries Internationally-respected – he has lectured on aspects of policing to officers in other countries
8	Has a track record of success – led investigations resulting in the arrest and conviction of a serial abductor and rapist
9	Known and trusted for his honesty – he led Operation Lancet – investigating alleged police corruption in another force
10	Free of racial prejudice – an expert on race relations, who gave evidence to the Macpherson Inquiry.
11	Has a wide and caring approach to his work – involved in providing social housing (homes for the poor)

Famous leaders

Famous leaders are often the leaders of countries, movements or large organisations. The most famous British leader of the last century was Winston Churchill:

FOCUS

The Right Honourable Sir Winston Leonard Spencer Churchill (1874-1965), the son of Lord Randolph Churchill and an American mother, was educated at Harrow and Sandhurst. After a brief but eventful career in the army, he became a Conservative Member of Parliament in 1900. He held many high posts in Liberal and Conservative governments during the first three decades of the century. At the outbreak of the Second World War, he was appointed First Lord of the Admiralty – a post which he had earlier held from 1911 to 1915. In May, 1940, he became Prime Minister and Minister of Defence and remained in office until 1945. He took over the premiership again in the Conservative victory of 1951 and resigned in 1955. However, he remained a Member of Parliament until the general election of 1964, when he did not seek re-election.

http://www.nobel.se/literature/laureates/index.html 2004 The Nobel Foundation

Churchill is famous for his leadership when he led Britain through World War II. He was not a good team player and his political career in peacetime had not been successful. As an individual he was sarcastic, ill-tempered and inclined to over-drink. He was hated in some parts of the country because he sent troops to fire on striking miners in Wales in 1911, and was in favour of putting down other strikes by force. He was a fierce nationalist who thought everything British was best, and would probably not have fitted in well with our modern multicultural society. At the end of World War II he was heavily voted out of office in the general election of 1945.

So why is he considered the greatest leader Britain ever produced?

He is admired for

- his determination that Britain would win the war, come what may
- his courage in staying in London and risking his own life by visiting bombed-out areas
- the wonderful and inspiring speeches he gave
- the respect and appreciation he showed to ordinary people
- his books, which won him the Nobel Prize for Literature in 1953.

Gandhi's leadership qualities appear very different from Churchill's. He was a deeply spiritual man, didn't smoke or drink, and dressed in a white robe symbolising poverty and purity. He didn't make sarcastic jokes at other people's expense. He was famous for carrying a spinning wheel around with him, which he used while talking to people to spin thread. Unlike Churchill, he never tried to solve a problem by encouraging the use of violence. Gandhi summed up some of his ideas in his list of "Seven Blunders Of The World That Lead To Violence":

Wealth without work

Science without humanity

Pleasure without conscience

Worship without sacrifice

Knowledge without character

Politics without principle

Commerce without morality

In fact, despite his pacifism, he shared many qualities with Churchill. These included

- putting the well-being of his country before his own safety
- unbreakable determination to do what he believed was right for his people
- courage and endurance: for example during his periods of imprisonment, and in hunger strikes
- an ability to think clearly and communicate with a wide audience
- imagination and foresight
- a deep sympathy with ordinary people

The importance of situation

With both Churchill and Gandhi, situation played a part in their greatness. If there had been no war, Churchill would have been remembered mainly as an eccentric and unsuccessful politician who was good at writing history books. And if India had not needed a leader during the struggle for

FOCUS

Mohandas (Mahatma) Gandhi (1869-1948), led the struggle for Indian independence from Britain, which colonised the country during the 1700s. Gandhi was a religious pacifist, and to obtain their goals he and his followers used 'passive resistance' and a philosophy called satyagraha, or 'defence by truth'.

Born in India, he studied law and spent some years as a young man working in South Africa. Here he saw how Indian immigrants were discriminated against by the whites.

When he returned to India he started campaigning for freedom. He used non-violent methods of civil disobedience including strikes, marches, hunger strikes and boycotts. He was arrested and imprisoned several times.

He also formed a political party, the Indian National Congress, and led a struggle to abolish India's caste system – which condemned some people, the 'untouchables' to permanent poverty.

During the Second World War, he continued campaigning for India's freedom – and was imprisoned. In 1944 he was released and negotiated for India's freedom from Britain. This was achieved in 1947 but quickly followed by the separation of Pakistan from India.

He became leader of India but was assassinated by a Hindu extremist in 1948.

independence, Gandhi might have been no more than an unremembered Indian lawyer.

Leadership v teamwork

Churchill and Gandhi were great leaders – but they were not great followers! In a public service most employees in leadership roles – e.g. police sergeants or leading firefighters – are sandwiched between superiors and subordinates. Their leadership qualities, used in managing and motivating subordinates, have to be matched with teamwork qualities of cooperation if they are to satisfy the demands of their superiors. This can lead to a conflict of roles which could undermine the officer's teamwork or leadership qualities – or both.

An example of this problem was seen in 2003 with Colonel Tim Collins, who was with the British army in Iraq. First he was famous for a highly motivating speech which he gave his soldiers. This speech was seen by President George W. Bush and hung up in the White House. Then Collins was accused by an American observer of a war crime (mistreating Iraqi captives). This accusation was investigated by the Ministry of Defence, and Collins was declared blameless. Later he left the army accusing them of excessive bureaucracy and interference with his work.

FOCUS

The 43-year-old colonel's rise through the ranks has not surprised his military peers.

One former colleague described him as a very professional soldier who was highly regarded by everyone who served with him.

To his men he is known as "Nails", a reflection of his strong character and unflinching determination.

The colonel's upbringing in Northern Ireland, where he was born in April 1960, played a central part in forming his future ambitions.

As a young schoolboy in Belfast he witnessed at close hand the terrible violence.

But from an early age he told his mother, Mary, that he wanted to be "a great soldier".

...

'He was a fairly regular, decent bloke, a good lad but obviously focused on what he wanted to do' Former classmate

...

Michael Ridley, principal of his old school, said recently, the school was proud of what he had achieved.

"Everybody who knew him was impressed with him and saw him as a very enthusiastic person."

BBC News website: Friday, 23 May 2003
http://news.bbc.co.uk/1/hi/northern_ireland/default.stm

CHECKPOINT ...

Research a leader who interests you (it does not have to be a political leader).

Theories about leadership qualities – Machiavelli and Weber

For as long as people could write they have written about leadership. To this day people who wish to learn about the subject can do so from the Bible, other holy books, history books or the works of William Shakespeare.

But two thinkers who particularly wrote on leadership were Niccolo Machiavelli (1469-1527) and Max Weber (1864-1920).

Machiavelli was a crafty man who thought that successful leadership involved the quality of being selfish, while trying to appear generous to other people. He put forward these views, amusingly and with a lot of clever arguments, in a book called *The Prince*. He claimed that leaders should be ruthless in getting what they wanted, and should be ready to deceive other people if necessary. His methods are still used by politicians – sometimes in the form of 'spin'.

Leadership qualities identified by Machiavelli are

- cleverness
- the ability to deceive others
- ruthlessness

Max Weber was a sociologist who studied bureaucratic leadership – a kind of leadership which is still used in large organisations such as the public services. He put forward six famous rules of bureaucratic (office) leadership:

1. The organisation should be split into departments governed by clear rules and regulations
2. There is a hierarchy where lower officials are supervised by higher ones

3 Management is based on official documents (files, codes of practice etc)
4 Officials have full training.
5 Officials work full-time.
6 Management follows rules.

Under this system the leadership qualities needed are

- the ability to understand the work and the regulations
- the ability to follow rules and to make other people follow rules.

> **!**
> **CHECKPOINT ...**
> In 2003/4 Humberside Police were criticised for deleting over ten records of alleged sex offences by Ian Huntley. Huntley had lived in Humberside before moving to Soham where he got a job as a primary school caretaker, and murdered two girl pupils – Holly Wells and Jessica Chapman – in August 2002. The head teacher of Soham Village College said he would never have employed Huntley if he had known of the allegations against him. Humberside Police said they deleted Huntley's records in order to comply with the Data Protection Act. What does this situation tell us about the strengths or weaknesses of bureaucratic leadership?

NHS Leadership qualities

The National Health Service has published a very useful guide to the leadership qualities it is looking for in its managers and leaders.

www.NHSLeadershipQualities.nhs.uk
(Most of what you need to know about leadership qualities)

The table below shows the some of the qualities explained.

Quality	Explanation
Self-belief	Inner confidence
Self-awareness	Knowing your strengths
Self-management	Self-control
Drive for improvement	Urge to make things better
Personal integrity	Honesty and openness
Seizing the future	Willing to bring about changes
Intellectual flexibility	Interest in solving problems
Broad scanning	Getting information from many sources
Political astuteness	Knowing the organisation
Drive for results	Determination to achieve aims
Leading change through people	Understanding and motivating people
Holding to account	Making sure others work well
Empowering others	Giving responsibility to others
Effective and strategic influencing	Networking; making partnerships
Collaborative working	Good teamwork

> **!**
> **CHECKPOINT ...**
> (a) Think of an example of each quality – in a public service context
> (b) Rank them in order of importance for a leader in a public service of your choice
> (c) Research other leadership qualities valued in the public service of your choice.

http://www.dti.gov.uk/mbp/bpgt/knowledge.pdf
(leadership in business)

http://www.mod.uk/mdp/aboutus/cc.htm

Leadership selection

Merit

> Establish and analyse different ways in which leaders are selected or emerge.

For this outcome, you need to explain how people become leaders. There are five main ways in which leaders emerge:

- by birth
- through education
- through promotion
- by appointment
- by self-appointment.

Birth

Many famous leaders have become leaders partly because they were born into rich and powerful families which had a tradition of leading. The father of Alexander the Great, who lived from 356–323 BC and conquered most of Europe and Asia, was the king of Macedonia. The father of George W. Bush, now President of the USA, was himself president between 1988 and 1993, and *his* father was a senator for the state of Connecticut. Many other leaders, such as Winston Churchill, the British wartime leader, or Imran Khan, the former Pakistan cricket captain and now a politician, were born into wealthy families. They became used to giving instructions (possibly to servants) at an early age, and this may well have helped them in their leadership roles later on.

Education

The British public school system (e.g. Eton, Winchester, Harrow) was set up to create a 'ruling class' of politicians, top civil servants, managing directors of companies and army officers. These schools, with their emphasis on sports, toughness, self-control, self-respect and academic excellence, have trained large numbers of society's leaders in the last hundred years. The same traditions form the basis of education at Welbeck College (the army's sixth-form college) and the Royal Military Academy at Sandhurst. In-service training in other uniformed services such as the police, fire service and prison service is also designed to identify and develop leadership qualities.

Promotion

In public service organisations such as the army and the police, promotion is the way in which leaders are chosen and developed. Police constables who can pass the necessary exams, give a good interview and have a good work record are promoted to sergeants. Further competitive examinations can qualify them as inspectors. But they are not actually promoted to inspector rank unless they have shown good leadership qualities as sergeants, and can give an impressive interview.

Appointment

This is similar to promotion, but the person is chosen for a leadership position by a committee or a person in an even higher position. Chief and assistant chief constables, for example, are appointed by the local police authority, following a consideration of their previous careers and an interview.

Election

This is the choosing of a leader by a system of voting – usually, in the UK, in secret.

LINK! Elections are explained in Unit 10 Democratic Processes, page 193.

Self-appointed leaders

These are people who put themselves forward as leaders and are accepted by their followers or colleagues. Hitler, Saddam Hussein and Napoleon were examples of this type – so are most gang leaders. But not all self-appointed leaders are bad: Bob Geldof, the rock star who led the LiveAid campaigns against world poverty in the 1980s, saved thousands of lives. And it appears that most of the great religious leaders of the past were self-appointed.

Distinction

Critically evaluate the selection process of a public services leader.

For this outcome, you need to:

- explain how potential leaders are identified by the public services
- explain how effective their methods for selecting leaders are.

Profile

An example of the kind of comments you could make when you 'critically evaluate' a selection process for leaders is given below:

Example of a critical evaluation

Aspect of selection process for an officer in the Royal Marines	Critical evaluation
Performance in the gym	Physical fitness, strength and agility are highly valued in the Marines, who have to be able to fight at short notice under difficult conditions. Unfit officers would lose authority and not get the obedience and cooperation they need.
An endurance run	Physical fitness is also part of the culture and traditions of the Marines, and is expected of all members of the service. It adds to the charisma of a Marines leader if he (women are still not allowed in the Royal Marines) is fit and strong. But such qualities may become less important in leadership as fighting grows more technological and mechanised.
Tarzan and assault courses	Assault courses help to build confidence, which is essential for an officer, who is in a leadership role.
Current affairs essay	Officers must be able to think clearly, express themselves well, and understand the wider context of what the Marines are doing.
Group discussion exercise	Royal Marines officers have to be able to listen as well as speak, and to cooperate as well as compete. Group discussions help to identify leadership qualities in an officer who has to be able to understand, relate to and inspire his men.
A three-minute lecture	This formal exercise tests ability to speak fluently and confidently in front of a group. Self-presentation skills, and the ability to be concise and self-disciplined are leadership qualities tested in this exercise.

These activities are all part of the three-day potential officers' course at Lympstone, Devon.

For this outcome, you should try to get information from recruitment departments and offices of public services. Visiting speakers with some leadership experience – such as a police inspector or an army officer – would be very helpful.

The selection of leaders can take place:

- in public service entry stages (e.g. army officers are selected around the age of 20, and they are leaders almost from the start)
- following a period of work at a more junior level (e.g. when leading firefighters are promoted to sub-officer, station officer or divisional officer).

Public services also produce leaflets about their selection processes, and you will find examples of them on the internet.

COOL SITES:

http://www.airmenaircrew.freeserve.co.uk/oasc/oasc_ppl.htm – gives a full account of selection processes for RAF officers, which last four days

http://www.met.police.uk/recruitment/chief_supt.htm – recruiting process for superintendents in the Metropolitan Police

A 'leader' can be regarded as anybody who is in charge of a team or other group of people.

A critical evaluation should include:

- a description of the selection process
- an explanation of important points which might not be immediately obvious
- a consideration of whether the activities in the selection process really would help to identify future leaders
- suggestions for altering and improving the selection process to make it more relevant to selecting leaders for that particular public service.

http://www.military-net.com/education/mpdlead.html – ideas about leadership, etc. in the US army, useful definitions

PERSONAL LEADERSHIP QUALITIES

Undertake a review of personal leadership qualities.

For this outcome, you need to identify and comment on your own leadership qualities.

This outcome asks you to outline your own leadership qualities. You should also *provide an example* of when you demonstrated each quality you mention. The reason for this is that in public service (e.g. police) application forms, and in interviews, you will be asked to explain why you are suitable for a particular job. If you have *evidence* to support what you say, this will be a great help to you.

It is up to you (perhaps with the help of your tutor) to decide what your leadership qualities are. All of us have more leadership qualities than we think – so you should not be too shy about putting forward leadership qualities for this outcome.

FOCUS

Leadership traits used in the US army

Bearing	Confidence
Courage	Integrity
Decisiveness	Justice
Endurance	Tact
Maturity	Coolness
Will	Improvement
Candour	Assertiveness
Competence	Empathy/compassion
Commitment	Sense of humour
Initiative	Creativity
Self-discipline	Humility
Flexibility	

Leadership qualities are sometimes called 'traits' of leadership.

CHECKPOINT ...

1. Discuss and reach agreement on what the leadership traits listed above actually mean.
2. Choose ten of them and find examples from your own life when you showed those traits.
3. Think of any other leadership traits which are missing from the list.

4 How would leadership traits in the National Health Service or the police differ (if at all) from the list above?

5 Make a list of leadership traits (you do not necessarily have to use any of those above) which you would like to develop in yourself.

Profile

This outcome could be covered in the form of a table (one row is given here as an example):

Name and explanation of leadership quality	When and where I showed it	Evidence which could support this
Bearing: This means making the most of your appearance and manner, so that you command respect from the public or your co-workers.	When I was working on the checkout in [——] supermarket, I took care to look smart and greeted customers politely and pleasantly.	My supervisor, Mrs Irene Braithwaite, stated this on my work placement report.

Merit

Analyse personal leadership qualities and identify needs for personal development.

For this outcome, you need to:

- examine your own leadership qualities
- suggest how they can be improved.

Leadership traits may or may not be inborn, but they can certainly be developed and improved. One of your main aims in the National Diploma in Public Services is to develop these qualities and skills.

An 'analysis' is a close examination of your strengths and weaknesses. This can also be called a 'self-appraisal' or 'self-assessment'.

For this outcome, you are asked to look closely at your own leadership qualities. This can be difficult: you need to be honest in your self-assessment. This does not mean being brutal. Never say anything like 'I was rubbish' because you will undermine your confidence, and if you made a sincere attempt it won't be true anyway! But you could say, 'I sometimes got confused and gave the wrong change while working on the [—] checkout', or 'I was hesitant and badly-prepared for my presentation'.

To identify needs for personal development, you should state what you could do to improve your leadership qualities. For example, if you are afraid to speak up in a presentation, you could consider joining a drama group, to build your confidence in front of an audience.

Distinction

Monitor and evaluate personal leadership development in relation to specified targets and objectives.

For this outcome, you need to:

- set out systematically and purposefully to develop and improve your own leadership qualities
- produce action plans designed to make you a better leader – and follow them
- follow and assess your own progress in improving your leadership qualities and skills.

This outcome could be met by doing things such as:

- a Duke of Edinburgh's Award
- joining the Cadets, Territorial Army or Special Constabulary
- being in sports teams, carrying out voluntary work
- taking part well in all interactive and leadership activities on your course
- prioritising Key Skills such as Communication, Working with others, Managing own learning and performance and Solving problems.

Ask your tutors for further advice!

Specified targets and objectives

- Targets are outcomes to be achieved to a particular level of competence within a given time (e.g. to show an improvement in self-discipline within three months – perhaps by learning to drive or by stopping smoking).
- Objectives are planned actions which will enable you to show your competences in a number of leadership traits such as assertiveness or flexibility (e.g. leading a group or making decisions on a residential).

Make sure you know whether you should set and specify these targets yourself, or whether you can get help from tutors or supervisors. In real life, e.g. in staff appraisals in the public service, the setting of such targets is a task shared between a worker and their line manager.

Negative traits

Many of us have qualities which prevent us from making the best of our leadership potential. You might wish to set targets which eliminate negative qualities as well as building on positive ones. The table on the next page may give you some ideas.

Profile

One possible way in which to 'monitor and evaluate personal leadership development in relation to specified targets and objectives' would be to set out all the traits you wish to develop in a chart. Choose, say, ten positive traits and arrange your chart as shown below.

Trait	Target	Objective	When achieved	Your evaluation	Assessor's evaluation	Assessor's signature
Bearing	Show improvement in personal presentation, especially in smartness and confidence	Go on a work placement with a public service, and show that I am punctual and smart	12–16 November while on a placement with Customs and Excise at Anytown.	I was punctual, smartly dressed, took a keen interest in what was going on and asked relevant questions.	Leroy was very keen and smart and made good use of his work placement with us.	*Jackie Kennedy (Personnel Officer)*

CHECKPOINT ...

List any negative leadership qualities you may have, and think of ways of getting rid of them!

Positive and negative leadership qualities

Positive leadership qualities	Negative leadership qualities
Takes part enthusiastically in all activities	Reluctant participation in activities
Fluency and clarity in giving information	Shows ignorance
Initiates conversation	Shows poor communication skills
Seeks new ideas	Is too bossy
Encourages others to speak and participate	Uses offensive language, e.g. sexist, racist, etc.
Listens accurately to others' contributions	Talks too much
Assertive but not aggressive	Absent too often
Good at 'networking' and setting up partnerships	Prefers to record activities rather than take part
Takes the opportunity to receive, give and co-ordinate information	Appears bored
	Shy
Avoids persuading people too obviously	Finds it hard to talk to strangers
Encourages group identity, e.g. 'we', not 'I'.	Too keen to make jokes
Shows keenness to plan and achieve	Shows contempt for leadership
Is flexible but not spineless	Bullying or aggressive
Meets agreed deadlines	Too willing to do as told
	Too eager to give own opinions
	Unwilling to listen
	Appears selfish or lazy
	Misses deadlines

Unit 4 Citizenship and Contemporary Issues

Grading criteria

PASSGRADE	Merit	Distinction
To achieve a pass grade the evidence must show that the learner is able to:	To achieve a merit grade the evidence must show that the learner is able to:	To achieve a distinction grade the evidence must show that the learner is able to:
• explain the term 'citizen(s)' and citizenship as defined by at least three public services and identify the differing groups of citizens found within society **75** • identify the qualities of 'good' citizenship and explain which qualities would make a positive contribution to the work of an individual in a named public service **78** • explain how environmental issues may affect the work of public services **80** • describe the main principles of the Human Rights Act, Equal Opportunities Legislation and individual rights and explain how two public services implement equal opportunities and human rights policies into their organisations **81** • describe the services provided to individuals and groups of citizens by statutory and non-statutory public services, the roles and responsibilities of the services and the differences between them in terms of relationships, consequences and influences **86** • explain how the statutory and non-statutory public services effect change and the roles of groups, personnel and information in the changes that take place **91**	• discuss how the rights of the individual 'citizen' may conflict with the needs of the community **77** • establish how two public services are addressing the main issues associated with equal opportunities and human rights policies **83** • analyse the services provided to individuals and groups of citizens by statutory and non-statutory public services and the need for these services **89**	• critically evaluate the need to protect the rights of the individual against the need to maintain the working of society as a whole **77** • evaluate, compare and justify the approach used by two public services to the main issues of equal opportunities and human rights **86** • critically evaluate the services provided to individuals and groups of citizens by statutory and non-statutory public services, justifying the need for these services **90**

Citizenship is a very ancient idea – but it never goes out of fashion. It is all about our rights and our responsibilities to other people. It is an idea which is at the heart of public service work.

This unit tells you about the theory and practice of good citizenship, and takes a good hard look at equal opportunities and human rights.

The unit is externally assessed, using an IVA.

CITIZENS AND CITIZENSHIP

PASSGRADE

Explain the term 'citizen(s)' and citizenship as defined by at least three public services and identify the differing groups of citizens found within society.

For this outcome, you will need to:

- find out what three or more public services mean by 'citizen' and 'citizenship' (in their words)
- explain what they mean in your own words
- name and briefly describe different groups of citizens found in Britain (or the country where you live).

FOCUS

Some definitions of citizenship

There are several ways of defining 'citizen' and 'citizenship'. Some are based on nationality; others are based on a person's rights and responsibilities in society.

Citizenship is ...

'the power to take part in the deliberative or judicial administration of any state.' – Aristotle

'the knowledge, skills and understanding to play an effective role in society at local, national and international levels' – QCA (the body in charge of the new citizenship curriculum in British schools)

'People who are closely connected with the United Kingdom (including the Channel Islands and the Isle of Man) and, in most cases, the British overseas territories are British citizens. British citizens have the right to live here permanently and are free to leave and re-enter the United Kingdom at any time.' – Home Office

Army citizenship requirements

'1 Applicants must have been born in the UK, Republic of Ireland or a Commonwealth Country.

2 At all times, since birth, applicants must have been a UK or Commonwealth citizen or a citizen of the Republic of Ireland.

3 They must normally have lived in the UK for five years immediately preceding the application. (In certain circumstances, particularly if the candidate is of UK origin, a shorter period of residency will be accepted.)'

Prison service definitions of citizenship (for recruitment purposes)

This extract shows the nationality requirements and some other citizenship requirements as defined by the prison service:

'1 You must be a British or Commonwealth Citizen, a British Protected Person, an EU National or an Icelandic or Norwegian National. Some EU family members may also qualify. All candidates must be free from immigration control and have indefinite leave to remain in the United Kingdom. For some posts candidates may be required to have been resident in the United Kingdom for three years.

2 At the time of appointment you must be aged between 18½ and 57.

3 You must not be an undischarged bankrupt.

4 You must not be a member of a group or organisation which the Prison Service considers to be racist.'

Source: Prison service website

Citizenship requirements for the London Ambulance Service

'No serious criminal convictions. All applicants will be subject to Criminal Records "Disclosure".'

Citizenship requirements for retained (volunteer) firefighters:

- 'of good character
- at least 18 years of age
- able to reach the Fire Station within 5 minutes from home or work
- amenable to discipline
- physically fit'

Source: Lancashire Fire and Rescue Service (Chorley) www.lancsfirerescue.org

From these definitions, it can be seen that citizenship is defined in more than one way:

- as the nationality of an individual
- as having political rights (e.g. voting)
- as being a responsible member of society.

http://www.ind.homeoffice.gov.uk/ – explains British citizenship in detail

http://www.hmprisonservice.gov.uk/corporate/dynpage.asp?Page=32

Aspects of citizenship

Type of citizen	Main characteristics
Community member	A community is any group of people outside the family who feel they have something in common, e.g. locality, interests, lifestyle or group aims. Examples: the inhabitants of Notting Hill, train-spotters, pro-life campaigners.
Consumer	Any person who buys goods or services.
Family member	Parents, brothers, sisters, children, aunts, uncles, cousins, etc.
Taxpayer	A person paying local or national taxes to pay for public services.
Voter	A person who votes in local, national or European elections – or any other ballot or referendum.
Worker	Workers can be self-employed, employed, full time, part-time, temporary, permanent, manual, white collar, public sector, private sector, paid and voluntary.
Pupil/learner	They may have limited citizenship because of age or nationality. But they have definite rights and responsibility within schools and colleges.
Young, middle-aged, elder	People between the ages of 18–70, broadly speaking, have the fullest citizenship rights and responsibilities. These rights are reduced if they are not British citizens, if they are prisoners, if they are young, if they are very old or if they are mentally ill.
Culture	This consists of 'norms' (the things most people do) and 'values' (the things most people think). Our lifestyles and beliefs, including such things as language, religion, ideas of right and wrong, food, etc. are all part of our culture. There is a historical link between nationality and culture.
Religion	Religion is part of culture, because it teaches norms and values. All religions encourage good citizenship – but they don't all agree about what it is.
Effect on public services	Public services exist to protect all citizens and help them to enjoy full rights and responsibilities within the law. But they sometimes discriminate against non-citizens (foreign nationals).
Morality	This is the rights and wrongs of an action or belief. Some public services, such as the police, prison service, ambulance service or armed forces, are constantly having to make moral decisions or choices. 'Good citizenship' suggests moral goodness – the desire to do right, rather than wrong.
Honesty	This is a moral quality. It means saying what you believe to be true, and not promising more than you can deliver.
Attitude	Attitude is emotion or beliefs which affect the way we act. It can be good or bad. Friendliness and kindness are attitudes – but so too is racism.

! CHECKPOINT ...

1 Which of the definitions (page 75) relates to:
  (a) nationality?
  (b) political rights?
  (c) responsible behaviour?

2 The Home Office is planning to introduce 'citizenship tests' for people applying for British citizenship. Find out about these tests. What are the human rights implications?

Merit

Discuss how the rights of the individual 'citizen' may conflict with the needs of the community.

For this outcome, you need to find and explain ways in which our freedom is limited by the need to respect other people's rights.

We have all been in classrooms where someone has wanted to 'mouth off' about something, and the rest of the class have wanted to get on with their work. This is a simple example of a situation where the rights of the individual (free speech) conflict with the needs of the community (to get on with their work).

How individual rights might confict with the needs of the community

In a free society, we should all be able to do what we want. But what happens if what we want to do is bad for everybody else?

The table below shows four individual rights given in the European Convention on Human Rights – 18 'articles' which support the human and individual rights we enjoy in the UK today. The right-hand column suggests ways in which these individual rights may conflict with the needs of the community (i.e. people in general).

CHECKPOINT ...

Look for other rights, either in the European Convention or in the United Nations Universal Declaration on Human Rights, and work out where they can conflict with community needs.

Distinction

Critically evaluate the need to protect the rights of the individual against the need to maintain the working of society as a whole.

For this outcome, you need to:

- decide which is more important: the freedom of individuals to do what they like, or the need to keep society running smoothly

Individual right (simplified from the European Convention on Human Rights)	Possible conflict with needs of the community
ARTICLE 2 Everyone has a right to life	It is OK to kill enemies in war because they threaten the community.
ARTICLE 5 Everyone has the right to liberty and security	Rapists and murderers can be locked up, because they are a danger to their communities.
ARTICLE 8 Everyone has the right to respect for his private and family life, his home and his correspondence.	The police have the power to demand e-mail, phone and internet records from phone companies and ISPs without a warrant in the Regulation of Investigatory Powers Act 2000. This is to protect the community against internet crime and terrorism.
ARTICLE 10 Everyone has the right to freedom of expression.	Nobody can make racist speeches (except in the House of Commons). The law against this type of free speech protects the community against racial violence.

- give reasons, explanations and examples to support your conclusions.

You may find it better to limit your investigations to one or two individual rights issues. Try to look at both sides of the argument in an unbiased way – except in the conclusion of your assignment, presentation, etc. where you should give your own *reasoned* viewpoint.

Useful sources of information are:

- newspapers such as the *Guardian* or *The Times*, which give in-depth analysis of this kind of problem
- police and prison officers whose work involves both upholding individual rights and society's workings.
- pressure groups such as Charter 88 or the Society for the Protection of the Unborn Child (you could write to them, visit their websites or invite speakers if they are available).

This is one of the most complex and difficult questions relating to public service work. All laws, which are for the benefit of society, also limit the freedom of the individual. The problem is to try to achieve 'proportionality' – a balance between respecting the individual's freedoms and society's needs for stability and security.

People find it hard to agree about where individual rights end and society's rights begin. This conflict between the individual's rights and society's needs can be on a huge scale. The Blair government justified the 2003 war in Iraq by claiming that stockpiles of weapons of mass destruction in Iraq posed a threat to western society. In the decision to go to war, the individual right to life of Iraqi civilians and soldiers was judged less important than the need to keep western society free from the threat of terrorism. The choice that Bush and Blair made in going to war divided opinion in their own countries and the rest of the world, and showed the complexity of moral questions involving individual rights and society's needs.

In war, the rights of the individual are always sacrificed to maintain the workings of society as a whole. This was seen most clearly of all in World War II where rationing, restrictions of travel, the suppression of free speech and political democracy all limited individual rights in order to maintain society. Around 300,000 British soldiers and 100,000 civilians were killed – not to mention at least 20,000,000 other people around the world. This enormous sacrifice is widely considered a price worth paying to ensure the survival of western democratic society.

In peacetime, there is still a conflict between the rights of the individual and the needs of society. Examples include:

- arguments on cloning, etc., where the rights of individual mothers are balanced against the risks to society of uncontrolled experimentation on human embryos
- the situation where individual privacy is threatened by the huge amounts of confidential information about us which is held on computer – in colleges, local government, police databases, etc.
- London's congestion charges. These limit the individual's right to travel by car, in the hope that London as a whole will benefit by having less traffic on the roads
- anti-terrorism and asylum laws, which limit the individual rights of terrorist suspects and economic migrants, in order to maintain the workings of British society as a whole.

The arguments you use will be based on such concepts as:

- morality: the study of right and wrong
- people's well-being, e.g. their comfort, wealth and security
- freedom: the right to do what we want
- justice: the right that we all have to be treated equally.

GOOD CITIZENSHIP

Identify the qualities of 'good' citizenship and explain which qualities would make a positive contribution to the work of an individual in a named public service.

For this outcome, you need to:

- find out what makes a person a good citizen
- show how good citizenship is needed to work in a given public service.

FOCUS

Another definition of citizenship

'... citizenship comprises three distinct but interrelated elements: social and moral responsibility, community involvement and political literacy.' – from *Education for Citizenship and the Teaching of Democracy in Schools,* the final report of the *Advisory Group on Citizenship 2002*

COOL SITE:

http://www.whsmith.co.uk/whs/go.asp?pagedef=/yso/citizen.htm

Examples of 'good citizenship' included in the 'elements of citizenship' are:

- **social and moral responsibility:**
  - obeying and upholding the law
  - reporting crimes you may have witnessed
  - volunteering, helping, caring
  - helping to solve disputes or problems among your friends or classmates, e.g. by conciliation
- **community involvement:**
  - participation in activities, e.g. sports, college societies, course activities, cadets, police youth groups/forums, etc.
  - organising activities from which others could benefit, e.g. charity fundraising, holidays with friends, inter-class sports contests, expeditions and outdoor activities
  - representing your class, e.g. on a staff–student committee
  - recognising, avoiding and combating discrimination and unfairness
- **political literacy:**
  - knowing your rights
  - taking an interest in politics, the news, local government and central government
  - voting in elections
  - awareness of social and economic issues
  - awareness of environment (litter, pollution, etc.)
  - awareness of community issues (drug abuse, social problems, sexism, racism, etc.)
  - consumer awareness; understanding money, not getting into debt, etc.
  - concern about people less fortunate than yourself, e.g. the poor.

Profile

Good citizenship qualities which would make a positive contribution to the fire service

Good citizenship qualities from the above list	Matching positive qualities mentioned in fire service recruitment booklet: *Start a new life – save someone else's*
Obeying and upholding the law	'Firefighters ... inspect premises to make sure they meet fire safety regulations and are up to standard for a fire safety certificate.'
Volunteering, helping, caring	All firefighters 'have self-discipline, commitment and a genuine desire to work with and for others.'
Participation in activities	'Firefighters have to work together. They also have to accept directions and use their initiative.'
Representing your class	Firefighters 'need the people skills to get that message (fire safety) across to audiences of all ages, in jobs and homes of all kinds.'
Awareness of the environment	'The work includes pumping out flood water, attending chemical spills and helping at road, rail and air crashes.'
Awareness of community issues	'Educating children, older people and other at-risk groups in the community in fire safety.'

! CHECKPOINT ...

Discuss with a friend how you could – realistically – become a better citizen. What could you do to put some of your ideas into practice?

Environmental issues

PASSGRADE

Explain how environmental issues may affect the work of public services.

For this outcome, you need to:

- explain how environmental problems or protection influence the work of public services
- explain how public services try to avoid damaging the environment more than necessary.

As more and more pressure comes on the environment from global warming, industrial and traffic pollution, waste disposal, population growth and the destruction of natural habitats, the public services – like many other organisations – are expected to play their part in easing the problem.

Environmental degradation is in many ways a global problem which requires global solutions. The framework for international action was laid down in the Kyoto Protocol in 1997, in which 38 industrialised countries promised to cut their emissions of greenhouse gases between 2008 and 2012 to levels that are 5.2 per cent below 1990 levels. In 2001, the USA withdrew from the Protocal, and in 2003 Russia, another major polluter, threatened to do the same. But other countries, including the UK, are still committed to cutting down on the production of CO_2 and other greenhouse gases.

British public services are working to recycle their waste and cut down on energy use. For example, in 2001 the Metropolitan Police made themselves more environment-friendly by:

- recycling packaging materials
- recovering lead and brass from used rounds in firearms training
- recycling some of the one and a quarter million aluminium drinks cans used each year throughout the Met
- setting up an interest-free season ticket loan scheme to encourage the use of public transport, rather than cars
- putting an environment site on the Met's intranet
- setting targets on atmospheric pollution, energy, water and waste management, transport and health and hygiene for the Metropolitan Police.

FOCUS

In 2003 the Ministry of Defence set itself targets in

- business travel
- water use
- waste
- energy
- biodiversity
- social impacts.

Source: www.mod.uk/dsef/index/html

The enemy are not the only targets for the Ministry of Defence.

In addition, most public services are actively involved in environmental protection. Examples include:

- Customs and Excise – combating the illegal trade in endangered species
- Police and Vehicle Inspectorate – stopping polluting vehicles, checking weights of loads, etc.
- environmental health officers – working with local authorities to combat noise and other forms of pollution

- fire service – cleaning up after chemical spillages; putting out forest fires
- Health and Safety Executive – reducing risks from hazardous chemicals, etc.
- HM Coastguards – checking and combating offshore pollution.

Environmental problems affect the work of some public services by making it more difficult. Traffic congestion on the UK's roads makes work for the police, and slows response times for the fire and ambulance services.

! CHECKPOINT ...

1 Research environmental impacts on public services by contacting a service of your choice and asking them about the problems they face.

2 Invite an environmental health officer to explain their work to you.

Equal opportunites and human rights

Describe the main principles of the Human Rights Act, equal opportunities legislation and individual rights and explain how two public services implement equal opportunities and human rights policies into their organisations.

For this outcome, you need to:

- give the main ideas in the Human Rights Act and equal opportunities law
- show what two public services do to put equal opportunities and human rights into practice.

For this outcome, there are many cool websites giving clear summaries of the laws. The full laws are on the HMSO website: http://www.hmso.gov.uk – read the 'explanatory notes' – it's easier than wading through the full Act!

FOCUS

The Human Rights Act 1998

The Human Rights Act came into force on 2 October 2000 and incorporates into UK law certain rights and freedoms set out in the European Convention on Human Rights, such as:

- the right to life (article 2)
- protection from torture and inhuman or degrading treatment or punishment (article 3)
- protection from slavery and forced or compulsory labour (article 4)
- the right to liberty and security of person (article 5)
- the right to a fair trial (article 6)
- protection from retrospective criminal offences (article 7)
- the protection of private and family life (article 8)
- freedom of thought, conscience and religion (article 9)
- freedom of expression (article 10)
- freedom of association and assembly (article 11)
- the right to marry and found a family (article 12)
- freedom from discrimination (article 13)
- the right to property (article 1 of the first protocol)
- the right to education (article 2 of the first protocol)
- the right to free and fair elections (article 3 of the first protocol)
- the abolition of the death penalty in peacetime (articles 1 and 2 of the sixth protocol).

Source: http://www.compactlaw.co.uk/hra.html Compact Law Ltd with permission

The Human Rights Act applies to public bodies such as the police, prison service, criminal courts and local authorities. Prosecution of a public body under the Act must take place less than a year after the alleged offence.

The Act must apply 'without discrimination on any ground such as sex, race, colour, language, religion, political or other opinion, national or social origin, association with a national minority, property, birth or other status'.

Equal opportunities legislation

These are laws which protect people against discrimination at work.

Sex Discrimination Act 1975

Under this Act it is unlawful to discriminate on grounds of sex or marital status in recruitment, promotion and training.

The Act deals with two kinds of sex discrimination – direct and indirect – and victimisation.

- Direct sex discrimination occurs when a person is treated less favourably on grounds of sex.
- Indirect sex discrimination occurs where a requirement or condition is applied equally to men and women, but the proportion of one sex that can satisfy the condition is much smaller than that of the other sex. The old physical entry tests for some fire services were an example of indirect sex discrimination.
- Victimisation occurs when an individual is discriminated against because they have exercised their rights under the Act.

COOL SITE:

http://www.eoc.org.uk/EOCeng/dynpages/Relevant_Legislation.asp

Race Relations Act 1976

This Act makes it unlawful to discriminate on grounds of race, colour, nationality or ethnic or national origin. It covers all aspects of employment, and the provision of goods and services.

- Direct discrimination is clearly on the grounds of race or colour, e.g. a job notice saying, 'No blacks need apply'.
- Indirect discrimination means applying restrictions or conditions which would apply more to one ethnic group than another. The old height limits for male police applicants ('must be over 5'8" ') were an example.

Victimisation of people who exercise their rights under this Act is also outlawed.

http://www.cre.gov.uk/legaladv/rra_regs.html

> **! CHECKPOINT ...**
>
> 1 There are a few cases under these Acts where sex and race discrimination are lawful, and some of them relate to public service. Find out what these exceptions are. Do you think they are justified?
>
> 2 The Asylum and Immigration Act 1996 makes it a criminal offence to employ a person who is not entitled to live or work in the United Kingdom. To what extent do you think this goes against the Race Relations Act?

Equal Pay Acts 1970 and 1983

This Act allows an individual to claim pay equal to that received by members of the opposite sex on the grounds that they are doing the same work, or work 'of equal value'. Its main aim is to ensure that women do not get paid less than men. Claims can be pursued through the Employment Tribunal.

http://www.eoc.org.uk/cseng/legislation/the_equal_pay_act_an_overview.asp

Disability Discrimination Act 1995

This Act requires employers to make 'reasonable adjustments' to premises or working practices to allow disabled people to be employed. Disability includes physical disabilities, sight or hearing impairment, learning difficulties, mental health problems and progressive conditions such as multiple sclerosis and AIDS.

http://www.disability.gov.uk/dda/

Age discrimination

This has been outlawed since 2003 by an EU Directive, and Parliament has an anti-ageism law planned for 2006. This will probably set the normal retirement age at 70, and give older people a right to continued job training. Many public services, e.g. the fire service, no longer have an upper age limit for applicants.

http://www.agepositive.gov.uk/findmenu.cfm?sectionid=55

Employment Equality (Sexual Orientation) Regulations 2003

These outlaw most discrimination against gays and lesbians – in employment, training and most benefits. This includes discrimination in the police and armed forces, and all kinds of bullying and harassment. Cases – as with other equal opportunities laws – will be tried at employment tribunals.

http://www.hmso.gov.uk/si/si2003/20031661.htm

How two public services implement equal opportunities and human rights policies

The aim of an equal opportunities policy is to ensure that no group of the population is discriminated against in recruitment, training, promotion or any other aspect of employment

For this outcome, you should collect recruitment literature, visit Home Office, ODPM and Ministry of Defence websites, and talk to public service workers about their experience of equal opportunities.

The fire and rescue service

This service is undergoing a period of rapid change and modernisation. This is especially true of its approach to equal opportunities.

The independent review of the fire service by Sir George Bain, published in 2002, said 'Firefighters are not a diverse group. The service is 98.3 per cent male and 98.5 per cent white. Of all the public services, its profile is the most skewed in this regard.'

To combat this imbalance the government is introducing sweeping changes. These include:

- changing recruitment literature to make it clear that the fire and rescue service (as it is now called) is serious about recruiting more women and more ethnic minority firefighters
- changing work practices to make them more attractive to women and applicants from ethnic minorities. This means changing the shift system to one which is 'more family friendly' (i.e. shorter shifts spread more evenly through the week) and getting rid of old-fashioned 'discipline regulations'
- carrying out audits and action plans to determine how far equal opportunities have been incorporated into the organisation – and how much still needs to be done.

Each fire and rescue service has to draw up a statement showing its commitment to equal opportunities.

www.lancsfirerescue.org.uk – equal opportunities statement

The prison service

Equal opportunities for prison service staff are implemented in recruitment, training, promotion and other aspects of work. The table on the following page explains some aspects of the equal opportunities policy.

COOL SITES:

www.20units.co.uk – prison service recruitment information

http://www.homeoffice.gov.uk/docs/raceequ_pubserv_nov02.pdf – race equality in public services

Merit

Establish how two public services are addressing the main issues associated with equal opportunities and human rights policies.

Aspects of equal opportunities policy in the prison service

Equal opportunities for prison officers (quoted from recruitment leaflet)	Explanation
'You should not be member of groups or organisations considered to have racist philosophy, principles, aims or policies.'	Applicants are checked through the Criminal Records Bureau. Such people would be unsuitable in the multi-ethnic environment of a prison.
'At the time of joining you must be between 18½ and up to 57 years of age.'	The age restrictions have been largely removed.
'Your employment will be conditional upon your declaring any membership of the Freemasons.'	This is to show that no special group of applicants will be favoured – as sometimes happened in the past.
'Applications from those who wish to work part-time or job-share are welcome.'	This removes discrimination which could affect women more than men.
'The Prison Service is an equal opportunities employer. We welcome applications from candidates regardless of ethnic origin, religious belief, gender, sexual orientation, disability or any other irrelevant factor.'	A clear statement showing that the prison service is putting equal opportunities into practice.
'The Prison Service operates a guaranteed interim scheme for disabled people (as defined by the Disability Discrimination Act 1995) who meet the minimum criteria for this appointment.'	Extra encouragement for disabled people to apply.

For this outcome, you need to build on the previous outcome by explaining what public services are doing to improve their record on equal opportunities and human rights.

'Establish' means that you need to find authentic, accurate and up-to-date material on what two public services are doing to improve their equal opportunities and human rights policies. Visits, visiting speakers, recruitment leaflets and the internet will all provide helpful information.

FOCUS

Definitions of equal opportunities and human rights

'"Equal opportunities" means the prevention, elimination or regulation of discrimination between persons on grounds of sex or marital status, on racial grounds, or on grounds of disability, age, sexual orientation, language or social origin, or of other personal attributes, including beliefs or opinions, such as religious beliefs or political opinions.' – Scotland Bill 1998

'"Human rights": the rights, liberties or freedoms conferred on, or guaranteed to persons by any agreement, treaty or convention to which the State is a party.' – Irish Human Rights Commission Bill 1999

These phrases have come to be used in particular contexts:

- 'Equal opportunities' is mainly about *the way people are treated at work*, e.g. in recruitment, promotion, the work done, conditions of service and fair pay.
- 'Human rights' is about *the way people are treated by the public services.*

How two public services address equal opportunities and human rights policies

The fire and rescue service

Equal opportunities

The fire and rescue service is:

- meeting diversity targets (recruiting more women and staff from ethnic minorities, so that the numbers reflect the diversity of the area served)
- creating a new adviser post to improve recruitment from under-represented groups (women and people from ethnic minorities)
- developing training and theatre-type presentations to improve firefighters' understanding of equal opportunities and diversity
- developing links with local racial equality councils
- modifying equipment, e.g. lowering 'vehicle mounted ladder housings' (this will make the equipment more suitable for women to use, and improve overall health and safety)
- improving internal communication within the service to help achieve equal opportunities targets
- setting up an Equality Forum chaired by the Chief Fire Officer to monitor progress.

Human rights

In respect of human rights, the fire service is:

- carrying out a 'cultural audit' within the service. This means interviewing staff in confidence and finding out about harassment, bullying and discrimination among fire service staff
- using the Combined Fire Authority's Equality Task Group – which consists of elected members, fire officers and representatives from local organisations – to help ensure that the whole community is being served equally.

The prison service

According to the 2002 annual report of the prison service, the following methods are being used to address the main issues associated with equal opportunities and human rights policies.

Equal opportunities

The prison service is:

- trying to recruit more women. In 2002 16 per cent of prison officers were female
- trying to recruit more people from ethnic minorities
- delivering race and diversity training to managers
- researching life–work balance issues (giving workers some control over when, where and how they work)
- setting up RESPOND (Race Equality for Staff and Prisoners Programme). 4.9 per cent of staff are from ethnic minorities. 6.3 per cent of staff promoted were from ethnic minorities. Both these figures are below the 9 per cent of ethnic minority people in the UK population at the 2001 census
- setting up RESPECT (Race Equality for Staff Network). Its aim is to eliminate racism in the workplace. RESPECT has 1850 members (out of 42,580 Prison Service staff)
- training managers in race relations
- actively recruiting disabled staff from 2004
- raising disability issues among staff.

Human rights

Human rights is an extremely complex issue in prisons. Almost all complaints to do with the treatment of prisoners are human rights complaints.

The essential problem in the UK's prisons is that they are over-crowded. This makes all attempts to respect the human rights of prisoners more difficult than they should be. But many of the public feel that prisoners, who have done wrong, should be made to suffer, and as a result spending money on prisons (or letting prisoners out early) is not politically popular. For that reason, and because the courts are getting tougher in their sentencing, the over-crowding is getting worse.

Prison over-crowding causes serious problems of security, health and prisoners' welfare.

1st officer: What are you reading that for, Bert?
2nd officer: I'm trying to find out how many prisoners you can get in a telephone box.

The 2002 annual report of Her Majesty's Chief Inspector of Prisons, Anne Owers, made the following recommendations, which the prison service will be expected to follow:

- far too many children are being kept in prison – they should be kept somewhere more suitable
- better education, rehabilitation and resettlement should be provided
- anti-bullying strategies must be improved – many prisoners feel unsafe
- more effort must be made to prevent suicide and self-harm
- there must be better risk assessments and monitoring of prisoners
- many (not all) staff must treat prisoners with more respect
- health care needs improving and co-ordinating better
- there must be better facilities and systems for treating prisoners who are mentally ill
- race relations liaison officers must be given more time to do their work
- arrangements for foreign nationals infringe their human rights and must be improved
- there need to be better arrangements for prison visits – especially from families
- foreign nationals should not be imprisoned when they have committed no offence
- prisoners are being locked up too long each day.

Many of these things are being done already, but because of the over-crowding they are not being done well enough.

Other ways in which the prison service is addressing human rights issues:

- The Commission for Racial Equality (CRE) has inspected the prison service's race relations policies and practices. The report should come out in 2003 and is expected to be critical.
- Diversity training has been introduced into the prison service. Four hundred Equal Opportunity Officers and Race Relations Liaison Officers have been trained.
- All staff will get 3 hours' training on diversity and race relations.
- The prisoner complaints system for racist staff behaviour has been revised to make it easier for prisoners to identify racism.
- A new report form has been introduced so that anyone inside a prison can report a racist incident.
- Prison officers have been banned from belonging to the BNP, National Front and Combat 18.

www.nelsonthornes.com/vocational/public_services – Unit 23 Custodial Care

Distinction

Evaluate, compare and justify the approach used by two public services to the main issues of equal opportunities and human rights.

For this outcome, you need to:

- explain in detail
- show the similarities and differences and
- consider any criticisms that might be made of the equal opportunities or human rights approach of the two services you have chosen.

The PROFILE on the next page indicates how you might do this for one issue, recruitment, in the fire service and prison service.

Equal opportunities and human rights is a wide and complex subject, and you will not have time to cover the whole field in depth. You may do better choosing certain topics, such as comparing the police and prison service in their treatment of foreign nationals, or the attitudes towards gay or disabled people in say, the armed forces and the ambulance service. When in doubt – ask your tutors!

PUBLIC SERVICES AND THE CITIZEN

Describe the services provided to individuals and groups of citizens by statutory and non-statutory public services, the roles and responsibilities of the services and the differences between them in terms of relationships, consequences and influences.

Profile

Issue	Evaluate	Compare	Justify
Recruitment	Both the fire service and the prison service are 'equal opportunities employers'. This means that all their recruitment advertisements, leaflets, etc. stress the fact that they welcome applications from all sections of the community. The problem is that their actual recruitment, and the people they already have working for them, do not reflect the communities that they serve. Less than 2 per cent of firefighters, and less than 5 per cent of prison officers belong to ethnic minorities – yet according to the 2001 census 9 per cent of the British population belong to ethnic minority groups.	The fire service has a worse recruitment problem than the prison service, when it comes to meeting equal opportunities targets. It has always been easy to recruit firefighters, with (according to the ODPM) 40 applicants for every vacancy. The physical and practical nature of the work has encouraged the fire service to pick and choose applicants according to male physical criteria (and aptitude tests which may be culturally biased towards white male applicants). The prison service has had far more criticism from the media (until 2002 when strikes put the fire service in the spotlight). Traditionally, prison officers have been suspected of brutality and a failure to understand the psychology and rehabilitation needs of prisoners. In the 1990s the prison service applied academic criteria to applicants, rather than rely wholly on their own entry procedures. In the interests of equal opportunities they are thinking of allowing disabled people to apply to be prison officers.	The fire service is now having to make strenuous efforts to address its recruitment imbalance. This will be an uphill struggle, not least because the public are more interested in the rescue abilities of the fire service than whether they fulfil ethnic and gender monitoring requirements. The fire service are employing diversity officers and advertising in media targeted at ethnic minorities. They are also decentralising so that fire stations become community fire stations, and they liaise actively with schools and youth programmes in the hope of getting more diverse recruits in the future.

For this outcome, you need to:

- describe what statutory public services do for people
- describe what non-statutory public services do for people
- show the differences in the scale and importance of what they do.

'Statutory' public services are those which have been set up by law. They include all the main professional public services, whether uniformed or non-uniformed. Their activities are covered by laws, they are supervised by central and local government and, though they may change in detail, they are an accepted and permanent part of the British way of life.

'Non-statutory public services' are charities and other organisations which have been started by people who see, and try to fulfil, a public need. Their aims are often more specialised or limited than those of statutory public services. There is no law which says they have to exist. Non-statutory public services often work in partnership with statutory public services, and get some funding from local or central government. Charities are monitored by the Charity Commission.

Examples of non-statutory public services are Citizens' Advice Bureaux, Samaritans and the Ramblers' Association.

http://www.charity-commission.gov.uk/

FOCUS

A non-statutory public service

The National Search and Rescue Dog Association (NSARDA) is an umbrella organisation for air-scenting search dogs in the UK. Its members are the search-and-rescue-dog associations which are located throughout the UK.

Each of the individual search-and-rescue-dog associations (SARDA) is a voluntary organisation responsible for training and deployment of air-scenting search and rescue dogs to search for missing persons in the mountains and high moorlands of the UK as well as the lowland, rural and urban areas.

www.nsarda.org.uk

CHECKPOINT ...

Make a list of ten non-statutory public services which operate in your local area, and find out what they do.

Because public service organisations have a tendency to work together and form partnerships, the distinction between statutory and non-statutory public services can become blurred.

Main roles of some statutory public services

Monarchy

The Queen is the official Head of State. Her role is ceremonial – except in the opening of Parliament, where she gives the Queen's Speech outlining the government's programme. She gives the Royal Assent to new laws (i.e. signs them) and has more or less regular meetings with the Prime Minister.

Her ceremonial role is important, as a national symbol around which patriotic feelings of 'Britishness' can be expressed (e.g. on money, stamps, etc. and in the names of public services, e.g. 'Her Majesty's Customs and Excise'). She symbolises a tradition of monarchy and nationhood going back to 1066, when the Battle of Hastings led to the first serious attempt in Britain to create an independent country. The Queen and the royal family are thought to stimulate the UK economy by using overseas visits to 'sell' ideas of Britishness and quality and by, in a sense, 'branding' British goods.

The Queen and the royal family are patrons of many charities, and deeply involved in the work of some non-statutory public services.

Parliament

Parliament is made up of two 'houses' – the House of Commons which contains 659 Members of Parliament (MPs) representing constituencies, or areas, of Britain, and the House of Lords.

LINK! See Unit 10, page 199.

The Cabinet (and ministers)

LINK! See Unit 10, page 199.

Local government

LINK! See Unit 10, page 199.

Law

Law is 'a rule of conduct or procedure recognised by a community as enforceable by authority' (*Oxford English Dictionary*). It is used to avoid or settle disputes, right wrongs and punish those who break their obligations to society. The aim of the law is to be fair, systematic and to act in the public interest. Criminal law, the police, the probation service and the prison service are all part of the criminal justice system. While the police enforce the law, members of the public can also enforce the law using solicitors and the civil courts, by prosecuting people or organisations that they believe have done wrong.

Roles of two non-statutory public services

FOCUS

The Citizens Advice Bureau

The Citizens Advice service helps people solve their legal, money and other problems by providing free, confidential, impartial and independent advice by influencing policy makers.

From its origins in 1939 as an emergency service during World War II, it has evolved into a professional national agency.

Every Citizens Advice Bureau is a registered charity reliant on volunteers. Citizens Advice Bureaux help solve nearly six million new problems every year which are central to people's lives, including debt and consumer issues, benefits, housing, legal matters, employment, and immigration. Advisers can help fill out forms, write letters, negotiate with creditors and represent clients at court or tribunal.

Source: www.adviceguide.org.uk

Samaritans

Samaritans' mission

Samaritans is available 24 hours a day to provide confidential emotional support for people who are experiencing feelings of distress or despair, including those which may lead to suicide.

Samaritans' vision

Samaritans' vision is for a society in which:

- fewer people die by suicide
- people are able to explore their feelings
- people are able to acknowledge and respect the feelings of others.

Source: http://www.samaritans.org/know/about.shtm#
© Samaritans

Main differences between statutory and non-statutory public services

Statutory public services are:

- set up by law
- paid for by the taxpayer
- matched by similar services in other countries
- huge employers (the Civil Service employs 500,000 people)
- run on wholly professional lines
- standardised throughout the country.

Non-statutory public services are:

- set up by individuals, not by Parliament
- numerous but usually small in scale
- paid for by members, donations from the public and government grants
- usually registered as charities
- sometimes international or national, but more often local
- small employers – or run by amateurs and volunteers (though their standards are often professional).

Merit

Analyse the services provided to individuals and groups of citizens by statutory and non-statutory public services and the need for these services.

For this outcome, you need to:

- examine closely what statutory and non-statutory public services do both for individuals and for groups of people
- show clearly when and why these services are needed.

For this outcome, you need to collect detailed information and make thoughtful comments about how the work of public services satisfies (or fails to satisfy) society's needs.

There is a risk of going into too much detail with this outcome. You will have to decide whether you wish to consider public services as a whole, or concentrate in more detail on one or two statutory and non-statutory public services. If in doubt – ask your tutors!

Why public services are needed

Public services exist to protect us, care for us, and look after our welfare. The needs they satisfy have always existed, ever since people started living together in settled communities over 3000 years ago. Such needs include the need:

- for protection against enemies and robbers
- to live in peace with one's neighbours
- for food and water
- for housing
- to make wealth and improve standards of living
- to improve public health
- for social activities
- for cultural, intellectual and religious fulfilment.

Profile

Protection against enemies – the service provided by the armed forces

The need for the armed forces is based on a history of conflict, since earliest times, between different communities. Conflict can be resolved by talking, but history seems to show that the time sometimes comes when people are no longer able or willing to talk – and war results.

The British armed forces are considered to provide an excellent service in defending the UK and acting as a deterrent against attack. Though less well equipped and funded than their American counterparts, they appear (at the time of writing) to have done a professional job in taking over southern Iraq. Their problems have stemmed mainly from being given unreasonable commands without the resources to carry them out. They have not been able to restore essential services or 'normality' around Basra – as yet.

There is a major argument going on as to whether British troops should be serving in Iraq in the first place. The United Nations have questioned the legality of the war, and, if it is true that the war is illegal, the British armed forces have been misused and both British soldiers and Iraqi civilians have lost their lives needlessly. This, of course, is not the fault of the British armed forces, but of the politicians who sent them to Iraq.

In recent years funding for the armed forces has gone down because the public have questioned whether there is the same need for them as there was in the past. This is mainly because of the end of the Cold War in 1989, when the threat from Communist Russia ended. In addition, within the ruling Labour Party, there has been a tradition of pacifism: that war is not a good way of solving international disputes. However, the majority of people are not pacifists, and the 'war against terror' beginning on 11 September 2001 may lead to an increase in the need, and the funding, for the armed forces.

COOL SITE:

http://www.local.dtlr.gov.uk/research/crosscut/mainrprt.pdf – a detailed report on statutory and non-statutory public services

Distinction

Critically evaluate the services provided to individuals and groups of citizens by statutory and non-statutory public services, justifying the need for these services.

For this outcome, you need to:

- make a reasoned judgement as to how effective statutory and non-statutory public services are
- explain why they are needed.

In this outcome, you need to look at the good and bad points of the work done by the public services, giving reasons for your views. You also need to show why their work is necessary. Remember that, for a **distinction**, you should use up-to-date, accurate information from a variety of sources. It might be useful to talk to someone from the public services and ask the following kinds of question:

- Do you think you provide a good service?
- What improvements would you make to the service, if you could?
- What are the main problems you meet in your work?
- Would you like the government to make changes to your service, and the way it is funded?
- What organisations or partnerships do you work with?
- What are the human rights issues connected with your work?
- What effects does the increasing diversity of society have on your work?
- What are the main complaints that you or your colleagues get in your work?
- How has your service changed since you started working for it?
- What do you think are the main changes or pressures your service will face in the next ten years?
- What do you think would happen if your service didn't exist?

! CHECKPOINT ...

Prepare your own list of questions, suitable for a particular public service (either statutory or non-statutory) that interests you.

PASSGRADE

Explain how the statutory and non-statutory public services effect change and the roles of groups, personnel and information in the changes that take place.

For this outcome, you need to:

- show how public services change themselves (responding to outside pressures)
- show how public services can act to change or improve society.

Changes in public services

Changes in the public services are the result of 'push' and 'pull' factors operating in a changing society.

Examples of 'push' and 'pull' factors

'Push' factors	'Pull' factors
Shortage of funding New or worsening social problems New health problems Changing priorities Complaints from the public, the media and politicians Dissatisfaction within the service Ideology of governments	People's wish to improve society or the quality of life Desire to improve human rights Seeing improvements in other countries (e.g. USA or Europe) which ought to be adopted in the UK New technology

Changing a statutory public service is not easy, simply because of the size of the organisation. The outcome says the public services 'effect' change (i.e. bring it about themselves), but many would say that they cannot change themselves, but always change in response to economic, social or political pressures from outside the services.

'Change' can be of many types. For example, let us look at recent changes in the fire service (see the table on the following page).

http://www.irfs.org.uk/docs/future/index.htm – Bain Report of the Fire Service, 2002

Changing a non-statutory public service is much easier, since the organisation is usually smaller, has not lasted as long as the fire service, has a far smaller budget and (normally) does much less complex and difficult work. As with statutory public services, the pressure for change may come from the bottom up, but change itself will happen from

Changes in the fire service

External pressures	Internal pressures	Ways in which change is being effected
1 A need to save money on public services, because of a downturn in the world economy, possibly linked to the Iraq War, the threat of terrorism and worries about the US economy 2 A change in the nature of Fire Service work: fewer fires but more rescues of other types; more fire prevention and public safety 3 A highly critical report: *Independent Review of the Fire Service* by Sir George Bain which made sweeping recommendations for change in the fire service 4 The decision of the government – for the above reasons – to make changes to the fire service	1 The need for firefighters to keep their jobs. 2 The traditions of the fire service which make firefighters unwilling to change 3 Strikes by the Fire Brigades Union, which may have added to the government's determination to change the fire service 4 Complaints from firefighters about shift patterns and bullying, which show up in surveys and confidential interviews	1 A new lead from the government 2 A new framework of duties – more fire prevention 3 Setting up cost-effective systems 4 Involving local government 5 New laws on the fire service's statutory duties 6 A change of structure (in the long term) to a regional one 7 More community involvement 8 A new 'culture of organic change' 9 Changes to be pushed through by inspectors and the Audit Commission (which monitors government spending) 10 Pay will be linked to reforms 11 Changed management and recruitment 12 Changes in conditions of service

the top down. Meetings are normally held at which issues such as funding and the future development of the organisation are discussed. An effective non-statutory public service usually has a democratic structure which ensures that decisions made will have majority support among members, stakeholders and users of that service.

CHECKPOINT ...

1 Contact someone who belongs to a non-statutory public service (e.g. Neighbourhood Watch) and ask them how and why changes come about in their organisation.
2 Research pressure groups and the changes they can bring about.

Changing society

Public services can change society by raising people's awareness of problems and how to deal with them. The police, for example, work to make people more aware of crime prevention and of good citizenship. Non-statutory public services, especially charities such as Barnardos, Greenpeace or Shelter, do valuable work in helping disadvantaged people, raising money for good causes and publicising social and environmental problems. In some cases, they act as pressure groups, using the media and public opinion to change government policy.

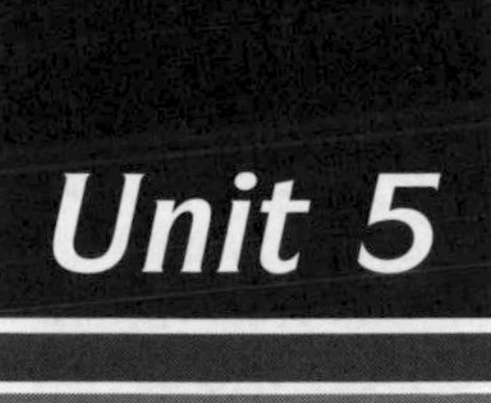

Unit 5 Diversity and the Public Services

Grading criteria

PASSGRADE	*Merit*	*Distinction*
To achieve a pass grade the evidence must show that the learner is able to:	To achieve a merit grade the evidence must show that the learner is able to:	To achieve a distinction grade the evidence must show that the learner is able to:
● summarise the history which has made Britain a multi-cultural society **94** ● describe the composition of the local community identifying their needs and the support available to them **97** ● describe how an identified public service has become more accessible to all sections of the community **99** ● explain how an identified public service has provided a 'user-friendly' service **101** ● describe the methodology used by a chosen public service to develop a diverse workforce **104** ● explain the working policies and procedures adopted by an identified public service to promote equality **106**	● analyse and evaluate the 'user-friendly' service provided by an identified public service **103** ● analyse the methodology used by a chosen public service to develop a diverse workforce **108**	● analyse and evaluate the success or failure of a chosen public service to develop a diverse workforce **108**

Imagine a time when your grandparents were young and it was rare to see a black or brown face in most parts of the UK, when race and sex discrimination were not against the law – and being gay was. Imagine a time when the words used to describe black people, gays or the disabled were all different. A time when the people who worked in the uniformed public services were nearly all white, and nearly all male. ...

How times change! Now, 8.7 per cent of the UK's population describe themselves as non-white. Race and sex discrimination are against the law, but being gay isn't. Society is diverse, and proud of it.

But some things never change. ... Or do they? That is what this unit is about.

MULTICULTURALISM

PASSGRADE

> Summarise the history which has made Britain a multi-cultural society.

For this outcome, you need to give a brief history of immigration and cultural change in the UK.

Definitions and background concepts

There are some words and ideas which crop up time and again when discussing diversity. To understand this outcome, you should read about them before going on to research the UK's multi-cultural history.

Multiculturalism

Multiculturalism is a set of ideas originating in America and Canada.

Multiculturalism is a word which may be going out of fashion, because it has given rise to so much disagreement and hostility. Definitions vary widely, but the agreed meaning is: *the co-existence of different races and cultures within the same country*.

Many difficult questions have been asked about multiculturalism such as:

- What is a 'culture'?
- Should cultures integrate or remain separate?
- Do any cultures have the right to demand (or expect) that other cultures should change?
- Does forcing 'multiculturalism' on people encourage the development of far right neo-nazi politics?

To some people, multiculturalism means 'the right of cultures to remain separate'. South Africa before 1989 was multi-cultural in this way. All ethnic groups were forced to have 'separate development', and there was strict segregation and denial of civil and human rights to non-white ethnic groups.

To other people, multiculturalism means the meeting of cultures and even the integration or joining up of cultures.

Neither of these views is helpful. The first kind of multiculturalism leads to unacceptable discrimination. The second kind forces people to leave their own cultures and traditions and accept a type of mixed culture whether they like it or not.

Diversity

In the UK, 'diversity' is now the preferred word because it recognises the differences between people, suggests that they are 'equal', and implies that they have a right to be different. Furthermore, because the word doesn't end in '-ism', it has a less ideological sound.

FOCUS

Definitions of multiculturalism

Multiculturalism is...

'of or relating to a social or educational theory or program that encourages interest in many cultures within a society rather than in only a mainstream culture' – *American Heritage Dictionary*

'a set of principles, policies, and practices for accommodating diversity as a legitimate and integral component of society' – Fleras, A. and Elliott, J.L. (1992), *Multi-culturalism in Canada: the Challenge of Diversity,* Nelson

FOCUS

Diversity: some definitions

'Diversity' (in this unit) can be defined as 'valuing difference'. Here is a more detailed definition:

'We value diversity, and are determined to ensure:

that we treat all individuals fairly, with dignity and respect;

that the opportunities we provide are open to all;

that we provide a safe, supportive and welcoming environment – for staff, for students and for visitors.' – Leeds University diversity policy

However, 'multiculturalism' will be used for this outcome because it is the word used in the 2002 Edexcel BTEC Specifications.

Culture

'Culture' (in this context) is 'the distinctive values and norms shared by a large and clearly-defined group of people'. Values are *beliefs*, e.g. of religion, right and wrong, and so on. Norms are types of *behaviour* accepted by the group, such as lifestyle, language, customs, dress and food.

- **Culture and ethnicity** Culture is often linked to ethnicity, which is why we talk, for instance, about Bangladeshi or British culture.
- **Culture and occupation** But we can also link culture to occupation (e.g. 'the culture' of fishing communities or police officers) and, more loosely, to social class (e.g. 'working-class culture').
- **Subcultures** 'Subcultures' are small cultures which are part of larger ones. The 'gay subculture' is an example of this. They also play their part in a multicultural or diverse society.

Society

For practical purposes, the word 'society' can be defined as 'all the people who live in a country, whatever their culture or ethnicity'.

Stereotyping

Stereotyping means thinking about people in an over-simplified and prejudiced way. The idea that all black people love music and sport is a stereotype based on the way black people are presented in the media. It becomes a problem for the public services, for example if the police stereotype black people as 'muggers' or 'druggies', and discriminate against them as a result.

Communication between cultural groups

In its full meaning (e.g. in the definition by Augie Fleras above) multiculturalism involves communities of different cultures communicating freely and without prejudice, while keeping their own identities. This is an ideal state of affairs, but there are problems:

- Communication involves transmitting (e.g. speaking, writing) and receiving (e.g. listening, reading), and the people who transmit are usually in a position of power and influence over those who receive. In an equal society, communication should be two-way. But in the UK, ethnic minorities are bombarded by British culture through the media, and are under pressure to conform as a result.
- Language is a major component of culture. People from a minority ethnic group are often at a disadvantage because they lack skills in the dominant language and have difficulty in communicating freely with people from the majority culture. If they become very good at the dominant language, it may mean that they have lost touch with their first language, and their cultural roots. Although as individuals they may profit from their skills, they may have lost something of the culture they were born into.
- Immigrants to a country often have to take the lowest paid jobs. This can lead to additional disadvantage for members of an ethnic minority culture. The average pay in the UK of people of Bangladeshi descent is much lower than that of people of British descent. Economic differences, as well as cultural differences, separate the Bangladeshi community from British mainstream culture.
- Colour can be a barrier to communication in a country like the UK which has a tradition of racial discrimination. Though colour discrimination is now outlawed, ethnic stereotyping is still common.
- Racism among the white British population reduces or degrades communication between the British and other ethnic groups. This is linked to fear, distrust and stereotypical thinking by some white people.

Population of Great Britain by ethnic group, 2001

Ethnic group	%	
White British	89	92
Other white	3	
Mixed background	1	
Indian	2	4
Other Asian background	3	
Black Caribbean	1	2*
Black African	1	
Other ethnic group	1	
Weighted base (000s) = 100%	57,034	
Unweighted sample	21,102	

* Including other Black groups not shown separately

Source: http://www.statistics.gov.uk/census2001/profiles/727-A.asp

Profile

A short history of the UK as a multi-cultural society	
Before 43 AD	The Iron Age: Britain was inhabited by Picts and Bell Beaker people. Later, Celts came from Europe and colonised the islands.
43–400 AD	The Roman occupation: main effect – the introduction of Christianity, though Paganism was still the norm.
400–1066	Britain was colonised by Angles, Saxons and Jutes. These Germanic peoples brought their language, Anglo-Saxon, which later developed into English. Vikings from Norway and Denmark occupied northern England.
1066	Battle of Hastings and the beginning of the 'Norman Conquest': Normans were ex-Vikings from northern France who brought their Old French language and culture into England. They became the ruling class, established Christianity and unified England. The Celts were driven into Wales, Scotland and Ireland, where their culture and languages still survive.
1066–1592	After 1066, there were no more invasions from Europe. But with increasing trade links between Europe, Africa and Asia, some Europeans, Africans and Jews came to live in Britain – mainly around London.
1592–1833	The period of the slave trade: West Africans were bought or captured by British merchants and taken to North America and the Caribbean to work in plantations. Some Africans were brought to Britain as servants. During this time many parts of Africa and Asia (especially India) were taken over by the British as colonies. They were ruled and exploited by the British. This led to an interest in colonial culture and crafts (especially pottery) in Britain. During this period there was also a strong French influence, first from 1640–60, the time of the English Civil War, when many rich English people fled to France and came back full of French culture, then around 1685, when tens of thousands of educated French Protestant refugees, called Huguenots, came to Britain.
1830–50	Many thousands of Irish people came to Britain to escape the potato famine. They built canals, railways and roads.
1851	The Great Exhibition at Crystal Palace, London: this was an immense celebration of the British Empire, its culture and its products. It marked, perhaps, the beginning of what we now think of as globalisation, and established Britain as the wealthiest nation in the world (a state of affairs which lasted for about 30 years). Exhibits came from India, Africa, Canada, China, Egypt, Persia, USA, Russia and many other distant and exotic places. The exhibition was visited by over 6 million people and made people aware of the world's cultures, though it also carried the message that 'British was best'. From 1851 to 1914 Britain was a great trading nation, and sent many thousands of people to work in its colonies. This colonisation prepared the ground for the later immigration of Commonwealth citizens into the UK, from the 1950s onwards.
1914–45	This period was dominated by two World Wars. Britain won both, but was seriously weakened. Hundreds of thousands of non-white soldiers from India, Africa and the Caribbean fought and died for Britain in these wars. The first race riots happened in London in 1919, but there was no large-scale immigration in the country as a whole. It was not until after 1945 that diversity as we now understand it began in this country.

1945–50	157,000 Poles, and many Italians, settled. The Poles were refugees from Communism, and settled in the UK to get a peaceful and secure life. In 1948 the first immigrants came from the West Indies. They, and immigrants from India and Pakistan, were urged to come by British employers. They were needed because thousands of British men had died in the war, and there was a shortage of labour to rebuild the economy. Also, non-white immigrants were prepared to work for lower wages than British workers.
1950–70	From 1955 to 1962 an average of 50,000 immigrants a year came into the UK from the West Indies and the Indian sub-continent (India, Pakistan and Bangladesh). Then, laws were changed to make immigration more difficult, so numbers began to fall. The immigrants settled in big cities, such as London, Birmingham, Manchester and Bradford, working in the public sector (especially transport and health care) and in the private sector (mills and factories). By 1970 1.4 million non-white people lived in the UK (though a third of these were not immigrants but people who had been born in the UK).
1970 onwards	Laws were passed which only allowed Commonwealth citizens of British, or partly British, descent to settle in the UK, so immigration of non-white people dropped. However, non-white Commonwealth citizens who had relatives living in the UK could still come, as could people who were intending to marry British citizens. (This was made much more difficult with the 1981 British Nationality Act.) An exception was made in 1972 when the Ugandan dictator Idi Amin expelled large numbers of Ugandan Asians who held British passports – 29,000 were allowed into the UK. Some Vietnamese refugees from the Vietnam War arrived in this decade. Later there were refugees from Romania and Afghanistan, fleeing the pro-Communist Najibullah government. There were also refugees from Africa (e.g. Nigeria and Somalia). In the 1990s conflict in Bosnia, Croatia and other parts of the former Yugoslavia caused a further influx of refugees. The general trend at the end of the 1990s and at the beginning of the twenty-first century has been more immigration by asylum seekers and 'economic migrants', counterbalancing a decline in the arrival of people from Commonwealth countries.

More on this subject can be found on the BBC and CRE websites, and in books on the history of UK race relations.

DIVERSITY

PASSGRADE

Describe the composition of the local community identifying their needs and the support available to them.

For this outcome, you need to say what groups of people live in your local community, and what services cater for them.

Support available to the local community

Within a local area, a great deal of support is available to the community. The support comes from all sorts of organisations and partnerships, including:

- statutory public services such as the police, the Post Office, water quality monitoring, and so on
- local government services (also statutory) such as education, environment services and social services
- companies which may be wholly or partly privately owned, such as bus companies, banks, water companies or Royal Mail
- a vast range of non-statutory support groups which get some kind of assistance or publicity from the local authority because they offer a public service. These include charities, self-help groups, religious organisations and societies to help particular ethnic groups
- branches of central government or the Civil Service such as Inland Revenue, courts and Jobcentres
- partnerships in which any of the above groups may be involved. Some of the partnerships, such as crime and disorder partnerships, are statutory because they were set up by law (Crime and Disorder Act 1998).

Information about your local community can come from a range of sources:

Source	What you might find
Friends, relatives, tutors, people you know	Ideas and advice on information-gathering
Your local library	Books, pamphlets and leaflets about your local community – including useful information from the local authority
Your local council	Publications about organisations, and services (both statutory and non-statutory) dealing with ethnic, community and cultural issues Visiting speakers who work with diversity Cultural, multi-cultural or community organisations which you could visit
Local organisations	Detailed information on groups of people living in the local community, and the issues that matter to them.
Other public services	Police, fire and other officers who have special responsibility for multi-cultural links, or diversity. They may help you gather information, and understand the main issues
The internet	Local authority and public service websites which contain a wealth of relevant information on multi-cultural issues Census 2001 returns for your local authority or electoral ward

For this outcome, you need to:

- make it clear where and how big your local community is
- describe the main occupations and economic activities, relating these to the people who live and work in the community
- give a detailed population breakdown, probably from 2001 Census figures. This must include information on ethnicity
- find out the needs of the community by talking to people who live or work there
- research support organisations which work with and for the local community.

COOL SITE:

http://www.statistics.gov.uk/downloads/census2001 – detailed information on ethnicity and local communities from the 2001 Census

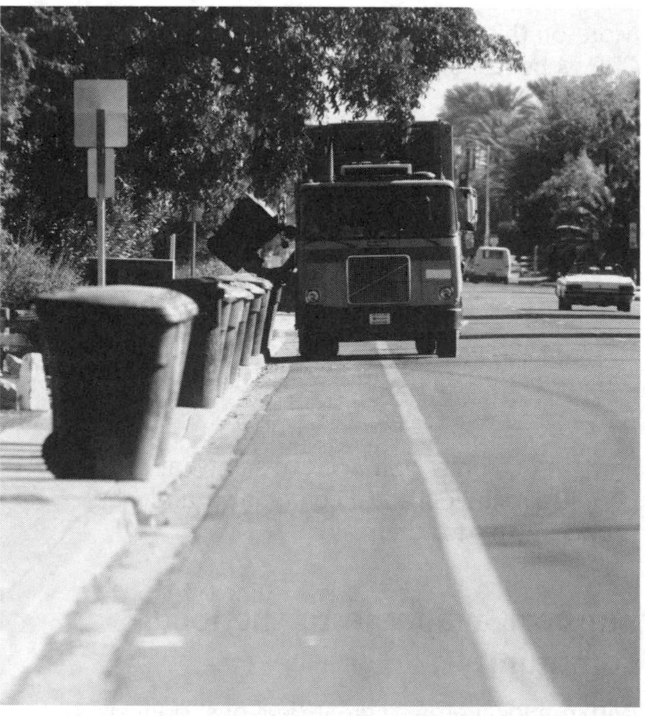

Refuse collection – a kind of local community support which we take for granted – unless it's not there!

FOCUS

Types of local support organisation

Arts and hobbies	Funding
Careers and employment	Health (a huge range, both general and for specific illnesses)
Charitable	Housing
Children and family	Older people
Community groups	Tourism
Council and public services	Religion
Councillors, MPs, political/pressure groups	Social organisations
Education	Sport
Environment	Women
Ethnic/national groups	Youth
Festivals	

An identified public service is one that you name and research. Ideally it should be a service which you can visit in person, but it doesn't have to be. The service you choose can be a local branch or force, e.g. the local tax office or police force. There is more on 'sections of the community' below.

'Accessible to' can be taken to mean a number of things, e.g.

- welcoming to the public
- willing to employ
- physically reachable
- open and accountable, as opposed to secretive.

It will help you to talk to a long-serving officer in a public service, who remembers what it was like twenty or so years ago. Some of your tutors may have relevant experience!

PUBLIC SERVICE AND EQUALITY

PASSGRADE

Describe how an identified public service has become more accessible to all sections of the community.

For this outcome, you need to:

- show what a public service has done to make it easier for people to contact it and get help
- pay special attention to groups of people who might have had difficulty contacting or getting help from the service in the past.

Accessibility of public services

In the past most public services were accessible to most people. But there were certain sections in the community which some public services were unable or unwilling to reach. As the PROFILE on the next page shows, things are changing.

Profile

How the West Yorkshire Police have become more accessible to all sections of the community

Section of the community	General accessibility	Accessibility for employment
Women	Crimes against women are taken much more seriously than they were in the past. Domestic incidents taken seriously	19.8 per cent of police officers in West Yorkshire are women. See Equal Opportunities statement below in FOCUS.
Ethnic minority groups	Outreach and better links with many community organisations. Interpreters available.	3.2 per cent of officers are from ethnic minorities. Recruitment literature invites people from ethnic minorities to apply.
Disabled people	Information given on disabled access to police stations	Disabled people now considered for civilian posts.
Gays and lesbians	Now have protection, e.g. in domestic incidents	West Yorkshire Police are an equal opportunities employer.
Young and old	Youth divert officers working in youth clubs, etc.; visits to schools. Child Protection Unit. High-visibility neighbourhood policing helps to reduce fears of older people	Applicants must be at least 18½ but there is no longer an upper age limit for applicants.
Mentally ill	Working with people who are mentally ill is only a priority if the people are a danger to themselves or others.	
The community as a whole	Many ways of contacting the police: • ring 999 • ring non-urgent number • invitation to comment on services through councillors • through Neighbourhood Watch schemes • in a public meeting with the police authority • through community forums at a rotating venue • at surgeries run by community beat officers (CBOs) outside the police station • by talking to any CBO (the West Yorkshire police have cycling CBOs because they are more accessible) • through a community safety initiative where high-visibility officers patrol, use flexible shifts and focus on problem areas in the towns • e-mailing a CBO.	

http://wypa.org – West Yorkshire Police Authority

http://www.homeoffice.gov.uk/rds/prgpdfs/prs138.pdf – Widening Access report – lots of detail

FOCUS

Equal opportunities in the West Yorkshire Police

Gender and ethnicity profile of employees as at February 2003

	White		Minority Ethnic		Unspecified		Total		
	M	F	M	F	M	F	M	F	Total
Divisional Policing	58.9%	15.9%	2.1%	0.6%	1.2%	0.1%	62.2%	16.5%	78.7%
Operational Support	14.2%	2.7%	0.3%	0.1%	0.7%	0.1%	15.1%	2.9%	18.0%
Other Support Department	2.7%	0.4%	0.1%	0.0%	0.1%	0.0%	2.8%	0.4%	1.1%
Police Total	75.7%	19.0%	2.5%	0.7%	1.9%	0.2%	80.2%	19.8%	100.0%
Support Total	38.1%	52.2%	0.9%	1.6%	3.5%	3.8%	42.4%	57.6%	100.0%

Equal Opportunities Statement

'It is the policy of West Yorkshire Police to provide equal opportunities in all aspects of employment. This policy is a commitment to make full use of the talents and resources of all our staff and to ensure that there is no unfair discrimination in the areas of:

Recruitment and Selection
Deployment
Specialisation
Promotion
Training
Facilities and Services.'

Source: West Yorkshire Police Authority

Providing a user-friendly service

PASSGRADE

Explain how an identified public service has provided a 'user-friendly' service.

For this outcome, you need to show what a public service has done to make it more welcoming to the public.

Public services have worked hard in recent years to provide a user-friendly service. Examples are:

- the fire service setting up community fire stations
- the police making themselves more accessible (see previous outcome)
- the army running residentials and 'Look at Life' days for young people.

But to cover this outcome, you need to think who the users of a public service really are, and what is meant by 'user-friendly'.

In the case of the police, the users are almost the entire public. Users come under two categories:

- anybody in the public who has any dealings with the police, including:
  - people who ask the police for information and help
  - people who report crimes
  - witnesses
  - suspects
  - people in custody or under arrest
  - interviewees
  - informants
  - staff of other public services who work with the police (e.g. prison officers, probation officers, social workers, etc.)
- people who might come in contact with the police in the future, including:
  - all children and young people, especially those who are at risk of becoming criminals, such as school truants or children being brought up in areas where crime levels are high
  - young people who might consider a career in the police
  - all the general public who may, at any time and for whatever reason, want to contact the police.

'User-friendly' means:

- accessible
- friendly
- quick and efficient
- reliable
- confidential
- considerate
- caring
- professional
- trustworthy
- honest.

There is a link between appearing to be user-friendly and having good public relations. People like to feel they have a good police force, and if the police are user-friendly the fact will spread by word-of-mouth.

An example of how the police make themselves more user-friendly to young people is the Bradford North Project, run by the West Yorkshire Police.

Other ways in which the police have come to provide a more user-friendly service over the years include:

- following the provisions of the PACE Act which is designed to ensure that the police treat suspects with fairness and respect
- following the Human Rights Act 1998 which makes the police ensure that they respect people's human rights and avoid all discrimination
- all the 'accessibility' points mentioned on page 100 above
- recruiting more members of minority groups, so that sections of the public are not put off by the 'white male image' that the police used to have (and to some extent still do).

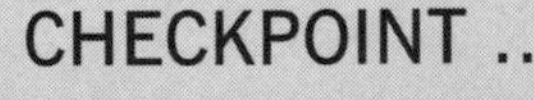

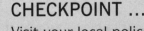

LINK! See page 30 for the PACE Act.

CHECKPOINT ...

Visit your local police station and ask what steps they have taken to become more user-friendly.

FOCUS

Bradford North Project

This project started out as a summer scheme and now provides activities throughout the year that help to prevent juvenile crime and reduce incidents of anti-social behaviour.

Other aims include the promotion of positive role models and forging closer links between the police and young people.

During the period April 2001–2002, activities undertaken in partnership with a wide range of local authority and voluntary sector partners include:

- residentials – local role models and young people looking at personal development and raising achievement
- residentials to reward community involvement
- army and RAF personal development away days for Year 10 and 11 students
- open access to the police station for the local community
- Country Trust away days for several primary schools visiting Skipton Castle, Bolton Abbey and the Falconry Centre at Settle
- recruiting volunteers to assist the local community and police
- Duke of Edinburgh Police Service course for 18 young people
- assistance for voluntary groups with funding applications
- £25,000 raised from the Key Fund, Neighbourhood Renewal, Yorkshire Building Society, and Awards for All. The money will be used to purchase outdoor equipment and run residentials
- young people directed to Millennium Volunteers
- work shadowing opportunities for young people
- half term and Easter activity schemes for local young people
- school trips to Leeds Armouries, Industrial Museum, Leeds Wall, canoeing, Alhambra Theatre and Leeds Playhouse
- crime prevention inputs to groups of young people
- training residential for community youth workers
- careers events
- two community mini buses managed.

Source: West Yorkshire Police

Merit

> Analyse and evaluate the 'user-friendly' service provided by an identified public service.

For this outcome, you need to choose a public service and explain how successful you think it has been in improving its service and image.

You must choose one particular public service that interests you. It can be either a statutory or non-statutory service. If you plan to work in a particular public service, you should choose that one.

- 'Analyse' means examine in detail, picking out and commenting on the main points.
- 'Evaluate' means you should consider the strengths and weaknesses of the service, and how far it can (or should) be improved.

It will help you to meet someone who works in your chosen public service, so you can discuss this outcome with them. Questions you might want to ask are:

- What have you done in recent years to make yourselves more user-friendly?
- What do you plan to do in the future to become more user-friendly?
- What are the advantages in having a user-friendly service?
- Are there any disadvantages in having a user-friendly service?
- How do you monitor the cost-effectiveness of your user-friendly service?
- Where do the ideas for making your service more user-friendly come from?

FOCUS

Measuring user satisfaction

The West Yorkshire police get constant feedback from the public about their service. But most of this is not recorded, and is not quantifiable (cannot be measured). However, they also carry out systematic research on whether their service is 'user-friendly' (i.e. satisfies the public) by sending out postal inquiries to victims of crime. This information is then tabulated and published in policing plans. Comparison figures for other forces are given, and a brief evaluation.

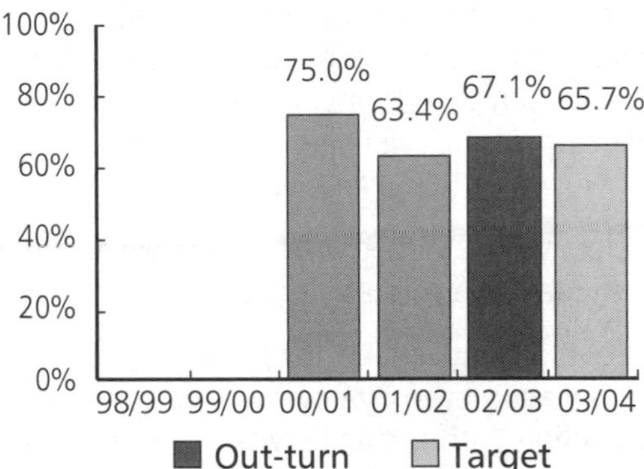

Percentage of victims satisfied with police initial response to a report of violent crime

Comparative figures for 2001/2002

Force	Victims satisfied
West Midlands	89.8%
GMP	86.8%
Northumbria	81.7%
South Yorkshire	79.4%
Merseyside	76.7%
West Yorkshire	*63.4%*

'Not all violent crimes are surveyed, those involved in serious or sensitive crimes are not considered appropriate to send out postal surveys, so the sample is predominantly of younger people involved in minor assaults. The out-turn of 67.1% is an improvement on last year. Efforts will continue to identify areas for service improvement by addressing the causes of dissatisfaction.'

Source: West Yorkshire Policing Plan 2003/4

http://www.policereform.gov.uk/natpoliceplan/npp_index.html – National policing plan, which covers this outcome in detail!

FOCUS

How user-friendly are the public services?

'An extraordinary 91% of users are satisfied with their GP and 90% of parents with their primary school, according to a Mori survey commissioned by the government.

However, satisfaction with the police has plummeted, from 73% in 1998 to 53% this year. They are also seen as one of the worst public organisations in terms of providing information to the public.

The survey of the government's so-called "people's panel", published yesterday, also shows falling satisfaction with trains, NHS hospitals, the fire service and council housing since the last survey two years ago.

Ministers will study the findings closely as they seek to persuade the electorate that services are improving.

The people's panel is a 5000-strong group of voters regularly surveyed by government. It has tracked satisfaction with public services over the past four years, but is being discontinued due to sampling difficulties.

Seven in ten or more users are satisfied with many other services: refuse collection (87%), street lighting (70%), NHS hospitals (76%), passport agency (79%), museums and art galleries (80%), local sports/leisure facilities (76%), libraries (86%), parks and open spaces (81%), provision of recycling facilities (75%), local nursery schools/classes (76%), local secondary schools (78%) and local adult education (81%).

The two services with the lowest levels of satisfaction are road maintenance and repairs (41% satisfied) and pavement maintenance (40%).

Since the first survey in 1998 satisfaction with the fire service has fallen to 42% from 78%. Dissatisfaction with the police has risen from 11% to 16% this year. Tenants' satisfaction with council housing service has fallen from 73% in 1998 to 49% this year.

Dissatisfaction with train companies has risen from 21% in 1998 to 31% in 2002. Answers showed public satisfaction with NHS hospitals had fallen from 78% to 71% in the past two years, and from 82% to 76% among users of the service.

Just under 80% agree that "you need a lot of determination to get something done about a complaint with a public service".'

Source: 'GPs and primaries get 90% approval', by Patrick Wintour, Guardian, *1 August 2002*

More on evaluation of user-friendly services

In the 1950s there was over 90 per cent satisfaction with the police in the UK and the service they offered. Despite the vast efforts which have been made in recent years (and are continuing to be made) satisfaction had dropped to 53 per cent by 2002 (see FOCUS above).

Possible reasons for this are:

- a change in national culture – after World War II, in the 1950s, people were much more deferential (prepared to obey authority) than they are now
- the public are now much more educated about the police and policing issues (mainly thanks to the media)
- poor policing in some inner cities has led to accusations of racism
- it is much easier to complain than it used to be – everyone has telephones, many people have computers, and the police positively welcome complaints
- methods for surveying complaints and public opinion are far more accurate and thorough than they used to be
- complaints against the police are now dealt with independently – in the old days the police investigated themselves.

COOL SITE:

www.pca.gov.uk – the Police Complaints Authority – an eye-opener!

POLICIES AND PROCEDURES TO ADDRESS CULTURAL ISSUES

Describe the methodology used by a chosen public service to develop a diverse workforce.

For this outcome, you need to show what a given public service has done to recruit from all sections of the community.

The diversity should extend through all ranks and types of worker/officer in the public service. It is no good getting an ethnic balance by employing lots of white police officers and black cleaners!

'Methodology' means ways, methods, plans, tactics and strategies (long-term plans) for making the work-force diverse.

'Diverse' means employing:

- a reasonably equal ratio of men and women
- staff from ethnic minorities, in a proportion matching the population mix of the area served
- gays and lesbians
- disabled people if they can do the job.

COOL SITES:

http://www.safety.odpm.gov.uk/fire/fepd/pdf/diversity.pdf
http://www.safety.odpm.gov.uk/fire/pdf/towards2.pdf

– everything you need to know about developing a diverse workforce in the fire service

Developing a diverse workforce in the fire service

The Fire Service has recently had to rethink its approach to equal opportunities and diversity issues. The main reason for this has been problems in recruiting a diverse workforce.

CHECKPOINT ...

Why do you think the fire service has had more difficulty than the other blue light services in recruiting a diverse workforce?

The fire service has decided to tackle the problem by starting from the top downwards. The government department responsible – the Office of the Deputy Prime Minister – set up an Equal Opportunities Task Group at the highest level, to plan a strategy and methodology for developing a diverse workforce.

How the planning was organised

The Equal Opportunities Task Group (EOTG) of the Central Fire Brigades Advisory Council for England and Wales organised a workshop involving the following diverse groups:

- government organisations and inspectors:
  - the Department for Transport, Local Government and the Regions (Fire Policy Division and HM Fire Service Inspectorate for England and Wales)
  - HM Fire Service Inspectorate for Scotland and the Home Office (Race Equality Unit)
  - Local Government Association
- the organisation of fire service leaders, the Chief and Assistant Chief Fire Officers' Association
- firefighters' 'grass-roots' organisations:
  - Fire Brigades Union (including the Black and Ethnic Minority Members National Committee, the Women's National Committee, and the Gay and Lesbian National Committee)
  - Networking Women in the Fire Service.

The workshop was facilitated by Opinion Research Services.

COOL SITE:

www.ors.org.uk/ – Opinion Research Services Ltd (ORS) is an applied social research company based at the University of Wales Swansea. ORS works with local authorities and public services.

Government organisations and inspectors

The first aim of the Equal Opportunities Task Group was to demonstrate that the fire service was serious about developing a diverse workforce. To do this, the Group wrote two books saying how it should be done. These books take the form of action plans.

The Group issued the following statement of intent.

FOCUS

Equal Opportunites Task Group statement of intent

'[The] following principles should be embedded into the ethos and culture of the [fire service] through its policies and practices:

- All communities should be involved in the service;

- The service should have a team culture that is open and inclusive at all times, at all levels;
- The contribution of all members of the organisation should be recognised and valued;
- Harassment and bullying are unacceptable;
- Culture should be based on trust not fear;
- Equal treatment and fairness is afforded to every member of the organisation;
- In service delivery, all members of the community are treated with equal fairness and respect.

The cultural change required by the fire service must actively engage the whole workforce, uniformed and non-uniformed, by getting people to think and act differently. To achieve this change every member of the fire service must treat colleagues with dignity and respect, irrespective of race, nationality, ethnic or national origins, religion, sex, marital status, sexual orientation or disability.'

Source: DTLR (2001), Towards Diversity II: Commitment of Cultural Change, *HMSO*

The second action plan, *Towards Diversity II*, published at the end of 2001, sets out the following methods for developing a diverse workforce:

- Fire service leaders should state their support for the 'core values' of equality and diversity (see Cool site! www.lancsfirerescue.org.uk).
- Minority officers should be used as 'minority role models'.
- Under-represented groups should be targeted for recruitment (using positive action but not positive discrimination).
- Monitor the views of the local community towards the fire service.
- Monitor the views of local minority groups towards the fire service.
- Carry out internal cultural audits (to detect any discrimination that may take place).
- Identify inappropriate practices.
- Give training to identify and eliminate bullying and harassment.
- Use non-discriminatory language and give training in equality and diversity issues.
- Each service should appoint an equality and fairness specialist adviser.
- Publicise and implement family-friendly policies (e.g. shorter shifts).
- Respect the privacy needs of men and women.
- Give provision for religious and cultural needs.
- Have mentoring and support schemes.
- Audit selection tests and remove the discriminatory ones (e.g. those where the physical requirements are above the national norms).
- Have rolling recruitment programmes and send back encouraging responses to all applicants.
- Give equality and diversity training to all recruits.
- Use positive action to encourage the promotion of minority officers.
- Use exit and follow-up interviews for those who leave the service.

FOCUS

Aspects of traditional fire service culture which are thought to have alienated minorities

- The term 'brigade'
- Priority of rank over role; rank markings
- Roll call; passing out parades; mess dinners
- Separate facilities ('officers and other ranks')
- Barracks style working/sleeping arrangements
- A culture of physique and endurance
- Some physical requirements, and implementation/use of current disciplinary regulations

Source: DTLR (2001), Towards Diversity II: Commitment of Cultural Change, *HMSO*

! CHECKPOINT ...

What is the difference between 'positive action' and 'positive discrimination'? Why can the fire service use one and not the other?

PASSGRADE

Explain the working policies and procedures adopted by an identified public service to promote equality.

For this outcome, you need to show how a public service has changed its working methods in order to treat everybody more equally.

skill POWER How to make notes

'Policies', for this outcome, are guidelines showing employees how to achieve organisational aims. 'Procedures' are systems of working in order to achieve organisational aims. The procedure puts the policy into practice.

To explain policies you have to say (a) what they mean and (b) what their purpose is. To explain procedures you have to say (a) what people do when carrying out these procedures and (b) why they do it.

For this outcome, you only need to investigate *one* public service.

Examples of policies and procedures

Equal opportunities policy

An equal opportunities policy is a statement detailing the intention of the public service to carry out equal opportunities in its recruitment and treatment of all employees. The equal opportunities statements which appear in recruitment literature (similar to the example on page 101) are short versions of the policy. Their aim is to make it clear to the public, to applicants and to employees that the organisation will not discriminate on the grounds of sex, race, disability, etc.

Grievance procedures

These are systems or channels through which employees in an organisation can complain about the way they are being treated by their colleagues or superiors. Common reasons for grievances are discrimination, bullying or harassment. Discrimination may take the form of being given boring duties or being overlooked for promotion.

The essential feature of the procedure is that the grievance (or complaint) is passed up the chain of command until it can be resolved. Grievances to do with sexual and racial harassment, or with matters relating to pay, are tried at a civilian employment tribunal.

The army has a well-developed grievance procedure which is explained at length in the cool site below.

COOL SITE:

http://www.army.mod.uk/linked_files/ag/servingsoldier/termsofserv/discmillaw/files/pdf/AGAI_Chapter_70_May_02.pdf – army grievance procedure

Other procedures supporting equality

- Child care facilities
- Trade unions. Trade unions look after the welfare of workers, and negotiate for improvements in pay and working conditions. In a serious dispute they organise industrial action or strikes – as with the Fire Brigades Union in 2002. Some public services, such as the police and armed forces, are not allowed to have trade unions or go on strike. The police have the Police Association which looks after the interests of officers, but cannot take industrial action. Trade unions offer useful advice – see the FOCUS below from the Fire Brigades Union, telling firefighters what to do if they are being bullied by colleagues.

FOCUS

Bullying – advice for firefighters from the Fire Brigades Union

'Actions that you can take yourself and that will help the Union take up your case include:

Log all incidents of bullying – dates, times, nature of incident, details of slurs, accusations, criticisms, etc., making sure you stick to the facts.

Write down your feelings at the time and your own response.

If you cannot confront the bully, try writing a memo to make it clear why you object to their behaviour and keep copies of the memo and any written reply.

Keep copies of all annual appraisals, and letters/memos relating to your ability to do the job. Try to get witnesses to bullying incidents – try to avoid situations where you are alone with the bully.

Find out if you are the only person being bullied or whether other people are also affected, and try to make a collective complaint.

Talk to colleagues and see if they will support you

Make sure that you know exactly what your job description is, so that you can check whether the responsibilities you are given match it.

Find out if your employer has a policy on harassment or unacceptable behaviour, which may cover bullying.

Make sure you keep the FBU representative whom you have asked for help, informed of all developments.

Stand firm and don't let yourself be a victim.'

Source: Fire Brigades Union

COOL SITE:

www.fbu.org.uk/index.php – plenty of low-down on the fire service!

Cultural and religious issues

Public services are addressing a number of cultural and religious issues in order to make themselves more attractive to applicants from ethnic minorities. An example relating to the Metropolitan Police is given in the FOCUS below.

FOCUS

How the Metropolitan Police have addressed one cultural issue

'Muslim police officers have welcomed the Metropolitan Police's decision to introduce a traditional headscarf as a uniform option for Muslim women.

The Association of Muslim Police hopes the move will encourage into the police Muslim women who had been deterred by the prospect of not being able to cover up in public.

The scarf or hijab – which covers the head, neck and shoulders – is worn by some Muslim women in public as a sign of their modesty and faith.'

Source: article by Cindi John, BBC News Online, 24 April 2001

Merit

Analyse the methodology used by a chosen public service to develop a diverse workforce.

For this outcome, you need to:

- obtain detailed up-to-date information about a public service and its commitment to diversity and equal opportunities (there's plenty on the internet about this!)
- classify and comment on the different ways used to recruit and keep a diverse workforce.

Profile

Points on the fire service's methodology in developing a diverse workforce

The methodology works best from the top down because firefighters are used to taking directives from above. They themselves would rather fight fires than sit round a desk devising equal opportunities policies.

The methodology aims to change the 'culture' of the fire service. The culture includes all the unspoken beliefs and assumptions, and all the ingrained behaviour patterns and traditions, that firefighters have developed during the past half-century or more. The culture has good and bad aspects. The good aspect is that firefighters are highly dedicated, efficient and professional. The bad aspect is that firefighters have a white, working-class, male culture, which tends to regard women and people from ethnic minorities as 'not quite up to the job'. This amounts to sexism and racism even where there is no intention of being sexist or racist. Both the government and the fire service are trying to change this side of the firefighters' culture (see page 105).

CHECKPOINT ...

As an exercise, try analysing other aspects of the list of methodologies given on page 105.

Distinction

Analyse and evaluate the success or failure of a chosen public service to develop a diverse workforce.

For this outcome, you need to:

- pick a public service and assess how successful it has been in recruiting, retaining and promoting women and minorities
- give evidence, reasons and explanations to support what you say.

FOCUS

Diversity in the fire service

'The service is 98.3 per cent male and 98.5 per cent white.' – Professor Sir George Bain, December 2002

For this outcome, you should choose a public service which has set out to develop a diverse workforce. Statutory public services are the best to choose, because they have had to set employment targets for ethnic minority employees, and you will be able to analyse and evaluate how successful they have been in meeting those targets.

You need to know:

- the numbers and percentages of women and people from ethnic minorities working in your chosen public service
- the employment targets for women and ethnic minority staff set by the employers. (In the case of the police or fire service, a general target is set by central government – the Home Office or the ODPM – and a more specific target is set by individual fire or police authorities.)

'Analyse' means:

- describe the diversity of the workforce of your chosen public service, using up-to-date, relevant data
- explain how that diversity has been achieved
- show what more needs to be done to achieve full diversity
- pick out and explain any other key points.

'Evaluate' means to judge, on the basis of your analysis, how successful the public service you have chosen has been in reaching its targets for a diverse workforce. In evaluating the success of your chosen public service to develop a diverse workforce, you should also consider the effectiveness of the methods they are using to recruit and retain diverse staff.

The PROFILE below gives an example of the kinds of arguments you can use for this outcome. But there are many more you could use, and what you say will depend on the service you choose!

COOL SITE:

http://www.homeoffice.gov.uk/docs/employmenttargets.pdf – targets for police, probation and prison services!

Profile

Statement by West Yorkshire Fire and Civil Defence Authority on its plan to develop a diverse workforce

'In line with the government's challenge, a number of targets are to be achieved by 2007:

- Employ 232 female firefighters.
- Employ 108 firefighters from minority ethnic backgrounds.
- Minimise the number of resignations from the service and compare their progression, in terms of holding rank, with other uniformed people within the service.

Currently there are 27 female firefighters, which equates to 1.48 per cent of the uniformed workforce and 33 firefighters from minority ethnic backgrounds, which equates to 1.81 per cent.

The number of firefighters from target groups has increased substantially since the introduction of positive action initiatives, which come within the framework of discrimination legislation, namely the Sex Discrimination Act 1975, the Race Relations Act 1976, the Race Relations (Amendment) Act 2000, and the Disability Discrimination Act 1995.

A key part of the positive action initiatives are 'Career Awareness Days' which offer the opportunity to all sections of the community within West Yorkshire to sample the recruitment tests and seek advice from qualified and experienced personnel on how to pursue a career within the fire service.

The use of a Community Development Worker and seconded firefighters has also strengthened the links within communities and schools in the region, which has helped promote the fire service as a career open to all.

The Fire Authority is committed to the principles of Equality and Fairness, both in the way it delivers its services to the people of West Yorkshire and to the way it recruits and retains its employees. To this end, the Authority has established policies and procedures, which ensure that all employees, applicants to the Authority, and service users are treated with dignity and respect.

In addition to this, the Authority reports on the Best Value indicators related to equalities. We are assessing ourselves against the Equality Standard for Local Government, which establishes how well we are mainstreaming equalities into service delivery and employment.

The Authority currently stands at Level 3.'

Source: West Yorkshire Fire Authority; http://fp.wyfcda.f9.co.uk/

Analysis and evaluation

According to the 2001 census, the minority ethnic population of West Yorkshire stood at about 7 per cent – little changed from the figure for 1991. In the statement given above, the West Yorkshire Fire Authority say 'The number of firefighters from target groups has increased substantially since the introduction of positive action initiatives'. Unfortunately, they do not say when they introduced their 'positive action initiatives', and though they say what the initiatives are now, they do not say what they were in the past. It is therefore not clear how long the service have been trying to meet the targets which they have set 'in line with the government's challenge'.

Although half the population are women, it is clear from the figures that the West Yorkshire fire and rescue Service do not intend 50 per cent of their firefighters to be women. If the 27 female firefighters they have at present equal 1.48 per cent of their uniformed workforce, then the planned 2007 total of 257 female firefighters (which they will have after they have recruited 232 more) is just under 14 per cent. If this is the government's target, why was it chosen?

In the case of firefighters from ethnic minority groups, there are at present 33, or 1.81 per cent. If 108 are recruited by 2007, the percentage of ethnic minority firefighters will then be around 5.9. This will still fall short of the proportion of ethnic minority people (7 per cent) in the population of West Yorkshire.

The figures suggest that the West Yorkshire fire and rescue service have not been successful in recruiting women or ethnic minority firefighters. They do not tell us whether the numbers are low because recruitment has been low, or because retention has been low. We also do not know whether the women and ethnic minority firefighters are all new recruits, or whether they are spread evenly through the ranks.

If the low level of diversity in the West Yorkshire fire and rescue service is typical of the country as a whole, the failure to recruit or retain people from minorities is a national problem, rather than a problem of the West Yorkshire service. According to Sir George Bain, nationally 1.7 per cent of firefighters are female and 1.5 per cent are from ethnic minorities. This suggests that West Yorkshire's figures are roughly in line with the national average.

If recruitment of women and ethnic minority firefighters has only begun recently, the figures are not as bad as they look, provided that those who have already been employed do not leave. As older firefighters retire, the service will gradually diversify. But since firefighters can stay in the career for 25 years, it may be 25 years before the service is as diverse as the society it serves – unless, over that period, more women and ethnic minority firefighters are recruited than are demanded by central government in their 'challenge'. In the case of ethnic minority applicants, this would mean recruiting more than the 7 per cent that would reflect the West Yorkshire population as a whole – a difficult task bearing in mind the fact that positive discrimination is illegal.

! CHECKPOINT ...

Why are some services, such as the NHS, far more effective in recruiting a diverse workforce than the fire service, the police or the armed forces?

Unit 6 International Perspectives

Grading criteria

PASSGRADE To achieve a pass grade the evidence must show that the learner is able to:	*Merit* To achieve a merit grade the evidence must show that the learner is able to:	*Distinction* To achieve a distinction grade the evidence must show that the learner is able to:
• describe international institutions, with particular reference to the structure and decision-making processes of the European Union showing how decisions made have affected UK public services **112** • summarise the common causes of war and conflict illustrating the spectrum of conflict and the changing nature of war **123** • explain how British public services are affected by war, conflict and terrorism **126** • summarise the threats posed by international terrorism and the effectiveness of counter-terrorist measures **127** • explain the key features of the United Nations Universal Declaration of Human Rights, showing how human rights are abused in at least three different countries **133** • explain how human rights issues affect the operations of at least three public services in the UK **135**	• analyse how decisions made at international level have affected the operations of UK public services **122** • compare the causes and effects of at least two contrasting international conflicts or wars since 1960 **125** • explain the threats posed by international terrorism and the effectiveness of counter-terrorist measures **127**	• analyse the threats posed by international terrorism and the effectiveness of counter-terrorist measures **127**

The fact that the UK is an island has protected us from a successful invasion by a foreign enemy for nearly a thousand years. Twenty-two miles of English Channel proved an insurmountable obstacle for the Spanish Armada, Napoleon and Hitler.

But times have changed and we can no longer hide behind the White Cliffs of Dover. Now, with globalisation – world trade, mass air travel, and everything the electronic media can throw at us – what happens in the rest of the world affects all of us in the UK too.

The public services are in the front line. The armed forces may be called upon to fight in any part of the world. International crime, from drug-running to people trafficking, is a major headache for the police and customs. Even the fire service is caught up in overseas events, sending specialist teams to disaster zones.

This is why you are studying International Perspectives.

INTERNATIONAL INSTITUTIONS

> Describe international institutions, with particular reference to the structure and decision-making processes of the European Union showing how decisions made have affected UK public services.

For this outcome, you need to:

- describe key international organisations – especially the EU
- explain the work of the main bodies in the EU
- show how what the European Union decides affects British public services.

As you can see from the definitions in the FOCUS box, there is some confusion about whether an institution is a set of norms and values governing a certain aspect of human behaviour, or whether it is an organisation which carries out a certain role in society. Professors in American universities prefer the first of these two meanings. But most ordinary people use the word in the second sense. *For the purposes of this outcome, it makes sense to accept both meanings*. Thus 'peace-keeping' by the United Nations is an institution because it is an accepted role of the United Nations. But the UN Security Council which authorises UN peace-keeping is itself an institution, because it is an officially recognised organisation with a beneficial public function.

FOCUS

Definitions of institution

An institution is ...

'(a) an established law, custom, usage, practice, organisation or other element in the political or social life of a people

(b) an establishment, organisation or association, instituted for the promotion of some object, especially one of public utility, religious, charitable, educational, etc.'

Shorter Oxford English Dictionary

'legal arrangements, routines, procedures, conventions, norms, and organizational forms that shape and inform human interaction.'

Richard B. Norgaard, 1992

Two big international institutions which affect British public services are the United Nations and the European Union.

The United Nations

Some basic facts are given in the FOCUS below:

FOCUS

The United Nations

'Organisation

In 1945, representatives of 50 countries met in San Francisco at the United Nations Conference on International Organisation to draw up the United Nations Charter. The Organisation officially came into existence on 24 October 1945, when the Charter had been ratified by China, France, the Soviet Union, the United Kingdom, the United States and a majority of other signatories. United Nations Day is celebrated on 24 October.

Charter

The Charter is the constituting instrument of the United Nations, setting out the rights and obligations of Member States, and establishing the Organisation's organs and procedures.

Purposes

The purposes of the United Nations, as set forth in the Charter, are to maintain international peace and security; to develop friendly relations among nations; to cooperate in solving international economic, social, cultural and humanitarian problems and in promoting respect for human rights and fundamental freedoms; and to be a centre for harmonising the actions of nations in attaining these ends.

Structures
The six principal organs of the United Nations are the: General Assembly, Security Council, Economic and Social Council, Trusteeship Council, International Court of Justice and Secretariat. The United Nations family, however, is much larger, encompassing 15 agencies and several programmes and bodies.

Budget
The budget for the two years 2000–1 is $2535 million. The main source of funds is the contributions of Member States, which are assessed on a scale approved by the General Assembly.

The fundamental criterion on which the scale of assessments is based is the capacity of countries to pay. In addition, countries are assessed for the costs of peace-keeping operations, which stood at around $2 billion in 2000.'

Source: http://www.un.org

The Secretary-General of the United Nations (Kofi Annan in 2003) is the main spokesperson for the UN. He heads the Secretariat (see below).

The UN General Assembly

This consists of delegates from all the 191 member states. Each country can send up to five delegates, who may be 'ambassadors to the United Nations', foreign ministers, etc. They discuss any world problem which is covered by the UN Charter and take appropriate action (i.e. make recommendations to the countries concerned, or refer the problem to the UN Security Council). Proposals are first put to a vote, and there has to be a two-thirds majority before the General Assembly will act.

The UN Charter (1945)

This is a major document setting out the constitution of the United Nations, the way it is to be organised, and its duties and responsibilities.

The UN Universal Declaration of Human Rights (1948)

This is the basis of all major human rights documents, including the European Convention on Human Rights and its five protocols, which came out in 1950, and the UK Human Rights Act 1998.

The UN Security Council

The Security Council is one of the main bodies of the United Nations and was set up in 1945. It has 15 members – five permanent and the rest non-permanent. The non-permanent members sit on the Security Council for two years. The five permanent members are the USA, China, France, Russia and the UK. The other members are chosen from different parts of the world, to provide a political balance and to give a voice to less wealthy or less powerful countries. The exact voting rules are stated in the UN Charter, which is available on http://www.un.org.

FOCUS

Role of the UN Security Council

Under the Charter, the functions and powers of the Security Council are:

'to maintain international peace and security in accordance with the principles and purposes of the United Nations;

to investigate any dispute or situation which might lead to international friction;

to recommend methods of adjusting such disputes or the terms of settlement;

to formulate plans for the establishment of a system to regulate armaments;

to determine the existence of a threat to the peace or act of aggression and to recommend what action should be taken;

to call on Members to apply economic sanctions and other measures not involving the use of force to prevent or stop aggression;

to take military action against an aggressor;

to recommend the admission of new Members;

to exercise the trusteeship functions of the United Nations in "strategic areas";

to recommend to the General Assembly the appointment of the Secretary General and, together with the Assembly, to elect the Judges of the International Court of Justice.'

Source: http://www.un.org

UN Economic and Social Council (UNESCO)

This council concerns itself with economic, social and human rights matters. It liaises closely with the Security Council, but cannot make any decisions about military action or peace-keeping. Its main function is to research problems and make reports.

The International Court of Justice

This is set up under Article 93 of the UN Charter. Its main function is to give legal advice, and to conduct war crimes tribunals such as that investigating Serbian war crimes at The Hague, in Holland.

The UN Secretariat

This is set up in Article 97 of the UN Charter. It is an independent organisation run by the Secretary-General, and does all the administrative work. Staff of the secretariat are chosen on the basis of their ability and honesty, and from as wide a range of countries as possible, to preserve the international and unbiased character of the United Nations.

NATO

The North Atlantic Treaty Organisation (NATO) was formed in 1949 at the Treaty of Washington. The original members of NATO were the UK, the USA, Canada, Belgium, France, Netherlands, Luxembourg, Denmark, Iceland, Italy, Norway and Portugal. These have since been joined by Greece, Turkey, Germany, Spain, Hungary, the Czech Republic and Poland. The purpose of NATO is to ensure military protection for member nations.

http://www.nato.int/

The European Union

The European Union (EU) is an association of European countries. Its aims are to:

- promote European unity
- improve living and working conditions for citizens
- foster economic development, balanced trade and fair competition
- reduce economic disparities between regions
- help developing countries
- preserve peace and freedom.

European Union Institutions

The European Union is a 'family' of nations which have agreed to cooperate for their own benefit – and for the long-term benefit of the rest of the world. It is not a union like the United States, because each member country retains many of its

EU member states and when they joined

Present members (2003) and year they joined		New members (after 2004)		Applicant countries	
Austria	1995	Cyprus	2004	Bulgaria	2007
Belgium	1957	Czech Rep.	2004	Romania	2007
Denmark	1973	Estonia	2004	Turkey	(to be considered later)
Finland	1995	Hungary	2004		
France	1957	Latvia	2004		
Germany	1957	Lithuania	2004		
Greece	1981	Malta	2004		
Ireland	1973	Poland	2004		
Italy	1957	Slovakia	2004		
Luxembourg	1957	Slovenia	2004		
Netherlands	1957				
Portugal	1986				
Spain	1986				
Sweden	1995				
UK	1973				

individual powers. On the other hand the ties are closer than those of the United Nations, which exists to solve world problems rather than bring about major changes in the laws or societies of member states.

The main aims of the European Union (EU) are to guarantee European peace and prosperity. But it also works to improve human rights, the environment, food standards, security and the fight against crime within its member states. The EU sees itself as having three pillars, or functions, supporting it (see below).

The EU consists of a number of 'institutions' which are designed to make sure that it carries out its aims in a fair, efficient, democratic and accountable way. These institutions take two forms:

- official bodies such as the European Parliament which follow agreed rules and carry out a range of agreed tasks
- decision-making processes which are used to settle disputes and help Europe to progress

Structure of the EU

The structure of the EU can be defined as its main official bodies and the ways they work together.

Official bodies

The European Parliament

The European Parliament consisted before 2004 of 624 MEPs (Members of the European Parliament). From 2004 to 2007 there will be 732 MEPs, and from 2007-2009 there will be 786. These MEPs are elected from the various member states of the EU. The number of MEPs each country elects is roughly linked to the population of the country. For example in 2005, the UK will elect 78 MEPs while Germany, the biggest EU country, provides 99 and Malta, the smallest, just 5.

MEPs belong to political parties, just as the MPs of national Parliaments like our own in Westminster do. In the European Parliament these MPs form groupings according to whether their policies are 'centre-right' (e.g. the Conservatives), 'centre-left'

The 'three pillars' of the European Union

The European Union

First pillar: the European Communities	Second pillar: common foreign and security policy	Third pillar: cooperation in justice and home affairs
EC • Customs union and single market • Agricultural Policy • Structural policy • Trade policy New or amended provisions on: • EU citizenship • Education and culture • Trans-European networks • Consumer protection • Health • Research and environment • Social policy • Asylum policy • External bordes • Immigration policy Euratom ECSC	Foreign Policy • Cooperation, common positions and measures • Peacekeeping • Human rights • Democract • Aid to non-member countries Security policy • Drawing on the WEU: questions concerning the securities of the EU • Disarmament • Finacial aspects of defence • Long-term: Europe's security framework	• Cooperation between judicial authorities in civil and criminal law • Police cooperation • Combating racsim and xenophobia • Fighting drugs and the arms trade • Fighting organised crime • Fighting terrorism • Criminal acts against children, trafficking in human beings

(e.g. Labour and LibDem), 'Green' – and so on. The European Parliament meets at different times in Brussels (Belgium), Strasbourg (France) and Luxembourg.

The European Parliament is the only main institution of the EU which is democratically elected.

The jobs of the European Parliament are

(a) to make laws. It makes these laws together with the European Council (see below)

(b) to supervise other EU institutions. It has the right to approve or reject members of the European Commission – Commissioners – (see below), and to influence the work of the Commission. In extreme cases it can sack the whole Commission.

(c) to influence – and finally accept or reject – the EU's spending plans. It shares this power with the European Council.

Full meetings of the European Parliament, called 'plenary sessions', take place once a month and usually last a week. The subjects to be debated (usually proposed new laws) are decided beforehand by special parliamentary committees, and the various political groupings of MEPs. The EU Parliament votes on these proposals, and if it accepts them they become law.

The European Commission

The European Commission is a body of senior politicians who are chosen by the following method:

(a) Member state governments choose a new Commission President

(b) The new Commission President nominates the other commission members

(c) The EU Parliament interviews each person nominated, and has the power to reject nominees if it wishes.

Before May 2004 there were 20 commissioners: this number has now risen to 30 to reflect the entry of new countries into the EU. After 2009 the number of Commissioners will drop to 27, and membership of the Commission will follow a rota so that every country has a representative on the Commission from time to time.

The role of the European Commission is to:

(a) put forward ideas for new laws

(b) make sure EU policies are put into practice, and to ensure that the budget (money) is spent properly

(c) work with the European Court of Justice in enforcing European law

(d) represent the EU when making agreements or having discussions with countries outside the EU

The EU Commission is based in Brussels and works full time. When planning new laws it takes advice from many people, including its own committees of advisers, and bodies such as the Economic and Social Committee and the Committee of the Regions (see below). The Commission only suggests new laws if it thinks they should apply to all EU countries.

The EU Commission also chooses development projects and plans the spending of EU money – a budget of over E100 million (about £70 million) a year.

If the Commission finds that a member country of the EU is breaking EU law (for example by giving government money to private industry) it sends a letter to the offending country accusing it of 'infringement'. If the country concerned does not satisfy the Commission, the Commission can refer that country to the European Court of Justice, which may impose heavy fines.

The Commission makes decisions by voting on issues. A simple majority – e.g. 16/30 – binds the whole Commission to supporting the decision.

The Council of the European Union

This – the third of the three main EU institutions – is made up of one government minister from each of the EU's member countries. It does not always have to be the same government minister: it depends what the Council are discussing.

Their discussions cover nine main subject areas:

- General Affairs and External Relations
- Economic and Financial Affairs
- Justice and Home Affairs
- Employment, Social Policy, Health and Consumer Affairs
- Competitiveness (Internal Market, Industry and Research)
- Transport, Telecommunications and Energy
- Agriculture and Fisheries
- Environment
- Education, Youth and Culture

If for example if they were discussing law and order (under 'Justice and Home Affairs'), Britain would send the Home Secretary, whereas if they were discussing education, Britain would send the Secretary of State for Education and Skills. Meetings take place once a month.

The roles of the Council of the European Union are

- to pass new laws (together with the European Parliament)
- to coordinate the economic policies of member countries
- to make agreements between the EU and outside countries and organisations – e.g. the USA or NATO.
- to approve the EU budget (how the EU spends its money)
- to improve EU security
- to improve cooperation between national courts and police forces in combating crime.

The European Economic and Social Committee
This is an advisory body: it cannot make new laws or exercise real power. It is made up of three groups of experts: employers' groups, workers' groups and pressure groups with special interests. After 2004 it will have 344 members drawn from all the member countries. Its roles are

- to advise the EU Council, Commission and Parliament on subjects such as employment and social welfare
- to get non-politicians more involved in advising the EU and in EU decision-making

The Committee of the Regions
This is also an advisory body. It contains (after 2004) 344 members drawn from every EU country, ranging from 24 from the biggest countries, such as Germany, France and the UK down to 5 from Malta. It has full meetings five times a year.

Its role is to study the effects of new EU proposals on different regions of the EU – to make sure all parts of the EU will be treated fairly under its laws.

The European Central Bank
This is based in Frankfurt. Its aim is to maintain price stability (stop prices from rising or falling too fast). It does this by

- controlling the money supply (i.e. controlling the numbers of euro coins and notes in circulation)
- checking price levels
- setting interest rates in the euro area (low interest rates encourage economic growth and spending; high interest rates discourage economic growth and spending)

The European Investment Bank
This bank supplies money to help pay for major projects or improvements in EU countries. The help it gives is mainly to do with economic development or social welfare, and is targeted at the poorer parts of the EU.

The Court of Auditors
This court, which has 550 employees, checks that EU money is spent properly, on the things it is supposed to be spent on. It produces accounts and tries to ensure that EU spending is 'transparent'.

The European Court of Justice
This court has one judge from each member state. Its job is to make sure that EU law is correctly understood and put into practice in each member country. It also oversees a 'Court of First Instance' which tries cases brought from all parts of the EU (usually cases about unfair business competition). The role of the European Court of Justice is:

- to give 'preliminary rulings' if there is a question of whether an EU country is interpreting EU law rightly or wrongly.
- to take court action against a member country which is suspected of not carrying out EU law correctly
- to take action to cancel an EU law which turns out to be bad or unjust
- to take action against any other EU institution which has broken or misapplied an EU law.

The European Ombudsman
The Ombudsman is an official with a large office. The Ombudsman's job is to investigate complaints by people or organisations in the EU about 'maladministration' – that is

- unfairness
- discrimination
- abuse of power
- withholding information
- unnecessary delay
- incorrect procedures.

EU decision-making processes

EU legislative decisions
These are top-level decisions within the EU government which result in the making of major new laws. They involve the European Parliament, the European Commission and the Council of the European Union. Such decisions are reached by one of three processes:

1 Co-decision. This is decision-making shared between the EU Parliament and the Council of the EU. Decisions made by this method often

Official bodies affecting public service work

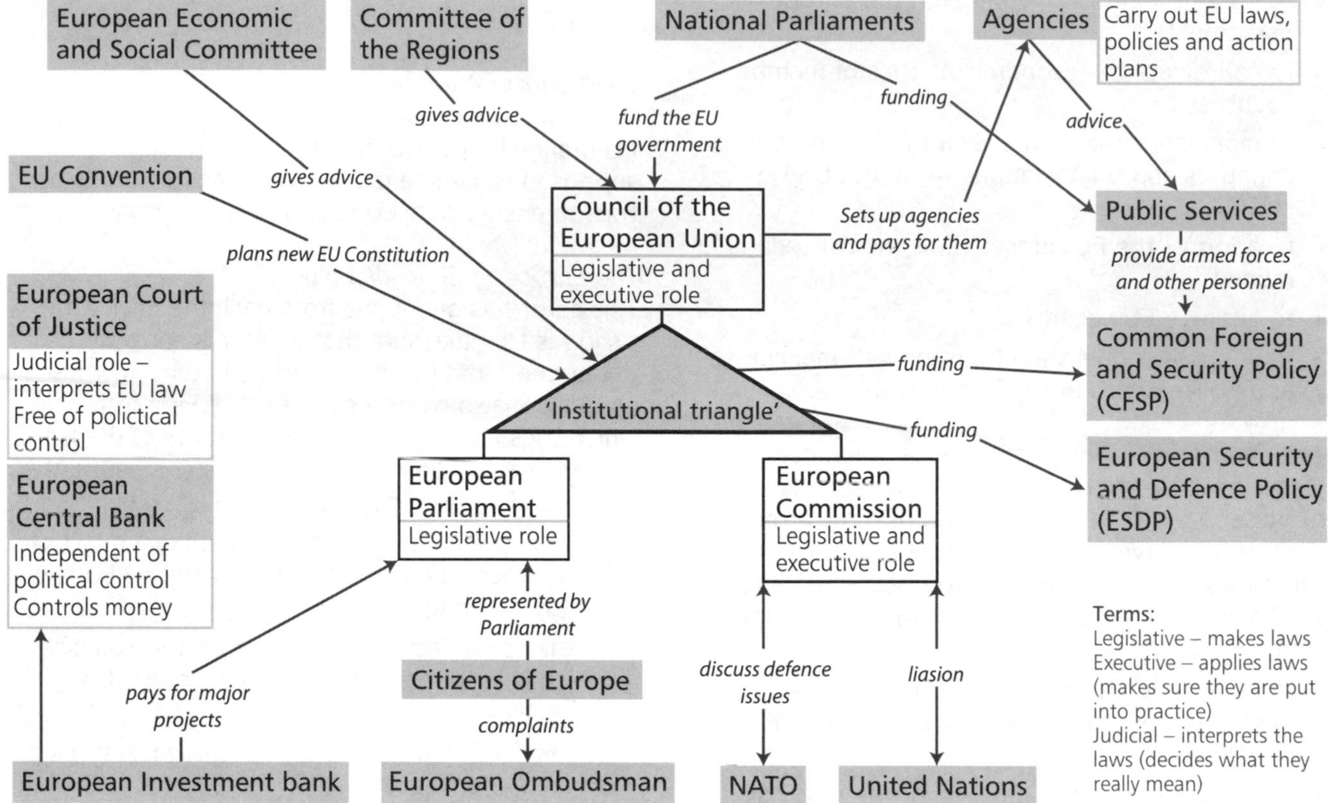

affect the public services, since they involve subjects such as:
- non-discrimination on the basis of nationality
- the right to move and reside
- the free movement of workers
- social security for migrant workers
- employment
- customs co-operation
- the fight against social exclusion
- equal opportunities and equal treatment
- health
- preventing and combating fraud
- data protection

2 Consultation. Under this system the Council consults the EU Parliament to find out what it thinks about proposals (ideas, often from the EU Commission) for new or changed laws. Areas which concern the public services and in which decisions can be made by consultation include:
- Police and judicial cooperation in criminal matters
- Discrimination on grounds of sex, race or ethnic origin, religion or political conviction, disability, age or sexual orientation
- EU citizenship
- Visas, asylum, immigration and other policies associated with the free movement of persons

3 Assent is the agreement by the EU Parliament to certain very important proposals from the Council of the EU. These decisions are mainly to do with money arrangements or new membership of the EU, and do not immediately affect the public services.

Some of these systems may change after May 2004, with the arrival of new member countries in the EU.

Two key principles of EU law

Subsidiarity

This principle aims to ensure that the EU doesn't pass a lot of unnecessary laws which interfere with the governing of member countries. It states that the EU should only make laws which can be applied to the EU as a whole. Laws on purely national issues should continue to be proposed and passed in national parliaments, and should not be binding on other member states.

Proportionality

This principle aims to protect people's basic freedoms. It states that new laws should be worded in such a way that the object of the law is achieved with minimum loss of other people's freedoms and rights.

Types of EU decision

The European Union makes many decisions which affect life – and the work of the public services – in member states. These decisions can be classified as follows (starting with the most important).

1 **Treaties**. These wide-ranging agreements are negotiated at big conferences. They update old European laws and make new ones, and usually signal a new stage in the evolution of the European Union. The decisions made at treaties are very major – e.g. the decision to start a new single European currency (the euro) at the Maastricht Treaty in 1992.

   Major as these decisions are, it is possible for countries to 'opt out' of treaty agreements without leaving the EU. Britain did this in 1992, leaving the choice open to join the euro at a later date.

2 **Regulations**. These are new laws agreed during treaties which must be adopted by member states. These laws are directly applied and do not need to be debated by the member states' national parliaments. An example is the Regulation implementing the Kimberley Process diamond certification scheme, which was adopted on 20 December 2002. This enabled all EU countries to combat trade in 'conflict diamonds' – from Sierra Leone – which were paying for a brutal civil war – a war which had cost the lives of some British soldiers who had gone in as peacekeepers.

3 **Directives**. These are EU laws which must be incorporated into the national law of member states after debate in their national parliaments. An example of a directive is Directive (COM (2002) 71) which compels member countries to provide short-term residence permits to victims of people trafficking who agree to give evidence in trials. Such a directive is needed to ensure that the procedures against people-trafficking are the same in all member states. If some states had harsher laws than others, it would lead to heavy pressure from illegal immigration in some parts of the EU, but not others. Other examples are the directives governing workers' rights, such as maternity leave.

4 **Individual decisions**. These EU decisions affect individual EU countries, or firms or individuals living in those countries. An example of such a decision was taken by the Council of the EU in 2002 to spend money on a UN scheme designed to cut off supplies of small arms and mines to Albania – to help promote peace and security in that region.

5 **Opinions and Recommendations**. These are decisions which are non-binding on member states (but the EU strongly advises them). For example the EU's Political and Security Committee (PSC) gives opinions to the Council of the EU on security threats, and these – if accepted – are then given out to member countries.

6 **Resolutions**. These are statements of long-term intentions to tackle a particular problem or achieve a long-term goal. An example is the Council Resolution of 1998 signalling for the first time the EU's intention to tackle the problem of organised, cross-border crime.

7 **Declarations**. These are comments, often on matters relating to political security. For example in 2002 the Council of the EU made a Declaration supporting democratic reforms agreed in the Turkish Parliament – reforms which might well help Turkey to join the EU in the future.

8 **Conventions**. These are complex agreements which are binding on member states at different levels. Their subject matter is specialised, but often has to do with human rights and freedoms. Many of their regulations are called protocols (guides for correct action). Conventions tend to grow and change with time, in response to changing political and social situations. An example which concerns the public services is the Schengen Convention of 1995, which allowed for free movement of EU Citizens across EU borders. Though good from a human rights point of view, this agreement makes cross-border crime easier and creates problems for immigration authorities. At present (2004) there is nervousness about large-scale movement of citizens from new EU countries into wealthier parts of the EU after enlargement in May 2004.

9 **Strategies and action plans**. These decisions have long-term objectives in specific areas and often involve the public services since they concern the fight against crime. An example is the EU Drugs Strategy for 2002–2004 which is a series of ideas designed to reduce drug trafficking and abuse in EU countries. The action plans linked the strategy set precise targets, stating dates and who is responsible; the EU Action Plan on Drugs defines actions to be undertaken during 2000–2004. Strategies and action plans state the various ways and levels at which the public services of different countries, e.g. Britain and France, need to cooperate to cut down on cross-border crime.

How European decisions have affected UK public services

European decisions have had major effects on UK public services, but these effects are not always obvious to the users of these services. Even to the people who work in public services, the fact that new laws or regulations come from Europe is not obvious, because new laws and regulations come from the British Parliament. However, a great many new laws and regulations passed by the British Parliament (or the Welsh and Scottish National Assemblies) are brought in because the EU has passed similar laws in Brussels.

The British Parliament has a committee called the European Scrutiny Committee. Its 16 members have a taxing job: to study the 1100 EU legal documents which come out each year and to decide which of them should be incorporated into British law. The important documents are debated by the European Standing Committee or by the House of Commons itself. The European Scrutiny Committee also keeps an eye on possible new developments, and subjects which are discussed by the Council of the European Union.

Many new Acts (major laws) and Statutory Instruments (minor laws) which are passed by the British Parliament in Westminster (London) are based on new EU laws. Three Acts of which this is true are

- the Antisocial Behaviour Act 2003, in which the police have a 'duty as a public authority to exercise their functions compatibly with the European Convention on Human Rights'
- the Crime (International Cooperation) Act 2003 based on the EU Schengen Agreement 1985 and the Agreement on Mutual Assistance in Criminal Matters 2000
- the Criminal Justice Act 2003, where the section on the trade in endangered species follows the European Council Regulation 338/97/EC on the protection of species of wild fauna and flora by regulating the trade therein.

Human Rights

The European Convention on Human Rights, a list of human rights articles (rules) accepted by all EU countries (and which will be included in the final EU Constitution), is now included in the British Human Rights Act of 1998. This Act controls the behaviour of all UK public services – uniformed and non-uniformed – but it might not have been introduced into the UK if other EU countries had not adopted it.

EU Agencies

The EU has set up many agencies – organisations of experts whose work influences UK public services. This is particularly true of agencies which support policing, the immigration services or armed forces cooperation.

Examples of these agencies (which have websites) are:

European Monitoring Centre for Drugs and Drug Addiction (EMCDDA)

European Agency for Safety and Health at Work (EU-OSHA)

European Monitoring Centre on Racism and Xenophobia (EUMC)

European Maritime Safety Agency (EMSA)

European Aviation Safety Agency (EASA)

These agencies help the relevant public services by giving expert advice and keeping databases of information – both personal (e.g. on leaders of race-hate organisations) and technical (e.g. methods of improving safety at sea).

Agencies fighting crime

These come under the heading of the European Crime Prevention Network (EUCPN). They include:

EUROPOL
This organisation helps national police forces – including Britain's – tackle cross-border crime in the EU. Its importance is increasing considerably with the enlargement of the EU in 2004. Its role is to combat:

- drug trafficking
- immigration networks
- vehicle trafficking
- trafficking in human beings including child pornography
- forgery of money and other means of payment
- trafficking in radioactive and nuclear substances
- terrorism

EUROPOL does not fight crime itself. But it supports the police forces of member states by:

- making it easier for national law enforcement agencies to exchange information
- providing operational analysis
- producing reports and crime analysis
- providing expertise and technical support for investigations and operations.

Eurojust – This agency, formed in 2002 and based in The Hague, helps national police forces to deal with organised crime, and also provides legal facilities to help extradite major players in organised crime and bring them to justice.

CEPOL – The European Police College (CEPOL) gives training in European and cross-border policing. This includes such matters as football hooliganism and money laundering.

The Convention on Mutual Assistance and Cooperation between Customs Administrations develops links and shares information and skills between the customs services of different EU countries.

OLAF is the EU anti-fraud office.

These organisations are all supported by an EU-wide agreement for cooperation between courts, called the European Judicial Network.

The civilian crime control measures are all funded by the EU under a number of schemes – one of these is ARGO, which funds research, development and programmes designed to control visas, asylum seekers and immigration issues.

Another measure is the European Arrest Warrant, which enables serious crime suspects to be handed over by any EU country to the EU country in which they are to be tried. This avoids the expensive and time-consuming process of extradition between EU countries.

There is also a common framework for dealing with the threat of terrorism.

None of these agreements and schemes prevent bilateral agreements – e.g. between Britain and France – to deal with specific problems, provided the aims of these agreements are legal within the EU as a whole. The closing of Sangatte refugee camp – agreed between Britain and France in 2002 to prevent asylum-seekers flocking round Calais to gain illegal entry into the UK – was an example of such an agreement.

Military cooperation

EU countries cooperate at many levels in military exercises and the sharing of military intelligence. But most of their cooperation is under the umbrella of NATO – since most EU countries are also members of NATO. In 1998 the agreement was made at St Malo in France that Europe would set up a Rapid Reaction Force of up to 60,000 personnel to deal with conflicts inside or outside Europe in which NATO was not involved. This, however, could not be deployed without the agreement of national governments. Military cooperation in the EU is at present limited partly by fear of American disapproval, and partly by the disagreements which took place before the 2003 Iraq War – in which Britain took a large role, while France and Germany strongly opposed getting involved.

COOL SITES:

http://europa.eu.int/eur-lex/en/com/rpt/2002/act0324en01/1.pdf – laws

http://europa.eu.int/eur-lex/en/about/pap/process_and_players2.html

http://europa.eu.int/eur-lex/en/about/abc/index.html

www.nelsonthornes.com/vocational/public_services/ – Unit 15 Public Services in Europe, for information on the institutions, structure and decision-making processes of the EU

Summary: How EU decisions have affected UK public services

The UK public services most immediately affected by European decisions are:

- the police
  - The police are affected by the Human Rights Act 1998, which is itself derived from the European Convention on Human Rights – a document written in 1950 and binding on member states.
  - The police and customs are affected by European crime-fighting initiatives such as Europol.
- the prison service, also affected by the Human Rights Act
- the armed forces – affected by the formation of a planned European 'rapid reaction force', whose aim is to take some of the burden off NATO when it comes to settling European military problems (e.g. in Kosovo in 1998).

Many recent British laws affecting public services have originated from European laws (see 'explanatory notes' on the HMSO website).

http://www.hmso.gov.uk/legislation/uk-expa.htm

How international decisions affect UK public services

Merit

Analyse how decisions made at international level have affected the operations of UK public services.

For this outcome, you need to:

- gather information about international decisions which have affected UK public services
- explain what these effects have been.

Relevant decisions could be legal decisions (e.g. by the EU, which change the way British public services work) or political decisions, such as the decision to go to war in Iraq. The PROFILE below looks in more detail at one international decision and its repercussions.

PROFILE

Closing the Sangatte refugee camp in 2002

The Red Cross set up the Sangatte refugee camp in a disused warehouse near Calais in 1999. Forty-five thousand refugees and asylum-seekers from countries such as Afghanistan, Iraq, Iran and the Balkans passed through the camp on their way to Britain, and 85 per cent stayed in the UK. After complaints from the UK, the French government finally closed the camp on condition that the UK took nearly all the 1300 refugees who were still in the camp when it closed and tightened its immigration policy.

The immediate effect on the UK and its public services was that they took the asylum-seekers remaining in Sangatte.

Other effects on public services:

- more policing of all channel ports, to discourage asylum-seekers from entering illegally
- more work for immigration officers processing the last 1300 Sangatte refugees
- more work for the National Asylum Support Service (NASS), organising accommodation and supplying £35 a week vouchers to asylum-seekers.

CHECKPOINT ...

1 What is the 'white list'?
2 What is the difference between asylum-seekers and economic migrants?
3 What problems would it cause the public services if the UK deported all new asylum-seekers?
4 What lessons can be learnt from the news report below?

FOCUS

'Violence erupted on a Wrexham housing estate last night as a local mob fought with asylum seekers for the second evening running.

The rioting was described as "racially motivated" by police who deployed more than 100 police officers from three forces to quell the trouble. At least 200 people were involved in the violence and police have charged two people with public order offences.

Gangs went on the rampage using sticks and snooker cues as weapons as tensions between local people on the Caia Park estate and Iraqi asylum seekers who had lived on the estate for a year without trouble erupted.'

Source: from article 'Race riots in Wrexham' by Naveed Raja, in the Mirror, *24 June 2003; http://www.mirror.co.uk/*

COOL SITES:

http://europa.eu.int/abc-en.htm

http://www.europarl.eu.int/addresses/institutions/websites.htm – things about Europe that your mother never told you

http://europa.eu.int/comm/justice_home/fsj/crime/fsj_crime_intro_en.htm – Europe and fighting crime

http://www.nato.int/

http://www.un.org/english/engtxt.htm

http://www.un.org/aboutun/chart.html – anatomy of the UN

http://www.un.org/peace/index.html – peace-keeping and peace-making

http://www.un.org/ha/index.html – refugees and disaster relief

WAR AND CONFLICT

PASSGRADE

> Summarise the common causes of war and conflict illustrating the spectrum of conflict and the changing nature of war.

For this outcome, you need to:

- describe briefly the main causes of war
- outline the different types of war
- show how war is changing.

The causes of war are extremely complex, and in any given war each side has a different view of the causes. The 2003 war in Iraq is a good example of this complexity, as the table below shows.

Different views on the causes of the 2003 Iraq War

Coalition view	Iraqi view
Threat of Saddam Hussein's weapons of mass destruction (he had already gassed Kurds at Halabja in 1985).	The Americans and British wanted to get their hands on Iraq's oil.
Iraq was sponsoring international terrorism, like the recent attacks of 9/11.	The coalition were anti-Islamic – Christians against Muslims.
War would make Iraq a democratic country – and more pro-western.	The coalition were acting on behalf of Israel.
War would free Shi'ite Muslims (in the Kurdish north and around Basra in the south) from victimisation by Sunni Muslims.	The war was part of an American plan for world domination.
They would get rid of Saddam Hussein, put a stop to human rights abuses – and the Iraqi people would be grateful.	The war was illegal, since there was no vote for it by the UN Security Council.
The West was serious about protecting its security and setting an example to other 'rogue states' such as Iran and North Korea.	Iraq had no weapons of mass destruction and no intention of threatening world peace.
Iraq had not cooperated with the UN weapons inspectors led by Dr Hans Blix.	Iraq had suffered 12 years of brutal trade sanctions.

*'Are you **sure** you can't see any weapons of mass destruction?'*

General causes of war may include:

- **human aggression** – the human race is naturally aggressive and has a psychological need for war
- **self-defence** This is the main legal justification for war, e.g. the Falklands Conflict 1982, when the UK recovered the Falkland Islands from Argentine invaders
- **perceived injustices in the past, e.g.** the six Arab–Israeli wars between 1948 and 1982, resulting from the creation of Israel in 1948, by the US and UK, out of Palestinian land
- **ethnic rivalries**, e.g. massacres in Rwanda in the 1980s caused by a power struggle between the ruling Tutsi and the majority Hutu
- **competition for economic resources**, e.g. fighting in Sierra Leone 1991–2002 over the diamond mines in the north-east of the country
- **religious conflict**, e.g. 'ethnic cleansing' of Bosnian Muslims by Christian Serbs in the 1990s in the former Yugoslavia

- **ideological differences** (differences about political systems) tend to cause war, e.g. the Vietnam War between communists and capitalists (backed up by the US), 1959–75.

COOL SITE:

http://www.infoplease.com/ce6/history/A0804479.html – the six Arab–Israeli wars

The spectrum of conflict and the changing nature of war

The 'spectrum of conflict' refers to the size and scale of wars, and the range of causes. The 'changing nature of war' refers to the different strategies and technology used in different conflicts. There is plenty of information on the internet if you use the name of the war as your search term.

The scale and nature of some recent conflicts

Name of war	Position in spectrum (1 biggest – 10 smallest)	Nature of war
Iran–Iraq War 1980–8 This war was fought by Iraq against Iran and took place along the border between the two countries, and around Basra	7. This war was serious because of the high death rate in a sparsely populated region, and because it paved the way for other wars. Iraq spent a lot of money and fell into debt; the invasion of Kuwait in 1991, followed by the 1991 Gulf War, was the result.	This was an old-style trench war, rather like World War I. About 1 million people, mainly young soldiers, lost their lives. Nothing was gained by either side. The war was partly religious, because most of the Iraqis who were fighting were Sunni Muslims, while the Iranians were Shi'ites. Young men were persuaded to fight and get killed by the promise of martyrdom. Iraq believed it owned some of the Iranian land. Saddam Hussein, the Iraq leader, bought many weapons from the west, and was supported by western leaders at this time.
Falklands Conflict 1982 A brief war with Argentina	10. This was a very minor conflict – with 255 British service personnel killed, and around 700–1000 Argentines. There were hardly any civilian deaths on the Falkland Islands, where 1800 people, of British descent, lived mainly as sheep farmers.	The conflict started with a misunderstanding: The UK had been negotiating with Argentina for 16 years to find a way to settle the dispute about who owned the Falkland Islands. The Argentine flag was raised on another island, South Georgia, then the Falklands were occupied. A British task force was sent and, after some fighting, the Argentines withdrew. The fighting was done by swift-moving infantry units who walked huge distances over rough moorland, covered by British air power.
Coalition versus Iraq 2003	8. So far (as of November 2003) 240 US personnel have been killed – many in peace-keeping activities. In the first month of war/occupation, 3240 Iraqi civilians died, according to figures given by hospitals. The figure for all Iraqis will be much higher.	This war showed the huge strategic and technological gap between the coalition, especially the USA, and Iraq. The use of smart weapons and electronic surveillance, some from satellites, minimised the risk to coalition fighters whose death toll was incredibly low by the standards of past wars. Civilian casualties were minimised by targeting official buildings only. There was a strong psychological element in the US tactics, with the dropping of leaflets and bombs intended to inspire 'shock and awe' in the Iraqis.

! CHECKPOINT ...

There have been many other wars since 1960. Choose one or two of them, analyse their causes, and sum up the way (strategy, weapons, etc.) in which they were fought.

Types of warfare

- **Conventional warfare** This uses tanks, shells, land-mines and large numbers of foot-soldiers. It is a wasteful way of fighting, with a high death rate. It was tried by the Iraqis against the British and Americans in 1991 – with disastrous results for them.
- **Use of air power** It can inflict great damage on the enemy while receiving few casualties in return. The main weapons are bombs and missiles. Air power is needed to protect land and sea forces, and to gather information.
- **Use of sea power** Battleships, destroyers and aircraft carriers are used to transport personnel and weapons to the 'theatre' of war. They can fire long-range missiles with pinpoint accuracy, and are hard to attack, if protected by an air force.
- **Weapons of mass destruction (WMD)** Chemical, biological and nuclear weapons, though outlawed by the Geneva Convention, are stockpiled by some of the richer nations. Chemical weapons were used by Saddam Hussein against the Kurds in 1985. Nuclear weapons were used by the US at Hiroshima and Nagasaki in 1945. Some of these weapons could be used by terrorists.
- **Guerrilla warfare** This is warfare by small, mobile groups. It works best in forested or built-up environments, and is a cheap and effective way of 'tying up' a much larger army. It was used by the North Vietnamese in the 1970s.
- **Terrorism** Terrorism is a method of fighting used by civilians when faced with overwhelming power. The aim of terrorism is to gain publicity and manipulate the world media. Its effectiveness is shown by the events after 9/11 – forcing the US and UK to go to war against much of world opinion. But as a war technique it has no value. Many terrorist attacks are suicide bombings – in which the terrorist organisation loses young, brave fighters in return for a few civilian lives.

Merit

Compare the causes and effects of at least two contrasting international conflicts or wars since 1960.

For this outcome, you need to:

- choose two or more different wars to research. They must have happened *after* 1960, they must be significantly different from each other, and they must involve at least two different countries
- show the similarities and differences between the causes of the two wars you choose and between their effects.

Though all wars are different, they have certain things in common:

- thousands, sometimes millions of deaths (mainly civilians)
- vast human suffering caused by injuries, bereavement and traumatisation
- mass starvation, illness and environmental disasters often result
- wars can have knock-on effects leading to other wars
- big companies make big profits rebuilding devastated countries.

Some international wars since 1960

Name and date of war	Countries fighting	Causes	Effects
Vietnam War 1954–75	South Vietnam and USA against North Vietnam (with help from China)	Communist North Vietnam wanted to take over capitalist South Vietnam.	North Vietnam won. Vietnam was cut off from the world for 20 years. The Vietnamese suffered great poverty. America kept out of foreign wars until 1991.

Six-day War 1967	Israel against Syria, Jordan and Egypt	Syria, Jordan and Egypt invaded Israel, to make a land for the Palestinian people.	Israel made huge advances and humiliated the invaders.
Yom Kippur War 1973	Israel against Syria and Egypt	Syria and Egypt tried to reclaim lost land.	Arab nations realised that Israel was there to stay.
Iran–Iraq War 1980–8	Iran against Iraq	Iran had an aggressive foreign policy, and Iraq felt threatened. The west encouraged Iraq to go to war by selling arms to Iraq.	Nobody won this war, but it impoverished Iraq, which had been rich up to then, and left them with a huge army.
Falklands War 1982	UK against Argentina	Argentina took over the Falkland Islands and South Georgia, which lie on the UK's route to the Antarctic, and have oil and fisheries wealth.	After Galtieri (the Argentine dictator) was replaced by Carlos Menem (an elected leader) diplomatic relations were resumed.
Gulf War 1991	USA, UK, France and Kuwait against Iraq	Iraq invaded Kuwait because the Iran–Iraq War had left them with no money but a big army, and because they felt they had an ancient right to Kuwait.	The defeat of Iraq. Twelve years of economic sanctions killed over 1 million Iraqis. Saddam Hussein stayed in power. Shi'ites rebelled in 1991, thinking the US would help them – but they didn't, so 30,000 or more Shi'ites died.
Iraq War 2003	USA and UK (with some Australian help) against Iraq	Iraq was thought to have weapons of mass destruction, and to be supporting international terrorism.	Iraq is being ruled by the Americans and British until either the UN or a democratic Iraq government step in.

Sources of information on wars:

- encyclopaedias (very useful!)
- books (often excellent, but you will need to pick out the main points)
- the internet (very good – but check for bias)
- television, museums, newspapers, etc. can be very good
- ex-combatants (if they are prepared to talk about them).

INTERNATIONAL TERRORISM AND COUNTER-TERRORISM

Explain how British public services are affected by war, conflict and terrorism.

For this outcome, you need to explain:

- how the public services are affected by the *threat* of war, conflict and terrorism
- how public services are affected when *actively involved* in war, conflict and terrorism.

How public services are affected

The threat of war, conflict and terrorism

The government and the public services respond to these threats by emergency planning, and training exercises. Central government lays down the ground rules for these plans in *Dealing with Disaster*, published by the Cabinet Office, and available on http://www.ukresilience.info/contingencies/dwd/.

The Civil Contingencies Secretariat is the government organisation responsible for planning a response to major terrorism, if it happens on British soil.

FOCUS

'We will define a major emergency as:
"any event or circumstance (happening with or without warning) that causes or threatens death or injury, disruption to the community, or damage to property or to the environment on such a scale that the effects cannot be dealt with by the emergency services, local authorities and other organisations as part of their normal day-to-day activities".'

Source: Dealing with Disaster, *The Cabinet Office*

The public services aim at a flexible and co-ordinated response to terrorist threats. This response is based on five principles:

- **Assessment** – determining the risk:
  - examining the design, working procedures and security arrangements of at-risk places such as airports
  - monitoring the global electronic 'chatter' from mobile phones, e-mails, etc., in which words and phrases connected with terrorism can be detected.
- **Prevention** – stopping it from happening:
  - patrolling
  - controlling people's movements
  - passing preventive laws giving the police wide powers, e.g. the Terrorism Act 2000.
- **Preparation** – planning, training and exercising to respond to a terrorist attack. The plans define the roles and responsibilities of each emergency service. Training and exercises show the services how to implement the plans, develop their skills, and identify possible problems.
- **Response** The first response is by the emergency services – police, fire and ambulance.
- **Recovery management:**
  - dealing with the 'physical, social, psychological, political and financial consequences of an emergency'
  - reviewing the preparation and response, and learning lessons.

The public services get extra money from the government to deal effectively with terrorist threats. This covers the cost of risk assessment, planning and training.

There is much more about this in Unit 14, Major Incidents, page 358.

Action outside the country

The effect of war, conflict and terrorism on the armed forces is that they may have to go abroad to fight, or carry out peace-keeping roles.

http://www.mod.uk/aboutus/keyfacts/index.html

When there is no war, the armed forces spend the bulk of their time preparing for one. They carry out strategic and tactical planning, and many exercises on the ground, the sea or in the air in many parts of the world. They develop the special skills needed for warfare in different environments, such as deserts, the arctic, jungles and built-up areas.

Summarise the threats posed by international terrorism and the effectiveness of counter-terrorist measures.

Merit

Explain the threats posed by international terrorism and the effectiveness of counter-terrorist measures.

Distinction

Analyse the threats posed by international terrorism and the effectiveness of counter-terrorist measures.

For these three closely-linked outcomes, you need to:

- pick out and state clearly the main threats posed by international terrorism

- discuss the nature of the threats, say why they are dangerous, and assess how dangerous they are (both to civilians and public services)
- state the main things which governments and public services do to fight, discourage or prevent terrorism
- reach a reasoned judgement on how well these 'counter-terrorist measures' work.

FOCUS

Terrorism

Terrorism is an action where:

- the use or threat is designed to influence the government or to intimidate the public or a section of the public
- the use or threat is made for the purpose of advancing a political, religious or ideological cause.

The action is terrorist if it:

- involves serious violence against a person
- involves serious damage to property
- endangers a person's life, other than that of the person committing the action
- creates a serious risk to the health or safety of the public or a section of the public
- is designed seriously to interfere with or seriously to disrupt an electronic system
- involves the use of firearms or explosives
- is action taken for the benefit of a proscribed organisation.

Source: Definitions above quoted from the Terrorism Act 2000

'violent acts ... intended to intimidate or coerce a civilian population, influence the policy of a government, or affect the conduct of a government' – FBI definition of terrorism

The word 'terrorist' is widely used by western governments, and by the public services. However, members of 'terrorist' organisations often prefer to call themselves 'freedom fighters', 'activists', 'soldiers' or 'martyrs'.

http://www.hmso.gov.uk/acts/acts2000/20000011.htm – the full Terrorism Act!

Moment of truth. Within days, George W. Bush had declared the 'war on terror'.

Terrorist organisations

These range from small groups of less than a hundred people to large organisations with mass support from local civilians.

FOCUS

Terrorist organisations

Four of the 25 organisations banned by the UK government:

- Abu Nidal Organisation (ANO): The principal aim of ANO is the destruction of the state of Israel. It is also hostile to 'reactionary' Arab regimes and states supporting Israel.
- Al Qaeda: Inspired and led by Osama Bin Laden, its aims are the expulsion of Western forces from Saudi Arabia, the destruction of Israel and the end of western influence in the Muslim world.
- Kurdistan Workers' Party (Partiya Karkeren Kurdistan): The PKK is primarily a separatist movement that has sought an independent Kurdish state in southeast Turkey.
- Basque Homeland and Liberty (Euskadi ta Askatasuna): ETA seeks the creation of an independent state comprising the Basque regions of Spain and France.

Source: Home Office 2003

http://www.homeoffice.gov.uk/terrorism/index.html

FOCUS

Hamas

'Hamas, the main Islamist movement in the Palestinian territories, was born soon after the previous intifada erupted in 1987.

The organisation opposes the Oslo peace process and its short-term aim is a complete Israeli withdrawal from the Palestinian territories.

Hamas does not recognise the right of Israel to exist. Its long-term aim is to establish an Islamic state on land originally mandated as Palestine – most of which has been contained within Israel's borders since its creation in 1948.

The grass-roots organisation – with a political and a military wing – has an unknown number of hard-core members but tens of thousands of supporters and sympathisers.

It has two main functions:

- It is involved in building schools and hospitals in the West Bank and the Gaza Strip, and in helping the community in social and religious ways.
- The military wing of Hamas – known as the Izzedine al-Qassam Brigades – has carried out a series of bloody attacks against Israeli targets.'

Source: article by Kathryn Westcott on BBC News Online, *19 October 2000*

CHECKPOINT ...

Research a terrorist group on the Internet, e.g. IRA, Al-Fatah or Al-Qaeda.

Threats posed by international terrorism

- **Dramatic atrocities** such as the attacks of 11 September 2001, in which 3021 people are thought to have been killed – 2801 at the World Trade Center, 180 at the Pentagon and 40 in Pennsylvania.
- **Other hi-jackings and strikes at vulnerable civilian targets** – especially airports, theatres (Moscow 2003) or (in Israel) buses. The worst terrorist attack in the UK was the Lockerbie bombing in 1988, when 270 people, including 189 Americans, died when Pan Am Flight 103 was blown up in mid-air over the Scottish borders.

FOCUS

An assassination

'Serbian Prime Minister Zoran Djindjic, a key leader of the revolt that overthrew Slobodan Milosevic, was assassinated in Belgrade Wednesday, throwing the country into a fresh political crisis amid bitter complaints about the power wielded by criminal overlords.

Mr Djindjic, an enthusiastically pro-Western leader, was shot dead as he entered government headquarters. Police said they had arrested two men in connection with the killing, but they were not sure they were the gunmen.

The future of democratic reforms was uncertain following the prime minister's death.

Speculation was rife as to who was behind the murder, but political leaders and observers said that shadowy mafia groups linked to former Yugoslav President Slobodan Milosevic's regime were most likely responsible.'

Source: article by Peter Ford on The New Republic Online, *13 March 2003; www.csmonitor.com*

FOCUS

Suicide attacks

'Suicide bombers are the most feared weapons in the arsenal of political activists. Unlike the bombing campaigns of the IRA or ETA, to give two examples, there is no telephone warning; the act itself and its resultant chaos announce the attack. While some attacks are successful against military targets, most are carried out against civilians. As a Hamas training manual notes, it is foolish to hunt the tiger when there are plenty of sheep around.

Since the technique was first perfected in the early 1980s, it has been grimly successful, most recently in the wrenching 11 September attacks in New York and Washington. While Sri Lanka and Palestine generate the most suicide bombings, the attacks against the USA dwarf all others in their planning, complexity and success. Individual suicide bombers present military and security officials with difficult detection and prevention problems for improvised explosive devices. Israel has developed a proactive approach with its "targeted killings" programme, but the long-term viability of such an operation remains to be seen.'

Source: from 'Suicide Bombing: The Penultimate Terrorist Act' by John Daly, reproduced with permission from Jane's Terrorism and Security Monitor, *17 September 2001*

- **Assassinations** An assassination is the killing of a person, especially a political leader, for suspected political reasons.
- **Suicide attacks** These are bombings and other attacks in which the terrorist plans to get killed.
- **Biological and chemical attacks** These are considered a serious risk for the future, since in theory biological and weapons are cheap, easy to carry and hard to detect. A very small amount of certain nerve gases, or anthrax spores, could kill large numbers of people. However, a good deal of expertise is needed to produce them and deliver them in such a way that they will kill people. Recent examples of biological and chemical attacks are the postal distribution of anthrax spores in the US in the autumn of 2001 (which caused two deaths), and the Tokyo subway attack by the Aum cult in 1995 when 12 people were killed by gassing.
- **Nuclear threats** The nightmare scenario is a 'suitcase' nuclear bomb, but terrorist organisations are not thought to have the resources or expertise to make one at present. There are some fears about 'dirty' nuclear weapons, in which conventional explosive delivers radioactive dust or gas.

Analysis of threats

The following points could be made:

- The chances of getting killed in a terrorist attack are much less than the risk of being killed on the roads. However, the danger is increased in city centres, airports and other public places.
- The people who carry out terrorist attacks do not have the resources to wage a war.
- Terrorism is essentially a psychological tactic, and its main large-scale effect is on people's minds.
- Terrorism affects world stock markets, causes wars and undermines world stability. Wars in Afghanistan and Iraq have followed the 11 September attacks – and there may be more. These wars have already killed many more people than were killed in 9/11. The Iraq War will soon have cost the US $100 billion – money which could have been spent saving lives or generating prosperity elsewhere.
- International terrorism is one kind of terrorism: 'ethnic cleansing' in civil war, e.g. in Rwanda in 1994 and in Bosnia-Herzegovina in the 1990s, is also terrorism – but this is unlikely to affect the UK directly.
- Terrorism causes unrest within countries and produces 'Islamophobia' – hostility to Muslims – a destabilising factor in British society.

Effectiveness of counter-terrorist measures

The 'war on terror'

This is being waged on many fronts. It includes actual war in Afghanistan and Iraq, strong diplomatic pressure on countries such as Syria, Saudi Arabia, Iran and South Korea, the 'road map' for peace between Israelis and Palestinians and other large-scale initiatives by western governments, NATO and the UN.

It is extremely hard to judge the effectiveness of these military, political, economic and diplomatic measures. Nobody knows how much terrorism there would be if the 'war on terror' had not been put into operation. War in Afghanistan failed to capture Osama bin Laden. War in Iraq may well have increased, not decreased, the threat of terrorism.

New laws on asylum and terrorism

- Terrorism Act 2000 (TACT)
- Anti-Terrorism, Crime and Security Act 2001 (ATCSA)

FOCUS

Terrorism Act 2000 (TACT)

'The Terrorism Act is the primary piece of UK counter-terrorist legislation and it has proved a vital tool in the fight against terrorism. Passed by Parliament on 20 July 2000, it came into force on 19 February 2001 in response to the changing threat from international terrorism, and replaced the previous temporary anti-terrorism legislation that dealt primarily with Northern Ireland.

These are some of the specific measures in the Terrorism Act:

- It outlaws certain terrorist groups and makes it illegal for them to operate in the UK (a process known as proscription), and specifically extends this proscription regime to include international terrorist groups, like Al Qaida. This is a tangible demonstration that we are serious in our fight against international terrorism and an effective deterrent against would-be terrorists.
- It gives police enhanced powers to investigate terrorism, including wider stop and search powers, and the power to detain suspects after arrest for up to seven days (though any period longer than two days must be approved by a magistrate).

- It creates new criminal offences, including 1) inciting terrorist acts, 2) seeking or providing training for terrorist purposes at home or overseas, 3) providing instruction or training in the use of firearms, explosives or chemical, biological or nuclear weapons.
- It provides additional powers applicable to Northern Ireland only, which must be renewed every year.

Anti-Terrorism, Crime and Security Act 2001 (ATCSA)

The Anti-Terrorism, Crime and Security Act was passed in the immediate aftermath of the 11 September attacks. It builds and expands on the Terrorism Act. However, the Terrorism Act is still the main piece of legislation that the police use operationally, on a day-to-day basis, to arrest and investigate terrorists.

These are some of the specific measures in the ATCSA:

- It prevents terrorists from abusing immigration procedures by allowing the Home Secretary to detain foreign nationals who are suspected of involvement in international terrorism but who cannot immediately be removed from the UK, until we can deport them.
- It strengthens the protection and security of aviation and civil nuclear sites, and tightens the security of dangerous substances held in labs and universities.
- It creates tough penalties for people seeking to exploit the events of 11 September by extending the law on hoaxes and increasing the penalties for crimes aggravated by racial or religious hatred.
- It cuts off terrorists from their funds by allowing assets to be frozen at the start of an investigation.'

Source: http://www.homeoffice.gov.uk/terrorism/index.html

Training the public services for terrorist incidents

The public services are increasing their training for terrorist threats. Many of their systems were refined in the 1970s and 1980s in Northern Ireland, and for routine threats, such as bombs, are very effective. The effectiveness of training for chemical and biological weapons attacks will not be tested until – or unless – they happen.

FOCUS

Bomb threats

'Certain key activities arise with the management of a bomb threat:

- police evaluation of the threat with a designated co-ordinator at the threatened location
- confirmation that a device exists at the threatened location
- consideration of cordons (dependent on the threat and possibly over 500 metres away)
- establishing a cordon
- potential evacuation to a safe distance
- rendering any suspect device safe
- gathering of forensic evidence
- recovery and re-occupation of the scene.'

Source: Dealing with Disaster, *The Cabinet Office*

COOL SITE:

http://www.ukresilience.info/contingencies/dwd/

Explaining and analysing terrorist threats and the effectiveness of counter-terrorist measures

To explain terrorist threats, you can:

- outline the political, economic, religious or ethnic tensions underlying the terrorism
- give (briefly) an account of some of the main terrorist attacks, showing the methods used, the targets chosen and the casualties suffered by both the victims and the terrorists.

To analyse terrorist threats, you can:

- examine more deeply the psychology and motivation of terrorists
- investigate types of chemical and biological weapon and how terrorists might use them
- decide whether the war on terror should concentrate on attacking terrorism itself, or on attacking the causes of terrorism
- address the question of whether the reaction of the world to terrorism is more dangerous than the terrorism itself
- assess the effectiveness of suicide attacks from the point of view of a terrorist organisation

- discuss the effect terrorism has on human rights law.

To explain the effectiveness of counter-terrorist measures, you can:

- outline the types of measures used and how they work
- state whether the measures prevent or deter terrorism or whether they deal with terrorism and terrorists after the attack.

To analyse the effectiveness of counter-terrorist measures, you can:

- classify the types of measures used
- judge in what situations the measures are most effective – and why.

Players in the 'war against terrorism'

Types of anti-terrorist measure	**Players**					
	Military	**Diplomatic**	**Media**	**Governments**	**Police**	**Emergency services**
Prevention	–	Negotiating over disputes; making treaties	Anti-terrorist propaganda; advertising security awareness, e.g. no knives on planes	Reducing differences in wealth; improving human rights	Building good relations with minorities; sharing information with other forces	–
Deterrence	Patrols; military build-up	Issuing threats or UN resolutions	Publicising the horror of terrorist attacks	Passing tough anti-terrorist laws	Providing a visible presence on the streets; being armed	–
Prediction	Intelligence gathering; spying	Intelligence gathering; listening to complaints by other diplomats	Receiving terrorist warnings	Analysing regional inequalities of wealth; ethnic disputes; historical injustices	Intelligence gathering; spying	Planning, preparing and exercising for a possible terrorist attack
Pre-emption	Striking at terrorists before they can act	Agreeing with terrorist demands before they act	–	Passing treaties which satisfy the terrorist sponsors' demands	Closing airports; 'flooding' an area known to be at risk	–
Response	Commando actions or war	Raising the matter with the UN, NATO or other governments	Use propaganda to get public opinion on side of government	Authorising war	Many roles, depending on casualties, etc.	Rescues, dealing with casualties, putting out fires, etc.

Detection	–	Liaising with intelligence services, who will be working to know more about the terrorists	–	Co-ordinating the search for terrorist cells; offering rewards	Intense activity to identify and capture terrorists and accomplices; intelligence-gathering; forensic work	Fire service may have a big role in investigating the scene, if fire is involved
Punishment	A punitive war	Organising diplomatic and trade sanctions	Mould public opinion so that people demand harsh penalties from the courts	Setting up internment camps; supporting tough courts – both internal and international	Preparing the case against the terrorists, so they can be prosecuted	Giving evidence to the police of the nature and scale of the attack
Review	–	Sharing intelligence with their governments; acting as a channel for information	Analysing and commenting on events; moulding public opinion; supporting or challenging the government	Consulting with all the 'players' to see how anti-terrorist measures can be improved	Police role is closely scrutinised by themselves and government, and lessons learned	A full debriefing and review of their response to the terrorist attack

Intelligence services

MI5, MI6 and other intelligence services monitor electronic communication, including phones and e-mails, to assess terrorist threats. They also use informers, share intelligence with other services such as the CIA, Mossad and European agencies and monitor all foreign language broadcasts.

! CHECKPOINT ...

1 Talk to emergency service workers about how they are trained to respond to terrorist threats
2 Ask your tutor to invite someone from the local authority emergency planning department to talk about co-ordinated disaster plans and civil defence in the case of a terrorist attack.
3 Visit disaster and emergency websites.

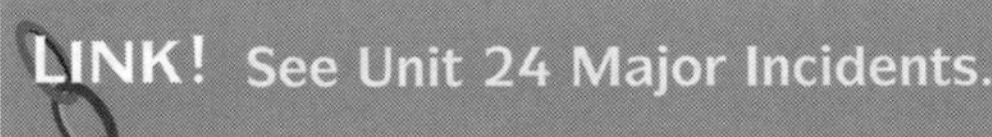

LINK! See Unit 24 Major Incidents.

HUMAN RIGHTS

Explain the key features of the United Nations Universal Declaration of Human Rights, showing how human rights are abused in at least three different countries.

For this outcome, you need to:

- explain the main points of the Declaration
- give examples of human rights abuses from three or more countries
- show how each human rights abuse you choose goes against an article in the Declaration.

Key features of the UN Universal Declaration of Human Rights

The United Nations Universal Declaration of Human Rights was published in 1948 by the newly-formed United Nations Organisation. It is the first and most important modern statement of human rights. All later statements, such as those by the European Union, follow its format and content.

It begins with a 'preamble' stating why understanding and promoting human rights is of the utmost importance.

The main declaration consists of 30 articles outlining the rights which every human being should have.

These articles cover:

1	Freedom	16	Marriage
2	Discrimination	17	Property
3	Security	18	Religion
4	Slavery	19	Free speech
5	Torture	20	Meetings
6	Law	21	Democracy
7	Equality	22	Welfare
8	Trials	23	Work
9	Arrest	24	Leisure
10	Fair trials	25	Affluence
11	Innocence	26	Education
12	Privacy	27	Culture
13	Movement	28	Public order
14	Asylum	29	Individuality
15	Nationality	30	Government.

Each article is a clear statement, several lines long and sometimes broken up into short sections.

COOL SITES:

http://www.un.org/Overview/rights.html – the full text of the UN Universal Declaration of Human Rights – about four pages

www.amnesty.org

www.hrw.org/

http://hrw.org/reports/2003/iraq0603/Iraq0603.pdf

LINK! There is more on human rights in Unit 4, page 81.

Abuse of human rights in different countries

There is no country in which human rights are not abused, to some extent.

Here are three examples of the kinds of human rights abuses being committed in different countries.

FOCUS

Human rights abuses in ...

Sudan

'In areas of Sudan, including in the capital Khartoum, incommunicado detention of political opponents, students and ordinary citizens as well as torture by the security forces remain common. Journalists are subjected to restrictions imposed by the security forces and civil society activists are routinely arrested, arbitrarily detained and harassed. Students and internally displaced persons have been injured or killed as a result of the use of excessive force by the police and security forces. Above all, the lack of judicial accountability of the security forces for any action they take, including acts of torture, is maintained in laws which are inconsistent with international human rights principles.'

USA

'Two thirds of the world's known executions of child offenders in the past decade occurred in the USA, including the only four in the past 18 months,' Amnesty International said. 'This is now the only country that openly continues to carry out such executions within the framework of its regular criminal justice system.'

Israel

'Extrajudicial executions are among the practices to which the Israeli army and security services have resorted for several years, without offering proof of guilt or right of defence. In addition to causing the death or injury of the targeted person, such attacks have resulted in the unlawful killing of scores and injury of hundreds of bystanders, including children. Amnesty International has repeatedly condemned these acts as unlawful and is gravely concerned at the increase of such practices in the past 32 months.'

Source: Amnesty International, July 2003

CHECKPOINT ...

Using the UN Universal Declaration of Human Rights as your guide, identify which articles are being violated in each of these extracts.

PASSGRADE

Explain how human rights issues affect the operations of at least three public services in the UK.

For this outcome, you need to:

- find out about human rights issues which affect the work of three or more UK public services
- show how the issues influence the ways the services work.

You could research this outcome by talking to people who work in public services, and by reading inspectors' reports of prisons, the police service, and so on. To some extent this outcome is already covered by the work you have done on equal opportunities.

All UK public services have to address human rights issues in:

- equal opportunities (see pages 81 and 85)
- in dealing with the public (check against UN Universal Declaration – as below)
- in dealing with an enemy (see the Geneva Convention).

Brief examples of how human rights issues may affect two public services are given on the next page.

CHECKPOINT ...

Examine the main provisions of the Police and Criminal Evidence Act (PACE), and how they fit in with the UN Universal Declaration of Human Rights.

COOL SITE:

http://hrw.org/reports/2003/iraq0603/iraq0603.pdf – the low-down on British forces in Basra – and human rights

Profile

How human rights issues affect an FE college

Action of college	Relevant UN article
College suspends or excludes student	Article 26: 'Everyone has the right to education.'
Student receives bad report	Article 12: 'No one shall be subjected to ... attacks upon his honour and reputation.'
Student not allowed to wear veil	Article 18: 'Everyone has the right to freedom of thought, conscience and religion [and] ... to manifest his religion or belief in teaching, practice, worship and observance.'

FOCUS

How human rights issues affect the army

A report by the American organisation, Human Rights Watch, made the following human rights criticisms of British troops in Basra:

- 'Failure to adequately prepare for the predictable breakdown in law and order following military operations and the fall of the civilian administration;
- Reliance on combat troops for police and security duties;
- Late and insufficient deployment of military police;
- Failure to deploy international civilian police;
- Failure to deploy international legal and judicial personnel;
- Failure to train adequately coalition forces on local law and customs;
- Failure to provide adequate protection for victims and witnesses regarding past and current crimes;
- Failure to secure evidence for investigations of past and current crimes;
- Failure to communicate with the local population on security issues.'

Source: from Basra: Crime and Insecurity under British Occupation, *Human Rights Watch, 2003 www.hrw.org/reports/2003/iraq0603a/*

Unit 7 Data Interpretation

Grading criteria

PASSGRADE	Merit	Distinction
To achieve a pass grade the evidence must show that the learner is able to:	To achieve a merit grade the evidence must show that the learner is able to:	To achieve a distinction grade the evidence must show that the learner is able to:
• demonstrate the extraction of data from at least two different secondary sources related to the public services 137 • analyse statistics from a chosen public service using at least two appropriate methods 142 • use appropriate software to store, retrieve, analyse and present information and numerical data 146 • explain what is meant by the term 'sampling' giving examples of different methods 147 • carry out research on an area related to the public services using an appropriate method of data collection 149 • interpret the results and present the information in appropriate textual, numerical and graphical forms from a report on a public service-related topic 153	• analyse and interpret data, and produce reasoned conclusions 139 • use statistics, and appropriate terminology, to show evidence of in depth research into data interpretation in a chosen public service 144 • use appropriate software effectively and justify conclusions in a coherent, well structured report 147 • interpret data in a chosen public service selecting and using an appropriate sampling method in carrying out research, giving reasons for choice 152	• analyse and evaluate the data received from the research into data interpretation in a chosen public service 153

A lot of public service work consists of gathering information and then passing it on to someone else.

Public service information doesn't just come in the form of words. Figures, charts, maps, diagrams, symbols and codes are all widely used. Much of this information – especially if it can be entered into a computer – is called **data**.

This unit is about finding, displaying, explaining and using different forms of information.

SOURCES OF INFORMATION

Demonstrate the extraction of data from at least two different secondary sources related to the public services.

For this outcome, you need to show that you know how to find information about the public services from two or more sources. These sources must *not* include speaking directly to people who work in the public services.

FOCUS

Definitions of data

Data are …

'known facts or things used as basis for inference or reckoning' – *Oxford English Dictionary*

'unprocessed information' – http://www.cetis.ac.uk/

Data is …

'information which

(a) is being processed by means of equipment operating automatically in response to instructions given for that purpose,

(b) is recorded with the intention that it should be processed by means of such equipment,

(c) is recorded as part of a relevant filing system or with the intention that it should form part of a relevant filing system, or

(d) … forms part of an accessible record …'

Data Protection Act 1998

Primary and secondary sources

FOCUS

Definitions

A primary source is 'firsthand testimony or direct evidence concerning a topic under investigation.' – Yale University Library

'Secondary sources offer an analysis or a restatement of primary sources. They often attempt to describe or explain primary sources.' – Bowling Green State University; http://www.bgsu.edu/colleges/library/infosrv/lue/basics.html

Sources of information on the public services

Primary sources	Secondary sources
The words of a visiting speaker who works in a public service	Hearsay evidence (i.e. anything said by a person about an event which they did not witness themselves)
Your own observations of public services, e.g. on work shadowing	All statistical graphs and charts, where information has been organised under headings
Raw unsorted data obtained from the public services	All statistics expressed in the form of percentages
Police notebooks	Television programmes, films or edited videos about fire, war, crime or any other subject related to the public services
Unedited interview tapes and video footage	Any encyclopaedias, magazines, newspaper reports and textbooks relating to public service
Photographs of actual events or real objects, e.g. fires, crashed vehicles, scenes of crime	Any website which summarises information, or puts it in a simplified form
Forensic evidence	
Unprocessed reply sheets from surveys	

CHECKPOINT …

Which of these are primary sources and which are secondary sources?

(a) a TV programme containing clips of spectacularly bad driving, taken from police cameras or CCTV.

(b) a book written by a Chief Constable telling the story of his own life
(c) fingerprints – after they have been lifted from a stolen car
(d) a bloodstained knife found by a dead body
(e) a speech by a barrister explaining why X is guilty of murder

Extraction of data

This means getting relevant information from a mass of information, much of which is not relevant, e.g. looking up a number in a phone book.

Data comes in three main forms:

- language, e.g. reports, letters, speeches, interviews, notes, audio tape recordings
- numerical, e.g. tables, lists of figures, statistics, measurements, quantities, weights
- graphical, e.g. diagrams, charts, graphs, photographs, video, pictograms, logos.

CHECKPOINT ...

Discuss with your friends what kinds of data are found in:
(a) a calendar
(b) a hazchem sign on a lorry
(c) today's horoscope
(d) a bar code.

To extract data we need to know two things:

- what data we are looking for
- where it is likely to be.

We need to know these two things because different kinds of data are usually found in different places as shown in the table at the bottom of the page.

Where to find secondary sources (i.e. your data)

A library

Your college library should have plenty of books, magazines and CD-ROMs related to the public services. If not, ask your tutor to ask the library to buy more material.

To use the library effectively:

- Understand the cataloguing system. The numbers on the books and magazines tell you what they are about.
- If the catalogue is computerised, practise using it until you have got it sussed.
- Look through the *contents* of a book or magazine (at the front) to see at a glance what the book is about.
- Use the *index* of a book (at the back) to find out if the information you want is in the book.
- If you can't find what you want, *ask the library staff*. They are paid to help.

Where data are found

Information wanted	Kind of data	Form of data	Possible source
Local recorded crime figures for one year	Numerical	Probably a table of figures	Annual report of local police force
Name of Defence Minister	Language	A name	Internet: http://www.number-10.gov.uk/output/Page2988.asp
Proportion of people in Ealing of Chinese descent	Graphical	Pie chart	*2001 Census Key Statistics for Local Authorities in England & Wales*, published by the Stationery Office, 2003

A computer

Use this to:

- access the internet. Useful public service sites include:

  www.homeoffice.gov.uk
  www.cabinet-office.gov.uk
  www.number-10.gov.uk
  www.homeoffice.gov.uk/rds
  www.hmprisonservice.gov.uk
  www.mod.uk
  www.open.gov.uk
  www.statistics.gov.uk/census2001
  www.met.police.uk
  www.nhs.uk
  www.hmce.gov.uk
- visit your local authority website – always packed with useful stuff!
- look at CD-ROMs, e.g. from the armed forces, or newspapers such as the *Guardian* and the *Times*.

The public services themselves

The secondary data they produce includes:

- recruitment leaflets/packs and the information they contain
- public information leaflets, e.g. about fire prevention
- leaflets and booklets about the local authority and the services it provides
- leaflets about legal rights (obtainable in Citizens' Advice Bureaux).

Your tutors and your college

Your tutors will be able to add to the ideas given above. Your college will have documents such as equal opportunities policies, evacuation plans, fire drills and health and safety documents which may be very useful!

! CHECKPOINT ...

1. What are the disadvantages of books or magazines as sources of data?
2. What are the good and bad points of the internet as a source of data?

Analysing data

Merit

Analyse and interpret data, and produce reasoned conclusions.

For this outcome, you need to:

- find your data
- 'analyse' data, – pick out the relevant points
- 'interpret' data – explain what it means, in a format which is different from the one in which the data was first presented, e.g. saying what a graph means, by using your own words.

Analysing and interpreting a table

Summary offences – other than traffic

	2001/02		2000/01	
	Adults	**Youths**	**Adults**	**Youths**
Offences				
Indecent Exposure	4	3	23	1
Simple Drunk	106	7	164	8
Drunk and Disorderly	662	63	593	41
Offences by Licensees	0	0	4	1
Breach of Peace	10	10	69	2
Offences under Bail Act	280	61	276	54
Depositing Litter	8	2	12	1
Firearms Offences	0	14	194	4
Urinating in Public	0	14	85	13
Begging	0	1	80	0

Bind over following Breach of Peace	0	0	50	1
Improper use of Telecom System	0	15	26	3
Gaming Offences	0	0	–	–
Railway Offences	0	3	13	2
Dangerous Dogs	0	0	20	1
Other Summary Offences	596	181	535	178
Totals	**1,666**	**374**	**2,144**	**310**

Source: North Yorkshire Police

The table above shows all the 'minor' crimes committed in North Yorkshire, during a two-year period – other than traffic offences.

The table tells us that:

- the total number of offences by adults was less in 2001–2 than it was in 2000–1
- only three types of offence by adults went up between 2000–1 and 2001–2 (drunk and disorderly, offences under the Bail Act and 'other summary offences')
- the total number of offences by youths went up in the same period
- there were ten types of offence by youths which went up in the same period
- in the years covered, many more cases of some kinds of offence were recorded in North Yorkshire than others, e.g. being drunk and disorderly, and offences under the Bail Act.

The table does not tell us ...

- some things which it appears to tell us at first sight!

To sum up – the conclusions *may* be right, but the data do not prove it!

CHECKPOINT ...

What is wrong with the following statements?

(a) The table shows that there is a low crime rate in North Yorkshire.

(b) Litter is not a serious problem in North Yorkshire.

(c) The table shows that the North Yorkshire police don't care about drugs.

Why some conclusions cannot be drawn with certainty – Conclusions which could be false

Conclusion	Why the conclusion could be false
'Crime levels in North Yorkshire are going down.'	Crime figures are not the same thing as crime levels. For example, in 2001–2 (a) crimes may not have been reported, (b) crimes may not have been recorded and (c) the police may have been less successful with their prosecutions. There may be fewer police, therefore fewer arrests and charges. The police may be less efficient, or they may have too much paperwork and therefore manage fewer prosecutions.
'The police have cracked the problem of dangerous dogs.'	It is true that the offences in 2001–2 dropped to zero. But it could be that the police have decided to change their priorities, or that dangerous dogs are now dealt with by dog wardens.
'Fewer people in North Yorkshire are indecently exposing themselves.'	We know that fewer people have gone to court for this offence. But, again, people may have stopped reporting the offence, or the police may have stopped acting on it. It could simply be that the weather was colder in 2001–2!
'There is a downward trend in offences by licensees.'	Not proven. Where there are very few cases (there were only five in the previous year), we do not have enough evidence to say that there is a 'trend'. Anyway, a trend normally continues over several years, and here we only have data for two years.

Other forms of data

Databases

A database is any large collection of information which is kept on computer. Its purpose is to store large amounts of information in such a way that it can easily be found again (**retrieved**).

Databases are widely used by public services to store information about individuals. When the police record a crime, they put the information about it on a database. The **fields** of information, e.g. what kind of crime it was, when it happened, where it happened, who the victim was, descriptions of suspects etc., are interlinked, so if one piece of information is looked up, all the other related information appears at the same time.

The usual software for making your own database is Microsoft Access.

Spreadsheets

Spreadsheets are like databases, only the information is in the form of figures. Spreadsheets store data about large numbers of people, and are used for calculating things like percentages, statistics and trends.

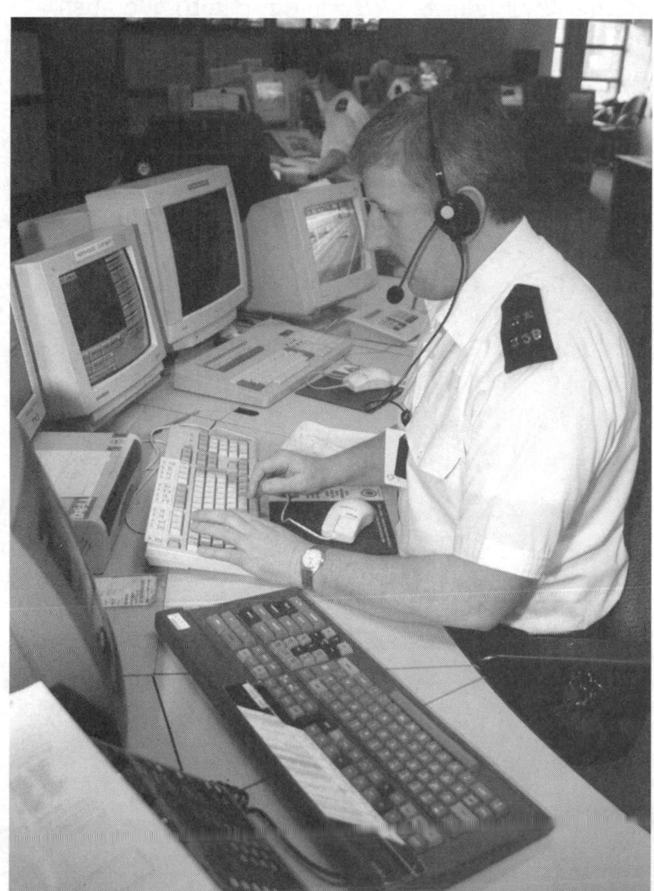

Information at their fingertips: a police control centre

The usual software for making your own spreadsheet is Microsoft Excel.

www.dbcc.cc.fl.us/fipse_sh/database.htm – a cool US site for beginners!

The figures on spreadsheets are never completely unsorted. When an immigration officer (for example) fills in a form, certain types of information are included, e.g. sex, date of birth, etc. This means that the information given by each immigrant is already being sorted into categories (or **fields**). These categories of information are kept separate when data is stored on a spreadsheet.

The following simple table is an extract from a table published by the Home Office which deals with immigration statistics.

Numbers of non-British people coming into the country, 1990–9

Year	Total	Males	%	Females	%
1990	161.2	81.0	50.2	80.2	49.8
1991	149.6	71.5	47.8	78.1	52.2
1992	116.4	53.0	45.5	63.4	54.5
1993	121.8	57.6	47.3	64.2	52.7
1994	135.3	64.1	47.4	71.2	52.6
1995	154.2	80.4	52.1	73.8	47.9
1996	168.5	86.0	51.0	82.5	49.0
1997	188.1	96.3	51.2	91.8	48.8
1998	221.1	108.0	48.8	113.1	51.2
1999	238.5	117.8	49.4	120.7	50.6

Source: from Table 4.2, Home Office RDS Occasional Paper 75, page 43

What most people would want to know is whether the numbers are increasing or decreasing – in other words, whether there is a *trend* over a period of time.

The trend *can* be seen by reading the figures in the 'Total' column. But it shows much more clearly if the column of figures headed 'Total' is put into a bar chart (histogram) where the numbers of people on the vertical axis are plotted against the years on the horizontal axis. The height of each bar clearly indicates the number of people entering the country, and – as the years run in sequence from left to right – the chart at the top of the next page gives an instantly recognisable image of yearly change.

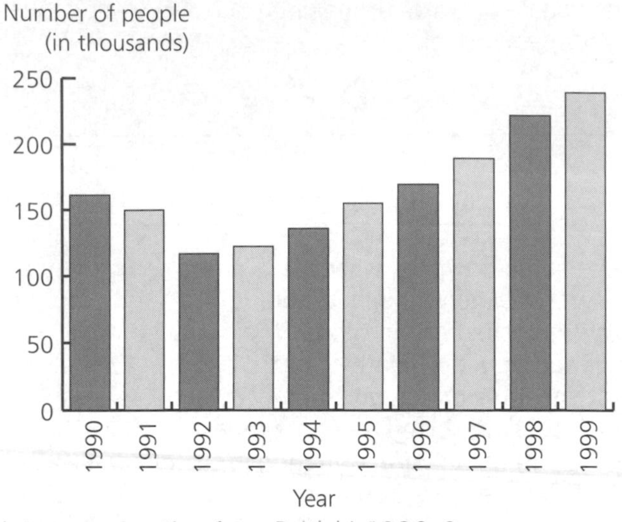

Internal migration (non-British) 1990–9

Source: based on figures from Table 4.2, Home Office RDS Occasional Paper 75, page 43

Analysis using other kinds of chart

Different kinds of data can be illustrated using different kinds of chart as summarised in the table on the next page.

CHECKPOINT ...

Search your library for examples of each of the charts mentioned in the table below.

Analysis by reasoning

Charts give a simple type of analysis – they highlight the main facts. More complex analysis – finding out underlying reasons for figures and trends – usually has to be done using words. This is especially true when you are analysing data to identify possibilities. The table below gives an example based on the bar chart above.

CHECKPOINT ...

The immigration figures (page 141) contain information about the numbers of men and women coming into the country between 1990 and 1999. What reasoned conclusions can you produce about those figures?

PASSGRADE

Analyse statistics from a chosen public service using at least two appropriate methods

For this outcome, you need to:

- find suitable statistics from a public service
- choose a particular aspect of the statistics that you wish to bring out
- present the statistics in such a way that the feature you want to bring out is made clear.

The statistics you analyse will normally take the form of a table of figures. You will be able to find such public service statistics on many websites, e.g. the Home Office, your local police authority, accident statistics from the HSE, and so on. An example of a suitable set of statistics is given on page 144.

If you wish to analyse this table by bringing out the trend in football-related arrests over a number of years, the best way to do it is to present the figures in the form of a bar chart, with the years along the horizontal axis and the numbers of arrests on the vertical axis. Once you have inputted the statistics into a computer, you will be able to do this easily.

If you wish to analyse the statistics to compare the numbers of arrests in different divisions taking place in any one year, a better method might be a pie

Example of analysis by reasoning

Analysis and interpretation of data	Reasoned conclusions
The chart shows that non-British immigration into the country declined before 1992 – the year when the number was lowest – and rose steadily after that. The highest inflow, in 1999, was over twice as high as the lowest.	The chart gives no reasons for this, but likely explanations are (a) changes in immigration law which affected the number of people coming into the country; (b) wars or political unrest in other countries which caused large numbers of refugees to come to the UK; (c) economic or employment changes in the UK or elsewhere which made the country more attractive to immigrants.

Data and suitable charts

Kind of data	Most suitable kind of chart
Numbers of different kinds of crime (as in the table on page 139)	Pie chart. This gives a clear visual comparison of crime numbers, etc. However, if there are more than, say, ten kinds of crime, the pie chart will start to look too complicated, and some of the 'slices' will be too thin.
The ethnic mix of a town, region or country	Pie chart. A pie chart is suitable because it gives a good visual impression, and because there are only about ten major ethnic groups in the UK.
Employment figures	Pictogram. This consists of rows of simplified pictures, in this case human figures where (typically) each figure might represent a thousand (or ten thousand) employees.
Variations in speed, temperature, growth charts, etc. Changes in inflation, house prices, trade figures. Crime or social trends over, say, ten years or more	Where a chart is representing values that change gradually over time, e.g. changes in air temperature over a given day, line graphs are best. This is because the figures are part of a continuous process. The line gives a rough idea of what the figure would be between the points plotted on the graph.
Raw, unprocessed data collected from a survey, etc.	Tables of figures. This gives the facts – analysis can come later. Huge numbers are often given in thousands, so that they don't look too long and confusing.
Organisation of public services or government departments	Tree diagrams are useful for showing the relationship between people or departments in an organisation. The lines between the people or departments indicate chains of command or responsibility.
Processes	These are best shown by flow charts or algorithms. Boxes containing the names of processes are joined up by arrows or lines. It is possible to include many choices or variables on such a diagram.
Data where two variables are plotted against each other, using information about individuals, etc.	Scatter diagram. Each bit of information is represented by a dot. A simple example would show the age and height of each individual in your class, but a similar diagram could be used to analyse political ideas against scales such as 'left-wing/right-wing' or 'tough/tender'.
Processing answers to closed (yes/no) questions on a questionnaire	The numbers of people answering 'yes' to a question (e.g. 'Do you feel safe when you go out at night?') can be recorded and expressed as a bar chart, pie chart or pictogram.
Gauging opinions or strength of feeling (of individuals)	This can be done on a three- or five-point scale, e.g. 'good, medium, bad'. This kind of information can then be presented on bar charts.
Data about buildings, machines, etc.	Plans and drawings which show the important information and leave out the rest. Technical drawing is an example; so too is a police officer's sketch of the scene of a RTA.
Data about the positions of places on the earth's surface	Maps
Data about the sea – depth, shipping lanes, etc.	Admiralty charts
Data about the weather at a given time	Weather maps

Football-related arrests, 10-year trend (League matches only)

Season	2002–03	2001–02	2000-01	1999–00	1998–99	1997–98	1996–97	1995–96	1994–95	1993–94
Attendances										
Total League	28,343,386	27,758,977	26,030,167	25,341,090	25,435,542	24,692,608	22,783,163	21,844,416	21,856,020	21,653,381
Arrests										
Premiership	1,636	1,318	1,623	1,461	1,543	1,438	1,759	1,697	1,723	1,630
Division 1	1,042	1,016	816	831	851	1,173	891	949	1,227	1,359
Division 2	687	648	601	586	641	468	626	506	674	7823
Division 3	330	278	351	25	315	228	301	289	226	456
Total	3,695	3,260	3,391	3,137	3,341	3,307	3,577	3,441	3,850	4,227

Notes: For comparisons and trends purposes arrests and attendances data relates only to League matches
Source of Arrests data 2001–2003 Football Banning Orders Authority
Source of Attendance data 2001–2003 Football Authorities
Source of all data 1992–2001 National Criminal Intelligence Service

Source: http://www.homeoffice.gov.uk/docs2/arrestbodata2002-3.pdf

chart. The 'pie' would have a segment for each division. The angle or size of the segment would represent visually the different numbers of arrests for each division.

You could do a written analysis by discussing the trends and quoting figures from the table which support your analysis.

Merit

> Use statistics, and appropriate terminology, to show evidence of in-depth research into data interpretation in a chosen public service.

For this outcome, you need to:

- show how data is used in a particular public service
- show what statistics are and how they are set out
- use the correct words to describe aspects of statistics
- show how public services use statistics.

Since data is a sensitive topic, you may need help from your tutor – to arrange a visit to a police control centre, or some other place where data is handled. If you are able to arrange a work placement with a public service, this will give you an excellent opportunity to research how the service collects and uses data.

The police, like many public services, now use linked or national databases to give them more access to more information. This helps them to catch criminals who commit crimes away from their home area.

Local and national government also make vast use of data. A work placement or visit to a local government office would fit in well with this outcome.

Data interpretation by central government can be studied on the internet.

www.homeoffice.gov.uk/rds/

www.statistics.gov.uk

Data interpretation by the public services is done in two stages:

- data analysis – sorting out the information
- presentation of the sorted data so it can be understood by their own employees, the government, the media and the general public.

Aspects of data interpretation

Tabulation

This is putting data into tables where information can be read both downwards and across. An example of a simple table is given at the top of the next page.

Children looked after by local authorities[1] by type of accommodation, England, 2001

	Number
Foster placements	38,400
With parents	6,900
Children's homes and hostels[2]	6,800
Placed for adoption	3,400
Living independently or in residential employment	1,200
Residential schools	1,100
Other	1,200
Total	**58,900**

1 Excludes children looked after under an agreed series of short-term placements
2 Includes local authority, voluntary sector and private children's homes and secure units.

Quoted in UK 2003, HMSO, 2002

Attributes

These are the items dealt with in the table. In the table above, 'placed for adoption' is an attribute. Attributes correspond to the 'fields' in the spreadsheet on which the data was first recorded.

Analysis

This is a more general process of sorting through data, often electronically, using (for example) Microsoft Excel. The aim is to identify patterns and relationships hidden in a mass of figures. The **parameters** (areas) in which data analysis is used include:

- association – the possible connection of one set of figures to another
- sequence or path analysis – possible chains of cause and effect, where one event causes another
- classification – searching for new patterns
- clustering – finding groups of interrelated facts
- forecasting – using patterns of data to predict future trends.

Percentages

Data is sometimes put into percentages to highlight inequalities or underlying facts about the data. Percentages are memorable, while real numbers are not.

Time series

This is data plotted against time, to show changes or trends taking place over a period of months or years. It can take the form of figures, bar charts or line graphs.

Averages

There are three kinds of average: mean, mode and median. Of the three, the mean is what people normally mean by the word 'average'.

Look at the following data:

The number of call-outs at Anytown Fire Station in one week

Sun	Mon	Tues	Wed	Thurs	Fri	Sat
14	6	9	9	13	11	5

- The mean is 14 + 6 + 9 + 9 + 13 + 11 + 5 divided by 7 = 9.57 approx.
- The mode is the number which appears most often = 9.
- The median is the number half way between the highest and lowest = 9.5.

Measures of dispersion

These are ways of showing how far individuals might deviate from the mean. They can be used for any collection of data which has a mean, e.g. scores in an army entry test, costs of road traffic accidents, speeds of response to fire service call-outs.

Range

This is the simplest measure of dispersion. It is the difference between the highest and lowest number in a collection of data. In Anytown Fire Station, above, the range for call-outs in the week surveyed is 14 – 6 = 8.

Percentiles

This term is used to describe the position of a number *relative to other numbers* (values) in a set of statistics. If a hundred soldiers take a test, and soldier X is in the lowest fifth percentile, that means at least 95 per cent got better marks than X.

Percentiles can be marked on a 'normal distribution curve' or 'bell curve' of the type which can be made whenever we carry out a big survey of things like people's heights or examination marks.

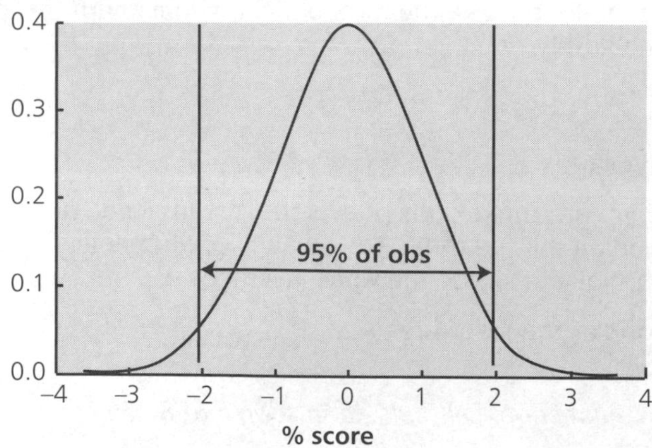

An example of a normal distribution curve

Variance

This is worked out mathematically as *the average squared difference of scores from the mean score of a distribution*.

Look at the following table:

	Students				
	A	B	C	D	E
Number of eggs eaten	2	3	1	5	4
Difference of scores	–1	0	–2	+2	+1
Squared difference of scores	1	0	4	4	1

The top two rows of the table show the number of eggs eaten by each of five public service students sharing a tent. The mean egg-consumption is 3. Two students eat less than the mean, and two eat more. Student B eats the mean. This is shown in the third row of the table.

The fourth row of the table shows the squared difference of scores (i.e. each difference is multiplied by itself).

The **variance** is the average of the figures in the bottom row – 10 divided by 5 – which works out at 2.

Standard deviation

The standard deviation is simply the square root of the variance. The square root of 2 happens to be about 1.4.

The higher the variance or the standard deviation, the more scattered the individual numbers are from the mean.

SOFTWARE APPLICATIONS

PASSGRADE

Use appropriate software to store, retrieve, analyse and present information and numerical data.

For this outcome, you need to collect and process data yourself.

You need access to an up-to-date computer with a Microsoft Excel software package on it – or something similar. Data can be typed into an Excel spreadsheet, or imported directly from the internet. It can be stored (saved) in spreadsheet form, or, of course, on saved web pages, until you need to analyse it.

- 'Retrieve' means find – and in this case it means finding information stored in a database or spreadsheet.
- 'Analyse' means to pick out information relevant to your purpose.
- 'Present' means to put the information you have selected into a form which is easily accessible and attractive to other people.

Detailed explanation on the use of software to process and present data is beyond the scope of this book. In any case, the packages available are changing and being upgraded all the time. However, the following points may be useful.

- If you haven't got one already, try to get a computer of your own. Even a cheap second-hand computer will improve your computer skills, give you confidence, and enable you to get your assignments done on wet Sunday afternoons.
- Your college should have a computer centre. Spend time in there learning how to use Excel and other kinds of software. Ask the staff if you get stuck!

- Always ask your tutor for help and advice if you need it.
- When producing charts always make sure that they are as big as you can reasonably make them, and are fully titled and labelled.
- Experiment with colours and visual effects to improve the impact of your charts.
- Proof-read any charts, graphs, diagrams, etc. that you produce to make sure that they don't contain errors – either of spelling or fact!
- Make it clear where you got the information from (e.g. Home Office website).
- Take a pride in what you produce on the computer. Older people (such as tutors and assessors) are easily dazzled by good computer skills: the result is better grades!

Written analysis

Graphics and charts sometimes need explaining in words to give a full analysis of the data they present. Such analysis could include:

- the main points shown in the chart, etc.
- the information which can *definitely* be derived from the data (e.g. that immigration rose between 1992 and 1999)
- information which is *suggested* by the data (e.g. war in Bosnia in the 1990s may have raised the immigration rate).

For this outcome, your written analysis should be word-processed. Pay attention to:

- paragraphs (they should be 'blocked' and average about 6–10 lines in length)
- font (12pt is about right) – choose a font that is legible
- all the usual stuff about spelling, grammar, sentence length and punctuation.

Merit

Use appropriate software effectively and justify conclusions in a coherent, well structured report.

For this outcome, you need to:

- show that you can input data accurately and efficiently into a spreadsheet
- analyse your data so that you can bring out the information which you wish to present in numerical, graphical and textual forms.
- present your data in a variety of forms, showing that you understand how to use the software. This means producing a range of attractive but clear tables, graphs or charts, fully labelled and titled.
- comment clearly and with relevance on the tables and charts, explaining what they show.

A 'coherent, well-structured report' is one which:

- is written in good English
- is well-presented – with a neat, orderly, businesslike appearance
- has a title page, introduction, findings, conclusions and recommendations
- starts off with a useful hypothesis, and concentrates on the job of proving or disproving that hypothesis
- includes all relevant information and excludes all irrelevant information
- explains difficult technical terms
- includes self-assessment in the conclusions section (i.e. what you have learnt, what you did well, and where you had difficulties).

'Justify conclusions' means explain your conclusions, and show how valid and reliable they are. If you think they are 'dodgy', you should give reasons why you think this, and suggest what you might have done to improve your conclusions.

See the SKILLPOWER on how to write a report on page 154.

GATHERING AND PROCESSING DATA

Explain what is meant by the term 'sampling' giving examples of different methods.

For this outcome, you need to:

- say what sampling is
- say why it is done
- show the different ways in which it can be done.

Sampling

Sampling is a process used when conducting surveys, market research and opinion polls. The aim is to survey a small group of people, and in doing so find out what a large group – normally the whole population – thinks or does. The advantage of sampling is that it saves time and money, since it would be impossible to survey everybody in the country. The disadvantage of sampling is that it is hard to choose a group of people who accurately reflect the population as a whole.

You can sample things instead of people, e.g. products on an assembly line, to check that the quality is steady. But we are more concerned here with sampling what people think, feel or do.

FOCUS

Key words

Target population – the people you want to know about (who are, of course, many more than the people you have in your sample)

Sampling frame – lists or maps from which the sample is chosen

Respondent unit – the person who answers the question

Unit of reference – the person the questions are about (it may be the respondent, or it may be some-one such as a child who cannot answer for itself)

Sample size – the number of people in the sample

Types of sampling

Probability sampling

In all these kinds of sampling, the chances of each person in the frame being chosen is the same (e.g. 1 in 10). This is the kind of sampling normally called 'random'. A computer program generating random numbers is used to make the choice.

Systematic or 'interval' sampling.
This method involves deciding how many people you are going to sample out of the frame you have chosen. If you wanted to sample, say, 100 out of a thousand, you would actually need a list of 1010 people, numbered from 1 to 1010. You would choose every tenth person for your sample. But to make it random, you would first have to obtain a number from 1 to10 randomly as the start of your sequence. If the number was four, the people you would choose would be numbers 4, 14, 24, 34 and so on – up to 1004.

Stratified sampling
For this you divide up the target population into groups called 'strata' (say on the basis of income, occupation or housing type). Having chosen your strata you then use probability or systematic sampling to pick the number of individuals you need from each stratum.

Cluster sampling
You divide the target population (possibly the whole country) into 'centres', e.g. towns, before selecting your random sample of those centres (e.g. 10 per cent of them). The same method could be used if you were surveying firefighters in, say, Hampshire. Your centres then would be fire stations within that county. But you might only visit ten fire stations, randomly selected. This saves time, money and effort and will bring results similar to those obtained if the whole country is the 'frame'.

Multi-stage sampling
You select a cluster within a cluster, e.g. certain postcode districts within certain towns. Both towns and postcode districts should be selected randomly. Within each postcode district selected there would then be yet another random selection – this time of individual interviewees.

Multi-phase sampling
This is a kind of sampling where, first, a large selection of people are interviewed briefly, e.g. on the phone. Later some of the first selection are followed up in depth, often with face-to-face interviews. In both phases of the sample, respondents can be randomly chosen by one of the methods mentioned above.

Non-probability sampling

This is the name given to all methods of sampling which do not require the generation of random numbers. They are easier and cheaper than probability sampling, but less accurate and credible because the choice of respondents can be (deliberately or accidentally) biased.

Convenience sampling
The kind of sampling done by market researchers in the street or in shops is convenience sampling. The people doing the survey interview people because they are there. They may well learn information of value, but it is not scientific, because the people are not randomly chosen.

Volunteer sampling
This is rather like asking people to ring up and say which Big Brother contestant they want to throw out. People select themselves to give data. The best use of this is where people volunteer for psychological experiments. It would be unethical to choose people at random for, say, personality tests, but it is not unethical to allow volunteers to choose themselves.

Judgement sampling
Here the researcher interviews and chooses the kind of people they wish to survey. This method is used for choosing focus groups who advise the government on policy issues and public opinion.

Quota sampling
This is any sample where people are surveyed in numbers which reflect their numbers in society as a whole. For example, a survey in the UK organised so that 52 per cent of those questioned were women, and 9 per cent came from ethnic minorities, would be using quota sampling.

Weighting
This is a way of altering the results of a survey (by about 1 or 2 per cent usually) to allow for factors which have distorted the truth in the past. For example, if a pollster asks people outside a polling station, on General Election day, how they have voted, some will refuse to say (for the very good reason that a vote is secret). Experience has shown that these so-called 'exit polls' give the impression that a higher number of people voted Labour than was actually the case. Weighting is therefore done to correct this imbalance and make the survey more accurate.

CHECKPOINT ...

Number these sampling systems in order of
(a) accuracy
(b) ease or cheapness.

COOL SITES:

http://www.statcan.ca/english/edu/power/ch13/probability/probability.htm

http://www.statcan.ca/english/edu/power/ch13/non_probability/non_probability.htm

PASSGRADE

Carry out research on an area related to the public services using an appropriate method of data collection.

For this outcome, you need to:

- choose a topic connected to the public services
- carry out your own research and collect your own data, in a way which is suited to the topic.

'Research' can be defined as 'the systematic and purposeful collection of data'.

The outcome gives you a wide remit: all it says about the subject of your research is that it has to be 'related to the public services'. It does not say that the research has to use primary or secondary data (see below); you can make your choice.

There are no restrictions on the kinds of public service you should research: they could be uniformed or non-uniformed, statutory or non-statutory, professional or voluntary. Nor does the outcome say that you have to target the research at the public service itself. For example, you could survey public opinion about the police without setting foot in a police station or even visiting a police website.

Some things are necessary, though, if you are carrying out research:

- You need to have a **subject area** which you are interested in and which is not too big and not too small.
- You need to frame a **hypothesis** which could either be confirmed or refuted by your research.
- You need to decide what **kinds of data** you wish to collect
- You need to choose appropriate **research methods**.

There are two main approaches to collecting data:

- traditional methods, such as forms and questionnaires, which are filled in either by the respondent or the researcher

- direct data capture, where data is inputted electronically, e.g. by barcode readers, scientific instruments linked to computers, the internet, and so on.

Advantages and disadvantages of methods of data collection

Method of collecting data	Advantages	Disadvantages
Forms and questionnaires	They are easy and cheap to print and distribute in small numbers. They are easily understood by respondents (if the wording is right).	They are expensive and difficult for dealing with large numbers of people, or quantities of information. The information is insecure, and hard to process accurately.
Direct data capture	It is a quick and very accurate way of collecting large amounts of data, widely used in the public services. It includes questionnaires where people shade boxes on forms which can be directly 'read' by the computer. Data is secure, and can be made to comply with the Data Protection Acts.	The initial technology is costly. It lacks the 'human touch' and is therefore not the best way of sampling the opinions of small groups of people.

There is also an intermediate form of data capture where information is inputted into the computer through the keyboard by the person asking the questions or conducting the survey.

Primary and secondary data

Primary data is new information that you have researched and collected yourself. It is primary because:

- no one else discovered that exact information before you did
- you know that it is 'true' because you researched and stored it yourself.

Secondary data is information that has been collected and processed by other people. It is secondary because:

- you are not directly connected with it (i.e. you have probably read it in a book or seen it on the internet)
- you do not know of your own knowledge that it is 'true'.

Hypotheses

Hypotheses are statements which are used as a basis or foundation for research. You should write a hypothesis before planning your own research, so that your research has a focus and a point.

The hypothesis takes the form of a single statement which may or may not be true, but which could be confirmed (shown to be true) or falsified (shown to be untrue) by your research.

Examples of hypotheses:

- 'Older people are more frightened of crime than younger people.'
- 'The police are less well-liked by people from ethnic minority groups than they are by people of British descent.'
- 'Most people would prefer to have the death penalty brought back for some serious crimes.'
- 'Congestion charging is more popular with women than men.'
- 'The fire service should spend more money on fire prevention and less on being a rescue service.'

Not all hypotheses are equally good. A good hypothesis:

- indicates clearly what you are planning to investigate
- does not try to cover too much ground
- is expressed in simple, straightforward language

- deals with something which is genuinely not known
- is capable of being shown to be true or untrue.

NB A hypothesis which can be shown to be false is just as good as one that can be shown to be true.

> **CHECKPOINT ...**
>
> 1 Which of the above hypotheses are more suitable for use in student research, and which are less suitable?
>
> 2 Which demand primary data (i.e. going out and getting the information yourself) and which demand secondary data (using information collected by other people)?
>
> 3 Write hypotheses connected with researching the work of your favourite public service.

Going out and asking people a lot of questions without thinking about it first is a recipe for disaster. You need information which is:

- **valid** (relevant to the area you are researching) – this means using good questions
- **reliable** (collected in a standard, systematic way under controlled conditions, so that the information you have got can be trusted) – this means using good sampling and data collection processes.

Methods of collecting data

There are two ways of surveying what people think:

- asking questions
- giving them a questionnaire or form to fill in.

There is nothing to stop you from using both methods in your research.

Asking questions

This is usually done in an interview. The researcher makes an appointment with the respondent and asks them a number of carefully prepared questions. You should get good results if you stick to the following rules.

- Arrive on time, suitably prepared and dressed for the occasion.
- Be polite. Explain what you are researching, and why. Show that you are interested in what your respondent has to say.
- Make sure that you have their willing permission to take notes or a tape recording.
- Prepare your questions carefully so that they will give you information on the things you want to know.
- Do not express your own opinions on any of the questions, or you may bias the respondent.
- Ask 'open questions', i.e. questions beginning with Where, What, How, Why, Who, When, Which. These encourage the respondent to speak at greater length.
- Do not allow the interview to run over time (unless you have a good reason and you are sure the respondent doesn't mind).
- Thank the respondent for giving their time and answering your questions.

Interviews versus questionnaires

Interviews	Questionnaires
Interviews collect information rather than data.	Questionnaires are the best way to collect data.
They are an excellent way of understanding people in depth, but they cannot be carried out in large numbers unless interviewing becomes a full-time job.	They are relatively easy to give out, fill in and collect.
Interviews give the respondent's personal opinions and experience, but they are hard to standardise, and the information gained is difficult to reduce to numbers.	Planning and writing questionnaires, and choosing who to give them to, is not easy, but it's much easier than interviewing people and recording what they say.
Interviews are good research tools for journalists and people who want to write stories – but they tell you about individuals, not the target population.	Information from questionnaires can easily be changed into data which gives information about more people than just the sample who filled in the questionnaire.
	The data from questionnaires can tell you something about the whole of the target population.

- If you have a number of interviewees, make sure you ask them all the same questions, otherwise the information you get will be 'patchy' and unreliable.

Questions for questionnaires

The following kinds of questions will give you quantifiable results, i.e. tables of figures, graphs and charts.

- **Closed questions**, e.g.

  Have you ever been the victim of a crime?

  (The answer can only be 'yes' or 'no'.)
- **Multiple choice questions**, e.g.

  Which of the following statements best represents your opinion?

  (a) All drugs should be legalised.

  (b) Cannabis should be legalised but not the others.

  (c) The present situation, with cannabis as a Class B drug, is the best.

  (d) All drug possession should be strictly penalised.

  (Tick the preferred statement.)
- **Questions showing a scale of preference or opinion**, e.g.

  Do you think the security arrangements at Anytown Football Ground are:

Excellent	Good	Fair	Poor	Very bad

(Tick the appropriate box.)

Using a questionnaire

A questionnaire is a written list of questions, often set out like a form with boxes for answers. Usually it is filled in by the respondent. It can, however, also be filled in by the person doing the survey, using the respondent's answers.

The following rules apply to questionnaires:

- Respondents should never be asked to put their names or personal details on the form.
- Pay attention to how you word your questions (see SKILLPOWER below).
- For large-scale questionnaires, it is best to use sheets that can be shaded and read by a computer. This saves a lot of work and ensures that answers can be recorded and processed accurately.
- If you are posting your questionnaires to people, include a stamped, self-addressed envelope.
- The more questionnaires you do, the more reliable your results will be.
- Give yourself time to process the results from your questionnaires.
- Always keep the completed forms in a safe place.

CHECKPOINT ...

Can you think of ideas for research related to the public services which would not involve questionnaires or interviews?

Merit

Interpret data in a chosen public service selecting and using an appropriate sampling method in carrying out research, giving reasons for choice.

For this outcome, you need to:

- follow up the research introduced and discussed on pages 149–52
- carry out public-service related research using a suitable sampling method
- interpret the data you have collected
- explain the methods you have used both in collecting and interpreting the data.

Your sampling should follow a system, and you should explain why you have chosen the sampling method you choose. Reasons might include:

- accuracy in representing the target population as a whole
- suitability for studying a public service of your choice
- convenience
- accessibility of the sample
- cheapness

- the presence of resources in the college which will help you in selecting or reaching your sample
- lack of bias
- ability of the sampling method to obtain valid and reliable data.

Interpretation of data is discussed in the two previous outcomes.

Distinction

Analyse and evaluate the data received from the research into data interpretation in a chosen public service.

For this outcome, you need to review the data you obtained in your research and comment on:

- your hypothesis. Did it say what you wanted it to say, and did it lead to meaningful and worthwhile research?
- the size of your sample. Was it big enough to give a reliable indication of the views, attitudes, etc. of your target population?
- the questions you asked. Did they gain information of a kind which really addressed the central issue covered by your hypothesis?
- your methods of data capture. How did you ensure that you inputted as much data as possible, as quickly and accurately as possible, into your spreadsheet or other storage system?
- your analysis of the data. Were you successful in picking out interesting and relevant trends, features or insights from your data, by appropriate analysis of the data through software applications?
- your presentation of your findings. Were you able to present your findings clearly, honestly and attractively, in suitable formats and with all necessary labelling and titles attached?
- the usefulness of your work. Did your research help you to understand (a) research methods, (b) data analysis and (c) some issue involving the public service of your choice?

CHECKPOINT ...

When undertaking research on a public service, consider asking someone who works in that service what sorts of data and research might be useful to them.

LINK!
See the SKILLPOWER on how to write a report on page 154.

PRESENTING INFORMATION

PASSGRADE

Interpret the results and present the information in appropriate textual, numerical and graphical forms from a report on a public service-related topic.

For this outcome, you need to:

- display the data you have collected in your research:
  - in words
  - in numbers
  - in charts or graphs
  - put all the above into a report, using suitable organisation and format.

The process (if you are using a questionnaire) is as follows.

Numerical stage

Having collected your completed questionnaires, you count, using tally marks, all the answers to all the questions on all the forms. This gives you raw figures for all the responses. You can then produce a table showing the total numbers of each response for each question.

If your questionnaires have boxes at the top for respondents to indicate such variables as age or sex, you can then, if you wish, break your figures down into figures according to age or sex.

Graphical stage

Your tables of figures can now be presented as bar charts, pie charts, pictograms, line graphs or in any other forms that seem appropriate. (See page 143.)

Textual stage

This means writing up your research so that your hypothesis, methods and findings are clearly stated and explained. You should try to show what your numerical and graphical information means, and whether it tends to support your original hypothesis or not.

The textual stage will almost certainly take the form of a report. Even if you are making a spoken presentation, it should still be organised as if it was a written report, so that both the process and the outcomes of your research can be understood.

'This is that feasibility study you asked me to write, Inspector, about whether we should get a coffee machine or not!'

skill POWER How to write a report

A report is a piece of writing, divided into sections, which clearly describes an investigation that someone has done. The sections are:

1 **Title page** Here you give the title of the report, e.g. 'Are older people more frightened of crime than young people?', the date the report was finished, the name of the author(s) and who it is intended for

2 **Contents** – a list of the sections of the report and their page numbers

3 **Introduction** This should give the purpose of the report (to support or falsify your original hypothesis) and explain briefly the methodology you followed, e.g. who you surveyed, why you chose that sample, the kind of questionnaire you used, the time you took over your research.

4 **Findings** Here you should have a copy of your questionnaire, the numerical tables showing the answers by all respondents for all questions, any other numerical tables, and any graphs, charts or diagrams highlighting various aspects of your findings. All the tables should have proper titles and notes attached so that it is clear what they represent. A brief description should be attached to each table or chart saying what you think the chart shows.

5 **Conclusions** Here you sum up the interesting points of your findings, and say whether they confirm or deny your hypothesis. If your findings are unclear, or if you had difficulties with your research, you should state it here, honestly and openly. If you would do the research differently next time – then say so and say why.

6 **Recommendations** In real-life reports recommendations are made. If you found (for example) that older people were more frightened of crime than young people, you might suggest things that the police or local government could do to make older people feel safer in their homes, and less afraid of going out at night.

7 **Bibliography** If you have used any books, documents, websites, etc. you should list them all here. If anyone has helped you, you can express thanks in this section as well.

The longest part of a report should be the findings.

Never try to put two sections of a report on the same page, even if the sections are very brief. It will make it look cramped and amateurish.

Since work for this unit has an IT dimension to it, you should word-process your report.

COOL SITE:

www.nelsonthornes.com – Unit 22 Signals and Communication Systems – more about reports!

Unit 8 The Uniformed Services

Grading criteria

PASSGRADE To achieve a pass grade the evidence must show that the learner is able to:	*Merit* To achieve a merit grade the evidence must show that the learner is able to:	*Distinction* To achieve a distinction grade the evidence must show that the learner is able to:
● outline the roles, purpose and responsibilities of two named uniformed public service organisations **156** ● describe the implications and positive and negative aspects of working in the uniformed services on a personal level **159** ● explain the range of jobs that are available in the uniformed services at operative level **163** ● compare the entry requirements for an officer in two different public services **164** ● describe the entry requirements and opportunities for career development in one of the uniformed services **165** ● outline the selection process for a job in one of the uniformed services **169**	● analyse the positive and negative aspects of working in the uniformed services **161** ● analyse the entry requirements and opportunities for career development in one of the uniformed services **165**	● evaluate and justify the entry requirements for career development in one of the uniformed services **169**

This unit explores who the uniformed services are. It looks at the jobs they do and the way they do them. And it gives you the opportunity to start planning your future career.

Now is the time to maximise your potential. That doesn't just mean passing your BTEC National Diploma in Public Services. It also means doing things which develop your fitness, character, maturity and confidence. This unit will show you what the public services are looking for in their applicants, and increase your chances of getting in.

ROLES, PURPOSE AND RESPONSIBILITIES

Outline the roles, purpose and responsibilities of two named uniformed public service organisations.

For this outcome, you need to:

- choose two uniformed public services
- say what their roles, purpose and responsibilities are.

The 'role' of an organisation is what it does on a day-to-day basis.

The 'purpose' of an organisation is its long-term objectives, which are laid down by law and in its mission statements.

The 'responsibilities' of an organisation are to do its work to the best of its ability, and have high levels of quality and accountability, i.e. to be good, and to be seen to be good.

As with many outcomes, this one is best achieved by meeting, talking to and listening to people who actually work in the uniformed public services (or who have worked in them in the recent past).

This is especially true of the *role* of a uniformed public service – what it actually does. Get it from the horse's mouth by:

- visiting as many public services as possible
- listening carefully to all visiting speakers, and taking notes
- asking questions about anything you don't understand
- getting work placements or work shadowing with uniformed public services
- doing voluntary work with a public service if you get the chance, e.g. joining the Cadets, the TA or the Special Constabulary.

Other sources are:

- television programmes – especially the 'fly-on-the-wall' documentaries about the police, etc.
- books and magazines – especially magazines such as *Police Review* and *Fire* which give an in-depth insight
- the internet – profiles on recruitment pages which are worth reading but may show the job through rose-coloured spectacles, and miss out the bad bits!

Nothing is quite as good as meeting the people who do the work!

For information on the purpose and responsibilities of uniformed public services, you should visit their web pages.

'Outline' the roles means describe them in a general way, covering the range of roles that each service does, but without going into too much detail. You should be guided by your tutor as to how much detail is needed.

Who are the uniformed services?

Statutory uniformed services

These are set up by law and are:

- the police
- the fire service (now officially called the Fire and Rescue Service)

- the ambulance service
- the army
- the Royal Air Force
- Her Majesty's Customs and Excise
- Coastguards
- the prison service
- the Royal Navy.

Non-statutory uniformed services

These are not set up by law. Therefore they are mostly private or voluntary, and include:

- the Royal National Lifeboat Institution
- door staff
- officers in private prisons
- community patrols which wear uniforms
- private security guards
- the Red Cross
- the Scouts
- the RSPCA
- school crossing patrols.

CHECKPOINT ...

There are many other people who do public service work and wear uniforms.

(a) How many examples can you think of?

(b) Why is their work not normally studied in depth in a BTEC National Public Services course?

Outlines of the roles, purpose and responsibilities of two uniformed public services

Police

Roles

The roles of the police include:

- investigation of serious crimes, such as murder, kidnap, fraud and paedophilia
- coordination of intelligence
- protection against terrorism and working for national security
- management of crime scenes and forensic investigation
- planning and training for major disasters and community safety
- maintaining public order
- dealing with road safety, serious and fatal collisions
- crime detection
- crime prevention
- armed response
- community safety.

http://www.devon-cornwall.police.uk/v3/homepage/index.htm

Purpose

FOCUS

MPS mission, vision and values

MAKING LONDON SAFE FOR ALL THE PEOPLE WE SERVE

Our Mission	Our Values	Our Vision
To make places safer To cut crime and the fear of crime To uphold the law	To treat everyone fairly To be open and honest To work in partnership To change to improve	To make London the safest major city in the world

Source: http://www.met.police.uk/about/mission.htm

The mission statement above outlines the purpose of the Metropolitan Police (the London Police force). The stress is on safety, since the public fear violent crime against the person more than other kinds of crime. There is also the promise to 'treat everyone fairly', recognising the diversity of London society and the need to police it in a non-discriminatory way. The idea of 'partnership' shows that the Metropolitan Police are part of 'joined-up government', where all agencies and public services work together for the good of the people.

The actions of the police are controlled by a number of laws ('Acts of Parliament'). The most famous of these laws is the Police and Criminal Evidence Act of 1984, which tells the police their 'powers' – what they can and cannot do when stopping, searching, arresting and questioning people.

Others are:

- the Police Act 1996 – about better local control of policing
- the Crime and Disorder Act 1998 – about partnerships between the police and other organisations
- the Terrorism Act 2000 – giving new powers to the police against suspected terrorists
- the Anti-Terrorism, Crime and Security Act 2001 – extra powers for dealing with terrorist money, suspected terrorists entering the country and terrorist weapons
- the Police Reform Act 2002 – setting up a national policing plan.

Responsibilities

The responsibilities of the police are to carry out their roles and purpose, and to provide the best possible service to the public. Points to note are as follows.

- The police's first duty is to the public rather than the government. This means that the Home Office, the government department in charge of the police, does not have direct control over what the police do. Each of the UK's 43 local police forces is responsible to its own police authority, a committee of councillors and others who make sure that local policing fits in with *local* needs.
- Each police force has its own mission statement, policing reports and policing plans. These are produced by the police authority. The authority keep the public well informed about the aims and purpose of their local police, and how well that purpose is carried out. The police responsibility to be accountable to the local community is statutory – laid down in the Police Act 1996.
- The police are regularly inspected by Her Majesty's Inspectors (HMIs) to ensure that they are giving good value for money. There is also an independent organisation, the Police Complaints Authority, which deals with complaints from the public. By investigating these complaints fully and fairly the PCA helps to ensure that the police carry out their responsibilities to the standard expected of them.

COOL SITES:

http://www.pca.gov.uk/ – complaints

http://www.wypa.org/welcome/whatwedo.htm – a police authority

Her Majesty's Coastguard

Role

Like the police, the Coastguard have several roles. The main one is given in the FOCUS below.

> **FOCUS**
>
> **Role of HM Coastguard**
>
> 'Her Majesty's Coastguard's primary role is to co-ordinate all civil maritime search and rescue activities around the 10,500 miles of UK coastline and 1000 miles into the North Atlantic, a total of 1.25 million square miles. 24 hours a day, Coastguard stations around the coast monitor the international maritime frequencies and respond to 999 emergency telephone calls.
>
> When a distress message is received at a Coastguard station, the Coastguard will instantly respond, formulating a search and rescue plan and mobilising resources. It may involve co-ordinating one of the 400+ Coastguard Response Teams or scrambling a Coastguard helicopter, calling on a lifeboat or other resources.'
>
> *Source: Maritime and Coastal Agency website http://www.mcga.gov.uk/aboutus/index.htm*

Other Coastguard roles include:

- responding to pollution incidents
- inspecting a sample of both British and foreign ships to carry out pollution risk assessments on them
- enforcing the laws on merchant shipping, especially laws on pollution, safety and manning (employment). They collect evidence of offences and can bring the offenders before the courts
- overseeing salvage operations (i.e. dealing with shipwrecks)
- investigating abandoned wrecks of ships.

Purpose

> **FOCUS**
>
> 'Our vision is to be a world-class agency that is committed to preventing loss of life, continuously improving maritime safety and protecting the marine environment:
>
> Safer Lives, Safer Ships, Cleaner Seas.'
>
> *Source: The Maritime and Coastguard Agency http://www.mcga.gov.uk/aboutus/index.htm/*

The main UK law governing the purpose of the Coastguards is the Aviation and Maritime Security Act 1990.

Responsibilities
The Coastguards are run by the Maritime and Coastguard Agency which is part of the Department for Transport. They are responsible to the public who use the sea or the coastline, but they do not have the same systems of local consultation that the police have.

To ensure that the public is properly served by the Coastguards, inspections and reviews are carried out of their activities. As they have a responsibility to the taxpayer to save money, as well as to the people who use the sea and coastline, they have been under pressure to become more cost-effective, especially by closing some of their centres.

CHECKPOINT ...

Investigate the roles, purpose and responsibilities of the public service that interests you most.

COOL SITES:

http://www.mcga.gov.uk/aboutus/index.htm

http://www.homeoffice.gov.uk/rds/prgpdfs/prs149.pdf – how the police spend their time ...

JOBS AND CONDITIONS OF SERVICE

PASSGRADE

Describe the implications and positive and negative aspects of working in the uniformed services on a personal level.

For this outcome, you are expected to explore the job satisfaction and dissatisfaction which can come from working in the uniformed services.

- 'Describe' means to give information about.
- 'Implications' are the effects that working in a uniformed service can have on someone's personal life.
- 'Positive' aspects give happiness and satisfaction; 'negative' aspects can cause stress, depression and dissatisfaction.
- 'Aspects' includes:
  - the work itself (Is it interesting and enjoyable?)
  - the pay (Is it good?)
  - promotions, rewards, etc.
  - the conditions of service (holidays, pensions, etc.)
  - working conditions (physical comfort, level and type of stress)
  - social aspects (relationships with colleagues).
- 'Personal level' is hard to define. It refers to one's own feelings of satisfaction or dissatisfaction. But it can also refer to the quality of one's relationships with other people – family, friends and colleagues. The 'personal level' is often contrasted with the 'professional level' but in fact the two are closely related – since 'job satisfaction' is experienced by the individual as a personal pleasure, but is linked to doing the job well.

This is another outcome which is best covered by talking to people who work in the public services. It may also be helpful to ask visiting speakers about the positive and negative effects of their work on their personal lives and happiness.

You should remember that everybody is different. If you talk to two soldiers about life in the army, they won't necessarily like or dislike the same things. For example, one may enjoy the camaraderie, being with 'mates', another may enjoy special training in skills such as skiing, while a third may enjoy the travelling. Because of these individual differences, you should try to get the opinions of a number of people, in different public services to cover this outcome. This will help you to get a balanced picture.

Details of pay and conditions of service can be found on the websites of uniformed public services. These change from time to time – always check that your information is up-to-date!

FOCUS

Job satisfaction: where it can come from

- **Intrinsic** (the job itself)
  - Mental: the challenge, solving problems, learning new skills, deeper understanding, research, etc.
  - Physical: fitness, exercise, training, testing yourself, sport, etc.
  - Emotional: sense of achievement, sense of fulfilment, serving others, rising to the challenge, leadership
  - Social: working with the community, teamwork, relationships with colleagues, meeting the public
- **Extrinsic** (outside the job, but dependent on it)

  Pay, status, holidays, good conditions of service, promotion and rewards

Job satisfaction is important. But you also need to know something about the following in order to cover this outcome.

Aspects of working in the uniformed services

Pay

Some starting salaries in 2003:

- teacher: £19,000
- nurse: £18,000
- trainee probation officer: £13,455
- soldier: about £11,500
- firefighter: £17,307 (but £25,000 after 2004)
- police: £18,666
- paramedics: £22,900
- army officer (graduate): £24,247.

Conditions of service

Here are some examples:

FOCUS

Hampshire Fire Service

'Annual Leave

Firefighters have 25 days annual leave each year and after 5 years' continuous service, they receive an additional 3 days. They will also receive paid holiday on, or in respect of, public holidays, and 2 extra statutory holidays. Maternity support leave and maternity leave are available and vary according to length of service.

Sick pay

Firefighters are entitled to full pay for up to 6 months if there is a good chance that they will eventually be able to return to work.

Hours of duty

A firefighter's normal week is one of 42 hours operating a shift system and limited overtime is payable when appropriate. Firefighters can be posted to day crewed and nucleus crewed stations where a different working pattern is applicable.

Pension scheme

The Fire Brigade offers a permanent job with an excellent contributory pension scheme to provide for your retirement. Currently the rate of contribution is 11% of a firefighter's annual salary (overtime and allowances are not pensionable pay).

Equal opportunities

The Fire Brigade is an Equal Opportunities employer. Applications are invited from women and men from all sections of the community, regardless of ethnic origin, colour, marital status, sexuality or religion, who have the necessary attributes for the job.'

Source: http://www.hantsfire.gov.uk/index.html

Paramedic

'You are likely to have to work regular unsocial hours. A rotating shift pattern, including nights and weekends, operates. You may be required for additional stand-by and on-call duties, especially in remote areas. You'll find meal breaks are often irregular.'

Source: www.prospects.ac.uk
Hampshire Fire and Rescue Service

Working conditions

This means the physical comfort and convenience of the place where the work is done.

Colleagues

You are likely to work in close contact with colleagues; there will be plenty of teamwork.

Prospects

The salary figures in the table below applied in 2003, but after the settlement of the firefighters' dispute, some of the lower rates should go up by about 16 per cent. This table, however, is typical of rank structures, pay differentials and 'promotion ladders' in the uniformed public services.

Career prospects in the fire service

Firefighter on entry	£16,941 per annum rising to (5th year) £21,531
Leading Firefighter	£23,055–£24,006
Sub-Officer	£23,643–£25,503
Station Officer	£27,426–£29,577
Assistant Divisional Officer	£28,908–£31,605
Divisional Officer Grade III	£30,960–£33,198
Divisional Officer Grade II	£32,874–£36,447
Divisional Officer Grade I	£36,312–£38,928
Senior Divisional Officer	£39,090–£42,168
Assistant Chief Officer	Receive various rates of pay
Chief Fire Officer	Receive various rates of pay
Firemaster	Receive various rates of pay

Source: Hampshire Fire and Rescue Service website; http://www.hantsfire.gov.uk/pay.html

Other benefits

These include:

- in-service training
- occupational health.

Equal opportunities

Typical figures for equal opportunities in the uniformed services, 2003

Uniformed public service	Percentage of female employees	Percentage of employees from ethnic minorities
Police	20.2 (constables only)	3.0
Fire service	1.7 (firefighters only	1.5
Prison service	17.4 (prison officers only)	3.5
Armed forces	8.0	1.4

These figures are likely to rise slowly in the coming years.

Positive and negative aspects of working in the uniformed services

Merit

Analyse the positive and negative aspects of working in the uniformed services.

For this outcome, you need to:

- examine job satisfaction, pay, conditions of service, working conditions and other aspects of work in the uniformed public services
- based on your information, say what you think are the 'good' and 'bad' aspects of uniformed service work.

For things like pay, prospects and job security it may be useful to make comparisons with national averages and with the private sector.

Job satisfaction

To research job satisfaction, you should talk to as many people as you can who work in the public services, asking them what they like and dislike about their jobs – and why.

Points to consider: job satisfaction in the uniformed services

Positive aspects?	Negative aspects?
Serving the community	The uniformed services are too male, and too white
Gaining the respect of fellow-citizens	Too much discipline for some people
Having a varied job	Shift work
Developing responsibility and leadership qualities	Dealing with difficult people
Working with people/ meeting people	Too much paperwork
	Physical risks, and the work

Showing initiative Much of the work is physical and outdoors, which is better than being stuck at a desk A steady job, with reasonable pay and good promotion prospects	can be shocking and distressing You have to behave responsibly even when off duty You cannot always choose where you live

Pay

The starting salary for most uniformed public services at officer level is close to the national average. At present, salaries in the public sector are rising faster than those in the private sector – but this is not normal. The pay is considered low in places like London where the cost of living is high – even though there is a London allowance ('London weighting'). Starting salaries are intended to reflect the amount of training and education needed before entry, and are supposed to be roughly comparable from one uniformed service to the next. Firefighters are paid less than most comparable services. This may be because they are unionised and allowed by law to strike; the police and the armed forces are not allowed to strike, and may get more pay to compensate them for the loss of this individual right.

Conditions of service

In most uniformed public services there are long shifts and some compulsory night work. Holidays, however, are on average longer than those in the private sector. Pensions are good, and retirement starts early – many police officers have retired by the time they are 50. Public service job security is good: you are less likely to get sacked than in the private sector.

The shift work can have an adverse effect on the health of employees in the uniformed public services. It can also put a strain on their families and their personal relationships.

http://www.irfs.org.uk/docs/future/index.htm – the text of the *Independent Review of the Fire Service* by Sir George Bain, 2002 – good bedtime reading

Working conditions

In the armed forces these can be harsh – think of the dust-storms in Iraq, and the complaints of poor rations that troops suffered at the beginning of the 2003 Iraq War! In the other public services, offices may be overcrowded or uncomfortable. However, the Health and Safety at Work Act 1974 has tended to standardise working conditions across the public and private sectors.

Physical danger

Uniformed service work is not the most dangerous there is: sea fishing is the worst. Construction and forestry, and even window cleaning, are more dangerous statistically than any public service work. Firefighting is the twenty-third most dangerous job, while policing is the twenty-fourth and the armed forces (excluding deaths from enemy fire) twenty-eighth. Nevertheless, these three jobs are far more dangerous than the average job.

Colleagues

Teamwork and cooperation with colleagues are vital in the public services. For most people, this teamwork and human contact is a great source of job satisfaction.

Prospects

There are good prospects for promotion in some public services, e.g. for officers in the armed forces, or in the prison service, where the work is expanding. Promotion prospects are worst in the more popular jobs – such as firefighting or policing – because fewer people leave, and there is more competition.

In-service training

The concept of 'lifelong learning' – constantly learning new skills to cope with technological and societal changes – has affected work in the uniformed public services. Officers at all levels in the uniformed services frequently undergo in-service training. This improves their promotion prospects and, in most cases, their job satisfaction.

Occupational health

There are occupational health schemes designed to keep officers in the uniformed services in good health. However, the jobs are stressful compared with many equivalent jobs in the private sector, and rates of absenteeism, and early retirement on health grounds, tend to be high. Forty-three per cent of firefighters retired early on ill-health grounds in 2000–1, according to the Bain Report. Many services, such as the prison and fire services, have repeat fitness tests for employees (e.g. yearly fitness tests), and many others have good gym and sports facilities for those who need or want to keep fit. Health and safety is taken very seriously in the uniformed public services – but then again, some of the work is dangerous!

Equal opportunities

The uniformed public services are equal opportunities employers. But some parts of the armed forces, e.g. the Royal Marines in the navy and the infantry in the army, still don't admit women. And in most other uniformed public services, women and ethnic minority groups are seriously under-represented. The services are making determined efforts to rectify the situation, but it may be a long time before they succeed.

Range of jobs at operative level

> Explain the range of jobs that are available in the uniformed services at operative level.

For this outcome, you need to:

- show the variety of different jobs for non-officers in the uniformed services
- explain what some of the jobs involve
- explain why there are so many different jobs.

'Operative level' means (in the armed forces) at a level below officer. It can also be taken to refer to *some* civilian jobs – mainly manual ones – in any uniformed service.

Civilian jobs

In organisations such as the police, many civilian jobs actually require high qualifications and specialised skills, e.g. IT skills or qualifications in social work. Forensic scientists are usually people with a scientific background (e.g. a degree in chemistry) rather than a police background.

Civilian police jobs which might be considered as 'operative level' would include people like cleaners, drivers, maintenance staff, traffic wardens, receptionists and other jobs not requiring special academic qualifications.

Armed forces operative level

Soldiers (privates) in the army and naval ratings (ordinary seamen) are examples of armed forces jobs which are at operative level. In the army, which employs around 100,000 people, there is a bewildering range of operative jobs. There is a sound reason for this: armies have to be self-sufficient when working abroad in a hostile environment (e.g. Iraq). They cannot depend on the goodwill of the local population, so if they want to get their hair cut or buy a Mars bar they have to do it within the army structure.

Army operative jobs come under the following headings:

- **Combat** – infantry soldiers, gunners, tank crew, etc. These people do the actual fighting on the front line.
- **Engineering** – technicians, fitters, engineers, surveyors, mechanics, armourers, bricklayers, electricians, etc. These do vehicle and weapons maintenance, build roads and bridges, put up buildings and keep the technology working.
- **IT/Communications** – aircraft technicians, military intelligence, signals, etc. They look after communications and the supply of information coming into and out of the army, while it is on operations (active service).
- **Logistics** – transport, petrol operative, port operative, chef, driver, storeman. This section keeps the army and its staff fully supplied with all their needs, even when they are posted thousands of miles from home.
- **Health care** – dental nurse, radiographer, environmental health technician, etc. They try to keep everybody in the army healthy.
- **Admin/finance** – military clerks. They look after pay and paperwork.
- **Specialist** – Royal Military Police, musicians. RMPs keep discipline and fight crime, mainly within the army itself. Musicians have ceremonial duties – often important for morale and the army's image.

COOL SITES:

http://www.army.mod.uk/careers/sitemap/index.html – army careers in a rather large nutshell

http://www.rafcareers.com/html/jobsrch/index.html – cool list of RAF careers

ENTRY REQUIREMENTS AND CAREER DEVELOPMENT

Compare the entry requirements for an officer in two different public services.

For this outcome, you need to:

- research the entry requirements for officers in two (uniformed) public services
- show the similarities and differences.

FOCUS

Entry requirements for a paramedic

A first degree in paramedical studies, completed in conjunction with the ambulance services, may give you immediate recognition as a paramedic although the profession is open to all graduates.

It is also open to all Diplomates [Higher National Diploma]. Although no specific subjects are required, life/medical science subjects provide relevant knowledge that may be an advantage when competing for an entry-level post.

A postgraduate qualification is not needed in order to become a paramedic. It is quite common to enter the profession without a degree or HND. Some ambulance services do particularly welcome applications from graduates, but there are no specific graduate entry schemes. Experience of dealing with the public, especially sick, disabled and elderly people, is valuable. A first aid certificate is useful evidence of your genuine interest in the work.

The requirements include:

- a clean current full driving licence for at least one year and often two, and preferably experience of driving vehicles larger than a car;
- a caring attitude to sick and injured people;
- a warm, outgoing personality and an enjoyment of working as part of a team;
- a responsible attitude and a serious approach to the work;
- good communication skills;
- the ability to remain calm in crises and make rapid decisions;
- good health, both physically and emotionally, normal colour vision, manual dexterity.

Minimum age of entry is 18 for an ambulance care assistant and 21 for paramedics. Although there is no mandatory upper age limit, some services operate age restrictions, while others recruit up to normal retirement age. Many services welcome applications up to the age of 45 for accident and emergency work, and up to 55 for non-emergency work.

Source: adapted from www.prospects.ac.uk
© AGCAS

FOCUS

Entry requirements for an RAF officer

'Age: Not less than 17 years 6 months

Our minimum requirement for commissioned officers is 2 A/A2 levels or 3 Scottish Highers passes, plus 5 GCSEs/SCEs (Grade C/3), including English Language and Maths. Graduates or qualified entrants may be offered enhanced promotion and starting pay. A number of specialisations – Engineer Officer, Catering Officer, Physical Education Officer, Legal Officer, Medical Officer, Dental Officer, Nursing Officer and Chaplain – require more specialist qualifications. You may apply a few months before you achieve the educational requirements. The minimum requirement for NCO aircrew is 3 GCSE/SCE passes (Grade C/3), including English Language and Maths. An elementary knowledge of science, in some cases physics, is also required

You must have been born in the United Kingdom, or a country which was, at the time, a member of the Commonwealth, or the Republic of Ireland. In addition, you must have been a citizen of one of those countries since birth. (This qualification is sufficient for the vast majority of branches; however, additional requirements may apply to certain specialisations.)

These conditions of entry were correct at the time of publication but may have changed. You should check with our careers information staff on current terms for joining.

All potential entrants (applicants) must appreciate that there are height, weight and size restrictions which may affect their application. In addition all candidates are expected to be physically fit with a body mass in proportion with their size (height).

The principles of equality of opportunity in employment, promotion and training – based on ability, performance, experience and aptitude – underpin all our personnel policies.

The RAF values every individual's contribution, irrespective of their race, ethnic origin, religion, gender, sexual orientation or social background. However, for reasons of combat effectiveness, women cannot join the RAF Regiment.'

Source: http://www.rafcareers.com/html/briefingroom/index.html

Comparison between paramedic and RAF officer entry requirements

Academic requirements

To become a paramedic, there are no fixed academic requirements, though they prefer graduates, especially with degrees in paramedical studies. Paramedics are employed by different employers (NHS trusts) and academic requirements vary slightly from place to place. Preference appears to be given to people with qualifications in life sciences (biology or human biology).

The RAF has strict academic requirements for officers (2 A-levels and 5 GCSEs at A–C including English and Maths). (This appears to exclude BTEC National Diplomas!) A distinction is made between commissioned (Pilot Officer upwards) and non-commissioned officers (Warrant Officer downwards).

http://www.raf.mod.uk/organisation/comstruc.html – RAF rank structure

Skills

Paramedic employers want people who are good drivers, with clean licences and, preferably, experience of driving larger vehicles. They also want people with good communication skills (listening, talking, reading and writing). The RAF do not mention skills.

Personal qualities

Paramedic employers want people who are caring, warm, outgoing, responsible, serious, calm, good decision-makers, good team workers and with good manual dexterity. The RAF are looking for 'ability, performance, experience and aptitude' – qualities which they do not define, but which they assess during recruitment.

Experience

Employers of paramedics want people who have experience of dealing with the public 'especially sick, disabled and elderly people'. They are looking for applicants who are 21 and above, or who choose being a paramedic as a second career (e.g. after nursing for some years). The RAF mention experience but say no more – probably because you only have to be 17 years and 6 months old to apply to become an RAF officer.

Nationality

No nationality requirements are given for paramedics. The requirements for RAF officers are strict, and rather complex where the Commonwealth is concerned. (Pakistan was not in the Commonwealth between 1972 and 1989, while South Africa was excluded between 1961 and 1994.) There are even stricter requirements (not stated) for certain branches of the RAF.

Physical requirements

Both services have physical requirements. For the paramedics what is needed is 'good health, both physically and emotionally'. The RAF have 'height, weight and size restrictions', require physical fitness and what (for them) is the right proportion between weight and height.

Equal opportunities

Both the paramedic employers and the RAF are equal opportunities employers. The RAF, however, have certain clothing and other restrictions which may, at times, infringe the religions and cultures of some people. The biggest difference is that women are not allowed in one branch of the RAF – the RAF Regiment.

PASSGRADE

Describe the entry requirements and opportunities for career development in one of the uniformed services.

Merit

Analyse the entry requirements and opportunities for career development in one of the uniformed services.

For the PASSGRADE outcome, you need to:

- set out the entry requirements for a uniformed service
- show how a person's career can progress once they have joined that service

- give the facts using appropriate words and format.

For the MERIT outcome, you need to:

- explain the entry requirements for one uniformed service – showing, for example, how they relate to the needs of the organisation.
- give details on how or why people are promoted, and how their work might change as their career develops.

Opportunities for career development include information about the rank structure and the system through which people are promoted. But 'career development' doesn't always mean promotion to a higher rank. It can mean specialising in a particular field of work – or moving from one specialisation to another (e.g. from Traffic to CID in the police).

It will help if you

- find a clear statement (from a recruitment leaflet or website) about the entry requirements for the service
- talk to someone who recruits for a public service
- examine not only what the recruitment leaflet says about requirements, but also consider some of the underlying implications for potential applicants (especially what types of long-term preparation they should consider)
- gain information from senior officers about promotion procedures and prospects in uniformed services.

FOCUS

Entry requirements for the prison service

'MINIMUM ELIGIBILITY REQUIREMENTS

In order to be eligible to apply, you must meet the following criteria:

- You must be a British or Commonwealth Citizen, a British Protected Person, an EU National or an Icelandic or Norwegian National. Some EU family members may also qualify. All candidates must be free from immigration control and have indefinite leave to remain in the United Kingdom. For some posts candidates may be required to have been resident in the United Kingdom for three years.
- At the time of appointment you must be aged between 18½ and 57.
- You must not be an undischarged bankrupt.
- You must not be a member of a group or organisation which the Prison Service considers to be racist.
- Your eyesight must meet the following standard: Snellen 6/24 in each eye corrected to 6/12 or better with contact lenses or glasses, or normal sight (Snellen 6/6) in one eye and up to Snellen 6/36 in the other corrected to Snellen 6/12 or better with visual aid.

  If you have any doubts about whether you meet the eyesight standard you are advised to seek professional advice. Ophthalmic opticians and most general practitioners or practice nurses should be able to indicate whether you meet the Snellen eyesight criteria.
- You must be capable of undergoing some physical exertion. You should therefore be physically fit and in good health. As part of the recruitment process you will be required to pass a medical examination and a fitness test.'

Source: Prison service website

http://www.hmprisonservice.gov.uk/

Profile

Nationality requirements

These exist because there might be security risks if prison officers came from a background which was anti-British. The EU has an action plan to ensure full labour mobility between member states by 2005; the prison service is supporting this by allowing people from other EU countries to work as prison officers in the UK.

Age

In recent years, the minimum requirement has been brought down from 21 to 18½ – in line with the police.

The upper age limit of 57 indicates (a) the determination of the prison service to avoid age discrimination, (b) that training a prison officer is expensive – if applicants were any older, the prison service would not get their money's worth for the cost of training them, (c) that the physical demands of being a prison officer are often not very great, and (d) that experience of life is useful in a prison officer.

Bankruptcy

An undischarged bankrupt is somebody whose debts are officially greater than their assets (the total value of what they own). Such people might (a) be of questionable moral character and (b) open to pressure, bribery or inducements from prisoners which could affect prison security.

Membership of racist groups

The prison service is showing its commitment to diversity by putting in this requirement. Most other public services would also not employ people who had a history of racist activism in, say, the BNP, National Front or Combat 18.

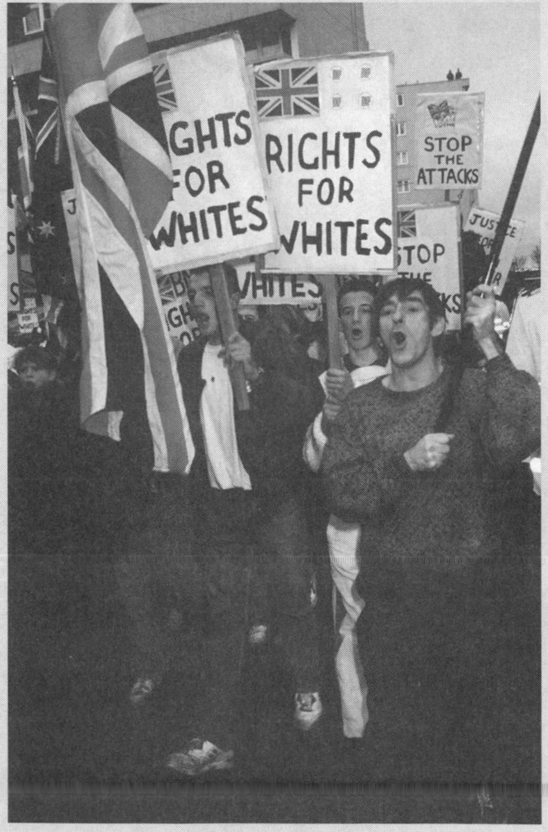

It is unlikely that any of these will ever get a job in the uniformed services.

Eyesight

The Snellen test is the normal eye-test that you take at an optician's. The test card has eight rows of letters, starting with big letters at the top and ending with tiny letters at the bottom.

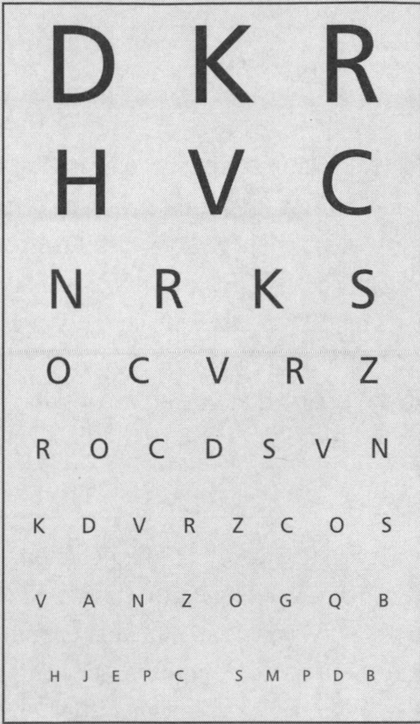

The Snellen test card

The Snellen test

Row number	Distance (metres) at which a person of 'normal' eyesight can read the letters
1	60
2	36
3	18
4	12
5	9
6	6
7	5
8	4

- 6/36 means that a line that can be read by a person of normal distance vision from 36 metres away, can be read by the person tested from a distance of 6 metres. (Such a person would be short-sighted, and would normally wear glasses.)
- 6/6 vision means that a person can read the sixth line down standing six metres away: this is normal good

eyesight. (This is the same as 20/20 vision; the measurement in the US is always done in feet, hence the higher numbers.)

- If someone is 6/12 in contact lenses, it means they can read the fourth line down, wearing contact lenses, at a distance of 6 metres.

To carry out the Snellen test you need a 6-metre line of sight – so a mirror is used if the test is done in a small room.

Prison officers need reasonably good eyesight to see down corridors, across an exercise yard, etc. and they should not be incapacitated if they lose their spectacles. Some public services are mistrustful of laser surgery to correct short sight: if you are thinking of having this done and want to join a public service, check out the situation first, just to make sure that you are not risking your career.

Physical exertion

The prison service take care not to frighten applicants off with talk of toughness – though they do value fitness. This approach is in line with their equal opportunities policies, and with the fact that, other things being equal, brain is more important than brawn in the prison service.

Opportunities for career development

The prison population is increasing all the time, and more prisons are being built. There are also private prisons. The opportunities for career development are therefore better than in services such as the fire service or the Coastguard, which are getting smaller.
Like some police forces the prison service have a 'fast-track' promotion scheme for ambitious and able young prison officers (see the table below). These officers *must* be graduates – in any subject. Officers who are not on the scheme will also get promoted if they have the right abilities and drive. But it will take them longer to get into prison management.

Career development on the fast track (Intensive Development Scheme) in the prison service

First nine weeks after acceptance into the service	A week's induction at the Prison Service College, followed by one week's observation at a prison. Then there are nine weeks' initial training at the PSC.
After initial training	First posting as a Prison Officer. It lasts nine months and includes the full range of officer duties. At the end of this period the Prison Officer's Promotion Exam is taken.
After about one year	Passing the Prison Officer's Promotion Exam is followed by a three-week management development course and a promotion assessment (interviews, etc.) to become a Principal Officer
The following year	12 months as a Principal Officer working at a different prison. This carries responsibility for a group of staff and for the running of a prison wing. There is continuous assessment throughout the year for promotion to Middle Manager
The next two years	After promotion to Middle Manager comes one month's training followed by two year-long placements. The first is not in a prison but could be at Headquarters. The second involves managing part of a prison. This means devising better regimes for prisoners, ensuring that staff give of their best, and looking after their welfare and progression.
After four years in all	If the placements are successful the officer becomes a Functional Head – and joins senior management.

Points to note:

- The prison service runs a two-tier system, and is clearly trying to recruit graduates into the service.
- Promotion to Principal Officer (the top grade of prison officer) is by examination, interviews and assessment of work done. Higher level promotions are done on the basis of interviews and assessment of work only.
- Fast-track prison officers have to be prepared to learn quickly, and move around the country.

http://www.hmce.gov.uk/about/career/progression.pdf – getting on in Customs and Excise!

! CHECKPOINT ...

1. What problems do you think a fast-track prison officer might face in the first five years of his or her career?
2. Why is the prison service so keen to recruit graduates?

Distinction

Evaluate and justify the entry requirements for career development in one of the uniformed services.

For this outcome, you need to:

- research entry requirements and career development in depth
- ask and answer searching questions about why the uniformed service of your choice has chosen the approach it has to entry requirements, promotion and career development.

Questions to think about

- What personality traits should an applicant to the prison service possess?
- What medical conditions, e.g. epilepsy, might bar applicants to the prison service, and why?
- Why is it vital to have a commitment to diversity and equal opportunities – for a person who wants to join the prison service?
- What would be the possible advantages to the prison service of recruiting more women?
- What is the drop-out rate among applicants to the prison service, and why do they drop out?
- What are the advantages and disadvantages of joining a fast-track promotion scheme?
- Why have the prison service chosen to have a fast-track scheme?
- Is the prison service right to ban officers from membership of certain political organisations?

COOL SITES:

http://www.homeoffice.gov.uk/justice/prisons/inspprisons/inspection.html

http://www.homeoffice.gov.uk/hmic/mps2002.pdf

www.nelsonthornes.com/vocational/public_services – Unit 23 Custodial Care

APPLICATION AND SELECTION PROCESS

PASSGRADE

Outline the selection process for a job in one of the uniformed services.

For this outcome, you need to describe the main features of one uniformed services selection process.

All the statutory uniformed services provide informative leaflets about their selection processes. These processes are often complex, consisting of several stages. The FOCUS gives an example.

FOCUS

Selection in the Sussex Police

'First complete and return the application form and medical questionnaire.

Your application form will be assessed against the entrance requirements and scored.

If successful, you will be invited to the next stage of the selection process. If your application is not successful we will write and tell you why.

The next stage will involve you in assessment tests and interview. You don't need to worry about these. You will receive plenty of information before the tests and you will find examples of the type of test you will face on our website at www.policecouldyou.co.uk. Typically these include written tests, ability tests, interactive role-play exercises and an interview. You will be assessed by trained assessors.

If you are successful at assessment, you will be invited for a medical examination and Fitness and Health. You will find details on the Fitness and Health and a suggested training programme on our website: www.policecouldyou.co.uk .

Appointment is subject to satisfactory reference checks and security vetting.

Note that the order of tests may vary.'

Source: http://www.sussex.police.uk/recruitment/index.asp

Each part of the selection process has a clearly defined purpose.

Application form

This is a long, detailed form! Its aim is to:

- see if you can write clearly, follow instructions, and are well organised
- gain an impression of your motivation, opinions and understanding of the job
- check that you fulfil age, nationality, health and background requirements
- ensure that you are prepared to work in a diverse, multi-ethnic setting
- find out if you have a criminal record (and if you are honest enough to say so – because they will check anyway!).

Assessment tests and interview

You have to spend a couple of days away from home to do these. They include:

- **the official Police Initial Recruitment Test (PIRT)** The PIRT has five sections (see the table below).
- The first four sections use question papers; the observation test uses video clips to test your memory and ability to notice details. There are time limits for all parts of the test ranging from 8 minutes for the checking test up to 25 minutes for the verbal reasoning test. You record your answers in pencil by shading a computerised sheet.

  The aim is to find out if you have the thinking skills police officers need.
- **interactive tests** These are role plays and group exercises. The aim is to reveal your resilience, problem-solving, respect for diversity, teamworking, personal responsibility and customer focus.
- **interview** You will be asked searching questions about
  - what you put on your application forms and why
  - your suitability and motivation for police work.

  The aim is to find out if your appearance, manner, confidence and maturity are what is expected of a police officer.

Fitness tests

The fitness tests vary in detail from force to force. The aim is to find out if you have the stamina, strength and agility for police work.

The PIRT test

Section of test	1 Verbal usage	2 Checking test	3 Working with number	4 Verbal reasoning	5 Observation
Testing ...	spelling and grammar	accuracy and speed	mental arithmetic	thinking clearly	noticing details

FOCUS

Fitness test

'Applicants will need to pass the Physical Fitness Test, which involves the following:

Press-ups – minimum of 30 in one minute.

Sit-ups – minimum of 30 in one minute.

Shuttle run – 20 metre shuttle run.

(The shuttle run requires applicants to run between two lines at a steadily increasing pace. Males must run for a minimum of 8 minutes and females for a minimum of 6 minutes.)'

Source: http://www.gloucestershire.police.uk/index/index.html

LINK! There is much more on fitness tests in Unit 9 Physical Preparation for the Uniformed Services.

Medical examination

The examination is carried out by a doctor and a nurse. They check your heart, abdomen, eyes, ears, mouth, blood pressure, pulse, height, weight, vision, colour vision, lung function, hearing and urine. The aim is to make sure that your health is good enough for the demands of the job.

Reference checks and security vetting

References (e.g. from your college and a workplace) will be followed up, and the referees may be contacted personally or by phone. The security vetting will check police and nationality records. The aim of this is to make sure that your character and background are suitable for the police.

CHECKPOINT ...

1. Find more information about selection processes from the recruitment departments of uniformed services. Ask your tutors to invite visiting speakers to tell you about them in detail. Also take any opportunity you have to do 'mock' entry tests and interviews for – or with – the public services.
2. Ask someone in a uniformed service what long-term preparation you can do to improve your chances of getting in.

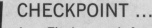

COOL SITES:

http://www.policecouldyou.co.uk/home/ – as recommended by Sussex Police – and others

http://www.police-information.co.uk/policebooks.html – ask your college library to buy these books

CHECKPOINT ...

The Secret Policeman, a BBC documentary about police recruits, caused a sensation in October 2003. Find out why – and watch it if you can get hold of a copy.

(a) What can police applicants learn from the programme and the public reactions to it?

(b) How might police application procedures change as a result of this programme?

Unit 9 Physical Preparation for the Uniformed Services

Grading criteria

PASSGRADE	Merit	Distinction
To achieve a pass grade the evidence must show that the learner is able to:	To achieve a merit grade the evidence must show that the learner is able to:	To achieve a distinction grade the evidence must show that the learner is able to:
• demonstrate the principles of standing-in **173** • plan and take part in a warm up and a cool down using the correct components in a safe environment **173** • organise and carry out a physical training session in a safe environment demonstrating health and safety awareness **175** • research, explain and undertake the range of uniformed service fitness tests **179** • explain the different types and methods of circuit training and techniques of running training **181** • explain the reasons for gym agility **183** • design, plan and complete a training programme in preparation for an entry test to a uniformed service incorporating the fitness types and techniques **185**	• explain the use of the components in a warm up and cool down **175** • analyse and evaluate the physical training session **178** • analyse the different types and methods of circuit training and the techniques used when running training **184**	• evaluate and justify own performance and the training programme **187**

If you want to join the uniformed services, physical preparation is very important. All the uniformed services except Customs and Excise have fitness tests for entrants, and the armed forces, fire and prison services also have repeat fitness tests for serving officers.

Many people who wish to work in the uniformed services are not sure they are fit enough to get in. The aim of this unit is to show you what levels of fitness are needed for the uniformed services, and to show you ways of building and maintaining your own fitness.

SAFE PRACTICE

Demonstrate the principles of standing-in.

It is likely that there is a misprint in this outcome in the 2002 Specifications: *BN011697 Guidance and Units for the Edexcel Level 3 BTEC Nationals in Public Services – Issue 1 – May 2002*, and that the outcome should read: 'Demonstrate the principles of standing'.

Standing properly, or having 'good posture' is a requirement for the uniformed services, partly because good posture is good for your health, flexibility, stamina and strength, and partly because standing well is needed on parade, or when working with the public. Standing properly suggests discipline, smartness and confidence – all of which are essential in the uniformed services.

What is posture?

Posture is the way you hold your body when you are sitting or standing.

Standing

You should stand with knees straight but not locked, stomach flat, ribs raised, shoulders and head erect. Imagine you are balancing a book on your head. Your weight should be evenly distributed on both legs.

Walking

'Walk tall' with your feet pointing straight ahead. Your arms should swing freely from your sides. Look straight ahead, rather than down.

Sitting

Sit up with both feet flat on the floor, your whole back against the chair back, and your head erect. Avoid hunching forward. Distribute your weight evenly on both buttocks.

CHECKPOINT ...

Is it right to judge people on their posture? What do you think?

http://ourworld.compuserve.com/homepages/Dr_John/posture.htm#content

http://www.spine-health.com/topics/cd/ergo/ergo03.html – to be read standing up!

Warming up and cooling down

Plan and take part in a warm up and a cool down using the correct components in a safe environment.

For this outcome, you need to plan a warm-up and cool-down for yourself, or for other people. Your tutor will guide you on this.

- A 'warm-up' is a short period of gentle activity immediately before starting a more vigorous activity. You should *always* have a warm-up before a training session, sports competition or strenuous game.
- A 'cool-down' is a short period of gentle activity following a period of strenuous exercise. Again, you should always have a cool-down following a training session or sports competition.

Warm-up

Purpose of a warm-up
The purpose of warming up is to:

- prevent injuries such as pulled muscles, tendons and ligaments which come from moving cold muscles too violently without warning
- enable you to function at peak power as soon as a game, race or training session starts
- focus your mind.

Effect of a warm-up

A warm-up:

- gets your blood flowing through your muscles to give them the heat, glucose and oxygen they need for hard physical activity
- lubricates muscles, tendons, ligaments and joints to increase flexibility and reduce the risk of pulling and tearing
- increases the adrenalin level in the blood, raises blood-sugar and oxygen levels and so prepares the mind for strenuous effort
- enables waste materials to be flushed out of the muscles more easily.

Most athletes do warm-ups which are partly sport-specific. This means that some of the movements in the warm-up are the same as the movements they will use in the main activity. An example is tennis players practising forehand and backhand strokes – at about three quarters of full power – in the minutes before a match starts.

Planning a warm-up

The total warm-up should last 10-15 minutes. When planning a warm-up, ensure that it has two phases:

1 a warming phase (lasting about 5 minutes)
2 a stretching phase (lasting 5–10 minutes).

Do not stretch before you are warmed up – it can lead to injuries. Sport-specific movements should be included, especially in the later parts of the warm-up.

The example in the FOCUS below is recommended by the fire service for circuit training and fire service drills. It is not sport-specific, but it is *activity-specific*, e.g. arm-swinging and side-bending would be used for hose-rolling.

FOCUS

Warm-up in the fire service

'Before every exercise session, always carry out at least a five minute warm up. This is to obtain the warming and loosening effects which prepare the body for more strenuous work, whether this is circuit training, running or Fire Service Drills. This prepares the body to:

Develop a state of mental alertness

Increase the pulse rate ready for more vigorous exercise to follow

Loosen and mobilise the joints and muscles

Exercise the major muscle groups of the body in turn.

These groups are:

Arms and Shoulders – Exercise can include arm circling, shoulder shrugging, arm swinging (outwards), arm shaking, and crawl strokes (as in swimming).

Trunk and Back – Exercises can include trunk rotation, side bending, dorsal raises and sit-ups.

Legs – Examples of exercises are knee bends (squats), side jumps and lunges. Finish with some gentle jogging on the spot – this uses the lower leg muscles and raises the pulse.

NOTE: Do not stretch before you are warmed up.'

Source: Hampshire Fire and Rescue Service; http://www.hantsfire.gov.uk/jobs/

Cool-downs

These need only take five minutes. They should include a little jogging or other light aerobic exercise, and some stretching. There should be a gradual decrease in the amount of energy used.

The aim of a cool-down is to help purify the muscles of lactic acid which builds up during a strenuous activity. If you cool down properly you will feel less stiff afterwards.

Safe environment

Check:

- that anybody taking part in a warm-up is fit and well
- that everyone is wearing suitable clothing. In a gym this would be: PE shoes with clean (non-marking) soles, track or running suits, shorts, t-shirts, sweatshirts, athletic socks
- that no dangerous jewellery is being worn
- that the floor and surrounding area is clean and clear of clutter of any sort
- if the warm-up is outdoors, that the weather and ground surface are suitable, and that everybody is suitably dressed.

When planning your warm-up and cool-down you should include the following information:

- the kind of activity they are associated with (could be a sport, a training activity or a job-related task)
- the age, fitness level and motivation of the people for whom your warm-up and cool-down are designed
- the purpose of each warm-up activity in relation to warming, flexibility, etc.
- each activity in the warm-up and cool-down and the time it takes
- the order in which warm-up activities take place, with warming activities coming before stretching, and less strenuous activities coming before more strenuous activities
- where the warm-up and cool-down will take place
- the fact that the warm-up and cool-down will take place immediately before and after the main physical activity
- safety considerations of clothing and environment.

Taking part

Four rules:

- Be enthusiastic, but not over-enthusiastic.
- Follow instructions.
- Stand well away from other people.
- Avoid stretching until you have warmed up.

Merit

Explain the use of the components in a warm up and cool down.

For this outcome, you need to explain the reasons for the different parts of a warm-up and a cool-down.

The 'components' are the different activities, e.g. shoulder-shrugging and arm-shaking, used in warm-ups and cool-downs.

Each of these activities is used for a purpose, and for this outcome you have to show you understand what that purpose is. You should be able to say:

- whether the activity is for warming, stretching or both
- why warming activities have to come before stretching activities
- which muscle-groups are being exercised, e.g. shoulder muscles, calf muscles
- exactly how the warm-up components should be carried out
- the kinds of injuries warm-up components might prevent
- how warm-up components prevent injuries (see page 173 above)
- the effects of a warm-up on blood-flow and mental alertness
- what sport-specific or activity-specific components are
- why they are included in a warm-up
- what components should be used in a cool-down
- how they should be carried out
- why they are used
- what the benefits of a cool-down are.

You should also be able to explain and justify the length of time spent on each component of a warm-up or cool-down. Some warming activities, such as jogging on the spot, will last much longer than some stretching activities, such as arm-shaking and trunk-rotation.

! CHECKPOINT ...

1. What value is there, if any, in breathing exercises?
2. What are the best ways of maintaining interest and keeping a mental focus during warm-ups?
3. Is it possible to evaluate the success of a warm-up and, if so, how would you do it (both for yourself and for other people)?

Organising a physical training session

Organise and carry out a physical training session in a safe environment demonstrating health and safety awareness.

For this outcome, you need to:

- plan and carry out a safe physical training session
- show that you understand health and safety for training sessions.

This outcome can mean organising and carrying out a physical training session for yourself or for other people. Follow your tutor's advice.

What you have to do

- Plan a number of physical activities – to be carried out on one occasion – which would help to make someone fitter or stronger.
- Carry out (or make someone else carry out) these activities.
- Pay full attention to health and safety in all four phases of the activity: (a) the planning, (b) the warm-up, (c) the training session itself and (d) the cool-down.
- Review the session afterwards (see the next outcome on page 178).

A physical training session must:

- last for a definite time, e.g. 1 hour
- consist of a structured group of activities
- have defined aims
- be part of a wider programme of increasing your fitness and strength. (But for this outcome you only need to organise and carry out one session.)

The activities must be:

- introduced by a warm-up and followed by a cool-down
- suited to the physical capabilities of the person doing them
- suited to the fitness/strength aims of the person doing them
- suited to the equipment, facilities and conditions available
- healthy and safe.

FOCUS

Definitions of fitness and strength

Fitness is...

'The ability to perform your normal daily tasks with vigour and alertness and without undue fatigue, with enough energy left in reserve to cope with any emergencies that may arise or to follow the leisure pursuits of your choice' – World Health Organisation

Aerobic fitness is ...

'the body's ability to take in, transport and use oxygen' – Fiona Whitfield, fitness instructor, Falmer Sports Complex, September 2000; http://www.studenthealth.co.uk/index.htm

Muscular strength is ...

'the amount of force that can be applied by a muscle during a single maximum contraction.' – www.sportsnutrition4u.com

Planning

When organising your physical training session you should do a written plan. Your plan should answer the following important questions:

Who is taking part in the session?

- Name?
- Age?
- What is their present level of fitness?
- What is their reason for wanting to become fitter and/or stronger?
- Are there any possible medical considerations?

Basic information

- When and where will the session take place?
- How long it will take?
- Who is taking part?
- What equipment or facilities will be needed?
- What personal clothing and equipment will be needed?

Health and safety

- Who is going to observe the session?
- What first aid is available?
- Are drinks available in case of dehydration?
- Is a training partner needed?
- Is any protective clothing needed?
- Will the weather be a factor?
- Has a risk assessment on both the venue and the planned activities been carried out?
- What will happen if something goes wrong?

The session itself

- What activities will be done?
- What is each activity designed to achieve?
- How long will each one take?

- Will there be any rest periods?
- What form will the warm-ups and cool-downs take?

After the session

- Will drinks, etc. be available?
- Are showers available?
- What will be done with equipment, etc.?

Review questions
For example:

- Was the session enjoyable?
- Could it be done on a regular basis, as part of a longer fitness programme?
- What did I do well?
- What could I do better next time round?
- What did I learn about my/our fitness needs?
- Did I notice any unforeseen health and safety problems?

Activities

There are many activities which can be used in training sessions. They fall into three main categories:

- **Aerobic activities** increase stamina. Such activities are good for your heart and the 'slow-twitch' muscle cells used for long periods of moderate physical activity. They also increase your lung efficiency, and make you less likely to get short of breath. Examples include: jogging, long-distance swimming, aerobics.
- **Anaerobic activities** increase strength. They develop your 'fast-twitch' muscle cells and build muscle bulk and strength. Examples include: weight-lifting, sprinting, shot-putting.
- **Flexibility activities** are stretching exercises which lubricate joints and stretch muscles, joints and tendons, so that you can bend more easily at the joints.

LINK! There's more on aerobic and anaerobic activities in Unit 18, Health and Fitness, page 300.

Choice of activities
The activities you choose for your training session should depend on:

- your present physical fitness
- your fitness needs, e.g. to improve endurance, or upper body strength
- your fitness aims, e.g. to participate in a sport or take a fitness test

Activities you can choose for your physical training session

Activity	Aerobic or anaerobic	Muscle groups trained	Number of repetitions or time spent
Running	Mainly aerobic	Thighs, calves, buttocks	4 minutes at a time for aerobic running; 100 m sprints for anaerobic running
Swimming	Aerobic	All	10 minutes – but you could spend much longer if you like swimming, and want a general aerobic exercise
Hamstring stretch	Flexibility	Hamstring (thigh muscle)	20–30 seconds. three times each leg
Abdominal stretch	Flexibility	Abdominal muscles	Maintain for 6–10 seconds, 15–20 repetitions
Sit ups	Anaerobic	Abdominal muscles	As many as possible
Press-ups	Anaerobic	Chest, arm and shoulders	As many as possible (must be done properly)
Pull-ups	Anaerobic	Biceps	As many as possible
Squats	Anaerobic	Hamstring/quadriceps	As many as possible
Step-ups	Aerobic	Legs, heart	Until you are short of breath

- the kinds of activity you enjoy
- the facilities or equipment available.

NB If you are organising a training session for other people, you need to know this information for all the people who are going to take part. (If you can, choose people of similar fitness – otherwise, make allowances for less fit people by letting them take rests, do activities of lower intensity, or do fewer repetitions.)

Guidelines

- If you are unfit, your first fitness need is for aerobic activities – usually to burn off excess fat and improve muscle tone.
- If you are fit, your fitness need may be to develop your strength – in which case you should put some anaerobic activities in your training session.
- It is not necessary to have a gym for a training session – you can use a playing field or a room with safety mats on the floor.
- A training session should aim to exercise as many muscle groups as possible, unless you are doing it for a very specific purpose.
- The rest period between each activity in your training session should be as short as possible.
- You should push yourself with each activity you do.
- Never train unless you are in good health, and always put health and safety first.

CHECKPOINT ...

1 What are the Latin names for the main muscles?
2 List the advantages and disadvantages of joining a commercial gym.
3 What are the advantages and drawbacks of weight training, if you want to become an army officer?
4 Why is it advisable to have a health check before a training session, if you have never trained before?

COOL SITE:

http://www.army.mod.uk/atr_pirbright/student_info/training_program/index.htm#Diet – army training

skill POWER

The plan of a training session can be set out as a table with the following headings:

Time spent	Activity	Equipment needed	Aerobic/ anaerobic	Muscles trained	Review

The review column should be filled in after your session, with comments on your performance and on the suitability of the activity.

If you are doing a one-off training session, you should try to exercise as many different muscle groups as possible.

Merit

Analyse and evaluate the physical training session.

For this outcome, you need to pick out and explain the good and bad features of the training session you did.

Why analyse and evaluate the session?

The purpose of analysing and evaluating the session is to:

- gain an idea of how well you performed the different activities
- assess the suitability of each activity
- find out how your planning and organisation can be improved.

Questions to be asked

Organisation

- Were the activities appropriate for you (or your group)?
- Was the length of the session right?
- Was the time spent on each activity right?

- Was the venue suitable?
- Was all the necessary equipment available?
- Had a risk assessment for the place and activities been carried out?
- Were the health and safety arrangements good?

Activities

- Were the warm-ups and cool-downs effective in preventing problems?
- Did you have a mixture of aerobic and anaerobic activities?
- Which muscle groups were trained?
- Were any muscle groups missed out?
- Which activities seemed most/least valuable?
- Were all activities enjoyable?
- If you were training a group, did you communicate instructions well?
- Were you (or your group) well motivated, and why?
- Was the transition between activities well handled?
- Did you notice any health and safety hazards during the training?

Review

- If there were other participants in your training session, how did you obtain their views on the effectiveness of the session?
- Did your participants (a) enjoy the training and (b) find it useful?
- What comments were made by your tutor or other people who attended/observed your session?
- If you did the training session again, what changes would you make?
- What did you learn about your own (or other people's) fitness needs from the session?

NB A careful review is needed for analysing your training session, and for planning a full training programme later in the year.

Uniformed Service Fitness Tests

Research, explain and undertake the range of uniformed service fitness tests.

Most uniformed services use fitness tests (a) for applicants and (b) for serving personnel (as yearly fitness checks).

For this outcome, you need to:

- find out as much as you can about the fitness tests done in the different uniformed services
- say why the fitness tests are used, and why they are appropriate for each particular service
- do the tests yourself.

The details given in the table below are correct at the time of writing, but subject to change.

Information about fitness tests can be obtained from:

- armed forces recruitment offices
- police recruitment departments
- the headquarters of your local fire and rescue service
- prison service recruitment information
- the internet.

Summary of fitness tests in the uniformed services

	Armed forces	Police	Fire service	Paramedics	Customs and Excise	Prison service	HM Coastguard
For applicants	Yes	Yes	Yes	Yes	No	Yes	At their discretion
Yearly repeat tests	Yes	No	Yes	No	No	Yes	No

COOL SITES:

http://www.fireservice.co.uk/physical.php

http://www.esfb.org/recruitment/recruitment_stage1.htm

https://www.royal-navy.mod.uk/static/pages/4472.html

http://www.lancashire.police.uk/policeofficers.html – but slalom test has been discontinued

http://www.royal-navy.mod.uk/static/pages/2928.html – Royal Marine Reserve – they do the Royal Marines' Commando test!

FOCUS

Prison officer fitness test

'To gain entry to the Prison Service as a Prison Officer you will need to pass the basic job related fitness test, which you will then also be required to pass on an annual basis throughout your career. The test and pass levels are the same for men and women, regardless of age. The standard of fitness required to reach the pass level reflects the physical demands of the job and is easily reached and maintained through regular aerobic exercise. Details of the test are provided below.

Fitness requirements and training

1 Grip Strength
This involves squeezing a dynamometer as tightly as possible to measure the strength of your forearm muscles and grip. Both hands are tested.

2 Endurance Shuttle Run
This test estimates your aerobic endurance and involves running at a progressively faster pace over a 15 metre course until you reach the required level. Inactivity is a key risk factor in coronary heart disease and can lead to other medical and physical problems such as obesity, diabetes, hypertension or injuries to the muscles or bones. Aerobic exercise and endurance are theretore essential, not just for the performance of your duties but for your health in general.

3 Dyno Strength
This measures the strength of the muscles in your upper body and upper arms. These are the muscle groups utilised most in controlling and restraining, pushing and pulling, and the test involves completing a series of pushes and pulls to reach a target level of force.

4 Speed Agility Run
This test measures both your ability to run at pace as well as to negotiate obstacles and change direction. Running at pace, often around objects and corners, is needed when responding quickly to an incident.

5 Shield Technique
This job specific test simulates the static position in which you are required to hold a shield (6 kg) during control and restraint techniques.'

Source: Prison service website
© Crown Copyright

For both the prison service and the police the test is 'job-related'. An explanation is given in the following FOCUS.

FOCUS

New police fitness test

'1 The adjusted job related fitness test will be carefully monitored and the standards validated. It will also be the subject of further research due to be carried out over the next year.

2 The new national job related fitness test consists of three elements:
endurance fitness – the new standard will be level 5 and 4 shuttles (5/4);
static (grip) strength – the pass level will remain at 32 kgs; and
dynamic strength – the pass levels will remain at 34 kgs push and 35 kgs pull.

3 The speed/agility element of the test has been removed. This element of the test was not directly job related and was the most difficult element for women.

The adjustment to the Job Related Fitness Test reflects recent research conducted by the Prison Service (who also use the JRFT).'

Source: Home Office (Bob Ainsworth), May 2003

Pass levels

For many British uniformed services, these are hard to come by, and subject to change. If you need to know these for certain, you are advised to contact the uniformed services directly.

! CHECKPOINT ...

Following criticism by inspectors there has recently been a move to standardise tests, and make the pass-rates easier in the civilian uniformed public services. Why is this – and do you think it's a good thing?

Undertake the range of uniformed service fitness tests

This means, 'take all the uniformed service fitness tests', but as there are a large number, it may cause difficulties. You should consult your tutor about this.

Tests must be done under controlled conditions, *with a qualified instructor present*. You must wear proper clothing: shorts, t-shirt, jogging bottoms, running shoes or suitable trainers. You must be in good health, and if you have not taken a fitness test recently, you should go to the doctor for a check-up.

Ask your tutor if fitness tests can be arranged with local uniformed services. They may be able to help out – and let you use their facilities.

Record all your test scores for future reference.

Fitness tests for the armed forces are more complex and varied than tests used for civilian uniformed services. Examples are shown in the table below, which relates to the Royal Marines Reserve – the volunteer branch of the Royal Marines.

FITNESS TRAINING

PASSGRADE

Explain the different types and methods of circuit training and techniques of running training.

For this outcome, you need to describe and give reasons for the different types of circuit training and running training.

Circuit training is training where you move quickly from one activity to the next, practising several activities in each session. It can take place in a gym, on a playing field or in a clean and well-carpeted room.

Circuit training is good for building general fitness, using a combination of activities designed to improve heart and lung capacity on the one hand, and muscular strength on the other. It can include activities to enhance other components of fitness too, such as speed, stamina, suppleness, skill (coordination) and agility. And it can easily be adapted to improve job-related fitness (the fire service do this with exercises linked to ladder climbing, hose-rolling or firemen's lifts). Circuit training is the best preparation for most uniformed service fitness tests.

Royal Marines Reserve fitness test

Activity	Description	Remarks
Gym tests	VO2 Max – Bleep test Press-ups Sit-ups Pull-ups	20 m shuttle runs 20 min – 60 max 2 minutes) 30 min – 80 max (2 minutes) 3 min – 6 max
Swimming	Breast stroke	At least 50 m
High obstacle test	Taking part in an abseil for example	Designed to test your confidence in dealing with heights
Three mile run	Run wearing training shoes	Complete the run within 22 and a half minutes
Obstacle course	Conducted either using gym course equipment or an actual assault course	Designed to test your stamina and agility

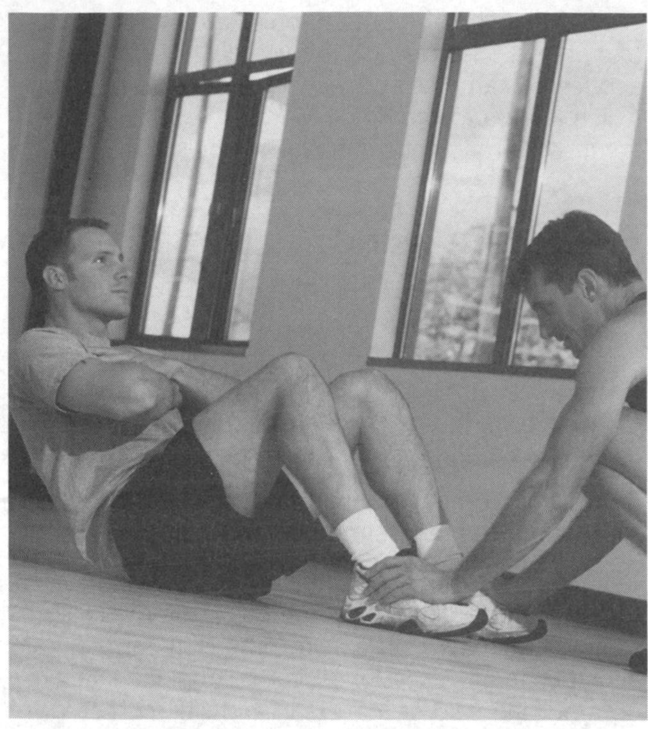

Circuit training can be used to improve any type of fitness.

Types of circuit training

For stamina

Suitable activities include stepping, running, fast walking, using the treadmill, working on an exercise bike, swimming. The aim is to raise the heart-rate to between 70 and 80 per cent of its maximum. If you are 16 your heart rate should be around 150 beats per minute while doing stamina training.

This is called 'aerobic training' – and it has the same aim as aerobics itself – to raise your heart-rate, improve your lung capacity, and develop your slow-twitch muscle fibres. It will increase your endurance, but not your strength.

> **FOCUS**
>
> **How to find your resting heart rate**
> Rest on a bed for about 15 minutes, then count your pulse for exactly 15 seconds. Multiply the figure by 4 and you get your resting heart rate in beats per minute.
>
> **How to calculate your maximum heart-rate**
> The easy way to do this (instead of running until you drop!) is to subtract your age from 220. So, if you are 17 your maximum heart-rate is 203.

For strength

Circuit training for strength requires a variety of activities in which sudden, forceful movements take place, using the maximum power in your muscles. Suitable activities include weight lifting, pull-ups, press-ups, sit-ups, squats and sprinting. Of these, weight-lifting is the most effective. Circuit training for strength is best done in a gym which has weights and other equipment designed to make you exert maximum force with your muscles.

This kind of training raises the heart-rate to 80–90 per cent of its maximum. It is called 'anaerobic training'. It develops the fast-twitch muscle cells and adds strength and bulk to your muscles. It builds your strength but not your stamina.

> **COOL SITE:**
>
> www.brianmac.demon.co.uk/ – incredibly cool site!

For speed

Speed training is a combination of flexibility, skill and strength training. Flexibility is improved by stretching and bending exercises; skill is achieved by studying and practising correct movements (running styles). Both these can be developed by low intensity (aerobic) training. But speed itself requires high intensity anaerobic training, running in explosive bursts over 40–100 metres. The anaerobic muscle-building intensity can only be achieved over bursts of 6 seconds. Anaerobic activities should begin immediately after the warm-up. There should be full recovery between sprints, but short sprints can be repeated up to ten times in a training session.

For flexibility/suppleness

Flexibility is the range of movement possible around joints. There are three main kinds of flexibility exercise. Static stretching means moving into the stretched position and holding that position for about 5 seconds. Abdominal, hamstring and calf stretches are examples. Dynamic stretches are stretching while the body is in continuous slow movement, as in *tai chi*. Training for flexibility can also be done with a partner, but there are risks of injury unless both partners are experienced. Flexibility training, like all circuit training, can be interspersed with aerobic activities such as jogging.

For skill

This kind of training is important for some public services – and for all sports, such as football, tennis and skiing – where skill as well as strength and speed are needed. Skills (e.g. bowling actions in cricket) have to be identified, and the correct actions learned before they can be practised. Coaching is needed for skill training. In a circuit, skill items can be interspersed with aerobic or anaerobic activities.

For agility

Agility is a combination of speed, strength, balance and coordination. It is a vital factor in competitive sports and armed forces training, but has apparently been removed from the police fitness test. Slalom-type exercises (running among obstacles with quick changes of direction) and balancing exercises can used to improve agility.

Useful concepts

Overload

'Overload' means pushing yourself beyond your limits to achieve greater fitness or strength.

Three types of overload

Type	Example	What it increases
More resistance	Lifting heavier weights	Strength
More repetitions	Running more laps	Stamina
More intensity	More repetitions done in the same time	Depends – strength or stamina

Endurance

Endurance means maintaining energy output over a long period of time. In marathon running, this means keeping aerobic activity going for over two (or more!) hours.

Cardiovascular training

This is training which concentrates on aerobic activities, getting the heart-rate up to about 70 per cent of its maximum and keeping it there for, say, half an hour or even longer. It benefits the heart, blood vessels and lungs.

Fartlek training

This is a kind of circuit training where all the activities are running – at different speeds. An example is shown below:

FOCUS

Astrand Fartlek

This is good training for 800 m:

- 10 minutes warm up jog
- Repeat 3 times – maximum effort for 75 seconds, 150 seconds jog run, maximum effort for 60 seconds, 120 seconds jog run
- 10 minute warm down jog.

Source: from Sports Coach website: www.brianmac.demon.co.uk

Gym agility

PASSGRADE

Explain the reasons for gym agility.

For this outcome, you need to:

- explain what agility is
- indicate how it can be developed and tested in the gym
- show how agility is relevant to the work of the uniformed public services.

Agility is a quality which is partly genetically determined. Fast reflexes, excellent balance, and the ability to move in explosive bursts of power may be inbuilt in some people. Nevertheless, agility can be trained and improved, given good motivation and the right exercises.

Higher than average agility is required in some uniformed service work. This is especially true in emergencies, such as rescuing someone from a burning building, hand-to-hand fighting or fleeing from danger on foot. The times when top agility is needed are rare, but it can save lives – your own or someone else's.

In the armed forces and fire service, routine work such as material handling tasks (lifting, lowering, carrying, pushing and pulling) are very important. These tasks require a combination of coordination, balance, strength and speed – in other words, agility.

Agility is trained and tested in the armed forces and the fire service. Assault courses, with their climbing, jumping and balancing components, are above all tests of agility.

Until 2003, most police forces had an agility test in their selection procedures. But the Home Office has decided that the agility of police entrants should no longer be tested, on the grounds that agility is not central to police work.

Agility is a component of 'performance-related fitness', and is therefore likely to be tested in any fitness test which includes job-related features, such as the fire service 'Breathing Apparatus test'. In this test, the candidate has to 'negotiate a 72-metre crawl way wearing a BA set (not started up) and a face mask that is unobscured at the first stage of testing and obscured at the second stage.' Agility is also a factor in the prison service shield test, and in skills such as 'control and restraint', which are needed in prison service work.

'He's practising for his fire service fitness test, Miss.'

Merit

Analyse the different types and methods of circuit training and the techniques used when running training.

For this outcome, you need to:

- do as much circuit training of your own as you can under the eye of an experienced, trained instructor
- note down different kinds of circuit training and try them – to see how well they suit you
- read about the theory of circuit training – in particular the difference between aerobic and anaerobic training
- show how different types of circuit training develop different components of fitness
- find out how to reduce the risks of certain problems and injuries which can result from the wrong kind of circuit training
- investigate how the needs for circuit training evolve in an individual who is becoming progressively fitter
- discover how frequently circuit-training sessions should be undertaken, and how to avoid overtraining
- talk to other people about their experiences of circuit training, its benefits and its drawbacks
- research how circuit training could benefit job-related fitness and strength as tested by the uniformed services
- comment in depth on different types of circuit training, especially their uses, what components of fitness they develop, their suitability for different people, their advantages and their drawbacks.

FOCUS

Components of fitness

- **Health components:**
  - cardiovascular fitness (a healthy heart, blood vessels and lungs)
  - body composition (the percentage of fat in your body)
  - flexibility (free movement at the joints)
  - muscular endurance
  - muscular strength

These are all linked to general health, strength and well-being.

- **Performance-related components:**
  - agility
  - balance
  - coordination
  - speed
  - power

These are linked to skill and effectiveness in sport or physical work.

Profile

Analysis of a circuit training routine

Activities

Treadmill, press-ups, squat jumps, sit-ups, squat thrusts, bench dips

Times

30 seconds' work on each exercise with a 30-second recovery between each exercise. 5 sets with a 3-minute recovery between each set. Each training session therefore lasts 45 minutes in all.

There should be a four-week cycle: an easy week, medium week, hard week and a recovery week. Progress should be monitored. If on-going improvement is needed there should be an increase in *repetitions* for more cardiovascular fitness, or an increase in *resistance* or *intensity* for more strength benefits.

This would be a good circuit for increasing both aerobic fitness and strength. However, it does not set out to improve agility, speed, flexibility or balance. It would be useful for improving general fitness before a public service fitness test, but it would not develop any performance related fitness.

Professional athletes need more focused circuits than this one, based on the requirements of their sport. And firefighters, for example, might prefer a circuit that develops special skills such as hose-rolling or ladder-climbing.

Undertake a training programme

PASSGRADE

Design, plan and complete a training programme in preparation for an entry test to a uniformed service incorporating the fitness types and techniques.

A training programme is a timetable of physical activities which is intended to build your fitness to the desired level within a fixed period of time.

For this outcome, you need to:

- make your major decisions for a training programme in the design stage
- work out the details and write them down in your planning stages (a) and (b)
- do the training programme
- keep a record of everything you do at each stage (this is needed for the next outcome).

Design stage

You need to decide:

- your present level of fitness, and your general fitness needs
- the aims of the programme. If the aim is to prepare yourself for the fitness entry test to a uniformed service, you should include activities which are done in the test. If not, you should base the aims of the programme on your fitness needs
- the length of the programme. For real life purposes (especially for a uniformed services fitness test), 12 weeks would be a good length. This should ensure a definite improvement in fitness or strength
- the frequency of training sessions. Three or four times a week is ideal for serious training. Less than this, and your gains will not be as great. More than this and you risk over-training.

Planning stage (a)

Work out:

- a number of circuit-training ideas to produce (say) four circuit training routines of increasing difficulty. These should be numbered 1–4. The increase in difficulty should not be too great between one circuit and the next, but circuit 4 should be at the level you want to be at when you finish your 12 weeks' training. The circuit must contain activities which will build the kind of fitness or strength you want. If you want to build flexibility, your circuit must contain stretching exercises. If you want to build strength, you must include weight-lifting
- a number of running ideas to improve cardiovascular fitness. These can be straightforward distance running, but if you want to increase strength as well you should include some fartlek training
- warm-up and cool-down exercises
- where you are going to do your training (e.g. Anytown Leisure Centre)
- when you are going to do your training (e.g. Monday evening, Wednesday evening, Saturday afternoon)
- how long each circuit training session should last (e.g. 45 minutes)
- what clothing or special equipment you need.

Safety

Carry out a risk assessment of the activities you plan to do, and the places where you intend to do them. Write down your findings, together with any health and safety precautions you intend to take.

If you have never done a training programme before, or if you are unsure about your health, see a doctor and have a check-up before you go any further.

Planning stage (b)

Write down your training programme so that you can follow it easily, and make notes on how well it is going. The plan could take the form of a grid, or timetable like the one below.

At the top of the next page are details of the four circuits. They aim for general fitness improvement – especially of the aerobic/cardiovascular type. Since

Profile

Name ______________________ Age ____

Present fitness __________________ Fitness needs/aim ______________

Week no.	Monday	Tuesday	Wednesday	Thursday	Friday	Saturday	Sunday
1 *Notes*	Circuit 1		Run			Circuit 1	
2 *Notes*	Circuit 1		Circuit 1			Run	
3 *Notes*	Run		Circuit 1			Circuit 1	
4 *Notes*	Circuit 2		Run			Circuit 2	
5 *Notes*	Circuit 2		Circuit 2			Run	
6 *Notes*	Run		Circuit 2			Circuit 2	
7 *Notes*	Circuit 3		Run			Circuit 3	
8 *Notes*	Circuit 3		Circuit 3			Run	
9 *Notes*	Run		Circuit 3			Circuit 3	
10 *Notes*	Circuit 4		Run			Circuit 4	
11 *Notes*	Circuit 4		Circuit 4			Run	
12 *Notes*	Run		Circuit 4			Circuit 4	

Your timetable should contain room below each week for notes recording your progress and comments.

The four circuits

Circuit no.	Press-ups	Standing squats	Lunges	Triceps press	Jog on spot	Dorsal raise	Sit-ups
1	10 reps followed by 10 step-ups	10 reps followed by 10 step-ups	10 reps followed by 10 step-ups	10 reps followed by 10 step-ups	30 seconds	10 reps followed by 10 step-ups	10 reps followed by 10 step-ups
2	15 reps followed by 15 step-ups	15 reps followed by 15 step-ups	15 reps followed by 15 step-ups	15 reps followed by 15 step-ups	40 seconds	15 reps followed by 15 step-ups	15 reps followed by 15 step-ups
3	20 reps followed by 20 step-ups	20 reps followed by 20 step-ups	20 reps followed by 20 step-ups	20 reps followed by 20 step-ups	50 seconds	20 reps followed by 20 step-ups	20 reps followed by 20 step-ups
4	25 reps followed by 25 step-ups	25 reps followed by 25 step-ups	25 reps followed by 25 step-ups	25 reps followed by 25 step-ups	60 seconds	25 reps followed by 25 step-ups	25 reps followed by 25 step-ups

they increase repetitions rather than intensity they would improve your aerobic fitness more than your strength.

The step-ups which follow each activity should be on to a 12-inch bench or step. Between each activity you should allow yourself a 2-minute rest.

Doing the programme

Carry it out as you have planned. If there are any problems (e.g. illness), let your tutor know. Check with your tutor that you are getting the evidence you need (e.g. a signed sheet) that you are completing the outcome.

Recording progress

Make notes in the spaces on your training timetable about each session soon after you have done it. Monitor your improvement using one of the methods given on the next page.

All the records you keep will be needed for the next outcome – the last in this unit.

CHECKPOINT ...

When athletes do a training programme they pay close attention to what they eat.

1 Research a healthy diet for someone who is training hard.

2 What differences do you notice between the diets of people who are training for stamina, and those who are training for strength?

3 How could you alter your own diet to take into account the fact that you are training?

http://www.hantsfire.gov.uk/jobs/fitness.html/ – top fitness tips for recruits!

Distinction

Evaluate and justify own performance and the training programme.

For this outcome, you need to:

- examine your own performance (in your training programme)
- decide what your fitness strengths and weaknesses are
- make recommendations for improving your fitness in the future
- assess the good and bad points of your training programme

- suggest ways your training programme could have been improved.

Your conclusions should be supported by evidence and reasoning.

Evaluating and justifying performance

How do you know if you did well or badly in your training programme? There are four questions you should ask yourself:

How much did I improve during the programme?

To be able to answer this question you need some quantitative (measurable) evidence. There are three possible ways of getting this evidence.

- If you are aiming to develop cardiovascular fitness, you could get this evidence by measuring your heart-rate immediately after a standard activity, e.g. stepping up and down on to a step of fixed height for one minute at a pre-determined speed. The lower the heart-rate, the fitter you are getting.
- If you are aiming for strength, you could judge your progress by your ability to lift heavier weights as the training programme progresses.
- You can also test your progress using an activity used in a public service fitness test, e.g. a bleep test or shuttle run (otherwise known as a multi-stage fitness test). By doing a shuttle run before your programme starts, and after it finishes, you can find out if your training programme would help you pass a public service fitness test. You could then include this finding in your evaluation of your training programme.

How do my scores (times), etc. compare with those of other people in my group?

The answer to this question may tell you something about your strength and fitness, as compared with that of other people of the same age as you. It won't tell you anything about the effectiveness of your training programme. This is not an accurate way of judging performance, and there is a risk of demotivating yourself or others by making unfavourable comparisons.

How does my improvement compare with that of other people in my group?

This is different from simply comparing fitness. If A improves more than B during a 12-week training programme, it could mean one or more of the following:

- A's training programme is better than B's.
- A has worked harder at his or her training programme than B has.
- A has been doing some other training outside the training programme.
- B is in poor health.
- B's programme concentrated on strength while A's programme concentrated on aerobic fitness.
- B was fitter than A to begin with.

It is easy to overlook the last of these possibilities – but it is one of the most important. Gaining fitness is rather like losing weight – it is easy when you start but gets progressively more difficult. A person who is totally unfit will benefit enormously from a simple training programme. But a top-class athlete has to really struggle to get that extra tenth of a second's advantage!

CHECKPOINT ...

Why is it more difficult to make gains in strength than to make gains in aerobic fitness?

How do my training programme scores compare with the pass levels for my chosen public service?

You can only answer this question if your training programme contains the same activities as the fitness test of your chosen public service.

Some public services do not issue pass levels for their physical entrance tests so you cannot always make this kind of comparison. Where a pass level for entrants is available, you can compare your performance with the standard they are looking for.

Evaluating and justifying the training programme

You should do this by asking yourself – and answering – these questions:

- Was the training programme really suited to my fitness level and needs?
- In what ways was it good, and in what ways was it inadequate?
- Was I able to follow the programme conscientiously?

- Did I enjoy doing the programme (why?) – or didn't I (why not?)
- Were there problems in setting up the programme and in the facilities available?
- Did I suffer any health or injury problems during the programme? Why?
- Did I make any adjustments to the programme as I went along – and why?
- Were the methods I used for recording progress adequate?
- Would the programme help me to get into a uniformed public service?
- Did the programme motivate me?
- Did other people make comments that I ought to 'take on board'?
- Should I continue fitness and/or strength training?

CHECKPOINT ...

1 For many kinds of training it is best to have a training partner. Why?
2 What are the qualities of a good training partner?
3 Does a fitness programme have to consist of circuit training, or would it be equally useful to do, say, a half-mile swim every day?
4 Some people overtrain. Why do they do it, and what are the symptoms – and dangers?
5 Why are fitness and strength training (normally) good for your health?
6 What are the symptoms of dehydration – and how is it prevented ... and treated?
7 You learn that your friend, who wants to be an army officer, is taking drugs to increase muscle bulk and strength. What would you say to them?

Unit 10 Democratic Processes

Grading criteria

PASSGRADE	Merit	Distinction
To achieve a pass grade the evidence must show that the learner is able to:	To achieve a merit grade the evidence must show that the learner is able to:	To achieve a distinction grade the evidence must show that the learner is able to:
• identify the main concepts of a representative democracy **191** • explain the workings of the voting process and systems **193** • describe the separation of powers, institutions of powers and the role of elected representatives **197** • summarise the structures of the British governmental system including the European dimension **199** • give an overview of the main beliefs of political parties **202** • identify the influence on the public services of the government in power **206** • research a political issue, giving your own balanced conclusions **207**	• demonstrate understanding of the importance of a representative democracy and problems with the present voting system **195** • briefly analyse the functions of the Houses of Parliament **200** • give a detailed understanding of the main ideologies of at least two political parties **204** • review and analyse appropriate recent information on a political issue **207**	• evaluate the present voting system and suggest alternatives which are fully justified and valid **197** • critically evaluate the ideology of two political parties **205** • review and evaluate a political issue, which demonstrates a wide variety of arguments and research, giving detailed and relevant conclusions with a reasoned evaluation of possible future events **207** • present information which is coherently organised with accurate use of political terms and logical arguments, giving own conclusions, which are fully justified and valid **208**

This unit explains what democracy is, shows how it works in the UK, and outlines its importance for the public services.

REPRESENTATIVE DEMOCRACY

PASSGRADE

Identify the main concepts of a representative democracy.

For this outcome, you need to find and explain briefly the main political ideas used in describing a democratic system.

FOCUS

Definitions of democracy

Democracy is ...

'government by the people or their elected representatives' – *Collins English Dictionary*

'government of the people, by the people, for the people' – Abraham Lincoln, US President, 1863. Lincoln was later assassinated.

'two wolves and a sheep debating about what to have for dinner' – popular American definition

'a system of government that meets three essential conditions: meaningful and extensive competition among individuals and groups (especially political parties) for all effective positions of government power, at regular intervals and excluding the use of force; a highly inclusive level of political participation in the selection of leaders and policies, at least through regular, free and fair elections, such that no major (adult) social group is excluded; and a level of civil and political liberties – freedom of expression, freedom of the press, freedom to form and join organizations – sufficient to ensure the integrity of political competition and participation.' – Diamond, L., Linz, J. and Seymour, M.L. (eds) (1988), *Democracy in Developing Countries*, Boulder: Lynne Rienner

'A representative democracy is defined as a political system where government is empowered by the consent of the people, power is exercised by elected officials, rights and liberties are guaranteed, and the government and people are under the rule of law.' – *Ohio Proficiency Test Fact Sheet Grade-Nine Citizenship*

http://www.darke.k12.oh.us/ss9prof.html – doesn't look promising, but it's full of brilliant definitions

FOCUS

Political words

anarchy – lack of leadership, a free-for-all

aristocracy – a ruling class of old, rich families (important in the UK up to 1999, when nine-tenths of the 'hereditary peers' were removed from the House of Lords)

authoritarian government – a government which does not allow freedom of speech

capitalism – an economic system where people pay little tax and are encouraged to get rich. The USA is the best example of a capitalist country. The UK is (very roughly!) 60 per cent capitalist and 40 per cent socialist.

communism – an extreme form of socialism, based on equality, collective ownership and workers' power

constituency – the area, town, etc. represented by an MP

democracy – rule by the people's elected representatives

despotism – the same as 'tyranny' below

elections – a system of voting to choose MPs

elite – any 'superior' or ruling group. Elitism is the giving of power to such a group.

dictatorship – a form of government with one leader who rules by decree (direct command), e.g. Iraq under Saddam Hussein

liberalism – *either* uncontrolled capitalism (US meaning) *or* government which allows free choice yet also tries to help the poor (modern UK meaning)

Marxism – communism or socialism based on the ideas of Karl Marx, e.g. of a 'class war' between 'the workers' and the 'bourgeoisie' (bosses)

Members of Parliament – people elected to represent a constituency

meritocracy – rule by the 'best people' ('clever', 'well-educated', etc.)

mob-rule – the type of democracy in which the people who shout loudest get what they want

monarchy – rule by a king or queen

oligarchy – rule by a small elite (group of rich, powerful or privileged people)

pluralism – a diversity of social, economic or political institutions or systems. The UK is a pluralistic country.

politics – how power is held, shared or used; the study of power and its use

representation – the process of sending people to a government assembly (e.g. Parliament) to speak up for (represent) local people

socialism – an economic system based on greater equality, and giving more power and wealth to ordinary people

theocracy – government where political leaders are also religious leaders, e.g. Iran

tyranny – rule by someone who grabs power and uses it selfishly and cruelly

Athenian democracy

Ancient Athens was the world's first democracy, with its first parliament. Politics and the idea of public service were invented there.

Many books have been written about Athenian democracy. You will find stuff about it in all encyclopaedias and on many cool websites. On the internet, search terms such as 'Athenian democracy' will also yield information on this interesting subject. You could also look up names such as Aristotle, Plato, Socrates, Solon, Cleisthenes and Pericles.

http://www.chs.harvard.edu/online_disc/athenian_law/lect_blackwell_intro_ovr.htm

http://www.bbc.co.uk/history/ancient/greeks/greekcritics_01.shtml

Representation

This is the process of communicating the ideas of ordinary people to the government. 'Representative democracy' means democracy with a system of representation.

In the UK, the people are represented by

- councillors – representation in local government
- Members of Parliament (MPs) – representation in central government
- the media, who publicise things that concern people
- pressure groups, who represent people who feel strongly about something, e.g. GM foods
- trade unions, who represent workers when negotiating with employers or the government, e.g. the Fire Brigades Union, UNISON
- charities, who publicise the problems of the poor
- political parties, who represent people with certain political opinions.

Other organisations such as the courts, opinion pollsters, the churches, community leaders and teams of government inspectors also have roles in representing the concerns of ordinary people to the government.

Political equality

This is the concept of 'one person one vote'. Every free British citizen aged 18+ is allowed to vote.

Political freedom

This is a human right. As well as the right to vote it includes:

- the right to believe what you want
- the right to join an organisation
- the right to demonstrate (i.e. march peacefully with banners, etc.).

Political pluralism

This is the system of having political parties. A political party (e.g. Labour, Conservative) is an association of like-minded people who tend to agree on how the country should be run. Different political parties have different ideas about how the country should be run.

More on political parties on page 203 below.

CHECKPOINT ...

Make a list of all the political parties which send MPs to Parliament.

'We've made a democratic decision that we're not going to do your assignment, sir.'

POLITICAL INSTITUTIONS

The voting process and systems

PASSGRADE

Explain the workings of the voting process and systems.

For this outcome, you need to explain:

- what voting is
- why voting is used
- different methods of organising votes
- different methods of casting and counting votes.

FOCUS

Definition of voting

Voting is ...

'a usually formal expression of opinion or will in response to a proposed decision; especially: one given as an indication of approval or disapproval of a proposal, motion, or candidate for office'
– *Webster's Dictionary*

Voting is a way of recording the opinions of a large number of people on a given question.

Examples of situations when voting is used in the UK:

- choosing Members of Parliament
- deciding Parliamentary debates
- choosing Members of the European Parliament
- choosing local councillors
- choosing mayors
- choosing trade union representatives
- choosing members of the boards of large companies
- finding out what people think about a major question (e.g. Should Britain join the euro?)
- finding out if a group of students want a day trip to Blackpool *or* to Alton Towers.

! CHECKPOINT ...

1 Voting in the UK is now almost always done secretly, but in the past, trade union ballots and others were often done with a show of hands. This system is still used in party conferences. What are its advantages and disadvantages?

2 Voting by texting and telephoning is used in TV programmes such as *Fame Academy* and *Big Brother*. Could this method be used in politics?

The act of voting to choose MPs and other representatives is called an election. (The words 'poll' and 'ballot' have a similar meaning.) Elections which take place in the UK include:

- general election – an election to choose all the MPs for the House of Commons
- by-election – an election to choose an MP for one constituency (if the sitting MP dies or resigns)
- local election – an election choosing councillors for local government
- European election – an election choosing members of the European Parliament
- referendum – a national poll organised by the government to find out what people think about a specific political issue (e.g. the euro)
- trade union ballot – a vote by trade unionists to decide whether to take industrial action, or to choose trade union officials.

Voting systems

Different countries or organisations have different voting systems. Here are some examples:

First past the post
The voting paper contains a short list of (say) five candidates and the political parties they belong to. There is one blank column next to the names. The voter puts one cross by the name of the candidate they want to see elected. The candidate with the most votes wins the election.

This system is used in British general and local elections.

Supplementary vote
The voting paper has a short list of candidates, this time with two columns next to them. Voters put one X in the first column for their first-choice candidate, and one X in the second column for their second choice candidate. If a candidate gets more than 50 per cent of all the first choice votes, they are elected. If not, the two candidates with the highest number of first choice votes are kept, and the rest discarded. All the second choice votes for the two highest candidates are allocated to the candidates they were given to. The candidate with the highest total number of votes (first and second choice) wins the election.

This system is used to elect the mayor of London.

Alternative vote
In this system there is only one column next to the names on the ballot paper. Voters rank the candidates in order of preference, i.e. 1, 2, 3, 4, 5. If a candidate gets over 50 per cent from first choice votes, that candidate wins. But if no candidate reaches the 50 per cent mark, the second choices for the last candidate are distributed to the other candidates, and counted as if they were first-choice votes. If there is still no candidate above the 50 per cent mark the second votes for the next lowest candidate are redistributed. This goes on until a candidate has more than 50 per cent of the vote – and becomes the winner.

This is the system used in Australia.

Single transferable vote
Each constituency (voting area) can elect several MPs. There may be 20 or more names on each voting paper. Voters rank the candidates in order of preference – 1, 2, 3, and so on.

A quota (or minimum number of votes needed for winning) is calculated before the votes are counted. The quota is the number of votes cast divided by the number of MPs allowed for the constituency plus 1.

Any candidate with enough first-choice votes to reach the quota is elected. Surplus votes for that candidate are ignored, but the second choice votes on those ballot papers are then treated as first choice votes and redistributed to the candidates they were given to.

Redistribution of second choice votes (first from elected candidates, then from the bottom candidates) goes on until enough candidates have reached the quota.

This system is used in the Irish Republic, and in Northern Ireland for European and local elections.

Closed party list system
Voters vote for a political party rather than a candidate, though lists of candidates are published for each constituency. The order of candidates is determined by the party's preference. Each constituency elects a number of MPs. After the election MPs are chosen from the party lists in the proportion in which the parties received votes in that constituency. So if a constituency was allowed to send 10 MPs to the national parliament, and five parties, A, B, C, D and E scored 30, 40, 20, 0 and 10 per cent of the votes respectively, Party A would have three MPs, Party B, four MPs, Party C, two MPs, Party D, no MPs and Party E, one MP.

This is the system used in Germany and Israel.

Open party list system
Voters vote twice, once for the parties, once for the candidates. The order of the candidates in the party lists then depends on the voters' preference, rather than the party's preference. But the number of MPs for each party depends on the party votes, not the candidate votes.

This system is used in Denmark, Finland, Italy, Luxembourg, Switzerland and the Philippines.

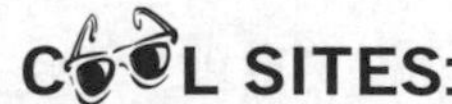

http://www.electoral-reform.org.uk/index.htm – top site giving advantages and disadvantages of each voting system

http://www.charter88.org.uk/home.html – cool but more technical

http://www.Georgetown.edu/faculty/kingch/Electoral_Systems.htm

Merit

Demonstrate understanding of the importance of a representative democracy and problems with the present voting system.

For this outcome, use your own words to explain:

- the rights and responsibilities which representative democracy gives people
- its effect on the economy (i.e. the creation and distribution of wealth)
- political stability
- human rights and diversity
- law, order and the public services
- the media
- a country's relationships with other countries
- strengths and weaknesses of representative democracy.

In a separate section, discuss the weaknesses of the voting system,

It can be assumed that 'the present voting system' referred to is the first-past-the-post system used in the UK for general and local council elections.

Importance of a representative democracy

Representative democracy is important first because most of the world's rich and powerful countries are representative democracies. These countries include the UK, the USA, the EU countries, Russia, Japan, South Korea, Canada, Mexico, Jamaica, Australia, New Zealand, India, South Africa, Chile and Brazil. Countries with little or no representative democracy, such as North Korea, Saudi Arabia, Somalia, Liberia, the Congo, Zimbabwe and Iraq, have serious political and economic problems.

Importance of representation

- It promotes political stability by allowing people to protest, complain and say what they think to the government, e.g. by voting, writing to their MP, demonstrating or going on strike.
- Representative democracies hold full and fair elections at 4–5 year intervals, so people can vote to change the government.
- Without representative democracy, there is a big risk that the government can only be changed through terrorism or civil war.
- It ensures that the government knows what people want, and that they try to do it.

Importance of political equality

- The fact that all adults are allowed to vote means that the poor, as well as the rich, have a say in choosing the government.
- Political equality is a necessary basis for a non-discriminatory society.
- It allows the government to reflect more accurately the wishes of different sections of the population – including women and ethnic minorities.

NB Young people (under 18), prisoners, people who are mentally ill and people who live in the UK but are not British citizens are not allowed to vote and so do not have this political equality.

Importance of political freedom

- It helps to guarantee human rights, by giving everyone a right to express their political views.
- Most representative democracies (but not the UK) have a written constitution which guarantees the rights of their citizens. The US Constitution, the new EU Constitution, and the French Constitution are examples.
- Political freedom gives citizens full human rights – the ones given in the United Nations Universal Declaration of Human Rights, or the European Convention.
- Political freedom also carries important responsibilities – if that freedom is to be permanent. These responsibilities are (a) to vote according to conscience, (b) to obey the law, and (c) to respect the community.
- It allows freedom of speech and expression, for individuals and for the media.

Importance of political pluralism

Pluralism, the mixture of capitalist and socialist systems, allows a country both to generate wealth (through free enterprise) and to distribute that wealth where needed (through taxation and effective public services).

Having different political parties with different ideologies, some capitalist, some socialist, gives people a real choice of government – rather than just 'more of the same'.

Weaknesses of representative democracy

These include:

- the risk of degenerating into mob-rule
- the fact that it can seem boring, incomprehensible or irrelevant, with the result that people don't bother to vote, and the government is therefore less representative
- the exploitation of poor countries by rich democratic countries
- the ease with which public opinion in democratic countries can be manipulated through the media by governments
- the inability or unwillingness of representative democracies to control global warming and protect the world environment.

> **!** CHECKPOINT ...
>
> 'Representative democracy is a luxury that only rich countries can afford.' How true is this statement?

Problems with the present voting system

The aims of a voting system are to register the views of the electorate (i.e. the whole population eligible to vote) as fully, accurately and cheaply as possible.

Problems with the first-past-the-post system as used in the UK are that:

- most votes are wasted, since they are cast for candidates who do not get elected
- candidates are chosen by the parties they belong to, not the public – so this aspect of the election is undemocratic
- there are big differences in the populations of different constituencies. A vote in a small constituency is worth more than a vote in a big constituency, since it takes fewer votes to elect an MP in a small constituency than in a large one
- smaller political parties are discriminated against in the present system. The table below shows the results of this discrimination on the three biggest parties in the 2001 General election
- If the parties had won seats in proportion to the total number of votes cast for them in the country, Labour would have done much worse, and the Conservatives and Liberal Democrats would have done much better than they actually did in 2001. This is the most obvious fault of the British voting system, and it has led to frequent calls for 'proportional representation' – systems of voting which would reflect more accurately the way the country voted. These were examined in great detail in the Jenkins Report of 1998.
- There can be a problem with constituency boundaries. These are redrawn about every ten years, by the Boundary Commission. The risk is that the boundaries will be redrawn to favour one party rather than another.
- The system encourages people to vote to get rid of the candidate they don't like, rather than to choose the candidate they do like. This is called 'tactical voting'.
- Parties can gang up to keep a third party out (see example).

How parties can gang up: Anytown East Constituency

Candidate	Herbert Whinge	Mona Lott	Titus Groan
Party	Labour	Liberal Democrat	Conservative
1992 Election votes	25,006	20,002	30,711
1997 Election votes	45,008	Did not stand	30,711

- In 1992 Titus Groan was elected as MP, because he got the most votes. Everybody who voted in 1992 wanted to vote in exactly the same way in 1997. But this time Labour won the seat

Results of 2001 General Election

Party	Percentage of vote	Number of MPs (Total is 659, but some MPs belong to other parties)	Number of MPs it should have been, if proportional to percentage of vote
Labour	40.7	412	268
Conservative	31.7	166	209
Liberal Democrats	18.5	52	122

because Mona Lott dropped out (knowing that her supporters all hated the Conservatives!). Of course it is rarely as simple as this – but this kind of undemocratic 'fiddle' is possible under the present voting system.

- The present voting system seems not to be popular with the voters. In 2001 only 59.4 per cent of people eligible to vote actually voted. A change of voting system might make more people bother to vote. The Australian system of compulsory voting has even been suggested.
- In the UK, you can get married or die for your country as a soldier when you are 16. But you are not allowed to vote until you are 18.
- In the present system people have to go out to polling stations and put a piece of paper in a box. This discriminates against people with mobility problems, or people who work during polling hours. Experiments are now being tried with postal voting, and further experiments with telephone, electronic or internet voting are being considered.

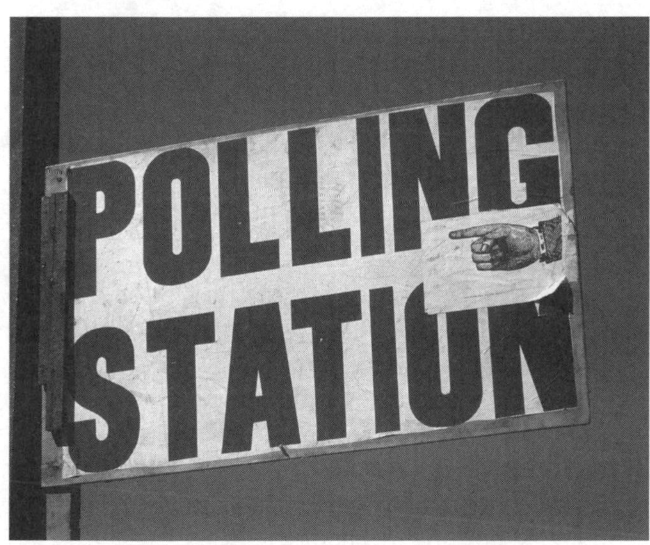

Without polling stations the UK wouldn't be a free country

> **!** CHECKPOINT ...
>
> Think about these questions:
> 1 Why do many young people not bother to vote?
> 2 What do you suggest to get people more interested in voting?
> 3 Why is it a good thing for the country if everybody votes?

Distinction

> Evaluate the present voting system and suggest alternatives which are fully justified and valid.

For this outcome, you need to:

- explain, with reasons, the strengths and weaknesses of the first-past-the-post system
- put forward other kinds of voting system which could be used
- state clearly why they would (or might) be better than the present system
- support your ideas fully, with convincing arguments.

A number of voting systems, already used in various countries, and even in some British elections, are given above. The strengths and weaknesses of the present system are given above on page 196.

To evaluate the present system, you should look at the following main questions:

- Does it choose the candidates that people really want?
- Does it give minority parties a fair chance?
- Does it encourage everybody to vote?
- In what ways can the system be fiddled, and is there a serious risk that the wrong candidate might 'win' by fraudulent means?
- Is it as cheap and efficient as possible?
- Can it be understood by the ordinary voter?

Separation of powers

> Describe the separation of powers, institutions of powers and the role of elected representatives.

> **FOCUS**
>
> **Definition of separation of powers**
>
> Separation of powers is ...
>
> 'limiting the powers of government by separating governmental functions into the executive, legislative, and judiciary' – *Hutchinson Encyclopaedia*

For this outcome, you need to:

- say what 'separation of powers means' and why it matters
- say what the 'institutions of powers' are, and outline what they do
- describe the role of MPs.

The separation of powers is the idea that a democratic government has three branches, or functions: the legislature, the judiciary and the executive.

Separation of powers

	Power		
	Legislature	**Judiciary**	**Executive**
What it does	Makes the law	Interprets the law	Carries out the law
Who does it	Parliament	The Lord Chancellor and the courts	Government ministers, departments, civil service and the police

In the UK, the separation of powers is not complete. This is mainly because the House of Commons has so much power that it can, in theory, override other branches of government. Another reason why powers are not fully separated is that government ministers are also MPs. The third problem is that the Lord Chancellor belongs to both the executive and the legislature. But his role is going to be abolished in 2004. If the new proposed Supreme Court is set up, and planned changes in the function of the House of Lords go through, the separation of powers in the UK will be greater in the future than it was in the past.

Separation of powers is necessary in a representative democracy. It is one of a number of 'checks and balances' which help control the government and prevent it from becoming a tyranny.

Institutions of powers

- **The legislature** is Parliament – the House of Commons and the House of Lords.
- **The executive** consists of the government, run by ministers, local government and public corporations, including the uniformed public services. The courts have executive roles in upholding the law, but judicial roles in questioning and interpreting the law.
- **The judiciary** consists of judges and lawyers who interpret the law, especially common law. They do not make new laws, but decide how the laws we already have should be applied.

LINK! Institutions are defined and explained on page 112.

The role of elected representatives

In Britain these elected representatives are called Members of Parliament (MPs). They are elected at general elections by the public in the constituency (area) they represent. Unless they die or resign they continue to represent their constituency for at least four or five years (the normal period of time between general elections). Often they are re-elected and serve for much longer than that.

Most MPs belong to a political party, and broadly agree with the views of that party.

MPs have a Code of Conduct which states that they must carry out their duties with selflessness, integrity, objectivity, accountability, openness, honesty and leadership. They must always act 'in the public interest'.

Their roles are to:

- represent their constituents, by letting Parliament know what their constituents think and by letting their constituents know what is going on in government
- raise issues in the House of Commons through oral questions, adjournment detates, early day motions and private members' bills
- present petitions (lists of names of people who feel strongly about an issue – such as a new law) from constituents to Parliament
- take part and vote in debates (i.e. give their opinions of government policies, new laws etc.). Normally MPs vote in support of their party, but they do not have to if this goes against their conscience. In such cases they can 'abstain' (not vote) or even vote against the wishes of their own party
- take office in government if asked to do so
- sit in parliamentary committees which specialise in dealing with certain problems and issues (e.g. Education and Skills)

- listen to local pressure groups
- listen to complaints and problems from constituents at a local 'surgery' (arranged time and place)
- help solve individuals' problems, especially where they concern central government, e.g. problems to do with income tax, the NHS, pensions and Home Office matters such as imprisonment or immigration. MPs do this by writing letters to government departments and officials, writing to government ministers or seeing government ministers personally.

THE STRUCTURE OF BRITISH GOVERNMENT

> Summarise the structures of the British governmental system including the European dimension.

For this outcome, you need to:

- outline the way the British government is organised
- give the main facts about the main players (people and institutions)
- show where the EU government fits into the British system.

This is a big subject, so note the word 'summarise'. Do not try to go into too much detail!

'Structures of the governmental system' are the organisations within it, and the relationships between those organisations.

http://www.parliament.uk/works/index.cfm

The organisations within government

The Prime Minister

Chosen by MPs of his (or her) party, the Prime Minister leads the government, runs Cabinet meetings, represents the country abroad at the highest level and makes major decisions such as whether to go to war. The Prime Minister has a second-in-command, the Deputy Prime Minister.

The Cabinet

The Cabinet consists of about 20 ministers, each of whom heads a government department (e.g. the Home Office or the Ministry of Defence). The Cabinet meets once a week to discuss major issues. The ministers are all senior MPs chosen by the Prime Minister.

The Treasury

The Treasury is the government department which controls government income and spending. It is headed by the Chancellor of the Exchequer, a senior minister who is also a member of the Cabinet.

Government departments and ministries

Each has a clearly defined role, e.g. Ministry of Defence. These are large organisations, each headed by a Cabinet minister and staffed by civil servants.

Parliament

Parliament is the name given to the House of Commons and the House of Lords, and the committees and institutions attached to these.

- The House of Commons is the most powerful body in British politics. In it the 659 MPs debate (discuss and vote on) new laws and any other major issues affecting the country.
- The House of Lords is sometimes called the Upper House, but it is less powerful than the House of Commons because its members are chosen, not elected. Its job is to scrutinise (examine) new laws referred to them from the House of Commons. It can criticise and delay bills but not veto them. The House of Lords can also act as a court, but this may stop in the near future. In 2003 there were 598 lords (including 26 Anglican bishops).

The Privy Council

This is a body of 474 senior MPs whose main job is to advise the Queen on her ceremonial duties or rights as a monarch.

Parliamentary committees

- **Standing committees** scrutinise the wording of new laws, making sure that they mean exactly what they say, and reflect both the wishes of Parliament and the best interests of the public.
- **Joint committees** have members from both the House of Commons and the House of Lords. They discuss some new laws and some general issues such as human rights.
- **Select committees** investigate problems in specific areas, e.g. whether the education system should be changed. They usually consist of about 15 MPs who are interested in their subject. They

produce reports and make recommendations to Parliament.

The Civil Service

These are public service workers – 500,000 up and down the country – who collect information for the government and, together with other public services, carry out the government's work. They range from highly paid experts and advisers to office workers and receptionists. HM Customs and Excise is a branch of the Civil Service.

Local government

This is regionally based and consists of local authorities, metropolitan councils, district councils, etc. It is overseen by the Office of the Deputy Prime Minister (which also oversees the fire service). Most decisions in local government are made by locally elected councillors, who debate local issues in much the same way as MPs debate national issues. Local government has a big say in local education, policing and health care. Civil servants put the councillors' decisions into practice.

Quangos

This acronym means Quasi-Autonomous Non-Governmental Organisations. They work with the government but are independent from it. Organisations such as the Commission for Racial Equality, which deals with race-related problems, Ofsted, which inspects schools and the Police Complaints Authority are examples. Their job is to monitor government systems and call for change if they think it is needed.

The monarchy

LINK! See Unit 4, page 88.

European Union

The EU is not part of the British government but it has a growing effect on the way the UK is governed and the kind of laws we have.

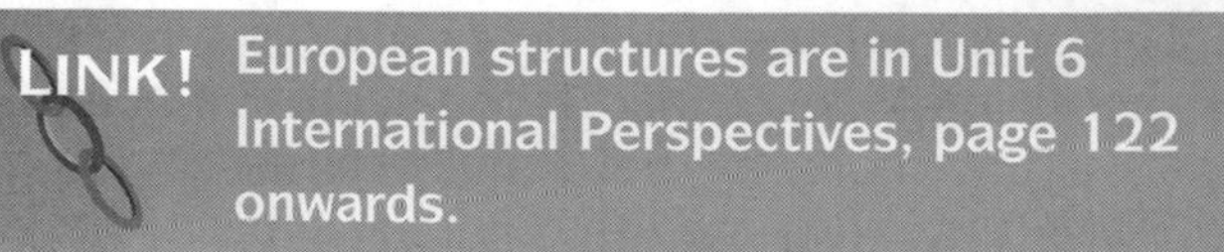
LINK! European structures are in Unit 6 International Perspectives, page 122 onwards.

www.nelsonthornes.com/vocational/public_services – Unit 15 Public Services in Europe

Functions of the Houses of Parliament

Merit

Briefly analyse the functions of the Houses of Parliament.

For this outcome, you need to:

- describe what is done in the House of Commons and the House of Lords
- pick out and explain some of the major functions.

FOCUS

Functions of Parliament

'The main functions of Parliament are:

- to pass laws;
- to provide (by voting for taxation) the means of carrying on the work of government;
- to scrutinise government policy and administration, including proposals for expenditure; and
- to debate the major issues of the day.'

Source: UK2003, *HMSO*

http://www.statistics.gov.uk/downloads/theme_compendia/UK2003/UK2003.pdf – brilliant!

There are two Houses of Parliament – the House of Commons and the House of Lords. This system of having two houses, one to balance the other, is typical of representative democracies and is called the *bicameral* ('two-room') system.

The House of Commons

The House of Commons is a debating room for the 659 British Members of Parliament, but when we talk about it we are really talking about the MPs themselves and their work. Features of the House of Commons are:

- It is *adversarial*, i.e. split into two sides: Government and Opposition. The Government is (in 2003) entirely drawn from the 412 Labour MPs, who have an overall majority in the House. The Opposition is led by the Conservative Party, who have 166 MPs. The LibDems (52 MPs) are also part of the Opposition, even though most of them agree more with Labour than with the Conservatives. There are other Opposition MPs from smaller parties. The total number of Opposition MPs is 247.
- A debate is a series of speeches arranged rather like the speeches of lawyers in a Crown Court. The subject of the debate is usually a new law, or a major national problem. There is a Proposer, an Opposer, and speakers from the floor (ordinary MPs from all parties, who can speak on either side of the argument). The debate ends with a summing up from both sides. Then MPs vote (by walking through a 'yes' or 'no' 'lobby') to decide (by a simple majority) whether the new law should be passed or not.
- Parliament creates new laws, and can abolish or change laws which have become out of date. The process is outlined in the table below.
- Prime Minister's Question Time. Every Wednesday afternoon there is a usually noisy debate at which MPs of all parties ask questions of the Prime Minister. The aim is to put his leadership to the test, and to question government policy. It is at Prime Minister's Question Time that the adversarial nature of the House of Commons can be seen most clearly.

The House of Lords

This 'upper' house is much less powerful than the House of Commons, mainly because its members are not elected. It contains many wise and experienced people who work hard to tidy up the laws proposed by the Commons, but it lacks clout. It is in the process of being reorganised by the Blair government – so watch this space!

Analysis

Your analysis could consider some of the following points:

- Does Parliament represent the people effectively, or is it out of step with the people, and out of date in its approach to lawmaking?

The 12 stages in the passing of a new Bill (i.e. law)

House of Commons	House of Lords
1 FIRST READING – brief introduction	
2 SECOND READING – full Commons debate on the Bill	
3 COMMITTEE STAGE – line-by-line examination of the wording	
4 REPORT STAGE – another debate on the changes made in committee	
5 THIRD READING – small changes	
	6 FIRST READING – no debate
	7 SECOND READING – full debate
	8 COMMITTEE STAGE – changes suggested
	9 REPORT STAGE – the Lords' changes are debated
	10 THIRD READING – review of the Bill so far
11 COMMONS CONSIDERATION – Lords' alterations are added to the Bill, unless the Commons don't like them. The Commons can override the Lords if they wish	
12 ROYAL ASSENT – The Queen signs the Bill and it becomes law	

- In a country where 9 per cent of people are from ethnic minorities, only 12 MPs out of 659 are from ethnic minorities (1.2 per cent).
- 118 MPs (18 per cent) are women.
- Opinion polls consistently show that most British people are in favour of capital punishment for certain crimes. But when MPs debate the matter they always reject capital punishment in any shape or form.
- Turn-out for general elections is going down, and at some recent by-elections has been below 30 per cent of those eligible to vote. Does this mean that people are bored with parliamentary democracy?

Political parties

Give an overview of the main beliefs of political parties.

For this outcome, you need to give the main ideas of a number of political parties on how the country should be run.

Learn about this outcome by
- contacting local councillors or your local MP asking for information about their parties' main policies
- visiting the parties' websites.

The beliefs of political parties are of two types – ideology and policies.

The difference between ideology and policies is that ideology is more theoretical and policies are more practical. The 'beliefs' of political parties are a combination of the two.

Before a general election, political parties put out a manifesto – a booklet explaining their policies, and what they would do if they won the election. Manifestos are a guide to the parties' beliefs, but they tend to be long-winded.

The beliefs of political parties change from time to time. This is because they have to keep up with public opinion – and with events. For example, after the attack on the World Trade Centre on 11 September 2001, all political parties strengthened their policies on terrorism.

FOCUS

Definitions of ideology and policy

Ideology is ...

'any systematic and all-embracing political doctrine, which claims to give a complete and universally applicable theory of man and society, and to derive therefrom a programme of political action.' – Scruton, R., 1982, *A Dictionary of Political Thought*, London: Macmillan, page 213

'a system of ideas, especially on social or political subjects' – *Webster's Dictionary*

Policies are ...

'the formal and informal decisions on how a public authority carries out its duties and uses its powers' – Commission for Racial Equality

Policy is ...

'a set of ideas or a plan of what to do in particular situations that has been agreed officially by a group of people, a business organization, a government or a political party' – *The Cambridge International Dictionary of English* (1995)

CHECKPOINT ...

1 Contact any political party and find out what their membership requirements and fees are.

2 Find out who your local MP is, which party they belong to, and when you can go and see them if you want to.

CHECKPOINT ...

Research the beliefs of (a) the British National Party, (b) the Green Party and (c) the Socialist Workers' Party. What implications do their beliefs have for the public services?

The main beliefs of political parties

Political party	Left or right	Main beliefs
Labour – a big political party, whose members don't all share the same beliefs!	Centre-left There is a touch of socialism	Public services should be well staffed and maintained Will consider redistributing wealth from rich to poor Broadly in favour of diversity Slightly pro-European Slight tradition of pacifism Will privatise, but unwillingly
Conservative – as with the Labour Party, Conservatives do not always agree among themselves	Centre-right Believes in capitalism	Public services should be made more efficient The rich deserve to keep their wealth Taxes should be lower Mildly interested in promoting diversity Mainly anti-European Not pacifist Keen on privatisation Tough on asylum-seekers
Liberal Democrats	Centre	Wants larger and better public services Neither socialist nor capitalist, but compassionate Prepared to raise taxes to pay for them More pro-European than other parties Relatively pacifist Some interest in diversity Compassionate on asylum-seekers
Scottish National Party	Centre-left	Wants more independence for Scotland, and closer links with Europe
Plaid Cymru	Left	Like the SNP but Welsh-orientated, and more socialist in tendency
Ulster Unionists	Centre-right	Supported by Protestants who want to keep links with rest of UK
Democratic Unionists	Right	Strongly Protestant party – rather anti-Catholic Against Sinn Fein
Social Democratic and Labour	Centre-left	Similar to Labour and with links to the Catholic community Closer to Ireland than UK
Sinn Fein	Left	The 'political wing of the IRA'; wants breakaway from the UK

Merit

> Give a detailed understanding of the main ideologies of at least two political parties.

For this outcome, you need to:

- select two or three political parties
- describe their ideologies fully
- indicate where the ideologies come from
- outline some practical effects of their ideologies.

Political ideologies are 'any systematic and all-embracing political doctrine' or 'a system of ideas ... on a political subject'. They are usually described as left-wing, centre or right-wing.

Sources of information

- Party manifestos
- MPs and councillors
- people who teach politics
- books on politics
- newspapers and TV programmes (news and current affairs)
- websites.

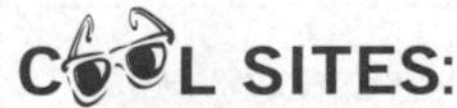

www.labour.org.uk/

http://www.conservatives.com/

FOCUS

Statements from Labour on ...

Crime

'We are investing record amounts in fighting crime and are reforming the criminal justice system to reduce the causes of crime and reforming policing to get more police on the street.'

Education

'... transforming secondary education, widening access to higher education, boosting adult basic skills, and extending free nursery places to all three-year-olds.'

Left, centre and right – a summary

Left-wing	Centre-left	Centre	Centre-right	Right-wing
Communists, Socialist Workers' Party, Leninists, Trotskyists, etc.	*Labour, Social democratic parties (e.g. in Germany), Socialists (France)*	*Liberal Democrats, (UK) Democrats (USA)*	*Conservatives (UK), Republicans (USA), UMP (France)*	*Nazis, Fascists, British National Party, National Front*
These parties oppose representative democracy. They believe in equality for all, power to the workers, etc. They are strongly anti-capitalist. Their ideas mainly come from Karl Marx, Lenin, Trotsky and other left-wing thinkers.	These parties support representative democracy. They seek to tackle poverty and injustice, and to help the working classes. They believe in taxing the rich. They don't like capitalism but will accept that it is sometimes not a bad thing. Ideas come partly from Marx, partly from the Labour leaders of the nineteenth/ twentieth century, e.g. Keir Hardie.	These democratic parties dislike socialism, but support equal opportunities. They are against ideology and prefer a 'pragmatic' (practical) approach. They support diversity and have mixed views on taxation. Political beliefs originated with the liberalism of nineteenth-century Whig Party and Methodism. and nineteenth-	These capitalist parties support representative democracy and privatisation of public services. They want to help the poor, but they also believe in keeping taxes low. They are nationalistic, keen on law and order, and don't like socialism. Political beliefs came from the views of landowners, bankers century mill-owners	These extreme right-wing parties are very nationalistic and openly racist. They are against immigration and against paying benefits to people who won't work. They hate socialists, support war and have tough views on crime. Ideologies come mainly from Hitler.

Transport

'Labour recognises that transport needs increased investment and to be a greater political priority than it has been for decades. That's why in July 2000 we published our £180 billion ten-year plan for transport ...'

Housing

'Labour is working to ensure that everyone has a decent home in a secure community, free from the fear of crime and with a safe and clean local environment.'

Poverty

'We are committed to halving child poverty in ten years, abolishing child poverty in a generation.'

Source: extracts from Labour Party website

FOCUS

Conservative policies

Tuition fees

'Conservatives will abolish tuition fees and axe Labour's plans for a £9,000 tax on learning.'

Public services

'Conservative-run councils deliver better public services, whilst still charging lower council taxes. Find out how Conservatives want to make your neighbourhood a better place to live.'

Council tax

'Council tax is going through the roof under Labour. Find out how much extra council tax you are paying under Labour with our council tax calculator.'

Congestion tax

'Conservatives oppose this unfair (Congestion) tax.'

Source: extracts from Conservative Party website

The statements quoted here are policies, but they are linked to underlying ideologies. The ideology of Labour is broadly left-wing, while the ideology of the Conservatives is broadly right-wing. However, the fact that most voters are centre, rather than left or right in their politics, means that both parties have included policies which supporters of the other party could identify with. They do this in the hope that voters will change over to them at the next general election.

Distinction

Critically evaluate the ideology of two political parties.

For this outcome, you need to:

- examine the ideologies of two parties carefully and critically, but without bias
- look for good and bad points, and reach a reasoned judgement
- show you fully understand and can define 'ideology'.

You can discuss any two political parties: they do not necessarily have to be British, and they do not have to be represented in Parliament.

This outcome can be interpreted in a number of ways. The ideology of a party can be criticised on the basis of:

- how well it serves the party
- how well it serves the people as a whole
- whether it is coherent or contradictory
- whether it is stable or keeps changing
- whether it is true to party traditions
- what its attitude is to specific issues, e.g. tax, human rights, diversity, the environment, etc.
- the attitude of the party to the public services.

To research for this outcome, you should keep up with the news, especially any announcements made by politicians. You will find it useful to compare what they say on the news with what they said in their last election manifesto. You should consider whether their party is trying to move to the right or the left, and what kinds of people they are trying to appeal to.

CHECKPOINT ...

Ideological change: research (a) the abandonment of Labour's policy of unilateral nuclear disarmament (1989) and (b) the 'dumping of Clause 4' (1999). Why and how did Labour benefit from getting rid of these pieces of 'ideological baggage'?

FOCUS

'Hidden ideology'

'The Tories said they were writing to all GPs and hospitals to establish what impact asylum seekers were having on the NHS. It was reported at the weekend that a doctor in North Staffs had cleared his normal patients off his register to make way for asylum seekers.'

Source: from 'Blunkett's race warning' by Philip Johnston, Daily Telegraph *Home Affairs Editor (filed 21/01/2003)*

CHECKPOINT ...

What does the FOCUS tell us about the ideology of the Conservative Party? What would the implications be for the public services, if the Conservatives got into power?

THE PUBLIC SERVICES AND POLITICAL ISSUES

PASSGRADE

Identify the influence on the public services of the government in power.

For this outcome, you need to research and briefly describe the effect of government policy on the public services.

Sources of information:

- public service employees
- newspaper reports on public service funding
- government reports
- other news websites, especially the COOL SITES given below.

COOL SITES:

http://www.guardian.co.uk/

http://www.homeoffice.gov.uk/

Different British governments have had different influences on the public services. The PROFILE gives an example.

Profile

The Labour government which took power in 1997 has had significant effects on the public services. These include:

- **'joined up government'** – the idea that public services should work together rather than in competition to serve the public. The clearest sign of this is the 'crime and disorder partnerships' introduced in 1998 for tackling petty crime.
- **increased funding** – see the FOCUS below. Increased funding benefits the public services. They can employ more staff, invest in better equipment and carry out their work more effectively.
- **the armed forces** Active service in Kosovo, Sierra Leone, Afghanistan and Iraq has raised the income and status of the armed forces and developed their skill and fighting/peace-keeping capabilities.
- **diversity** The Labour government is tackling the problem of lack of diversity in the public services.
- **asylum-seekers** Wars involving British armed forces have raised the numbers of refugees and asylum-seekers coming to the UK. This means more work for the police, the immigration service, the National Asylum Support Service which processes asylum-seekers and the social services and housing departments of some local authorities.
- **community wardens** This government scheme for uniformed volunteer patrols to support the police was given £65million funding in 2003. Two hundred and forty-five schemes were set up around the country – but the service will be stopped in 2005.
- **privatisation of prisons** This government initiative to raise the prison population without spending taxpayers' money has run into difficulties – see page 22.

FOCUS

'UK anti-terror efforts get £330m

A £330m boost to the UK's anti-terrorism effort will be spent on equipment capable of detecting radioactive material being smuggled through Britain's ports.

The money – earmarked in Gordon Brown's 2003 Budget – will also be used to upgrade testing facilities for substances capable of being used in a chemical or biological terror attack.

Home Secretary David Blunkett was quick to welcome what he labelled a "boost in the fight against terrorism".'

Source: BBC News Online, 9 April 2003

COOL SITES:

http://www.asylumsupport.info/asylumcity.pdf – asylum-seekers – housing

http://www.homeoffice.gov.uk/ – the mother of all public service sites!

http://www.homeoffice.gov.uk/docs2/pocc.html – inner-city riots

Research and review a political issue

PASSGRADE

Research a political issue, giving your own balanced conclusions.

For this outcome, you need to:

- find information on a news report or problem involving politics
- explain what it is about in your own words
- give your view, with reasons.

Merit

Review and analyse appropriate recent information on a political issue.

For this outcome, you need to:

- collect recent information on a political news story or problem
- explain the main ideas, principles and issues involved
- give your opinion, with reasons and explanations.

Check with your tutor that the issue you choose is recent enough!

Distinction

Review and evaluate a political issue, which demonstrates a wide variety of arguments and research, giving detailed and relevant conclusions with a reasoned evaluation of possible future events.

For this outcome, you need to:

- collect relevant, up-to-date information on a political issue
- examine the issue in detail, showing the arguments on different sides
- reach reasoned, balanced conclusions about the rights and wrongs of the situation
- explain the implications of the issue for the future.

Political issues are events, disputes or problems which make news and involve the government, local government, politicians – or public services. Examples are:

- racism in the public services, e.g. the Metropolitan Police and the murder of Stephen Lawrence, or the treatment of Superintendent Ali Dizaei
- Northern Ireland (the Good Friday Agreement, power sharing, suspension of Stormont, changes to the RUC, etc.
- genetically modified foods – the environmental, health and economic effects, together, perhaps, with the ethical issues of patenting genes, and of globalisation.

Other examples of on-going political issues are:

- terrorism and how to combat it
- asylum-seekers
- racism
- discrimination against women
- the Iraq situation
- whether the UK should adopt the euro
- the energy crisis
- police attitudes to drugs.

For covering these three linked objectives, you should bear in mind the following points:

- A fresh, new political issue is better than one which is getting out of date.
- Newspapers such as the *Daily Telegraph*, the *Guardian*, *The Times*, the *Observer*, the *Independent* and the *Sunday Times* are good sources of information.

- The internet is excellent, but watch out for biased sites (especially on immigration).
- If you can talk to someone who is actively involved in the issue, it should help you very much.
- A political issue always involves at least two opposed points of view. For these outcomes, *always give both sides of the argument* – before giving your own reasoned judgement.
- The merit and distinction outcomes need more depth. Think about ideological differences, moral issues, economic issues, the main personalities involved and how different participants are trying to gain a political advantage from the situation. Think about short-, medium- and long-term effects. Consider, too, how the media are treating the issue, and whether they are taking sides.
- List your sources, and acknowledge people who have helped you.

CHECKPOINT ...

Keep a scrapbook of newspaper cuttings about political issues, and use the information you collect as an up-to-date basis for covering these outcomes.

Distinction

Present information which is coherently organised with accurate use of political terms and logical arguments, giving own conclusions, which are fully justified and valid.

This outcome has no content. It refers to

- the quality of your research, and the information you get from it
- the way you organise your information, so as to bring out its meaning(s)
- your use of appropriate vocabulary, showing a familiarity with, and understanding of, the language of politics
- the way you link ideas so as to show how the different aspects of your chosen political issue are related to each other (e.g. the various pressures which make people – and political parties – think and act as they do on the issue concerned)
- the way you highlight the key issues and distinguish fact from opinion
- the way you explore the implications of the issue, especially for the future, showing how it could affect ordinary people and the public services, as well as politicians.

Unit 11 Expedition Skills

Grading criteria

PASSGRADE To achieve a pass grade the evidence must show that the learner is able to:	*Merit* To achieve a merit grade the evidence must show that the learner is able to:	*Distinction* To achieve a distinction grade the evidence must show that the learner is able to:
● explain the advantages and disadvantages of a range of suitable maps to be used during an expedition including a full description of the meanings of conventional map symbols **210** ● produce a complete and accurate route card for open country (which covers at least eight kilometres and five legs) and use this, with some guidance, to complete the eight kilometre journey **212** ● demonstrate a range of practical navigation skills including knowledge and use of map, compass and techniques (with some guidance) **214** ● describe the equipment and materials taken on an expedition **218** ● describe and comment on the effectiveness of a range of different types and designs of personal, group, and safety equipment used in walking and camping **219** ● prepare and carry out a camping and walking expedition of at least 25 kilometres which includes camping for at least two days and one night **221** ● experience two other outdoor pursuits and analyse the benefits of outdoor pursuits **223** ● describe the current issues around access to the countryside, explaining the work of one agency and one statutory body involved in promoting and protecting the countryside **223**	● explain the choice of equipment and materials taken on an expedition **220** ● analyse and evaluate the design and properties of materials used and the selection and care of equipment **220** ● demonstrate the use of highly competent, accurate, safe skills when walking, navigating and camping **222** ● explain the benefits of outdoor activities **223** ● analyse the benefits of outdoor activities and the issues around access to the countryside by detailed investigation into the work of one agency and one statutory body involved in the promotion and protection of the countryside **226**	● justify the decisions made in the choice of materials used and the correct selection and care of equipment when taking part in the camping expedition **221** ● demonstrate and evaluate practical skills used in walking, navigating and camping **222** ● evaluate the benefits of outdoor activities and the issues around access to the countryside by detailed investigation into the work of one agency and one statutory body involved in the promotion and protection of the countryside **226**

An expedition is a journey into open country, which lasts more than one day and where you carry your own necessities.

Expeditions are an essential form of training for the armed forces – and can be used in other uniformed services too. As well as teaching survival skills and developing fitness, expeditions are used for team-building and leadership training in many organisations. Your experience in this unit will be a great help to you when you apply to join a uniformed service.

Expeditions have also become a major part of tourism – and fit, adventurous people now take expedition holidays in many parts of the world.

In this unit, you'll learn how to plan and carry out a camping and walking expedition lasting at least two days and one night. You'll learn how to do it in safety and comfort, respecting the environment – and with some exciting outdoor activities thrown in.

Read this!

Being on an expedition is potentially dangerous. So ...

- If you have any health worries, tell your tutor.
- Follow *all* safety instructions and advice.
- Do not do anything that could put yourself or others at risk.

NAVIGATION SKILLS

Maps

PASSGRADE

Explain the advantages and disadvantages of a range of suitable maps to be used during an expedition including a full description of the meanings of conventional map symbols.

For this outcome, you need to:

- learn to read two or more different kinds of map used for expeditions
- explain their good and bad points
- give the meanings of the symbols.

If you go on an expedition, you will need a map. It must be the right kind of map, and you must know how to use it.

The two main map-making companies are the Ordnance Survey (an agency linked to the government's Department of the Environment, Transport and the Regions) and Harvey.

Map symbols and how to use them

A map is basically a drawing of part of the earth's surface seen from directly above. In an OS or Harvey map the map is drawn to scale, so that a given length on the map corresponds to a given

Four kinds of map, and their suitability for expeditions

Map type and scale (if shown)	Comments: advantages and disadvantages
OS Outdoor Leisure 1:25 000	This is a favourite large-scale map for walking and rambling. **Advantages:** • Distances are easy to judge, thanks to the National Grid blue squares (each side 1 km). • Grid references can be given. • Plenty of relevant detail shown – contours, tracks, walls, cliffs. • Good information on terrain and land use – types of woods, rough ground, bogs, etc. are all shown. • Very suitable for shorter walks (e.g. 8 km). **Disadvantages:** • Almost too much detail for a beginner; also the fine details – especially contour heights – are hard to see in bad light. • The area covered by the map is quite small, so you may have to buy two maps if you want to go on a long expedition. • The maps are rather large and fragile, and hard to handle in wet, windy weather. • Relatively expensive.

<table>
<tr><td>OS Landranger
1:50 000</td><td>This is a medium-scale all-purpose map.
Advantages:
• The scale is large enough for it to show most relevant detail needed for expeditions.
• Distances are easy to judge thanks to the National Grid blue 1 km squares.
• Grid references can be given.
• Contours are clear.
• Maps more robust than 1:25 000.
• It is suitable for very long walks (e.g. 25 km).
Disadvantages:
• Small features of interest to walkers such as walls, minor paths, etc. are omitted.
• Less detail about land use than the 1:25 000.
• Relatively expensive.</td></tr>
<tr><td>Harvey walking maps
1:25 000 and
1:40 000</td><td>These maps are specifically made for walkers.
Advantages:
• Information given is chosen for tourists, ramblers and walkers.
• Information is printed more clearly and simply than information on OS maps.
• The scale 1:40 000 is a good scale for long-distance walking.
• Cheaper than the equivalent OS maps.
• Relatively weatherproof.
• Contain information on camping, food and walking/clothing tips.
Disadvantage:
The 1:25 000 contain less detail about walls, etc. than the equivalent OS maps.</td></tr>
<tr><td>OS Travel maps</td><td>Motoring maps, completely unsuitable for walking expeditions. The scale is too small, contours are inadequate, and there is not enough information for walkers.</td></tr>
</table>

distance on the ground. (For example, on a 1:25 000 map, 4 cm on the map = 1 km on the ground.)

On a map all irrelevant information is left out, and relevant information is shown by symbols which are easy to see and use. Each symbol stands for something. Most symbols look like a simplified form of the thing they represent – streams are blue lines, for example, and houses are tiny rectangles. These symbols are all explained at the side of the map.

Contours are different, because they do not stand for objects on the ground. Contours are brown lines joining places of equal height above sea level. The lines are numbered with their height in metres above sea level. The top of the number is uphill. If contours are close together, the slope is steep; if they are wide apart, it's gentle, and if there are no contours at all, the land is flat.

The blue lines (horizontal and vertical) make up 1 km squares called the national grid. This grid has three functions:

- It tells you at a glance how long one kilometre appears on the map (the length of one side of a blue square).
- It shows you which is north (always up the vertical line to the top of the map).
- It enables you to pinpoint any location in the UK to within 100 metres by using 4 letters and 6 figures. (How to do this is clearly explained, with an example, at the bottom right-hand side of any Ordnance Survey 1:50 000 or 1: 25 000 map.) National grid references, as these letters and figures are called, are used for planning expeditions, or in rescuing people from a mountain.

http://www.scoutingresources.org.uk/mapping_coordinates.html

As well as national grid numbers, there are numbers identifying lines of latitude and longitude along the sides of an OS 1:25 000 and 1:50 000 map. Their meeting points on the 1:50 000 map are shown by tiny crosses called graticule intersections. Though it is rarely necessary to do this, these figures and crosses enable you to pinpoint a place without reference to the National Grid.

LINK! See page 214 in this unit for map skills.

CHECKPOINT ...

1 Practise writing grid references for a range of places on a map – then ask a friend to find the places your grid references relate to.
2 Test your knowledge of conventional symbols, e.g. for a public right of way, marked footpath, county boundary, public house, etc.

Making and using a route card

Produce a complete and accurate route card for open country (which covers at least eight kilometres and five legs) and use this, with some guidance, to complete the eight kilometre journey.

For this outcome, you need to:

- plan and draw up a full accurate route card (8 km and 5 legs)
- follow it.

A route card is a piece of paper which outlines, in table form, the route of a walk. It gives all the information the walkers need, and which rescuers would need if they had to set out, even in darkness and fog, to find them.

The card divides a walk up into 'legs' (sections). It gives 6-figure grid references for the start and end of each leg. It also gives distances, directions (or bearings), gains and losses of height, estimated walk times, rest periods, an estimated time of arrival, and a contingency plan (escape) to be used if someone gets hurt, the weather turns bad, or it gets dark and you don't have a torch.

Your card for this outcome must contain all necessary information, and it must be accurate. Grid references, distances and changes of height must all be correct, and the time estimates must be realistic.

The route you plan must be on open country (moorland, downland or other unfenced land). It may include some footpaths. Check with your tutor.

To produce a route card you should bear the following factors in mind:

- average walking speed of your party
- the terrain (land surface)
- height changes and steepness of slopes
- weather and light conditions
- weight carried.
- Add 30 minutes for every 300 metres climbed for a fast party; add 40 minutes for a medium party and 50 minutes for a slow one.
- Add about 20 minutes for every 300 metres descent. Very steep and rocky slopes will add to these delays.
- Halve all speeds on snow or at night. Add 5 minutes per kilometre for wet or windy weather. Add 5 minutes per kilometre for every 5 kilograms of extra load.
- Poor equipment, e.g. boots with slippery soles, will also slow you down, especially on steep or rough ground.

Safety planning for an 8 kilometre walk

For a fit, experienced and well-equipped walker, 8 kilometres is an easy walk (in good weather) which should take less than two hours. Even so, there are precautions to be taken for safety and comfort. These include:

- giving a copy of your route card to your tutor or instructor
- taking and using a suitable map
- taking safety equipment such as a whistle, compass, phone, and torch
- taking spare clothes (say a fleece and a waterproof)
- carrying a small first aid pack with sticky plasters and paracetamol

Walking speeds – rough guide

Nature of group	Roads and smooth tracks	Rough tracks	Moorland
Fast	6 kph (3½–4 mph)	5 kph (2½–3½ mph)	3 kph (2 mph)
Medium	5 kph (2½–3½ mph)	3 kph (2 mph)	2½ kph (1½ mph)
Slow	3 kph (2 mph)	2½ kph (1½ mph)	2 kph (1 mph)

Profile

Here is a specimen route card, based on the extract from the OS 1:25 000 map on page 214.

Leg	From - to (grid reference)	Details of route	Direction and bearing	Distance (leg) (m)	Cumulative distance (km)	Height (m)	Walking time	Rests (minutes)	Total time	Estimated time of arrival	Escape
1	339072 339083	Leave car park, walk NW along road with church on right through Grasmere. Turn right at police station after 500 m. Walk NNE for 600 m to public phone.	NW 305 for 500 m then NE 040 for 600 m	1100		+10	20 mins	10 (for shopping)	30	1000	Go back
2	33908[illegible] 34108[illegible]	200 m up minor road to right of pub, left at junction. 100 m to where track goes up from right hand side of road	NE 040	300	1.4	+10	5 mins	0	5 mins	1005	Go back
3	34108[illegible] 34308[illegible]	300 m up steep track, wood on right, to where track forks.	ENE 070	300	1.7	+50	8 mins	0	8 mins	1013	Go back
4	34308[illegible] 34809[illegible]	Take left fork which curves right after 100 m; follow track up steep slope for 350 m to ford across stream; track rises ESE, ENE and then N to a cairn.	NNW 335, then NE 045	1000	2.7	+350	1 hour	20	1hr 20	1133	Go back
5	3480[illegible] 3561[illegible]	Walk NE up rounded ridge following straight path with crest of ridge 50 m to left. After 1100 m (when another path comes in from right) bear slightly left – NNE – for 400 m to summit of Green Rigg (Greatrigg Man cairn)	NE 040, then NNE 015	1500	4.2	+260	1 hr 10 mins	15 at top of Great Rigg	1hr 25 mins	1258	Go back
6	3561[illegible]4 3560[illegible]3	Walk south 400 m to junction of paths. Follow left path for 1.7 km due south along mainly level ridge to Heron Pike, a small rise at end of ridge.	S 180 for 400 m, then 170 for 1300 m, then 190 for 400 m	2100	1.1	– 154	1 hr 10 mins	10 on Heron Pike	1hr 20	1318	Cut straight down hillside to right (290) in emergency until stream is reached. Follow stream down.
7.	356[illegible]33 343[illegible]35	Turn sharp right following straight path 600 m down steep hillside to stream in V-shaped valley. Follow path on left (south) bank of stream – pine trees on left – to path junction.	WNW 290	1000	7.3	– 480	1hr	10	1hr 10	1428	Follow planned route, keeping to path
8.	343[illegible]85 339[illegible]83	Follow path down (the one taken at start of walk) to public telephone.	WSW 250	600	7.9	– 60	10 mins	0	10 mins	1438	Follow planned route
9.	339[illegible]83 339[illegible]72	Walk back through Grasmere the way we set out.	SW 220, SE 125	1100	9.0	– 10	20 mins	30 for more shopping	50 mins	1528	Follow planned route

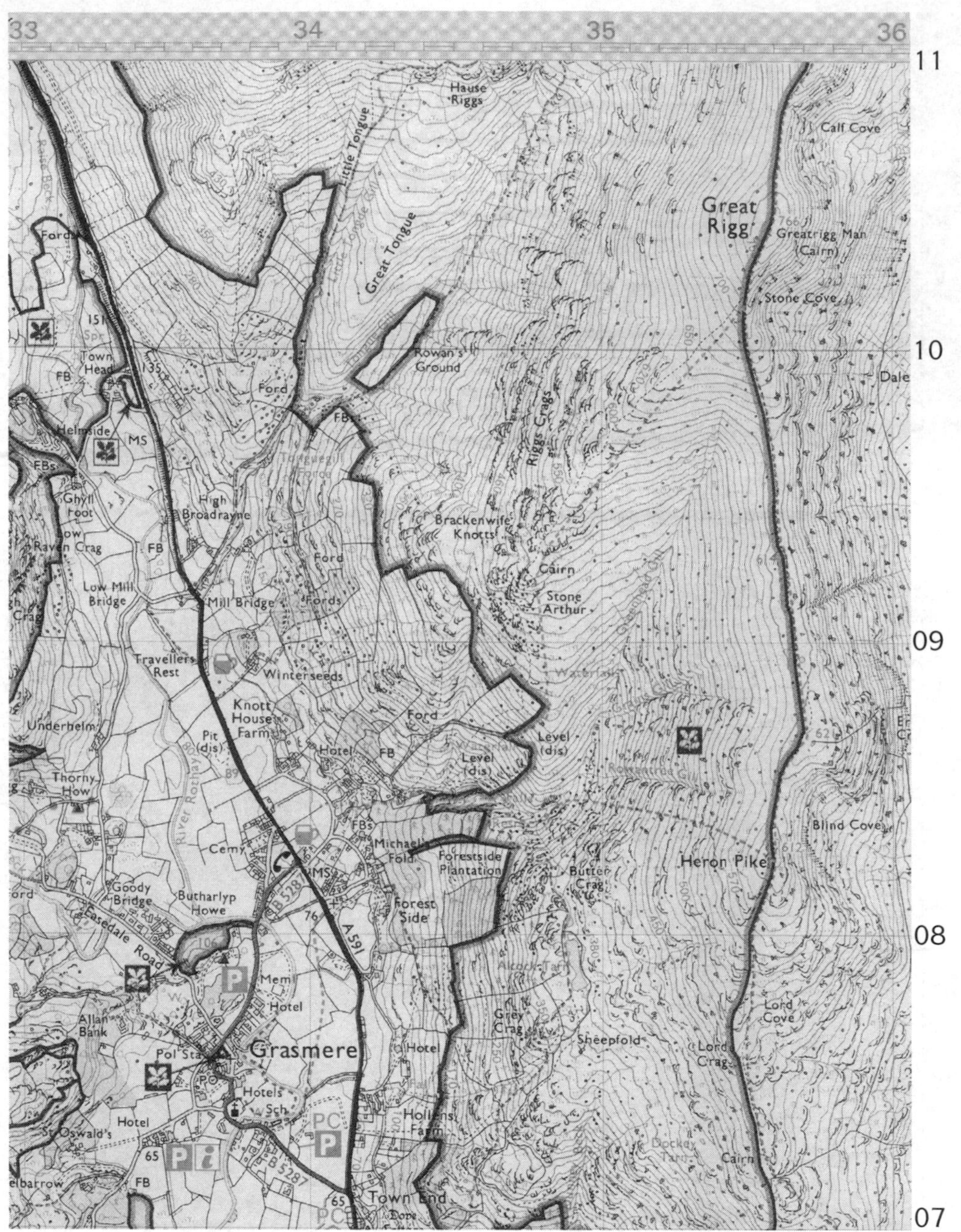

An extract from Outdoor Leisure map 7, 1:25 000, Grasmere area. Reproduced by permission of Ordnance Survey on behalf of The Controller of Her Majesty's Stationery Office, © Crown Copyright 100036771

- carrying food, water or soft drinks
- checking that your boots don't hurt.

Do not carry any unnecessary weight.

PASSGRADE

> Demonstrate a range of practical navigation skills including knowledge and use of map, compass and techniques (with some guidance).

For this outcome, you need to use a map, compass and some navigation skills correctly.

Map skills

Planning

Make sure you know the scale of your map. Work out rough distances using the 1 km squares of the national grid. To work out exact distances, place a piece of thread carefully along the route of your walk, then measure it against the scale at the bottom of the map, or against a ruler. On a 1:50 000 2 cm = 1 km; on a 1:25 000 map 4 cm = 1 km. You can also mark off each leg against the edge of a piece of paper in pencil, then measure the marked lengths on the paper with a ruler.

Reading a map out of doors

If you know where you are, and can see landmarks which are marked on the map, you don't need a compass. Stand so that you are facing a landmark and hold your map in front of you so that your landmark (say a hilltop) is in the same direction on the map as it is in reality. Identify other landmarks on the map by using what you can see in front of you as a guide.

If you are inexperienced, you should keep the map open (or consult it frequently), identifying the features you see as you go along.

Map care

Maps are fragile. They should be kept open at the place you want in a clear map-case, if possible, so that they don't get wet, and you can look at them without handling them. If you don't have a map-case, carry the map in a plastic bag to protect it from rain. Make sure you know how to open and fold the map before going out. Never write or draw on a map.

Compass skills

Features of a standard Silva-type compass:

- **transparent base-plate** You can put the compass on the map while setting the map and working out bearings. Because you can see through the base plate you can accurately place the pivot of the compass needle over your present position on the map, and point the direction of travel arrow towards your destination on the map.
- **orienting lines** These are used to align your compass with the vertical blue lines (eastings) on the map so that you can 'set the map' (see below).
- **roamer scales** These can be used for estimating tenths (or even hundredths!) when working out a grid reference.

FOCUS

Getting a travel direction from a map

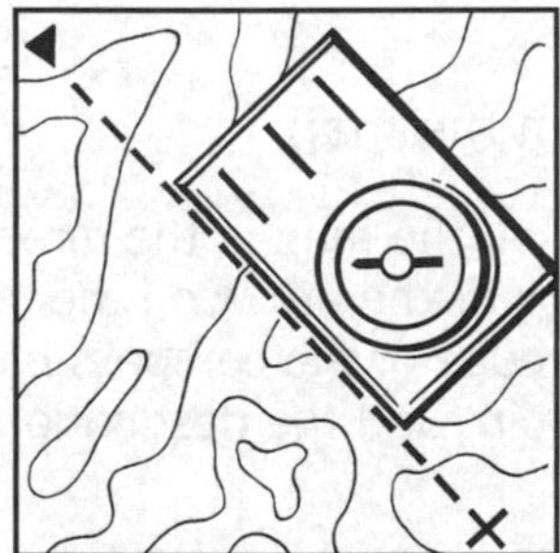

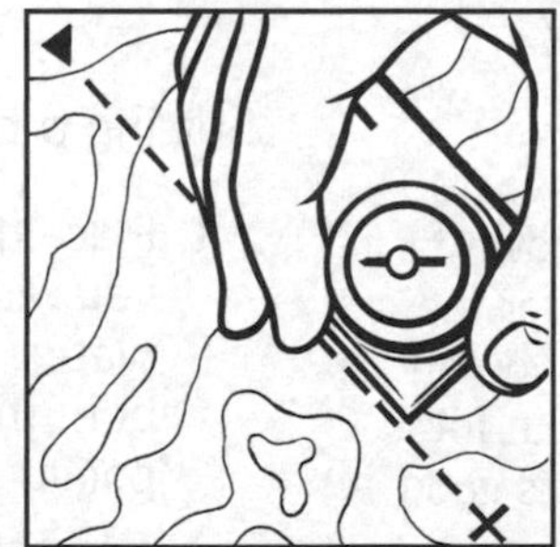

1 (a) Place the compass on the map so that the long edge connects the starting point with the desired destination.

(b) Make sure that the direction arrows are pointing from the starting point to the place of destination (and not the opposite way).

2 (a) Hold the compass firm on the map in order to keep the base plate steady.

(b) Turn the rotating capsule until the North–South lines on the bottom of the capsule are parallel with the North–South lines on the map.

(c) Be sure that the North–South arrow on the bottom of the capsule points to the same direction as North on the map.

3 (a) Hold the compass in your hand in front of you. Make sure that the base plate is in horizontal position, and that the direction arrows are pointing straight ahead.

(b) Rotate your body until the North–South arrow on the bottom of the capsule lines up with the magnetic needle, and the red end of the needle points in the same direction as the arrow.

(c) The directional arrows on the baseplate now show your desired travel direction.

Source: www.suuntousa.com/products_compuse.htm

- **'tachometer'** This may be the pedometer or odometer (see below)
- **calibration** This is the marking of degree or 2-degree intervals round the compass face. 2-degree intervals are easier to read and accurate enough for normal navigation in the UK.

FOCUS

Using a roamer

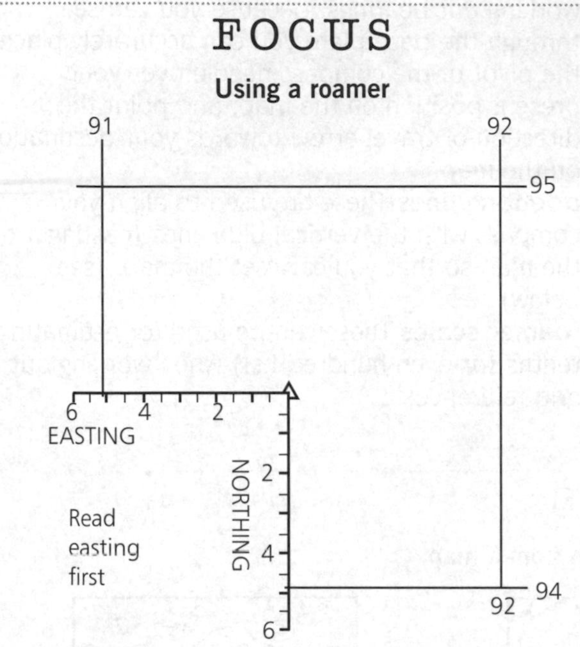

A roamer is a small – usually transparent – card marked with units of the proper scale as shown in the figure. With the roamer, the reference for the hilltop is 91519449. The roamer can give you an estimated reading to within 10 metres. But for practical purposes a 6-figure grid reference is good enough!

Source: http://maps.nrcan.gc.ca/maps101/index.html

COOL SITES:

http://www.silva.se/outdoor/index.htm

www.learn-orienteering.org/old

www.chasetrek.org.uk/tutorial/compass.html – clear, useful explanations

www.suuntousa.com/products_compuse.htm

http://www.harbach.4ever.org.uk/snowdonia/navigation/map.htm

http://maps.nrcan.gc.ca/maps101/grid_ref.html – seriously cool!

Setting the map

1. Put the map on a flat surface.
2. Place the compass on the map.
3. Align the orienting arrow/lines in the housing (capsule) of the compass with the vertical grid lines on the map.
4. Turn compass and map together until the red end of the needle is on top of the orienting arrow.
5. The map is now set, i.e. pointing north.

FOCUS

Bearings

Bearings are the usual way of describing direction. The face of the compass, and the circle of the horizon, can both be divided into 360° (the standard unit for measuring angles). North is 0°, and then the degrees are counted in a clockwise direction (as they are marked round the face of the compass). Thus east is 90°, south is 180°, and so on. Bearings are always given in three figures, even if the first one (or two) figures are zero, e.g. 007, 026, 289, etc.

Setting a bearing from the map

1. Place the compass on the map in the direction you wish to go (look at the arrow on the base plate), so that the edge of the compass passes both the starting point and the destination point.
2. Turn the compass housing until it lines up with the grid lines (eastings).
3. Read off the compass bearing (the number on the top dial which is next to the direction arrow).

COOL SITE:

http://www.chasetrek.org.uk/tutorial/compass.html

Setting a bearing from compass to map

1. Point the compass direction arrow towards the feature you want to take a bearing of (the reference point).
2. Keeping the compass still, turn the compass capsule until the orienting arrow is aligned with the N on the compass. This gives you the grid bearing.

3 Place the compass on the map with the long edge passing through your present location.
4 Rotate the compass around your position until the orienting lines inside the capsule align with the grid lines, with the orienting arrow pointing to the north of the map.
5 The edge of the compass which is on your position should now pass through, or towards, your reference point.

Other ways of describing direction

- Less accurate. Use the four points of the compass (cardinal points), e.g., north, east, etc., and the 'intercardinal' points, such as north-east, east-north-east. But if you want anything more accurate than this you should use bearings.
- More accurate. For aiming guns, etc., the armed forces use a system of describing direction which is more accurate than bearings. They use a unit called 'mils'. A circle is divided into 6400 mils. One degree equals 17.8 mils.

Magnetic variation

This is the angle between grid north (the direction of the 'easting' lines) and magnetic north, which is 4° west of true north. If you transfer a bearing from compass to map remember to *subtract* 4° from your compass bearing to get the bearing on the map.

Other navigation skills

Judging distance walked

This is done by:

- referring to the map
- timing your walking, and referring to the guidance figures given above on page 212.
- counting your paces, having first got a figure for your *average* pace length
- using a pedometer, an instrument which counts your paces and tells you how far you've walked.

Handrailing

Following a feature such as a road, wall, ridge or stream to get to your destination (which must lie near the feature). Instead of reading the compass or looking at your map, you simply follow the feature

Attack points

These are landmarks which you pass on the way to your real destination.

Collecting features

These are landmarks beyond your destination, e.g. mountains, which you can take bearings of to ensure you are walking in the right direction.

Aiming off

This technique is useful when making for a destination (e.g. a hut or bridge) which is on a road or a river. You deliberately aim to the left or right of your target, so that you know which way to turn when you reach the road or river.

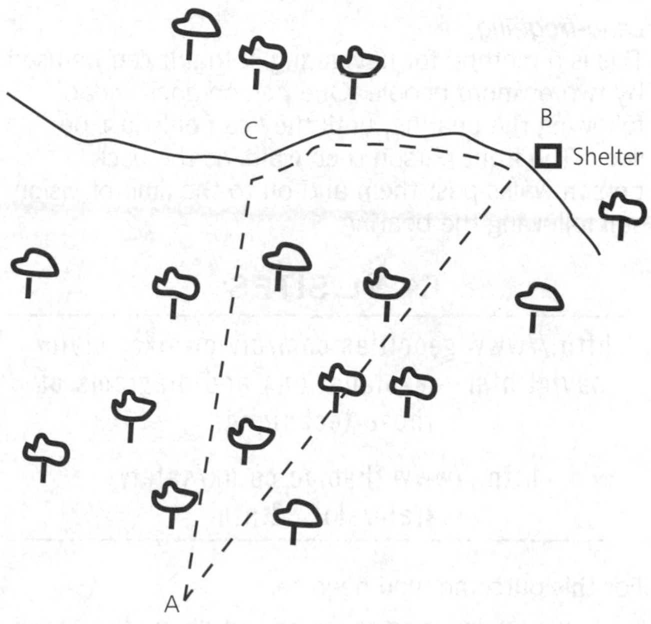

Aiming off

Spiral searches

This is a way of searching for a cairn or other feature in thick fog.

Method:

1 Mark your present position.
2 Walk 10 m north.
3 Walk 10 m west.
4 Walk 20 m south.
5 Walk 20 m east.
6 Walk 30 m north.
7 Walk 30 m west.
8 Walk 40 m south.
9 Walk 40 m east.
10 Walk 50 m north.
11 Walk 50 m west.
12 Walk 30 m south.
13 Walk 30 m east.
14 You should now be back at your starting point, if your search failed.

Walking on a bearing
This is a technique for walking in the right direction in fog or darkness.

1 Take your bearing and face the way you want to go.
2 Note a feature on the ground, e.g. a stone or tuft of grass, at the limit of visibility.
3 Walk to that point, stop and look for the next feature which is on your bearing.
4 Repeat the process.

Leap-frogging
This is a method for navigating in fog. It can be used by two or more people. One person goes ahead, following the bearing, until they can only just be seen. The front person then waits as the back person walks past them and on to the limit of vision, still following the bearing.

COOL SITES:

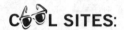

http://www.geocities.com/civicwalker/civic/navigt.htm – explanations and diagrams of these techniques

http://www.thebmc.co.uk/safety/train/skill_2.htm

For this outcome, you need to:

- show you can read maps accurately and confidently
- use the compass and take accurate bearings
- show awareness of your own safety and that of others while walking in open country
- be safe, tidy and considerate when camping.

! CHECKPOINT ...

Why not practise expedition skills in your own time – either with an organisation such as the cadets, on the Duke of Edinburgh's Award Scheme, or simply for your own pleasure? There are many parts of the UK and the near continent where you can go walking in open country, or treat yourself to a cheap camping holiday with your friends.

COOL SITE:

http://www.thebmc.co.uk/safety/advice/advice_1.htm – details on mountain safety

EQUIPMENT

Describe the equipment and materials taken on an expedition.

For this outcome, you need to:

- make a list of each item you would take on a two-day camping expedition in which you walk at least 25 km.
- describe two aspects of commonplace items, e.g. shorts (they should be strong and comfortable)
- describe three or four design features of specialised items, e.g. rucksack (capacity in litres, weight, frame, pockets, straps, materials, waterproofing, etc.).

See SKILLPOWER below for more detail.

You are expected to describe the items listed above for this outcome. The specifications state that you should pay most attention to specialist equipment. The table on the following page summarises the guidelines.

Try to use *pictures and annotated diagrams* when you cover this outcome. This will save you time and give more information.

Detailed information about expedition equipment can be obtained from shops, manufacturers' brochures or the internet.

Equipment checklist

- **Personal equipment**: boots, socks, thermals, fleeces, walking trousers, shorts, shirt, overtrousers, walking jacket, hat, gloves, gaiters, rucksack (day-sack and framed sack for backpacking) rucksack liner (or rucksack cover) compass, knife, cord, walking poles, map and map case, flask and bottle/hydration system, watch, trowel, head torch with spare batteries and bulb, route card, food plus hot and cold drinks, money, tissues

Summary of guidelines

Type of equipment	Design features	Correct usage	Properties of materials used	Cleaning and care	Factors influencing choice for person and conditions
Simple, e.g. cutlery, plates, survival bag	Basic information, e.g. size and weight	Be brief!	Weight, flammability – little detail needed	Simple notes only	Lightness, cheapness, size, safety, warmth, etc.
More complex, e.g. walking trousers, walking pole, carry mat	Explain at least two design features	Explain	Give properties of at least two different materials used, e.g. weight, waterproof	Explain one or more methods of cleaning and care	Give at least one factor, e.g. comfort, weight, warmth, cost, convenience, size
Complex and/or specialised, e.g. boots, walking jacket, rucksack, tent	Explain at least two types; cover four or more design features	Explain three or more points of correct usage	Compare properties of at least two materials used, e.g. advantages and disadvantages of each	Explain at least two factors in cleaning and care	Include at least three factors influencing choice, e.g. durability, insulation, protection

- **Camping equipment**: tent, sleeping bag and liner, compression sack, insulation mat, stove, pans and fuel, matches/lighter, knife, fork and spoon, plate, mug, sterilisation tablets/water filters, camp rations, toiletries, pan cleaning equipment, soft shoes
- **Safety**: accident procedure and how to summon help, whistle (international distress signal and response), survival bag, group shelter, mobile phone, personal first aid kit (containing items to treat common walking injuries and personal medication where appropriate), sewing/repair kit, waterproof paper and pencil, insect repellent, sun screen, sunglasses, survival rations, spare clothing, weather forecast (and, if appropriate, rope and flares).

Source: BN011697 Guidance and Units for the Edexcel Level 3 BTEC Nationals in Public Services – Issue 1 – May 2002

COOL SITES:

http://www.cotswold-outdoor.com/
http://www.interhike.com/camping.equipment.gear/
http://www.ukcamping.co.uk/
http://www.field-trek.co.uk/ft1/news.asp – good technical info

CHECKPOINT ...

1. Find out where and when your planned expedition for this unit is going to take place.
2. Which of the above items would you not take on your expedition – and why?
3. Which items not mentioned in the above list would *you* consider taking?
4. What items have been missed out of the above list?

PASSGRADE

Describe and comment on the effectiveness of a range of different types and designs of personal, group, and safety equipment used in walking and camping.

For this outcome, you need to examine the 'effectiveness' (fitness for purpose) of different kinds of walking and camping equipment.

- 'Personal equipment' is equipment belonging to you, or for your own use.
- 'Group equipment' is material such as ropes or large tents which will be used by more than one person.
- 'Safety equipment' includes survival bags, whistles, flares, first aid kit, sun-block, etc.

COOL SITE:

http://www.walkingbritain.co.uk/features/index6.shtml

Ways of researching this outcome:

- use a wide range of equipment yourself
- ask other people about the equipment they use
- look for product reviews, consumer assessments of equipment, etc. – in outdoor magazines or the internet.

You should:

- collect information about tents, boots, jackets, waterproof trousers, sleeping bags and rucksacks from suppliers or the internet. Find out about design, materials, size, type of use intended, weight, bulk, durability, waterproof qualities, heat insulation and price. Notice any gadgets, and also any features which might cause problems in a snowstorm on a mountain! Discuss the good and bad aspects of the products with the shopkeeper, if you get a chance
- on your residential, survey your classmates or companions about what equipment they use and what they think of it (and be prepared to give similar information to them)
- question your tutors and outdoor instructors about the kinds of equipment they think are best (or worst) – and why
- if you get the chance to meet armed forces personnel who use outdoor equipment on training exercises, find out what they consider to be the best equipment for different conditions.

'When I told you to bring flares I didn't mean that kind!'

Merit

Explain the choice of equipment and materials taken on an expedition.

Merit

Analyse and evaluate the design and properties of materials used and the selection and care of equipment.

For these outcomes, you need to:

- state – with reasons – why you have chosen the equipment you have for your own expedition
- give the good and bad features of equipment you have chosen and used on an expedition
- give guidelines for looking after equipment, explaining why care is needed.

Choice of equipment

The table at the top of the next page summarises the factors that should be considered when choosing equipment for an expedition.

Care of equipment

For this you normally follow the manufacturers' instructions.

Factors to take into account when explaining choice of equipment

Boots	Rucksack(s)	Jacket	Sleeping bag	Tent	Stove
Comfort Size Waterproofing Durability Sole grip Protection Lightness Ease of fastening Price	Capacity (65+ litres needed for full expedition) Is additional day-sack needed? Weight Pockets Waterproof? Straps? Frame? Price	Size Comfort Waterproofing Lightness Hood Pockets Fastenings Zip quality Insulation (i.e. will it protect you against cold and wind?) Price	Size Weight Warmth (i.e. what is its 'tog' rating?) Filling (e.g. terylene or down?) Hood How small will it pack? Price	Size (is it big enough for the number of people?) Can you put it up? Fireproof? Weight Are all pegs, guy-ropes, etc. with it? Strength Waterproofing Performance in wind Price	Type Weight Size Fuel Safety Ease of use Does it need cleaning? Price of stove and fuel

Profile

Care of tents

- Avoid all risk of fire.
- Always dry a tent before you pack it up.
- Count pegs, poles, etc. so you don't lose them.
- Don't let your guy ropes get tangled.
- Don't pitch tents too close together.
- Never fall or tread on a tent.

! CHECKPOINT ...

Research the correct care of all major equipment that you will be using on your expedition. Write yourself brief notes for each item.

Distinction

Justify the decisions made in the choice of materials used and the correct selection and care of equipment when taking part in the camping expedition.

For this outcome, you need to:

- state clearly why you chose each item you used on your expedition
- give reasoned criticisms of the suitability of your equipment
- outline how you cleaned and cared for each major item
- show that you fully understand the pitching and packing of tents, use of cookers and camping safety and hygiene.

PLANNING AND CARRYING OUT AN EXPEDITION

PASSGRADE

Prepare and carry out a camping and walking expedition of at least 25 kilometres which includes camping for at least two days and one night.

For this outcome, you need to:

- make sure that all arrangements involving transport, payment, etc. are covered
- get all the things you need bought, collected and packed
- walk for at least 25 kilometres in at least two days
- camp for at least one night.

Much of the practical planning may be done by your college, or some other organisation. Let the organisers know if you run into any problems.

25 kilometres is 16 miles.

Prepare

Assuming the transport is arranged by the college, preparing usually means making lists, often in groups who will be sharing tents and cooking. You will be assessed on your preparation, so the following points are worth noting:

- If you are in groups, choose companions you will get on with.
- If there are any potential problems (e.g. money or health), see your tutor as soon as possible.
- Be enthusiastic and interested. Don't sit back and let everyone else make the decisions and do the work. Make an effort to be present at all group or team meetings.
- Offer to do your share of the work, if the preparation is a group effort.
- Keep copies of lists and decisions so that you know what you and everybody else is doing.
- If you have never camped before, make sure your tutor checks your list of what you are taking with you.
- Arrange to borrow anything you haven't got and don't wish to buy.
- Get all paperwork done: your organisers will need (a) signed consent forms, (b) contact names and telephone numbers (parents or next of kin), (c) your doctor's address and phone number.
- Provide any other information needed by the organisers of your expedition. Check that you are insured.

Carry out

For this outcome, you should have a number of qualified and experienced tutors or instructors supervising what you do. As well as carrying out walks adding up to 25 km in length, you will take part in other outdoor pursuits (see below). Here are some ground-rules:

- Always put safety first.
- When in doubt, consult your tutors.
- If you are unhappy about anything, say so.
- If you are ill or injured, tell your tutor and get treatment.
- Check your equipment each morning before setting out on any activity.
- Take part in all activities cheerfully and willingly.
- Be helpful and considerate towards other expedition members.
- Be well disciplined and cooperative.

Merit

Demonstrate the use of highly competent, accurate, safe skills when walking, navigating and camping.

Distinction

Demonstrate and evaluate practical skills used in walking, navigating and camping.

A wilderness close to home: people die every year in the Scottish Highlands, often because they don't know how to navigate.

For this outcome, you need to:

- show very good practical skills in walking, navigating and camping
- explain and assess the importance of each of the skills you have used
- appraise (judge) your own performance honestly, suggesting ways in which you may be able to improve or develop your skills.

OUTDOOR PURSUITS

PASSGRADE

Experience two other outdoor pursuits and analyse the benefits of outdoor pursuits.

For this outcome, you need to take part in two outdoor pursuits, as well as walking and camping.

'Outdoor pursuits' include activities such as mountain-biking, kayaking, caving, potholing, sailing, orienteering, water-skiing, horse-riding, gorge walking, rock-climbing, abseiling and canoeing. There may also be problem-solving activities – such as building temporary bridges or searching for 'injured strangers'. What you do will depend on where you go for your expedition, and what kind of facilities or equipment are available.

The benefits of outdoor pursuits include:

- **teamwork skills** – how to motivate, encourage, help, guide, cooperate, follow instructions and requests, share responsibility, resolve minor disagreements, etc.

  These skills are developed in any shared group activity such as camping, cooking, rock-climbing, caving, etc.
- **leadership** – how to organise, guide, advise, command, explain, listen, inspire, take responsibility, reward – or rebuke – by making appropriate comments. These skills are developed in group activities. Everyone should be able to take on a leadership role at one time or another
- **individual achievement** – trying new experiences, and succeeding at them, e.g. abseiling for the first time
- **physical fitness** – aerobic fitness developed by hard walking up steep hills; other kinds of fitness including skill-based components through water-skiing, kayaking, etc.
- **mental stability** – taking things in your stride without panicking; overcoming fears, e.g. of heights, through rock-climbing
- **self-reliance** – trusting your own judgement, e.g. when map-reading and planning.

! CHECKPOINT ...

Other benefits of outdoor pursuits can include: developing problem-solving skills, building relationships, improving own performance, communication skills, confidence building, stress relief, enjoyment, inner peace.

For each benefit, relate it to any outdoor activity you have done, and show in what way that outdoor activity has brought about that particular benefit.

Merit

Explain the benefits of outdoor activities.

For this outcome, you need to:

- give more detail on exactly how outdoor activities benefit people mentally, physically, emotionally and spiritually
- draw on your own experience, by saying what you have gained from each of the activities you have done during your expedition
- explain how each outdoor activity would benefit an applicant to a named public service, e.g. that rock-climbing would benefit someone wishing to join the fire service by improving agility and balance, and by instilling confidence in working at a height.

USING AND PROTECTING THE COUNTRYSIDE

PASSGRADE

Describe the current issues around access to the countryside, explaining the work of one agency and one statutory body involved in promoting and protecting the countryside.

For this outcome, you need to:

- say what is meant by access to the countryside, and why it can cause problems
- outline the rights and responsibilities of walkers

- outline the law of trespass
- choose one statutory and one non-statutory service connected with the use and/or conservation of the countryside – and say what these services do.

Access

The issue of access to the countryside – allowing ramblers, walkers and other members of the general public on to what is legally private land – has caused problems since the 1932 'mass trespass' on the moors of Kinder Scout by walkers from the Manchester area. Farmers prefer not to have large numbers of strangers wandering around their land. Walkers and other users of the outdoors think differently; they want the 'right to roam'.

The law was changed by the Countryside and Rights of Way Act in 2000 to give walkers more access to open countryside. 'Open countryside' means mountains, moors or downland, not enclosed fields. The right will be fully granted in 2004, when areas to be designated under the Act have been mapped by the Countryside Agency (see below).

Under civil law, walkers only have a right to cross private enclosed land if they use a 'right of way'. A right of way is a legally recognised track. Farmers have a legal responsibility to keep rights of way in a usable condition.

There are three kinds of right of way:

- foot only (public footpaths)
- foot and horse (public bridleways)
- any traffic (byways open to all traffic, including cars, etc.).

Rights of way are marked on most OS 1:25 000 and 1:50 000 maps.

Trespass

Trespass is normally a common law civil offence, not a criminal offence. If you go on a farmer's land and they tell you to get off because you are trespassing, they have a right to ask you to leave by the shortest possible route (and you should carry out their request). They do not have a right to threaten you. If however, two or more people camp on land without permission and it appears that they will be there for some time, they can be evicted by the police under the Criminal Justice and Public Order Act 1994.

http://www.ca-mapping.co.uk/mapping/Regional/1/R1.htm

http://www.naturenet.net/law/

Responsibilities of walkers and campers

FOCUS

The Country Code

Enjoy the countryside and respect its life and work.

Guard against all risk of fire.

Close and fasten all gates behind you.

Keep your dogs under close control at all times.

Keep to public paths across farmland.

Use only gateways or stiles to cross fences, hedges and walls.

Leave livestock, crops and machinery alone.

Take all litter home with you.

Help to keep all waterways clean.

Protect wildlife, plants and trees.

Take special care on country roads.

Avoid making unnecessary noise.

Promotion and protection of the countryside

Now that 30 million Britons live in towns, the countryside has value not only as a place where farmers grow food, but as a tourist attraction. This was vividly seen in the 2000–1 foot and mouth epidemic. The rural economy suffered a 'double whammy', losing approximately £355 million in the livestock sector, and a massive £3 billion in income from tourism. The government was attacked afterwards for doing too much to help livestock farmers while letting tourism, a much bigger earner, suffer huge losses as the countryside was 'closed down'.

Promotion of the countryside means developing the countryside as a leisure resource, and building visitor centres, footpaths and other facilities to attract holidaymakers. If the countryside is not promoted rural communities will become even more disadvantaged, and degenerate into a mixture of ghost villages and second homes.

But the other side of the coin is that the countryside is damaged by economic development. The environmental pressures are immense, and the beauty of the landscape, and its wildlife, are suffering as a result. Promotion of the countryside brings mass tourism, a rash of new building, road-widening schemes, wind-farms, signposts, footpaths and bridle paths and the loss of that peace and beauty which attract people to the countryside in the first place.

> **!** CHECKPOINT ...
> Can there be both promotion and protection of the countryside? What do you think, and why?

Agencies and statutory bodies which protect and promote the countryside.

Many bodies which aim to protect the countryside also promote it, and many which aim to promote it also try to protect it. Here are two of them.

FOCUS

The Ramblers' Association

'The Ramblers' Association is Britain's biggest organisation working for walkers, a registered charity with 139,000 members across England, Scotland and Wales. We've been looking after Britain's footpaths and defending its beautiful countryside for more than 65 years by:

- **protecting** Britain's unique network of public paths – all too often, they are illegally blocked, obstructed and overgrown. We work with local authorities to make them a pleasure to walk on.
- **providing** information to help you plan your walk and enjoy it in safety and comfort.
- **increasing** access for walkers – our work is helping to establish statutory rights of access to our countryside.
- **safeguarding** the countryside from unsightly and polluting developments so that walkers can enjoy its tranquillity and beauty.
- **educating** the public about their rights and responsibilities and the health and environmental benefits of walking so that everyone can enjoy our wonderful heritage.'

Source: The Ramblers' Association
www.ramblers.org.uk

http://www.ramblers.org.uk/ – lots of good stuff

FOCUS

The Countryside Agency

'The Countryside Agency is the statutory body working to:

- make life better for people in the countryside; and
- improve the quality of the countryside for everyone.

The Countryside Agency will help to achieve the following outcomes:

- empowered, active and inclusive communities;
- high standards of rural services;
- vibrant local economies;
- all countryside managed sustainably;
- recreational infrastructure that's easy to enjoy;
- a vibrant and diverse urban fringe providing better quality of life.'

Source: The Countryside Agency

http://www.countryside.gov.uk/reception/default.htm

> **!** CHECKPOINT ...
> 1 The government has suggested it might change the Countryside Agency and set up other bodies to develop or protect the countryside. Research this point to make sure that your information is up to date
> 2 Research the issues around fox-hunting – is it exploitation or conservation of the countryside?

Profile

The work of the Countryside Agency is much more far-reaching than that of the Ramblers' Association. This is only to be expected, because it is a statutory organisation, i.e. set up by the government and largely paid for by taxpayers' money. The Countryside Agency works both to protect and develop the countryside, looking after rural people, their economic development and the protection of the environment. Its aim is to help all who live and work in the countryside, or who go there to enjoy themselves. It does this by giving grants and advice, by forming partnerships with local people, community groups and charities, by researching rural needs and by producing action plans. It wants to help rural communities to diversify from farming and get more involved in tourism and says, 'We also work to encourage proper provision for walkers, riders and cyclists.' In this sense its work supports that of the Ramblers' Association.

The Ramblers' Association is a charity and pressure group supporting people who walk for pleasure and recreation. It is a non-statutory organisation and most of its money comes from members' subscriptions. It works to keep pathways open, organise holidays and social activities, and support the preservation of the countryside (in ways which do not discriminate against walkers!).

Merit

Analyse the benefits of outdoor activities and the issues around access to the countryside by detailed investigation into the work of one agency and one statutory body involved in the promotion and protection of the countryside.

For this outcome, you need to:

- examine outdoor activities and access to the countryside
- explain why outdoor activities can be good for the people doing them, and for the people living and working in the countryside
- study the work of one statutory and one non-statutory organisation involved in the development and/or the conservation of the countryside.

For the first part of this outcome, you should:

- explain the skills needed in each outdoor activity, and how the activity develops those skills
- examine closely how communication and teamwork skills are developed by outdoor activities
- state the personal benefits these skills bring
- explain the professional advantages a person working in the public services might gain from skills used in outdoor activities.

For the second part of this outcome, you should:

- research how outdoor activities benefit local industry and the rural economy
- discuss the economic benefits to the countryside of the establishment of bunk-houses and field centres, and the setting up of shops to sell walking, potholing or climbing equipment
- examine more closely the work of the Countryside Agency, outlining how it reconciles its development role with its protection role
- clarify what the Countryside Agency means by 'empowered, active and inclusive communities'.

Distinction

Evaluate the benefits of outdoor activities and the issues around access to the countryside by detailed investigation into the work of one agency and one statutory body involved in the promotion and protection of the countryside.

For this outcome, you need to:

- build on the previous one
- explain the advantages and disadvantages of outdoor activities, both for participants and for those who live and work in the countryside
- explain the advantages and disadvantages of opening up the countryside to the public
- assess the work of a statutory and non-statutory body (organisation) which either 'markets' or protects the countryside.

For this outcome, you might also:

- examine whether outdoor activities really do bring the benefits people claim
- consider the damaging psychological effects outdoor activities can have: for example the way they encourage obedience and conformity
- think about the cultural bias of outdoor activities, e.g. encouraging 'macho' or 'quasi-military' ideas

of strength, competition, manliness, etc. which can be counterproductive in modern society

- question the lack of emphasis of outdoor activities in appreciating the beauty of nature and the spiritual benefits nature can bring
- evaluate the physical dangers of outdoor activities (From 1985–2003, 47 British children died on school trips involving outdoor activities, and in 2001–2, 29 people died on Scottish hills with the rescue services being called out 300 times.)
- assess the direct environmental damage they cause, e.g. litter, destruction to wildlife (rare plants and resting birds), damage to rock faces and potholes
- assess their indirect environmental damage, e.g. the commercialisation of the countryside, turning it into a kind of adventure playground.

Your comments should not all be negative. From a public service point of view, outdoor activities are considered to be a very good thing. For this outcome you should be able to say why, in some depth and detail. Your aim is to give a balanced account, supported by evidence and reasoning, of the good and the not-so-good aspects of outdoor activities.

Detailed investigation into the work of one agency and one statutory body involved in the promotion and protection of the countryside

From the organisations and websites listed below, you should be able to choose suitable organisations to research.

Statutory bodies

- http://www.countryside.gov.uk/ – the Countryside Agency
- Defra
- English Heritage
- English Nature
- the Forestry Commission
- the Centre for Ecology and Hydrology

Non-statutory bodies

- http://www.uknature.pwp.blueyonder.co.uk/organisa.html – nature organisations
- http://www.dudley.gov.uk/council/plan_app/nature/Local%20conservation%20orgs.htm
- http://www.countrylovers.co.uk/orgs/ctryorgs.htm#natrgs – countryside organisations

! CHECKPOINT ...

1. Find out about the work of the British Mountaineering Council and the Mountain Leader training which they give.
2. Research Mountain Leader Training Boards.
3. Find someone who has a mountain leader award and ask what skills and knowledge the training gave them.
4. If you are interested, consider doing such a course yourself.

COOL SITES:

These sites give easy access to information for much of this unit.

http://education.guardian.co.uk/schooltrips/story/0,10621,665483,00.html – interesting article

http://www.teachersupport.org.uk/index.cfm?p=1507 – young people and outdoor activities

https://www.yha.org.uk/website-yhauk/pdfs/ypoa.pdf – a balanced view from the YHA

http://www.thebmc.co.uk/default.asp – good general information

http://www.ukmtb.org/contacts.htm#BMC

http://www.mountaineering-scotland.org.uk/documents/mountain%20accidents.pdf –*Strategies for Improving Mountain Safety*, by Strathclyde University Faculty of Education – a detailed and fascinating report

Unit 12 Human Behaviour

Grading criteria

PASSGRADE	Merit	Distinction
To achieve a pass grade the evidence must show that the learner is able to:	To achieve a merit grade the evidence must show that the learner is able to:	To achieve a distinction grade the evidence must show that the learner is able to:
• explain the approaches to psychology 229 • describe your own personality type and associated traits 234 • explain the evolution of behaviour 236 • describe personality types and related behaviour and the treatment of abnormal behavioural types 238 • explain the different types of interview 240 • demonstrate and evaluate your own techniques in an interview situation 241 • explain the difference and similarities between verbal and non-verbal communication and the importance of the use of the senses in each 242	• Analyse the approaches to psychology found in colleagues and customers 233 • analyse what makes a good interviewer and interviewee 242 • analyse the different types of communication used in public services 244 • evaluate communication styles in relation to speech and behaviour 245	• analyse and evaluate how the different approaches to psychology will have an effect on individuals and the organisation 233

This unit is all about the way people act – individually and in groups.

Human behaviour, as a subject, is closely linked to psychology, which means 'the study of the mind'. This is because the main evidence of how people's minds work comes from the way they behave.

This unit will help you to understand human behaviour – both in relation to your own life and to public service work.

APPROACHES TO PSYCHOLOGY

Explain the approaches to psychology.

For this outcome, you need to outline the main 'schools of thought' in psychology in your own words.

FOCUS

Definition of psychology

Psychology is ...

'the science of mental life' – William James (a classic definition from the nineteenth century)

'the scientific study of the mind and its activities, both normal and abnormal' – *Collins Dictionary*

'the science of behavior and mental processes' – Myers, D.G. (2002), *Exploring Psychology*, Bedford, Freeman and Worth

COOL SITE:

http://www.gpc.peachnet.edu/~bbrown/psyc1501/psychology/definition.htm

There are four main approaches to psychology: behaviourist, psychoanalytic, humanistic and cognitive. Many psychologists combine two or more of these approaches. Psychology is also influenced by ideas such as feminism and Marxism, and by the use of medicine and surgery ('clinical psychology').

The behaviourist approach

This approach was pioneered by Ivan Pavlov (1849–1936). J.B. Watson (1878–1958) and B.F. Skinner (1904–90). Behaviourists argue that all behaviour is caused by something else – in other words, behaviour is the *response* to a *stimulus*. They also believe that behaviour can be tested scientifically in conditions that can be reproduced. Behaviourism was the first serious attempt to make psychology into an experimental science, in the same way that physics and biology were experimental sciences.

Behaviourism is not interested in mind, consciousness or thoughts, but in actions. Behaviourists have often used animals for their experiments, mainly because animals are less complicated than human beings, and not affected by things like language and culture. Pavlov is famous for his experiments with dogs, in which he discovered that dogs could learn, by a process which he called 'conditioning'.

Pavlov discovered *classical conditioning* (in which a dog could be made to associate a sound with food so that it salivated when hearing the sound, even when no food was present).

B.F. Skinner later identified another type of conditioning: *operant conditioning* (in which a pigeon, for example, learnt to peck a lever in order to get a food reward).

Classical conditioning involves no link between the dog's response and a reward (i.e. the dog does not get food because it salivates). Operant conditioning links the response, the pecking of a lever, to a reward (a seed). The animal has to do something to get its reward.

J.B. Watson attempted to show conditioning in human beings. In 1923 he trained a child to be terrified of furry objects by clanging a metal bar behind the child every time it held a furry toy.

Assessment of behaviourism

Against:

- It tends to oversimplify people and view them as animals.
- It can lead to inhumane experiments.
- It could lead to brainwashing and indoctrination of children (or even adults).

For:

- It shows the importance of environment in determining our behaviour.
- It has led to improvements in housing and education.
- It shows that people are not always to blame for their actions.

- It encourages things like crime prevention and positive crime reduction or youth diversion schemes.

The psychoanalytic approach

This approach was put forward mainly by Sigmund Freud (1856–1939), the most famous of all psychologists. He based it on his studies of mentally ill people. Although Freud was interested in behaviour, he didn't study it 'scientifically' like the behaviourists did, and he never experimented with animals. To understand the mind, he used a technique called 'free association', in which words were given to his patients, and they had to tell him about the ideas, images and memories those words produced in their minds. This procedure of finding and interpreting thoughts by free association Freud called 'psychoanalysis' – 'sorting out' the mind.

Freud believed that much human behaviour, including mental illness, resulted from events which happened in early childhood whose memory had been 'repressed' but which came out in 'neuroses' (mental problems) later in life. He divided the mind into two parts – the *conscious* and the *unconscious*. The conscious mind was the thoughts, ideas and memories that we were aware of; the unconscious mind was all the stuff we had repressed – forced ourselves to 'forget' (in Freud's view very little was truly forgotten). Freud believed that mental illness, and lesser problems such as mistakes, slips of the tongue or bad dreams, were caused by the unconscious mind stirring up the conscious mind. And Freud thought he could cure mental illness if he could reveal the hidden problems of the unconscious mind to the conscious mind of the patient.

Unlike the behaviourists, Freud thought it was possible to understand not just human behaviour, but also the mind itself. Apart from the idea of the conscious and unconscious mind, he had many other famous ideas about the mind (some of which he gave Greek and Latin names). They include:

- **Instinct**
  - Eros – the urge for sex, the life-force
  - Thanatos – the 'death-wish'
  - Libido – the urge for bodily pleasure
- **Infantile sexuality**
  - Oral stage, e.g. thumb-sucking
  - Anal stage, e.g. retention
  - Phallic stage – awareness of penis
  - Oedipus Complex – the secret wish of the male child to kill his father and make love to his mother
  - Castration Complex – irrational fear of castration
  - Penis envy – the desire of young girls to be boys

Freud believed all these existed in the under-fives, and that, in repressed form, they could cause mental problems in later life.

- **Structure of the mind**
  - Id – the sexual energy hidden in the unconscious mind
  - Ego – the self we know
  - Super-ego – the 'conscience', guarding the ego from the id
- **Mental illness** Freud saw this as a power-struggle between the three parts of the mind. The super-ego tried to fight the id in ways which were destructive to mental health. These ways included:
  - repression – pushing desires forcibly back into the unconscious mind
  - sublimation – changing 'bad' desires into something more socially acceptable
  - fixation – obsessively stuck at one of the stages of infantile sexual development
  - regression – return to an earlier, more childlike stage of development.

Assessment of Freud

Against:

- Freud is condemned by many psychologists as 'unscientific' because his theories cannot be put to the test.
- There is little objective proof that psychoanalysis can cure mental illness.
- Psychoanalysis can be damaging to patients and their families, e.g. causing allegations of child sex abuse without providing any objective evidence.
- Freud has been accused of being obsessed with sex.
- His theories are seen as 'phallocentric' – male-orientated – and undervaluing or ignoring women.

For:

- Freud did a great deal to make people interested in psychology.
- Many of his theories are accepted, even though they cannot be proved.
- Psychologists started studying sex, instead of pretending it didn't exist.
- He had an immense effect on the arts, the media (e.g. advertising, film) and on the way we think about other people.
- His ideas are important in criminal psychology and offender profiling.

http://www.utm.edu/research/iep/f/freud.htm

The humanistic approach

The humanistic approach to psychology is more straightforward than the others. It states that:

- we are who we think we are. Humanism is 'phenomenological' in the sense that it accepts the individual's view of the self and of the world as being essentially valid
- we have free will and can therefore control who we are and what we do if we want to
- we have positive qualities and that we all have the capacity to grow and become better
- when looking at ourselves and other people we should consider the present and the future, rather than dwell on the past.

The main humanist psychologists were Carl Rogers and Abraham Maslow.

Carl Rogers (1902–87) said it was important to:

- accept other people without criticism; in other words to give them 'unconditional positive regard'
- have a positive 'self-concept'; that is to consider oneself to be of value.

Rogers believed that lack of 'unconditional positive regard' (genuine respect and liking with no strings attached) from others, and a 'negative self-concept' (feelings of worthlessness) were at the root of many mental illnesses. He developed a system of counselling which was designed to build self-esteem and a positive self-concept in people who were suffering from depression, anxiety and other mental problems.

Abraham Maslow (1908–70) developed the hugely influential 'hierarchy of human needs'.

LINK! See page 54 for a diagram and explanation of Maslow's hierarchy of human needs.

This was humanistic in that it stressed the individual's potential for self-development, and presented a positive and optimistic view of the human condition.

Assessment of humanism

Against:

- It seems to offer no new insights into either human behaviour or the human mind.

For:

- It has more common sense and less theory than other approaches to psychology.
- It presents people as being in some sense 'basically good'.
- It is effective in counselling, either of young people in schools and colleges, or in the public services when employees are suffering from stress.
- It has had a very good effect on management and working conditions in all areas of employment – especially the public services.

FOCUS

Transactional analysis

This is a system of therapy which blends the psychoanalytic and humanistic approaches. Its inventor, Eric Berne (1910–70), who wrote a famous book called *Games People Play*, identifies three 'ego states', which he calls 'adult', 'parent' and 'child'. These ego states define roles that people adopt in relation to each other. The parent and child ego states are seen as damaging both to relationships and to personal development, because they lock people into 'games' (repetitive behaviour patterns) such as giving advice all the time ('Why don't you ...?') or playing tit for tat ('Now I've got you, you SOB!'). People who are trapped into these behaviours are seen to be following a harmful 'life script'. Transactional analysis means analysing the individual's use of 'strokes' or individual actions which made up the 'games'. The aim of transactional analysis is to help people overcome these restrictive and harmful behaviours through therapy, and to lead them towards an 'I'm OK, you're OK' attitude, where people respect and value each other for what they are.

http://www.itaa-net.org/ta/keyideas.htm – groovy '70s stuff!

The cognitive approach

Cognitive psychology looks at how we learn and develop. Its chief researchers have been Jean Piaget, Albert Bandura, Noam Chomsky and Jerome Bruner.

Jean Piaget (1896–1980) made a great contribution to the study of child development. He was particularly interested in the nature of 'intelligence', and the changing forms that intelligence took as a child grew older. He discovered that children think in different ways at different ages, and use different 'schemas' (ways of processing ideas) as they grow up. He identified four stages of intellectual development, summarised in the table below.

Piaget's four stages of intellectual development

Stage	Age	Characteristics
1 Sensorimotor	0–2	Develops mental skills mainly through coordinating movements and senses.
2 Pre-operational	2–7	Children can imagine things they cannot see, but cannot use deductive reasoning.
3 Concrete operations	7–11	Children use deductive reasoning and can differentiate their views from those of other people.
4 Formal operations	After 11	The ability for abstract thought develops.

Albert Bandura was born in Canada in 1925. He developed a version of cognitive psychology called 'social learning theory' (or 'social cognitive theory'). The theory states that human behaviour is determined by a range of factors: the situation the person is in, the way other people behave, and the knowledge and feelings of that person. These factors all influence each other by a process which Bandura called 'reciprocal determinism'. He believed that people were free to decide their actions, but in a framework of environmental and personal factors which limited their range of choice. Bandura believed that personality, knowledge and skills were all learned – but in a social context, through interactions with other people and groups. He found that imitation played a key role in this kind of learning, and has researched on the ways people pick up violent behaviour from TV and films. He has also studied the effects of rewards and punishments on human behaviour.

Jerome Bruner (born 1915), working in the 1960s, developed a 'cognitive learning model' to explain how people learn new ideas and skills. He showed that learning was an active, organised, internal process, rather than a matter of 'trial and error' He suggested that people's minds contained both learned and inbuilt 'structures' which helped to arrange new stimuli into their own unique classification. These structures enabled predictions to take place about new learning, and these predictions greatly facilitated the learning process.

Bruner linked learning ability with language acquisition, and with the ability to think analytically, using steps which can be explained to other people. Bruner was also interested in leadership, which he believed would increasingly need to include an ability to solve problems.

Noam Chomsky (born 1928) is famous for his studies on how children learn language. He believed that all children have an inborn grammar ('universal grammar') in their minds which gave them a special ability to learn any language. This ability, which Chomsky called the 'Language Acquisition Device' (LAD), was different from all other cognitive (learning) abilities. The language acquisition device determined the order in which children learn different types of words, grammatical functions and sentence structures (i.e. it told them what order to put words in so that they made sense).

Assessment of the cognitive approach

Against:

- It tends to test, classify and label people.
- It stresses genetic factors, so it's open to accusations of racism.

For:

- It has contributed much to teaching and learning theory, and therefore improved the quality of education.
- It is the basis of public service psychometric testing.
- It is the basis of public service training methods.
- It is effective in treating phobias and (together with drugs) post traumatic stress disorder.

Free will versus determinism

Free will is the ability to choose or decide our own actions. Determinism is the belief that our actions are caused by other factors, e.g. the environment.

Free will underpins our notions of justice. Our ideas of crime and punishment are based on the belief that criminals choose to do wrong, through their free will. Without free will, right and wrong or good and evil would be meaningless and no action would be any better than any other.

On the other hand, research shows that certain types of individual (e.g. those who come from criminal backgrounds) are more likely to commit crimes than the average person. This suggests our will is not completely free because what we do can be *determined* by the people, things and ideas around us. When, as Shadow Home Secretary, Tony Blair famously said that Labour would be 'tough on crime and tough on the causes of crime' he was recognising that an action like crime has two causes – a direct cause (an act of free will for which the individual is to blame) and an indirect cause (e.g. poverty, bad parenting or mental illness) for which the individual is not to blame.

Free will and determinism appear to contradict each other – yet it seems we need both ideas if we are to fully explain and understand human behaviour.

'It wasn't me wot done it, guv. It was me environment!'

COOL SITES:

http://www.psy.pdx.edu/PsiCafe/KeyTheorists/Bruner.htm#Research

http://www.hull.ac.uk/php/cetag/2b5camps.htm – cool!

http://www.personalitytype.com/types/enfj.html

http://www.longevitywatch.com/PersonalityTypes.htm

Merit

Analyse the approaches to psychology found in colleagues and customers.

For this outcome, you need to research and comment on the use colleagues and customers make of psychology.

You should decide from the outset:

- what group(s) of people you are going to research
- what kinds of information you want to obtain:
  - If you want quantitative information, which you can analyse using graphs and charts, you must ask closed questions (e.g. 'yes/no' questions, or questions to be answered on a three- or five-point scale of preference).
  - If you want in-depth information from fewer respondents (e.g. your college counsellors), you should ask open questions about their own interests and preferences, and their reasons for them.

Your analysis should seek to find out things like:

- how relevant your respondents find psychology to their daily work
- what kinds of psychology are used in teaching or learning
- how shops use psychology to attract customers
- what psychological methods of motivation are used in the armed forces
- what the police know about crowd psychology
- how psychology has helped the fire service to tackle malicious false alarms
- what kinds of psychology operate in courtrooms and trials
- the role of psychology is sports and fitness coaching and training.

Take care to collect and record your data in an accurate and professional manner, and to draw reasoned conclusions which relate clearly to the evidence you have collected.

Distinction

Analyse and evaluate how the different approaches to psychology will have an effect on individuals and the organisation.

For this outcome, you need to:

- examine the use and importance of different approaches to psychology:
  - for the behaviour of individuals
  - for the workings of an organisation
- explain why different approaches are used for different kinds of work
- draw conclusions about the effectiveness of these approaches – both for individuals and for organisations.

The organisation does not have to be a public service, but public services make extensive use of psychology both in their dealings with the public and with clients, and for the productivity and welfare of their employees.

Examples of the kinds of things you could consider are:

- the use of psychological theories of motivation such as those of Maslow and his followers, to get the maximum productivity from a workforce
- the use of transactional analysis and game theories to achieve better results, with less conflict, in police interviews
- the relevance of research on conformity and obedience (Asch and Milgram, for example – see page 253) to discipline and drill in the armed forces
- the use of cognitive psychology for teachers, lecturers and instructors in a public service
- types of counselling used in occupational health, e.g. to help people with stress at work, or with post traumatic stress disorder
- psychological theories and research underlying psychometric testing
- training in the probation and prison services to deal with clients with abnormal behaviour patterns
- psychological aspects of crowd control at football matches
- whether psychological theories of human attraction are used when selecting police officers
- psychological profiling of offenders such as arsonists or serial killers.

BEHAVIOURAL TYPES

Describe your own personality type and associated traits.

For this outcome, you need to:

- identify your personality type (you could use the system given below)
- describe its main characteristics.

FOCUS

Definitions of personality

Personality is ...

'...enduring patterns of perceiving, relating to, and thinking about the environment and oneself ... exhibited in a wide range of important social and personal contexts.' – American Psychiatric Association. DSM-IV-TR, Washington, 2000

' the distinctive character or qualities of a person, often as distinct from others ...' – *Oxford English Dictionary*

'psychological characteristics of an individual that are general, enduring, distinctive, integrated and functional' – Peterson, C. (1997), *Psychology: A Biopsychosocial Approach* (2nd edition), New York: Longman

This is a complex outcome. It is based on the idea that all of us have personalities, and that personalities can be classified according to type.

CHECKPOINT ...

What are the possible dangers of describing or labelling our own personalities?

Psychologists have made a number of such classifications for two main purposes: career guidance and health predictions.

Careers guidance

The Myers–Briggs Personality Indicator identifies your personality type through your answers to four key questions, each of which has two possible answers.

As a result of choosing one of the options to each of the questions you should end up with four letters. (Note that N is used for 'Intuition' to avoid confusion with Introvert.) There are 16 possible combinations, and these correspond to the 16 personality types identified by this method:

The Myers–Briggs Personality Indicator

Question	Choice of answers	Diagnosis
1 Where, primarily, do you direct your energy?	(a) Outward, to other people. I am active, sociable, outgoing, and prefer doing things to thinking about them. (b) Inwards, towards my own interests and aims. I am a private, quiet person who likes to think before acting.	(a) Extrovert (E) (b) Introvert (I)
2 How do you prefer to process information?	(a) I prefer information based on facts or experience; I am a practical person who prefers to live in the present. I am realistic and like to enjoy life. (b) I am interested in new ideas and possibilities; I like to be imaginative and to change and develop. I am idealistic and I want to make the world a better place.	(a) Sensing (S) (b) Intuition (N)
3 How do you prefer to make decisions?	(a) I like to analyse and think things through in an objective way. I am logical, critical and like to make my decisions coolly, weighing everything up. I take a long-term view when making up my mind. (b) I am a sympathetic person who likes to make decisions quickly. I tend to be subjective and guided by my feelings and my values (what I believe to be right). I am guided by immediate needs more than long-term benefits.	(a) Thinking (T) (b) Feeling (F)
4 How do you prefer to organise your life?	(a) I like to have system, structure and order in my life – with things under control. I tend to be firm and decisive. (b) I take life as it comes and am flexible and spontaneous. It doesn't worry me if things aren't clear-cut or if I don't really know where I'm going.	(a) Judgement (J) (b) Perception (P)

ESTJ	INFP	ESFP	INTJ
ESFJ	INTP	ENFP	ISTJ
ESTP	INFJ	ENFJ	ISTP
ENTJ	ISFP	ENTP	ISFJ

Using this system it is also possible to gain a picture of the role you prefer to play in a team, as shown in the table. The names given to the team roles are not jobs as such. They are labels intended to suggest the roles that might suit your personality type.

It is possible that our personality types change as we develop, undergo new experiences or take on more responsibilities.

http://www.teamtechnology.co.uk/consultancy.html

How team roles match the Myers–Briggs personality types

Team role	Personality type
Coach	ESFJ/ENFJ
Crusader	ISFP/INFP
Explorer	ENTP/ENFP
Innovator	INTJ/INFJ
Sculptor	ESFP/ESTP
Curator	ISFJ/ISTJ
Conductor	ESTJ/ENTJ
Scientist	ISTP/INTP

Source: http://www.teamtechnology.co.uk

Teams – they may look alike, but they all have different personalities.

Health predictions

Another, much simpler, division of personality types is into A, B and C:

- Type A – keen, ambitious, in a hurry and easily annoyed
- Type B – non-competitive, easy-going, rarely angry
- Type C – have emotions such as anger, but they hide and repress them.

These come from studies made in 1960 by Gallup and Hill and in 1977 by Woodruff. The researchers wanted to find out whether there was a link between personality type and the length of people's lives. They discovered that Type A were four times more at risk of heart attacks than the population as a whole. Type B stood a better chance of enjoying good health and living for a long time. Type C were thought to be at more risk, not from heart attacks but from cancer.

http://www.longevitywatch.com/index.htm

Evolution of behaviour

Explain the evolution of behaviour.

For this outcome, you need to explain what makes people behave in the way they do.

> **FOCUS**
>
> **Definitions of behaviour**
>
> Behaviour is ...
>
> 'anything a dead man cannot do' – Malott, R.W., Whaley, D.L. and Malott, M.E. (1994), *Elementary Principles of Behavior* (2nd edition), Englewood Cliffs, NJ: Prentice-Hall
>
> 'the way somebody/something acts or functions in particular situations' – *Oxford Advanced Learners Dictionary*
>
> 'anything that an organism does involving action and response to stimulation' – *Webster's Dictionary*
>
> NB If you are researching behaviour on the internet, note that the Americans spell it 'behavior'.

Behaviour has two main origins. One is 'innate' – built into us at birth. The other is learned. For many years psychologists have argued about which of the two is more important. These arguments are called the 'nature–nurture debate' (nature being the innate factors, and nurture the learned). While it is clear that some behaviour is innate in all of us, the real argument comes in discussing things like intelligence, which could either be inherited, or developed by our environment. The jury is still out on this question.

Innate behaviour

This includes:

- early reflexes, such as the cry of a baby at birth, sucking, gripping and 'walking' reflexes which pass after the first few days

- actions governed by the autonomic nervous system, such as breathing and excretion. Later in life we learn some control over these functions
- 'blueprints' or 'templates' which influence learning, such as Chomsky's language acquisition device and Piaget's developmental stages (see above)
- drives such as hunger and the need for sex and parenthood (the drives are innate but the expressions of these drives are mainly learned)
- complex qualities such as 'intelligence' may be partly innate.

> **CHECKPOINT ...**
> If a boy is good at football and his father is good at football, has he inherited the ability, or is he good because his father plays football with him in the park from an early age?

Learned behaviour

Learned behaviour evolves through interaction with other people. The individuals, groups and institutions which give us our learned behaviour are called 'agencies of social control'. These are the main ones:

- family
- peer group
- education
- religion
- the media
- the law.

These agencies form our behaviour through a process called **socialisation**, which could be defined as 'the preparation of the individual for social life'. Socialisation is a learning process which comes about by imitating role models, conforming to other people's expectations – and by some direct instruction. The process is aided by the use of sanctions: rewards and punishments which may be formal, informal or vicarious (using other people as examples).

Socialisation gives us both **norms** (accepted behaviour) and **values** (accepted beliefs). These norms and values together make up our **culture**.

The family

The family is the most influential agency of social control. It:

- gives us our early socialisation – learning how to eat, excrete, speak, dress
- instils norms and values about gender, ownership of property, morality, customs and a wider view of the world.

The sanctions of the family are informal:

- Negative sanctions include smacking and grounding; milder sanctions might be a telling-off or simply a 'look'.
- Positive sanctions include thanks, presents, cuddles, smiles, etc.

The peer group

The peer group consists of our 'equals' – our friends and colleagues. We keep a peer group throughout life, but its influence is greatest in childhood, adolescence and early adulthood. It:

- helps us to define our characters, identities and roles in relation to other people
- gives us the social skills needed to live away from the family
- develops skills to do with relationships and sex
- teaches us norms and values which may conflict with those of the family (i.e. parents)
- is often blamed by parents, teachers, social workers and police for leading young people into crime.

The sanctions of the peer group are informal:

- Negative sanctions: mockery, bullying, sarcasm, 'nasty looks', etc.
- Positive sanctions: laughing at jokes, any 'friendly' behaviour, helping someone out, etc.

Education

Education teaches us rules (of behaviour, games, etc.). It also:

- gives us knowledge and culture
- teaches us about citizenship
- classifies and labels us (e.g. through reports and exam results)
- provides entry into the world of work
- is accused by some of socialising us into middle-class, restrictive norms and values.

The sanctions of education are often formal, but can be informal:

- Negative: detention, suspension, lines, low grades, tellings-off, etc.
- Positive: praise from teachers, high grades, appointment as prefects, class or team captains.

Religion
Religion:

- teaches moral values and norms
- has values which are often traditional, like those of the family
- is less powerful in a largely secular (non-religious) society like the modern UK.

The sanctions of religion are formal and informal (they vary from religion to religion):

- Negative: expulsion from church, condemnation or criticism from someone in authority, 'displeasing God', threat of 'going to hell'
- Positive: approval from other church members, 'pleasing God', full acceptance into the church (e.g. confirmation), promise of 'going to heaven'.

The media
The media:

- give values and norms from outside our social circle
- create a sense of nationality, and our position in wider society
- give us a fuller awareness of our culture
- teach the political side of citizenship
- present norms and values on lifestyle, relationships, sex, violence, etc.
- influence our ideas on gender roles
- provide role models and ideal identities
- develops us as consumers.

The sanctions of the media are vicarious – we see them applied to others and learn from this:

- Negative: someone we identify with is punished
- Positive: someone we identify with is rewarded.

The law
The law deters us from committing any act which has been deemed by society as unlawful. Its sanctions are formal and negative, involving a wide range of sentences from the courts.

Abnormal behaviour

Describe personality types and related behaviour and the treatment of abnormal behavioural types.

For this outcome, you need to:

- describe extroverts and introverts and how they behave
- outline some of the main features and treatments of mental illness.

LINK! There is material on 'normal' personality types on pages 234–37 above.

'Abnormal behavioural types' refers to mental illness, and to personality disorders such as kleptomania and paedophilia, which the law does not consider to be mental illnesses, since it treats such activities as crimes.

Abnormal behavioural types are classified in America through a system called DSM IV and by the United Nations in a similar system called ICD10. These systems are vastly complex, but the main groups of abnormal behaviour come under these headings given in the FOCUS.

FOCUS

Categories of abnormal behavioural types (i.e. 'mental illness')

Disorders usually first diagnosed in infancy, childhood or adolescence

Cognitive disorders; Mental disorders due to a general medical condition

Substance-related disorders

Schizophrenia and other psychotic disorders

Mood disorders

Anxiety disorders

Somatoform disorders; Factitious disorder; Dissociative disorders

Sexual and gender identity disorders

Eating disorders; Sleep disorders

Impulse control disorders not elsewhere classified; Adjustment disorder

Personality disorders

COOL SITES:

Two top sites for mental illness and its treatments:

http://www.sane.org.uk/Sitemap.htm

http://www.nami.org/Hometemplate.cfm

Treatment of abnormal behavioural types

The treatment is different for different kinds of abnormal behaviour. Often a number of treatments are tried. Information about some of them is given below:

Medication

Twenty-five per cent of drugs prescribed through the NHS are for drugs affecting mood and behaviour. The main types of drugs are shown in the table below.

The main types of drugs and the illnesses they treat

Type of drug	Illness treated
Antipsychotics	Schizophrenia
Antimuscarinics	Parkinsonism (trembling, etc.)
Antidepressants	Depression
Antimanics	Manic depression (extreme mood swings)
Hypnotics	Sleep disorders
Anxiolytics	Stress

Unfortunately many of these drugs have serious side effects – especially confusion, drowsiness, blurred vision and sexual problems. Secondary drugs are often prescribed to treat the unwanted side effects of the main drug. However, drug treatment is becoming increasingly successful and widely used.

Psychological methods (psychotherapy and counselling)

Humanistic counselling
This can be carried out by people such as nurses and teachers. Its aim is to relieve temporary distress and to help the person sort out their own problems in a caring and supportive atmosphere. Humanistic counselling involves listening and prompting, not telling or advising. The aim is to enable people to help themselves. It requires a limited amount of training, and is effective in minor cases.

Cognitive and behavioural methods
These methods are used to treat phobias, anxiety, post-traumatic stress disorder and unwanted behaviour patterns. The cognitive side involves the patient learning to recognise the thoughts and emotions which are linked with the behavioural problem, e.g. the fears and wishes underlying an eating disorder. The behavioural side breaks down the problem and tackles the easy bits first, by a process of learned behavioural change.

> **FOCUS**
>
> **Summary of psychological methods used to treat abnormal behaviour**
>
> *Purpose of treatment*
> - Relief of distress
> - Helping people adapt to new situations
> - Restoration of function
> - Reconstruction of long-term patterns of thinking and behaviour
>
> *Techniques used*
> - Counselling
> - Cognitive and behavioural methods
> - Psychodynamic methods
>
> *Numbers of patients involved together*
> - Individual (the sufferer alone)
> - Couple (married or cohabiting)
> - Family (when children are also involved)
> - Group (usually 8 to 10 unrelated patients)
>
> *Source: Sane*

Psychodynamic therapy
This Freudian method tries to overcome abnormal behaviour by finding and neutralising its source in the unconscious mind. It uses free association (see page 230). The therapist tries to build up an emotional rapport with the patient, so that 'transference' (a sort of off-loading of the problem) can take place.

None of these methods can be guaranteed to 'cure' abnormal behaviour, but in many cases they are extremely helpful.

Physical methods

ECT
Electro-convulsive therapy has been used to treat schizophrenia and other serious disorders. It involves passing electric shocks through the brain.

Aversion therapy
This behaviourist method uses pain or some other form of strong negative sanction to treat abnormal

behaviour. It has been tried with homosexuals and paedophiles – linking pain with images of homosexual sex or child abuse.

Lobotomy
This is an operation occasionally used to 'treat' schizophrenia by cutting out a small part of the front of the brain.

Other surgery
Where behaviour abnormality is caused by a brain tumour, or brain damage resulting from an accident or injury, surgery can lead to complete recovery.

Apart from surgery to remove brain tumours or repair brain damage, the physical methods of treating abnormal behaviour are now rarely used in the west. They are criticised on human rights grounds, and because they are dangerous and ineffective.

INTERVIEW SKILLS

Explain the different types of interview.

For this outcome, you need to:

- list the different types of interview
- explain the purpose and main features of each one.

An interview is a formal question and answer session. In some interviews you ask the questions, and in some you answer them.

The PROFILE below gives brief explanations of three types of interview.

CHECKPOINT ...

Other types of interview include: appraisal, one-to-one interviews, research interviews, police interviews, 'brains trusts', psychometric testing, group interviews. Many of your tutors and employers will know all about them, and there is plenty of information about interviews on the internet.
Carry out research (using interviews or other methods) to find out what each of these is, how they are carried out, what their purpose is – and any other interesting points.

COOL SITES:

http://pcw.co.uk/Careers/Features/Psychometrics/index.jsp – psychometric testing

http://www.graduatecareersonline.com/advice/employability/psychometrics.asp – tip-top tips

CHECKPOINT ...

With a friend, discuss the kinds of interview listed above – especially with reference to:
(a) who asks the questions, and why
(b) whether the questions are likely to be 'closed' or 'open'.

Profile

Three types of interview

Type of interview	Purpose	Explanation
Job interview	To interview an applicant to determine their suitability for a job	Usually one interviewee and two or more interviewers (an 'interview panel')
Disciplinary interview	To be given a verbal warning by someone in authority	Often part of a formal disciplinary procedure in a college or workplace
Exit interview	To find out why an employee is leaving	Employers do this to assess themselves as employers, or discover if there is a problem or grudge

Interview techniques

Demonstrate and evaluate your own techniques in an interview situation.

For this outcome, you need to:
- have a practice interview
- assess your performance in the interview.

There will be three stages:

1. Preparation for the interview
2. The interview itself
3. Appraisal and self-appraisal.

The following points refer to job interviews.

1 Preparation

- Research the organisation and the job you are applying for. If you are applying for a job in the West Midlands Police, find out everything you reasonably can about the West Midlands Police, the work they do, the area, its social, ethnic and economic mix, and its crime patterns. Get hold of the latest West Midlands policing report and policing plan, study their mission statement and find out what their priorities are. Know the superficial facts too, such as the name of the Chief Constable and the address of headquarters.
- Have your own career action plan which should include (a) a list of your strengths in relation to the kind of job you want to apply for, (b) a list of weaknesses, (c) a career action plan saying what you hope to achieve in the next five years.
- Have an accurate and up-to-date CV. Use it to help you fill in the application form. Be accurate and neat on the form, follow all instructions exactly, and be very thoughtful about the longer answers you give (e.g. your autobiography, if there is one).
- List all the questions you would expect the interview panel to ask. *Then write down the answers you would give to each question*. Most questions will relate to the 'applicant requirements' sheet in the recruitment pack, or to what you yourself have put in your application form.
- Know when and where the interview will take place, and how you will get there. Make sure you have suitable interview clothes, and make any necessary adjustments to your appearance. Have a good night's sleep and breakfast before the interview. Get to the interview place with 20 minutes to spare, so that you feel ready for anything when the interview starts.

CHECKPOINT ...

Discuss among yourselves and with your tutors the right kind of image to present, and clothes to wear, at a public service job interview.

2 The interview

- Arrive on time.
- Be polite and pleasant to everybody you meet in the building
- Shake hands, smile and make eye contact with your interviewer(s).
- Do not sit until you are invited to.
- Sit up straight and keep your hands away from your face.
- Answer questions honestly and directly, giving reasons or examples to support what you say.
- Be friendly without being casual, and confident without being arrogant.
- Pay attention to all members of the interviewing panel, not just the one who is asking the questions.
- Have some questions of your own to ask (e.g. about the organisation, or where you might be working).
- Offer to shake hands at the end of the interview.

3 Appraisal and self-appraisal

- Make quick notes immediately after the interview about what you think you did well, and where you could have done better. Note any questions that gave you problems.
- For the purposes of this outcome (*but not in real life*!), find out from your interviewer what your strengths and weaknesses were – and note the comments.
- When evaluating your own techniques, use a checklist like the one at the top of the next page to make sure you haven't missed anything out.

CHECKPOINT ...

Design an exercise to enable you and the rest of your group to assess each other's handshakes.

Interview appraisal – checklist

Preparation	Interview
Form	Punctuality
CV	Appearance
Knowledge of job	Greeting and conclusion
Prediction of questions	Quality of answers
Preparation of answers	Speech and body language

http://www.alec.co.uk/interview/

http://www.pwcjobs.com/index.php3?PageIdentifier=24

Qualities of good interviews and interviewees

Analyse what makes a good interviewer and interviewee.

For this outcome, you need to explain the qualities and skills of:

- a good interviewer
- a good interviewee.

skill POWER

You will get useful ideas for this outcome from training videos for job applicants, and by asking recruiters for public services what makes a good interviewer and interviewee.

Points to consider

To analyse how good an interviewer is you should:

- make notes on how effectively they set the scene for the interview (e.g. arranging the furniture so that it puts interviewees at their ease, or prevents confrontational body language)
- study the content and wording of the questions asked. Do the questions ask for the right information, in the right way, and are they put together so that they lead naturally on from one part of the interview to the next?
- decide if the interviewer tests the interviewee's character, e.g. by asking difficult questions in order to find out if the interviewee keeps cool under stress (how appropriate this is depends on the job being applied for)
- note how the interviewer uses non-verbal communication. Does the non-verbal communication (NVC – see next page) help to bring out the knowledge and qualities of the interviewee?
- assess if the interviewer gives a good image of the organisation they represent
- notice if the interviewer asks any questions which are 'out of order', e.g. with a racist or sexist agenda.

To analyse how good an interviewee is, focus on:

- the NVC and general manner and self-presentation of the interviewee. Does the person seem confident and well-organised?
- the clarity and relevance with which questions are answered
- the ability of the interviewee to think on their feet, or to deal with questions they don't know the answers to
- evidence of good motivation and interest in the job
- evidence of knowledge and good preparation
- the ability to ask suitable questions of their own at the end of the interview.

TYPES OF COMMUNICATION

Explain the difference and similarities between verbal and non-verbal communication and the importance of the use of the senses in each.

For this outcome, you need to:

- explain what verbal and non-verbal communication are
- show the differences and similarities
- show what senses we use for each.

'Verbal communication' is communication which uses words. The words can be either spoken or written, but most people think of spoken words when they use the word 'verbal'.

'Non-verbal communication' (NVC) is communication which doesn't use words. It especially means gestures, expressions and clothing – but might include smells and non-verbal noises (e.g. grunts).

The main aspects of verbal communication

Aspects of verbal communication	Use of senses
Language Languages are distinctive bodies of words and grammar used by large numbers, often millions, of people. Many people have a first language, or mother tongue, and then have second or third languages as well.	Sense of hearing; awareness of loudness and pitch; sense of timing. Sight used for reading and writing.
Dialect Dialects are regional variations in languages, usually with different words and grammatical structures. They have largely died out in the UK.	Same as for language, but grammar and vocabulary restricted. Mainly spoken.
Accent This refers to the sounds with which words or parts of words are pronounced. It can include intonation (stress) and pitch.	Accents are regional, and can be heard by the trained ear.
Register Register is the formality or informality of speech – ranging from received pronunciation ('Queen's English') through standard English to colloquial English and slang.	Heard in choice and sound of words. Register is the 'poshness' of speech.
Function The words we use ('lexis') and the order we use them in ('syntax') varies with the function or purpose of speech or writing, e.g. the word order in questions and statements is different.	Knowledge and experience are needed to understand and use different language functions.
Audience This is an important aspect of verbal communication. An effective communication is one which is suited to its audience (listener or reader).	Experience and a 'social sense' are used to assess the needs of an audience.
Speech v. writing Speech is a defining characteristic of the human species. Writing started about 4000 years ago. It is used to express, store and communicate ideas. Writing, like speech, has register, function and audience – but tends to be more formal than speech.	Sight. Font, layout and handwriting have a visual effect – and aid comprehension by creating expectations in the reader.

The main aspects of non-verbal communication

Aspects of non-verbal communication	Use of senses
Appearance Our appearance is often the first thing other people notice about us. Psychologists have shown that first impressions matter – and this is one reason why people care so much about their (and other people's) appearance.	Sight. Sex, age and race are usually registered first before other details.

Expression Most facial expressions are temporary but in some people are seen as permanent (e.g. 'he looks conceited'). Expressions are partly reflexes (e.g. blinking at bright lights) and partly learned through agencies of social control (see page 237).	Expressions are registered by sight and classified according to an 'index' which we have in our minds.
Eye-contact This is an important way in which people monitor or control their interactions with others. Eye-contact is needed when presenting to a group, and is important at job interviews.	Registered by sight.
Pose, movement and posture convey mood, age, personality, power and status relationships, sexual attraction, etc.	Registered by sight.
Clothing carries a wide range of social, personal and professional messages. Uniform is used to depersonalise the individual and stress membership of an organisation.	Registered by sight – awareness of colour, texture, form and cut.
Proxemics This is the aspect of NVC linked to personal territory and space. Each of us has a preferred 'personal space'. Dominance, aggression and cultural identity can be expressed in this way.	Registered by sight, sound and – sometimes – smell.
Smell Perfume is used to send signals of attractiveness or sexual availability; some after-shave smells suggest dominance. Other smells suggest poor hygiene – hence the popularity of deodorants.	Sense of smell.

COOL SITE:

http://www.cultsock.ndirect.co.uk/MUHome/cshtml/nvc/nvc3a.html

CHECKPOINT ...

1 Research gestures and other forms of NVC to find out what they all mean.
2 Talk to someone who works in a uniformed service, e.g. a police officer, and ask them what importance they attach to NVC.
3 Review your own use of body language. Are there any ways in which you could change it in order to present yourself more effectively?
4 What are the differences and similarities between verbal and non-verbal communication and the messages they send?

Communication in public services

Merit

Analyse the different types of communication used in public services.

For this outcome, you need to:

- examine the use of listening, speaking, reading, writing and NVC in the public services
- pick out the special communication skills which are valued in the public services, and show why they are valued.

The ideal way to research this would be to spend some time work-shadowing in a public service, and making notes on all the communication – spoken, written and non-verbal, that you come across.

Failing this, you can question someone who works in a public service.
Types of communication you would encounter include those shown in the table at the bottom of the page.

Your analysis should consider the use of different methods for different types of communication, e.g. Why is the phone used for one communication, while a letter is used for another?

CHECKPOINT ...

1 What conclusions can you draw from the different registers of verbal and written communication?

2 What differences do you see in the communication used by people of different rank in an organisation? Are there differences when communicating with people who are more senior or less senior in the organisation?

3 How do communications between women, or involving women, differ from those between men only?

Styles of communication

Merit

Evaluate communication styles in relation to speech and behaviour.

For this outcome, you need to:

- study the different ways in which people speak and behave with each other
- examine their different purposes and results
- find out which ways of speaking and acting are most effective in achieving their aims.

Audio and video recordings, and written transcripts of conversations and dialogues will help you to evaluate (judge) communication styles and how they relate to behaviour.

Television documentaries – especially of the 'fly-on-the-wall' type – would also be a useful source of material for this outcome.

'Styles' means things like formality and informality, or assertiveness and aggression. For example 'Could I trouble you to open that window please?', 'Open that damn window for God's sake!' and 'Would you please open that window?' all carry a similar message but the styles are very different.

Types of communication ideas for analysis

Speaking	Listening	Writing	Reading	NVC	Other
Briefings Speeches Lectures Presentations Advice Commands Requests Questions Explanations Comments Phoning Jokes	Record the way people listen and respond to each type of spoken communication, e.g. how they listen on the phone and how they listen to a briefing.	Reports Memos Letters Notices Leaflets Publicity Notes made from spoken or written communications	Investigate what people read, why they read it, and whether they skim, scan, speed-read or read slowly and carefully.	Where people sit, how they use space, what they wear, their gestures and expressions, eye-contact. Décor and furnishing of rooms; corporate image.	Technological communication Telephone Radio E-mails Texting Fax Teleprinter Using databases Graphical and numerical presentation of data

Assertive, aggressive, passive, passive–aggressive

These four styles of communication have been identified by managers in many fields of work as a factor in whether there are good relationships in the workplace. The styles are:

- **assertive** You say what you want, why you want it, and what will happen if you don't get what you want. This is all done in a polite tone of voice, without any unnecessary explanation, and without any empty threats. The aim is to get your own way, not to humiliate the other person.
- **aggressive** This style of communication uses threats and intimidation. The person raises their voice, is rude, and may use bullying tactics.
- **passive** In this style of communication the person is too meek and apologetic, and acts as if every problem is their own fault.
- **passive–aggressive** This is where people try to express aggression in roundabout and manipulative ways, for example by gossiping, delaying things unnecessarily, distorting the truth and generally being underhand.

For example, your tutor (who is strict but fair) tells you off because you are a day late with your assignment. The reason it is late is because you went to your aunt's funeral. The four styles of response might be:

- **assertive** Hand in the assignment and tell the tutor that it's late because you were at your aunt's funeral.
- **aggressive** Tell the tutor to go and take a running jump.
- **passive** Say that you're very sorry and hand in the assignment without mentioning your aunt's funeral.
- **passive–aggressive** Go to the tutor's line manager and say that the tutor is discriminating against you.

Degrees of formality

In all forms of communication there are levels of formality. Whether writing or speaking, we communicate more formally with strangers, or with people of a higher social and professional rank. Formal communication uses standard English, and may even include formal words such as 'sir' or 'madam'. 'Please' and 'thank you' are used more frequently in formal communication. We are, of course, informal with our friends and family.

Formality shows itself in NVC as well – in the clothes people wear, the gestures they use, and the way they move.

Unit 14 Understanding Discipline

Grading criteria

PASSGRADE To achieve a pass grade the evidence must show that the learner is able to:	*Merit* To achieve a merit grade the evidence must show that the learner is able to:	*Distinction* To achieve a distinction grade the evidence must show that the learner is able to:
• explain the need for discipline in at least two public services **248** • describe the main features of conformity and obedience **251** • identify and explain three factors which influence conformity and three factors which influence obedience **255** • describe the qualities needed for self-discipline in a given public service **256** • explore the possible effects of lack of self-discipline in the given public service **258** • explain the meaning of authority in relation to the public services **259** • identify and explain four types of authority **260**	• analyse the role of discipline in public service **250** • analyse two conformity and obedience studies and evaluate their application in the public services **252** • explain in detail how these qualities are necessary for the effective operation of a given public service **257** • analyse the positive and negative effects of blind obedience to authority **261**	• evaluate the application of the role of discipline in the public services **251** • analyse two conformity and obedience studies and evaluate their application in the public services **252**

Discipline is fundamental to public service work. The following of rules and orders, the exercise of self-control, the ability to put the needs of others before one's own needs and the readiness to face danger are all aspects of this very important quality.

Another side of discipline is the use of sanctions and punishments within a service: it may be a system of verbal and written warnings, or something more elaborate like the army discipline code.

We call discipline a quality, but in many ways it is more like a skill: it has to be learned and developed through training and experience. To be disciplined should not be thought of as a weakness, for it is only through discipline – or self-discipline – that any of us can focus our energies and fulfil our potential in life.

In this unit, you will learn about discipline and how to develop discipline within yourself.

ROLE OF DISCIPLINE

PASSGRADE

Explain the need for discipline in at least two public services.

For this outcome, you need to:

- explain what 'discipline' means
- discuss discipline with people who work in public services
- show how it is used in two or more public services
- explain why those public services need discipline.

FOCUS

Definitions of discipline

Discipline is ...

'the practice of training people to obey rules or a code of behaviour' – *Oxford Dictionary*

'the individual or group attitude that ensures prompt obedience to orders, and the initiation of appropriate action in the absence of orders' – US Marine Corps

Discipline in the army and police

Some aspects of army and police discipline are given in the following FOCUS sections.

FOCUS

Army discipline

'0309. To be effective on operations, the Army must act as a disciplined force. Commanders must be certain that their orders will be carried out, and everybody must be confident that they will not be let down by their comrades. Lives may depend on it, as may the success of the mission. Discipline is the glue that holds soldiers together when threatened; it is the primary antidote to fear. Supported by team loyalty, regimental spirit, pride, trust and professionalism, discipline keeps soldiers from yielding to the human stress of battle. The best discipline – which the Army expects from every soldier and which training aims to elicit in them, is self-discipline: innate, not imposed. Good discipline does not stifle individuals, but rather it enables them to achieve more than they would expect of themselves without it. Good discipline means that soldiers of all ranks are trained to obey their orders under the worst conditions of war, and to do so with imagination and resource. Because discipline is so vital to success on operations, commanders must be able to enforce it when necessary. That requires clearly understood rules and a military legal system which can deal with offences such as absence, desertion or insubordination which are not found in civil law. And if it is to work in war, such a system must be in place in peace, for it cannot be turned on and off at will. Discipline must therefore be rigorously but fairly upheld by all those in positions of authority, and self-discipline must be deeply rooted.'

Source: The Military Covenant, *Chapter 3*
© Crown Copyright

COOL SITES:

http://www.army.mod.uk/servingsoldier/usefulinfo/index.html

http://www.army.mod.uk/servingsoldier/usefulinfo/valuesgeneral/adp5milcov/ss_hrpers_values_adp5_3_w.html#discipline – what army discipline is really all about

FOCUS

Police code of conduct

'Honesty and integrity

1 It is of paramount importance that the public has faith in the honesty and integrity of police officers. Officers should therefore be open and

truthful in their dealings; avoid being improperly beholden to any person or institution; and discharge their duties with integrity.

Fairness and impartiality

2 Police officers have a particular responsibility to act with fairness and impartiality in all their dealings with the public and their colleagues.

Politeness and tolerance

3 Officers should treat members of the public and colleagues with courtesy and respect, avoiding abusive or deriding attitudes or behaviour. In particular, officers must avoid: favouritism of an individual or group; all forms of harassment, victimisation or unreasonable discrimination; and overbearing conduct to a colleague, particularly to one junior in rank or service.

Use of force and abuse of authority

4 Officers must never knowingly use more force than is reasonable, nor should they abuse their authority.

Performance of duties

5 Officers should be conscientious and diligent in the performance of their duties. Officers should attend work promptly when rostered for duty. If absent through sickness or injury, they should avoid activities likely to retard their return to duty.

Lawful orders

6 The police service is a disciplined body. Unless there is good and sufficient cause to do otherwise, officers must obey all lawful orders and abide by the provisions of Police Regulations. Officers should support their colleagues in the execution of their lawful duties, and oppose any improper behaviour, reporting it where appropriate.

Confidentiality

7 Information which comes into the possession of the police should be treated as confidential. It should not be used for personal benefit and nor should it be divulged to other parties except in the proper course of police duty. Similarly, officers should respect, as confidential, information about force policy and operations unless authorised to disclose it in the course of their duties.

Criminal offences

8 Officers must report any proceedings for a criminal offence taken against them. Conviction of a criminal offence may of itself result in further action being taken.

Property

9 Officers must exercise reasonable care to prevent loss or damage to property (excluding their own personal property but including police property).

Sobriety

10 Whilst on duty officers must be sober. Officers should not consume alcohol when on duty unless specifically authorised to do so or it becomes necessary for the proper discharge of police duty.

Appearance

11 Unless on duties which dictate otherwise, officers should always be well turned out, clean and tidy whilst on duty in uniform or in plain clothes.

General conduct

12 Whether on or off duty, police officers should not behave in a way which is likely to bring discredit upon the police service.'

Source: Statutory Instruments 1999, No. 730, 10 March 1999, HMSO

COOL SITES:

http://www.hmso.gov.uk/
http://www.hmso.gov.uk/si/si1999/99073002.htm#end – more on police discipline

All uniformed services have discipline requirements, regulations and procedures which should be obtainable from them, or on the internetWhy the army needs discipline:

- to achieve trust between soldiers
- because lives depend on it
- because the success of operations depends on discipline
- to control fear
- to keep up morale
- to allow individuals to do their best
- to enable orders to be obeyed 'with imagination and resource'.

Why the police need discipline:

- for the same reasons that the army needs discipline – *and*
- to reassure the public and to inspire confidence
- to get the respect and cooperation of the public
- to be fair in their treatment of all sections of a diverse society.

CHECKPOINT ...

Make similar lists on the need for discipline in other uniformed services.

Merit

Analyse the role of discipline in public service.

For this outcome, you need to:

- collect information on how discipline is used in public service work
- explain why discipline matters.

Under this outcome, you will be expected to be able to define – or explain – a number of key words as they would be used in the context of public service discipline. Then you are expected to show how the theory and practice of discipline are used to help fulfil the aims of a public service organisation.

'Role' is:

- the normal actions of a person or group of people within an organisation (e.g. 'the role of the fire investigation team')
- the use made of an idea within an organisation (e.g. 'the role of discipline in the prison service').

FOCUS

Definition of role

An individual's role is ...

'a set of norms and expectations applied to the incumbent of a particular position' – Banton, 1965

Public service discipline has a lot to do with following rules, regulations and procedures.

FOCUS

Some more definitions

Rules are ...

'a prescribed guide for conduct or action' – *Webster's Dictionary*

'general norm[s] mandating or guiding conduct or action is a given type of situation' – Baldwin, R. (1995), *Rules and Government*, Oxford: Clarendon Press

A regulation is ...

'a set of "incentives" established either by the legislature, Government, or public administration that mandates or prohibits actions of citizens ... Regulations are supported by the explicit threat of punishment for non-compliance.' – OECD, 1994

Procedure is ...

'the internal processes, methods, and operational considerations required on a day-to-day basis to implement policies' – *Athabasca University Policy Manual* (Canada), 2000

The difference between rules and regulations is that rules come from within an organisation, while regulations come from outside the organisation (and therefore have the force of law).

CHECKPOINT ...

Which of these notices gives a rule, and which gives a regulation?

(a) MOBILE PHONES MUST BE TURNED OFF IN CLASS
(b) NO SMOKING
(c) WHAT TO DO IN CASE OF FIRE

The role of discipline in public service is shown in:

- the wearing of uniforms (to suggest that the individual is less important than the organisation)
- the disciplinary nature of initial training (in which the repeated following of orders, systems and procedures is intended to create a habit of discipline)
- the importance attached to outward signs of discipline such as neatness, cleanliness and punctuality
- the stress on fitness, which is a sign of self-discipline
- the rank structure which facilitates communication and makes it clear who is responsible for what
- the wide use of rotas, duty rosters, notices and timetables so that people have no excuse for being late or disorganised
- the use of marching, saluting and other drills, especially in the armed forces – these both train and express discipline
- the use of ceremonies for new recruits
- oaths of allegiance and other forms of words designed to strengthen loyalty
- traditions of loyalty, belonging and *esprit de corps* (team spirit)

- the use of sanctions (positive: rewards, promotion or medals for good discipline; negative: warnings, punishments and sentences for poor discipline)
- the enforcement of no-drugs policies
- codes of practice and discipline regulations, covering powers, responsibilities and duties, usually laid down by government.

Distinction

Evaluate the application of the role of discipline in the public services.

For this outcome, you need to:

- collect detailed information on how discipline is encouraged, enforced and shown in the work of different public services
- try to get some informed criticism of discipline in one or more public services. The aim of this outcome is not only to show how well discipline works, but also to investigate discipline problems
- assess whether public service attitudes to discipline are changing – and if so, why
- find out how the misuse of discipline can lead to harassment, bullying, discrimination or human rights violations.

Collect information for this outcome by

- talking to people who work in the public services
- joining organisations such as the Cadets, TA, RAF Auxiliaries or Special Police
- visiting websites.

FOCUS

Discipline in the fire service

'We recommend that the Discipline Regulations should be repealed and be replaced by a system based on modern good practice. We suggest that the ACAS Code of Practice on Disciplinary and Grievances Procedures would be a good basis for such a system.'

Source: Bain Report on the Fire Service, 2002

COOL SITES:

http://www.irfs.org.uk/docs/future/index.htm – Bain Report

http://www.fbuberkshire.co.uk/hand_book_discipline_regs.htm – 1985 Fire Service Discipline Regulations

http://www.acas.org.uk/publications/pdf/CP01.pdf – cool ACAS code!

http://www.acas.org.uk/a-z_index.html – the whole site is cool

CHECKPOINT ...

1 Obtain copies of the 1985 Fire Service Discipline Regulations and the ACAS Code of Practice on Disciplinary and Grievance Procedures. What are the main differences?

2 Other things you could do:

(a) Gather information on discipline in comparable public services in other countries. For example, how does discipline in the British police or army compare with that in their American, Irish, French or Pakistani counterparts?

(b) Outline the dangerous effects of indiscipline and low morale, e.g. police corruption and brutality, or the human rights abuses carried out by Serbian militia in Kosovo in the late 1990s.

The internet is the most accessible and up-to-date resource for this information, especially the websites of human rights organisations such as Human Rights Watch and Amnesty International.

CONFORMITY AND OBEDIENCE

Describe the main features of conformity and obedience.

For this outcome, you need to:

- say what 'conformity' and 'obedience' mean
- indicate the main differences between them.

FOCUS

Definitions

Conformity is ...

'yielding to group pressures' – R.D. Crutchfield, 1954

'going along with one's peers' – Stanley Milgram

'the tendency to change our perceptions, opinions, or behavior in ways that are consistent with group norms' – Brehm, S.S., Kassin, S.M. and Fein, S. (1999), *Social Psychology* (4th edition), Boston: Houghton Mifflin, page 213

Some researchers think there are two main types of conformity:

- 'normative influence', i.e. fear of rejection by the group (we conform to their behaviour only when in a group situation) – as in Asch's study below
- 'informational influence', i.e. we think others are correct – as in studies by Deutsch and Gerard (1955).

Obedience is ...

'behavior change produced by the commands of authority' – Brehm, Kassin and Fein (1999), page 232

'an immediate response to fulfil the commands in every situation, whether in accordance or contradiction to one's desire' – Imam Al-Banna

The main difference between conformity and obedience is that:

- in conformity we do what (we think) others want us to do *without having to be asked*
- in obedience we *do what we are told*.

An applicant for the army who gets his hair cut before an interview is conforming. An infantryman who gets his hair cut because his corporal has said 'Get your hair cut!' is obeying.

Features of conformity and obedience in the uniformed services

Conformity

- Uniforms are worn.
- Employees are proud of the service they belong to.
- They identify with its ethos, norms and values.
- They willingly accept the rules, regulations and procedures of the job.
- They have a sense of belonging.
- They feel loyal to their team or unit.
- The needs of the group come before the wishes of the individual.

Obedience

- Orders are expected to be obeyed.
- There is a rank structure, in which higher ranks give orders or directives to lower ranks.
- The commands of the superior officer take precedence over the personal wishes of the subordinate.

Merit

Analyse two conformity and obedience studies and evaluate their application in the public services.

Distinction

Analyse two conformity and obedience studies and evaluate their application in the public services.

NB In the May 2002 Specifications BN011697, the merit and distinction outcomes are the same.

For these outcomes, you need to:

- examine the main points of two conformity and obedience studies (experiments)
- judge how relevant they are for the public services.

Conformity studies

Muzafir Sherif: 1935 and 1937 – study of 'norm formation'

The aim of this experiment was to find out if people would think differently if they were in a group than they would as separate individuals.

The subjects (people being experimented on) were told to sit in a completely darkened laboratory. Then a spot of light appeared on a screen 15 feet in front of them. They were told that the light was going to move – and they had to estimate how far it moved. The experiment was repeated a hundred times for each subject. Each time they did the experiment their estimate was recorded. After a few wildly varying estimates, most of the subjects settled down to a fairly consistent estimate each time they did the experiment. But although each subject tended to standardise their own estimates to a figure that remained much the same, different subjects arrived at different standardised figures. Thus subject A might say the spot of light moved 3 inches each time, while subject B estimated the spot moved 6 inches each time.

In the next version of the experiment, groups of subjects did it together, and made group estimates of how far the light spot had moved. Each group tended to reach an agreement quite quickly on how far the light spot moved.

In fact, the spot never moved – the subjects' eyes 'played tricks on them'. They were seeing a 'psychokinetic effect' (imaginary movement). But what interested Sherif was (a) the way the subjects standardised their own estimates of light movement when tested as individuals, and (b) the way they reached a 'group norm', an agreement close to the average of the original estimates by individuals in the group.

Solomon Asch 1951, 1952 and 1956 – conformity of individual to group

Subjects were told they were going to do an experiment about 'visual perception'. In the first phase of the experiment, the subjects were – separately – shown cards with three straight lines of different length on them. They were also given another card with a 'standard' line on it (which was the same length as one of the three lines on the first card). The subjects had to say which of the three lines was the same length as the standard line. The task was easy and 95 per cent of the subjects got it right.

In the second phase, the subjects were placed at a table round which several other people were sitting. Sets of cards showing three lines of different length and a standard line were given to all the people at the table. They were then asked, in turn, to say which of the three lines matched the standard line. Unknown to the subject, the other people round the table had all been trained by Asch. The experiment was arranged so that the subject always answered after the others. For the first two rounds the 'fake' subjects gave the right answer (and so did the subject of the experiment). After that, the fake subjects gave consistently wrong answers. It was found that in 37 per cent of the rounds, on average, the subject gave the same wrong answer as the other people sitting round the table – even though the same subject had always identified the correct line when tested by themselves.

Asch tried his experiment with many different groups of people. It showed that there was a clear tendency for some people to conform to group pressure.

Obedience studies

Stanley Milgram 1960–3

In Milgram's obedience experiment the subject had to play the role of a teacher, while another person (secretly trained by Milgram) played the role of student. Subjects were volunteers recruited through a newspaper advertisement, and they were paid for taking part. Milgram told the subjects that the experiment was about learning.

The 'teacher' had to read word-pairs and the 'learner' had to indicate from a list of four words which one was originally paired with a word read by the teacher. The 'learner' was wired up to a piece of equipment which was said (by Milgram) to give electric shocks. The 'teacher' was instructed to give the 'learner' an electric shock if he or she gave a wrong answer. (There was no electric shock, but the teacher was led to believe that there would be one.) A dial on the front of the fake machine gave voltages up to 450 volts (a fatal voltage). The dial also stated how severe each shock would be – and 'teachers' were given a 45-volt shock before the experiment so that they would know what kind of pain they were inflicting on the 'learner'. With each wrong answer the 'teacher' was told to increase the shock.

In discussing the experiment with psychiatrists and students, Milgram was told that the subjects ('teachers') would not give shocks above 135 volts. But the truth turned out to be very different. Milgram found that 65 per cent of subjects gave shocks up to 450 volts if he told them to – even though the learner, on the other side of a screen, was shouting and begging them to stop.

Milgram varied his experiments and discovered that the subjects were more obedient if he stood closer to them while instructing them to give electric shocks. They were also more obedient when the experiment was carried out at Yale University, the American university where he worked, than when it was done in a disused warehouse. But even in the warehouse, the obedience rate was 48 per cent, i.e. 48 per cent of subjects went up to the limit of a 450-volt electric shock.

The experiment was later tried in many countries – and in all of them there were unexpectedly high levels of obedience – ranging from 63 per cent in Jordan to 85 per cent in Germany.

http://www.le.ac.uk/psychology/

Charles K. Hofling 1966

Hofling's experiment used hospital nurses as 'subjects'. First he met nurses on 22 different wards to warn them of the dangers of a supposedly new drug 'Astroten'. 'Astroten' was actually harmless glucose tablets. The maximum dose – 10 mg – was clearly labelled on the box.

Later, a 'Dr Smith' – who was not known to the nurses – phoned a nurse on each of the 22 wards instructing them to give 20 mg of Astroten to a 'patient' who was 'in urgent need of the drug'.

'Dr Smith' was asking the nurses to break three basic rules of nursing:

- never to give more than the maximum allowed dose of a drug
- never to give drugs without written authorisation ('Dr Smith' said he would 'come round in ten minutes' and do this).
- never to accept instructions by a stranger on the phone. (The nurses had no way of knowing that 'Dr Smith' was a genuine doctor. After all, anybody can ring up and say they are 'Dr Smith'.)

In Hofling's experiment the nurses were observed following the phone call from 'Dr Smith', and 21 out of 22 nurses followed 'Dr Smith's' instructions.

http://www.nursesnetwork.co.uk/ – Hofling

Analysis

To analyse studies like these you should ask the following questions:

- What was the hypothesis of the experiment likely to have been? For example, with the Hofling experiment the hypothesis could have been: 'Nurses will obey any instructions, however unreasonable, if they think they have been given by a doctor'.
- Did the experiment succeed in demonstrating the truth or falsehood of the hypothesis? (It doesn't matter if the hypothesis was true or false, but it does matter whether the experiment was a valid way of 'proving' or 'disproving' the hypothesis.)
- Are there any ways in which Hofling's experiment could have been better designed?
- Could the findings of the experiment apply to all public services? For example, could a police superintendent phone a constable and ask them to beat up a suspect in the cells – and, if so, would the 'superintendent' be obeyed?
- Can the public services learn good practice from the experiment, e.g. by training employees not to accept blindly orders or requests? Or would the questioning of every non-routine order lead to time-wasting, inefficiency and bad staff relationships?
- What are the human rights implications of the experiment (a) with regard to the blind following of orders which may be cruel or unjustified and (b) with the nurses who unknowingly took part as 'subjects' in Hofling's experiment?

Application of these studies in the public services

These experiments, carried out in America 50 years ago or more, were inspired by people's horror and incomprehension of what had happened in the German extermination camps at Auschwitz, Belsen and elsewhere during World War II.

Though British public services have never carried out genocide, the studies suggest that any public service might have done if they had been subjected to the same political pressures as the German services were in the early 1940s.

The experiments showed that:

- the need to conform will make many people distort the truth or mistrust their own judgement (Sherif's experiment)
- the need to conform will either muddle people's thinking, or make them lie to avoid the disapproval of the group (Asch's experiment)
- people will obey 'bad' commands if they respect or fear the source (Milgram and Hofling's experiments).

The application of the experiments is that public services:

- now train their recruits in human rights awareness, so that they will not obey unreasonable orders blindly
- have systems to identify and eliminate destructive forms of obedience and conformity such as racism and bullying (see FOCUS below)
- are more aware of the risks of 'false confessions' of crime suspects resulting in suspects' desire to conform and obey.

FOCUS

Dealing with racism and bullying

'any statement of core values should make plain that bullying and harassment are unacceptable. Fire services should take steps to regularly communicate these policies to all members of the workforce in order to re-emphasise the unacceptability of such behaviour and ensure that all staff are aware of the policies.' – DTLR (2001), *Towards Diversity II: Commitment of Cultural Change*, HMSO (fire service employers' viewpoint)

'We discovered a prison which was itself imprisoned in its own past – locked into unsuitable but historic buildings and, more importantly, into an outdated culture of over-control and disrespect for prisoners. This preface, and much of the report that follows, focuses on that culture, as we believe that tackling it is fundamental to the future and development of the prison.' – from *Report on An Unannounced Follow-up Inspection of HM Prison Dartmoor, 17–21 September 2001* by HM Chief Inspector of Prisons

COOL SITES:

http://www.fbu.org.uk

http://www.odpm.gov.uk/stellent/groups/odpm_fire/documents/page/odpm_fire_601265.pdf

http://www.homeoffice.gov.uk/docs/dartmoor01.pdf – giving Dartmoor the hard word

www.nelsonthornes.com/vocational/public_services/ – Unit 23 Custodial Care

Other famous cases showing the dangers of conformity:

- the videoed beating of Rodney King by Los Angeles police in 1991, followed by riots and a racist trial
- the Metropolitan Police response to the murder of Stephen Lawrence in 1993.

COOL SITES:

http://www.law.umkc.edu/faculty/projects/ftrials/lapd/lapd.html – Rodney King beating

www.official-documents.co.uk/document/cm42/4262/4262.htm – Macpherson Report 1999

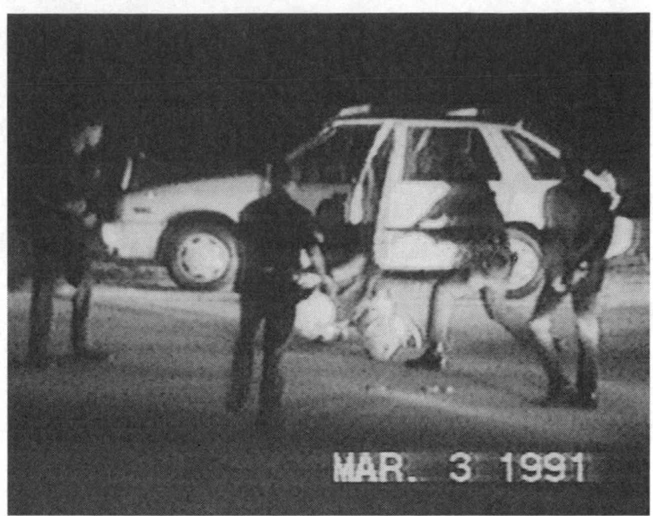

The beating of Rodney King – conformity of the wrong type

CHECKPOINT ...

1. Does the culture of obedience and conformity in the uniformed services increase the risk of racism and bullying?
2. The law states that schools and colleges are liable for racism and bullying which take place among their pupils or students. Is this fair – or should it be the pupils and students who take the blame? What do you think?
3. Institutionalised racism was defined by Sir William Macpherson as: 'The collective failure of an organisation to provide an appropriate and professional service to people because of their colour, culture or ethnic origin.' What, in your view, has this got to do with conformity and obedience?

PASSGRADE

Identify and explain three factors which influence conformity and three factors which influence obedience.

For this outcome, you need to:

- explain three things which make people more likely to conform to a group
- explain three things which make people more likely to obey an order.

This outcome invites you to look at the findings of researchers such as Asch and Milgram in a little more detail. Both researchers repeated their experiments with numerous small variations in order to find out what factors would make people more or less likely to conform or obey.

Factors influencing conformity

Through his experiments Asch identified the following factors which influenced the willingness of people to conform to group norms (i.e. the decisions of the rest of the group):

- **group size** There is greater conformity of the individual to the norms of the group as the group size increases to 4 or 5. Above 5, the tendency of the individual to conform to the group remains roughly constant.
- **the presence of an ally** An individual is much less likely to conform if there is someone else in the group who isn't conforming.
- **awareness of the group norm** An individual is more likely to conform if they are quite clear that the group norms are different from their own. If there is uncertainty about the group norm the individual feels under less pressure to conform.

Factors such as age, gender and culture might influence conformity, but experiments on this have tended to be inconclusive.

Factors influencing obedience

- **Status of the person giving the commands** There is greater obedience if the person giving the orders is of obviously higher status than the person responding to the orders. Milgram found that subjects were more obedient if the experimenter giving the orders was (a) wearing a white coat – the symbol of a scientific researcher – while giving the commands or (b) inside the buildings of Yale University – which has a famous tradition of research.
- **Proximity of the victim** Milgram's findings suggested that if obeying an order meant that someone else was going to be hurt, the person receiving the order was more likely to obey it if the person who was being harmed by the order was not visible to them. The obedience level of Milgram's 'teachers' was 65 per cent if they were in another room from the 'learner', 40 per cent if they were in the same room and only 30 per cent if the 'teacher' had to physically place the 'learner's' hands on a metal shock plate.

*'You **will** hand in your assignment tomorrow!'*

- **The gradual increase of the harm being done by the 'bad' orders** Milgram found that his 'teachers' were more likely to give the maximum shock to the 'learner' if they were told to inflict weak electric shocks at first, and gradually build up to the powerful ones.

Milgram's experiments were carried out in many countries, and it appears that culture, gender and ethnicity do not affect obedience levels very much.

SELF-DISCIPLINE

PASSGRADE

Describe the qualities needed for self-discipline in a given public service.

For this outcome, you need to say what types of self-discipline are needed in a particular public service.

FOCUS

Definition of self-discipline

Self discipline is ...

'taking control of your mind, your habits, and your emotions. Self-discipline is the ability to do what you should do, when you should do it, whether you want to or not.' – Napoleon Hill, author of *Think and Grow Rich*, 1937

The qualities needed for self-discipline in a public service are much the same as those needed for any other work or, indeed, in our everyday lives.

The best way to look at the self-discipline requirements of public service work is to look at a public service disciplinary code. From it we can work out what should be done by a self-disciplined officer in that service.

Check out the Police Code of Conduct on pages 248–9. It is clear from it that the self-discipline qualities needed in the police are:

1. Honesty and integrity
2. Fairness and impartiality
3. Politeness and tolerance
4. Patience and self-control
5. Conscientiousness, diligence, punctuality
6. Obedience to lawful orders and regulations; supportiveness to colleagues
7. Trustworthiness and ability to keep confidential information
8. Courage – especially when owning up to own faults
9. Carefulness with police property
10. Sobriety: not consuming alcohol on duty
11. Cleanliness, neatness and tidiness
12. Respectable behaviour.

The self-disciplined police officer also avoids:

- bullying
- abusing their authority
- drugs
- exploiting other people in personal relationships
- damaging their own health
- getting deep into debt
- giving way to emotion
- boasting and showing off
- racist and discriminatory talk or behaviour
- covering up for friends and colleagues who break the law.

All these are linked to *the need to think ahead and consider the possible consequences of an action.*

Merit

Explain in detail how these qualities are necessary for the effective operation of a given public service.

For this outcome, you need to:

- choose a public service
- take each of the self-discipline qualities you have described for the previous outcome and show how each quality helps people to do their job well.

The qualities you choose must be applicable for that public service. An ability to withstand physical pain and hardship would be a self-discipline quality for the Royal Marines, but is less important in the prison service. On the other hand, qualities needed for the police are also needed for Customs and Excise.

The PROFILE below takes two self-discipline qualities as an example. Then it explains how they are needed for Customs and Excise work:

Profile

Two qualities of self-discipline needed for Her Majesty's Customs and Excise

Quality	Why it is needed for the effective operation of HM Customs and Excise
Honesty and integrity	Honesty means that you do what you say you will do, and what you are paid to do. It also means you won't tell lies or deliberately hide the truth (except to carry out your duties). Integrity means that you cannot be bribed, corrupted or tempted. Customs officers who are dishonest or who lack integrity could get involved in corrupt behaviour, such as taking bribes to let people who are carrying smuggled goods through customs. They could secretly help smuggling gangs (taking large kickbacks), or simply steal the prohibited goods, e.g. drugs or weapons, that they seized at the port. Criminals could pay them for tipping them off about customs operations which could result in their capture. Even one or two dishonest customs officers could do great damage to the reputation, effectiveness and morale of the service.
Fairness and impartiality	The public that customs officers work with is extremely diverse, since the travellers at airports and sea ports arrive from all parts of the world. There will very often be

cultural and ethnic differences between the customs officers and the people they deal with. But the officers must be fair and impartial, treating everybody the same (but with cultural sensitivity) – while doing their job of detecting smuggling and other problems. They must be aware that some smugglers, such as drug mules, are victims as well as criminals. They must also remember that travel is a stressful experience for many people, and that having their bags searched may make them angry even if they have nothing to hide. Customs officers are, in a sense, ambassadors for the country: they are the first people visitors meet on arrival in the UK. If they are unfair or partial it speaks badly for the country as a whole, and would leave a very disagreeable first impression for foreign travellers.

CHECKPOINT ...

Write similar explanations for qualities needed for self-discipline in a public service of your choice.

PASSGRADE

Explore the possible effects of lack of self-discipline in the given public service.

For this outcome, you need to describe what might happen if employees in a particular public service lacks self-discipline.

The effects of lack of self-discipline in a public service can be very serious. They can be considered under two main headings.

Lack of self-discipline in one individual

Effects on that individual

- The individual may be distrusted, disliked or ignored by colleagues.
- Their promotion prospects may be blighted.
- Any good work the person does is undervalued.
- The individual receives disciplinary action.
- The individual may receive counselling, if the lack of self-discipline is thought to be 'curable', or the result of, say, personal or family problems.
- The individual may be suspected of alcohol or drug abuse.
- The individual may be sidelined into jobs carrying no real responsibility.
- The individual may be dismissed or discharged from the service.
- If the individual's lack of self-discipline leads to the injury or death of a colleague, it could result in lifelong feelings of guilt, and in prosecution.

Effects on colleagues and the service as a whole

- Colleagues do not trust the individual, and prefer not to work with them.
- Colleagues may cover up for the individual's shortcomings (this means extra work for them).
- The service receives complaints from the public which somebody has to deal with, when they could be doing something more useful.
- Colleagues complain about the individual to supervisory officers, who then have to do something.
- Colleagues grow to dislike, distrust, avoid and ignore the individual.
- There is a general lowering of morale among people who know the individual.
- There is a health and safety risk for colleagues – and in rare cases colleagues could die as a result of errors made by an individual who lacks self-discipline.

Effects on the public

- The public are unimpressed by a public service employee who lacks self-discipline.
- It reflects on the service, and they think that everybody working for the service lacks self-discipline.
- Members of the public could complain to the service, to an MP, an ombudsman, a complaints authority for that service, or to the media.
- Members of the public could be put at risk, injured or killed.

Lack of self-discipline among many members of the service, or in the service as a whole

This can be disastrous for the public service, and the public it serves.

- It leads to poor staff relations with frequent harassment, intimidation, dereliction of duty and general slackness.
- There is public fear, distrust and contempt for the service.
- The service abuses its power, and is racist, sexist and discriminatory.
- There can be serious human rights abuses, e.g. with the Serbian militia in Kosovo in the late 1990s, with the Taliban and Ba'ath Party secret police in Afghanistan and Iraq, with the Israeli armed forces' assassinations of Hammas officials (2003) and with the US treatment of alleged Al-Qaeda prisoners at Guantanamo Bay following the Afghanistan war in 2001.

You should

- ask people who work in public services about the problems caused by colleagues who lack self-discipline
- investigate disciplinary codes for different public services, and the kinds of procedures, punishments and sentences outlined in the Armed Forces Discipline Act 2000 and the Armed Forces Act 2001
- find out how services such as the army teach, or 'inculcate', self-discipline
- visit human rights websites to discover the appalling results when there is no culture of self-discipline in a public service.

Authority

Explain the meaning of authority in relation to the public services.

For this outcome, you need to say what authority means, in the public services.

FOCUS

Definitions of authority

Authority is ...

'Power or right to enforce obedience; moral or legal supremacy; the right to command, or give an ultimate decision' – *Oxford English Dictionary*

'power which is recognised as legitimate and justified by both the powerful and the powerless' – Max Weber 1864–1920; Henderson, A.M. and Parsons, T. (1947), Max Weber: *The Theory of Social and Economic Organization*, NY: The Free Press

'that which implies obedience in a context of freedom' – Arendt, H. (1961), *Between Past and Future*, Viking Press

'a right to tell others, within certain limits that will vary from case to case, what to do' – McMahon, C. (1994) *Authority and Democracy: A General Theory of Government and Management,* Princeton, New Jersey: Princeton University Press

As is always the case, definitions of key words vary. From a public service point of view, authority is an agreed right to tell someone what to do.

There is sometimes a confusion between authority and power, but they are not the same thing. A bank robber has the power to make someone lie down on the floor, because he has a gun, but he does not have the authority to do that. Power is an ability: authority is a right.

In most public services, authority means 'the right to enforce'. The police have the right to enforce the law, and prison officers have the right to enforce the prison regime.

But 'enforce' does not mean the same as 'use force' – except as a last resort. The authority of the police comes mainly from the threat of sanctions that can be applied by law, e.g. sentences and fines. 'Reasonable force' is allowed by law for making an arrest or for self-defence. Even the armed forces are expected only to use 'minimum force' – and to limit the deaths both of civilians and enemy soldiers.

Types of authority

Identify and explain four types of authority.

For this outcome, you need to name and explain four kinds of authority.

Max Weber (1864–1920)

Weber, a German sociologist, identified three types of authority based on *where they came from*, summarised in the table.

Weber's views are generally accepted in the west. But not all thinkers agree with this classification. Marxists see 'authority' as a con-trick, allowing the rich to keep an undeserved power over the poor. Feminists see authority as a power-game for men, and male-dominated institutions. Anarchists believe that all authority is a bad thing.

Weber's three types of authority

Type of authority	Where it comes from
Charismatic	Personality, strength, intelligence or beauty, e.g. Arnold Schwarzenegger
Bureaucratic	Knowledge or expertise, e.g. Gordon Brown
Traditional	Customs, such as giving respect to older people or to traditional chiefs, e.g. The Queen

Rensis Likert (1903–81)

Likert was an American expert on leadership, management and teamwork. He identified four types of authority, based on *how they were used*, summarised in the table below.

Likert's four types of authority

Type of authority	Superiors' attitude to subordinates	Types of motivation used	Who has responsibility	Communication and teamwork
Exploitative–authoritative (dictatorial)	Dictatorial: decisions imposed from above 'Slave-driving' approach	Threats	Top management has all the responsibility; lower levels have none	Little communication and no teamwork between different levels
Benevolent–authoritative (authoritarian)	A master–servant relationship with decisions imposed from above 'Paternalistic' approach Subordinates trusted a little	Rewards	Top management take and feel all the responsibility	Little communication and not much teamwork between different levels
Consultative	Superiors have a good deal of trust in subordinates	Rewards and some involvement in decision-making	Many personnel feel responsible for achieving goals (though superiors feel it most)	A good deal of communication, and moderate teamwork, between different levels
Participative	Superiors have complete confidence in subordinates	Motivated by economic rewards and shared goals	All levels of personnel have and feel real responsibility	A high degree of communication and teamwork between all levels

COOL SITES:

http://cbae.nmsu.edu/~dboje/teaching/503/weber_links.html

http://www.accel-team.com/human_relations/hrels_04_likert.html

Application of Likert's ideas in public services

Likert's ideas are part of a general movement away from authoritarian management which started in the 1960s. Now the Civil Service, the NHS, local government and education are mainly organised on consultative or participative lines, with authority spread through the organisations, rather than concentrated only at the top levels.

The armed forces, the fire and rescue service and the prison service tend to be more authoritarian – though even in these uniformed services the dictatorial approach has gone out of fashion.

CHECKPOINT ...

Talk to a person who works in a public service to see what their views on authority in their public service are.

Positive and negative effects of blind obedience to authority

Merit

Analyse the positive and negative effects of blind obedience to authority.

For this outcome, you need to:

- explain what blind obedience is
- pick out and comment on the good and bad effects of blind obedience.

'Blind obedience to authority' means carrying out commands, however unreasonable, without questioning them.

Blind obedience is said to have been a factor in:

- the 'Jonestown massacre' – the mass suicide or murder of 913 members of a religious cult of (mainly) Americans in Guyana in 1978. The cult was called 'the People's Temple'. It is thought that the cult members killed themselves on the orders of their leader, the Rev. Jim Jones
- the Waco massacre when 74 people died (through suicide, murder or accidental shooting) during an FBI siege and shootout at Waco, Texas. The dead were followers of a charismatic and ruthless cult leader called David Koresh, and belonged to the Branch Davidian sect
- killings or suicides in the Order of the Solar Temple, a 'millenarian cult' (believing in a day of reckoning or Judgement Day). These took place in 1994 in Switzerland, France and Quebec (French-speaking Canada). The leader was a charismatic man with a criminal record for illegal gun ownership called Luc Jouret. Approximately 100 people died. Members of the order believed that the Hale-Bopp comet, visible in the sky at that time, would take them to a new and better life on the star Sirius
- suicide bombings in Israel, Gaza, the West Bank and Baghdad
- the attacks of 11 September 2001 in America
- the Holocaust in World War II in which around 6 million Jews were murdered by the Nazi authorities in Germany. Many of the murderers defended themselves at the Nuremberg War Trials of 1945–9 with the famous words, 'We were only following orders'
- human rights abuses and mob violence carried out under the mental state of 'groupthink' (see FOCUS).

FOCUS

Groupthink

'This is defined as "a mode of thinking that people engage in when they are deeply involved in a cohesive group, when the members' strivings for unanimity override their motivation to realistically appraise alternative courses of action."'

Source: Irving, J. (1972), Victims of Groupthink: Psychological Study of Foreign-Policy Decisions and Fiascoes *(2nd edition), Boston: Houghton Mifflin.*

COOL SITE:

http://sol.brunel.ac.uk/~jarvis/bola/index.html

Positive effects

It is hard to think of any positive effects of 'blind obedience'. But many people who die in acts of blind obedience believe that they will go to heaven, or a better place than this world.

Suicide bombers succeed in killing people because it is hard to defend soft, or civilian, targets against this sort of attack. The tactic is a successful terror tactic in the sense that it gains publicity and causes fear and anger.

The effect of the Holocaust has only been positive in that it has inspired the world to try to make sure that such a crime never happens again.

http://www.ushmm.org/wlc/en/index.php?lang=en&ModuleId=10005143 – the Holocaust

Negative effects

Blind obedience is overwhelmingly negative in its effects. It dehumanises people and can make them behave in ways which are unimaginably callous and brutal. It by-passes the brain, and turns people into the equivalent of machines or robots.

It is hard to know whether obedience is blind or not, because we cannot see into other people's minds. Acts which seem reasonable to some people (e.g. going to war in Iraq) seem like blind obedience to those who thought the war was unnecessary or morally wrong.

Blind obedience has a range of negative effects. In suicide attacks, the first negative effect is the deaths and maiming of innocent people. Next there are the psychological effects on the grieving families and friends. Long-term effects include the fear and inconvenience that millions of people have to put up with because of the security risks, and security measures, that result from terrorism. Last and worst are the knock-on effects of further terrorism and 'the war against terror'. The money spent on this 'war' – over $100 billion from America alone so far – could have been spent on saving lives instead of ending them, but for the effects of 9/11.

Suicide bombers are usually in their early twenties and have often been university students. They rarely have a criminal record. Their young lives are wasted because of their blind obedience. From a military point of view it is a doomed tactic, since the organisations they die for are losing their bravest young people, and sapping their own strength as a result.

CHECKPOINT ...

1. Research the mental illness called 'automatism'. What problems could it cause the public services?
2. Is there any age at which a child should be blindly obedient?

Unit 16 Dealing with Accidents

Grading criteria

PASSGRADE To achieve a pass grade the evidence must show that the learner is able to:	*Merit* To achieve a merit grade the evidence must show that the learner is able to:	*Distinction* To achieve a distinction grade the evidence must show that the learner is able to:
• compare two different types of fire situations and two different types of accident situations **264** • explain how the public services deal with a range of accidents, fires and rescues and their involvement in fire and accident safety measures **267** • explain the central role of the fire service when dealing with fires, accidents and rescues **268** • explain in detail four measures that can be taken to prevent fires and accidents **269** • detail the role of public services in fire and accident prevention **272** • explain the need for different types of fire and accident safety legislation **275**	• analyse the causes of four different types of fire and accident situations **265** • analyse the involvement of the fire service in fire and accident safety measures **274** • analyse the major aspects of fire and accident safety legislation **278**	• evaluate and justify the involvement of the fire service in fire and accident safety measures **274** • evaluate the major aspects of fire and accident safety legislation **280**

An accident is any misfortune causing death, injury or damage to property. We've all experienced accidents, or known people who have. They are unexpected and can be frightening, unpleasant, inconvenient, distressing or tragic, depending on their seriousness and how closely we are involved. A minor accident can be forgotten in a few hours; a serious one can ruin lives.

'Accidents will happen', goes the old saying, and though they usually surprise us, we can be absolutely certain that they will continue to happen. We are so certain that we even have public services to deal with them.

And that's why you are studying this unit.

TYPES AND CAUSES OF ACCIDENTS AND FIRES

Compare two different types of fire situations and two different types of accident situations.

For this outcome, you need to:

- choose two different types of fire, and two different types of accident
- state the differences in their severity, causes and effects.

Your best sources of information on fires and accidents are:

- your local fire and rescue service.
- the internet. There are many good fire service websites, some of which will be given in the cool sites below. The government department in charge of the fire service is the Office of the Deputy Prime Minister
- the Institution of Fire Engineers. This organisation publishes the Fire Service Manuals. You should ask your college to buy them if they do not already have them
- the Health and Safety Executive – the key government agency engaged in accident prevention
- the Royal Society for the Prevention of Accidents (RoSPA).

http://www.odpm.gov.uk/

http://www.ife.org.uk/Retail/pubs.html

http://www.hse.gov.uk/pubns/ohsingb.pdf

http://www.rospa.co.uk

Types of fire

This is a classification of fires used by fire services:

- Primary fires – fires in buildings or vehicles
- Secondary fires – outdoor fires such as grass fires
- Chimney fires.

They classify primary fires into different types, according to where they take place, and whether they started accidentally or deliberately.

Percentages for different types of primary fire in the area covered by the Avon Fire Brigade, 2000–1

	Property		Transport	
	Dwellings	Other	Road	Other
Accidental	17%	10%	9%	5%
Deliberate	4%	12%	41%	2%

Source: Avon Fire Authority Annual Report 2000/1

Types of accident

Safety organisations such as RoSPA classify accidents as in the table below.

Injuries treated in UK hospitals, 1994–6

Road	Work	Home	Sport	Other
10%	23%	33%	13%	20%

Source: RoSPA, Accidents in the United Kingdom, *March 2002*

> **!** **CHECKPOINT ...**
>
> These are not the only ways of classifying fires or accidents into different types.
>
> 1 With a friend, note down as many types of fire and accident as you can think of
>
> 2 Search for classifications of accidents on health and safety internet sites.

How fires are caused

Fires are fast chemical reactions which give off dangerous amounts of heat. They are caused by the coming together of three essential factors, known as the fire triangle.

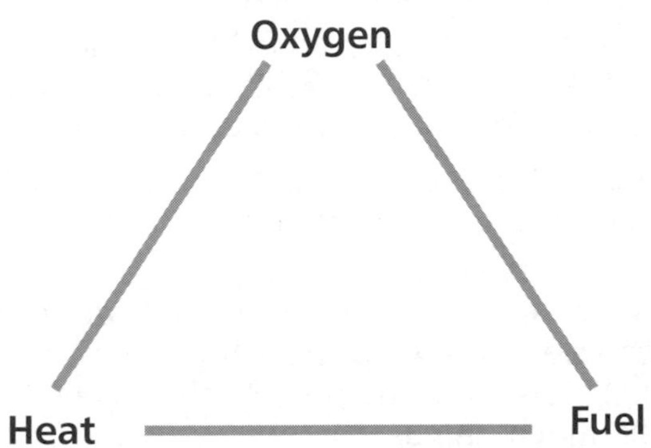

The fire triangle

Heat, oxygen and fuel are the three requirements of any fire. Putting out a fire involves getting rid of one or more of these requirements.

The process of burning is called **combustion**. Under the influence of heat, suitable chemicals combine rapidly with the oxygen in the air, in a reaction known as oxidation.

The equation below shows what happens when methane (CH_4 – the main constituent of natural gas) burns. The nature of the reaction (the joining of chemicals to produce other chemicals) is shown in the form of an equation:

$$CH_4 + 2O_2 = CO_2 + 2H_2O$$

A molecule of methane is made of one carbon atom attached to four hydrogen atoms. At room temperature it can mingle with oxygen atoms and nothing happens. But at the temperature of a match flame, or an electrical spark, a violent reaction takes place. The methane molecule joins with two pairs of oxygen atoms, and there is a sudden release of heat. If there is enough methane and enough air, in the right mixture (5–14 per cent methane), there is a violent explosion. The methane changes into carbon dioxide (one atom of carbon joined to two atoms of oxygen) and water vapour.

In an ordinary gas fire, the methane is burnt off safely, but the reaction is the same.

http://energyconcepts.tripod.com/energyconcepts/combustionfluegasses.htm – a hot site!

How accidents are caused

The main causes of accidents are:

- human error
- equipment or materials failure.

A car crash could be due to many factors, e.g. poor lighting, bad road design, brake failure, driver tiredness or drunkenness, the driver being distracted, a cat running across the road, black ice, etc. But each of these is essentially either human error or equipment/materials failure.

Merit

> Analyse the causes of four different types of fire and accident situations.

For this outcome, you need to:

- choose four different cases of fire and four different accidents
- research and explain their causes.

Reports on fires and accidents can be found in your local paper, or on fire service websites. More detailed and analytical accounts of major fires can be found in *Fire* magazine.

http://www.fire-magazine.com/#

The PROFILE gives an example of the kind of analysis that can be done for this outcome.

Profile

Just before 2 p.m. on Tuesday 19th August, firefighter crews from City Centre and Low Hill stations and the Special Rescue Unit (SRU), based at Kirkdale, were called to an incident in Richmond Street, Liverpool city centre.

A 15 ft high section of wall that was being renovated by two workmen collapsed from a height of 30 ft.

The workmen were caught under the partial collapse of the second floor wall of the adjoining building. One of the men, a 52 year old, dragged himself from the rubble, but a 40 year old man was trapped underneath.

Analysis

Each year there are between 80 and 100 deaths in the construction industry, and approximately 5000 major injuries. Fifteen per cent of deaths in construction are caused by falling objects (including walls). In 2001–2, 32 per cent of all deaths to workers in the UK were in the construction industry.

The cause of this accident was a wall falling while it was being renovated. This kind of accident is likely to happen in cities like Liverpool, where there are many old Victorian buildings, which people want to conserve because they are part of the UK's cultural heritage and history. As these buildings are now over 100 years old, the ravages of time, damp and air pollution have rotted the mortar. Changes in the water table, or subsidence from collapsing sewers, old mines, and other causes may have weakened the foundations. Renovating such buildings is a hazardous job, and requires special knowledge and skills.

Builders know that renovation is dangerous work, and should carry out a risk assessment before they start. In this case it is not clear whether such an assessment was done – but if it was, it seems that the danger of the wall collapsing was not fully appreciated. This could have been due to hidden dangers in the wall, or a lack of skill, knowledge or care in whoever did the assessment. In any event, the accident could have been avoided if the dangers had been recognised and the job tackled in a different way.

http://www.merseyfire.gov.uk/pages/latestnews/detail.asp

http://www.ukconstruction.com/default.asp?f=l&p=HSEPriorities.asp

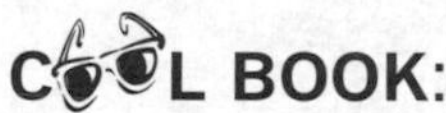

Statistics of Workplace Fatalities and Injuries – Construction (HSE)

Here is another situation:

Monday, July 14, 2003

A neighbour turned firefighter after he tackled a blaze at Holy Trinity Primary School, Freshfield, with a garden hose.

The roof of the school, in Lonsdale Road, had caught fire at around 11.30 p.m.

A fire service spokesman said: 'Somebody had deliberately set fire to a wheelie bin next to the school which had then spread to the roof. There was not too much damage.'

CHECKPOINT ...

Write your own analysis of the causes of the fire at Holy Trinity Primary School. Questions you could consider are:

- How would the fire service know that the fire had been started deliberately?
- What kind of person had probably started the fire?
- What would be the possible motives for starting the fire?
- What actions might have prevented this fire from happening?
- What physical or chemical factors were at work in this fire?

PRACTICAL WORK OF PUBLIC SERVICES IN DEALING WITH ACCIDENTS AND FIRES

PASSGRADE

Explain how the public services deal with a range of accidents, fires and rescues and their involvement in fire and accident safety measures.

For this outcome, you need to:

- arrange to meet members of the police, fire and ambulance services.
- ask your tutor to invite visiting speakers to talk about emergency service responses to accidents, fires and rescues.

Other services you might want to contact are:

- HM Coastguard
- the armed forces
- mountain rescue groups.

COOL SITES:

http://www.ukemergency.f9.co.uk/p109.htm – on-line descriptions of RTAs and the emergency service response

http://www.basics.org.uk/

http://www.tameside.gov.uk/tmbc1/emergency/rolesexternal.htm

Typical response to a serious road traffic accident (tanker crash)

In serious road traffic accidents (RTAs), there is a combined response from the emergency services – fire, ambulance and police all having a role to play.

The combined response would normally follow a 999 call that would go through a shared control centre, automatically alerting all three blue light services. The fire service would aim to be at the scene in 5–20 minutes (depending on whether the accident was in a big town or out in the country).

Fire service response

1. Bring two pumps (containing firefighting equipment), from different directions, and an emergency tender (containing equipment for first aid and for cutting people out of crashed vehicles).
2. Assess what the tanker is carrying, using the orange HAZCHEM placards, and any indication of what extinguishing agent (foam, powder, etc.) should be used.
3. Call for more backup – and technical help – if needed.
4. Approach the crash downhill and downwind.
5. Prevent fire spread, e.g. by using water jets to cool the tanker or anything else which is dangerously hot.
6. Carry out snatch rescues – perhaps of the driver, or people at serious risk in nearby houses.
7. Damp down or divert gases and vapours with a wall of spray, if the gas reacts to water.
8. Keep some of their vehicles in 'fend-off' positions to protect rescue workers from other traffic, if the accident has happened on a motorway.
9. Investigate the accident (together with the police and, perhaps, health and safety [HSE] inspectors).
10. Take part in debriefing.

Police response

1. Save lives in conjunction with the other emergency services.
2. Coordinate the emergency services where necessary (though if fire is involved in the accident, the fire service may do this as they are more aware of the hazards).
3. Protect and preserve the scene – including controlling traffic and any crowds that might gather.
4. Investigate the accident – together with others (e.g. the fire service fire investigation team) if appropriate.
5. Collect and communicate information on casualties.
6. Identify any dead victims on behalf of the coroner.
7. Prevent crime (if necessary).
8. Liaise with families (if necessary).
9. Restore normality at the earliest opportunity.

Ambulance service response

1. Assess the scene, call for backup if needed, contact receiving hospitals.

2 Give primary care to any injured people; stabilise the condition of crash victims, e.g. by giving painkillers or by hydrating them.
3 Continue to give care while the fire service is cutting out trapped accident victims.
4 Prioritise casualties ('triage') if there are many of them, and not enough ambulances to take them immediately to hospital.
5 Organise parking and loading points for other ambulances.
6 Take casualties to hospital.

Central role of the fire service

Explain the central role of the fire service when dealing with fires, accidents and rescues.

For this outcome, you need to give reasons why the fire service (now fire and rescue service) does most of the work in dealing with fires, accidents and rescues.

This central role is based on a number of factors – all important.

Firefighters themselves.

According to Sir George Bain's *Independent Review of the Fire Service* (2002) there are on average 40 applicants for every vacancy for a firefighter. Application procedures are extremely tough. Even before they are trained, firefighters are well above the average in fitness, strength, dexterity, practical intelligence and motivation.

Their training

Firefighter training covers a wide range of skills and knowledge including rescue drills, pump operations, rail incidents, advanced first aid, fire safety, health and safety, physics and chemistry of combustion, ship incidents, tactical ventilation, aircraft incidents, and manual handling.There are two years' probation. After this, appraisal and training in new techniques continues throughout their careers.

Skill and commitment

Firefighters take a pride in their work. They are also very brave. The following quotation from the *Independent Review of the Fire Service* sums it up:

FOCUS

Skill and commitment in the fire service

'Two firefighters undertook an arduous three-hour rescue of a man trapped 35 feet down in a cramped bunker containing lime. The limited space and difficulty of removing lime dust, whilst wearing breathing apparatus, made the rescue extremely difficult. Both officers received burns to their face, neck and wrists before successfully completing the rescue and had to undergo decontamination and hospital treatment.

Chief Fire Officer's commendation'

Source: http://www.irfs.org.uk/docs/future/index.htm

Equipment

Modern firefighting is highly mechanised and uses state-of-the-art equipment.

FOCUS

The special equipment units of the Hampshire Fire and Rescue Service carry ...

'Additional equipment of a type already carried on Water Tenders and Water Tender Ladders (e.g. Breathing Apparatus, Chemical Protective Clothing, Thermal Imaging Cameras)

Larger versions of equipment being carried on Water Tenders and Water Tender Ladders (e.g. Road Traffic Accident cutting gear, Positive Pressure Ventilation fans)

Additional equipment of a type carried on other Specialist Appliances (e.g. portable main scheme radios, monitors, tabards)

Equipment which is unique to these vehicles (e.g. radiation monitoring equipment, decontamination shower, Akro Props, Disc Cutters, Aqua Vac, Air Bags)'

NB This list is not complete.

Source: Hampshire Fire and Rescue Service

COOL SITES:

http://www.hantsfire.gov.uk/index.html

http://www.odpm.gov.uk/stellent/groups/odpm_fire/documents/page/odpm_fire_022968.hcsp

'I only use it for sharpening pencils these days.'

Fire and accident prevention

The fire and rescue service is very active in fire prevention and in raising community awareness of the risks of fires and accidents. The main things the service does are to:

- inspect buildings used by the public to give fire certificates, or to upgrade standards so that they can get fire certificates
- advise the building, furniture and other industries on fire risks and ways of designing out fire
- visit schools and colleges to educate young people about fire risks and safety awareness
- set up outreach centres so that the wider community can find out more fire safety and fire service work
- work in partnership with local authorities to produce emergency plans for possible disasters
- carry out exercises and disaster simulations with other public services in order to develop skills to deal with major incidents, where a combined service response is needed
- work with large chemical firms and other places which have special fire prevention or firefighting needs
- constantly update their own knowledge and skills in dealing with possible civil threats of all kinds
- run young firefighter or fire cadet schemes for children and young people who want to know more about the fire service
- produce and distribute information leaflets on all aspects of fire safety and accident prevention.

http://www.fireservice.co.uk/incidents.php

Resources

The fire and rescue service covers the whole of the UK and has a long history. It is very much part of the nation's tradition, and has wide popular support. It is a statutory public service controlled and legislated for by the government. About £2 billion is spent on the fire and rescue service each year, and it saves the country at least £7 billion in fire damage and accident costs.

PREVENTION MEASURES

Explain in detail four measures that can be taken to prevent fires and accidents.

For this outcome, you need to:

- explain four ways of preventing fires
- explain four ways of preventing accidents
- show how the methods work.

'Preventing' fires and accidents means any of the following:

- not allowing them to happen in the first place.
- giving warnings of danger
- using methods to reduce the severity of the fire or accident after it has happened
- assessing risks so that people can avoid them
- educating people on safety awareness.

There are two principles of prevention:

- preventing the cause
- preventing the effects.

Some examples are shown in the table on the next page.

Examples of prevention measures

Categories of prevention	Examples of preventing the cause	Examples of preventing (or lessening) the effects
Physical Designing machines, cars, roads, buildings, furniture, clothing, etc. so that they are less hazardous to use	Traffic lights, road markings, street lighting, road widening and redesigning Safe building design with handrails, good ventilation; safe electrical installation	Seat-belts, crush zones, airbags and head-rests in cars Fire doors, fire extinguishers, smoke alarms, sprinklers and fire escapes in buildings
Chemical Using materials which are non-flammable and non-hazardous	Putting stenching agents in town gas Using non-flammable building materials	Avoiding toxic plastic foam upholstery, lead-based paints and asbestos Using fireproof fabrics
Risk assessment Checking the work and home environment, in a systematic way, for possible dangers – then acting to remove or lessen those dangers	Checking for risks – and then removing the cause, putting up warning notices or telling people about the dangers, installing machine guards	Checking for dangers – and then reducing the risk, e.g. by using non-slip tiles on stairs, soft floors under playground equipment or wearing protective clothing
Educational and occupational Teaching people about dangers and how to avoid or minimise them. How to get help; health and safety training at college and work Health and safety laws.	Leaflets showing correct practice, e.g. manual handling Notices and leaflets about avoidable risks Staff training in how to use machines, etc. Learning how to drive Giving responsibility to people for their own and others' safety	First aid training, leaflets, etc. Information on what to do in case of a fire, bomb warning, etc. Accident recording, reporting and analysis procedures Making sure people know how and where to get help

CHECKPOINT ...

Think of two more examples to put in each section in the above table.

Measures (methods) to prevent fire and accidents can be taken from any of the categories or types shown above. You have a wide choice, and there is plenty of information, which can be found:

- in health and safety handbooks
- in safety leaflets
- on the internet
- in the brochures or websites of manufacturers of safety equipment.

The example of smoke alarms is given in the PROFILE on the next page.

FOCUS

BSI

'Standards exist to make life safer and more efficient and to facilitate trade.

Standards cover every area of life from technical guidelines for the aerospace industry to specifications for "making things happen" – the management of diverse issues like CCTV systems, customer loyalty and even skateparks.

British Standards pioneered the development of these, along with BS 5750, which has become ISO 9000, the world's most popular management system series.'

Source: http://www.bsi-global.com/group.xalter

Profile

Smoke alarms

A smoke alarm is a device which gives warning of a fire by detecting the smoke, and emitting a loud noise.

Smoke alarms work on two principles: (a) optical and (b) ionisation.

Optical smoke alarms

Optical smoke alarms are based on the principle that if you shine a light into a cloud of smoke, the smoke glows. Such alarms contain a light source and a light detector. The detector detects the light from the source only if it is reflected (or scattered) by smoke.

In the diagram, light is deflected by the smoke onto the sensor, which then sets off a loud warning noise.

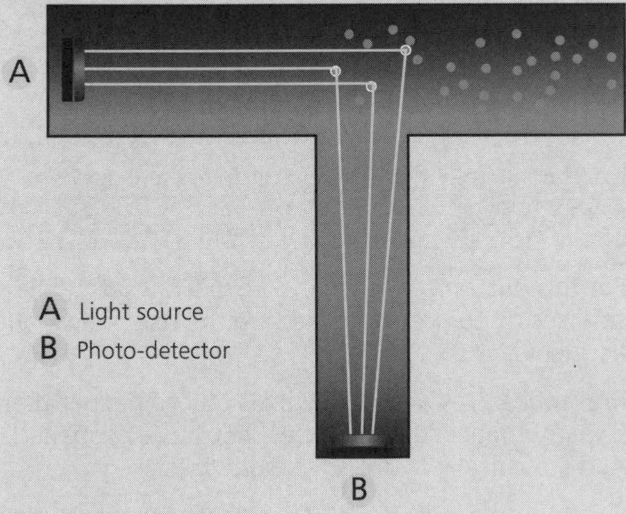

An optical smoke alarm

Ionisation smoke alarms

This kind of smoke alarm contains two metal plates attached to the positive and negative terminals of a battery, and a tiny amount of a radioactive isotope (an element that gives off high-energy subatomic particles). The radioactivity ionises nitrogen and oxygen atoms in the air inside the alarm by knocking electrons off them so that they have a positive charge. These positively charged atoms stick to the negatively charged metal plate. Normally this process allows a small electric current to pass through the air from one plate to another.

But if smoke enters the alarm, it interferes with the ionisation process and blocks off the electric current. An electronic sensor built into the alarm registers the drop in current, and sets off a loud warning noise.

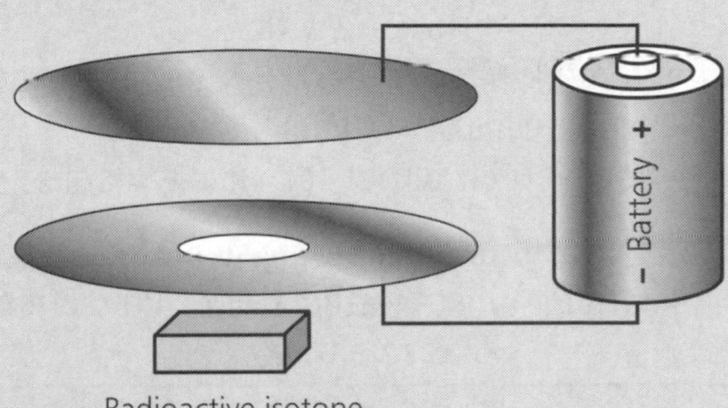

An ionisation smoke alarm

The design of British smoke alarms is overseen by the British Standards Institution (BSI – see FOCUS on previous page), which specifies their quality and reliability. The BSI controls the quality of nearly all other safety equipment made or marketed in the UK, and publishes the information in a large series of booklets called British Standards.

The BSI give advice on how and where different kinds of smoke alarm should be installed in BS 5446 and BS 5839. They recommend that optical smoke alarms are best installed in 'circulation spaces' such as hallways and landings, while ionisation alarms are more effective in places like living rooms and dining rooms. The optical ones are more sensitive, but are also more likely to cause false alarms.

The effectiveness of smoke alarms, which were introduced about 30 years ago, has been clearly shown by statistics from many countries (see FOCUS below).

Smoke alarms are one of the cheapest and most effective forms of fire protection. They cannot prevent fires starting, but they have saved hundreds of thousands of lives in different parts of the world, since they were invented. The optical ones cost about £10, while the ionising type cost about £20.

FOCUS

'In the USA, 15 of every 16 homes (94%) in the U.S. have at least one smoke alarm. One-half of home fire deaths occur in the 6% of homes with no smoke alarms.' – National Fire Protection Association, USA

COOL SITES:

http://www.tlc-direct.co.uk/Main_Index/Fire_and_Smoke/Smoke_1/index.html
– commercial outlet for smoke alarms

http://www.nfpa.org/catalog/home/index.asp
– American site – National Fire Protection Association

When explaining measures to prevent fires and accidents:

- if it is physical:
  - describe the technology
  - explain its purpose
  - show how it's used
  - give information, if available, about its effectiveness and cost
- if it is chemical:
  - explain the relevant chemical properties
  - explain the other points as in (a) above
- if it is to do with risk assessment:
  - describe the procedure and any legal background (LINK! Page 273 below)
  - any other relevant points
- if it is educational:
  - discuss what methods, techniques and 'teaching aids' are used to get the message across
  - discuss the word-use, layout and visual presentation of any printed material
  - describe the 'audience' (i.e. the target group)
  - explain any other relevant points.

COOL SITES:

http://www.highwaycode.gov.uk/index.shtml
– The Highway Code – search this site for ways to prevent car accidents!

http://www.rospa.com/CMS/index.asp
– lots of stuff about accidents!

The role of public services

PASSGRADE

Detail the role of public services in fire and accident prevention.

For this outcome, you need to explain what public services do to prevent or reduce the risk of fires and accidents.

Preventing fires and accidents is much cheaper than trying to deal with them after they have happened. And statistically it saves far more lives

For these reasons, fire and accident prevention plays a much bigger part on public service work than it used to.

You'll get the best information for this outcome from serving firefighters, police officers, mountain rescue teams and the local authority. But there is plenty of background stuff on the internet which is useful too.

Fire and accident prevention by the fire and rescue service

The fire and rescue service approach fire and accident prevention from a number of angles.

Community fire safety
This involves meeting as many people as possible – from all sections of society – and raising awareness

of fire safety. It includes outreach working, educating the public, distributing leaflets, door-to-door canvassing, home fire safety checks and fitting of smoke alarms. Community fire safety officers visit schools and colleges, mount exhibitions, run 'fire cadet' schemes, hold open days and take part in community events.

Legislative fire safety

The fire and rescue service inspects workplaces and buildings used by the public to make sure that they comply with fire safety laws. They issue fire certificates when those buildings are up to the legal standard of fire safety. The law may be changed in the near future (see below, page 279).

Emergency planning

This means planning, preparing and training for possible large-scale emergencies such as explosions, terrorist attacks, floods and major chemical spills. The planning is done in conjunction with the local authority, other emergency services, the local health service, the suppliers of water, gas and electricity and any other organisation, public or private, statutory or non-statutory, which might be involved.

LINK! More in Unit 24 about major incident plans (page 359) and disaster simulations (page 360)

Research and development

The fire and rescue service advises builders and manufacturers about the fire safety of construction methods, building materials, and other substances such as fabric and plastics. Research is carried out by the Fire Service College at Moreton-in-Marsh – often in conjunction with manufacturing industry or with universities.

http://www.fireservice.co.uk/

http://www.fireservicecollege.ac.uk/

Accident prevention by the police

The police have a special responsibility for road safety – but they often work in partnership with other agencies as the FOCUS shows.

FOCUS

Police roles in accident prevention

In Spring 1999, a new partnership was formed building on previous effective liaisons. Northamptonshire Police, Northamptonshire County Council, Highways Agency, Northamptonshire Health Authority and Northamptonshire Magistrates Court, all came together with one aim in mind: To reduce the number of road casualties and increase public awareness of the problem by forming a casualty reduction strategy.

Source: www.northantspolice.com

Measures taken by such partnerships include:

- roadbuilding schemes to make roads safer
- improvement of traffic lights and road signs
- using speed cameras and laser guns
- SID machines – radar units with a large speed indicator built in
- free car safety checks and eyesight tests
- drink-driving campaigns
- high visibility police traffic patrols
- publicising of 'red routes' which have most accidents
- publication of accident statistics
- printing of road safety leaflets and posters.

Accident and crime prevention can overlap – as the FOCUS shows.

FOCUS

Police advice

'Pickpockets

They like stations and trains, where people are often in a hurry and slightly careless of their possessions. Keep your valuables secure on you – wallets and purses in inside pockets; bags carried forward, with your hand on them.

If you have a heavy bag or box, don't dump it several feet away from you. It will get in the way of other people and may cause an accident. Also, you run a greater risk of having it stolen – it only takes seconds to snatch something when the train stops at a station.

Put big or heavy items on the rack above your head (if there's room) or on an empty seat, where you can keep an eye on them.'

Source: Metropolitan Police

http://www.met.police.uk/index.htm – The ultimate crime prevention site

Local authorities

Many services offered by local authorities are to do with fire and accident prevention. Examples are given in the table below.

Examples of fire and accident prevention by local authorities

General accident prevention	Road accident prevention
Anti-social behaviour unit	Abandoned vehicles
Asbestos disposal	Car parks and parking
Blocked sewers and drains	ROSS street care
Chemical toilet emptying service	School crossing patrols
Clinical waste collection	Road safety
Child protection register	School transport to and from home
Contaminated land	Street lighting and signs
Council house repairs	Traffic calming
Dangerous buildings and structures	
Dead animals – removal and disposal	
Dog wardens – complaints about dogs	

Local authorities employ environmental health officers who are concerned with accident prevention in the sense that they check on noise hazards, hygiene in restaurants and similar matters which pose a risk to the public. Local authorities also employ traffic wardens who reduce the risk of accidents by enforcing parking regulations.

Through fire and police authorities (committees of elected councillors), local authorities try to ensure that the fire service and the police carry out adequate fire and accident prevention work for the good of local people.

Merit

Analyse the involvement of the fire service in fire and accident safety measures.

Distinction

Evaluate and justify the involvement of the fire service in fire and accident safety measures.

For these outcomes, you need to:

- collect information from
  - your local fire station
  - reports or action plans produced by your local fire authority
  - reports and fire authority plans on the internet
- explain in detail what the fire service does to promote fire and accident safety
- identify and explain their priorities
- examine trends (changes in fire and safety measures – either in recent years or planned for the near future)
- note successes, failures, problems and opportunities
- find out the cost of fire and accident safety measures, and state why (or whether) you think they are money well spent.
- assess the importance of fire and accident safety measures in fire service work (both for the public and for fire service personnel).

It would be useful to ask firefighters themselves how effective they think their fire and accident safety measures are.

http://www.lancsfirerescue.org.uk/best_value.htm – excellent

FOCUS

Lancashire Fire and Rescue Service

'The Lancashire Fire and Rescue Service carry out the following fire and accident safety measures:

- Issuing fire certificates
- Improving response times by setting targets
- Chip pan fire campaign
- Enforcing fire safety legislation to ensure that public buildings, etc. meet fire prevention standards
- Working with young firesetters to prevent deliberate fire setting

- Child Safe – an education scheme involving primary schools
- Home Safe – this involves using health visitors to be the 'eyes and ears' for the fire service when they are visiting vulnerable people
- Home fire safety checks upon request, to give advice and raise awareness of the risks and what to do in the event of a fire
- Supplying and fitting smoke alarms in private homes where needed. During 2002/2003 we fitted, free of charge, 12,726 smoke alarms
- Young firefighters scheme involving the 12–18 years age group
- "Abuse it! – Lose it" – reducing malicious calls from mobile phones which can divert valuable fire-fighting resources to deal with a hoax
- Working to encourage the fitting of sprinklers in homes, industrial buildings and schools
- Using data to identify areas where the greatest number of fires occur, in order to target resources more effectively.'

Source: Lancashire Combined Fire Authority

Under the Crime and Disorder Act 1998, the fire service has a statutory duty to take part in crime reduction strategies. Areas directly involving the fire service are: arson, malicious fire calls, attacks on firefighters, and vandalism affecting fire service efficiency e.g. damage to rising mains, fire fighting lifts and staircases, hydrants and public phone boxes (999).

CHECKPOINT ...

Carry out a fire safety check on your own home – using the standards the fire service themselves would use.

FOCUS

Money matters – the cost of running one of the UK's 50 fire and rescue services

'For the financial year to 31 March 2004, the Lancashire Fire and Rescue Service is expected to incur expenditure totalling £57.413 million which will be funded in the main through contributions of £51.273 million from Lancashire County Council (approx. 81%), Blackburn with Darwen Borough Council (approx. 9%) and Blackpool Borough Council (approx. 10%) who receive funding from central government grants, council taxes and business rates. The balance of £6.140 million is income raised from a variety of services performed by the Brigade, plus employee pension contributions to the Firefighter's Pension Scheme. The total cost of £51.273 million, excluding these notional charges, equates to an estimated cost per head of population for the coming year of £36.22 per year.'

Source: Lancashire Combined Fire Authority, Best Value Plan, 2003/4

The cost of fire safety compared with the cost of firefighting

Areas of expenditure level	2002/3 (£000s)	2003/4 (£000s)
Firefighting and rescue operations	39,809	40,920
Community fire safety	3,232	3,762

Source: Lancashire Combined Fire Authority

FIRE AND ACCIDENT SAFETY LEGISLATION

Explain the need for different types of fire and accident safety legislation.

For this outcome, you need to show why different types of fire and accident safety laws are needed.

Fire and accident safety legislation protect us against:

- fires (accidental and deliberate)
- accidents
- dangers on the roads
- dangerous, negligent or careless human behaviour
- terrorist attacks.

Such laws are needed because:

- human behaviour is often dangerous
- modern technology and materials are dangerous if misused.

Fire and safety laws:

- penalise dangerous, criminal or risky behaviour (e.g. give stiff sentences to drink-drivers and arsonists)
- regulate technology, the workplace and the environment generally, to make them less dangerous (set standards for workplace safety, vehicle safety, electrical installation and for the design, materials, etc. of manufactured goods)
- encourage positive action to make us protect ourselves and others (e.g. using smoke alarms and safety belts, enabling fire services to operate, learning first aid, etc.).

Safety laws

In the last 60 years, Parliament has passed many laws about fire and accident safety. The three big ones are the Fire Services Act 1947, the Health and Safety at Work Act 1974 and the Fire Precautions Act 1971.

Fire Services Act 1947

This marks the beginning of the modern fire service. It states that each fire service has to provide:

- a fire service for its geographical area
- training of its firefighters
- arrangements to receive calls and mobilise fire crews
- water supplies
- the giving of fire safety advice.

The Act also allows the equipment and resources of the fire brigade to be used for marine and offshore firefighting and for special service, e.g. rescues from road traffic accidents, dealing with spillage of substances and calls to flooding.

Health and Safety at Work Act 1974

This is the most important safety law. It covers all buildings which are workplaces or are used by the public.

LINK! Find the main points on page 278.

Fire Precautions Act 1971

This law made fire prevention one of the central roles of the fire service, by making them issue certificates of fire safety to buildings which were workplaces or used by the public.

FOCUS

Other fire and accident laws

- *Management of Health and Safety at Work Regulations 1999:* require employers to carry out risk assessments, make arrangements to implement necessary measures, appoint competent people and arrange for appropriate information and training.
- *Workplace (Health, Safety and Welfare) Regulations 1992:* cover a wide range of basic health, safety and welfare issues such as ventilation, heating, lighting, workstations, seating and welfare facilities.
- *Health and Safety (Display Screen Equipment) Regulations 1992:* set out requirements for work with visual display units (VDUs).
- *Personal Protective Equipment (PPE) Regulations 1992:* require employers to provide appropriate protective clothing and equipment for their employees.
- *Provision and Use of Work Equipment Regulations (PUWER) 1998:* require that equipment provided for use at work, including machinery, is safe.
- *Manual Handling Operations Regulations 1992:* cover the moving of objects by hand or bodily force.
- *Health and Safety (First Aid) Regulations 1981:* cover requirements for first aid.
- *The Health and Safety Information for Employees Regulations 1989:* require employers to display a poster telling employees what they need to know about health and safety.
- *Employers' Liability (Compulsory Insurance) Regulations 1969:* require employers to take out insurance against accidents and ill health to their employees.
- *Reporting of Injuries, Diseases and Dangerous Occurrences Regulations 1995 (RIDDOR):* require employers to notify certain occupational injuries, diseases and dangerous events.
- *Noise at Work Regulations 1989:* require employers to take action to protect employees from hearing damage.
- *Electricity at Work Regulations 1989:* require people in control of electrical systems to ensure they are safe to use and maintained in a safe condition.

- *Control of Substances Hazardous to Health Regulations 1999 (COSHH):* require employers to assess the risks from hazardous substances and take appropriate precautions. In addition, specific regulations cover particular areas, for example asbestos and lead, and:
- *Chemicals (Hazard Information and Packaging for Supply) Regulations (CHIP 2) 1994:* require suppliers to classify, label and package dangerous chemicals and provide safety data sheets for them.
- *Construction (Design and Management) Regulations 1994:* cover safe systems of work on construction sites.
- *Gas Safety (Installation and Use) Regulations 1998:* cover safe installation, maintenance and use of gas systems and appliances in domestic and commercial premises.

Source: HSE
© Crown Copyright

New fire and accident safety laws come in every year. They come in two forms:

- Acts of Parliament (major new laws)
- statutory instruments (minor laws, or additions to Acts).

The Acts outlaw unsafe behaviour; the statutory instruments legislate against unsafe products.

FOCUS

New fire and accident safety Acts since 2000

2000

- The Nuclear Safeguards Act – Special powers shared with other countries to limit the risk of illegal trade in nuclear materials.
- The Football Disorder Act – This allows the police to withdraw passports or place banning orders on known football hooligans.

2001

- Anti-terrorism, Crime and Security Act
- The Private Security Industry Act – Ensures that criminals do not work as security guards, door staff, etc.

2002

- Police Reform Act – Helps to tackle antisocial behaviour which is a risk to the public.
- Football Disorder Amendment Act – Strengthens police powers to deal with football violence.

2003

- Aviation Offences Act – Prevents drunken, disorderly and dangerous behaviour on planes.
- Marine Safety Act – Reduces risks of marine pollution and makes it easier to fight fires at sea.
- Railways and Transport Safety Act – Strengthens the British Transport Police; imposes alcohol limits on all train employees, sets up a rail accident investigation branch; also introduces laws to keep roads clear in winter.

FOCUS

Recent statutory instruments

- The Traffic Signs (Amendment) General Directions 2003 – temporary traffic signs
- The Nuclear Industries Security Regulations 2003 – security of radioactive materials
- The Farm Waste Grant (Nitrate Vulnerable Zones) (England) Scheme 2003 – protecting water supplies
- The Creosote (Prohibition on Use and Marketing) Regulations 2003 – banning a toxic product
- The Products of Animal Origin (Third Country Imports) (England) (Amendment) Regulations 2003 – limiting risks of human and animal disease
- The Cosmetic Products (Safety) Regulations 2003 – protection from toxic chemicals
- The Miscellaneous Food Additives (Amendment) (England) Regulations 2003 – toxic/allergenic additives
- The Ammonium Nitrate Materials (High Nitrogen Content) Safety Regulations 2003 – limiting explosion risks (and terrorist access to a bomb-making chemical)
- The Pedal Bicycles (Safety) Regulations 2003 – protection against cycle accidents
- The Motor Vehicle Tyres (Safety) (Amendment) Regulations 2003 – road safety
- The Contaminants in Food (England) Regulations 2003 – public health
- The Offshore Installations (Safety Zones) (No. 2) Order 2003 – risk of fires and accidents near oil rigs.

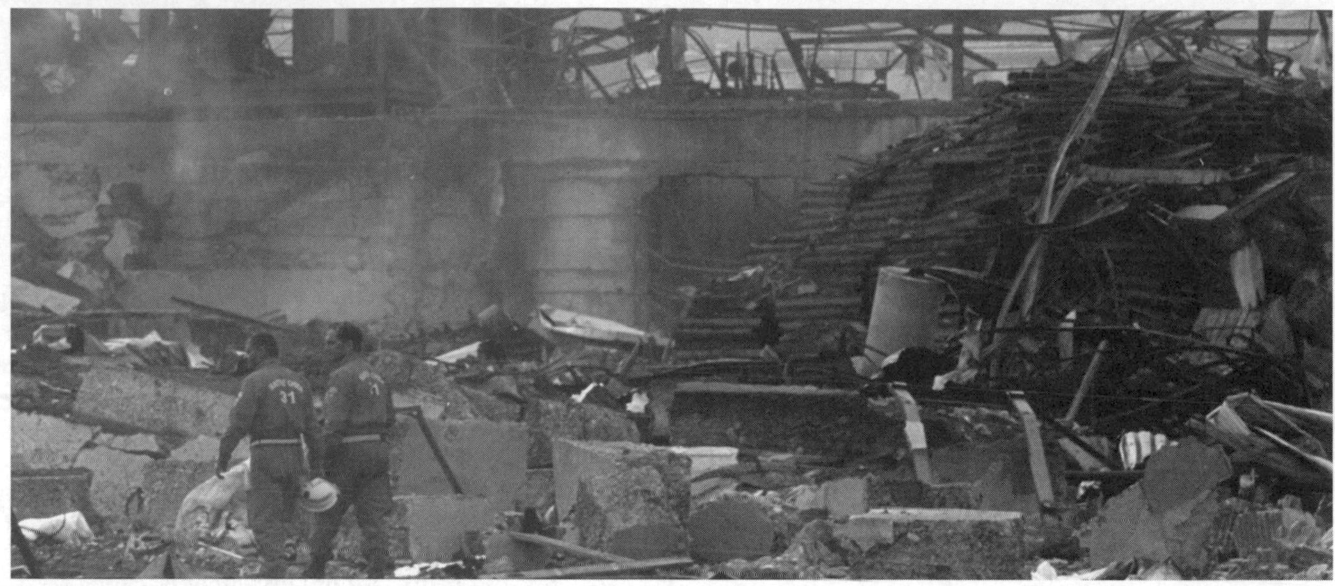

Why safety regulations are needed. Devastation at Toulouse, France, after the ammonium nitrate explosion of 2001

Merit

Analyse the major aspects of fire and accident safety legislation.

For this outcome, you need to:

- examine the main laws which protect us from fires and accidents in detail
- identify the key points of the laws and explain why they are important.

The Health and Safety at Work Act 1974

This act was brought in to simplify British health and safety law and bring it up to date. Before 1974, health and safety was covered by a lot of different laws, mainly Factory Acts, which had become old-fashioned and confusing.

The Health and Safety at Work Act defined the safety responsibilities that employers have towards employees and members of the public, and that employees have to themselves and to each other.

Since 1974, the provisions of the Act have been added to. The main points now are:

- National control of safety is in the hands of the Health and Safety Commission, a committee of about ten people appointed by the Secretary of State for Transport, Local Government and the Regions.
- Enforcement of safety is the responsibility of the Health and Safety Executive. The HSE has a staff of 4000 people – mainly inspectors, policy advisers, technologists, scientists and medical experts.
- Employers must:
  - provide a safe, healthy workplace
  - provide adequate welfare and health facilities
  - give information and training in health and safety
  - carry out full risk assessments – and eliminate or minimise those risks
  - write a health and safety policy and display it clearly
  - appoint a competent safety officer
  - have safety consultations with employees' safety representatives
  - set up emergency procedures
  - provide adequate first aid
  - record accidents and report serious ones to the Health and Safety Executive (HSE).
- Employees must:
  - take reasonable care of themselves and others
  - cooperate with the employer on health and safety
  - use work items and protective equipment correctly
  - not misuse anything connected with health, safety or welfare.

COOL SITES:

http://www.hse.gov.uk/ (a big, safe site)

http://www.safety.ed.ac.uk/resources/pdf/law.pdf

http://www.iee.org/Policy/Areas/Health/hsb04.cfm

FOCUS

A safe workplace

- is clean, well-aired, well lit and of a comfortable temperature
- contains suitable, well-maintained work equipment
- has no unnecessary exposure to hazardous substances
- minimises fire, noise, electrical, handling and radiation hazards
- provides free protective clothing or equipment whenever needed
- has clear safety signs wherever needed.

Analysis

The Health and Safety at Work Act does not claim that it is possible to have a completely safe workplace. It states that the workplace should be 'as safe as reasonably practicable'.

The Act saves lives – but it doesn't save *all* lives. In 2000–1, 291 workers were killed in accidents at work, and 445 members of the public died in accidents which happened in places covered by the Health and Safety at Work Act (including fairgrounds, railways and schools).

The Health and Safety at Work Act is enforced by local authorities and the inspectors of the Health and Safety Executive.

HSE inspectors can:

- give advice
- issue improvement notices – the source of danger must be remedied in a specific time
- issue prohibition notices – the dangerous activity must be immediately stopped
- prosecute in the criminal courts, leading to fines of up to £20,000 in the magistrates' courts, and unlimited fines in the Crown Court. In some cases prison sentences can result
- hand the matter over to the police if there has been a death – and the police can charge the offender with manslaughter.

In 1999–2000, 17,400 improvement and prohibition notices were issued and 2500 charges brought by the HSE.

! CHECKPOINT ...

What are RIDDOR, HAZCHEM and COSHH? How are they put into practice? Ask a safety officer (perhaps at your college) to advise you on this.

The Fire Precautions Act 1971

This Act authorises the fire service to inspect premises for fire safety, demand alterations if the premises are unsafe, and – if they are safe – to issue a fire certificate. A fire certificate is simply a form which, when filled in, specifies:

- the use or uses of the premises which the certificate covers
- the means of escape in case of fire with which the premises are provided
- the means for ensuring that the means of escape can be safely and effectively used at all times
- the type, number and location of the means for fighting fire with which the relevant building is provided
- the type, number and location of fire alarms
- information on any explosive or highly flammable materials which may be stored or used in the premises.

The Act covers all workplaces, including schools, colleges and places of entertainment and sport.

The law in this area is likely to change. The government has published *A Consultation Document on the Reform of Fire Safety Legislation* (2002) outlining plans to scrap the system by which the fire service issues fire certificates. If the new law is passed, it will place more responsibility on owners and managers of buildings for fire risk assessments than they have at present.

CHECKPOINT ...

Find out whether fire safety law has changed. Then (if it has) outline changes.

www.odpm.gov.uk
– for the consultation document

http://www.fire.org.uk/fpact/s1.htm

Distinction

Evaluate the major aspects of fire and accident safety legislation

For this outcome, you need to:

- assess how successful fire and safety legislation are at eliminating fires and accidents
- explain the limitations of fire and safety legislation
- determine the true cost of fires and accidents
- compare the cost of accident prevention with the cost of accidents.

FOCUS

The cost of accidents v. the cost of safety

'The HSE have estimated that over 30 million working days are lost due to workplace accidents, and that when all the costs are properly taken into account, the total cost of work accidents and work related ill-health, to society as a whole, is likely to be between 10 and 15 billion pounds sterling a year – equivalent to between 1.75% and 2.75% of the GDP of the UK.'

Source: IEE (2003), The Costs to Industry of Accidents and Ill-health, Health & Safety Briefing 3

In 2001–2, the Health and Safety Commission cost the taxpayer about £605,000, while the Health and Safety Executive cost about £203,304,000.

COOL SITES:

http://www.hse.gov.uk/statistics/overpic.htm

http://www.iee.org/Policy/Areas/Health/hsb03.pdf

FOCUS

Deaths and injuries – fires 2002

'The total number of fire deaths rose to an estimated 612 from 578 in the previous 12-month period. Of these, 471 deaths occurred in dwelling fires compared with 458, in the previous 12 months.

The number of injuries in fires fell by 3% to 16,700 from 17,200 in the previous 12 months. Injuries in dwelling fires fell by 1% to 13,600.'

Source: http://www.odpm.gov.uk

Profile

Major aspects of fire and accident legislation

In the home

Many more people die in house fires than in other kinds of fire. This is partly because people spend more time at home than anywhere else. But another factor is that private houses are not directly protected by fire safety laws. It is not compulsory to get the fire service to check the fire safety of your house.

There is some indirect protection because fire safety laws apply to the materials and construction of houses, the professional installation of gas and electricity and the making of soft furnishings. But in the UK there are no effective laws against homeowners doing their own dangerous DIY installations.

Although fires and accidents in the home cause many injuries and deaths it is unlikely that the law will be changed, partly because of the cost of changing it, and partly because of a general feeling that people should be free to do what they like in their own homes.

At work

There is much more fire and accident legislation for workplaces than there is in the home. But the chart on the next page suggests that there is no realistic chance of eliminating accidents, however much fire and safety legislation is brought in. Between 1992 and 2002, the rate of fatal injuries per 100,000 workers went down, but the line appears to be bottoming out – or even rising again.

Statistics do not prove that it is legislation which brings down the accident rate. A fall in accident numbers could be the result of using more machines and fewer people at work – or of cut-backs in dangerous industries such as construction or fishing.

The cost of enforcing safety law in the workplace is tiny compared to the cost to individuals and the country of industrial accidents. The law can therefore be said to be cost-effective.

But fire and accident safety legislation has one overriding weakness. It only demands safety 'as far as is reasonably practicable'. In other words, safety is less important than making money. The attitude to road safety is a case in point. Nobody ever suggests banning the motor car because about 3500 people are killed on the UK's roads each year.

Nevertheless, even if only a very few lives are saved by fire and accident safety legislation, it is surely worth the money and effort spent on it.

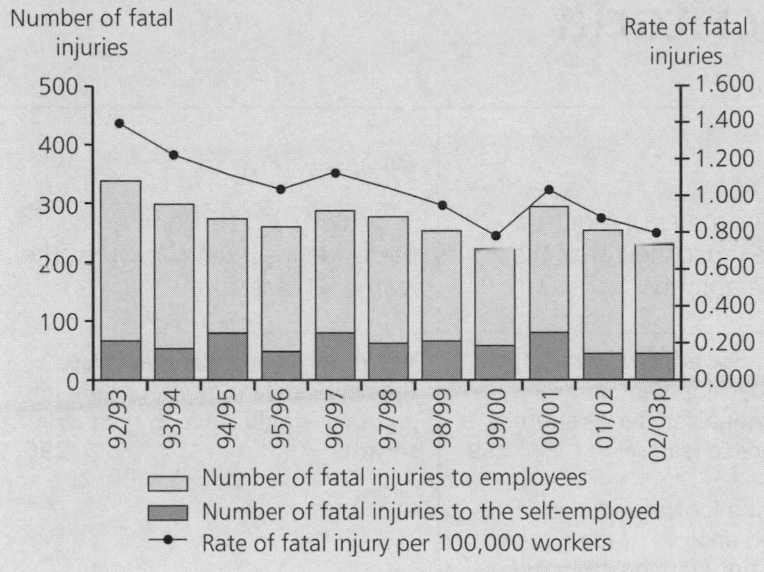

Number and rate of fatal injury to workers, 1992/3–2002/3 (figures for 2002/3 are provisional)
Source: http://www.hse.gov.uk/statistics/overall/hssh0203.pdf
© Crown Copyright

Teamwork in the Public Services

Grading criteria

PASSGRADE	Merit	Distinction
To achieve a pass grade the evidence must show that the learner is able to:	To achieve a merit grade the evidence must show that the learner is able to:	To achieve a distinction grade the evidence must show that the learner is able to:
• explain in detail the major theories which support the development of teams in public service **283** • explain clearly the stages of team development **287** • analyse and evaluate the roles of individual team members **288** • describe the types of teams which operate within two public services **290** • accurately describe the characteristics of effective teams **293** • produce examples of good practice in relation to two teams within a specified public service **293** • explain, using appropriate examples, the barriers to teamwork that may exist in two public services **297**	• summarise effectively the stages of team development and roles that individuals undertake within public service teams **289** • present a logical and well structured analysis of the types of the teams operating within the public services **292** • make considered comments about the skills, attributes and characteristics of effective public service teams **295** • analyse and evaluate the barriers to team work in public services **297**	• critically analyse and evaluate the development of effective teams and their significance to the public services **296**

Human beings have always been teamworkers. In the Stone Age our ancestors hunted and gathered in teams – it was safer and more productive than hunting and gathering alone. Now, as well as working in teams, we take much of our pleasure in teams – for sport and recreation. Even the family could be seen as a team.

Public services are no different. If you study an organisation chart of a uniformed public service you will see that the service is divided into departments, sections, units and teams. The names may differ but the purpose is always to break the organisation down into manageable groups which have identifiable jobs and purposes – so that people can work successfully.

DEVELOPMENT OF TEAMS

Explain in detail the major theories which support the development of teams in public service.

For this outcome, you need to:

- explain the main theories about teamwork
- give details about how they apply to public service teamwork.

Since the start of the twentieth century, there has been a great deal of research on teams, team-building and teamwork. This research, powered by the needs of industry and war, has given rise to many theories on the subject.

Some major theorists – and their ideas

Peter F. Drucker

Peter F. Drucker (1909–) is one of the greatest modern management theorists. He says that a team must have:

- **a plan or mission** This must relate to the needs, opportunities, strengths and values of the organisation it belongs to. It must 'focus on what the institution really tries to do'. The mission is the real reason for the team's existence. The primary job of the leader is to define and promote this mission, so that all members of the team can sincerely believe in it and work for it.
- **a marketing strategy** The team has to know who it is serving or working with. For example, if the team is dealing with young offenders, it has to know, understand and reach out to young offenders if it is to have any chance of producing a 'changed human being who has more power to achieve' (which is the real objective of having such a team in the first place).
- **money** In the case of a statutory British public service, this is mainly funding from central or local government. But if the organisation is voluntary (e.g. a charity), a team will have to decide how to obtain money for its work.
- **people** who have the enthusiasm and commitment to be effective team-workers and who can make a real contribution to the team's success.

> **FOCUS**
>
> **Definitions of 'team'**
>
> A team is ...
>
> 'a group of individuals working together for a common purpose, who must rely on each other to achieve mutually defined results' – Capezio, P. (1998), *Winning Teams*, Franklin Lakes, NJ: Career Press
>
> 'a small number of people with complementary skills who are committed to a common purpose, a set of performance goals, and an approach for which they hold themselves mutually accountable.' – Wergin, J. (1998), *The Collaborative Department*, AAHE
>
> 'a group with a common goal' – Bill Gates, CEO, Microsoft
>
> Teamwork is ...
>
> 'doing something together' – Robbins, H. and Finley, M. (1995), *Why Teams Don't Work*, Robbins & Robbins
>
> 'the coming together of a group of people who are: committed to achieving defined results, vested with the authority to make decisions, and willing to be held jointly accountable for achieving results' – USAID (foreign aid organisation)
>
> A workplace team is ...
>
> 'a number of persons, usually reporting to a common superior and having some face to face interaction, who have some degree of interdependence in carrying out tasks for the purpose of achieving organizational goals' – French, W.L. and Bell, C.H. (1995), *Organizational Development* (6th edition), Prentice-Hall.

Drucker puts forward ideas about team structures and dynamics as well. In a recent article 'There's three kinds of teams' (1995), Drucker uses sports comparisons to define them as follows:

- the **baseball team**, in which each individual has a single, clear role. Team members remain in that role at all times, e.g. a surgeon's team carrying out an operation.
- the **football team**, in which individuals work together in a less specialised way – though they still have definable roles, e.g. a team of paramedics at an accident.
- the **tennis doubles kind of team**, in which members have a 'primary' but not a 'fixed' position. They cover their team-mates, adjust to their strengths and weaknesses – and to changing demands, e.g. a unit of marines on active service.

Drucker believes that management and teamwork are judged by results, and that value and service must come first. Results, he says, come from exploiting opportunities, not solving problems. Effective teams are driven by a desire to succeed, not a fear of failure. The aim of team leaders should be 'not how to do things right, but how to find the right things to do.'

Relevance of Drucker's theory to public service
His ideas that teams should have a clear mission, defining hoped-for results, and that the best teams are 'pursuing the greater good' (trying to make people's lives better) have been taken up by all British public services. The stress on 'quality' of service comes from Drucker.

COOL SITE:

http://drucker.org/leaderbooks/drucker/time-of-change.html

COOL BOOKS:

Drucker, P. (1966), *The Effective Executive*, HarperCollins

Drucker, P. (1986), *The Frontiers of Management*, E.P. Dutton

Meredith Belbin

Belbin (1926–), a British researcher, has carried out influential studies in team roles. These he defines as: 'a tendency to behave, contribute and interrelate with others in a particular way'.

The roles he has identified are:

- **action-oriented roles** – Shaper, Implementer, and Completer Finisher
- **people-oriented roles** – Coordinator, Teamworker and Resource Investigator
- **cerebral roles** – Plant, Monitor Evaluator and Specialist.

See the table on the next page.

Relevance to public service:
Belbin's idea that every team member can contribute something distinctive and different, to the benefit of the whole team, has encouraged public service teams to work more imaginatively – and shown the importance of democratic leadership.

http://www.belbin.com/belbin-team-roles.htm

Belbin, R.M. (1993), *Team Roles at Work*, Butterworth-Heinemann

K. Lewin

Lewin (1890–1947) was a psychologist who studied group dynamics (how people work and interact in a group). He researched:

- why groups often find it hard to get things done
- communication within the group
- how group membership influences people's view of society outside the group
- relations between one group and another
- how individuals respond to being members of groups
- how to train group leaders to make groups work better.

His theories include:

- **driving forces and restraining forces** Lewin believed teams were driven forward by what they wanted (or needed) to achieve, but restrained (held back) by negative forces such as laziness or lack of confidence. Teams had to maximise the driving forces and minimise the restraining forces, in order to be well-motivated.
- **field theory** A 'field' is the totality of factors that a person feels influence their behaviour. To

understand teams and their members, the members' fields, 'lifespace' or backgrounds have to be understood.

- **interdependence of fate** A team couldn't begin to give of its best until its members saw that their future was linked to that of other team members. Once they realised this, the team could 'bond'.
- **task interdependence** This was the awareness on the part of team members that their future was in some way dependent on achieving their team tasks. Once they realised this, a team was committed to its work.
- **group dynamics** This idea states that groups of people, by interacting and learning through theory and practice, can develop themselves as individuals and as a team or group. Lewin used 'basic skills training groups' or 'T-groups' (see FOCUS) to research this. He believed in the importance of:
  - **feedback** – the group members told each other what they had learnt or achieved through a shared activity
  - **unfreezing** – challenging the values and beliefs of group members in order to 'reorientate' them towards the goals of the group, or towards a new way of thinking
  - **participant observation** – active group members observed what was going on in the group and drew conclusions from it
  - **cognition aids** – exercises or explanations which helped the group to understand themselves and the way they interacted.

Belbin's team roles

Team-role type	Contributions	Allowable weaknesses
Plant	Creative, imaginative, unorthodox Solves difficult problems	Ignores incidentals Too pre-occupied to communicate effectively
Coordinator	Mature, confident, a good chairperson Clarifies goals, promotes decision-making, delegates well	Can often be seen as manipulative Off loads personal work
Monitor Evaluator	Sober, strategic and discerning Sees all options Judges accurately	Lacks drive and ability to inspire others
Implementer	Disciplined, reliable, conservative and efficient Turns ideas into practical actions	Somewhat inflexible Slow to respond to new possibilities
Completer Finisher	Painstaking, conscientious, anxious Searches out errors and omissions Delivers on time	Inclined to worry unduly Reluctant to delegate
Resource Investigator	Extrovert, enthusiastic, communicative Explores opportunities Develops contacts	Over-optimistic Loses interest once initial enthusiasm has passed
Shaper	Challenging, dynamic, thrives on pressure Drive and courage to overcome obstacles	Prone to provocation Offends people's feelings
Teamworker	Co-operative, mild, perceptive and diplomatic Listens, builds, averts friction	Indecisive in crunch situations
Specialist	Single-minded, self-starting, dedicated Provides knowledge and skills in rare supply	Contributes only on a narrow front Dwells on technicalities

FOCUS

Aims of T-groups

- Improve interpersonal skills.
- Increase sensitivity to your own feelings.
- Increase understanding of the effect of your behaviour on others.
- Increase sensitivity to others' feelings.
- Increase ability to give and receive feedback.
- Increase ability to handle conflict.
- Increase members' understanding of small group interaction.

Lewin saw this learning process as a kind of dialectic – a way of thinking which resolves conflict and differences by stating two or more points of view and reaching an agreement (synthesis) between them.

- **leadership styles** – authoritarian, *laissez-faire* and democratic.
- **action research** This is the method of group learning and development which forms the basis of much of your BTEC assignment work! Linked to cognitive psychology (see page 231 it states that group learning follows the stages: idea – plan – act – evaluate – change basic plan. The process is repeated and progresses from one 'learning event' to the next.

LINK! The leadership styles, identified and described by Lewin, are fully explained in Unit 3 Leadership, page 49.

Relevance to public service
Public services owe the idea that different leadership styles are needed for different situations to Lewin. Group therapy, based on T-groups, is an important aspect of some kinds of counselling, and is used to help prisoners and people who are mentally ill. Lewin's ideas are widely used in training, education and counselling to overcome phobias and post-traumatic stress disorder.

COOL BOOKS:

Lewin, K. (1935), *A Dynamic Theory of Personality*, New York: McGraw-Hill

Lewin, K. (1948), *Resolving Social Conflicts*, New York: Harper & Brothers

B. Tuckman and N. Jensen

Tuckman's theory of team development is perhaps the most easily understood of all such theories. It takes the form of a sequence of rhyming words, which Tuckman then explains. The stages are:

1. **Forming** At this stage the groups is just getting to know each other. People are unsure of their roles or the roles of other people, and the first priority is to get to know the other members of the group. Very little important work gets done.
2. **Storming** This is a stressful time when the team is not fully 'up and running' and there is a good deal of conflict (either open or hidden) between the members. There is a struggle to be 'top dog'; each individual is fighting to get the role they want – and nobody really trusts anybody else.
3. **Norming** Team members begin to trust each other and to feel that they are really part of the team. Conflicts have been resolved, and people either agree or have agreed to differ. Communications have improved and information is now freely shared.
4. **Performing** The team is now doing its best work: everybody knows what they are doing and has the confidence to do it. There is maximum communication and cooperation.
5. **Adjourning (or Mourning)** Tuckman (with N. Jensen) added this stage as an afterthought, since most teams, however successful, do not last for ever. The members change or the main work is finished and often there is a sense that the team has 'lost its way'.

Relevance to public service
Tuckman and Jensen have explained how teams evolve and what problems they can encounter. In public services, this enables leaders and managers to be more understanding of the stresses teams can encounter as they establish themselves. They have also helped team members to understand their own feelings, stresses and inner conflicts.

COOL BOOK:

Tuckman, B. and Jensen, N. (1977), 'Stages of small group development revisited', *Group and Organisational Studies*, 2, page 109

John Adair

Adair (1934–) has worked on team-building with the British armed forces. In his books he describes a good team as having:

- a common task
- a high quality of leadership
- a shared historical background
- participation from all members
- cohesiveness (sticking together)
- a supportive atmosphere
- clear defined standards
- a structure suitable for the task.

Other qualities of an effective team are that:

- people care for each other
- people are open and truthful
- there is a high level of trust
- decisions are agreed
- there is a strong team commitment
- conflict is faced up to and worked through
- people really listen to ideas and to feelings
- feelings are expressed freely
- process issues (tasks and feelings) are dealt with.

Relevance to public service
Adair's ideas, which are clear and accessible, provide a good foundation for understanding teamwork. His experience working with the armed forces has helped him to formulate practical ideas which are of great use in military team-building and exercises.

COOL BOOK:

Adair, J. (1993), *Effective Teambuilding*, Gower Publishing

Mike Woodcock

Mike Woodcock is concerned with the skills of team-building, and has published successful books full of team-building exercises. The qualities his books aim to develop are:

- managing the self
- competence at tasks
- unselfish, mature values (beliefs and feelings)
- focusing on goals
- belief in ongoing self-development
- problem-solving skills
- the ability to have new, creative ideas
- leadership skills
- organising ability
- desire to help others
- constructive attitude to the team
- ability to learn from experience.

Mike Woodcock believes it is important not to judge other people, yet at the same time to be hard-working and dedicated.

http://www.dancinglion.co.uk/tcarticleeight.html

Relevance to public service
Mike Woodcock has updated some of the 'lateral thinking' (creative thinking) techniques of the 1970s and his ideas are widely used for training teams, and developing team spirit, in the public services.

C. Margerison and R. McCann

Margerison and McCann have done a lot of work classifying personality types according to their preferred team/group roles (see the table below). The basic idea is that people should recognise their teamwork strengths and take on roles which come naturally to them if they are working in a team. In addition, leaders who are choosing teams can choose team members whose group roles fit in well with other people's group roles.

Relevance to public service
There is a link between the work of Margerison and McCann and that of Meredith Belbin, outlined above. Margerison and McCann throw light on preferred methods of working and communication in teams; their classifications make it easier to train and develop teams in the public services.

http://www.tms.com.au/welcome.html
– full of good ideas

PASSGRADE

Explain clearly the stages of team development.

For this outcome, you need to show clearly how a new team develops.

Tuckman's ideas are widely-accepted, and focus most directly on *stages* of team development (see page opposite).

Margerison and McCann's group roles

Reporter–Adviser	Supporter, helper, tolerant; A collector of information; Dislikes being rushed; Knowledgeable; Flexible
Creator–Innovator	Imaginative; Future-oriented; Enjoys complexity; Creative; Likes research work
Explorer–Promoter	Persuader, 'seller'; Likes varied, exciting, stimulating work; Easily bored; Influential and outgoing
Assessor–Developer	Analytical and objective; Developer of ideas; Enjoys prototype or project work; Experimenter
Thruster–Organizer	Organizes and implements; Quick to decide; Results-oriented; Sets up systems; Analytical
Concluder–Producer	Practical; Production-oriented; Likes schedules and plans; Pride in reproducing goods and services; Values effectiveness and efficiency
Controller–Inspector	Strong on control; Detail-oriented; Low need for people contact; An inspector of standards and procedures
Upholder–Maintainer	Conservative, loyal, supportive; Personal values important; Strong sense of right and wrong; Work motivation based on purpose

Source: TMS website

Resources

You will find plenty on team development on the internet.

CHECKPOINT ...

1 Think of a team you belong to (or have belonged to in the past). Did it develop in the way Tuckman outlines?
2 Compare your experience of team development with that of your classmates. Does it appear that all teams develop in the way Tuckman outlines? Or are there other ways in which teams can develop?
3 Does your own class work together as a team to achieve the task of passing your BTEC qualification? Which theories, of those outlined above, might help you and your class to be successful during your course?
4 Ask someone who works in the public services what theories of teamwork they follow.

PASSGRADE

Analyse and evaluate the roles of individual team members.

For this outcome, you need to:

- recognise the differences between:
  - the ideas of Belbin, and Margerison and McCann, who consider that team members can be classified into type, *or*
  - the ideas of Adair and Woodcock who believe that shared values and skills – such as truthfulness or organising ability – are at the basis of individual roles
- choose one of them as the basis of your evaluation
- take part in a team activity and evaluate your own role and those of your team-mates.

CHECKPOINT ...

1 The theories of Belbin, Margerison and McCann are a form of labelling. What are the dangers of labelling?
2 The ideas of Adair and Woodcock suggest that team roles can be learnt. Is this true in your own experience?

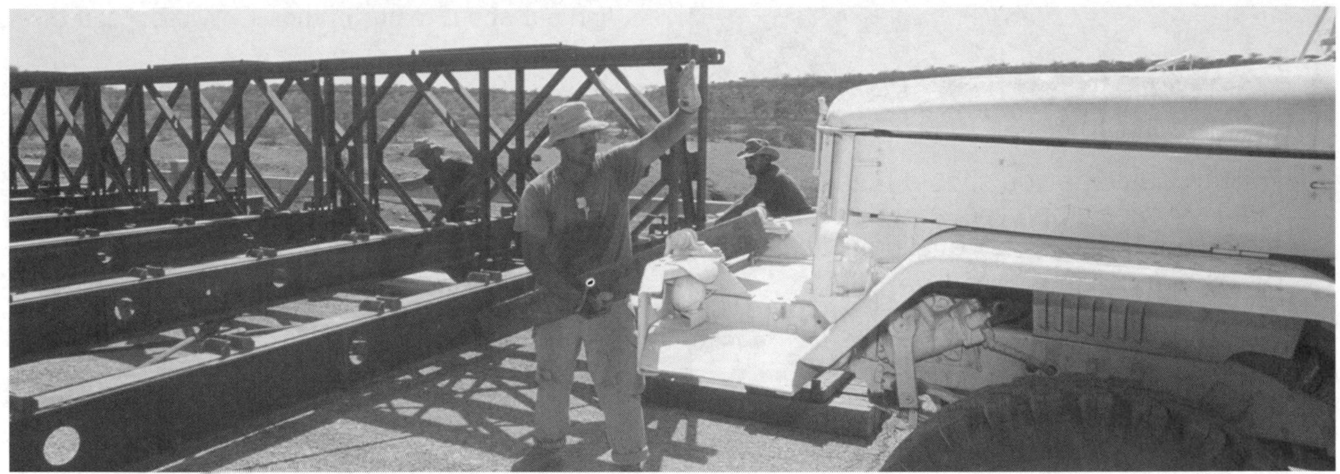

If everybody had the same role, the job wouldn't get done.

The easiest way to cover this outcome would probably be to use Belbin's classification. If, say, your team was building a raft, you could use his system to assess the roles of each team member. If X was telling everybody what to do, that person could be identified as a 'coordinator'; if Y was doing the job of lashing all the pieces of wood together, then Y would be a 'completer-finisher'. Your analysis and evaluation should explain how each team member's behaviour related to their team role, and how the team as a whole benefited (or not) from the way they carried out their role.

Merit

Summarise effectively the stages of team development and roles that individuals undertake within public service teams.

For this outcome, you need to:

- give an outline of team development
- state the roles of people in public service teams.

'Summarise' means give a description stating only the key points, and omitting examples and unnecessary explanations.

Tuckman's theory of team development is itself a summary, and you will find many statements of his theory on the internet. If you decide to use his theory you may want to stick to the names he gives each stage – 'forming', 'norming', etc. However, when saying what these mean, you should *use your own words as far as you can* – but without changing the sense of what Tuckman is trying to say.

But Tuckman's theory is not the only theory of team development. Lewin's ideas of action research also involve team development as the team passes through the various stages of the learning experience. The sequence: idea – plan – act – evaluate – change basic plan – repeat sequence is a good way of describing the development of a team which is performing a major task.

The difference between Tuckman's theory and Lewin's theory is that Tuckman views team development from the standpoint of group members – each stage linked not only to the achievement of tasks, but also to the emotions experienced by team members. Lewin, on the other hand, takes a cognitive view, describing the team's learning process in completing its tasks.

To summarise the roles that individuals undertake within public service teams, you need to find out about teams in different public services. You need to distinguish between:

- roles given to individuals by group leaders, e.g. choosing A to collect money because they are known to be reliable
- roles taken on 'naturally' by team members, e.g. B becomes the team's 'shaper' because she can motivate the other team members
- roles based on special skills, e.g. C is the secretary because he's the only person who can spell
- roles which come from outside the team, e.g. D has been chosen as team leader by Inspector Buggins.

! CHECKPOINT ...

Which of above roles corresponds most closely to the view of roles taken by Belbin or Margerison and McCann?

For this outcome you should meet a public service employee, and discuss the teamwork they do. Ask questions like these:

- What team(s) do you belong to?
- What is the purpose of the team?
- How many members does it have?
- Do different team members have different roles?
- Are their roles given by the team leader, or chosen by team members themselves?
- Are the roles based on the skills or the personalities of the team members (or both)?
- How many working hours a week do you spend with your team?
- Has the team changed or developed while you have been in it?
- Is the team permanent or temporary?

Using the notes you have made, then pick out all the information you have on (a) team development and (b) roles of individuals within teams.

You may also get ideas for this outcome from teams you have participated in yourself. This could include sports teams, work teams in a part-time job, voluntary work, or teams you have formed when doing group assignments or other college-based activities.

TYPES OF TEAMS

PASSGRADE

Describe the types of teams which operate within two public services.

For this outcome, you need to:

- visit two public services or get visiting speakers from two services
- find out about teams in those services – and the kind of work they do
- obtain an organisational plan of the public services you wish to discuss.

Points to remember:

- Teams exist at all levels of a public service organisation.
- Every public service worker belongs to at least one team.
- Some teams link one organisation to another (e.g. crime and disorder partnerships).
- Some teams work together all the time (e.g. watches in the fire service); others meet occasionally (e.g. health and safety committees).
- Some teams are permanent; some are temporary.
- Teams may also be called sections, units, groups, departments, squads or crews.
- Most teams are identified by their role.

Police teams

The FOCUS on the next page shows how teams are organised in the Essex Police

Management teams

The teams chaired by the Chief Constable, the Deputy Chief Constable and the Assistant Chief Constables oversee the effective development and running of Essex Police. They make major decisions about the priorities and work of Essex Police as a whole.

Specialist teams

The teams at the bottom of the chart are specialist teams, each concerned with a separate aspect of police work. Some are groups of teams (focusing on different tasks or working in different parts of the county). For example, in Community Safety there are drug action teams and youth offending teams. Civilian police employees can also belong to such teams. Police teams sometimes liaise closely with other teams (e.g. social workers or probation officers) outside the police.

Prison teams

Prisons, too, have management and specialist teams, as shown in the second FOCUS on the next page.

FOCUS

Chief Officers' areas of responsibility, Essex Police

'Essex Police is led by Chief Constable David Stevens with support from his Deputy, ACC Charles Clark and three other Assistant Chief Constables. Each has particular areas of responsibility involving the chairing of several key executive decision meetings and the overall command for a number of specialist and territorial policing units.'

Chief Constable
Chair of:
Chief Officers Management Group
Force Tactical Group
Force Strategy and Performance Group

Deputy Chief Constable
Responsibilities:
Chair of
Force Development Board
Information Technology
Professional Standards
Corporate Support
Media and Public Relations

Assistant Chief Constable
Responsibilities:
Chair of Operational Policing Policy and Programme Board
Territorial Policing
Mobile Support Division
Force Information Room
Special Constabulary
Traffic Wardens

Assistant Chief Constable
Responsibilities:
Chair of Crime Policy and Programme Board
Crime Division
(including Community Safety)
Criminal Justice Department

Assistant Chief Constable
Responsibilities:
Chair of Human Resources and Support Services Policy and Programme Boards
Financial
Administration
Procurement
Legal Services
Property Services
Transport Services
Personnel & Training

Team structure in Essex Police
Source http://www.essex.police.uk/pages/about/a_acpo.htm

FOCUS

Teams in prisons

Teams in Feltham Young Offenders' Institution

Team	Function
Outreach Team	Monitors risk of suicide and self-harm
Children's Society (outside charity)	Advises and secures bail
Youth Offending Teams	Information, documentation of inmates
PE Department	Physical activities for inmates
Vocational Training Team	Training inmates in work skills
Management Team (Governor, Deputy Governor and three principal officers)	Has overall control of the management and development of the prison
Induction Unit (1 senior officer and five prison officers)	Does all the paperwork and arrangements connected with new inmates
CARAT	Drug and alcohol misuse service
Visitors' Centre	Support and refreshment for families, etc.

Source: based on information in A Full Announced Inspection of HMYOI Feltham, 14–23 January 2002, *by HM Chief Inspector of Prisons*

Merit

Present a logical and well structured analysis of the types of the teams operating within the public services.

For this outcome, you need to:

- explain different types of teams
- show how they work together.

This should be done in a 'logical' way. This means your analysis must:

- be easy to follow
- show how work is divided, how teams liaise, and how they are managed.

The structure of your analysis should follow the organisational structure of the public service whose teams you are analysing.

Profile

Teams in Merseyside Fire and Rescue Service

Merseyside Fire & Civil Defence Authority

- Clerk to the Authority
  - Legal & Democratic Services
- Chief Fire Officer
  - Deputy Chief Fire Officer
    - Operational Delivery & Fire Safety
  - Assistant Chief Fire Officer Human Resources
    - Human Resources
  - Assistant Chief Fire Officer Service Support
    - Service Support
  - Corporate Support
- Treasurer
  - Treasury

Structure of Merseyside Fire and Rescue Service

Source: Merseyside Fire and Rescue Service website; http://www.merseyfire.gov.uk/pages/org_chart/org_chart.htm

The most logical and structured way of analysing the types of team in an organisation is by dealing with them from the top downwards. The advantage of this method is that it shows the chains of command and the different types of team more clearly.

- The Fire and Civil Defence Authority controls the money supply and the overall development of the Merseyside Fire and Rescue Service. It makes major decisions on the service's priorities. The 18 Members of the Authority are elected Members nominated by the five constituent District Councils.
- **Senior management teams** (chaired by the Chief Fire Officer) ensure that the wishes of the Fire Authority are carried out in the most effective possible way.
- **Middle management teams** (chaired by Deputy or Assistant Chief Fire Officers) specialise in the management of different sections of the Merseyside Fire and Rescue Service. They organise spending and staffing, and put into practice the strategic planning of the senior management teams. They communicate information both up and down the organisation.

- **Other management teams** These specialise in various areas such as human resources and service support. Their role is to put into practice the tactical planning by middle management, and to ensure the smooth running of operations.
- **Operational delivery** These teams do the practical work – fire prevention, firefighting, communications, maintenance, staff welfare, salaries, and so on. Watches are general purpose teams which can respond fast to call-outs and are highly adaptable. This suits the varied and unexpected nature of firefighting. But there are also specialist operational teams composed of experts, e.g. the Petroleum and Explosives Team and the Incident Investigation Team. These teams are composed of people with special expertise in their field. Supervisory officers monitor the workings of operational teams, and act as a link between them and management.

CHARACTERISTICS OF EFFECTIVE TEAMS

PASSGRADE

Accurately describe the characteristics of effective teams.

For this outcome, you need to describe correctly and clearly what makes teams successful.

The characteristics of effective teams are not exactly the same in all parts of public service work. For example, an effective team of marines needs to be at the peak of physical fitness. But fitness hardly matters for a team of probation officers!

However, most effective teams have certain characteristics or qualities which help their success (see the table on page 294).

PASSGRADE

Produce examples of good practice in relation to two teams within a specified public service.

For this outcome, you need to:

- meet people who work in a public service team
- ask them what aspects of teamwork they feel they do well – and why
- take a record of what they say.

! CHECKPOINT ...

Visit the inspectors' reports for police and prisons on the Home Office web-site, and find examples where good practice in teamwork has been praised by Her Majesty's Inspectors.

Profile

AYT 124: Army Youth Team, Duke of Wellington's Regiment

Aims of the team:

- To take young people for days out or residentials
- To give young people an experience of 'adventurous activities' such as mountaineering, potholing and canoeing
- To provide young people with a taste of army life and teamwork
- To present the army in a good light to young people who might want to join

Good practice:

- Understanding the client group (young people) and knowing how to treat them in a friendly and motivating way
- Excellent knowledge and skills in adventurous activities – and the facilities available in North Yorkshire and the Lake District
- Fully qualified and experienced in the theory and practice of health and safety
- Different team members specialise in different skills – such as rock climbing, canoeing or potholing
- Able to adapt their plans at short notice to poor weather, or the needs of the client group
- Reliable and trustworthy in the timing and organisation of activities
- Respecting the diversity of their clients

Some characteristics of effective teams

Characteristic	Description
Culture	The culture of a team is the norms and values of its members, *in relation to the way they work and support the team*. It doesn't matter how different people are in their own time, as long as their team culture is the same.
Team identity	'Identity' here means 'that which makes the team different from every other team'. Team identity is a sense of belonging to the team, and a pride in its work. Lewin calls it 'an interdependence of fate'; the army calls it *esprit de corps*. Team identity is often shown by wearing badges, uniforms or, in football, the team strip.
Social cohesion	Social cohesion means sticking together, and spending time together. Watches in the fire service, for example, spend long periods of time together. A team with social cohesion gets on well, and gains job satisfaction from the pleasure of working in company with team-mates.
Mutual support	In the armed forces, this consists of physical back-up when under attack. It also consists of doing your fair share of heavy and boring work, e.g. loading trucks. Psychologists have shown how 'social facilitation' (Zajonc, 1965) – mutual support – makes people work harder. A close-knit team gives mutual support of a different kind when dealing with shocking or stressful events (e.g. when firefighters find a dead child in a house fire).
Level of trust	Trust means knowing that you, and your team-mates, are going to do the right thing in a difficult situation. Teams which work in dangerous conditions – warfare, disasters, etc. – need high levels of trust in their comrades. Trust is linked to knowledge and skill in the job. It is also linked to more ordinary good qualities such as punctuality and reliability.
Maintenance of morale	Good morale means believing in yourself and what you are doing. Bad morale is a feeling of hopelessness, failure, despair or weakness. Good morale makes people work hard and cheerfully, even under difficult or dangerous conditions. It is the sign of an effective team.
High level of co-operation	In an effective team communications are good, everybody knows what they are supposed to do, and everybody is willing to help everybody else.
Role identification	'Role identification' means knowing, understanding and being committed to your role (job) in a team. It makes for effective teamwork.
Delegation	When a leader asks or tells a team member to do work which the leader would normally do, it is delegation. This spreads the workload and gives team members responsibility. It shows trust, is good for the subordinates' personal and professional development, and can make the team more productive – and therefore more effective.
Task orientation	This means concentrating on the work the team has to do, and not allowing yourself to be distracted.
Commitment to the achievement of aims/ objectives/targets	Commitment means determination to succeed. Uniformed public service work can be very difficult or dangerous – especially in emergencies, warfare, etc. Effective teams show commitment under such circumstances.
Collective responsibility	In an authoritarian team structure, the leader takes responsibility since the team are simply following his or her orders. But in a democratic team structure, such as we find in many public services, especially the non-uniformed ones such as local government or teaching, everybody in an effective team takes responsibility for decisions made.
Recognition of efforts	In an effective team, members respect each other, and praise them for their good work. Leaders value the team's work, and show that they value it.
Enhanced mental security	'Unity means strength' and a team that is loyal and focussed is good for the confidence of its individual members.

COOL SITES:

http://www.homeoffice.gov.uk/justice/prisons/inspprisons/annual.html

http://www.homeoffice.gov.uk/hmic/hmic.htm

FOCUS

'Finally, the external exercise area for the Vulnerable Prisoner Unit was a pleasing garden area that had been created from what was virtually a derelict, stone littered yard. The part we saw was evidence of hard work, commitment and creative imagination by those concerned with the transformation of this area – further evidence that in this corner of Dartmoor there were positive forces at work.'

Source: from Report on An Unannounced Follow-up Inspection of HM Prison Dartmoor, 17–21 September 2001 by HM Chief Inspector of Prisons

Merit

Make considered comments about the skills, attributes and characteristics of effective public service teams.

For this outcome, you need to:

- ask people who work in the public services about what they think good teamwork means
- collect public service recruitment material which describes the teamwork skills, attributes and characteristics (qualities) they are looking for in applicants
- read inspectors' reports commenting on public service teamwork (available on government websites)
- collect your findings and draw conclusions about the skills and qualities of good public service teams.

Profile

Teamwork at Feltham Young Offenders' Institution, 2002

Team attributes mentioned	Comments
'excellent partnerships', 'the team was well regarded', 'staff communication strategy'	The inspectors thought teams were effective if they worked in partnership with other teams, or communicated well with them
'innovative work'	The inspectors liked teams which came up with original solutions to problems.
'responded positively', 'positive dynamics', 'committed and enthusiastic'	'Positive' means forward-looking, open to new ideas, and well motivated. These teams were confident and keen to make the prison a better place.
'taking decisive action', 'an air of purposefulness and professionalism', 'work was being rigorously carried out', '... arranged more quickly in greater numbers', 'productive and inclusive reviews'	Effective teams are energetic and get plenty of work done.
'a realistic strategic plan', 'good remedial programme and monitoring system', 'detailed community supervision plan'.	Effective public service teams are 'realistic' – they set out to do what is possible. They are 'strategic' because they can see ahead and plan for the future. Their work is well-organised and 'detailed', not skimped and slapdash.
With the inmates, teams 'demonstrated concern' and carried out 'positive and inclusive reviews'.	Effective teams care about their clients, and work for their good. They are never prejudiced or vindictive, even when the clients are difficult to work with.

Source: team attributes quoted from A Full Announced Inspection of HMYOI Feltham, 14–23 January 2002, by HM Chief Inspector of Prisons

Distinction

Critically analyse and evaluate the development of effective teams and their significance to the public services.

For this outcome, you need to:

- examine the methods used to develop effective teams
- assess the importance of such teams for public service work.

You will get useful information from:

- appraising your own experience of teams and the way they develop
- any teamwork or group problem-solving exercises you have done on your course
- people who train teams in public services
- PTIs in the armed forces
- books on team development (see the management section of your college or local library)
- websites on teamwork.

The two FOCUS extracts to the right show the significance of effective teams in the public services.

COOL SITES:

http://www.guardian.co.uk/crime/ – very useful research site for almost anything linked to the public services

http//www.victoria-climbie-inquiry.org.uk – this site is about an 8-year-old girl who was murdered by relatives. The *Report of the Victoria Climbié Inquiry* by Lord Laming (2003) tells the detailed story of ineffective teamwork and its tragic results.

Other major events which show poor teamwork in public services include:

- 1981 – the Brixton Riots
- 1989 – the Hillsborough Disaster
- 1993 – the murder of Stephen Lawrence
- 1999 – the publication of the *Home Office Thematic Review of Fairness and Equality in the Fire Service*
- 2000 – the murder of Damilola Taylor.

FOCUS

Effective teams

'Police were today assessing more than $6bn (£4.4bn) worth of suspect US bonds seized together with a hoard of drugs during a raid on a suspected Colombian drug ring operating out of Britain.

The national crime squad (NCS) swooped on addresses in north London and Essex during two raids in July and August. They found the suspect bonds, 55,000 ecstasy tablets, 15 kilos of amphetamine powder, a couple of kilos of ecstasy powder, a pill press and a negligible amount of cocaine. They also seized goods, including cars, houses and furniture, estimated to be worth about £7m.

If the bonds prove genuine, the raids will become one of the biggest hauls in criminal history.'

Source: Press Association article 'Police seize "Columbian" drugs and bonds hoard', 5 September 2003; http://www.guardian.co.uk/crime/

Ineffective teams: a lack of good practice

'1.16 ... during the days and months following her initial contact with Ealing Housing Department's Homeless Persons' Unit, Victoria was known to no less than two further housing authorities, four social services departments, two child protection teams of the Metropolitan Police Service (MPS), a specialist centre managed by the NSPCC, and she was admitted to two different hospitals because of suspected deliberate harm. The dreadful reality was that these services knew little or nothing more about Victoria at the end of the process than they did when she was first referred to Ealing Social Services by the Homeless Persons' Unit in April 1999. The final irony was that Haringey Social Services formally closed Victoria's case on the very day she died. The extent of the failure to protect Victoria was lamentable. Tragically, it required nothing more than basic good practice being put into operation. This never happened.'

Source: http//www.victoria-climbie-inquiry.org.uk

It is hard to exaggerate the importance of having effective public service teams. They:

- achieve their aims and meet their targets
- recognise and solve difficult problems
- provide a good quality of service
- save money
- enable us to live in peace and comfort, free of fear

- enable us to be educated and healthy
- save lives.

From the point of view of those working in the public services, effective teams:

- are good for the reputation of the services
- raise morale
- give job satisfaction.

CHECKPOINT ...

Read about public service teamwork that really goes wrong.

http://www.amnesty.org – Amnesty International

http://www.hrw.org/ – Human Rights Watch

'I'd like to welcome you all to our new Traffic team. Hands up those of you who can drive.'

BARRIERS TO EFFECTIVE TEAMWORK

PASSGRADE

Explain, using appropriate examples, the barriers to teamwork that may exist in two public services.

For this outcome, you need to explain, using examples, the problems that can sometimes affect teamwork in two public services.

Barriers to teamwork are factors which prevent teams from achieving their aims effectively. Some of these are things like lack of money or time; others relate to poor skills, poor leadership or unsuitable choice of team members.

The PROFILE on page 298 gives a range of barriers to effective teamwork and examples of how they might affect two public services.

CHECKPOINT ...

Carry out a similar explanation of the following barriers to teamwork:

(a) non-cooperation of individuals
(b) unwillingness to share knowledge
(c) time wasting
(d) competition/self-interest/hostile criticism within the team.

Merit

Analyse and evaluate the barriers to team work in public services.

For this outcome, you need to:

- examine more deeply the barriers to teamwork in public services
- assess their seriousness
- suggest how they might be overcome.

This outcome gives you an opportunity to explore some of the more difficult, and less usual, types of teamwork. Below are some ideas about barriers to teamwork researched for the US army, to help them integrate better into European peace-keeping forces.

The research identified barriers to teamwork existing between US troops and their European counterparts while on peace-keeping missions in places such as Bosnia Herzegovina.

Researchers identified two kinds of barrier – cultural and organisational. 'Cultural' refers mainly to the norms and values (i.e. the preferred way of working and thinking) in the team, though nationality apparently plays a role as well. 'Organisational' barriers were the result of bad planning.

Profile

Barriers to effective teamwork in two public services

Type of barrier	What it is	How it could affect public service work
Poor communication	Failure to listen, speak, read or write effectively. Poor receptive skills (listening and reading) mean information is not received. Poor productive skills (speaking and writing) mean information is not given out.	(a) In a police drugs raid, poor communication would lead to confused planning, putting the success of the raid at risk. (b) In battle, soldiers could get lost or killed following such misunderstandings.
Need for leadership to direct/control work	If teams don't have effective leaders, members are unsure of what to do and how to do it.	(a) In a police drugs raid, officers would lack confidence. (b) In battle, soldiers would have to retreat.
Role ambiguity	Team members don't know what they – or other people – are supposed to be doing.	(a) In a police drugs raid, this would cause confusion. (b) In battle, it could risk fellow soldiers, e.g. through 'friendly fire'.
Resource constraints, e.g. finance, personnel time/training/development	Lack of money, people, time and expertise. Teams are unprepared for the work or don't have time to complete it. They feel undervalued so morale is low	(a) In a police drugs raid, these constraints lead to poor preparation and morale. (b) In battle, soldiers have poor skills, equipment and morale. They are less effective and risk being killed.
Lack of commitment to aims objectives/targets	This means not caring enough about the team's aims or work. Either the team or the aims need changing.	(a) In a police drugs raid, officers could make mistakes. (b) In battle, soldiers would be unwilling to fight.
Personal/hidden agendas	This means infighting, backbiting, and status games by team members. Instead of being assertive, they are aggressive, passive or passive-aggressive.	(a) In a police drugs raid, officers would try to show off, or not back each other up. (b) In battle, soldiers would quarrel about what to do.

Cultural barriers

Power distance

This means the difference in status between the team leader and members. Where the power distance is low, there is more 'equality' in the team. This increases collaboration, but can make teamwork slower or less focused. Where the power distance is high, leaders are more authoritarian. This can mean that the team is afraid to be creative, and that higher status members are afraid to ask for clarification of things they don't understand. Where team members have different ideas of power distance they can be uncertain of their role and importance in the team.

Tolerance of uncertainty

People with a low tolerance of uncertainty like to know all the rules and facts before they act, to minimise the risk of mistakes. This means they can waste time searching for rules and structures instead of getting on with the job. People with a high tolerance of uncertainty prefer thinking on their feet and getting down to work, even if they are unsure of some details. They act fast, but can make serious mistakes due to slapdash preparation. Where team members have different tolerances of uncertainty, they will find it hard to agree on preparation and planning.

Individualism versus collectivism

Some people prefer individual effort and task achievement, rather than building relationships with the rest of the team. Others put relationship-building first, and have a more collective approach to teamwork. Individualists and collectivists find it hard to work together in a team. Individualists feel that collectivists waste their time, while collectivists feel that individualists ignore their ideas. The US researchers felt that American soldiers were individualists, while European soldiers were collectivists. To work together effectively they had to resolve these differences.

Concrete thought patterns versus hypothetical thought patterns

Hypothetical thinkers throw up lots of ideas; concrete thinkers prefer one clear, practical plan. Where concrete and hypothetical thinkers are in the same team, it can lead to conflict because their ways of solving problems are incompatible. Hypothetical thinkers feel the concrete thinkers are slow, while concrete thinkers feel the hypothetical ones are 'evasive'.

Organisational barriers

- **Differences in previous training, especially in cultural awareness** Soldiers from countries such as Holland had received a great deal of cultural awareness training, while most American soldiers had received none.
- **The habit of putting people in teams 'to get experience'** This was harmful to team development because the people gaining experience didn't – or couldn't – pull their weight, and were resented by the other team members.
- **Placing people in teams when they didn't speak the same language as other team members (usually English)** British or American soldiers were not trained how to speak in the presence of soldiers whose first language was not English, and made things difficult by using slang and colloquialisms.

COOL SITE:

www.asc2002.com/summaries/i/IP-06.pdf – for an abstract of paper: Bowman, E.K. and Pierce, L.G. (2002), 'Cultural barriers to teamwork in a multinational coalition environment', *Proceedings of the 23rd Army Science Conference*, Orlando, Florida, 2–5 December

Ways of overcoming barriers to teamwork

- Better choice and training of leaders
- Better choice of team members
- Better training and preparation of team members, using team-building exercises of the type developed by John Adair or Mike Woodcock (see pages 287–8)
- Proper consideration – by the team or its supervisory officers – about the team's role
- Analysis of tasks and whether they are really feasible
- Democratic methods of leadership which enable problems to be aired and resolved
- Strategies to eliminate bullying, sexism and racism from the team
- Analysis of team ethos and preferred working methods of team members
- Ensuring that teams have resources they need
- Giving appreciation and moral support to team members

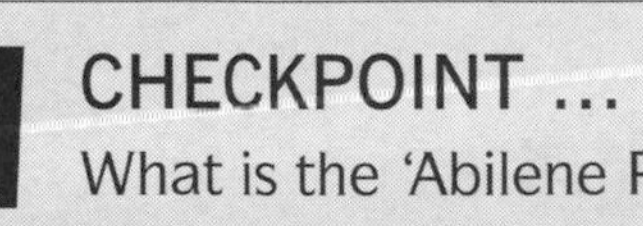

CHECKPOINT ...

What is the 'Abilene Paradox'?

Unit 18 Health and Fitness

Grading criteria

PASSGRADE To achieve a pass grade the evidence must show that the learner is able to:	*Merit* To achieve a merit grade the evidence must show that the learner is able to:	*Distinction* To achieve a distinction grade the evidence must show that the learner is able to:
• detail muscular, cardiovascular and respiratory systems associated with health and fitness **301** • describe the effects of lifestyle, balanced diet and good nutrition on health and fitness **306** • describe the effects of the principles of fitness in relation to performance **312** • review, explain and compare a number of fitness testing methods **313** • explain the principles of fitness testing methods **315** • complete and record a number of fitness testing methods and evaluate the results **317**	• analyse the skeletal system in relation to health and fitness **305** • analyse the effects of lifestyle, balanced diet and good nutrition on health and fitness **311** • analyse and evaluate the reliability, validity, accuracy and safety of the fitness testing methods explained **315**	• justify the need for a healthy lifestyle and a balanced diet to ensure health and fitness **311** • justify the use of fitness testing methods for entry to the public services **318**

Most uniformed public services will only recruit fit and healthy people. So anybody who wants to join a uniformed service should try to improve their health and fitness.

The need for fitness is obvious in the armed forces or the fire service. But even in the police or prison service, it helps to be fitter and stronger than average. Health is equally important – the shifts are long, and the work can be tiring. The public services don't want employees who are going to be off sick all the time.

Of course, none of these are the *real* reason for getting healthy and fit. Health and fitness make you feel good and look good. They put a spring in your step. They are the bedrock of a happy life.

FOCUS

Definitions of health and fitness

Health is ...

'the state of optimal physical, mental, and social well-being, and NOT merely the absence of disease or infirmity' – World Health Organisation

Fitness is ...

'the ability to perform your normal daily tasks with vigour and alertness and without undue fatigue, with enough energy left in reserve to cope with any emergencies that may arise or to follow the leisure pursuits of your choice' – World Health Organisation

BODY SYSTEMS

Detail muscular, cardiovascular and respiratory systems associated with health and fitness.

For this outcome, you need to describe the systems and explain briefly how they work.

Body systems are groups of organs which work together.

The muscular system

The muscular system contains around 640 muscles and makes up 40–50 per cent of our body weight. It contains two kinds of muscles:

- **voluntary muscles**, which we can control (e.g. leg and arm muscles)
- **involuntary muscles**, which we cannot control (e.g. heart muscles, muscles in blood vessels and muscles round our intestines, etc.).

Muscles are bundles of specialised cells, which change the nutrients they receive through the bloodstream into energy. In the relaxed state the muscle cells are long and thin, but when we move the muscle the cells contract and become much shorter. It is this process of contraction which enables us to move.

Voluntary muscles are arranged in pairs, so that when one muscle has contracted, another muscle can straighten it out again. For example, the biceps at the front of the upper arm contracts to bend our arm; the triceps at the back of the upper arm contracts in order to straighten our arm again.

Many muscles are attached to bones by tendons. The muscle is therefore able to move the bone, and we ourselves can move in a controlled way.

Voluntary muscles contain two main kinds of cells:

- **slow twitch cells**, which don't tire easily and which we use for most of our movements, including walking, jogging and other aerobic activities
- **fast twitch cells**, which give us a short burst of strength (e.g. for weight-lifting), but which get tired easily.

How muscles work

Muscles work through the release of chemicals which give energy. The source of energy is the food we eat. Carbohydrates, fats and protein all provide energy – once they have been broken down into simpler chemicals:

- Carbohydrates break down into glucose in the blood and are stored in muscle cells, ready for use, as glycogen.
- Fats break down into fatty acids which combine with glycogen and provide stored energy.
- Proteins break down into amino acids which can also release some energy.

The changing of stored, chemical energy into muscular movement is achieved with the help of chemicals called enzymes. Stored chemicals such as glycogen are broken down by enzymes into ATP – adenosine triphosphate. It is from the breakdown of ATP that muscular energy is released.
There are three 'pathways' by which energy from ATP is released, and the pathway used depends on how suddenly the energy is needed:

- The **immediate pathway** is a series of rapid chemical reactions which give energy for the first five seconds.

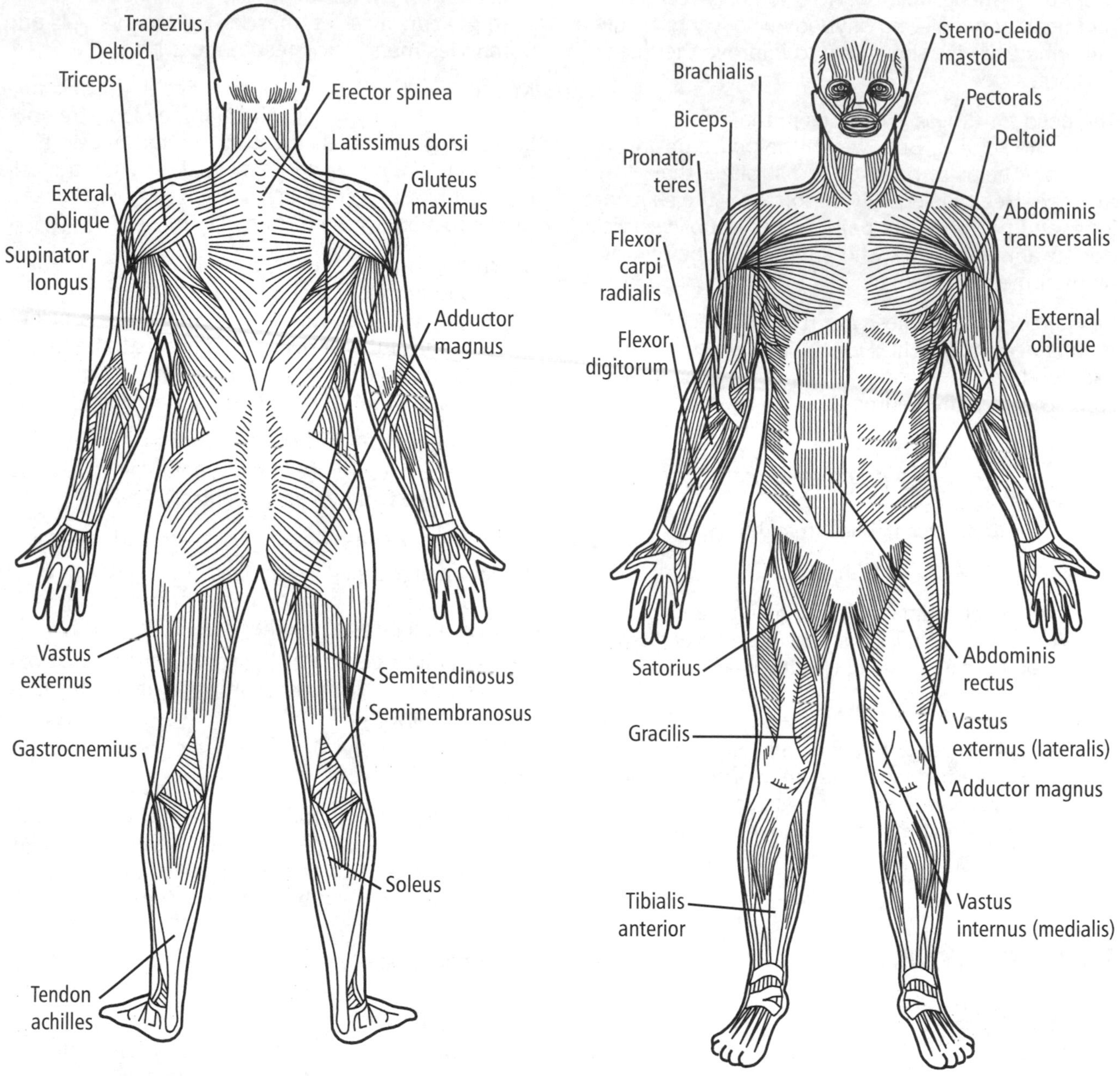

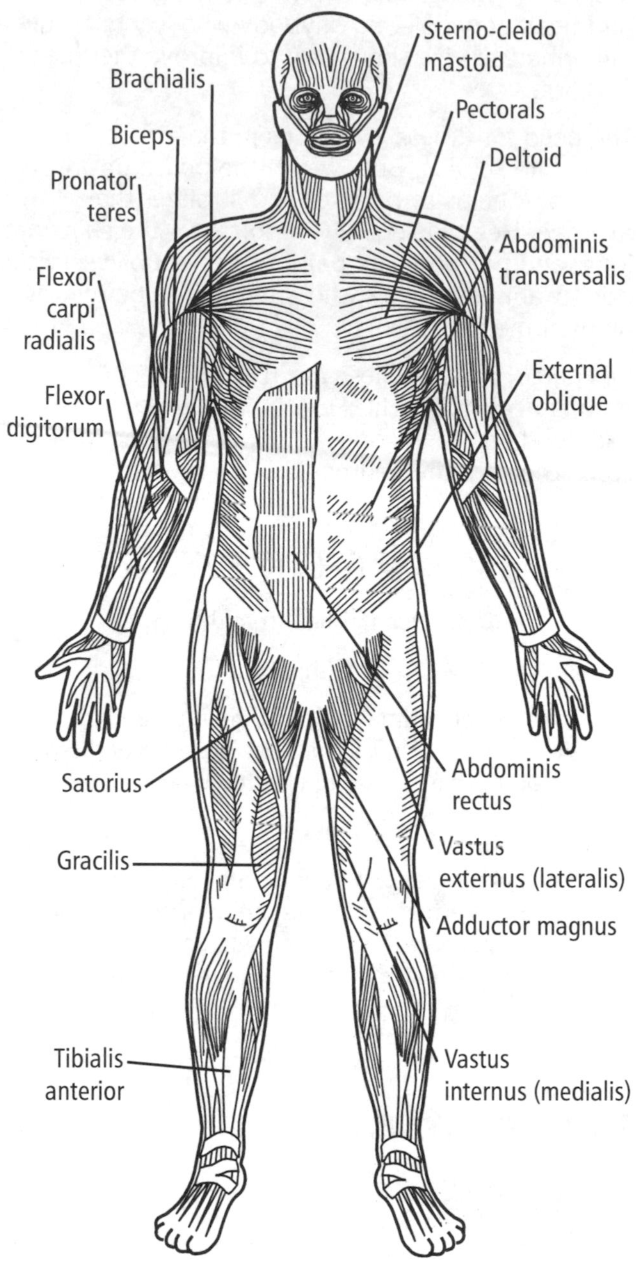

The muscular system

- The **anaerobic pathway** is another series of rapid reactions which can keep going for about two minutes.
- The **aerobic pathway** uses oxygen to break down the ATP and will last for hours.

The total amount of energy released through the anaerobic pathway is vastly greater than that released by the other two, faster pathways, but for sudden powerful movement, such as weight-lifting, it is the first and second pathways that are used.

Immediate and anaerobic reactions take place in the fast-twitch cells; aerobic reactions happen in the slow-twitch cells. The use of the three pathways is of significance in fitness and strength training. The immediate and anaerobic reactions lead to muscle growth and increased strength. The aerobic reactions improve fitness by increasing the body's ability to take in and use oxygen over a period of time.

! **CHECKPOINT ...**

The diaphragm is the muscle that controls breathing. Is it voluntary or involuntary?

The cardiovascular system

The cardiovascular system is made up of the **heart** and **blood vessels**.

The heart

The heart is a muscular pump that pumps about 9000 litres of blood round the body every day. In an average lifetime, it beats 2.5 billion times. It consists of four main chambers (two atria and two ventricles) and has a number of large blood vessels running in and out of it.

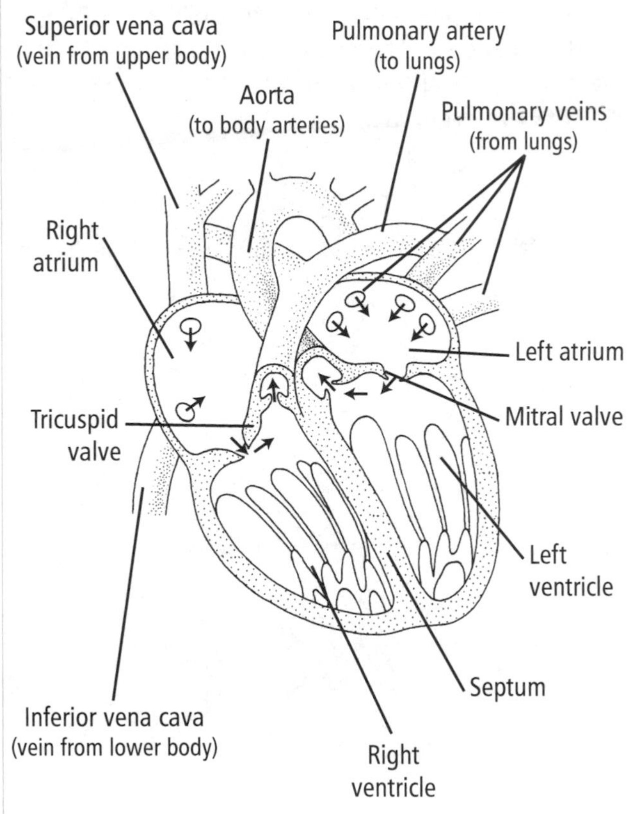

The cardiovascular system

Blood flow in and out of the heart is controlled by the way the heart beats and by the opening and closing of valves. Blood enters the heart through the vena cava into the right atrium. From the right atrium the blood flows into the right ventricle and is pumped to the lungs. There the blood loses waste gases and takes in oxygen. The oxygen-rich blood comes back from the lungs through the pulmonary veins to the left atrium. From there the blood goes through the mitral valve to the left ventricle. The left ventricle pumps blood into the aorta and so into the circulatory system.

The beating of the heart is automatic, triggered by cells in a part of the heart called the sinus. But the brain controls this automatic beating, raising the speed at times of activity or stress, and lowering it when we relax. Average heartbeat is around 70 beats a minute, but it can beat much faster.

LINK! See Unit 9 Physical Preparation for the Uniformed Services, page 182.

Blood pressure varies with each beat of the heart, which is why, when you have a blood pressure reading on a sphygmomanometer, you get two figures – typically 120/80. The first figure is the systolic pressure (when the heart is pushing blood out); the second figure is the diastolic pressure, when the heart is relaxed and filling up again. Blood pressure goes up if you are stressed, or exercising hard, and goes down afterwards.

Blood

Most of us have between 5 and 6 litres of blood in our bodies. This feeds all the living organs and tissues in our body – supplying nutrients (glucose and other chemicals), oxygen, water and minerals such as salt. It also carries chemicals called hormones, produced by a range of glands such as the adrenal glands, pituitary gland, thyroid gland, ovaries and testes. These determine our moods, growth, levels of activity and sexuality.

Blood is 55 per cent plasma, a clearish liquid which carries salts, minerals and living cells around the body. Most blood cells are red, and carry a chemical called haemoglobin which supplies oxygen and nutrition to the cells. But many blood cells are white – and these protect the body by killing and devouring bacteria. There is a third kind of cell – platelets – which enable the blood to clot, so that we do not lose too much when we bleed. In addition, blood transports antibodies – chemicals produced in the body to protect us against poisoning and infection.

Most blood is made (and recycled) in the bone marrow of the thighbones (femur), but it can be made in the liver as well.

Blood vessels

These are tubes made of smooth muscle which carry blood away from the heart, through all parts of the body, and then back to the heart again. Factors such as temperature, food and alcohol prompt the blood vessels to dilate (get wider) or constrict (get narrower) to regulate the flow of blood to different parts of the body.

There are three kinds of blood vessel – **arteries**, **capillaries** and **veins**.

Arteries
Arteries lead out from the heart. They have strong walls to withstand the pressure changes caused by the heart's beating. The blood in them is bright red because it is full of oxygen freshly delivered from the lungs. (There is one exception: the pulmonary artery, which takes stale blood out of the heart to the lungs to be re-oxgenated.)

Capillaries
Away from the heart, arteries split into tiny blood vessels called capillaries. They are so small that the microscopic blood cells can only move along them one at a time. Capillaries supply tiny but adequate amounts of nutrition, oxygen, etc. to all the body's cells. In return for this, they take waste materials away with them – substances such as carbon dioxide and urea.

Veins
Capillaries then join up into blood vessels called veins which carry used (dark red) blood back to the heart. (The exception is the pulmonary veins which carry bright red oxygen-rich blood from the lungs to the heart.)

The respiratory system

This consists of the **mouth**, **nose**, **trachea**, **lungs** and **diaphragm**. Through it we breathe in air, which is about 20 per cent oxygen – and oxygen is essential for the body's metabolism.

Normally we breathe through the nose, which provides some protection from infection, foreign bodies such as insects and extremes of temperature. Air passes through the larynx, down the trachea (windpipe) and then into the two bronchi (the tubes which go into each lung). The bronchi divide into many smaller tubes called bronchioles which go into each lung. They end in 600 million tiny air-sacs called alveoli.

Each alveolus has capillaries in its walls. Carbon dioxide is taken from the blood in these capillaries, and replaced with oxygen. This 'exchange of gases' is the basis of breathing. Air going into the lungs is rich in oxygen; air leaving the lungs contains carbon dioxide. An average pair of lungs, fully inflated, contains over five litres of air.

Oxygenated blood from the lungs goes straight back to the heart along the pulmonary veins, and is then pumped out to all parts of the body.

The lungs are delicate organs which are well protected by the ribcage. Underneath the lungs is a sheet of muscle called the diaphragm. When we breathe in, the diaphragm contracts and (if we breathe in deeply) the ribcage rises. Both of these actions pull air into the lungs. When the diaphragm relaxes, or we lower the ribcage, air flows out of the lungs again.

Air leaving the lungs passes through the larynx, where it can make noises by vibrating flaps of tissue called vocal cords. By moving our tongue and palate (the back of the mouth) we can change these noises into speech.

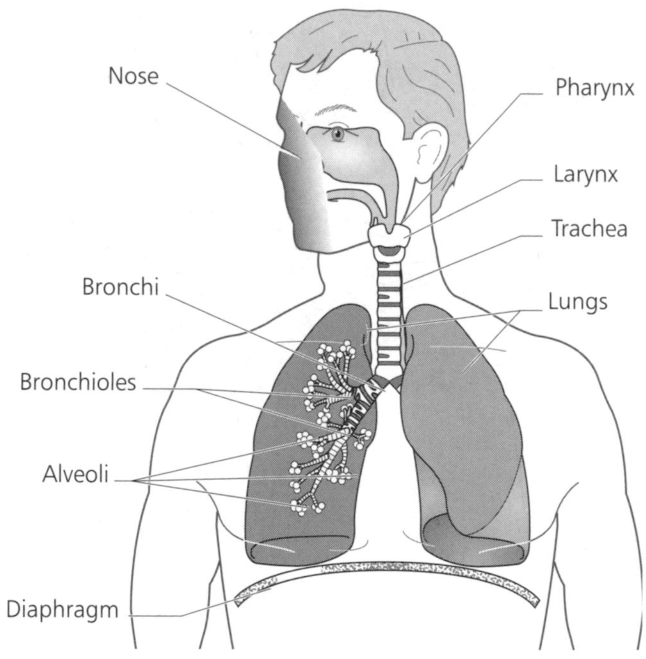

The respiratory system

http://www.fortunecity.com/greenfield/rattler/46/haemopoiesis.htm – all about blood

http://www.health.gov/dietaryguidelines/dga2000/document/frontcover.htm

www.nlm.nih.gov/medlineplus/foodnutritionandmetabolism.html

http://www.bbc.co.uk/science/humanbody/body/factfiles

The skeletal system

Merit

Analyse the skeletal system in relation to health and fitness.

For this outcome, you need to:

- describe the bones, what they are made of, what they do and how they are joined together
- relate all these to health and fitness.

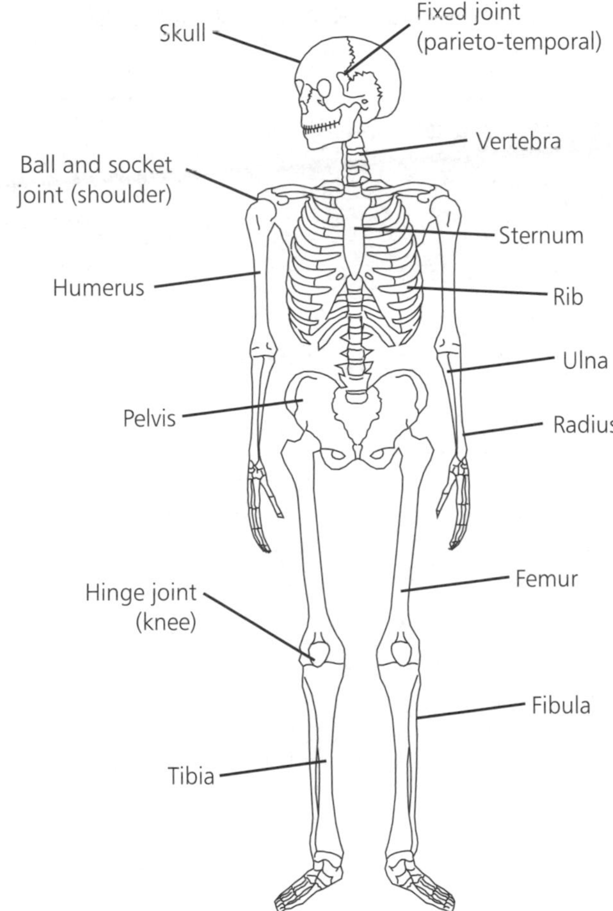

The skeletal system

An adult has 206 bones, most of them joined up to form the skeleton. The biggest is the femur, or thighbone, and the smallest is in the ear.

Bones are living organs, made of water, a protein called collagen which makes strong elastic fibres, calcium, phosphorus, magnesium and sodium. Young children's bones contain a lot of cartilage, and have areas in them called growth plates which only harden fully when growth stops – in the late teens or early twenties, usually sooner in women than in men.

Living bones contain blood vessels and nerves, and are built up in concentric layers like the trunk of a tree. They are hard on the outside and have a lighter, spongy interior. The biggest bones, especially the femur, are hollow and contain bone marrow. Marrow is red in children, and is used for making blood. In adults, some of the red marrow turns into yellow marrow, a fatty substance which can no longer make blood cells.

The spine

The spine, or backbone, contains 26 bones called **vertebrae** and is divided into five main sections:

- cervical vertebrae – the first seven vertebrae in the neck
- thoracic vertebrae – twelve vertebrae in the upper back, attached to the ribs
- lumbar vertebrae – five in the small of the back
- sacrum – five joined vertebrae in the lower back
- coccyx – four joined vertebrae at the very bottom of the spine.

The spine holds our upper and lower bodies together and protects the spinal cord, the biggest nerve in the body, which runs inside it.

The skeleton in relation to health and fitness

- Bones hold us together and enable us to move. They support and protect the soft parts of the body.
- Bones make blood cells which are essential for transporting nutrients round the body, and for protecting us against disease.
- Bones store calcium and other essential minerals, which can be released into the bloodstream if we need them (though this can weaken the bones).
- Bones grow as we do. In children they are soft, with a high proportion of cartilage, which is why, for example, children should not try weight-training until they are 14 years old.
- Exercise strengthens the bones, helping the deposition of calcium and other minerals. Activity also produces synovial fluid, which lubricates moveable joints and protects the bone and cartilage from wear and tear.
- A healthy diet is important for bone growth and strength. Children who are starved stop growing, though they catch up if they are properly fed before too much damage is done.
- Broken bones will repair well, provided they are set so the new growth will be in the right place.
- Old people are at risk from osteoporosis (brittle bones) and osteoarthritis (joint pain caused by bone deformities).

FOCUS

Joints

Bones are linked by joints – and there are several kinds.

Types of joint

Type of joint	Description	Example
Immovable joints	Fit together in jagged lines called sutures	Skull-bones
Slightly movable joints	Tightly tied by cartilage	Ribs attached to breast-bone (sternum)
Ball and socket joints	Round ball fits into round cup. Move in any direction. Some rotation	Shoulder and hip joints
Condyloid joints	Elliptical ball and socket. Movement in any direction but no rotation	Knuckles
Saddle joints	Concave and convex surfaces on both bones. Movement in most directions	Base of thumbs
Pivot joints	Round end of one bone fits into a ring in the other. Allows rotation	Neck bones
Hinge joints	Move only in one direction	Elbows, knees
Gliding joints	Flat surfaces allow compression of joint only	Some small bones in wrists and ankles

Joints are tied together by **ligaments** (cords of the protein, collagen), to avoid dislocation.

Body types

In the 1940s an American psychologist called William Sheldon identified three main body types ('somatypes'). These were:

- **ectomorphs** – thin people
- **mesomorphs** – muscular or 'medium-built' people
- **endomorphs** – well-built people.

Sheldon's somatypes are still widely used when talking about health and fitness. Different body-types seem to be suited to different sports. Distance and marathon runners, for example, are ectomorphs; sprinters and long-jumpers are mesomorphs, while shot-putters and hammer-throwers are endomorphs.

Uniformed public services usually like applicants to be of an 'appropriate weight for their height'. This gives mesomorphs an advantage in the physical selection tests.

CHECKPOINT ...

Some scientists dislike the idea of somatypes. Why?

LIFESTYLE AND NUTRITION

Describe the effects of lifestyle, balanced diet and good nutrition on health and fitness.

For this outcome, you need to show how the way people live and what they eat affects their health and fitness.

FOCUS

Definition of lifestyle

Lifestyle is ...

'a more or less integrated set of practices maintained by an individual, not only because such practices contribute to fulfilling practical needs, but also because in a material form and in a special way, they tell something about people's self-identity' – Giddens, A. (1991) *Modernity and Self-identity: Self and Society in the Late Modern Age*, Cambridge: Polity Press, page 256

'a general way of living based on the interplay between living conditions in the wide sense and individual patterns of behavior as determined by sociocultural factors and personal characteristics' – World Health Organisation

- 'Lifestyle' is the way we normally live our lives, e.g. how we spend our time, what we eat and what we do for leisure.
- A 'balanced diet' means regularly eating the right amount and types of food for long-term good health.
- 'Good nutrition' is food which promotes long-term health.

What determines lifestyle?

Lifestyle depends on many factors – age, sex, job, wealth, interests, personality and culture. The type of lifestyle we choose as adults is deeply influenced by the way we have been socialised during our upbringing. Family, peer group, education, the media, religion and law – all the main agencies of social control (see page 237) – help to determine our lifestyle. Genetic factors probably play a part too – our physique, our hormones – perhaps even inherited psychological characteristics. Finally, there are environmental factors such as where we live: the lifestyle of Londoners is different from that of people living in the Scottish Highlands.

Healthy and unhealthy lifestyles

In the modern UK, most of us can choose whether we lead healthy lives or not. We cannot guarantee good health, but we can maximise our chances of good health by choosing a healthy lifestyle and diet.

Our knowledge of what is healthy and what isn't is based on:

- extensive scientific research – on laboratory animals, tissue cultures, etc.
- collecting and interpreting health data from hospitals, doctors and even undertakers all over the world
- many surveys of lifestyle and health.

Balanced diet and good nutrition

A balanced diet means regularly eating the right amount of the five food groups.

The five food groups

Group	Examples	Balanced quantity
Bread	Bread, potatoes, rice, pasta, maize, yam, cassava	6–11
Vegetable	Peas, beans, carrots, turnips, onions	3–5
Fruit	Oranges, apples, pears, grapes, melon, pawpaw, mango	2–4
Meat	Beef, lamb, pork, fish, (nuts, beans, lentils)	2–3
Milk	Milk, butter, cheese	2–3

Checklist: healthy and unhealthy lifestyles

Healthy	Unhealthy
Taking enough exercise – 30 minutes or more vigorous activity at least four times a week	Too little exercise – or (rarely) getting obsessed and over-exercising
Having a balanced diet – eating the right amounts of the five food groups (see above)	Not eating a balanced diet (most commonly, eating too much fat and sugar)
Getting the right amount of sleep (about 7 hours a night for most people)	Going without sleep or – rarely – sleeping too much
Taking reasonable care over hygiene, warmth, etc.	Neglecting hygiene – including food hygiene
Having regular medical and dental check-ups	Not bothering to go to the doctor or dentist
Being the right weight for your height	Being under- or over-weight
Mental health: being with people you like, enjoying work – and play	Depression – letting things get you down; thinking badly of yourself
Avoiding health risks	Doing things which are unhealthy – e.g. binge drinking, drug abuse, risky sex

NB The figures in the right-hand column show the *proportions* of food that make up a balanced diet. The amounts of food people need vary, but the proportions of each food group are much the same for most people.

CHECKPOINT ...

Some classifications have a separate group for fats and sugars. Why? What place do fats and sugars have in a balanced diet?

Nutrition

FOCUS

Definitions of nutrition

Nutrition is ...

'a process whereby living organisms utilize food for maintenance of life, growth and normal function of organs and tissues and the production of energy' – World Health Organisation

'the science of food, the nutrients and other substances therein, their action, interaction, and balance in relation to health and disease and the processes by which the organism ingests, digests, absorbs, transports, utilizes and excretes food substances' –Council on Food and Nutrition for the American Medical Association

COOL SITE:

http://www.nal.usda.gov/fnic/foodcomp/Data/HG72/hg72_2002.pdf – US nutrition guide

COOL BOOK:

Manual of Nutrition, 10th edition, HMSO, 1995 (previously published as MAFF Reference Book 342), ISBN 0112429912

Nutrition can be described as 'the scientific study of food and its effects on people'. Nutrients are the chemicals in food which the body can use. There are four main nutrient types and some non-nutrients which we also need (see the tables below and on the next two pages).

Vitamins

The table on page 310 shows the source and the importance of different vitamins.

Food and energy

The energy content of food is normally measured in kilocalories (often called calories for short).

The number of calories we need each day depends on three main factors: age, sex and lifestyle. The facts can be summarised as:

- People in their late teens and early twenties need most calories.
- Men need more calories than women.
- Active people need more calories than inactive people.

CHECKPOINT ...

Do big people need more calories than small ones? What do you think – and why?

Non-nutrients that we need

Non-nutrient	Sources	Effects	Other points
Water	Taps, drinks, in fresh fruit and vegetables and in many other foods We need about two litres of water (either pure or in drinks) each day.	Water is the body's main content by weight, and used for all metabolic processes.	Drinks containing caffeine or alcohol are diuretic – they can make you urinate and may. increase your need for water.
Salt	Occurs naturally in all foods	Needed for nerve signals, brain activity and many other functions	Too much salt raises blood pressure.
Fibre (roughage)	Fruit, vegetables, wholemeal bread and other unrefined foods	Helps digestion and absorption of nutrients	Protects against bowel cancer Helps excretion

Four main nutrient types

Nutrient type	Sources	Effects	Other points
Carbohydrates – these are starches (complex carbohydrates) and sugars (simple carbohydrates)	Starches: • cereals such as wheat, rice, oats and maize • starchy root crops such as potatoes, cassava and yams • bananas Sugars: • sugar cane and beet • fruit and vegetables • honey	Carbohydrates give us energy. The body changes carbohydrates into glucose, for fast energy, and glycogen for steady energy.	Complex carbohydrates release energy steadily for several hours. Sugars release energy fast, for a short time. Too much sugar can cause diabetes and obesity.
Proteins	Meat, fish, beans, lentils, pulses, nuts, eggs and milk	Proteins give energy and are used in building and repairing our bodies. Digestion changes them into amino acids.	Vegetarian diets can be low on essential amino acids. Too much meat protein may be a cancer risk.
Fats – animal fats are 'saturated'; vegetable oils (uncooked) are mostly 'unsaturated'	Butter, margarine, oils, cream, whole milk, cheese, fatty meat, oily fish, chicken skin, lard, etc. Used in making cakes, biscuits, crisps, chips, fried food and pastry	Fats provide 'fatty acids' on digestion and release large amounts of energy. Fat can also be needed for healthy nerves, and to help digest protein.	Eating too much fat makes some people obese. Saturated fats can lead to cholesterol being deposited in blood vessels, and heart disease.
Vitamins – these are complex organic chemicals	Found in many different foods – especially foods which are fresh, unprocessed and natural (see below)	Vitamins are needed for growth, energy, vitality, and good function of nerves.	Lack of vitamins ('vitamin deficiency') can cause serious illnesses.
Minerals, e.g. calcium, iron, iodine, magnesium (mainly in compound form)	Found in tiny quantities in a wide range of fresh foods	Minerals are needed for many functions, e.g. bone growth and blood formation.	Sometimes poisonous in excess. The government publishes recommended intakes.

Vitamins: sources and effects

Vitamin and RNI* per day	Good sources	Health effects
Vitamin A 700 micrograms	Liver, eggs, green leafy vegetables, fruit, carrots	Good for vision and the development of tissues. Serious deficiency causes blindness and death.
Vitamin B6 1.4 milligrams	Chicken, fish, pork, bananas, wholewheat bread and other unrefined cereals	Releases glucose, and therefore energy, from glycogen stored in muscle cells.
Vitamin B12 1.5 micrograms	Shellfish, liver, kidneys, egg yolk, meat, poultry, fish, cheese and milk	Breaks down amino acids (from proteins) and fatty acids (from fats). Deficiency causes serious nerve and brain damage.
Vitamin C (also called ascorbic acid) 40 milligrams	Citrus fruits, berries, melons, tomatoes, potatoes, green peppers and leafy green vegetables Also present in fresh milk and meat	Used in nerves, the production of hormones, the formation of collagen (the tough protein in ligaments and tendons); may reduce cataracts, cancer and heart/circulation disease; possible protection against colds. Deficiency leads to scurvy, which causes internal bleeding. Massive doses from tablets may encourage kidney stones.
Vitamin D 7 micrograms	Milk, oily fish such as salmon and mackerel, bread, cereals and egg yolks The skin makes its own vitamin D in sunlight – and people who never expose their skin to sunlight are at more risk of vitamin D deficiency.	Regulates calcium and phosphorus in bones, keeping them strong. May protect against some kinds of cancer, e.g. prostate. Deficiency causes the disease rickets, and bone and muscle weakness.
Vitamin E 4 milligrams	Vegetables and seed oils including soybean, safflower, and corn oil, sunflower seeds, nuts and wholewheat bread Leafy vegetables also contain some vitamin E.	Protects tissues and may reduce some visible signs of ageing. Deficiency causes muscular wasting, anaemia, nervous problems and problems with the immune system.
Vitamin K 1 microgram	Spinach, kale, broccoli, kiwi, cabbage, liver, soya products and olive oil Vitamin K is also made by bacteria in the intestines.	Deficiency causes poor blood clotting and, in later life, bone problems: osteoporosis and osteo-arthritis.

*RNI = Referent Nutrient Intake (UK) = recommended daily allowance

Daily calorie requirements

Age: 16–22	Active	Sedentary
Men	3000	2500
Women	2200	2000

Different foods contain different amounts of energy. The highest are fats and oils, followed by starches and sugars (carbohydrates), followed by proteins such as meat and fish. The lowest are fruit and vegetables. A few sample figures are given in the table below.

Energy content of some foods

Food	Quantity	Calories
Whole milk	1 cup	150
Raw eggs	1 cup	211
Margarine	1 cup	1626
Olive oil	1 cup	1909
Lamb	3 oz	305
Potatoes	1 cup	134
Cabbage	1 cup	33
Apple	1	81

NB 3.5 oz = 100 grams. A 'cup' is the size of an 'average' mug, or a clenched fist.

COOL SITES:

http://www.independentpharmacy.co.uk/public/health/vitaminguide.html

http://www.primusweb.com/fitnesspartner/library/nutrition/snacking.htm

http://www.bbc.co.uk/food/healthyeating/dairy.shtml

http://www.pueblo.gsa.gov/

http://www.nutrition.org/nutinfo/ – vitamins explained!

Merit

Analyse the effects of lifestyle, balanced diet and good nutrition on health and fitness.

For this outcome, you need to identify and give reasons for the most important effects.

In your analysis you should answer some of these questions:

- What is the difference between health and fitness – if any?
- How does being fit improve your health, and how can good health help your fitness?
- What are the benefits of regular exercise?
- What are the risks of over-training?
- What are the effects of smoking, alcohol and drugs on heath and fitness?
- What are 'complex carbohydrates' and why are they the best source of energy?
- How important is it to watch your weight?
- What is the best way of controlling your weight?

! CHECKPOINT ...

Carry out an audit of your own lifestyle and diet. What changes of lifestyle and diet could you carry out in order to get an improvement in health and fitness?

Distinction

Justify the need for a healthy lifestyle and a balanced diet to ensure health and fitness.

For this outcome, you need to show clearly why you must have a healthy lifestyle and a balanced diet to make sure you are healthy and fit.

Points you could develop include:

- Nothing can ensure health and fitness, but a healthy lifestyle and balanced diet can maximise a person's chances of being healthy and fit.

Diet

- It is easier to have a balanced diet than a healthy lifestyle. Diet is less complex than lifestyle.
- Planning a balanced diet is easy using the food group system. All you need is the right amount of the right nutrients with enough fibre and fluids.
- Diets for losing or gaining weight are never balanced – and may lead to health problems.
- Complex issues about body image, weight loss, eating disorders and consumer pressures have made dieting into a multi-million pound industry (but it may not help health and fitness).

- There are public health fears that people in the UK and the US are eating too much fatty or sugary food – risking obesity and diabetes.
- Governments now issue advice on healthy diets, and the proper intake of vitamins and minerals (the Reference Nutrient Index in the UK; the Recommended Daily Allowance in the US). Doctors and dieticians give reliable advice on diet.
- Research shows that a balanced diet reduces the risk of heart disease and cancer – the two worst killer diseases.

http://www.nal.usda.gov

Lifestyle

Factors which increase the risk of heart disease, cancer and other health problems include:

- environmental pollution
- smoking
- stress
- soft drinking water
- alcohol and drug abuse
- lack of exercise.

> **! CHECKPOINT ...**
> Which of the above are lifestyle *choices*?

Elements of a healthy lifestyle

- A balanced diet
- Good housing
- Plenty of aerobic exercise
- Lack of money worries
- Enough sleep
- A varied and/or interesting life
- Mental activity
- A clean environment
- Work that is challenging, but not stressful in a negative way
- Low or moderate alcohol consumption
- Satisfying personal relationships
- Having a degree of control over your life
- An optimistic, generous outlook

Healthy lifestyle is a holistic thing. There should be physical, emotional, mental and spiritual nourishment. If any of these are missing, something is wrong with the lifestyle. But it is hard to lay down rules for lifestyle, since we are all different. The lifestyle must suit the individual.

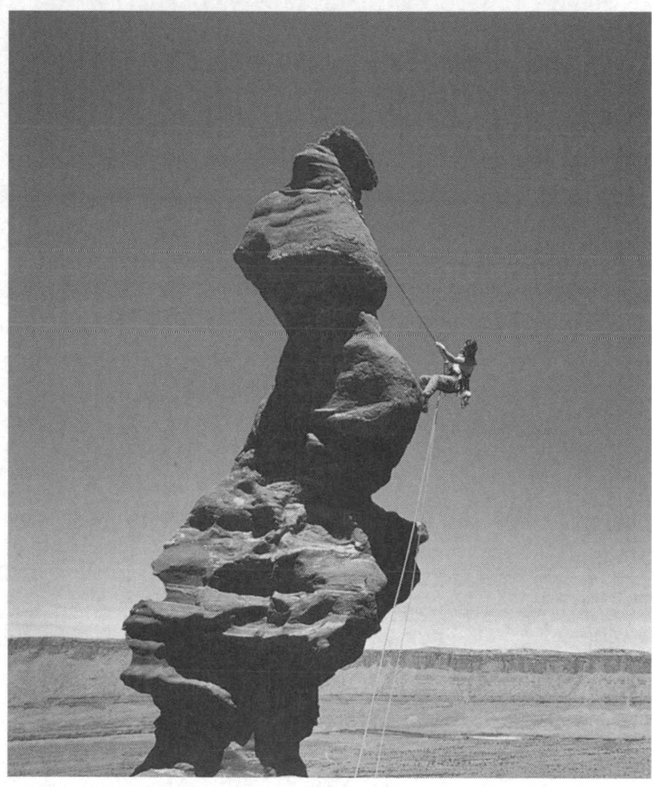

The rewards of health and fitness

PRINCIPLES OF FITNESS

PASSGRADE

> Describe the effects of the principles of fitness in relation to performance.

For this outcome, you need to describe the different aspects of fitness, and how they affect what we can do.

'Principles of fitness' are also called 'components of fitness'. They are sometimes called 'the five Ss' (though there are more than five – and they don't all begin with 's'!).

'Sleep', which appears in the 2002 Specifications, is not a component of fitness – but it is a necessary part of becoming fit. A healthy body needs rest just as much as it needs exercise!

FOCUS

Principles of fitness

General fitness is ...

'a set of attributes that people have or achieve that relates to the ability to perform physical activity' – US Department of Health and Human Services, 1996

Cardiorespiratory fitness (also known as stamina) is ...

'the ability of the body's circulatory and respiratory systems to supply fuel during sustained physical activity' – US Department of Health and Human Services, 1996

Muscular endurance (the other kind of stamina) is ...

'the ability of the muscle to continue to perform without fatigue' – US Department of Health and Human Services, 1996

Strength is ...

'the ability of the muscle to exert force during an activity' – US Department of Health and Human Services, 1996

Body composition is ...

'the relative amount of muscle, fat, bone, and other vital parts of the body' – US Department of Health and Human Services, 1996

Agility is ...

'the ability to change direction without the loss of speed, strength, balance, or body control' – Frank Costello, strength and conditioning coach for the Washington Capitals ice hockey team

Suppleness is ...

'the range of motion around a joint' – US Department of Health and Human Services, 1996

Speed is ...

'the ability to move the body or parts of the body through a given range of motion in the least amount of time' – USA Track & Field

Power is ...

'the ability to perform quickly an activity that requires strength' – Chris Parsons, 2003

Skill is ...

'the ability of muscles to function harmoniously and efficiently, resulting in smooth coordinated muscular movement' – Chris Parsons, 2003

COOL SITE:

http://www.evh.k12.nf.ca/cparsons/Active%20Living.htm

'Health' principles of fitness are to do with how well the body works. They include stamina, muscular endurance, body composition, strength and suppleness.

'Performance-related' principles of fitness are linked with learnable skills, such as coordination, agility and speed.

Different principles (or components) of fitness are used for different activities – whether they are sport-related or job-related. For example marathon-running requires a very high level of cardiorespiratory fitness, while hose-rolling requires cardiorespiratory fitness, speed and skill.

CHECKPOINT ...

Choose a range of sports and public service tasks, and decide which principles of fitness are needed in each case. Then check your findings with a friend.

FITNESS TESTING

PASSGRADE

Review, explain and compare a number of fitness testing methods.

For this outcome, you need to:

- describe several tests
- say what kinds of fitness they test
- say if they are specific to certain parts of the body
- say if they are used in public service fitness tests
- indicate if they are difficult or costly to carry out
- decide if they depend on effort and motivation
- compare them for accuracy, validity and reliability.

There are a range of fitness testing methods, depending on the type of fitness being tested. The table below gives nine common ones.

Nine common fitness tests

Test	How it's done	Kind of fitness it tests
Multi-stage fitness test (a.k.a. 'beep test'; 'shuttle run')	Run between two lines 20 m apart in time to a bleep, until you can no longer keep up with the speed set.	Aerobic fitness
Abdominal curl test (sit-ups)	Lie on a mat with knees bent, feet flat on floor and arms folded across the chest. Raise your body until you are sitting up straight, then lie back again. Record the number of sit-ups achieved in 30 seconds.	Strength of abdominal muscles
Press-ups	Lie face down on the floor. Place your hands flat under your shoulders. Then, keeping your toes on the floor and your legs and body straight, push upwards on your hands till your body is raised and your arms are straight. Lower and repeat.	Upper body strength
Heaves (pull-ups)	Hang from a beam with the arms fully extended. Heave yourself up until your chin clears the top of the beam. Lower yourself until you are hanging again with your arms straight, then repeat.	Bicep strength
Sit and reach flexibility test	Sit down with your legs in front of you and feet 30 cm (12 inches) apart. Your feet should be on the 38 cm (15 inch) mark on the tape, and the zero on the tape should be towards your body. Place your hands on top of each other so that the fingers are aligned, then bend forwards slowly, reaching forwards with your hands kept together. The score is the furthest point reached on the tape after three attempts.	Flexibility (suppleness)
Grip test (uses a dynamometer for measuring grip)	Grip the dynamometer and squeeze as hard as possible. You are allowed two attempts with each hand. Your scores are recorded.	Hand grip strength
Kasch Boyer/ Harvard step test	(a) The Kasch test lasts for 3 minutes, and a 12-inch step is used. You step on to the step and down again at a timed speed. After 3 minutes you step down and your heart-rate is monitored for the next minute. The rate of decrease of heart-rate after the stepping has ended is a measure of aerobic fitness. (b) In the Harvard test you step up and down at 30 steps per minute for 5 minutes or until exhausted. You sit down and the heart-beats are counted for 1 to 1.5, 2 to 2.5, and 3 to 3.5 minutes.	Cardiovascular fitness
Vertical and horizontal jump test	(a Vertical. Chalk your fingertips, stand by a wall, and mark how high you can reach (without standing on tiptoes). Re-chalk your fingertips, then jump as high as you can from a standing position, and mark the wall again. Record the difference in height between the two sets of chalkmarks. (b) Horizontal. Stand with your toes behind a line. Jump forward as far as you can, keeping your feet together. Record the distance between the line and the heel of your back foot.	Power
Calliper skin-fold test	This test is done with a pair of callipers which are used to pinch the skin and the fat under it, and get a thickness measurement. Using tables, and knowing the person's height and weight, it is possible to calculate their 'body fat percentage'	Body composition

'Sam did very well in the vertical jump test.'

FOCUS

Aerobic fitness

'Cardiovascular endurance, or aerobic fitness, is the ability to exercise continuously for extended periods without tiring, and is an important component of many sporting activities. A person's aerobic fitness level is dependent upon the amount of oxygen which can be transported by the body to the working muscles, and the efficiency of the muscles to use that oxygen. The best test for aerobic fitness is the maximal oxygen uptake (VO_{2max}) test.'

Source: http://topendsports.com/testing/main.htm

PASSGRADE

Explain the principles of fitness testing methods.

For this outcome, you need to explain:

- the aim of each test
- how it is done
- how fitness is measured and recorded.

Profile

Multi-stage fitness test

The main aim of the test is to assess the amount of oxygen a person's body can process.

This test grows progressively more difficult by decreasing the time allowed to run between the two lines. A CD or other recording is used to regulate the time between beeps. This means that a beep test score is standardised, and the result is reliable.

The beeps get faster each minute in order to differentiate clearly the fit from the very fit. Each minute is a level, and the test can go on to level 23. A score of 9.6 would mean the person being tested had dropped out after 9 minutes (i.e. at level 9) and 6 runs between the lines.

Abdominal curl test

This is designed to test both stamina and the strength of the abdominal muscles. During the test, these are the muscles which do the work. The test is easy to carry out and measure, and tests an identifiable muscle-group.

CHECKPOINT ...

Explain the principles for the other test methods listed.

Merit

Analyse and evaluate the reliability, validity, accuracy and safety of the fitness testing methods explained.

For this outcome, you need to:

- think about the fitness tests covered in the previous outcome
- assess how trustworthy, suitable, precise and safe they are.

FOCUS

Dictionary definitions

Reliable – 'trustworthy, safe, sure'

Valid – 'well-founded and applicable; sound and to the point'

Accurate – 'precise, correct'

Source: The Shorter Oxford Dictionary

- 'Reliability' means the tests can be trusted because the conditions under which they are carried out are controlled.
- 'Validity' means that the tests measure what they claim to measure.
- 'Accuracy' means that the test gives an exact measure of what the person being tested has done.
- 'Safety' means the risk of injury or harm.

Profile

Analysis and evaluation of three fitness tests

Test	Reliable?	Valid?	Accurate?	Safe?	Evaluation
Multi-stage fitness test	Yes, if the lines are measured properly, the CD is not distorted, the floor is in good condition and the person tested wears standard kit.	Not really. It claims to measure aerobic fitness but there is skill and agility needed for turning and the higher levels test strength.	It is accurate if measurements, e.g. of time and number of shuttles are correctly recorded.	Not very safe: it may push unfit people beyond their limits and lead to a heart attack.	The test records performance, but ignores motivation. It someone isn't trying, it does not give a true picture of their fitness.
Abdominal curl test	Yes, as long as the test is carried out under standard conditions. But encouragement, etc. by onlookers, makes it less reliable if it's given to some people being tested and not others.	It claims to test the strength of abdominal muscles. But it also tests aerobic fitness and muscular endurance. Easier for short people – doubtful validity.	If 30 seconds are given and the curls are counted, they can be counted accurately. But mistakes can be made in counting, telling the time and recording the score.	Moderately safe: people may still push themselves too far. Risk of pulled muscles without proper warm-up. Needs a helper to keep feet on floor.	This only tests the ability to do a lot of abdominal curls in a short time. It confuses aerobic fitness and strength.
Calliper skin-fold test	Not very. There are many differences in the way this test is carried out – 1,3,4 or 7 parts of the body are used by different testers. Not all testers are equally skilled at using the callipers, and people gain fat on different parts of the body.	This is a valid test, because it claims to give a measure of body composition, and that is what it does – if it is carried out correctly.	Callipers are much less accurate than the expensive electronic devices for body fat measurement on the market. Callipers can be up to 8 per cent wrong. Unskilled testers may pinch too much or too little tissue between the callipers.	Physically safe but psychologically damaging to people with body image worries. Skin-fold tests have been blamed for encouraging eating disorders in America.	Body composition my be unrelated to an individual's aerobic fitness and strength. Skin-fold tests do not measure a performance.

CHECKPOINT ...

1. Analyse and evaluate other tests.
2. Consider these questions:
   (a) There are two tests given above which do not depend on motivation, i.e. trying as hard as you can. Which are they?
   (b) Which of the nine tests listed in the table on page 314 is the most accurate? Give your reasons.
   (c) Which of the tests could also be used in a training programme for public service fitness tests?
   (d) Are the fitness tests above equally suitable for men and women? What do you think – and why?
   (e) Comment on the following statements:
   'It is possible to have a reliable test of aerobic fitness, but not possible to have a reliable test of strength.'
   'A fitness test only records a performance on a given day; it cannot give a picture of a person's real fitness.'

PASSGRADE

Complete and record a number of fitness testing methods and evaluate the results.

For this outcome, you need to:

- undergo fitness tests yourself
- test the fitness of other people
- record the results
- comment on the results and, if appropriate, make recommendations.

It might be possible to do this outcome in pairs. Follow your tutor's guidance.

Whether you are being tested or carrying out tests on other people, you *must* follow safe practices at all times, and ensure that a qualified and experienced instructor is present.

If you have *any* health worries, or have never taken fitness tests before, tell your tutor, see a doctor and have a proper health check before you start.

skill POWER

- Make sure you have all equipment, clothing and facilities available for your fitness tests when you plan to complete them.
- Wear the right clothes and use the right equipment.
- There must be a qualified and experienced instructor present whenever fitness tests are being carried out.
- You must follow safe practices at all times (e.g. warm up before the test session, and cool down after it). See Unit 9 Physical Preparation for the Uniformed Services, page 173.
- Never take a fitness test if you are injured or feel unwell.
- Be prepared to push yourself when being tested, but stop at once if you feel ill.
- Keep a full and honest record of all fitness test performances. This could be like the fitness record sheet below.

Name ....
Date ....

Test activity	1st attempt	2nd attempt	3rd attempt	Signed by
Abdominal curl				
Press ups				

A fitness record sheet

Evaluation

- Of your own performance:
  - How well did I do by my own standards?
  - How well did I do compared with my partner or other class members?

- How well did I do in comparison with the requirements of a public service fitness test?
- How do I feel about my own performance?

- Of the way you tested someone else:
  - How reliable, valid and accurate were the tests?
  - Did I plan the tests well?
  - Were they carried out correctly?
  - Was safe practice followed at all times?
  - What would I have done if the person had been injured?

Distinction

Justify the use of fitness testing methods for entry to the public services.

For this outcome, you need to explain:

- why public services use fitness tests
- why different services use different tests
- any problems raised by the use of fitness tests, and how they might be resolved.

For their entry procedures public services use:

- general fitness tests
- job-related fitness tests
- a combination of the two.

You need information on fitness testing for several public services. The PROFILE gives one example.

Profile

Cumbria Fire Service (2003) fitness test methods

Test item	Justification	Comments
General test		
The Chester step test	'measures your aerobic capacity'	An accurate, valid and reliable general fitness test
Strength tests		
Handgrip test	'gives an indication as to an individual's upper body strength'	Assumes a link between hand strength and upper body strength
Leg/back pull test	'designed to determine the combined lifting strength of your back and legs'	Depends on motivation – not fully accurate
Work-related tests		
Ladder haul	'give us a measure of your potential to perform specialised tasks related to carrying out firefighting'	Accurate assuming good motivation. Risks of injury without practice and warm-ups
Hose running	'give us a measure of your potential to perform specialised tasks related to carrying out firefighting'	Accurate assuming good motivation. Risks of injury without practice and warm-ups
Claustrophobia test	'give us a measure of your potential to perform specialised tasks related to carrying out firefighting'	Tests fear of confined spaces
Acrophobia test	'give us a measure of your potential to perform specialised tasks related to carrying out firefighting'	Tests fear of heights

Source: http://www.cumbria.gov.uk/fireservice/default.asp

General justification
These tests would successfully select fit and well-motivated people for the fire service.

Potential drawbacks

- Possible injury risks for poorly-prepared candidates (but the fire service stresses the need for preparation)
- Some may cause problems for female recruits.

Conclusion
Some fire and rescue service fitness tests may change in the light of recent government moves to make the fire service more accessible to female and ethnic minority recruits. But a high standard of the right kinds of fitness will always be needed.

CHECKPOINT ...

Do you think it is important that all police officers are physically fit and strong? What are the reasons for your opinion?

LINK! Information on fitness tests for prison officers, the police and the Royal Marines Reserve can be found in Unit 9, Physical Preparation for the Uniformed Services, pages 180 and 181.

Unit 20 Outdoor Activities

Grading criteria

PASSGRADE To achieve a pass grade the evidence must show that the learner is able to:	*Merit* To achieve a merit grade the evidence must show that the learner is able to:	*Distinction* To achieve a distinction grade the evidence must show that the learner is able to:
● describe, using correct terminology, the personal, group and safety equipment the discipline requires **321** ● describe the design features and discuss the importance of the properties of materials used **323** ● demonstrate the correct choice, transport, usage, care and checking of required equipment **323** ● demonstrate the full range of practical skills (on land and on water or on rock) to the level indicated in outcome 2 **324** ● help to plan and then safely carry out two longer or four shorter trips, journeys or routes, following appropriate codes, guidelines and agreements **329** ● demonstrate correct emergency techniques and know how to use appropriate emergency/safety equipment **332** ● demonstrate effective navigation skills (showing knowledge and use of map/chart, compass and techniques) sufficient to complete the journeys or routes, with some guidance **335**	● demonstrate competent, safe and environmentally friendly practical skills **328** ● show independent competence in the production and use of a route card/itinerary with some variation in accuracy **331** ● analyse the risks inherent in the activity and show understanding by applying their knowledge unprompted in practical situations **333**	● demonstrate very competent practical skills **329** ● show independent competence in the production and use of a route card/itinerary with no variation in accuracy **331** ● evaluate the requirements for accuracy and safety in the activity **334** ● discuss possible options which could be taken in a hypothetical emergency situation and suggest appropriate action, showing skill and understanding through evaluating and synthesising knowledge and justifying conclusions **334**

The purpose of this unit is to introduce you to a range of adventurous outdoor activities. It will give you practical experience in canoeing, kayaking, dinghy sailing and rock climbing.

In addition, it will show you how to research and assess the types of equipment used, and how to do your own planning before carrying out these activities. You will learn about safety, first aid and care of the environment.

The benefits of the unit for people wishing to have careers in the public services are obvious: you will experience activities which are important in the armed forces and relevant to other services. And – much more important – you will develop teamwork, leadership skills and confidence which should stand you in good stead for the future!

EQUIPMENT

PASSGRADE

Describe, using correct terminology, the personal, group and safety equipment the discipline requires.

For this outcome, you need to:

- choose one of the outdoor activities covered in the unit
- find out all the equipment and special clothing you need
- divide it into personal, group and safety equipment
- describe it, using the right words for different parts/aspects of the equipment.

The Specifications provide a list of personal, group and safety equipment for the activities covered in the unit. The full list is given below.

FOCUS

Equipment checklist

- **Boat features:** boat fittings (foot rests, seat and back-strap, buoyancy, end grab or toggle, rope, drainage hole and bung, hatch and cover, pump or bailer and sponge, compass, deck lines, dry bag and barrel, portage wheels/straps/trolley/trailer, skeg/rudder, towing system)
- In addition the **sailing option** to cover: spars, foils, sails and parts of sails, standing rigging, running rigging, mast fittings and bow fittings, anchor
- The **climbing option** to include: ropes (dynamic and non-dynamic,) harnesses, leadrack and normal range of attachments (slings, karabiners, belaying devices, chocks and friends), rucksack, chalk bag
- **Personal and safety equipment:** life jacket/buoyancy aid, wet suit, dry suit, waterproof jacket and trousers, spray deck, cagoule, salopettes, thermal clothing, fleece clothing, warm weather clothing, non-restrictive clothing for climbing, non-slip footwear/wellingtons/wetsuit boots/climbing boots, knee pads, paddle leash, spare clothing, first aid kit, map and map cover, food and hot drink, watch, torch, compass, hat, gloves, pogies, helmet, whistle, flares, insect repellent, sunscreen, sunglasses

Source: BN011697 Guidance and Units for the Edexcel Level 3 BTEC Nationals in Public Services – Issue 1 – May 2002

CHECKPOINT ...

Are there any important items missing from this list? What are they and why are they important?

Most of these items are best researched using:

- manufacturers' catalogues (available from outdoor shops or through the post)
- websites of manufacturers or retailers
- websites of organisations or clubs involved in these activities.

Your information about equipment should be in the form of:

- annotated diagrams or photographs (see example below)
- brief written or spoken descriptions (perhaps with examples of the equipment).

You could present your information as wall charts, fact-sheets, class presentations, mock sales talks, mock brochures or videos.

Selecting relevant information

The kind of information you give about equipment could include some or any of the following:

- design features of the equipment which help it to do its job properly
- the terminology or technical words used to describe the essential features of the equipment
- how the equipment should be used
- the properties of the material from which the equipment is made (e.g. waterproofing qualities, thermal insulation, toughness, lightness)
- what kind of people the equipment is designed for
- what kind of weather or other conditions the equipment is designed for
- how to transport the equipment
- how to take good care of the equipment, either in use or storage
- how to check the equipment before, during or after use.

For this outcome, there is a lot of ground to cover, so you should be selective about the amount of information you supply about different kinds of equipment. Not all of the kinds of information listed above need to be given for each type of equipment! The BTEC guidelines on this are summarised and explained in the table below.

What the 'information headings' mean

Example(s) – the normal, correct name of the equipment you are describing

Types – different models, styles, names, etc. of equipment

Design features – size, shape, convenience, safety, strength, multi-purpose

Correct usage – information on the purpose of the equipment and how it is used

Properties of materials – weight, strength, elasticity, waterproofing, insulating qualities, safety factors

Cleaning and care – how to look after the equipment so that it stays in good condition

Factors influencing choice – cost, size, aims and level of interest of user, safety, comfort, weight, appearance, ease of replacement, convenience, after-sales care

BTEC guidelines: amount of detail needed

Information headings	Simple equipment	Medium equipment	Complex equipment
Examples	Pogies Baler Chalk bag	Dry bag Thermal clothing Spray deck	Climbing harness Paddle
Types	Brief description or illustration (one type)	Description or illustration (one type)	Explain two types.
Design features	Very brief	Explain two design features.	Explain three design features.
Correct usage	Note	Describe	Explain three points of correct usage.
Properties of materials used.	Say what they are normally made of.	Explain the properties of materials used.	Explain in more detail the properties of materials
Cleaning and care	Very brief	Outline cleaning . and care	Explain two factors in cleaning and care.
Factors influencing choice	Very brief – one note or sentence	Explain one factor which would influence a person's choice of this equipment.	Explain three factors which would influence a person's choice of this equipment.

Source: information based on BN011697 Guidance and Units for the Edexcel Level 3 BTEC Nationals in Public Services – Issue 1 – May 2002, page 196

PASSGRADE

> Describe the design features and discuss the importance of the properties of materials used.

For this outcome, you need to:

- gather manufacturers' information on some of the more 'hi-tech' outdoor equipment listed
- describe the design of the equipment and its suitability for the intended use
- explain why the materials of which the equipment is made are suitable for its use.

'Design features' are to do with the shape, parts and function of equipment.

The 'properties of materials used' relates to the quality, behaviour and suitability of the metals, plastics, fabrics and other materials that the equipment is made of.

http://www.voyageur-gear.com/
– kayaks, etc.

http://www.hnh.dircon.co.uk/links.htm
– full list of cool links

http://www.bealplanet.com/indexfr.html
– ropes

Profile

Stinger II climbing rope made by Beal

This is a rope made for general purpose rock-climbing and mountaineering.

Design features

The rope consists of a sheath (outer layer) and a core. A special process is used to link the two together so that the sheath doesn't slip or loosen from the core. The function of the sheath is to make the rope easier to hold, and to protect the core from abrasion on rock ledges. There are variations in the tension of the sheath at the ends of the rope to protect against wear (which is always worse at the ends). There is a black mark at the middle of the rope to make it easier to avoid accidents which can result if the rope's length is misjudged. The rope is 9.4 mm in diameter, which makes it easy to roll up, thread through karabiners (clips), etc.

Materials

The rope is made of an artificial fibre called polyamide. This fibre is light, strong, elastic and heat-resistant up to a temperature of 230° C. It stretches by 10 per cent under a weight of 80 kg. Lightness is important because climbers often have to carry their ropes up a mountain before they can begin climbing. Heat resistance matters because friction heat is generated through abseiling and a rope which is not heat-resistant could be weakened or snapped in this way. Elasticity is essential in a climbing rope, for if a climber falls they can suffer internal injuries if the rope stops their fall too suddenly. The rope is water-resistant: this makes the rope less damaging to the hands, and keeps it light to carry, even if the weather turns wet.

PASSGRADE

> Demonstrate the correct choice, transport, usage, care and checking of required equipment.

For this outcome, you need to:

- choose equipment which is suited to a particular purpose
- pack and carry equipment correctly
- use equipment correctly
- take care of equipment
- check for wear, damage, missing pieces, dirt, etc. before and after use.

To get information:

- listen carefully and note what your tutors and instructors have to say about these topics
- research in shops and collect equipment brochures
- visit websites, and note the useful ones
- talk to people who are interested in your chosen outdoor activity
- note your own impressions of any outdoor equipment you use yourself
- practise taking care of outdoor equipment yourself.

Profile

Stinger II climbing rope

Choice

Make sure the rope is undamaged, that it is long enough, that it is intended for climbing, and that it is not too heavy for you to carry.

Transport

Coil rope correctly and carry in a rope sack.

Usage

- For climbing and abseiling.
- Doubling as a top rope must be through a karabiner – to ensure the rope is not damaged or weakened by friction on a rough surface such as rock or tree-trunk.
- Avoid fast abseiling.
- Don't use with damaged karabiners which could have sharp edges in them.
- Make sure the rope is long enough for the climbing pitch.
- Learn and use the correct knots (double fisherman's knot, tape knot or figure of 8 loop).

Care

- Protect against sharp edges, e.g. pitons and ice axes.
- Don't let two ropes rub together inside a karabiner – it causes friction burning.
- Keep the rope clean, e.g. by laying it on the rope-sack, not the ground.
- Store away from heat.
- Avoid contact with petrol, oils or acids.
- If you need to wash it, dry it in a cool shady place.
- Never lend a climbing rope to anyone else.

Checking

- Check for damage to the sheath and especially the core (do not use if the core is damaged).
- Ensure that no one has had a serious fall on the rope (this will have damaged it).
- Check that the rope is no more than four or five years old (less if it has been used frequently).

You will find it useful to do this kind of breakdown with any major piece of equipment which you will be using for your outdoor activity.

PRACTICAL SKILLS

Demonstrate the full range of practical skills (on land and on water or on rock) to the level indicated in outcome 2.

For this outcome, you need to:
- carry out the activity to the necessary skill level (see below)
- ensure that you have evidence that you have carried out the activity.

It is highly likely that you will carry out your outdoor activity as part of a college programme, or using organisations such as the army or an outdoor recreation centre. This is the ideal situation, since you will have trained, experienced instructors who will also be able to collect all the evidence needed by tutors, assessors and verifiers to prove that you have indeed met this outcome.

If you want to use activities for this outcome that you have *not* carried out with the college (e.g. with cadets, scouts or in other circumstances), you *must* discuss this with your tutors well in advance – and agree with them on the kinds of evidence (e.g. videos, photographs, signed sheets) you need to provide.

To be successful in this outcome, you need to carry out the chosen activities in a safe, responsible manner. This means you should:
- learn how to use the relevant equipment
- take all opportunities to improve your skills
- follow all instructions promptly and carefully
- look after your own safety
- not endanger anyone else.

And ...
- make sure your personal equipment is in order, e.g. that you have enough clothes and food. In both rock-climbing and boating, you may find yourself hanging around in the cold and wet before it is your turn. Always expect the conditions to be worse than they look.

If there are any problems they should, if possible, be dealt with well in advance. For example, you should:
- inform your tutors of any health or injury problems
- tell your tutors if you have any other reasons why you cannot do an activity.

If you think you are in difficulties, say – or shout!

Skill levels

The Specifications define the skills you are expected to have in your chosen activity. These skills are given in the tables below, with a few notes for guidance.

Source: the data in the skills tables on pages 325–27 are taken from BN011697 Guidance and Units for the Edexcel Level 3 BTEC Nationals in Public Services – Issue 1 – May 2002

http://www.seakayak.ws/kayak/kayak.nsf/NavigationList/NT0000090A – paddle your own canoe

http://www.sbkc.ie/Level%202%20Kayak%20Proficiency%20Award.doc

http://www.kcs.dircon.co.uk/mainSite/pages/stars/star1.htm – good tips

Skills on water in kayak or canoe

Skill	Explanation	Skill	Explanation
Launch	Get the boat into the water	Sculling draw	Figure of 8 stroke for adjusting position
Enter	Get into the boat	Pry stroke	A stroke used to move the boat sideways, away from the paddle
Disembark	Get out of the boat on to dry land	J stroke	Stroke for paddling long distances
Recover	Get ready for the next paddle stroke	Swim with boat	Swimming with kayak – keeping behind it!
Forward and reverse paddling in a straight line	Paddling forwards and backwards	Capsize drill	What to do if the boat falls on its side in the water
Stopping	Stopping the kayak with a paddle stroke	Rescue of swimmer and return to craft	Rescuing a swimmer from a kayak
Forward and reverse sweeps	Strokes used for turning	'All in' rescue	Multiple rescue of capsized kayakers by other capsized kayakers
Low brace turn	Stroke to stabilise the canoe	Breaking in and breaking out	Getting in and out of the fast current in white water
Stern rudder	Stroke to steer the boat at the back	Securing boat	Making kayak safe after getting out
Bow rudder	Stroke to steer the boat at the front	Stowing of equipment	Packing equipment on boat
Low brace support	Stroke for turning	Trimming the craft	Setting the angle right, e.g. front up, front down or level, as desired
High brace support	Stroke to prevent a capsize	Propulsion by one means other than paddle	E.g. a canoe pole, for pushing against a shallow bottom
Draw stroke	A stroke of the paddle pulling the boat sideways	Use of tow line and throw line	Tow line – rope with floats to help disabled kayak Throw line – an emergency rope to throw out to another canoe

Skills on water in a dinghy

Skill	Explanation	Skill	Explanation
Launch	Get the boat in the water	Heaving to	Technique for sailing slowly upwind
Secure and recover	Fixing and storing the boat	Getting out of irons	Sailing towards the wind
Leaving shore or moorings	Setting off	Sail setting	Getting the sails right
Coming ashore	Getting off the boat on to land	Trimming	Adjusting sails in a strengthening wind
Coming alongside another boat	Coming sideways to the side of another boat	Balancing the boat	Positioning yourself and others to balance the dinghy
Close haul	See 'Points of sail' page 15, on www.nelsonthornes.com/vocational/public_services/ – Unit 19 Nautical Studies	Boat trim	Getting the boat level from front to back in the water
Close reach	See 'Points of sail' as above.	Centre-board position	Adjustable board below the keel of the boat – stops boat going sideways
Beam reach	See 'Points of sail' as above.	Course made good	See page 6, on www.nelsonthornes.com – Unit 19 Nautical Studies
Broad reach	See 'Points of sail' as above.	Course to steer	See page 6, on www.nelsonthornes.com – Unit 19 Nautical Studies
Run	See 'Points of sail' page 15 on www.nelsonthornes.com – Unit 19 Nautical Studies	Paddling/rowing round a triangular course	Using paddles or oars and steering the boat
Tacking	See 'Points of sail' as above.	Rules of the road	'Lane discipline' on water
Gybing/jibing	See 'Points of sail' as above.	Drills for man overboard and capsize 19 Nautical Studies	See page 16, on www.nelsonthornes.com – Unit
Luffing up	Sail shaking as the boat turns into the wind		
Bearing away	Turning the boat away from the wind		

Skills on land

Skill	Explanation	Skill	Explanation
Storage and checking of equipment	Packing; checking everything is there and in good condition	Tying knots: figure of 8, bowline, round turn and two half hitches, clove hitch, Italian hitch, stopper knot, fisherman's knot	See page 14 on www.nelsonthornes.com – Unit 19 Nautical Studies
Transport or carry the equipment correctly	Moving equipment safely, without damage	Rigging the boat	Arranging the sails
Weather awareness	See page 8 www.nelsonthornes.com – Unit 19 Nautical Studies	Aerodynamics Hydrodynamics Mechanics	See FOCUS below.

FOCUS

Aerodynamics, hydrodynamics and mechanics

These are subjects you would have to study if you want to get a scientific understanding of the movement of boats.

- **Aerodynamics** – the way things (e.g. sails) move in currents of air (e.g. wind), includes turbulence, wind resistance, the angling of sails to get the desired movement of the boat
- **Hydrodynamics** – the way things (e.g. boats) move in water, includes movements of waves, currents, turbulence, drag, angling of paddles or rudders
- **Mechanics** – the way objects move in response to the forces acting upon them (e.g. in levers, pulleys and machines), balancing, centre of gravity of boat, strains, stresses, etc.

COOL SITES:

http://www4.tpg.com.au/users/battagli/NHSC-TL1_Course.PDF

http://www.wellesley.edu/Athletics/pe/sailing/

http://www.geocities.com/ajl397/sailing.html – cooler than cool

Skills for rock-climbing

Skill	Explanation	Skill	Explanation
Belay techniques and devices	Ways of protecting yourself from falling	Movement on rock	The basics of climbing, balance and using handholds
Setting up belays (direct and indirect)	Direct – climber protected by rope round rock Indirect – climber protected by rope attached to rock and another climber	Hand jamming	Jamming hand or fist in crack
Selection of single and multiple anchors	Place to attach belay/rope for protection (e.g. jutting rock)	Mantle-shelf moves	Gripping a horizontal hold between thumb and fingers
Top and bottom rope systems	Protecting the climber with someone at the top, or bottom, holding a rope	Side pulling	Gripping vertical holds by twisting hands sideways
Lowering	Letting a climber down a small rock face on a rope, without doing a full abseil	Lay backing	Leaning back to press feet against rock
Roping up	Two or more climbers joined by a rope	Back and footing	Resting back on one wall and feet on the other
Runner placements	Projections where nylon loops and clips for holding rope can be fixed	Traversing	Moving sideways across a rock face
Bringing second climber up	When the second climber on a rope moves up towards the leader	Bridging	Pressing feet on opposite sides of a gap
Holding falls	Holding a climber who falls	Finger jams	Where the climber presses fingers into narrow cracks
Abseiling (fixed and releasable systems)	Technique for descending cliffs	Crimps	Handhold gripped with knuckles raised
Use of safety rope/self protection systems	Ways of using ropes to prevent falls	Smears	Friction footholds
Appreciation of different rock types	See FOCUS below.	Foot jams	Cracks just wide enough to hold the foot

FOCUS

Rock types

Rock that is suited to climbing is usually hard, relatively unbroken, dry, free of excess vegetation, and high enough to offer a challenge. Natural rock faces are usually preferred to quarries.

Different rock types

Type	Origin	Names	Where found in UK	Climbing qualities
Igneous	Volcanic eruptions or underground volcanic activity	Gabbro Granite Rhyolite Basalt	Scottish Highlands and islands, Lake District, North Wales, Devon and Cornwall	Gabbro, rhyolite – very good Granite, OK but limited Basalt poor
Sedimentary	Laid down in seas, deltas, swamps and some sandy deserts	Limestone Chalk Gritstone Sandstone Shale	Pennines, South Wales, South and east England	Gritstone – quite good Limestone – OK Sandstone, poorish Chalk and shale unsuitable
Metamorphic	Originally sedimentary but hardened by intense heat and pressure	Schist Gneiss Marble Slate	Scotland, Wales, some sea cliffs in Devon and Cornwall	Variable – generally worse than igneous rock

COOL SITES:

http://www.rockclimbing.com/articles/term.php – rock-climbing dictionary

http://www.bdel.com/community/articles/72.html– runners

http://www.planetfear.com/climbing/features/technical/belaydevices1.html

http://www.rocksport.co.za/climbing/belaying.htm

Merit

Demonstrate competent, safe and environmentally friendly practical skills.

For this outcome, you need to carry out your chosen activity safely, showing a good skill level and avoiding damage to the environment.

The word 'competent' means that you can do an activity fairly well, with reasonable confidence.

To achieve this level, you should:

- pay attention to all instructions and guidance in the activity
- make sure you understand the theory and technical vocabulary of the activity, so that you can understand and follow instructions
- practise strokes, moves, etc. which require skill, checking that your technique is right
- identify errors or weaknesses and try to correct them
- be enthusiastic, yet careful, in what you do
- ensure that you carry out all safety checks and procedures
- know how to use equipment
- take all necessary care of equipment
- understand and be able to carry out navigation
- understand factors such as weather, nature of rock
- avoid causing environmental damage, e.g. by dropping litter

- follow the country code (see page 224)
- behave in a responsible manner at all times.

! CHECKPOINT ...

1. What are the main types of environmental damage caused by:
   (a) kayaking/canoeing?
   (b) dinghy sailing?
   (c) rock climbing?
2. How seriously should these problems be taken?

Distinction

Demonstrate very competent practical skills.

For this outcome, you need to be skilled in all strokes, moves and other physical aspects of the activity.

This means being well-coordinated, showing good judgement and timing, and being fit and strong enough for the activity. To achieve this outcome, you need to practise your chosen activity as much as possible.

If you are enthusiastic, and if you can join a club or association that carries out the activity, you will maximise your chances of reaching this level of practical skills

PLANNING AND CARRYING OUT JOURNEYS AND EXPEDITIONS

Help to plan and then safely carry out two longer or four shorter trips, journeys or routes, following appropriate codes, guidelines and agreements.

For this outcome, you need to:

- choose:
  - journeys on water in kayaks, canoes or dinghies
  - long walks to a climbing place
  - rock climbs (any combinations available or allowed by your instructors)
- carry these out as stated in the Specifications, by your tutors, and by any laws or regulations.

The Specifications lay down clear guidelines (see the FOCUS below).

FOCUS

Journeys and expeditions using safe and environmentally friendly practice

'*Journeys and expeditions:* on placid, or on grade 1 or 2 water, or in conditions not exceeding 3 on the Beaufort wind scale, or in open country to reach the venue for a climb, plan and carry out two longer journeys of at least 8 kilometres, or at least four shorter trips, or four graded climbs (in different locations if possible). The climbs should be on rock and not on an indoor climbing wall, although the latter could be incorporated into the learning experience. Following factors to be demonstrated: suitable choice of venue and routes, plan of trip, access arrangements and local by-laws, weather and tide restrictions, risk assessment, navigation skills and use of compass (see outcome 4) group awareness, leadership, care and respect for the environment.'

Source: BN011697 Guidance and Units for the Edexcel Level 3 BTEC Nationals in Public Services – Issue 1 – May 2002

Explanation

- Journeys on water will be in still or fairly calm conditions.
- Walks will be in open country (free of walls or fences). There must be either two walks of at least 8 km each, or four shorter walks (length not given).
- Four graded climbs (of a grade not worse than 'severe'). If possible these will be on different crags, or in different climbing areas.

Information on planning boat trips is given in Unit 19 Nautical Studies, on www.nelsonthornes.com/vocational/public_services/
Information on planning walks is given in Unit 11 Expedition Skills, page 212.
Information on leadership is in Unit 3 Leadership.
Information on group awareness is in Unit 17 Teamwork in the Public Services, page 283.

Fun – but a lot of planning goes into it!

FOCUS

The Beaufort Scale *1 knot = 1.15 miles per hour = 1.85 kilometres per hour*

Beaufort force	Wind knots	kph	Description	Land effects	Sea condition
0	0	0	Calm	Smoke rises vertically	Sea like a mirror
1	1–3	1–5	Light air	Smoke slants	Ripples
2	4–6	6–11	Light breeze	Wind felt on face; leave rustle	Small wavelets.
3	7–10	12–19	Gentle breeze	Leaves in constant motion	Large wavelets.
4	11–16	20–28	Moderate breeze	Small branches move	Small waves, fairly frequent white horses.
5	17–21	29–38	Fresh breeze	Small trees sway	Moderate waves, many white horses
6	22–27	39–49	Strong breeze	Large branches moving	Large waves; white foam crests
7	28–33	50–61	Near gale	Whole trees moving	Sea heaps up and white foam blown in streaks
8	34–40	62–74	Gale	Breaks twigs off trees; affects walking	Moderately high waves, crests break into spray
9	41–47	75–88	Strong gale	Slight damage to buildings – tiles and chimney pots	High waves. Dense foam. Spray may affect visibility
10	48–55	89–102	Storm	Trees uprooted; widespread structural damage	Very high waves. The surface of the sea mainly white. Visibility affected
11	56–63	103–117	Violent storm	Very damaging	Exceptionally high waves. The sea is completely covered with long white patches of foam. Visibility affected
12	64+	117+	Hurricane	Extremely damaging and dangerous	The air is filled with foam and spray. Visibility very seriously affected

http://www.met-office.gov.uk/education/historic/beaufort.html – windy site

FOCUS

Grading of rock climbs

Moderate

Difficult

Very difficult

Hard very difficult

Mild severe

Severe

Hard severe

Mild very severe

Very severe

Hard very severe

Extremely severe

NB There are many ways of grading rock climbs. This one is the simplest to understand.

Merit

Show independent competence in the production and use of a route card/itinerary with some variation in accuracy.

For this outcome, you need to plan, write and use your own route card or itinerary (journey information).

- 'Independent competence' means you should produce your route-plan without help.
- 'Some variation in accuracy' means that it is still possible to achieve this outcome even if you make some small mistakes.

Route cards

For a planned journey on foot over open country, you should produce a route card. This process is fully explained on page 212.

Plotting a course

For a journey on water where navigation is needed, follow the planning procedures (dead reckoning, etc.) outlined in Unit 19 Nautical Studies (on www.nelsonthornes.com). These techniques apply to large lakes or coastal waters.

River journeys

For kayaking on white water, you will probably be with an instructor who knows the river. With the help of the instructor, and using or drawing your own large-scale map, you could produce a route plan showing the main rapids, noting their characteristics and giving estimated times of arrival.

Safety

When planning an outdoor activity:

- take the weather forecast, time of year and sunset times into account in your planning. Factors such as wind, rain, river levels, snow, fog and darkness can have serious effects
- know your own and your group's personal fitness and skills – and plan accordingly.Take into account the weight you are carrying if you are on foot
- the quality and type of equipment you are using may be a factor (e.g. footwear)
- make 'escape' or 'contingency' plans – ways of ending your journey and getting quickly back to safety if something goes wrong. (Example on page 213.)

A route should be neither too easy nor too hard for your party. It should offer a challenge – yet put safety first!

Distinction

Show independent competence in the production and use of a route card/itinerary with no variation in accuracy.

For this outcome, you need to:

- be able to plan routes
- produce route or itinerary cards
- work to a high, consistent standard of accuracy
- do these things *without help or guidance from other people*.

LINK! There are details on land and sea route planning in Units 11 and 19.

SAFETY

> Demonstrate correct emergency techniques and know how to use appropriate emergency/safety equipment.

For this outcome, you need to:

- show what to do in various kinds of emergency
- show a knowledge of the kinds of first aid sometimes needed for outdoor activities
- show that you can use the relevant kinds of emergency equipment.

Outdoor activities can be dangerous. The way to deal with such dangers is (a) avoid them if at all possible and (b) use correct emergency techniques and safety equipment if things go wrong.

Due to lack of space, it is not possible to describe emergency techniques fully in this book. You should have access to a range of specialist first aid books, and books on boat and mountain safety.

COOL SITE:

http://www.walgreens.com/library/firstaid/

> **!** CHECKPOINT ...
>
> Research and practise:
> (a) EAR (expired air resuscitation)
> (b) CPR (cardio-pulmonary resuscitation)
> (c) the recovery position.

Using emergency equipment

Learn about and practise using the kinds of equipment listed in the FOCUS.

First aid

Problem	Recognition	Treatment
Hypothermia (too cold)	Shivering, slurred speech	Get person in a warm place; remove wet clothing; call a doctor.
Hyperthermia (too hot)	Sweating or fatigue or no sweating and high temperature	Move to cool place; loosen clothing; make person drink cool water and/or sports drinks; give something salty. If the person has a high temperature, call the doctor at once.
Hyperventilation (fast breathing)	Fast breathing; anxiety	Encourage sufferer to breathe into a bag, or to breathe slowly, and relax.
Drowning	Unconscious or in trouble in the water	Get victim out of water; do rescue breathing; call doctor.
Burns (primary, secondary and dry)	Pain, redness, obviously damaged skin	Stop cause of burn; douse burn in cold water; call doctor unless the burn is minor; give nothing to eat or drink.
Blisters	Sore skin on feet with fluid gathering	Cover with plasters; cut the walk short; wash them when you get the chance. Keep clean and dry.
Shock	Weakness, trembling, rapid shallow breathing	Lay person face down. Raise feet slightly. Loosen tight clothing. Keep the person warm. Call for medical help.
Sprain	Twisting of ankle or knee, followed by pain	Keep the limb still. Apply ice. Use elastic bandage or wrap. Call the doctor unless you are sure the sprain is minor.
Dislocation	Pain; kneecap, shoulder or other bone out of place	Call a doctor. Put ice on the joint. Keep the person's affected area still, and tie it up so it can't move. Don't try to replace the joint yourself.
Fracture	Pain; limb out of shape; bone sticking out	Immobilise fracture; call doctor; apply ice unless there is an open wound; give painkiller.
Cuts and grazes	Skin broken by minor falls, barbed wire, etc.	Wash affected area. Put antiseptic on. Cover with plaster. See doctor if it isn't getting better. Have a tetanus injection if you haven't had one recently.

FOCUS

Emergency equipment mentioned in the Specifications

Emergency food and warm drink

Flares

Global positioning systems (GPS)

Group shelter

Radio and mobile phone

Repair kit

Rope

Spare clothing

Spare paddle

Strobe

Survival bag

Throw bag

Torch

Tow line

Waterproof paper and pencil

Whistle

'Who cares if we're lost? You've got a radio and I've got a strobe. Let's party!'

Avoiding water-borne diseases

- Avoid bathing in water which contains raw sewage, farm slurry, green algae, industrial or other pollutants.
- Do not bathe near old buildings, barns or other places where there may be rats.
- Do not drink from streams unless they are on mountains above the highest fields, and the water is clear and running fast.
- Do not drink from lakes or ponds.
- If you have to drink dirty water, boil it first, or use water purifying tablets.

Merit

Analyse the risks inherent in the activity and show understanding by applying their knowledge unprompted in practical situations.

For this outcome, you need to:
- carry out a risk assessment of an outdoor activity
- show awareness of safety while doing the activity.

Kayak risks

- **Current** At sea this is dangerous. It can carry you quickly away from the shore – without your knowing – and into danger. In rivers, do not go into fast currents until you have gained basic skills.
- **Unsuitable clothing** Wetsuits or drysuits should be worn to reduce the risk of hypothermia.
- **Lack of safety equipment** Flares, strobes and whistles can be kept in a drybag to raise the alarm.
- **Lack of experience** You have to go into more difficult water in order to get better at the activity, but you should do this step by step. Become good at kayaking in easy conditions before attempting more difficult ones.
- **Drowning** This can happen if your kayak capsizes. Learn to do braces and Eskimo rolls to avoid the risk of getting trapped under water. Also, know how to swim!

Climbing risks

- **Falls** Take care when walking on steep slopes and rocky terrain. If you are roped, make sure that you and your companions fully understand belay techniques.
- **Falling rocks** If you dislodge a rock, shout 'Below!' – even if you think nobody is there. Do not walk or climb directly above other people. If

you are in a party on a steep slope, keep close together.

- **Hypothermia** Poor planning, going out in bad weather, wearing insufficient clothing or not carrying enough food can all cause this. Never attempt more climbing than you can do in the time available. Carry a whistle or phone in remote country.
- **Getting lost** Stay with your group.

Navigation risks

These are avoided by learning the skills listed in the FOCUS below. See more in Unit 11 Expedition Skills.

Small boat safety

- Never take risks.
- Learn to swim.
- Tell someone where you are going.
- Look after your boat.
- Check the weather forecast.

Distinction

Evaluate the requirements for accuracy and safety in the activity.

For this outcome, you need to:

- understand the theoretical and planning aspects of the activity
- explain their importance.

You should be able to describe and explain:

- all aspects of navigation and planning
- the equipment needed for the activity
- possible dangers, their causes, and ways of either avoiding those dangers or minimising their effects
- relevant first aid
- the emergency services and safety organisations connected with the activity.

COOL SITES:

http://www.scoutbase.org.uk/library/hqdocs/facts/pdfs/fs120603.pdf – wet, cold site! Check it out!

http://www.mountaineering-scotland.org.uk/safety/index.html

FOCUS

Navigation skills checklist

- Setting the map
- Contour interpretation
- Taking and following a compass bearing (in detail and as a rough guide)
- Estimating distance travelled by timing and by pacing
- Route choice. Selection of features on the map which can be identified on the ground to create navigational legs along a route that avoids major hazards and is practical to follow
- Identifying 'catching features' so that you will know what the ground will be like if you have overshot your target
- Relocation strategies – in case you lose track of where you are
- Map scales and measuring distances on the map
- Aspect of slope or direction of linear features
- Symbols
- Aiming off, attack points, collecting features, handrails
- Grid references

Source: http://www.mountaineering-scotland.org.uk/safety/index.html

Distinction

Discuss possible options which could be taken in a hypothetical emergency situation and suggest appropriate action, showing skill and understanding through evaluating and synthesising knowledge and justifying conclusions.

For this outcome, you need to:

- show a full understanding of safety, emergency, rescue and first aid procedures
- be able to apply this knowledge in exercises or simulations of accidents
- be able to explain all these procedures to other people
- be able to decide – and explain – which measures are most suitable for particular emergency situations.

> **!** CHECKPOINT ...
> Some organisations, e.g. St John Ambulance, run free first aid courses. Research these and, if you do not have a current first aid qualification, get one!

NAVIGATION SKILLS

PASSGRADE

> Demonstrate effective navigation skills (showing knowledge and use of map/chart, compass and techniques) sufficient to complete the journeys or routes, with some guidance.

For this outcome, you need to:

- for map and compass information, read the relevant sections of Unit 11 Expedition Skills
- for the boating skills, look at Unit 19 Nautical Studies on www.nelsonthornes.com
- practise using map and compass in a variety of situations
- prepare a route card (see page 213).

FOCUS

Navigation skills

The following appear in the 2002 Specifications:

'Skills and equipment: types of maps and charts i.e. suitable for chosen activity, familiarity with range of conventional symbols used on maps and charts. Compass features and uses, magnetic variation, calculating bearings, finding position, travelling on a bearing, use of transits, measurement of distance covered, correcting for wind and tide, buoyage and lights. Construction and effective use of route/itinerary cards/planning sheets. Interpretation of weather forecasts. Use of Global Positioning Systems (GPS).'

Source: *BN011697 Guidance and Units for the Edexcel Level 3 BTEC Nationals in Public Services – Issue 1 – May 2002*

Navigation skills are easy to learn – but you need practice to be confident. If you are working for this outcome in a group, make sure that you do some navigating or map-reading yourself.

Unit 21 Criminology

Grading criteria

PASSGRADE To achieve a pass grade the evidence must show that the learner is able to:	Merit To achieve a merit grade the evidence must show that the learner is able to:	Distinction To achieve a distinction grade the evidence must show that the learner is able to:
● give a detailed explanation outlining the theories and other contributory factors which may explain criminal activity or deviant behaviour **337** ● identify the vulnerable members of society describing factors which may increase the fear of crime **339** ● explain the role of the public services and other agencies to assist victims of crime using appropriate examples **341** ● undertake relevant investigations to explain the methods of reporting and recording crime **346** ● describe clearly the role of various types of court, the Crown Prosecution Service and other associated agencies **348** ● identify and describe in detail local safer community initiatives involving multi-agency partnerships **350**	● give a detailed description of how data analysis may be used to tackle crime **343** ● analyse the methods used to effectively tackle crime **344** ● provide a clear explanation of the support given to witness in court **348** ● effectively summarise the structure and funding of specified multi-agency partnerships involved in safer community initiatives **351**	● carry out independent research to explain the financial implications to society – the cost of crime **346** ● evaluate a strategy or initiative to tackle current crime trend(s) **353**

From earliest history, there is evidence of crime and the fear of crime. There are Iron Age graves showing that people died of violence; the Ancient Greeks wrote plays about crime, and the world's religions have plenty to say about good and bad behaviour, and how people should respond to it. In the modern UK, preventing and fighting crime costs billions of pounds, and the cost is going up all the time. A number of public services – the police, the courts, the prison service, the security industry and the probation service – depend for their very existence on crime. When people are attacked, the ambulance service takes them to hospital, and nearly half of all fires are started deliberately.

No wonder we are fascinated by crime. We get our entertainment from it – in the form of books, television, news and films. It seems there is a little bit of the criminal in all of us.

Criminology is the study of crime, and how society deals with it. Understanding how and why crime is committed, how crime affects people, how crimes can be detected and how they can be prevented are all important questions, both for society as a whole and for the criminal justice system in particular. It may not take a thief to catch a thief, but it certainly takes people with an interest in criminology to do something worthwhile about the problem of crime. So read on ...

THEORIES AND EFFECTS OF CRIME

Give a detailed explanation outlining the theories and other contributory factors which may explain criminal activity or deviant behaviour.

For this outcome, you need to:

- explain what is meant by 'criminal activity' and 'deviant behaviour'
- explain the main theories of why some people commit crimes
- explain factors which might make people commit crimes.

Crime and deviance are both types of behaviour which are not accepted by society. Crime is usually defined as 'actions against the law', though some people prefer to take a wider or more religious view – as in the Gormley quote above. This wider view of crime is based on a theory called 'restorative justice'. However, from a police standpoint, the idea of crime being acts which are against the law is more immediately applicable to their work.

FOCUS

Definitions of crime and deviance

Crime is ...

'an act punishable by law, as being forbidden by statute or injurious to the public welfare' – *Oxford English Dictionary*

'an offence against human relationships' – John Gormley, Irish MP

Deviance ...

'Social groups create deviance by making the rules where infraction constitutes deviance and by applying these rules to particular people and labelling them as deviants.'– Becker, H.S. (1997), *Outsiders*, New York: The Free Press

Why people commit crime

Many attempts have been made to explain why some people commit crimes and others do not. They come under two categories (a) underlying or 'distal' causes and (b) immediate or 'proximal' causes.

Gender and age

Men are at least twice as likely to commit crimes as women. Reasons for this include cultural factors (learned social behaviour) and biological (hormonal and physical) factors. The highest rate of criminal activity for both sexes is between the ages of 16 and 24. This is thought to be due to social and cultural factors such as the power of the peer group at this age, physical and biological factors (physical strength and learning ability are at their peak in this age group), and perhaps the influence of the media (e.g. role models, such as Eminem, who glorify an aggressive lifestyle).

Criminal careers

Most crimes, especially against property, are committed by a small number of habitual offenders. In a famous American study, 6 per cent of an age-group of boys born in 1945 accounted for 52 per cent of arrests for that age group.

COOL BOOK:

Wolfgang, M.E., Figlio, R.M. and Sollin, T. (1972), *Delinquency in a Birth Cohort*, Chicago: The University of Chicago Press – the American study mentioned above

Biological factors

This is the belief that a tendency to criminal behaviour is inborn.

- Lombroso (1835–1909), Sheldon and Goring believed there was a link between criminality and appearance. (For example, Sheldon [1949] concluded that criminals were more likely to be mesomorphs than ectomorphs [see page 306].)
- Criminal behaviour has also been linked to XYY chromosomes in men (instead of the usual XY combination), following studies by Jacobs at Barlinnie Prison, Glasgow, in the 1970s.
- The presence or lack of chemicals in the body has been suspected of increasing the likelihood of a person's acting in a criminal manner. Lead, cobalt and vitamin B deficiency may be factors, according to Lesser (1980). Young boys who are hyperactive (due to chemical imbalance) are thought to be at more risk of offending later in life.

Family factors

Certain kinds of family upbringing appear to make people more likely to commit crimes. These include:

- neglect
- harsh or abusive behaviour by parents
- deviant or criminal behaviour by parents
- family disruption and break-up.

A combination of these family factors is more likely to lead to crime than just one of them, and the most damaging of all is neglect.

COOL BOOK:

Loeber, R. and Stouthamer-Loeber, M. (1986), 'Family factors as correlates and predictors of juvenile conduct problems and delinquency', in Tonry, M. and Morris, N. (eds), *Crime and Justice: An Annual Review of Research*, Vol. 7, Chicago: The University of Chicago Press, pages 29–149

School record

Children who do badly at school, who are disruptive, or who truant are all at more risk of committing crimes. Low scores in 'intelligence tests' are statistically linked with criminal behaviour.

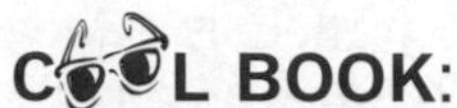
COOL BOOK:

Maguin, M. and Loeber, R. (1996), 'Academic performance and delinquency', in M. Tonry (ed.), *Crime and Justice: An Annual Review of Research*, Vol. 20, Chicago: The University of Chicago Press, pages 145–264

Delinquent peers

These are 'friends' who lead young people into crime. Where family influence is weak, peer influence is stronger. The peer group communicates deviant or criminal values, and teaches criminal skills.

COOL BOOK:

Klein, M.W. (1995), 'Street gang cycles', in Wilson, J.Q. and Petersilia, J. (eds), *Crime, San Francisco*: ICS Press, pages 65–90

Poverty and unemployment

These are statistically linked to high crime figures, though it is not clear if criminals themselves are poor, or if they live in economically disadvantaged areas. It may also be that the police pick on poor or unemployed people. Prisoners in British gaols are more likely to be poor and unemployed than the population as a whole. Poverty may give an encouragement for theft, and unemployment leads to poverty. In some parts of the world, there are high poverty and unemployment, but low crime rates.

Alcohol and drugs

Crimes of violence and road offences are linked to alcohol abuse. Psychological experiments have shown that alcohol increases aggression; criminal assaults and vandalism are more common around pubs and areas with high rates of drinking have high rates of violence. Drugs are linked to crime because drug-users need to steal to pay for drugs, and drugs gangs use crime to increase business.

COOL BOOK:

Stevenson, R.J. (1996), *The Impact of Alcohol Sales on Violent Crime, Property Destruction and Public Disorder*, Sydney: NSW Bureau of Crime Statistics and Research

Opportunities for crime

Crime rates are highest where there are opportunities for crime, and where criminals think they can 'get away with it'. The drop in crime rates observed where CCTV is installed, or where neighbourhood watch groups are set up, shows this link. Repeat victimisation suggests that offenders target people or places who offer better opportunities for crime. Poor policing, and a lack of community awareness or interest, also increase crime opportunities. Much crime prevention consists of reducing the opportunities for crime.

Organised crime

Gangs are linked to:

- a culture clash between cities and disadvantaged communities coming from rural backgrounds. The 'family' values of gang members are more important than the 'civic' values of law and order
- a youth subculture which cuts young people off from other parts of the community
- the prohibition of alcohol, drugs or sex
- ghetto living
- race or ethnic discrimination.

Cloward, R.A. and Ohlin, L.E. (1960), *Delinquency and Opportunity: A Theory of Delinquent Gangs*, New York: The Free Press

Economic cycles

In the UK, there is a link between crime rates, crime types and the performance of the country's economy. When the economy is in recession (low wages and productivity), crime against property (theft) goes up. When the economy is booming (higher wages and productivity, and more money in people's pockets), crime against property goes down, and crime against the person (e.g. assault, rape) goes up. Possible reasons are that in times of boom, people have less need to steal because they have what they want, but there is more drinking, and people go out more, so there is more crime against the person.

Field, S. (1999), *Trends in Crime Revisited*, Home Office Research Study 195, London: Home Office

Time of day

There is more crime against the person in the evenings, but some other kinds of crime, e.g. burglary, are higher at other times of day. These variations are mainly due to alcohol consumption and better opportunities for crime – but there may be other factors.

> **CHECKPOINT ...**
> Which of the above causes would you say are proximal and which are distal?

Vulnerable members of society

> Identify the vulnerable members of society describing factors which may increase the fear of crime.

For this outcome, you need to:

- explain briefly which groups of the population are most at risk of being victims of crime
- say which kinds of people are most frightened of crime and why
- outline other factors which might make people fear crime.

The vulnerable members of society are those who are most likely to be victims of crime.

> **FOCUS**
>
> **Four kinds of crime (statistically speaking)**
>
> - Unreported crime – crime that happens, but is never reported to the police
> - Reported crime – crime that is reported to the police
> - Recorded crime – crime that the police record (i.e. write down and add to their reported crime figures)
> - Detected crime – crimes that the police 'solve'

The main source of information about who is vulnerable to crime, and who fears crime, is *Crime in England and Wales*, a book published each year by the Home Office. This contains crime figures obtained by two methods:

- from the British Crime Survey, carried out by questioning and interviewing 40,000 people throughout the country each year
- from police figures of recorded crime.

The crime figures from the two sources are very different, mainly because many victims of crime never report the crime to the police.

The twin-track approach gives valuable information on what proportion of crimes are reported to the police, and the use of in-depth interviews for the British Crime Survey enables researchers to find out more about fear of crime, and how it affects people's lives.

The chart below shows who are the vulnerable members of society, as regards the risk they run of being victims of violent crime – 4.1 per cent of adults suffer some form of violent crime in a year, according to the respondents of the British Crime Survey. But if those adults are broken down into categories, it appears that some types of adult are more likely to be victims of violent crime than others. The most vulnerable, in this sense, are young men aged between 16 and 24. Fifteen per cent of them claim to have suffered some sort of violent crime in 2002–3.

Other vulnerable groups are separated people, single people, single parents and 'private renters' – people whose accommodation is rented from a private landlord.

This chart says that the people are vulnerable, not that they suffer fear of crime. It could be argued that people who fear crime, and show it by locking their houses and rarely going out at night, or never going to the pub, are less likely than average to be victims of crime. Young men who get out and about, and go to places where fighting is likely to happen, may well be at more risk of being attacked. Their lack of fear (if this is what their behaviour shows) is linked to an increased risk of becoming victims of violent crime.

Crime in England and Wales 2002/2003 contains information about the fear of crime. The chart on the next page summarises that information.

This chart suggests that fear of crime is evenly spread throughout the age groups. However, since older people suffer less crime than younger people, but have the same fear of it, their level of fear could be seen as higher. They still feel vulnerable, even though their risk of being crime victims is relatively low. See the FOCUS below:

FOCUS

Older people's view of crime

'Older people's risk of suffering from a household or a personal crime is much lower than for the other age groups. Older people are more likely to report violent incidents of crime and much less likely to be repeatedly victimised than the other age groups.

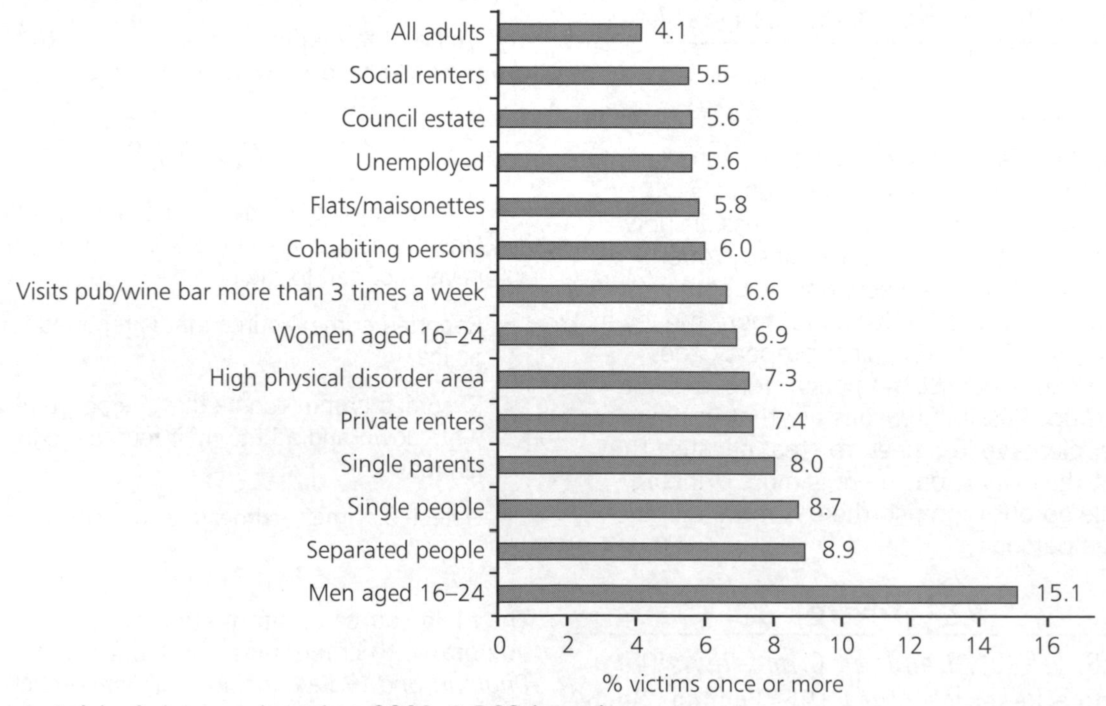

Adults most at risk of violence, based on 2002–3 BCS interviews

Source: Crime in England and Wales 2002/2003, *Home Office, Figure 5.5*

- Older people have similar levels of worry for most crime types to those of other age groups despite their lower levels of victimisation.
- Older women are more likely than older men to worry about fear of household or personal crime. Those that perceive their health to be bad or very bad also worry more about crime than those that perceive their health to be fair to very good. This may help to explain why older people have disproportionate levels of fear, given their relatively low levels of victimisation, as they also tend to suffer from worse health than the other age groups.'

Source: Crime, Policing and Justice: The Experience of Older People, *Home Office, August 2002*

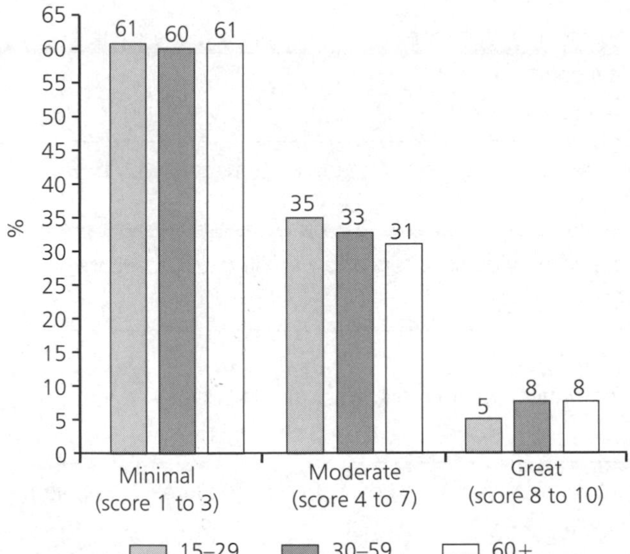

Effect of fear of crime on quality of life for different age groups, 2002–3

Source: Crime in England and Wales 2002/2003, *Home Office, Figure 8.8*

Some other groups of people show big differences in the fear of crime. The following table summarises some of the main findings.

COOL SITES:

http://www.homeoffice.gov.uk/rds/bcs1.html – British Crime Survey

http://www.homeoffice.gov.uk/rds/pdfs2/hosb802.pdf – older people's views of crime

CHECKPOINT ...

1. The table suggests that women fear crime more than men, and that people on low income fear crime more than people on high income. Note down as many reasons as you can which *might* explain these findings.
2. How does the treatment of crime in the media increase fear of crime?
3. Do politicians try to increase our fear of crime – and, if so, why?

Assisting victims of crime

Explain the role of the public services and other agencies to assist victims of crime using appropriate examples.

For this outcome, you need to:

- state what the public services and other organisations do to help victims of crime
- say why they do what they do
- give relevant examples.

Victims of crime suffer in many ways, depending on the nature and seriousness of the crime, and on the nature and circumstances of the victim. Their suffering includes:

% feeling very worried

Type of person	Burglary	Mugging	Physical attack	Rape	Theft of car	Out after dark
Men	12	9	7	5	15	5
Women	17	19	22	23	17	21
Low income	22	24	20	20	25	27
High income	10	9	10	11	12	6
All adults	15	14	15	15	16	13

Source: figures from British Crime Survey

- physical suffering, e.g. injury
- mental or emotional suffering, e.g. fear, bereavement, post traumatic stress disorder, etc.
- financial loss.

The government and the public services work hard to assist crime victims. There are also organisations outside the statutory public services which can help the victims of crime. The following table outlines the main roles of the main organisations which help victims of crime.

CHECKPOINT ...

1 Talk to local police, Neighbourhood Watch, Victim Support, etc. about the help given to crime victims. Ask them for examples of the kind of help given.

2 Research the measures brought in by the courts and the police to protect child victims of crime.

Roles of organisations who help victims of crime

Organisation	Role
Police	Investigate crimes Identify offenders Provide evidence to the Crown Prosecution Service so that offenders can be prosecuted in a criminal court Enforce Court Orders (see below)
NHS	Give primary care – and hospital treatment if needed – to people who have been injured in a crime
Crown Prosecution Service	Prepare the police case, and provide solicitors and barristers to prosecute offenders
Courts	Hear cases and sentence offenders Make Court Orders which protect victims, e.g. Restraining Orders; Sex Offender Orders
Criminal Injuries Compensation Scheme	Arrange compensation to victims who have been physically injured in a violent crime
Civil courts	Arrange compensation for financial losses which result from crime
Insurance companies, etc.	Cover the cost of criminal losses. Most insurance companies are private organisations, and will only compensate people who have taken out an insurance policy (e.g. on house contents) with them.
Victim Support	Counsel, advise and help crime victims
Rape Crisis Group	Give support for rape victims – one of a number of groups helping victims of specific crimes
Government and media	Central government passes laws and introduces schemes which help crime victims. One recent idea is that of a 'fines surcharge' of up to £30 which will be used specifically to help crime victims. Local government encourages police and voluntary schemes for safer communities, which protect crime victims and reduce the risks of 'repeat victimisation'. The media influence public opinion and politicians by focusing on the victims of crime, and campaigning (in most cases) for harsher penalties against offenders – something which many victims understandably want.

3 Find out what help or protection is available for victims of race or homophobic crime.

COOL SITES:

http://www.homeoffice.gov.uk/docs/victimsofcrime.pdf

http://www.cjsonline.org/library/pdf/18890_victims_and_witness_strategy.pdf

http://www.homeoffice.gov.uk/docs/childcon.pdf

Tackling crime

Merit

Give a detailed description of how data analysis may be used to tackle crime.

For this outcome, you need to:

- give plenty of relevant information about crime data
- explain how analysing crime data shows crime trends, hot-spots, etc.
- show how the data enable the police to target crime prevention towards high-risk areas.

'To tackle crime' means both to prevent and detect crime.

'Data analysis' is the interpretation of crime and other statistics. It is used to tackle crime in two ways:

- to provide evidence that there is a crime problem
- to analyse whether measures to tackle crime are really working.

'Data' can be defined as systematically collected information.

Using data analysis

Repeat victimisation is crime which targets the same individuals or property again and again. Huddersfield was chosen for a project to study this because the crime pattern was a problem in the town. The main points of the project report, *Biting Back II*, are summarised below.

FOCUS

Reducing repeat victimisation in Huddersfield

The project report sets out the police tasks necessary for areas wishing to implement a divisional repeat victimisation scheme.

- Quantification of repeat victimisation, and determination of how well this is reflected in recorded crime data.
- Routine identification of repeat victims, by the first officer attending, and establishment of Cocoon Watch and Police Watch.
- Purchase of equipment for temporary installation with burglary victims.
- Decision as to allocation of resources to victims, including identification of suitable targets for installation of high-tech equipment, for example videos and alarms.
- Training and oversight of police, and liaison with local authority.
- Monitoring and modification of scheme in the light of developments, including the purchase of new equipment.

The project was characterised by effective partnerships, particularly with the local authority, Victim Support, the university and the victims themselves.

The achievements of the project were:

- a reduction in crime – domestic burglary fell by 30 per cent and theft from motor vehicles fell by 20 per cent
- reduced levels of repeat domestic burglary
- no evidence to suggest that domestic burglary was displaced rather than prevented
- an increase in arrests from temporary alarms, from 4 per cent of installations to 14 per cent
- improved quality of service to victims.

Source: Chenery, S., Holt, J. and Pease, K. (1997), Biting Back II: Reducing Repeat Victimisation in Huddersfield, *Crime detection and prevention series, Paper 82, Home Office*

Data analysis was used before, during and after this successful crime prevention project. Analysis was carried out first on local crime statistics to identify the nature and scale of the repeat victimisation problem. Establishing that there really was a problem made it possible for the police, the local authority and others to raise the money and appoint the staff to set up the scheme and tackle the problem. Analysis was used during the project to identify all repeat victimisation crimes – as the FOCUS below explains.

FOCUS

Data analysis in practice

'An analyst interrogated the Crime Information System (CIS) daily, looking for the "hidden" repeats, drawing to the co-ordinator's attention any crime scene officer comments, looking for information that would assist in initiating the correct response, and printing out the daily crimes. A second analyst was assigned to the crime pattern analysis (CPA) system, designed by West Yorkshire Police, piloted in the Huddersfield division at the same time. A daily download of offences from the force CIS took place. This had the capacity to identify repeats, however many repeats were unrecognised by CPA for various reasons. The roles of the two analysts were closely interlinked and many victims would have been neglected if the "repeats" were solely identified from CPA. The analysts shared an office and relevant skills.'

Source: Chenery, S., Holt, J. and Pease, K. (1997), Biting Back II: Reducing Repeat Victimisation in Huddersfield, *Crime detection and prevention series, Paper 82, Home Office*

After the project, data analysis was used to determine if it had been successful or not. This was a complex procedure, since it involved discovering whether crime really had been reduced, or whether it had merely been displaced to other nearby areas.

Merit

Analyse the methods used to effectively tackle crime.

For this outcome, you need to explain methods of tackling crime in a logical way, showing how they connect up.

There are three main ways of tackling crime:

- tackling the causes of crime
- preventing crime
- detecting crime and catching offenders.

Useful sources of information are:

- crime prevention officers
- police involved in crime detection, e.g. Scenes of Crime Officers, CID
- newspaper reports of crime, especially in papers such as the *Daily Telegraph* and the *Times* which have detailed crime coverage
- television news and crime reports (use a notepad to get down the main points)
- *Police Review*, and other magazines dealing with criminology
- internet sites – especially the Home Office and Metropolitan Police websites, but there are also many other good sites, e.g. local authority sites
- people involved in Neighbourhood Watch schemes.

This outcome is very wide, and could cover not only tackling crime, but also tackling 'the causes of crime'.

Tackling the causes of crime

These are measures which are not directly linked to crime, but which might have the effect of reducing crime. They include alleviating poverty, and providing work and training for the unemployed. Any schemes involving education, urban renewal, parenting classes, a different approach to citizenship teaching, tackling drugs, lengthening the school day, censoring sex and violence in the media, changing the legal system, altering sentencing and imprisonment, redefining crime and decriminalising certain activities might have the effect of reducing crime. Unfortunately, the effectiveness of these measures takes a long time to assess, and some of them might be expensive, unpopular, or an infringement of human rights.

Crime prevention

There are different types of crime prevention. They include:

- technology used to deter crime, e.g. rape alarms, pepper sprays, visible burglar alarms, CCTV
- technology used to prevent crime, e..g. locks, high fences, fastening property to desks and walls, keeping valuables in a safe, etc.
- technology used to make crimes easier to detect. e.g. marking property with invisible pens, installing microchips in valuable items, using 'smart water', etc.
- behaviour which deters crime, e.g. using plug-in timer switches, closing curtains, leaving lights on, walking in well lighted streets and avoiding eye-contact with strangers

- behaviour which prevents crime, e.g. not going out
- behaviour by police, e.g. 'high visibility' policing, patrolling of 'at risk' areas, community policing
- publicity which deters crime – warning notices either to the public or to potential criminals, e.g. 'Guard dogs operating'
- design which discourages crime, e.g. designing houses, streets and gardens so that they do not provide hiding places for burglars, muggers, etc.
- rewarding non-criminal behaviour, e.g. youth clubs, schemes for involving 'at risk' young people in adventurous or enjoyable activities, providing more facilities for young people, teaching the benefits of good citizenship
- community measures such as Neighbourhood Watch, police drugs forums
- partnerships between police, the local authority, schools, other public services, etc. in crime and disorder partnerships and other crime prevention schemes
- media roles – news reports of crime; articles on crime prevention
- intelligence-gathering – anything from listening to informers to monitoring communications, e.g. telephone tapping to catch criminals before or during their crimes
- proactive crime prevention such as 'stings', infiltration of gangs, and setting other traps for criminals.

http://www.met.police.uk/youth/MetPoliceYouthStrategy-MAIN.pdf

Crime detection

This means investigating crimes to find out who did them, and questioning, searching and arresting suspects. The methods used in crime detection are governed by the Police and Criminal Evidence Act 1984 (available on the Home Office website).

When detecting a crime, the police carry out some or all of the following actions:

- securing the scenes of crime
- stopping and searching people suspected of carrying out crimes
- searching premises and vehicles
- detaining and questioning suspects
- identifying suspects
- interviewing suspects and witnesses
- charging suspects with crimes
- collecting and filing evidence
- gathering relevant computerised data
- sending their evidence to the Crown Prosecution Service, who organise and conduct the prosecution of the accused person.

The police gain their evidence from witnesses, confessions and from evidence found at the scene of crime, or elsewhere. The methods used for analysing and evaluating this evidence are carried out in a laboratory, and are called forensic science. Although police forces have fingerprint teams, most forensic scientists are civilians and many of them work for the Forensic Science Service, which is not part of the police.

FOCUS

Aspects of forensic science

- Analysis of evidence, e.g. glass, paint, bloodstains, tool patterns, accelerants in fire debris, fingerprints, DNA, footprints (bare and shoes), dust, hair, wounds, tyre imprints, substances
- Collecting, tagging, bagging and processing evidence so that it doesn't get lost, spoilt or confused
- Document analysis – forgeries, handwriting, etc.
- Examination of computers, disks, etc.
- Firearms identification (guns and bullets)
- Odontology (analysis of dental records, tooth-marks, etc.)
- Psychology and offender profiling
- Taphonomy (study of decay of dead bodies)

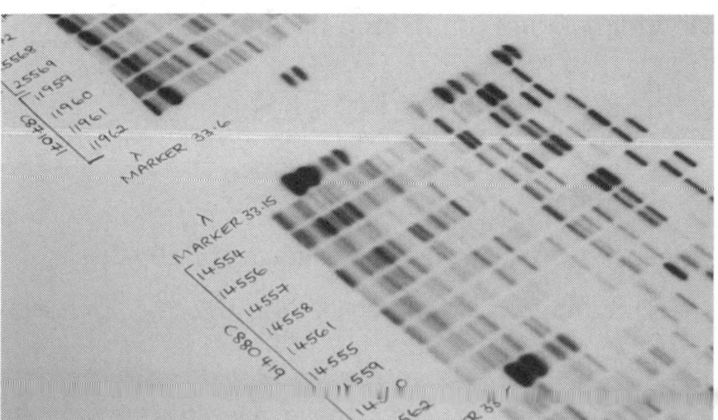

DNA analysis is a powerful forensic tool. DNA is found in all body tissues and most fluids. The only people who share the same DNA are identical twins.

The cost of crime

Distinction

Carry out independent research to explain the financial implications to society – the cost of crime.

For this outcome, you need to:

- find out what crime, and fighting and preventing crime, cost the taxpayer
- find out about the costs of insurance against crime.

Researching the cost of crime is quite a complex matter. It includes the cost of:

- having a police force
- Customs and Excise, the probation service and the prison service
- insurance against crime
- time lost at work through crime
- replacing stolen goods and repairing criminal damage
- all fire service work linked to arson
- benefits to prisoners' families (if they result from the breadwinner's imprisonment)
- all forms of crime prevention, security guards, etc.

and:

- the medical costs to people injured in crimes
- the costs to the National Health Service of physical and psychological injury or illness caused by crime
- the human cost of the suffering caused by crime.

Not surprisingly, figures on the cost of crime are rather variable. The government makes estimates, but not every year. Home Office research in 2000 found that crime cost £60 billion a year, and wounding alone cost £15.6 billion a year.

FOCUS

The cost of crime

- Each murder costs an average of £1.1m.
- Each wounding costs an average of £19,000.
- The average car theft costs £4800.
- Fraud costs £14 billion.
- Criminal damage costs on average £510.

Source: BBC News, 22 December 2000; http://news.bbc.co.uk/hi/english/uk/default.stm

Suggested methods of research

- Visit the Home Office website.
- Search the internet trying 'cost of crime uk'.
- Contact the police for information.
- Contact insurance companies.

REPORTING AND RECORDING CRIME

Undertake relevant investigations to explain the methods of reporting and recording crime.

For this outcome, you need to:

- research the different ways of telling the police about a crime
- find out how and when the police record crimes.

To research this outcome, you should talk to the police, get them to talk to you, or visit police websites.

Reporting crime

The table on the following page summarises the various ways of reporting crime.

http://www.met.police.uk/contact/crime.htm

Recording crime

When the police hear about a crime, and they are sure that it has happened, they record it. It helps them to solve crimes if they have as much data about them on their computers as possible – not least because many crimes are carried out by career criminals, and knowing about their *modus operandi* (way of working) helps the police to track them down.

Before 2002, different forces had different methods and priorities for recording crime. But in that year

Methods of reporting crime

Situation	Method of reporting
Emergency	Call 999. Say which emergency service you want, where you are, why you are calling – and your name and phone number. This method should only be used if a crime is happening or there is immediate danger.
Minor, non-urgent crime	Online reporting at http://www.met.police.uk/contact/onlinecrime.htm
Computer- and internet-related crime	http://www.iwf.org.uk/ – They will contact the internet service provider and the police. This works for child pornography all over the world, and for obscenity and criminally racist British-hosted material. The Metropolitan Police deal with hacking and virus writing, but not auction fraud.
Domestic violence	Call 999 if there is immediate danger, or a Community Safety Unit, where they have specially trained staff. Domestic violence can also be reported through housing associations or advice bureaux.
Frauds, con-trick, scams	Contact the local police, but not on 999 unless the case is urgent.
High value fraud	Ring the Metropolitan Police and ask to be put through to the Fraud Squad.
Internet fraud	Contact the Metropolitan Police, who may be able to do something.
Phone scams	Contact http://www.icstis.org.uk/ – Independent Committee for the Supervision of Standards for Telephone Information Services. Also useful to contact the telephone regulator, Oftel, at http://www.oftel.gov.uk/
Homophobic crime	999 or the Community Safety Unit
Paedophile pornography	Contact the Metropolitan Police. There's a free helpline, or ring CRIMESTOPPERS on 0800 555 111.
Racial crime	999 or the Community Safety Unit
Rape and sexual crime	999 or phone Project Sapphire (the Metropolitan Police rape and sexual assault unit).
Terrorism	999 for emergencies, bomb-threats, etc. or the anti-terrorist hotline: 0800 789 321.

the government laid down standards for crime recording by the police. The aim of this was to get a clearer picture of crime in different parts of the country, and to measure the efficiency of police forces in tackling it. These government standards are called the National Crime Reporting Standard.

The system now used by Nottinghamshire Police is a good example of how crime recording is done, following the new standard (see the following FOCUS).

FOCUS

Fast, accurate data capture

'Nottinghamshire police officers now use simple-to-complete multi-page crime forms. When they return to the station they simply scan the form either using a fax machine, a scanner or a digital sender. The images of the forms are transmitted to the centralised data capture system at the force HQ. [The software identifies] what form type it is, and therefore how to read and recognise the data. This data can include hand printed and machine printed characters, bar-codes and tick-boxes. ...

Any freeform areas such as notes, comments, sketches or diagrams are either keyed from image, or the image itself is simply clipped as a digital image for storage with the data. Once validated, the form data is output to the force's main crime recording system. ...

To further streamline and assist the data capture process, some forms are available electronically. Officers can open PDF versions of forms from the force intranet for completion and submission on-line. These forms are received and processed in an identical way by [the system's software]. This is particularly useful for updates or amendments.'

Source: from material provided by DRS Data & Research Services plc; www.drs.co.uk

As well as enabling the same recording system to be used by all police forces in the country, the National Crime Reporting Standard reduces bureaucracy, and increases the accuracy of the information stored by the police. The greater accuracy is the result of using direct data capture, which cuts down the risk of human error.

THE JUDICIAL SYSTEM

Describe clearly the role of various types of court, the Crown Prosecution Service and other associated agencies.

For this outcome, you need to:

- say what kind of work each court specialises in
- state the difference between civil and criminal courts, and between different kinds of criminal court
- distinguish between magistrates and judges, and explain how juries work
- outline the jobs done by the main people working in the courts
- indicate the limits of sentencing for the magistrates' and Crown courts
- describe what the Crown Prosecution Service do.

LINK! This outcome is covered in Unit 2 Law, pages 36–38. You will be able to get extra information from your local magistrates' court, and from the Court Service website.

COOL SITES:

http://www.courtservice.gov.uk/you_courts/criminal/index.htm – all you need to know about the courts

http://www.cps.gov.uk/ – Crown Prosecution Service

Merit

Provide a clear explanation of the support given to witness in court.

For this outcome, you need to explain the protection and help that witnesses can get in court.

The criminal justice system depends on witnesses – people who are prepared to come forward and testify in court to what they know about crimes. Being a witness can be an unpleasant or even frightening experience, and if somebody testifies against organised criminals their life may be at risk. For example, Alan Decabral was shot dead after testifying in court against the killer Kenneth Noye in 2000.

In the US, where they know about gangsterism and career criminals, there are laws to compel the authorities to support and protect witnesses. This is not the case in the UK, except where children are concerned.

Witness support can be given by:

- the court itself
- Victim Support (a charitable organisation)
- a solicitor
- the police.

Witness support – the courts

A witness is a person who knows something about the events leading up to a court case, and who is in a position to testify to what they have seen, or what they know. There are two kinds of witness:

- witnesses of fact – people who may have seen a crime, or know something important about it
- expert witnesses – people who have special knowledge about something to do with a crime, e.g. firearms experts.

Witnesses give their evidence both in the form of written statements and as spoken testimony, under oath or affirmation, in court.

The courts give guidance about the duties and rights of witnesses in a leaflet called 'I have been asked to be a witness – what do I do?' Support in the sense of advice is therefore readily available. Barristers in the Crown Court are under instructions to put witnesses at their ease as much as is reasonably possible – but they may still end up asking awkward questions, either to help the prosecution case, or the defendant. If a witness thinks they might be at risk from giving evidence in court (which is a public place), they should let the court know well in advance, so that some form of protection can be arranged. Under normal circumstances, it is not possible to refuse to be a witness.

Witness support by Victim Support

The Witness Service, a branch of Victim Support, helps witnesses in many ways (see the FOCUS below).

FOCUS

The Witness Service

'The Witness Service can offer:

- Someone to talk to in confidence
- A visit to the court and, where possible, a look round a court room before you are called as a witness
- Information on court procedures
- A quiet place to wait before and during the hearing
- Someone to accompany you into the courtroom when giving evidence
- Practical help, for example with expense forms
- Support and practical help for any person accompanying a witness
- To put you in touch with people who can answer specific questions about the case (the Witness Service cannot discuss evidence or offer legal advice)
- An opportunity to talk about the experience of giving evidence following the case
- Referral onwards for further help'

Source: http://www.victimsupportwestyorkshire.org.uk/whatwedo.htm

The Victim Support Witness Service aims to take the stress out of being a witness, but it cannot give any legal help.

Witness support from a solicitor

A solicitor could give legal help and advice to a witness who was unsure of their position in relation to a case where they were to testify. This could well be the case if the witness feels that they themselves may have broken the law. Matters discussed between a witness and their solicitor would, like all discussions between lawyers and their client, be 'privileged communications'. This means the content of those discussions does not have to be revealed to anyone, even in court. If the witness cannot afford to hire a solicitor themselves, they can apply for – and get – legal aid.

Witness support from the police

The police can give support and protection whenever a witness feels that they or their family are in danger as a result of their testifying in court.

FOCUS

Support from the police

'Britain's senior policeman has promised full protection to witnesses who can help solve the gang-land murder of a seven-year-old girl and her father in north west London. ...

The Metropolitan Police Commissioner, Sir John Stevens, said that anyone who came forward would be able to name their terms for cooperation, even if that meant them being resettled abroad. ...

Sir John spoke amid continuing outrage about the killing of Toni-Ann Byfield who was gunned down in her father's bedsit in Harrow Road on Sunday.

Sir John revealed that the force has expanded its use of witness protection schemes in an attempt to persuade more informants to give evidence against gunmen in London. Reciprocal agreements with Jamaica, South Africa, Romania and Bulgaria mean those who fear from their safety can begin new lives thousands of miles away.

He said police are already receiving "good cooperation" from the local community and said those who help the police will be taken care of, adding: "I give my word on that."'

Source: article 'Police promise protection to informants on killing of girl, 7' by Hugh Muir, Guardian, 18 September 2003

Police protection can range from a police presence at court, to the construction of a completely new identity for a witness who is at risk.

We'll give you complete protection. We'll even give you a new identity.
Oooh! Can I be David Beckham?

> **!** CHECKPOINT ...
> Do you think witnesses should be excused from giving evidence if they are at risk of being murdered?

COOL SITES:

http://www.courtservice.gov.uk/using_courts/witness/index.htm – lots of stuff about witnesses

http://www.bigissueinthenorth.com/Magazine/witness_protection.html – the human cost of witness protection

CRIME REDUCTION

PASSGRADE

> Identify and describe in detail local safer community initiatives involving multi-agency partnerships.

For this outcome, you need to name and describe partnership schemes intended to make the streets and local neighbourhoods safer.

Modern public services work in partnerships – and there are many partnerships working to improve community safety and the quality of life in all parts of the UK. Some of these partnerships have been made a legal requirement by the Crime and Disorder Act 1998.

> **FOCUS**
>
> **The Crime and Disorder Act 1998**
>
> 'The Crime and Disorder Act 1998, placed a statutory duty upon Local Authorities and the Police, along with the Health Authorities, Probation Service and others, to form Crime and Disorder Partnerships to work together to develop and implement a strategy to reduce crime and disorder in their area.'
>
> *Source: Leicester Partnership against Crime and Disorder,* 2002–2005 Strategy

> You can get information about crime and disorder partnerships from your local authority – and indeed you will find the information you need for this outcome by searching the internet using the words: 'crime and disorder partnership uk'. However, to learn how these partnerships really work, you should do some active research and try to meet someone who works in one.

Partnerships, like teams, are basic units in public service organisation, and within big partnerships you will find smaller ones. Any partnership with two or more agencies (public services, charities, private organisations, etc.) is a **multi-agency partnership**, and therefore relevant to this outcome. Crime and disorder partnerships are by no means the only partnerships which work for safer communities. Organisations such as the Metropolitan Police's Community Safety Unit are also partnerships (see the FOCUS at the top of the next page).

A large partnership such as the Leicester Partnership against Crime and Disorder has a mission statement and clearly defined aims. The aims are:

- reducing the opportunities for crime to occur
- tackling disorder and anti-social behaviour

FOCUS

Metropolitan Police Community Safety Unit

'The Community Safety Unit (CSU) is responsible for the investigation of hate crimes within the Borough of Hammersmith and Fulham. This includes racist crime, domestic violence, homophobic crime and hate mail. The unit is staffed by both male and female officers who are specially trained to deal with these crimes. It is also responsible for maintaining the register of missing persons. The unit is committed to working in partnership with both the statutory and voluntary organisations in the borough to improve the quality of life for the residents.'

Source: http://www.met.police.uk/hammersmithandfulham/community_safety_unit.htm

- improving methods of crime detection
- improving services to victims
- reducing the fear of crime
- tackling domestic violence and racial harassment
- combating the use of drugs.

The members of the partnership are:

- Leicester City Council
- Leicestershire Constabulary
- Leicestershire and Rutland Probation Service
- Leicestershire Health Authority
- Leicestershire Police Authority
- Leicester City Youth Offending Team
- Leicestershire Fire and Rescue Service
- Leicester Victims of Crime Support Scheme
- Leicestershire Chamber of Commerce and Industry
- Voluntary Action Leicester
- Leicester Racial Equality Council
- Leicester Magistrates Courts
- Neighbourhood Watch
- Crown Prosecution Service
- Leicester Witness Cocoon.

http://www.met.police.uk/youth/MetPoliceYouthStrategy-MAIN.pdf

For this outcome, you should also try to describe:

- a few initiatives (schemes) set up by the partnership
- the way in which the partnership is split up into smaller teams
- the twin-track approach (some activities are crime prevention, others are 'diversion': schemes to encourage responsible, positive behaviour through sport, recreation and other challenging and enjoyable activities)
- where the money comes from
- how the partnership judges the success or failure of its schemes.

Merit

Effectively summarise the structure and funding of specified multi-agency partnerships involved in safer community initiatives.

For this outcome, you need to:

- outline the organisation of particular partnerships working for safer communities
- explain what they cost and where they get their money from.

The structure of multi-agency partnerships is based on the links between them. Each partner is itself a team, and all the partners work together to make the partnership a team as well. This is a challenge, of course, because it means that public services or organisations which have their own culture (way of thinking and working) have to adapt and get used to the cultures of other partners.

Partnerships frequently produce organisation charts, like the one below, to show how they work together. One of the key features is that such structures are less authoritarian than, say, the rank structure within a single public service such as the police. In the Leicester example, the Leicester Partnership against Crime and Disorder is 'first among equals', but it doesn't tell the other partners what to do: they work together in a democratic and consultative way to reach an agreed solution to the town's problems. Under the 1998 Crime and Disorder Act, all public bodies have a duty to consider crime and disorder and how to minimise it in their planning – so in that sense all the partners are working together to achieve the same aim.

Each partner works in the same way. There is a cycle of development which consists of:

- gathering information about problems
- producing an action plan to tackle the problems within a time frame of (say) two years. The action plan also states who is responsible for doing what

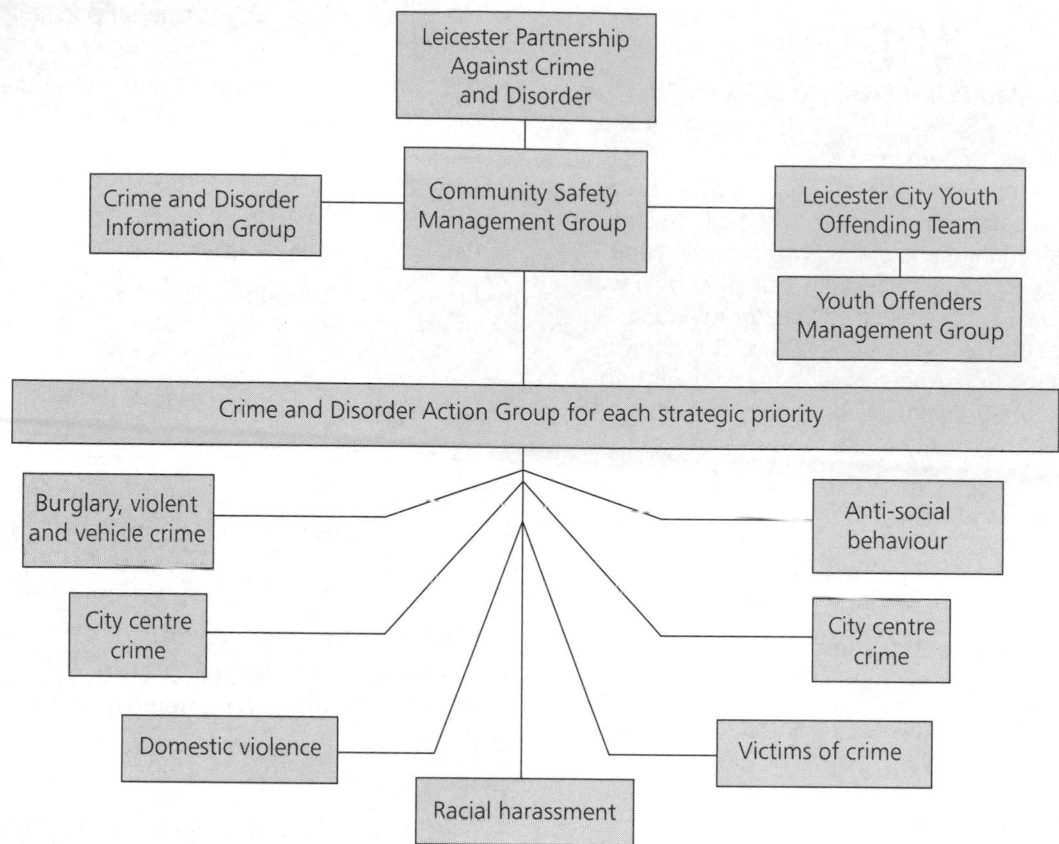

The organisational structure of the Leicester Partnership against Crime and Disorder
Source: Reproduced with kind permission from Leicester Partnership against Crime and Disorder, 2002–2005 Strategy

- carrying out the actions which have been planned
- reviewing progress.

The review stage leads on to further information-gathering, and the cycle is repeated, only this time, if the first aims have been achieved, a different set of aims is chosen. Action plans are compared and coordinated by the Partnership against Crime and Disorder to ensure that two different agencies (partners) are not overlapping and doing the same work. But at the same time, the Partnership against Crime and Disorder has to ensure that there are no gaps in the provision – in other words, that every possible type of crime and disorder is being covered. In a wider sense, the structure reflects the political idea of 'joined-up government' which is popular at present (2003). The idea comes from the problems encountered in cases such as that of Victoria Climbié (see page 000), where a child died because agencies which were supposed to be working together in partnership failed to do so, and her plight was never recognised.

Funding

Funding is the supply of money needed to pay for a public service. Partnerships are not expensive, however, because they do not usually employ people or pay their salaries directly. Most people who work in partnerships are paid by their own employers, e.g. police officers working with a crime and disorder partnership are still paid their police salaries in the normal way.

Crime and disorder partnerships are funded by grants from the Home Office under the Safer Communities Initiative.

The total sum allocated by the Home Office for crime and disorder partnerships in 2002–3 was £20 million. Leicester received £143,000. The figures for each town or city were based on their crime figures, so places with high crime figures got more money. The money is 'ring-fenced', which means it cannot be spent on anything except crime and disorder reduction agreed by the partnership. Capital and revenue spending must be recorded separately: if a partnership buys a computer (capital expenditure) it must not be counted along with money to pay a secretary (revenue expenditure).

Crime and disorder partnerships are allowed to receive money from other sources, such as private industry, if this is possible – as long as it is spent in agreed ways that reduce crime and disorder.

COOL SITE:

http://www.crimereduction.gov.uk/safercommunities1.pdf

Distinction

Evaluate a strategy or initiative to tackle current crime trend(s).

For this outcome, you need to:

- research a scheme for tackling crime which is operating at the present time
- find out what it costs
- make a reasoned judgement on how effective you think it is.

'Strategy' means a major or long-term plan.

An 'initiative' is a new idea.

'Evaluate' means that you have to discuss whether or not the aim of the plan is good, how effective it might be, the plan's effect on individual freedoms, and whether it seems like good value for money.

Every crime and disorder partnership set up under the 1998 Crime and Disorder Act has a written strategy setting out the partnership's aims and how they hope to achieve them. The strategy contains action plans and targets.

To evaluate the strategy you need to describe or quote from it. Best of all, you could have a copy of it and refer to the points it contains as you discuss it. A small example of the kind of evaluation you might do is given in the PROFILE on the next page.

Evaluating an idea is not the same as simply saying that it's a good one. For this outcome, you should also look at possible drawbacks and problems in crime and disorder – or other – partnerships. Ask yourself some of the wider questions, e.g.

- Are these partnerships stereotyping young people as troublemakers?
- Do they take a negative view of dealing with crime, concentrating too much on punishment and not enough on providing interesting and rewarding activities for young people?
- Are they a political ploy to convince people that the government are taking crime seriously, so that they get more votes at the next election?
- Are they a way of getting more policing on the cheap?
- Do partnerships have the effect of spreading responsibility – so that, in the end, nobody is responsible for tackling crime?

Profile

Priority	Responsibility
Priority 1 Reduction of domestic burglary violent crime and vehicle crime	*Police* The police are already involved in a number of established burglary reduction initiatives and are well placed to coordinate the network of local crime and disorder action groups as they are already involved in a large number of local partnerships and multi-agency groups in Leicester.
Priority 2 Reduce crime in the city centre	*Police* The police are already involved in a number of multi-agency groups working towards reducing crime in the city centre.
Priority 3 Domestic violence	*Leicester Domestic Violence Forum* The multi-agency Domestic Violence Forum was established in 1995 to facilitate a closer working relationship between the statutory and voluntary sectors to ensure a more accessible and comprehensive service for all victims of domestic violence.

Evaluation: Priority 1

The aim of reducing rates of burglary, violent crime and vehicle crime is clearly one that most people would consider to be a good one. All of these crimes cost society a great deal of money, and cause suffering to the victims. However, responding to these kinds of crime is what the police have always done, and including this in the strategy implies that the police have not been giving these crimes enough attention until now. 'Coordinating a network' of local crime and disorder action groups is apparently an additional task, and if it was to be done effectively it might need a large increase in resources, i.e. money and staff. It appears that the police, as well as having to fight crime, now have to chair meetings and explain crime prevention to a lot of other people, when their time might be better spent out on the streets fighting crime.

There is also a problem of information flow between people from different agencies, and though it is a good thing to improve this flow, communicating between agencies can be hard and time-consuming work. If information is communicated too well, it may cause problems under the Data Protection Act 1998: most police information, after all, is supposed to be confidential.

Another problem with partnerships is that the member organisations may not see eye-to-eye about various problems or schemes, and this could lead to in-fighting and time-wasting arguments. Being part of a partnership can put pressure on agencies to behave in ways which they don't like, and which go against their principles.

The setting of too many targets may also be a bad thing, since it encourages people to fake the figures in order to meet the targets, and reduces crime-fighting to an exercise in ticking boxes.

Unit 24 Major Incidents

Grading criteria

PASSGRADE To achieve a pass grade the evidence must show that the learner is able to:	*Merit* To achieve a merit grade the evidence must show that the learner is able to:	*Distinction* To achieve a distinction grade the evidence must show that the learner is able to:
● describe in detail three recent disasters or major incidents and, with examples, the three main ways in which disasters or major incidents are caused **356** ● describe the main features of a major incident plan detailing the organisations involved in major incident planning in Britain **358** ● explain the nature and value of disaster simulations **360** ● explain the role of three emergency services and three organisations outside the emergency services in a given disaster scenario outlining possible command and communication problems which may arise between agencies, giving possible solutions **361** ● describe a range of long-term environmental or health problems which could follow three given types of disaster **367** ● explain the roles of three organisations dealing with these situations **369**	● analyse the role played by the emergency and other public services in a recent disaster **364** ● analyse the environmental or health problems following one recent disaster **370**	● evaluate how the emergency services review their response to a given disaster scenario **366** ● critically analyse the impact on processes, procedures, communications, legislation, roles and responsibilities of one disaster **370**

Most of us, if we are lucky, go through life without ever experiencing a major disaster. The UK does not have real hurricanes or major earthquakes. Floods, when they happen, do not come without warning, and droughts, though serious for farmers, do not claim thousands or even millions of lives as they do in Africa. Terrorist acts have occurred, but mainly in Northern Ireland, and the risk of those has decreased considerably.

Nevertheless, disasters do happen, even in the UK. The Paddington rail crash, the Hillsborough disaster and the foot and mouth epidemic of 2001 were all, by British standards, very serious incidents demanding a much greater and more complex public service response than ordinary day-to-day crime and accidents.

Even though disasters are so rare, the public services prepare and train for them – in case they happen. And to gain wider knowledge, as well as help other people, British public services send teams of firefighters and soldiers to bigger disasters overseas, such as the Turkish earthquake of 1999 or Hurricane Mitch, which struck Honduras, Central America, in 1998.

EFFECT OF DISASTER AND MAJOR INCIDENT SITUATIONS

Describe in detail three recent disasters or major incidents and, with examples, the three main ways in which disasters or major incidents are caused.

For this outcome, you need to:

- choose three recent disasters or major incidents
- describe what happened in detail
- state the three main types of cause of disasters
- give examples of disasters linking them to their main causes.

For this outcome search the internet and CD-ROMs of newspapers, etc. for accounts of recent disasters. You should keep a scrapbook of disaster press cuttings.

FOCUS

Definition of a major incident

'A major incident is any emergency that requires the implementation of special arrangements by one or all of the emergency services and will generally include the involvement, either directly or indirectly, of large numbers of people.'

'There are many serious and protracted incidents which do not meet the criteria for a major incident but which would nonetheless warrant a co-ordinated effort from the services involved. Recent events such as the national fuel dispute, foot and mouth outbreak and severe flooding in some outlying London boroughs have met these criteria.'

Source: London Emergency Services Liaison Panel, Major Incident Procedure Manual *(6th edition), Metropolitan Police Service Emergency Procedures, Policy Unit, HQ Public Order Branch, New Scotland Yard, Broadway, London SW1H 0BG*

It is worth noting that the words 'disaster' and 'major incident' are used more in connection with peacetime than wartime. Thus the attacks of 11 September 2001 on the World Trade Center in New York were certainly a major incident – because although they were described by President George W. Bush as 'an act of war', they happened in peacetime.

For this outcome, you should keep an eye on the news and collect newspaper accounts of major incidents and disasters, in any part of the world. You can also get plenty of information about recent disasters on the internet.

Disasters and their causes

There are three main types of disaster, caused by:

- human behaviour (whether deliberate or accidental)
- a failure of technology
- natural events.

Of the three examples in the PROFILE opposite, one is of each type.

Though wars are not themselves classified as disasters, many of the world's worst disasters are associated with wars or unrest in many parts of the world, e.g. Israel/Palestine, Zimbabwe, Iraq, Liberia, Sudan, Congo, etc. This is because wars bring economic devastation and large-scale problems with refugees and displaced persons.

PROFILE

Examples of disasters

Incident, place and date	Number killed	Cause of major incident	Effects (and other points)
12 November 2002: bombing of Paddy's Bar and the Sari night club Kuta Beach, Bali, Indonesia There were two separate bombs, moments apart. The buildings collapsed and became infernos. Many people were badly burnt and injured.	Thought to be 202. The team worked on identification of remains until February 2003. The exact number will always be uncertain, and three bodies remained unidentified in February 2003. 88 Australians, 38 Indonesians, 26 Britons killed and people from many other nationalities.	The bombing was carried out by five members of the Jemaah Islamiah organisation, a militant group thought to have links with Al Qaeda. The bombing was a politically-motivated terrorist act, with westerners as the target. The root cause is the world political order.	(a) The wounded, and the families and friends of the dead and wounded, have their lives changed for ever. (b) The economy of Bali, based on tourism, suffers and in a wider sense Indonesia suffers economically and politically. (c) The west's 'war on terror' is given a boost.
25 July 2000: Concorde The supersonic passenger plane built by the UK and France in collaboration in the 1970s, crashed at Gonesse, near Paris, shortly after take-off from Charles de Gaulle Airport.	All 109 passengers and crew were killed, together with four people on the ground. Many more could have died, but the pilot swerved to avoid the centre of Gonesse just before the crash.	The crash cause was hard to determine. The plane had flames coming out of the back shortly after take-off. After two years, a report concluded that a piece of metal punctured the front tyre, and lumps of flying rubber broke the fuel tanks. It was claimed the metal was fixed on as a 'repair' in America.	(a) Concorde was grounded for over a year while tests and alterations were carried out to the whole fleet, both in the UK and in France. (b) The plane was never popular again, and started making a loss. The last Concorde flight was in 2003. (c) Families of the dead are still waiting for compensation.
September 2003: Hurricane Isabel struck North Carolina and Virginia in the eastern US Very heavy rain and winds of over 100 miles an hours caused great devastation, leaving 4.5 million people without power and contaminating water supplies.	17 people dead in six states. Causes of death included falling trees, electrocution, drowning and weather-related traffic accidents. Cost of the damage could be $1 billion (roughly £600 million).	Hurricanes are deep areas of low pressure formed over warm seas between America and Africa. The earth's rotation gives a 'spin' to the rising air, creating a violent storm over 300 miles across. Winds reached 160 mph in Isabel, but dropped as the storm hit land. Exceptionally high tides did much damage.	(a) Loss of life – but this was relatively small because the US is well-prepared for storms of this type. In Honduras, Central America, 15,000 people died in a similar storm in 1998, because the people there were poor, badly housed, and had no warning. (b) Widespread destruction of property.

Economic blockades and trade sanctions only add to the misery and death-toll. As if these problems were not bad enough, they are often made worse by natural disasters such as drought.

CHECKPOINT ...

1 Though these disasters are human-caused, technologically-caused and natural, there are other factors which made each one more or less serious than it might have been. With a friend, discuss what these factors are.
2 Do any disasters have only one cause?

CHECKPOINT ...

1 Which of the disasters below have directly affected Britain?
2 How predictable are the kinds of major incident listed below?

http://www.uneptie.org/pc/apell/disasters/lists/disastercat.html

http://www.keele.ac.uk/depts/por/disaster.htm

DISASTER PLANNING AND PREVENTION

Describe the main features of a major incident plan detailing the organisations involved in major incident planning in Britain.

For this outcome, you need to:

- find a major incident plan
- describe the main points in it
- list the main organisations involved.

Disasters and causes

Type of disaster (and examples)	Causes (or suspected causes)
Terrorist attack, e.g. 9/11, Lockerbie 1989, Tokyo subway gas attack 1995, bombing of UN HQ Iraq 2003	Deliberately caused disasters, intended to create fear and provoke reaction or over-reaction. Motive political or religious.
Poor crowd management, e.g. Hillsborough disaster 1989, Kumbh Mela drownings in Godavari River, India 2003	These disasters are caused by failures to control large crowds of people. Death results from stampedes, followed by crushing and suffocation.
Industrial, e.g. Prestige oil spill 2002, Toulouse explosion 2001, Bhopal 1984, Enschede 2000 fireworks factory	Various causes – mainly lack of safety checks (trying to maximise profits by doing things on the cheap).
Forest fires, e.g. Portugal, Spain, France 2003	Drought, lightning and arson
Floods – many examples, e.g. South Russia 2002, Haiti 2003, Algeria 2001	Heavy rain (global warming?), melting snow; clearing of forests so rain runs off too fast; poor rescue facilities.
Volcanoes, e.g. Mt Pinatubo, Philippines 1991	Splitting of earth's crust due to movement of tectonic plates. Poor forecasting of eruptions. Deaths increased by mudslides.
Earthquakes, e.g. Turkey 1999, Bam, Iran 2003	Movements of fault-lines and tectonic plates in earth's crust; poor building methods.
Drought, e.g. Pakistan 2000	Possibly caused by climate change linked to global warming.
Diseases, Aids/HIV; SARS; vCJD	'New' viruses entering human population through lifestyle changes and infection from animals.

At the time of writing, there are three national major incident plans. All have been set up by central government departments.

Local authorities are also required by law the have emergency planning departments, and to have their own major incident plan.

These can be found on the internet (see cool sites on the next page), and on local authority websites.

Major incident plans

Major incident plans are usually written documents structured into sections, like any other official report. Each section is itself divided into subsections, or paragraphs, which are clearly titled and numbered so that the reader can see at a glance which part of the major incident plan deals with which aspect of the subject.

FOCUS

Main features of a major incident plan

The London Emergency Services Liaison Panel's, *Major Incident Procedure Manual* (6th edition) is structured as follows.

Introduction

The plan begins with an introduction stating the need for emergency planning, and the background to the particular major incident plan.

Then there is a definition of major incidents, a statement of how an emergency is declared (it can be declared by any member of the emergency services, in the first instance), and an outline of the four stages an emergency passes though:

- the initial response
- the consolidation phase
- the recovery phase
- the restoration of normality.

Sections

After this, the plan is broken into sections detailing the roles and duties of all the emergency services (and any other organisation which might be involved). The sections are:

- main functions of the emergency services and other agencies (e.g. police, fire and ambulance)
- actions by first officers at the scene (for each of the blue light services and the medical incident officer)
- scene management (cordoning off the area, vehicle access, control centre, etc.)
- command and control (initial control, and under the gold, silver and bronze commands)
- gold and silver coordinating groups (management of the most serious major incidents)
- communications systems (police, fire, ambulance and others)
- casualty clearance (sorting of casualties, caring for survivors, role of coroner, information, etc.)
- helicopters – guidance for different services
- investigation of disaster (evidence, police role, 'debriefing')
- safety (especially for emergency workers)
- local authority role (giving assistance, organising logistics, etc.)
- other assistance (voluntary sector, utilities [gas, water, electricity], military help)
- welfare support
- media liaison (press statements, release of information, etc.)
- occupiers of property within the disaster zone (their rights of entry, etc.).

All these sections are broken into subsections.

Appendices

These are small sections at the end. They give extra advice and information about specific types of emergency:

- chemical, biological, radiological and nuclear devices
- railway incidents
- aircraft incidents
- River Thames incident
- flooding
- military assistance.

Glossary

A list of special words related to disasters and emergencies. The meanings of these words are explained.

COOL SITES:

http://www.ukresilience.info/terrorism.htm

http://www.doh.gov.uk/epcu/nhsguidance.htm

http://www.environment-agency.gov.uk

PASSGRADE

Explain the nature and value of disaster simulations.

For this outcome, you need to show how role-plays and 'mock disasters' are used to educate and train emergency workers.

A 'disaster simulation' is a role-play of a disaster. It is the equivalent of training exercises carried out by the armed forces. Most disaster simulations are based on possible chemical incidents,or terrorist attacks. They vary in scale from fire drills and practice evacuations to major exercises like the one described below.

FOCUS

Exercise at Bank Underground Station, Sunday 7 September 2003

'The Emergency Services took part in an exercise at Bank Underground Station and at University College Hospital on Sunday 7th September. This exercise was part of an ongoing exercise programme and was not a response to a specific threat.

The exercise aim was to test specific elements of the operational response to a chemical attack on the Tube. The emergency services carried out their roles and responsibilities as they would in response to such an incident, in accordance with the arrangements in the London Emergency Services Liaison Panel (LESLP) *Major Incident Procedure Manual.*

The exercise was used to test protocols for collaboration between the emergency services in the use of detection and identification equipment to maintain safe cordons.

The London Fire Brigade tested their capability to perform search and rescue by appropriately protected personnel, of casualties from an immobilised train in a tunnel. Central stockpiles of equipment were deployed to supplement that carried on appliances as they would be in an incident. New lightweight aluminium stretchers were also used.

Police personnel practised the use of personal protective equipment in a realistic scenario. Police from the Metropolitan Police Service, the City of London Police and British Transport Police were involved in the exercise.

The London Ambulance Service conducted triage of casualties by personnel in appropriate personal protective equipment. They exercised the deployment of appropriate antidotes.

Clinical and Mass decontamination were carried out by the London Ambulance Service and the London Fire Brigade respectively. The NHS carried out decontamination for "casualties" who had notionally made their own way to University College Hospital. Police were additionally supporting decontamination at Bank and at University College Hospital.'

Source: UK Resilience; http://www.ukresilience.info/home.htm

The value of such exercises is to:

- educate and train the public services in disaster response
- improve teamwork between different public services
- give training in using new systems or equipment
- experiment with new ideas of disaster management, or learn lessons from real major incidents elsewhere in the world
- enable the organisers to find ways of improving the response
- enable individual members of the emergency services to appraise their own performance.

The need for such exercises stems from the fact that terrorist incidents are rare. Exercises based on chemical or radioactive leaks and plane crashes also need to be carried out so that people who have never had to deal with them will know what to do if one happens. Training for more common disasters such as motorway pile-ups and major fires goes on all the time, but not usually through full-scale disaster simulations.

! CHECKPOINT ...

Contact your local emergency services or emergency planning department, and find out how civilians (such as public service students) can get involved in disaster simulations of the kind described above.

INTER-AGENCY COOPERATION

> Explain the role of three emergency services and three organisations outside the emergency services in a given disaster scenario outlining possible command and communication problems which may arise between agencies, giving possible solutions.

For this outcome, you need to:

- explain what three emergency services and three non-emergency services do in a major incident
- show how the services work together
- outline the command structure
- explain possible difficulties of communication
- suggest solutions to problems relating to who is in control, and to communication between different services in an emergency
- do all these things in relation to 'a given disaster scenario'. This means you should carry out these tasks or requirements in relation to a specific disaster which you have researched, or to an imaginary disaster, such as flooding, perhaps set in your own town. Ask your tutor for advice if you are unsure.

Your best source of information is your local authority emergency planning department. Ask your tutor to arrange a visit, or a visiting speaker.

The most useful websites are (a) the Metropolitan Police and (b) UK Resilience, a new website set up by the Civil Contingencies Secretariat – a part of the Cabinet Office. The Secretariat (a small department) was established in 2001 as a response to the threat signalled by the 11 September attacks in America. Other sites are run by police forces and local authorities.

http://www.wiltshire.police.uk/planning/index.htm

http://www.ukresilience.info/home.htm

Roles of three emergency services

Police

On arrival at a major incident the police (or whatever other service is first on the scene) assess the situation. While others are starting rescues, one officer reports the following information back to command, summed up in the word CHALETS:

Casualties – numbers of injured, uninjured and dead

Hazards – fire, chemicals and other dangers

Access – how emergency vehicles can get in and out

Location – the exact position of the incident

Emergency services – those already present and those needed

Type of incident – train, aircraft, chemical, bomb, etc.

Safety – safety of self and other rescue workers.

After making this initial report, the police role is to:

- coordinate the activities of other rescue services
- save and protect life
- search for survivors
- preserve the scene, and evidence for possible inquiries and prosecutions (unless the disaster is natural)
- set up cordons to protect the public and help the emergency services
- manage safety (e.g. controlling traffic and the public)
- issue public warnings (e.g. to keep indoors, shut the windows, and listen for instructions on local radio or TV)
- carry out searches if necessary
- collect, label, seal, store and record evidence
- assist others, such as the Health and Safety Executive, in their inquiries
- process casualty information
- remove the dead and act for the coroner (who has to investigate the cause and circumstances of deaths)
- deal with the media, giving interviews or keeping them out of the way
- supervise the return of the scene to normality (if possible)
- take part in any criminal proceedings, inquiries and reviews afterwards.

Fire service

The role of the fire services is to:

- rescue trapped people
- prevent the incident getting worse (e.g. by setting up firebreaks or cooling down oil-tanks)
- deal with released chemicals or decide exclusion zones

- help the ambulance service with handling casualties
- help the police to recover bodies
- supervise the health and safety of other rescue workers
- supervise access to the danger area itself
- help with decontamination – especially if large numbers of people have been exposed to chemical or biological agents
- work on fire investigation (if any)
- take part in debriefing and reviews.

Ambulance service

The role of the ambulance service is to:

- coordinate with hospitals to find out where casualties of different types should go
- give emergency medical attention at the scene
- determine the seriousness and types of casualties, so the most urgent ones get first treatment
- transport the injured to hospital
- get help from voluntary aid societies such as the Red Cross, if needed.

Explanation

Each emergency service concentrates on the activities for which it has been trained, and where it has most expertise. The police usually have overall control for the management of a major incident, but where there are fires burning, or chemicals spilling, the fire service are in charge (at least around the disaster site itself). Where the incident involves agriculture, the Ministry of Agriculture, Fisheries and Food has overall control, and in the case of a major health threat (such as the SARS virus in 2003) the main responsibility lies with the Department of Health.

Police, fire and ambulance services are the main emergency services in most circumstances. At sea, however, the Royal Navy and HM Coastguard play the main role, though the police may still oversee the operation. In terrorist attacks, the police have the major role at and around the scene, but where there is a major threat (e.g. at an airport), the army are brought in – as in a 2003 terrorist threat at Heathrow where 400 troops, some in armoured vehicles, were patrolling.

Role of non-emergency services

Medical services

- Hospitals with major accident and emergency departments receive casualties.
- Other hospitals may take patients transferred from the receiving hospitals, to make more room for casualties.
- A Medical Incident Officer oversees ambulance service activity at the scene of the major incident.
- The NHS gives advice to the public if there is (or may have been) large-scale exposure to chemical, biological, radiological or nuclear materials.
- Doctors, primary care trusts, community nurses, pharmacists, mental health personnel should all be on hand if needed, and should be involved in major incident planning.

HM Coroner

- The coroner's job is to determine the time, place and cause of violent, sudden and mysterious deaths. (The coroner relies on medical specialists to give expert opinions.)
- A coroner's court hearing is called an inquest.
- The coroner gives authority (usually to the police) for bodies to be moved from the scene of the incident.
- The coroner orders post-mortems.
- The findings of the inquest will help to determine whether a public inquiry or a police investigation will be carried out afterwards.

Local authorities

Large local authorities have a wide role in major incidents. This includes:

- coordination and planning (with the emergency services, local utilities such as gas, electricity and water, local companies, central government departments, the Environment Agency and voluntary groups)
- providing support for people in the area (e.g. emergency accommodation, restoration of supplies)
- providing normal services for people outside the disaster area
- coordinating the response of the voluntary sector and local firms (who have a big role to play in events like major storms and flooding)
- setting up temporary mortuaries if the death-toll is high

- restoring the environment when the major incident is over
- getting help from other local authorities if needed
- getting help from central government where needed.

Explanation

Non-emergency services are less likely than the rescue services to work at the scene of the incident, if it is something localised such as an explosion or major fire. Nevertheless, it is a statutory requirement that they deal with disasters (i.e. it is laid down by law).

Normally volunteers are kept away. But the bigger the disaster, the more likely it is that volunteers will have to take part, e.g. by helping in evacuation centres, feeding people and giving out blankets.

> **CHECKPOINT ...**
>
> In the Kegworth plane crash (1989), where a Boeing 737 came down on the M1, motorists leaped out of their cars to give first aid to casualties (38 died on the spot, and 74 were seriously injured, with eight dying later). Lives were saved by their prompt actions. What do you think are the rights and wrongs of volunteers getting involved in major incidents?

Communication and command problems

In theory, these should not exist, since the police usually have the controlling and coordinating role in a major incident, and because communication should have been practised in multi-agency disaster simulations. In practice, some communication and command problems are likely to happen.

Some command and communication problems are unforeseeable or hard to resolve at major incidents.

These can lead to tragic results – the needless deaths of many firefighters, for example, in the 2001 attacks on the World Trade Center. In major world disasters command and communication problems are made worse by

- the scale and horror of the event
- the suddenness and unexpectedness of the event
- noise, panic, poor visibility and other factors which make communication difficult or impossible
- the difficulty of communicating with the general public
- failure to grasp the essentials of the situation (e.g. when some people were told to go back to their workstations on 9/11).

In Britain, command and communication problems can be minimised as the table below shows:

Possible problems and solutions

Possible communication and command problems	Possible solutions
Not knowing who is in charge	There is a planning system laid down by the government. The police are in charge unless there is a fire or chemical incident. Command structures must be clear and linked to the seriousness of the event. See below for more on this.
Failure of communications equipment	Police communications centres alert the other services as a matter of course. Radio and other technology is used – including mobile phones which are more reliable and adaptable than traditional radio equipment. See the FOCUS below.
Unsure of own roles and those of other emergency workers	Simulations and training are the best ways of ensuring that emergency workers know their and other people's roles.
Duplication of effort (two or more teams trying to do the same job and getting in each other's way)	Efficient and clear command systems and supervision will help to resolve this problem. Such teams need training and practice in working together.
Culture or language differences between different services	Where 'culture' means differences in work practices, training together will help. Wider culture and language barriers may affect international emergency relief, e.g. at major earthquakes. Again, training, practice and proper briefing of teams before they go overseas should help.

FOCUS

Communication methods used in major incidents

- Radio
- Land line
- Mobile phone
- Text messaging
- Pager
- Fax
- Email
- Geographical information systems (GIS)
- CCTV
- Databases
- Video conferencing
- Public television networks
- Public radio networks
- Internet

Command frameworks

There are three command frameworks. Their use depends on the type, size and seriousness of the incident.

- **Operational Command** is used for incidents which are major, but routine. These might include motorway pile-ups and serious fires. They are major incidents, but dealing with them is included within the normal training and expertise of the three 'blue light' services. Resources to deal with these incidents do not normally need to be brought in from outside the area.
- **Tactical Command** is used when more resources are needed to deal with the incident than can be normally supplied (e.g. bringing in large numbers of appliances from neighbouring fire services). Serious floods and similar events can come in this category. Special local authority planning is needed to deal with such an event, and there may be bigger risks than those covered by Operational Command.
- **Strategic Command** is used for the biggest and most unusual major incidents. These may well be a national problem, such as the BSE outbreak of the late 1980s and early 1990s or the foot and mouth epidemic of 2001. The role of strategic command is to:
  - set up systems for the overall management of the incident
  - develop policies for dealing with media interest
  - ensure good communication with and cooperation between tactical managers
  - provide major resources, perhaps over a long period of time
  - make big decisions which might have long-term effects
  - plan a long-term and permanent recovery from the incident.

These frameworks of management are sometimes called Gold (Strategic), Silver (Tactical) and Bronze (Operational).

Merit

Analyse the role played by the emergency and other public services in a recent disaster.

For this outcome, you need to:

- collect information about a recent disaster
- show in detail how the emergency and other services responded
- draw conclusions – where possible – about why the various services acted as they did.

Since disasters are few and far between, your best research source will probably be the internet – since it gives you access to information on all recent world disasters. It is also a good idea to collect newspaper reports on major incidents – both in the UK and overseas.

Some uniformed services send teams out to help in disasters: for example the Duke of Wellington's regiment sent a team to Honduras to help build temporary bridges and other infrastructure after Hurricane Mitch had laid waste the country in 1998. British firefighters went to Turkey to help after the 1999 earthquake, in which up to 35,000 people died. If you can find local public services which have done this sort of work, and they are prepared to speak about it, they will be an excellent resource. There may also be charities such as the Red Cross and Save the Children who can give you material on their role in disaster relief. But note that the outcome asks you to analyse the role played by emergency and other public services in a recent disaster (in other words, a specific disaster – not disasters in general).

- 'Recent' can be taken to mean 'in the last 15 years', since the 2002 Edexcel BTEC specifications for BTEC National in Public Services mentions disasters such as Kegworth which took place in 1989 in the 'content'. Disasters which took place between one and five years ago are suitable for study, because you can then gather information about the aftermath and what the public services have done to tackle long-term effects.

- 'Public services' can be anything from the UN, national governments, the armed forces and major charities all the way down to small charities or individual efforts (e.g. by pop singers or film stars).

Profile

The role of emergency services and other organisations in the floods of autumn 2000

According to the Environment Agency's report on the floods, there was a major combined public service response to the floods, which included many gold and silver command frameworks. The Environment Agency says:

'A particularly notable feature of the autumn 2000 floods was the tremendous collaborative effort of all the various agencies and organisations who have a role to play during a flood event. They included the Environment Agency, local authorities, the voluntary sector, Police, Fire and Ambulance services, RNLI, British Waterways and the Armed Services. Suppliers, contractors, consultant engineers and the utilities also provided considerable support. The floods rigorously tested the incident management and emergency procedures established by all organisations.'

Source: Lessons Learned: Autumn 2000 Floods, *Environment Agency*

'I'm not coming until EastEnders has finished!'

FOCUS

Who did what in November 2000

- Aftercare – local authorities, voluntary groups (counselling frightened children, etc.)
- Assessment work and repair – Environment Agency
- Clearing sewers and checking water purity – water companies
- Dealing with flooded railways – Railtrack (now Network Rail) overseen by Strategic Rail Authority
- Evacuation – initiated by police and local authorities
- Flood emergency plans – local authorities
- Flood forecasting – Environment Agency and Met Office
- Flood warnings – Environment Agency; National Flood Warning Centre
- Insurance – the Association of British Insurers put pressure on the government to improve flood management
- Protection of evacuated property and traffic control – police
- Publicising flood warnings – media (including the internet)
- Rescues – mainly fire service
- Research – Environment Agency and MAFF
- Sandbagging – public and uniformed services including armed forces; many volunteers and ordinary citizens
- VIP visits – politicians
- Voluntary groups – looking after evacuated people, etc.

To analyse these in more detail, you could:

- contact your local authority and ask them about their flood emergency plans
- visit the Environment Agency website and download their reports.

COOL SITES:

http://www.environment-agency.gov.uk – the coolest, wettest site!

http://www.hambleton.gov.uk/hambleton/news.nsf – useful local perspective

http://www.environment-agency.gov.uk/commondata/105385/126637 – major flood report 2001

Distinction

Evaluate how the emergency services review their response to a given disaster scenario.

For this outcome, you need to:

- examine how emergency services record and assess their own response to a disaster or a simulated disaster
- reach conclusions as to why this process is done, and how effective it is in achieving its aims.

Ask your tutor to invite a visiting speaker who is concerned with training rescue workers, or who has experience of being trained.

Disasters are disasters, but they are also 'learning curves'. The fact that disasters are not common means that it is all the more important to review every aspect of them when they happen, so that valuable lessons can be learnt. These lessons are not only valuable to the emergency services who have dealt with a particular disaster. They are important to rescue services all over the world – who may one day be faced with a similar disaster. Today's real disasters form the scenarios for tomorrow's training exercises.

To learn from disasters there has to be:

- a record kept of what happened and what was done to deal with it (this should include video records if possible)
- thorough debriefing of all emergency personnel involved in the incident. (If the incident is very big, then there should be debriefing of as many key workers as possible, including volunteers.) It is important that no blame or judgement is passed at this time
- knowledge of the views of the public and the media
- an audit of what the emergency services' response cost
- comparison of the performance of the emergency services with performances of emergency services in other, similar incidents or in training simulations
- a self-assessment for each phase of the emergency services' response
- a full written report on the response to the major incident.

A review of the emergency services' response to a disaster is carried out by the services themselves. It involves a process called 'debriefing', which is explained in the FOCUS below.

FOCUS

Debriefing

'2.5.1 Debrief

Debriefing provides an opportunity for everyone involved in an exercise to comment on the organisational response. In retrospect it is nearly always possible to identify things that could have been done better. Criticisms should be constructive and not attempt to apportion blame. When debriefing identifies what went well, individuals should be congratulated and good practice disseminated. Debriefing may be in large or small groups. It is easier to admit to failures within your peer group than when others are present. There should be an opportunity to provide written comments. Whatever the form of the debrief, it should take place as soon as possible after the event.

The purpose of debriefing is to capture the lessons learned for subsequent analysis. A debriefing session after a major incident or exercise, if necessary with other agencies, will help to:

- inform future training
- improve procedures
- collect evidence for any enquiry
- identify and respond to the needs of staff.

Following debriefing it is important to distinguish between lessons arising from the specific incident or exercise and those that are generally applicable. It is easier to plan for the last incident that occurred than the next one!

You may identify issues that need to be addressed by other organisations. If so, inform other agencies or senior management or the Department of Health as appropriate.

The person responsible for the major incident plan must arrange a debrief after every incident or major exercise.'

Source: Department of Health

After a major disaster, especially one where crimes may have been committed, or mistakes made, or lessons have to be learnt, there is a public inquiry. An example of this was the inquiry by Lord Cullen (a Privy Councillor and eminent judge) in 2000 into the 1999 Paddington rail crash. At the same time the police, the Health and Safety Executive and a scientific adviser carried out their own investigations. The purpose of the police investigation was to decide if criminal charges should be brought. The purpose of the HSE investigation was to look at safety issues. The purpose of the scientific adviser's investigation was to look at signalling systems. During these inquiries (especially the main public inquiry) the response of the emergency services was reviewed – for example to see if they could, or should, have saved more lives.

COOL SITES:

http://www.doh.gov.uk/epcu/pdf/chap2.pdf

http://www.lanmic.org.uk/Reports/DeBrief.htm

http://www.ubht.nhs.uk/edhandbook/Major%20Incident/wgh_%20majincidplan.doc

THE IMPACT OF DISASTERS

Environmental and health problems

Describe a range of long-term environmental or health problems which could follow three given types of disaster.

For this outcome, you need to:

- explain what is meant by long-term 'environmental or health problems'
- describe a number of long-term environmental and health problems following three different types of disaster.

The exact meaning of 'long-term' is a matter of opinion, but 'long-term environmental or health problems' could be defined as those which persist more than a year after a disaster. For this outcome you should therefore research disasters which have happened more than a year ago.

The most convenient source of information is the internet – especially for overseas disasters, or for research based in the USA. Search terms such as 'disaster long term effects' should yield fruit!

Visiting speakers from local authority emergency planning departments may be able to give you good information in a British context.

Long-term environmental problems are those which involve agriculture, wildlife, pollution (air and water), risk of climate change and the physical appearance of the disaster area. Long-term health problems can involve many kinds of illness, ranging from malnutrition to cancer, and include mental health effects. Some short term health problems such as dysentery and cholera may persist and become long-term problems if the infrastructure damage (e.g. to water supplies) caused by disasters such as hurricanes and earthquakes is not repaired.

Terrorist attacks in built-up areas (World Trade Center)

Every disaster is different in its long-term effects. One that you will hear a lot about is the 2001 destruction of the World Trade Center in New York. Whole books can be written about the long-term effects of that attack: what follows is the briefest of summaries.

Long-term environmental effects

These are slight considering the seriousness of the event. The site has been cleaned up, leaving a space called Ground Zero (a phrase originally used for the explosion sites of hydrogen bombs). The Twin Towers may be replaced by other skyscrapers. There was serious air pollution in the attack itself and during the clean-up operation which is having long-term health consequences on firefighters and public service workers.

Long-term health effects

These consist of:

- **injuries** There were very few of these considering the scale of the attacks. If the attacks had been bomb attacks there would have been many lacerations, burns and more serious injuries. On 9/11, the vast majority of victims were killed outright.
- **problems caused by dust, smoke and gas inhalation** These could be serious for all those involved in the clean-up operation, and for civilians living or working in surrounding parts of the city. At Ground Zero fires burned for a long time, and the smoke, dust and rubble from the collapsed buildings contained many substances which are toxic in dust or gas form. The table below gives information on toxic materials found in collapsed buildings.
- **mental health problems** Head injuries in terrorist attacks can cause brain damage, and physical injuries may cause depression. But the most widespread mental health problems result from delayed shock. These problems take many forms but, because they are the result of shock, are called post traumatic stress disorder (PTSD). Symptoms of PTSD include depression, anxiety, irritability, feelings of numbness, headaches, stomach problems, dizziness, chest pains, sleep problems, anger, guilt, nightmares and problems with relationships. If these symptoms start over three months after the traumatic event, and if they last more than one month, they can be diagnosed as PTSD. The illness can last for six months or more. It is treated with combinations of anti-depressant drugs, and cognitive-behavioural therapy which teaches sufferers to recognise and overcome the symptoms before they get disabling.

COOL SITES:

http://ehpnet1.niehs.nih.gov/docs/2001/109-11/editorial.html

http://www.nimh.nih.gov/anxiety/ptsdfacts.cfm

Hurricane Mitch 1998 (Honduras, Central America)

The effects of this hurricane were typical of the effects of hurricanes, typhoons, cyclones and major flooding in developing countries.

Environmental effects

- Agriculture and the infrastructure (roads, water and electricity) were both seriously damaged by the powerful hurricane.
- Drinking water was contaminated and cholera became endemic in some parts for at least a year afterwards.
- Farmland was permanently damaged by raging rivers and mudslides.
- Many thousands of cattle died.
- Deforestation occurred on the Caribbean coast of Honduras.
- People have left the land to build poverty-ridden shantytowns in Tegucigalpa, the capital of Honduras.
- In the longer term, rebuilding may lead to a better infrastructure than before.

Toxic materials found in collapsed buildings

Chemical	Health effects	Source
Asbestos	Mesothelioma and lung cancer	Insulation, fire retardants, applied to steel beams
Benzene	Cancer and leukaemia	Burning plastics
Biohazards	Hepatitis and AIDS	Body parts and blood
Chromium	Cancer, skin ulcers	TVs, computer monitors
Copper	Kidney and liver damage	Electric wiring and cables
Diesel fumes	Asthma	Trucks and machines
Dioxins	Cancer, birth defects, etc.	Burning PVC on cables
Freon	Destroys lungs	Burning fridges and air-conditioners
Lead	Brain and nerve damage	Monitors, rust-proof paint
Mercury	Damages nerves	Thermometers
Particulates	Asthma, cardiovascular disease	Concrete dust, smoke, soot, diesel fumes, etc.
Polychlorinated biphenyls	Cancer, reproductive problems	Transformers and electrical equipment
Sulphur dioxide	Causes lasting lung damage	Many burning materials

Health effects

- Increased poverty, worse nutrition
- Thousands of people made homeless – forced to move to the city and live on the streets or in dirty shantytowns with no sewerage
- Water-borne diseases such as cholera (leads to vomiting, diarrhoea, dehydration and, sometimes, death)
- High incidence of colds, skin diseases, respiratory infections and conjunctivitis (some of these would be minor if treatment was available)

Foot and mouth epidemic 2001 (UK)

This major incident had huge economic costs to the UK – £3–4 billion in 2001, mainly due it its impact on tourism. An estimated 15–20,000 jobs were lost because of it. Foot and mouth disease does not kill most animals, but causes ulceration and weight-loss in sheep, cows and pigs, and becomes endemic (impossible to get rid of) if allowed to establish itself. The disease is highly infectious, and can be spread by the wind. Had it become endemic all meat trade from the UK would have ended.

Environmental effects

- The slaughtering of over 4 million animals caused environmental problems. These included the release of smoke, dioxins and particulates into the air when the carcasses were burnt, and water pollution incidents when the carcasses were buried.
- The reduction in animals reduced the problem of overgrazing, but caused an increase in the spread of bracken on British hills. Bracken is considered to be carcinogenic to farm animals that try to eat it.

Health effects

- Foot and mouth disease can be caught by humans, but is easily cured.
- Dioxins from burning sheep are toxic (see page opposite).
- Water polluted by rotting carcasses could cause illness if not boiled.
- People made unemployed by foot and mouth disease would be more prone to many illness, including psychological illness. (There is a statistical link between unemployment and poor health.) Suicide rates among British farmers are much higher than the average for the population as a whole.

Nevertheless, both health and environmental effects of foot and mouth are minor compared with those of many other types of major incident.

Foot and mouth – a disaster which caused no human deaths, yet brought the rural economy to its knees

PASSGRADE

> Explain the roles of three organisations dealing with these situations.

For this outcome, you need to choose three organisations which deal with the long term effects of disasters, and explain what they do.

Since the disasters themselves are tackled by the emergency services (in ways which you have covered in a previous outcome, page 361), it can be assumed that this outcome is asking you to research organisations which help to deal with the *long-term effects* of major incidents.

The kind of organisation dealing with the long-term effects of a major incident depends on (a) the type of incident and (b) where it takes place. The effects of a terrorist incident in a rich country are dealt with in a very different way from, say, the effects of a flood in Bangladesh, or a drought in Sudan.

Roles of organisations dealing with the long-term effects of disasters are summarised in the table on the next page.

Organisations dealing with the long-term effects of disasters

Type of disaster	Organisations dealing with long term effects – and examples	Reconstruction, rehabilitation work or preventive work
Terrorist attacks in rich countries	FEMA (Federal Emergency Management Authority), Federal Screening Program – Mt Sinai Medical Center, New York	Screening firefighters and construction workers for effects of dust inhalation at Ground Zero. So far, 12,000 out of 30,000 workers examined. 19% have PTSD and 48% have ear, nose and throat problems.
Natural disasters in poor countries (mainly famine relief)	United Nations, UNICEF (United Nations Children's Fund), UNHCR (United Nations High Commission for Refugees), OCHA (Office for the Coordination of Humanitarian Affairs), World Food Programme, USAID, Government and non-governmental aid organisations, e.g. Oxfam, Red Cross, Red Crescent, Médecins sans frontières	These organisations collect information about food and water needs, then try to organise and coordinate shipments of aid. Some UN agencies and non-governmental organisations such as Oxfam try to set up sustainable agriculture and water projects to prevent famine in the future.
Foot and mouth	DEFRA (Department for the Environment, Food and Rural Affairs), the Countryside Agency, army, police, WHO, EU	The army burnt carcasses; the police enforced exclusion zones to prevent infection spreading, the Countryside Agency reported on the problem, DEFRA organised compensation to farmers.

Further information can be found on the websites of these organisations.

http://www.reliefweb.int/w/rwb.nsf – the low-down on disaster relief

Merit

Analyse the environmental or health problems following one recent disaster.

For this outcome, you need to:

- collect information about the environmental or health effects of a disaster
- make it clear what has caused those effects
- explain what the public services and others have done about those environmental or health effects
- state how far the environmental or health effects are ongoing, or whether the problems have been solved
- indicate any benefits the disaster may have brought, either to the environment or to people's health
- explain what measures could be taken to prevent or reduce the problems happening in future disasters.

NB Most disasters bring both environmental *and* health problems.

Different types of disasters bring different kinds of environmental or health problems. Some events cause their worst problems thousands of miles away from where they happen.

The wider effects of a disaster

Distinction

Critically analyse the impact on processes, procedures, communications, legislation, roles and responsibilities of one disaster.

For this outcome, you need to examine in detail the

The effects of two disasters

Event	Environmental effects	Health effects	Other effects
Attacks of 11 September 2001	Destruction of buildings and some pollution	Death of about 3000 people; injuries, PTSD, other illnesses of rescue workers	Political effects have led to war in Afghanistan and Iraq; many thousands of civilians dead and injured
El Nino (a warm sea current in the Pacific, which appears every few years – could be a natural event, or the result of global warming)	Abnormal weather in many tropical regions – causing droughts and desertification in Africa	Famine – deaths of hundreds of thousands of people: the health of millions damaged by malnutrition	Research by US government agencies – e.g. National Oceanic and Atmospheric Administration and NASA in an attempt to explain and predict 'El Nino events'; world concern on climate change

wider effects of a disaster.

For example, if you were examining the results of a major train crash:

- 'processes' would be the general principles of the way trains, track and signalling were timetabled, used and maintained. It would also include computerisation, signalling methods and any other safety systems on the railways
- 'procedures' would be rules, regulations and working practices that railway workers – drivers, track repairers, signal staff, etc. – were supposed to follow
- 'communications' would refer to the way signalling and the passing of information were used to try to ensure safety
- 'legislation' would be laws (e.g. relating to safety checks, driver training or passenger behaviour on trains) that might need changing
- 'roles' refers to who does what on the railways
- 'responsibilities' would relate to the duties different organisations or workers have for ensuring safety.

For the outcome, you have to choose one disaster and examine all these aspects. In the case of a train crash, the railways themselves are a public service, so everything you find out will relate to the work of the public services. (*The Ladbroke Grove Rail Inquiry 2000*, published by the HSE, gives a great deal of information on this topic for the railways, but does not review what the rescue services did in this train crash.)

In the case of, say, the foot and mouth outbreak of 2001, even though foot and mouth is a disease, it can only be controlled or eliminated by the public services working together, e.g. by controlling the movement of livestock, inspecting their feed, and checking the movement of animals and meat in and out of the country. Some disasters, especially that of 9/11, have very far-reaching effects, and you will only be able to summarise them.

When in doubt – as ever – ask your tutor for advice!

CHECKPOINT ...

David King, the UK government's chief scientific adviser, said in 2004 that climate change was a far greater threat to the world than international terrorism. What are the arguments for and against this view?

Bibliography

Note to users

These details and links were correct at the time of going to press. However, websites have a habit of changing, so as time passes some information may either be deleted or may appear on a different site. Sometimes a search using keywords may be more successful than one using the web address.

Whenever you research the public services, always use the most recent information available. Government documents are frequently updated – typically every year – and new relevant material appears all the time.

Unit 1

HM Treasury (2003) Public Expenditure Statistical Analyses 2003 www.hm-treasury.gov.uk/Documents/Public_Spending_and_Services/Public_Spending_Data/pss_pss_pesaindex

Macpherson, Sir William of Cluny (1999) The Inquiry into the matters arising from the death of Stephen Lawrence (Macpherson Report) TSO http://www.archive.official-documents.co.uk/document/cm42/4262/sli-pre.htm

Sackman, S. A. (1991) *Cultural Knowledge in Organisations*. Newbury Park, CA: Sage.

Dharwadkar, S., Bidanda, B. and Cleland, D. (1994) Shared Manufacturing Assistance Center Project: A New Product Development, Chapter in *The Global Project Management Handbook*, ed. Cleland, D and Gareis, R., McGraw Hill.

Gray, R. (1998) *Organisational Culture: A Review of the Literature*. Anglia Business School.

Prison Privatisation Report International. PPRI appears 6 times a year. It is written by Stephen Nathan and published by PSIRU, University of Greenwich, London SE10 9LS, UK.

Bain, Professor Sir George (2002) *Independent Review of the Fire Service* www.irfs.org.uk/

UK 2003 The Official Yearbook of the United Kingdom of Great Britain and Northern Ireland. London: TSO http://www.statistics.gov.uk/statbase/Product.asp?vlnk=5703&More=N

Unit 2

Police and Criminal Evidence Act (1984) HMSO (with updates) http://www.homeoffice.gov.uk/crimpol/police/system/pacecodes.html

Road Traffic Act (1988) HMSO http://www.legislation.hmso.gov.uk/acts.htm

Crime and Disorder Act (1998) HMSO http://www.legislation.hmso.gov.uk/acts.htm

Queen's Regulations (1975) http://www.army.mod.uk/linked_files/ag/servingsoldier/termsofserv/discmillaw/QR%20(Army)%20incl%20A26%20Mk2.doc

Army Act (1955) http://www.army.mod.uk/militarylaw/army_act2.htm

Social Trends 33 (or latest) The Stationery Office Available free online at www.statistics.gov.uk/socialtrends http://www.statistics.gov.uk/

Unit 3

Ministry of Defence (2002) The Military Covenant http://www.army.mod.uk/servingsoldier/usefulinfo/valuesgeneral/adp5milcov/ss_hrpers_values_adp5_0_w.html

Franken, R. (1994) *Human Motivation*. Pacific Grove, CA: Brooks/Cole.

Gellerman, S. W. (1992) *Motivation in the Real World*. Dutton Books: New York.

McDougall, W. (1933) *The Energies of Men: A Study of the Fundamentals of Dynamic Psychology* xix+395+8(list) 1933 (2nd edn. revised. 1st–13th Oct. 1932) London: Methuen d/w 1982

Morgan, G. (1997) *Images of Organization* (2nd edn.) Thousand Oaks, Calif: Sage.

Harper (1954) *Motivation and Personality* (3rd edn.) NY: Addison-Wesley, 1987.

McGregor, D. (1960) *The Human Side of Enterprise*. New York: McGraw-Hill.

Herzberg, F., Mausner, B. and Snyderman, B. B. (1959) *The Motivation to Work*. New York: Wiley.

Alderfer, C. (1972) *Existence, Relatedness, & Growth*. New York: Free Press.

Zajonc, R. B. (1965) Social facilitation. *Science* 149: 269–74.

Cottrell, N. B., Wack, D. L., Sekerak, G. J. and Rittle, R. H. (1968) Social facilitation of dominant responses by the presence of an audience and the mere presence of others. *Journal of Personality and Social Psychology* 9, 245–250.

Prokopenko, J. (1987) *Productivity Management: A practical handbook*. International Labour Organisation.

Prokopenko, J. and North, K. (eds) (1996) *Productivity and Quality Management: A modular programme*. International Labour Organisation.

Churchill, W. (1930) *My Early Life: 1874–1904*. Eland Books (new edn. June 2000).

Churchill, W. (1948–53) *Memoirs of the Second World War: An Abridgement of the Six Volumes of the Second World War with an Epilogue by the Author on the Postwar Years*. 1088 pages Reprint edition (September 1991). Houghton Mifflin Co.

Rose, N. (1995) *Churchill: The Unruly Giant*. Free Press.

Merton, T. (ed.) (1965) *Gandhi on Non-Violence* by Mohandas Karamchand Gandhi. W. W. Norton & Company.

Parel, A. J. (ed.) (1997) *Hind Swaraj and Other Writings,* Cambridge University Press.

Jack, H. A. (ed.) (1995) *The Gandhi Reader: A Sourcebook of His Life and Writings*. Grove/Atlantic.

Machiavelli, N. (1515) *The Prince: And Selected Discourses*. Bantam Classics Series (1990).

Weber, M. (1947) *Max Weber: The Theory of Social and Economic Organization*. Translated by A. M. Henderson and Talcott Parsons. NY: The Free Press.

NHS Leadership Centre (2002) *The NHS Leadership Qualities Framework*. NHS Leadership Centre – www.NHSLeadershipQualities.nhs.uk

UNIT 4

Rhodes, P. J. (ed.) (1984) *Aristotle: The Athenian Constitution*. Penguin Classics.

Aristotle (c340BC) *Politics*. Dover Publications Incorporated (2000).

European Convention on Human Rights http://conventions.coe.int/treaty/en/Treaties/Html/005.htm

UN Universal Declaration of Human Rights http://www.unhchr.ch/udhr/lang/eng.htm

Advisory Group to the Secretary of State for Education and Employment (2002) Citizenship for 16–19 Year Olds in Education and Training DFEE http://www.des.gov.uk/citizenship

Kyoto Protocol in 1997, Kyoto Protocol to the United Nations Framework Convention on Climate Change – http://www.unfccc.de/resource/docs/convkp/kpeng.html

Human Rights Act (1988) – http://www.legislation.hmso.gov.uk/acts.htm

Sex Discrimination Act (1975) – http://www.pfc.org.uk/legal/sda.htm

Race Relations Act (1976) – http://www.homeoffice.gov.uk/comrace/race/raceact/index.html

Equal Pay Acts (1970) and (1983) http://www.eoc.org.uk/EOCeng/dynpages/Relevant_Legislation.asp

Disability Discrimination Act (1995) – http://www.legislation.hmso.gov.uk/acts.htm

EU Directive on Age Discrimination Council Directive 2000/78/EC

http://europa.eu.int/smartapi/cgi/sga_doc?smartapi!celexapi!prod!CELEXnumdoc&lg=en&numdoc=32000L0078&model=guichett

EU Charter of fundamental rights (2000) – http://www.europarl.eu.int/charter/default_en.htm

Employment Equality (Sexual Orientation) regulations (2003) www.hmso.gov.uk/si/si2003/20031661.htm

Bain, Professor Sir George (2002) *Independent Review of the Fire Service* www.irfs.org.uk/

Annual report of the prison service (2002) http://www.hmprisons.gov.uk/corporate/dynpage.asp?Page=1052

HM Inspectorate of Prisons for England and Wales (2003) Annual report of HM Chief Inspector of Prisons for England and Wales 2002–2003. Anne Owers (HM Chief Inspector of Prisons) – http://www.homeoffice.gov.uk/docs/annual_report.pdf

Woodhouse, L. (2002) A Review of Local Authority Statutory and Non-Statutory Service and Policy Planning Requirements, Local and Regional

Government Research Unit Department for Transport, Local Government & the Regions – http://www.local.dtlr.gov.uk/research/crosscut/revwrprt.pdf

UNIT 5

Fleras, A. and Elliot (1992) *Multiculturalism in Canada: the Challenge of Diversity*. Nelson.

Census (2001) information: Office for National Statistics http://www.statistics.gov.uk/downloads/census2001

Crime and Disorder Act (1998) – http://www.legislation.hmso.gov.uk/acts.htm

Police and Criminal Evidence Act (1984) – http://www.homeoffice.gov.uk/crimpol/police/system/pacecodes.html

Human Rights Act (1998) – http://www.legislation.hmso.gov.uk/acts.htm

Home Office (2002) National Policing Plan http://www.policereform.gov.uk/natpoliceplan/npp_index.html All Different All Equal a Thematic Review by HM Fire Service Inspectorate (September 1999) Her Majesty's Inspectors.

HM Fire Service Inspectorate (1999) *Thematic Review into Fairness and Equality in the Fire Service.* HMSO http://www.odpm.gov.uk/stellent/groups/odpm_fire/documents/page/odpm_fire_601081.pdf

ODPM (2004) *Government Response to ODPM: Housing, Planning, Local Government and the Regions Committee's Report on the Fire Service.* HMSO http://www.odpm.gov.uk/stellent/groups/odpm_fire/documents/page/odpm_fire_027780.pdf

Office of the Deputy Prime Minister (2001) *Toward Diversity: promoting cultural change. The Fire Service equal opportunities action plan*, 1 June 2000 to 31 May 2001 http://www.odpm.gov.uk/stellent/groups/odpm_fire/documents/page/odpm_fire_601079.pdf

ODPM (2001) *Toward Diversity 2: commitment to cultural change. The second Fire Service equal opportunities action plan.* Dec2001http://www.odpm.gov.uk/stellent/groups/odpm_fire/documents/page/odpm_fire_601265.pdf

Ministry of Defence (2002): Army terms of service Chapter 70 Management and Resolution of Complaints 2002 http://www.army.mod.uk/linked_files/ag/servingsoldier/termsofserv/discmillaw/files/pdf/AGAI_Chapter_70_May_02.pdf

Bain, Professor Sir George (2002) *Independent Review of the Fire Service* www.irfs.org.uk/

Home Office (2003) *Milestone Report. Staff Targets for the Home Office, the Prison, the Police and the Probation Services* – http://www.homeoffice.gov.uk/docs/employmenttargets.pdf

UNIT 6

UN Charter (1945). http://www.un.org

The UN Universal Declaration of Human Rights (1948) http://www.unhchr.ch/udhr/lang/eng.htm

European Union Charter of Fundamental Rights (2000) the European Parliament, the Council and the Commission http://www.europarl.eu.int/charter/pdf/text_en.pdf

UK Human Rights Act (1998) www.hmso.gov.uk/acts.htm

Treaty of Washington http://www.nato.int/docu/basictxt/treaty.htm

Schengen Agreement (1985) http://ue.eu.int/ejn/data/vol_c/9_autres_textes/schengen/indexen.html europa.eu.int/scadplus/leg/en/lvb/l33020.htm (summary)

Schengen Convention (1990–95) http://europa.eu.int/comm/justice_home/fsj/freetravel/frontiers/fsj_freetravel_schengen_en.htm (introduction) http://europa.eu.int/smartapi/cgi/sga_doc?smartapi!celexapi!prod!CELEXnumdoc&lg=EN&numdoc=42000A0922(02)&model=guichett (full text)

Schengen – brief explanation – http://www.auswaertiges-amt.de/www/en/willkommen/einreisebestimmungen/schengen_html

EU Treaties and Constitution http://europa.eu.int/eur-lex/en/search/search_treaties.html

European arrest warrant http://europa.eu.int/comm/justice_home/news/laecken_council/en/mandat_en.htm

Terrorism framework decision
http://europa.eu.int/comm/justice_home/news/laecken_council/en/terrorism_en.htm

EU cooperation on asylum and immigration
http://europa.eu.int/comm/justice_home/news/laecken_council/en/asylum_en.htm

St Malo Agreement 1998 http://www.iss-eu.org/chaillot/chai47e.html#3
http://europa.eu.int/comm/publications/booklets/eu_glance/22/en.doc

European Convention on Human Rights
http://conventions.coe.int/treaty/en/Treaties/Html/005.htm

National Asylum Support Service –
http://www.asylumsupport.info/nass.htm

Cabinet Office (2003) Dealing with Disaster
http://www.ukresilience.info/contingencies/dwd/

Terrorism Act (2000) –
http://www.hmso.gov.uk/acts/acts2000/20000011.htm

Terrorism publications –
http://www.homeoffice.gov.uk/terrorism/index.html

Suicide Bombing: no warning and no total solution – John Daly 17 September 2001 *Jane's Terrorism and Security Monitor*
www.janes.com/security/international_security/news/jtsm/jtsm010917_1_n.shtml

Road map for Middle East peace
http://www.state.gov/r/pa/prs/ps/2003/20062.htm
Anti-Terrorism, Crime and Security Act (2001) (ATCSA)

Amnesty International www.amnesty.org/

Geneva Convention (one for civilians; the other for prisoners of war)
http://www.unhchr.ch/html/menu3/b/92.htm
http://www.unhchr.ch/html/menu3/b/91.htm

Office of the United Nations High Commissioner for Human Rights http://www.unhchr.ch/

Human Rights Watch (2003) *Basra: Crime and Insecurity under British Occupation*
http://hrw.org/reports/2003/iraq0603/

UNIT 7

Data Protection Act (1998) –
http://www.legislation.hmso.gov.uk/acts.htm

National Statistics online (2003) 2001 Census Key Statistics for Local Authorities in England & Wales
www.statistics.gov.uk/StatBase/Product.asp?vlnk=10150
http://www.tso.co.uk/bookshop/bookstore.asp?Action=Book&ProductId=0116216433&AF=A10071
The Stationery Office

Home Office (2001) RDS Occasional Paper 75 – International migration and the United Kingdom: Recent patterns and trends –
http://www.homeoffice.gov.uk/rds/pdfs/occ75intro.pdf

Statistics on Football-Related Arrests & Banning Orders Season 2002–2003. Home Office
http://www.homeoffice.gov.uk/docs2/arrestbodata2002-3.pdf

UK 2003 The Official Yearbook of the United Kingdom of Great Britain and Northern Ireland. London: TSO
http://www.statistics.gov.uk/statbase/Product.asp?vlnk=5703&More=N

Social Trends
www.statistics.gov.uk/products/p5748.asp
Annual Abstract of Statistics
www.statistics.gov.uk/statbase/Product.asp?vlnk=94&More=N

UNIT 8

Police Review – Jane's Information Group.
http://www.janes.com/company/catalog/police_review.shtml

Fire Magazine (2004) dmg world media (uk) Ltd.
http://www.fire-magazine.com/

The Police Act (1996) HMSO –
http://www.legislation.hmso.gov.uk/acts.htm

The Crime and Disorder Act (1998) HMSO –
http://www.legislation.hmso.gov.uk/acts.htm

The Terrorism Act (2000) HMSO –
http://www.legislation.hmso.gov.uk/acts.htm

The Anti-Terrorism, Crime and Security Act (2001) HMSO – http://www.legislation.hmso.gov.uk/acts.htm

The Police Reform Act (2002) HMSO –
http://www.legislation.hmso.gov.uk/acts.htm

Police and Criminal Evidence Act (1984) –
http://www.homeoffice.gov.uk/crimpol/police/system/pacecodes.html

Metropolitan Police website Home:
http://www.met.police.uk/
Careers: http://www.metpolicecareers.co.uk/home

Coastguard information –
http://www.mcga.gov.uk/c4mca/mcga-home.htm

Home Office (2001) Police Research Papers 149 Diary of a police officer – http://www.homeoffice.gov.uk/rds/prgpdfs/prs149.pdf

Retained (voluntary) firefighters http://www.hantsfire.gov.uk/jobs/retained.html#What%20is%20a%20Retained%20Firefighter

Health and Safety at Work Act (1974) London:HMSO, 1974, reprinted 1991– http://www.healthandsafety.co.uk/haswa.htm

Health and Safety Executive – www.hse.gov.uk/http://www.hse.gov.uk/pubns/ohsingb.pdf

Roberts, Dr S. E. Hazardous occupations in Great Britain. *The Lancet* 360 (9332) p.543 http://www.thelancet.com/home *quoted in* http://news.bbc.co.uk/1/hi/health/2195847.stm

NHS Careers – http://www.nhscareers.nhs.uk/nhs-knowledge_base/data/5118.html

Customs and Excise: Career progression chart – http://www.hmce.gov.uk/about/career/progression.pdf

Prison inspections – http://www.homeoffice.gov.uk/justice/prisons/inspprisons/inspection.html

Inspectors' Report – Metropolitan Police 2002/2003 http://uk.sitestat.com/homeoffice/homeoffice/s?docs.document&ns_type=pdf&ns_url=[http://www.homeoffice.gov.uk/hmic/mps2002.pdf]

Police recruitment information – http://www.policecouldyou.co.uk/default.asp?action=article&ID=1

UNIT 9

'Sports Coach' website: www.brianmac.demon.co.uk

UNIT 10

Diamond, L., Linz, J. and Seymour M. L., (eds) (1988) *Democracy in Developing Countries*. Boulder, Lynne Rienner.

US Constitution – www.usconstitution.net/

French Constitution – http://www.assemblee-nat.fr/english/8ab.asp

Draft EU Constitution – http://europa.eu.int/futurum/constitution/index_en.htm

The UN Universal Declaration of Human Rights (1948) http://www.unhchr.ch/udhr/lang/eng.htm

European Convention on Human Rights http://conventions.coe.int/treaty/en/Treaties/Html/005.htm

UK 2003 The Official Yearbook of the United Kingdom of Great Britain and Northern Ireland. London: TSO http://www.statistics.gov.uk/statbase/Product.asp?vlnk=5703&More=N

Scruton, R. A. (1982) *Dictionary of Political Thought*. London: Macmillan.

Commission for Racial Equality – www.cre.gov.uk/

Labour – www.labour.org.uk/

Conservative – www.conservative-party.org.uk/

Liberal Democrats – libdems.org.uk/

Immigration and Nationality Directorate – http://www.ind.homeoffice.gov.uk/

National Asylum Support Service – http://www.asylumsupport.info/nass.htm

Community Cohesion: A Report of the Independent Review Team (2002) http://www.homeoffice.gov.uk/docs2/pocc.html (Inner city riots)

Text of the Good Friday agreement (Northern Ireland peace plan) http://www.nio.gov.uk/agreement.htm

UNIT 11

Ordnance Survey – www.ordsvy.gov.uk/

Harvey Maps – www.harveymaps.co.uk/

British Mountaineering Council – http://www.thebmc.co.uk/

Countryside and Rights of Way Act (2000) – http://www.legislation.hmso.gov.uk/acts.htm

Criminal Justice and Public Order Act (1994) – http://www.legislation.hmso.gov.uk/acts.htm

Countryside agency – http://www.countryside.gov.uk/index.asp

Ramblers association – www.ramblers.org.uk/

Department for Education and Employment (1998) Health and safety of pupils on educational visits – http://www.dfes.gov.uk/h_s_ev/hspv.pdf

Sharp, B. (2001) Strategies for Improving Mountain Safety, Analysis of Scottish Mountain Incidents 1996/99. University of Strathclyde Faculty of Education. www.mountaineering-scotland.org.uk/safety/bobsharp.html

UNIT 12

Myers, D. G. (2002) *Exploring Psychology*. Worth Publishing.

Pavlov, I. (1926) *Lectures on Conditioned Reflexes: Twenty-Five Years of Objective Study of the Higher Nervous Activity Behavior of Animals*. (Reprint edn. 1980) Pinter Pub Ltd.

Watson J. B. (1913) Psychology as the behaviorist views it. *Psychological Review*, 20: 158–177.

Skinner, B. F. (1974) *About Behaviorism*. New York: Knopf.

Freud, S. (1900) *The Interpretation of Dreams* (Translated by A. A. Brill 1913). Macmillan: New York.

Freud, S. (1900) *The Interpretation of Dreams*. Standard Edition, 4 & 5. London: Hogarth Press, 1953.

Rogers, C. (1961/1995) *On Becoming a Person: A Therapist's View of Psychotherapy* Introduction by Peter Kramer, M.D. Houghton Mifflin Co.

Maslow, A. (1954) *Motivation and Personality*. NY: Harper.

Berne, E.(1974) *Games People Play*. Penguin Books.

Piaget, J. (1954) *The Construction of Reality in the Child*. New York: Basic Books.

Bandura, A. (1977) *Social Learning Theory*. Englewood Cliffs, NJ: Prentice-Hall.

Chomsky, N. (1975) 'On Cognitive Capacity,' Chapter 1 of *Reflections on Language*. New York: Pantheon. Reprinted in Block 1981.

Bruner, J. (1960) *The Process of Education*. Cambridge, MA: Harvard University Press (reprinted 1977).

American Psychiatric Association (2000) *DSM-IV-TR*, Washington.

Peterson, C. (1997) *Psychology: A biopsychosocial approach* (2nd edn). New York: Longman.

Myers, S. P. (1997) *Influencing People using Myers Briggs*. Consulting Psychologists Press Inc – http://www.teamtechnology.co.uk

Personality and longevity (Types A, B and C) – http://www.jr2.ox.ac.uk/bandolier/booth/hliving/personHD.html.

Malott, R. W., Whaley, D. L. and Malott, M. E. (1994) *Elementary Principles of Behavior* (2nd edn). Englewood Cliffs, NJ: Prentice-Hall.

Mental illness information – http://www.sane.org.uk/Sitemap.htm any

Psychometric testing – http://pcw.co.uk/Careers/Features/Psychometrics/index.jsp http://www.graduatecareersonline.com/advice/employability/psychometrics.asp

Non-verbal communication (NVC) – http://www.cultsock.ndirect.co.uk/MUHome/cshtml/nvc/nvc3a.html

http://www.bbc.co.uk/worldservice/learningenglish/work/workskills/wsu5.shtml

Hinde, R. A. (ed.) (1975) *Non-verbal Communication*. Cambridge University Press.

UNIT 14

The Military Covenant (2002) MoD http://www.army.mod.uk/servingsoldier/usefulinfo/valuesgeneral/adp5milcov/ss_hrpers_values_adp5_0_w.html

Statutory Instruments (1999) No. 730. Police code of conduct HMSO – http://www.hmso.gov.uk/stat.htm

Banton, M. (1965) *Roles*. London: Tavistock.

Baldwin, R. (1995) *Rules and Government*. Oxford: Clarendon Press.

Bain, Professor Sir George (2002) *Independent Review of the Fire Service* www.irfs.org.uk/

Fire Service Discipline Regulations (1985) http://www.fbuberkshire.co.uk/hand_book_discipline_regs.htm

ACAS (2001) *Disciplinary and Grievance Procedures*. New edition 2004 Draft Acas Code of Practice http://www.acas.co.uk/publications/pdf/cp01.2.pdf

Discipline and Grievances at Work – advisory handbook http://www.acas.co.uk/publications/h02.html

Handbook on Discipline and Grievance at Work http://www.acas.co.uk/publications/pdf/CP01.pdf

Crutchfield, R. S. (1954) A new technique for measuring individual differences in conformity to group judgement. *Proceedings of the Invitational Conference on Testing Problems*. pp.69–74. Cited in Gross, R. (1996) *Psychology, The Science of Mind and Behaviour* (3rd edn). Hodder & Stoughton, London p.479.

Brehm, Kassin and Fein (1999) *Social Psychology* (4th edn). Boston: Houghton Mifflin, p.213.

Deutsch, P. T. and Gerard, H. (1955) A study of normative and informational social influences on individual judgment. *Journal of Abnormal and Social Psychology*.

Al-Banna, S. M. Hasan (2000) *Imam Shahid Hasan al-Banna*. Awakening.

Sherif, M. (1935) A study of some social factors in perception. *Archives of Psychology*, No. 187.

Sherif, M. (1936) *The Psychology of Social Norms*. New York: Harper.

Asch, S. (1958) Effects of Group Pressure upon the Modification and Distortion of Judgments, pp.174–83 in *Readings in Social Psychology* (3rd edn), edited by Eleanor E. Maccoby *et al.* New York: Holt, Rinehart & Winston.

Asch, S. (1952) *Social Psychology*. New York: Oxford University Press.

Milgram, S. (1974) *Obedience to Authority; an experimental view*. New York, Harper & Row.

Hofling, Charles K., Brotzman, E., Dalrymple, S., Graves, N. and Pierce, C. M. (1966) An Experimental Study in Nurse–Physician Relationships. *Journal of Nervous and Mental Disease*, 143, 171–180.

Arendt, H. (1963) *Eichmann in Jerusalem: a Report on the Banality of Evil*, London, Faber & Faber.

Office of the Deputy Prime Minister (2001) *Toward Diversity: promoting cultural change. The Fire Service equal opportunities action plan*, 1 June 2000 to 31 May 2001 http://www.odpm.gov.uk/stellent/groups/odpm_fire/documents/page/odpm_fire_601079.pdf

ODPM (2001) *Toward Diversity 2: commitment to cultural change. The second Fire Service equal opportunities action plan*. Dec2001http://www.odpm.gov.uk/stellent/groups/odpm_fire/documents/page/odpm_fire_601265.pdf

HM Chief Inspector of Prisons (2001) An Unannounced Follow-up Inspection of HM Prison, Dartmoor – http://www.homeoffice.gov.uk/docs/dartmoor01.pdf

Rodney King beating – http://www.law.umkc.edu/faculty/projects/ftrials/lapd/lapd.html

Macpherson, Sir William of Cluny (1999) The Inquiry into the matters arising from the death of Stephen Lawrence (Macpherson Report) TSO http://www.archive.official-documents.co.uk/document/cm42/4262/sli-pre.htm

The Napoleon Hill Foundation (1994) *Napoleon Hill's Keys To Success: The 17 Principles of Personal Achievement*. New York: Penguin.

Armed Forces Discipline Act (2000) http://www.legislation.hmso.gov.uk/acts.htm

Armed Forces Act (2001) http://www.legislation.hmso.gov.uk/acts.htm

Weber, M. (1947) *The Theory of Social and Economic Organization*. Translated by A. M. Henderson & Talcott Parsons. NY: The Free Press.

Arendt, H. (1961) *Between Past and Future: Six Exercises in Political Thought*. Cleveland: Meridian Books.

McMahon, C. (1994) *Authority and Democracy: a general theory of government and management*. Princeton, New Jersey: Princeton University Press.

Likert R. (1967) *The Human Organization: Its Management and Value*. New York: McGraw-Hill.

Irving, J. (1972) *Victims of Groupthink: psychological study of foreign-policy decisions and fiascoes* (2nd edn). Boston: Houghton Mifflin.

Unit 16

Institution of Fire Engineers. (Manuals of Firemanship, etc.) Cool site! http://www.ife.org.uk/Retail/pubs.html

Health and Safety Executive – publications: http://www.hse.gov.uk/pubns/ohsingb.pdf

Royal Society for the Prevention of Accidents (2002) *Accidents in the United Kingdom* – March 2002 – http://www.rospa.co.uk

Fire Magazine – http://www.fire-magazine.com/#

Statistics of Workplace Fatalities and Injuries – www.hse.gov.uk/

Tameside MBC (2003) Emergency Plan http://www.tameside.gov.uk/tmbc1/emergency/roles external.htm

Bain, Professor Sir George (2002) *Independent Review of the Fire Service* www.irfs.org.uk/

Office of the Deputy Prime Minister (2003) *Our Fire and Rescue Service* http://www.odpm.gov.uk/stellent/groups/odpm_fire/documents/page/odpm_fire_022968.hcsp

Office of the Deputy Prime Minister (2004) *Draft Fire and Rescue National Framework: 2004/05* http://www.odpm.gov.uk/stellent/groups/odpm_control/documents/contentservertemplate/odpm_index.hcst?n=4084&l=1

Fire and rescue service information: http://www.fireservice.co.uk/

Fire and rescue service incidents: Incident Pages – http://www.fireservice.co.uk/incidents.php

British Standards Institution: British Standards for smoke alarms: BS 5446 (2003) and BS 5839 (2002) – http://www.bsi-global.com/group.xalter

Fire research in USA: National Fire Protection Association (USA) http://www.nfpa.org/Research/index.asp

Highway Code (2001) http://www.highwaycode.gov.uk/index.shtml

Emergency Training College, Easingwold, near York – http://www.fireservicecollege.ac.uk/

Northamptonshire road traffic safety – www.reducingroadcasualties.com

Fire Services Act (1947) HMSO – http://www.fire.org.uk/fsact/intro.htm

Health and Safety at Work Act (1974) – www.healthandsafety.co.uk/haswa.htm

Fire Precautions Act 1971 HMSO – http://www.fire.org.uk/fpact/

The Nuclear Safeguards Act (2001) – http://www.legislation.hmso.gov.uk/acts.htm

The Football Disorder Act (2001)– http://www.legislation.hmso.gov.uk/acts.htm

Anti-Terrorism, Crime and Security Act (2002) – http://www.legislation.hmso.gov.uk/acts.htm

The Private Security Industry Act (2002) – http://www.legislation.hmso.gov.uk/acts.htm

Police Reform Act (2002) – http://www.legislation.hmso.gov.uk/acts.htm

Aviation Offences Act (2003) – http://www.legislation.hmso.gov.uk/acts.htm

Marine Safety Act (2003) – http://www.legislation.hmso.gov.uk/acts.htm

Railways and Transport Safety Act (2003) – http://www.legislation.hmso.gov.uk/acts.htm

The Motor Vehicle Tyres (Safety) (Amendment) Regulations (2003) – http://www.hmso.gov.uk/stat.htm

The Traffic Signs (Amendment) General Directions (2003) – http://www.hmso.gov.uk/stat.htm

The Nuclear Industries Security Regulations (2003) – http://www.hmso.gov.uk/stat.htm

Health and Safety Law – what you should know http://www.safety.ed.ac.uk/resources/pdf/law.pdf

Health and Safety Executive: General information on workplace health and safety http://www.hse.gov.uk/

RIDDOR http://www.hse.gov.uk/a-z/r.htm#REPORTING

HAZCHEM http://www.hse.gov.uk/a-z/h.htm#h-goods

COSHH http://www.hse.gov.uk/a-z/c.htm#coshh

A Consultation Document on the Reform of Fire Safety Legislation (2002) www.odpm.gov.uk

IEE (2003) – The Costs to Industry of Accidents and Ill-health Health & Safety Briefing 3 http://www.iee.org.uk/Policy/Areas/Health/hsb03.pdf

Lancashire Fire and Rescue Service: Best Value Performance Plan (2003/4) http://www.lancsfirerescue.org.uk/files%20for%20Downloads/BV%20Plan%202003%202004.pdf

The Crime and Disorder Act (1998) HMSO – http://www.legislation.hmso.gov.uk/acts.htm

UNIT 17

Capezio, P. (1998) *Winning Teams*. Career Press, Franklin Lakes, NJ.

Wergin, J. (1998) *The Collaborative Department*. (AAHE).

Robbins, H. and Finley, M. (2000) *The New Why Teams Don't Work*. Berrett-Koehler.

French, W. L. and Bell, C. H. (l995) *Organizational Development* (6th edn). Prentice-Hall.

Drucker, P. F. (1966) *The Effective Executive*. HarperCollins.

Drucker, P. F. (1986) *The Frontiers of Management*. EP Dutton.

Belbin, R. M, (1993) *Team Roles at Work*. Butterworth-Heinemann http://www.belbin.com/belbin-team-roles.htm

Lewin, K. (1935) *A Dynamic Theory of Personality*. New York: McGraw-Hill.

Lewin, K. (1948) *Resolving Social Conflicts*. New York: Harper and Brothers.

Tuckman, B. and Jensen, N. (1977) Stages of small group development revisited, *Group and Organisational Studies*, 2, 109.

Adair, J. (1993) *Effective Teambuilding*. Gower Publishing.

Team-building – http://www.dancinglion.co.uk/tcarticleeight.html

Woodcock, M. and Francis, D. (1994) *Teambuilding Strategy*. Gower Publishing Ltd.

Woodcock, M. (1989) *Team Development Manual*. Gower Publishing Limited.

Team management – http://www.tms.com.au/welcome.html (full of good ideas)

Margerison, C. and McCann, D. (1995) *Team Management* (2nd edn) *Practical New Approaches,* Other information on – http://www.mb2000.com/Team.htm

Essex Police – www.essex.police.uk/ Merseyside fire and rescue service – www.merseyfire.gov.uk/

HM Chief Inspector of Prisons (2001) Report on an unannounced follow-up inspection of HM Prison Dartmoor, 17–21 September 2001 http://www.homeoffice.gov.uk/justice/prisons/inspprisons/inspectionreports/w.html

HM Chief Inspector of Prisons (2002) Report on a full announced inspection of HMYOI Feltham, 14–23 January 2002 www.homeoffice.gov.uk/docs/imbfeltham2002.pdf

Bowman, E. K. and Pierce, L. G. (2002) Cultural Barriers to Teamwork in a Multinational Coalition Environment, Army Research Laboratory, Fort Sill, OK (USA).

Laming, Lord (2003) Report of the Victoria Climbié inquiry – www.victoria-climbie-inquiry.org.uk/

HM Fire Service Inspectorate (1999). Thematic Review into Fairness and Equality in the Fire Service, HMSO http://www.odpm.gov.uk/stellent/groups/odpm_fire/documents/page/odpm_fire_601081.pdf

Amnesty International – http://www.amnesty.org

Human Rights Watch – http://www.hrw.org/

Unit 18

World Health Organization (2003) World Health Report 2003 http://www.who.int/entity/whr/order/en (Summary) http://www.who.int/entity/whr/2003/en/overview_en.pdf

Information on blood http://www.fortunecity.com/greenfield/rattler/46/haemopoiesis.htm

Food, nutrition and metabolism – www.nlm.nih.gov/medlineplus/foodnutritionandmetabolism.html

BBC – The Human Body – http://www.bbc.co.uk/science/humanbody/body/factfiles

Sheldon, W. H. (with the collaboration of Stevens, S. S. and Tucker, W. B.) (1940) *The Varieties of Human Physique: An Introduction to Constitutional Psychology*. New York: Harper.

Giddens, A. (1991) *Modernity and Self-Identity. Self and society in the late modern age*. Cambridge: Polity Press.

Food and Nutrition Information Center http://www.nal.usda.gov/fnic/foodcomp/Data/HG72/hg72_2002.pdf

Nutrition and health http://www.nutrition.gov/home/index.php3

Ministry of Agriculture, Fisheries and Food (1995) *Manual of Nutrition* 10th edn. The Stationery Office.

Parsons, C. Healthy living and fitness – http://www.evh.k12.nf.ca/cparsons/Active%20Living.htm

The ultimate health advice website: US Department of Health and Human Services http://www.hhs.gov/

Rob's Home of Fitness Testing – http://www.topendsports.com/testing/index.htm

Unit 20

Outdoor activities website – http://www.hnh.dircon.co.uk/links.htm

Nealy, W. (1997) *Kayak: A Manual of Technique*. Menasha Ridge Press.

McGuffin, G. and McGuffin, J. (2003) *Paddle Your Own Canoe*. Stoddart Publishing.

Long, J. (2003) *How to Rock Climb!* (How to Climb Series). Globe Pequot Press.

Stevens, J. (1999) *Start Sailing: The Basic Skills*. Fernhurst Books.

Kayak websites – http://www.seakayak.ws/kayak/kayak.nsf/NavigationList/NT0000090A http://www.sbkc.ie/Level%202%20Kayak%20Proficiency%20Award.doc

First aid on mountains – http://www.survival-center.com/med-faq/

Lyme disease – http://www.brecon-beacons.com/lyme-disease.htm

Countryside agency publications – http://www.countryside.gov.uk/Publications/Index.asp

http://www.mountaineering–scotland.org.uk/safety/index.html

http://www.scoutbase.org.uk/library

UNIT 21

Gormley, J. (Irish MP) (1998) Speech on restorative justice in the Dail (Irish Parliament) http://www.irlgov.ie/debates/25jun98/sect5.htm

Becker, H. S. (1963) *Outsiders: studies in the sociology of deviance*. London: Free Press of Glencoe.

Wolfgang, M. E., Figlio, R. M. and Sellin, T. (1972) *Delinquency in a Birth Cohort*. The University of Chicago Press, Chicago.

Lombroso, C. (1876) The Criminal Man – published in Italian and partly translated in Lombroso, C. (1911) *Crime: its causes and remedies*. Boston: Little, Brown and Company.

Sheldon, W. H. (with the collaboration of Stevens, S. S. and Tucker, W. B.) (1940) *The Varieties of Human Physique: An Introduction to Constitutional Psychology*. New York: Harper.

Goring, C. (1913) *The English Convict*. Montclair, NJ: Patterson Smith.

Jacobs, P. A., Melville, M., Ratcliffe, S., Keay, A. J. and Syme, J. A cytogenetic survey of 11,680 newborn infants. *Ann Hum Genet* 1974;37: 359–376. (about XYY chromosomes)

Lesser, M. (1985) *Nutrition & Vitamin Therapy*, Thorsons.

Loeber, R. and Stouthamer-Loeber, M. (1986) Family Factors as Correlates and Predictors of Juvenile Conduct Problems and Delinquency, in *Crime and Justice: An Annual Review of Research*, vol. 7. eds M. Tonry and N. Morris, The University of Chicago Press, Chicago, pp.29–149.

Maguin, M. and Loeber, R. (1996) Academic Performance and Delinquency, in *Crime and Justice: An Annual Review of Research*, vol. 20, ed. M. Tonry, The University of Chicago Press, Chicago, pp.145–264.

Klein, M. W. (1995), Street Gang Cycles, in *Crime*, eds J. Q. Wilson and J. Petersilia, ICS Press, San Francisco, pp.65–90.

Stevenson, R. J. (1996) *The Impact of Alcohol Sales on Violent Crime, Property Destruction and Public Disorder*, NSW Bureau of Crime Statistics and Research, Sydney.

Cloward, R. A. and Ohlin, L. E. (1960) *Delinquency and Opportunity: A Theory of Delinquent Gangs*. The Free Press, New York.

Field, S. (1999) *Trends in Crime Revisited*. Home Office Research Study 195, Home Office, London.

Home Office (2003) Crime in England and Wales 2002/2003 http://www.homeoffice.gov.uk/rds/crimeew0203.html

Simmons, J. and colleagues (2003) *Crime, Policing and Justice: the experience of older people*. Home Office RDS.

Home Office (2002) Crime report page http://www.homeoffice.gov.uk/rds/bcs1.html

Chenery, S., Holt, J. and Pease, K. (1997) *Biting Back II: Reducing Repeat Victimisation in Huddersfield* (Crime detection and prevention series, Paper 82, Home Office).

Metropolitan Police Youth Strategy –http://www.met.police.uk/youth/MetPoliceYouthStrategy-MAIN.pdf

Police and Criminal Evidence Act (1984) HMSO (with updates) http://www.homeoffice.gov.uk/crimpol/police/system/pacecodes.html

Reporting crime to the police – http://www.met.police.uk/contact/crime.htm

Home Office (2002) National Crime Recording Standard (ACPO) http://www.homeoffice.gov.uk/rds/pdfs2/countrecstan03.pdf

Crime and Disorder Act (1998) HMSO http://www.legislation.hmso.gov.uk/acts.htm

Leicester Partnership against Crime and Disorder (2002 Strategy) http://www.crimeanddisorder.leicester.gov.uk/default.htm

Community safety – http://www.met.police.uk/hammersmithandfulham/community_safety_unit.htm

Home Office under the Safer Communities Initiative. Documents? Cool site: http://www.crimereduction.gov.uk/safercommunities1.pdf

I have been asked to be a witness – what do I do? (leaflet) http://www.courtservice.gov.uk/cms/media/ex341.pdf

Victim Support http://www.victimsupportwestyorkshire.org.uk/whatwedo.htm

Personal account of witness protection http://www.bigissueinthenorth.com/Magazine/witness_protection.html

Data Protection Act (1998) – http://www.legislation.hmso.gov.uk/acts.htm

UNIT 24

London Emergency Services Liaison Panel (2003) *Major Incident Procedure Manual* (6th edn) Metropolitan Police Service.

Emergency Procedures, Policy Unit, HQ Public Order Branch, New Scotland Yard – http://www.met.police.uk/leslp/LESLP_Man.pdf

OPOCE (Office for official publications of the European communities) (2003). Europe's environment: the third assessment. Environmental assessment report No 10. Chapter 10 Technological and natural hazards – http://reports.eea.eu.int/environmental_assessment_report_2003_10/en

Cabinet Office (2003). Dealing with Disaster http://www.ukresilience.info/contingencies/dwd/

Draft civil contingencies bill – http://www.ukresilience.info/ccbill/index.htm

Measures against terrorism – http://www.ukresilience.info/terrorism.htm

NHS (1998) Planning for major incidents: the NHS guidance http://www.dh.gov.uk/assetRoot/04/07/15/48/04071548.pdf

NHS Handling major incidents – an operational doctrine – http://www.dh.gov.uk/assetRoot/04/07/18/11/04071811.pdf

Flood reports – http://www.environment-agency.gov.uk

Disaster plan, Wiltshire – http://www.wiltshire.police.uk/planning/index.htm

Health Consequences of the 11 September 2001 Attacks http://ehpnet1.niehs.nih.gov/docs/2001/109-11/editorial.html

Information on post traumatic stress disorder – http://www.nimh.nih.gov/anxiety/ptsdfacts.cfm

Cabinet Office (2001) Inquiry into the lessons to be learned from the foot and mouth disease outbreak of 2001 – http://www.cabinet-office.gov.uk/fmd/nav/report.htm Foot and Mouth Outbreak of 2001

Relief Web – Information on disasters world-wide – http://www.reliefweb.int/w/rwb.nsf

Environment Agency (2001) Report on major floods – 2001 – http://www.environment-agency.gov.uk/commondata/105385/126637

Lord Cullen (2001) The Ladbroke Grove rail inquiry part 1 http://www.hse.gov.uk/railways/paddrail/lgri1.pdf

The Ladbroke Grove inquiry part 2 (Paddington rail disaster) http://www.hse.gov.uk/railways/paddrail/lgri2.pdf

Health and Safety Executive separate inquiry into Paddington crash http://www.hse.gov.uk/railways/paddrail/ladbroke.pdf

Weston Area Health NHS Trust Major Incident Plan (2001) http://www.ubht.nhs.uk/edhandbook/Major%20Incident/wgh_%20majincidplan.doc

Index